Slow
Burn

Slow Burn

The Great American Antismoking Scam
(And Why It Will Fail)

Don Oakley

Eyrie Press
Roswell, Georgia

Library of Congress Cataloging-in-Publication Data

Oakley, Don, 1927-
Slow Burn : the great American antismoking scam, and why it will fail / Don Oakley.
p. cm.
ISBN 0-9619465-3-9 (pbk. : alk. paper)
1. Antismoking movement—United States. 2.. Smoking—United States. 3. Science—Social aspects—United States. 4. Law—Social aspects—United States. I. Title.
HV5751.025 1999
362.29'67'0973—dc21 98-55531
CIP

Eyrie Press
Roswell, Georgia
Printed in the United States of America

'Tain't what we don't know that hurts us so much.
It's what we know that ain't so.

— Artemis Ward

A strong conviction that something must be done
is the parent of many bad measures.

— Daniel Webster

CONTENTS

Preface

When U.S. Surgeon General Luther L. Terry's historic—and today virtually enshrined—report, *Smoking and Health*, was released in mid-January 1964, I had just two weeks before been made chief editorial writer for Newspaper Enterprise Association, a newspaper features service in Cleveland, Ohio.

There had been scuttlebutt for some time that the SG was going to drop a bombshell on tobacco but I'd paid little attention to it. When it actually happened it was as a bolt from the blue to me. Sure, I'd heard about "smoker's cough" or "smoker's hack" for years and we frequently referred to cigarettes as "coffin nails," but that was just joking. I was innocently unaware that there had ever been any really serious concern within the medical establishment about any possible health dangers from smoking.

Thus the report shook me—a little bit. Heck, I'd already been smoking at least a pack a day for 18 years and "coffin nails" had never hurt me or anybody I knew. They'd never even so much as made me have to clear my throat.

But 18 years was a lot of years and a lot of cigarettes. And this was, after all, a verdict bearing the imprimatur of the nation's highest medical authority, *the surgeon general of the United States* no less: smoking causes lung cancer (and other bad things).

I liked to smoke. It was not welcome news.

Not for a second did it enter my mind that the report could be anything but the product of rigorous research and careful analysis by dedicated and disinterested men of science, many of whom were smokers themselves for all I knew. Not for a second did I consider that their findings could be anything less than unassailable fact.

At 36 I was still just a snot-nosed kid, journalistically speaking, and although I had written editorials before as a staff writer for NEA, this was one of the first in my new capacity. Yet so little importance did

I attach to the report that I ran the editorial about it as the second of two I wrote that day to fill my column. (The lead editorial was about the latest crisis in Panama over ownership of the canal.)

Anyway, I sat down at my typewriter and lit a cigarette and tried to think of something meaningful to say that the editors of our 800-some subscribing newspapers could use. All I knew about the SG's report was what had come over the United Press teletype machine that day. (It was not until 1996, 32 years later, that I obtained the actual report and saw for myself what it said.)

Rereading that editorial now after more than three decades, I am struck by what a lightweight treatment it was of what turned out to be a truly watershed event in American social history. It was only about 250 words in all.

"Human beings are sometimes more rationalizing than rational," I intoned in my opening sentence. "They usually find excuses for doing what they want to do."

Those who want to smoke will do so, I elucidated, despite release of the government's report. "They will seize on the fact that there is still no 'absolutely proved' cause-and-effect relationship between smoking and lung cancer and other diseases. There never will be such 100-percent proof, for medical science is not that exact nor cancer that simple. Smokers are now officially on notice, however, that they puff at their peril."

I predicted that the report would probably result in an overall decline in cigarette usage, a severe dip at first, a slow recovery later, which is what happened during the first year after the report. But I never conceived that within the next few years tens of millions of smokers would give up the habit (or even less conceivable, in the face of what the report eventually set into motion, that millions of others would take it up).

My most naïve statement was, "Tobacco men can be happy about one thing: the worst is over. It is to be hoped that they will now cease blowing up statistical smoke screens to try to prove that cigarettes don't hurt anyone and concentrate their resources on finding out just what it is in tobacco that is injurious."

There I displayed not only my poor predictive ability but an ignorance, albeit a forgivable one, of the chemical complexity of tobacco smoke, which at latest count is supposed to contain some 4,000 individual constituents, give or take a thousand, of longer or shorter duration and greater or lesser carcinogeneity.

I take no pride in the fact that I may have been one of the first writers in the country to use the words "smoke screen" in connection with the tobacco industry—a phrase that to this day continues to be belabored in a never-ending stream of newspaper and magazine articles on smoking, along with an infinite number of variations such as "up in smoke," "blowing smoke," "snuffing out," "no butts about it" and so on ad nauseam. I do not recall having had any grounds for such an allegation against the industry. Whether I did or not, it was essentially a cheap shot intended to demonstrate the "independence" of my views on the issue.

I concluded with: "Men have been comforted by the weed for several hundred years. They will beat a path to the door of anyone who can give them a healthy smoke."

Again I was too naïve at that time to realize that the tobacco industry dared not admit to trying to design a "healthy" or "safe" cigarette, for that would be tantamount to conceding that the cigarettes it had been peddling for decades were *un*healthy and *un*safe and be an open invitation to the plaintiffs' bar to "Come sue us."

"The worst is over."(!) I certainly did not foresee that over the coming years the surgeon general's report would launch an accelerating stream of indictment after indictment and attack after attack against smoking, each more damning than the last . . . the growth of a veritable industry devoted to helping people stop smoking . . . the mandatory placing of health warnings on cigarette packages and printed ads . . . the banning of cigarette commercials from radio and television . . . the "secondhand smoke" hysteria and resulting smoking bans in restaurants and workplaces . . . the attempt by the Food and Drug Administration to regulate nicotine as a drug with the goal of banishing cigarettes entirely . . . the publicly applauded mugging of the tobacco industry by 40 state attorneys general, and on and on. In sum: the transformation of a congenial and well-nigh universal pleasure into a socially unacceptable practice with, ultimately, the relegation of smokers to an outcast minority, alternately despised and pitied—but nice to have around as easy and convenient prey for exploitation by tax-and-spend politicos.

Least of all—*least of all*—did I foresee the emergence of a powerful and militant antismoking movement, whose cutting edge is led by an extremist fringe of fanatics who are not above the use of fear, fraud and mendacity in their crusade against smoking and smokers.

Now, 32 years later, in retirement, I light yet another cigarette and reach again for whatever editorial skills I ever had and begin what will be a highly personal journey into the past, present and possible future of smoking—for two reasons: to examine for myself, in the light of my own observation and experience and common sense, the evidence against smoking and, more importantly, to raise a voice against the fanatical antismokers and their ilk and the danger they pose to the rights and freedoms of all Americans, smokers and nonsmokers alike.

* * *

UPDATE: The foregoing was committed to my word processor in late 1996, when I began the actual writing of this book and at which time I lived in the greater Atlanta, Georgia, area. The original subtitle I planned for it was "America's Insane Crusade Against Smoking (And Why It Will Fail)."

Shortly before the book was ready for press, wiser heads prevailed upon me either to eliminate the "Insane" or to substitute some milder adjective for it, like "Misguided" or "Misdirected." Something not so "in your face" that would not alienate potential nonsmoking readers.

I resisted the idea. The antismoking crusade *is* insane. Anyway, I'd used the words "insane" and "insanity" several times in the text and I wasn't about to go back and tone them down. But then it occurred to me: the crusade is also a monumental scam that the antismoking establishment has perpetrated on a trusting public—a pseudoscientific con game of the worst kind because at least some of its leaders fervently believe it themselves. Thus I finally decided on the present subtitle. It is both a play on the American Cancer Society's annual "Great American Smokeout" and an accurate characterization of much of the evidence that undergirds and fuels the ongoing and never-ending crusade against smoking.

"Scam" also suggests that this book is some kind of exposé—which it is.

Don Oakley
Gainesville, Virginia
January 1999

Introduction

Everything you read in the press is 100-percent true—except for those instances of which you have personal knowledge.

— Unknown

THERE ARE LITERALLY thousands of what are called "newsgroups" or "usergroups" on the Internet. Not to be confused with e-mail, most of them are meeting places where people with a common interest in any of a variety of subjects—history, a hobby, a recreation or almost anything—gather together electronically. Many of them are labeled "alternate" groups, one of which is "alt.smokers." It is supposed to be a forum where people who smoke can exchange talk about what they smoke and why they do so and generally discuss matters involving their habit. Unfortunately, alt.smokers is regularly "flamed" by others with a contrary purpose, a "flame" being a nasty, rude and meanspirited message.

The following flames posted to alt.smokers by persons whose hatred of smoking is matched only by their unacquaintance with good English are cited by Joe Dawson on his Internet page, "Essays on the Anti-Smoking Movement."[1]

From rka@ix.netcom.com:

> I am an invironmetal [*sic*] activist and would shove your fags up you [*sic*] ass in an [*sic*] heartbeat to save the ozone. I mean if it takes the abliteration [*sic*] of and [*sic*] addictive drug to do so, then by myself(god) [*sic*] do it.

From rlm@interlog.com:

> Die. Do it now. You are completely worthless. You have nothing to contribute to society. You are nothing but a drain on our resources. If I was as fucked up as you are I would buy a gun and blow my brains out. And I'd do it "right now."

From hhh3@crux2.cit.cornell.edu):

> I'd say that taking a dump in public would be more justified and less offensive than sucking on a cancer stick in public. Shitting cannot be avoided, but drug abuse can be. The smell of shit (with the exception of mine) although offensive, does not kill people. Take your drugs in private, it is the only logical option—besides quitting. Cigarettes are a very vile and repulsive drug delivery system.

From kendall@io.org:

> Non-smokers are complaining, and being heard . . . hence the anti-smoking legislation of the past few years. And we're not done yet. Not until smokers are forced to congregate under disused railway bridges on the edge of town to indulge their horrid habit.

From sylvain@accent.net:

> Smokers should be killed on sight!

From dcitron@gate.net:

> No, it's not really a nasty habit. It's a feelthy [*sic*], self-destructive, childish, inconsiderate, stupid, polluting, breathtaking, oxygen-depriving, Kevorkianistic, self-indulgent, polluting [*sic*], breath-fouling, addictive, brain-cell-killing, emphysema-inducing, peer-group-impressing, ozone-depleting, politically incorrect habit, laden with Freudian phallic symbolism.

"Dcitron," a frequent interloper at alt.smokers, also likes to append this "signature" to his messages: "Smokers! Don't kill yourself by inches—Get FAST-FAST-FAST relief! Call Dr. Kevorkian today!"

Out of morbid curiosity, I looked into alt.smokers myself and had no trouble finding other examples of the low regard, to put it mildly, in which smokers and smoking are held by some persons expressing themselves from the relative anonymity of their computer keyboards.

From rlm@intercom.com (again):

> Smoking kills. If you smoke you are either a moron or a murderer or more likely both. And soon you will either be dead or be caged. And maybe in some states you will be executed. Hopefully it will be televised, although furiously sucking on that last cigarette may fuzz up the video somewhat.

From Steve.Jungersen@worldnet.att.net:

> I know the mention of human excretion generates large numbers of denials from the smokers but many of us non-smokers

consider being around smokers to be just as bad as being around someone defecating. This is something we all do but we do it in private. I see very few people pissing in front of a restaurant simply because their [*sic*] is no non-pissing sign posted. This is what we want for smoking. Smoke only in designated areas. I would be happy to fight the battle to place smoking cubicles throughout the area.

From geoffm@netcom.com:

Good manners to a nonsmoker means refraining from dousing smokers with fire extinguisher efflux or buckets of stale dogpiss. Good manners to smokers means quitting now before you either make yourself a pariah in an increasingly sane and nonsmoking world or else die in screaming, writhing, cathetized [*sic*], cancerous agony that even morphine won't be able to block . . . The fact of the matter is that maintaining a habit of deliberately inhaling hot, chemically irritating smoke into one's formerly clean, pink lungs is fucking STUPID, and those who perish from doing so represent natural selection in action. You deserve to die, and when you're lying there helpless in your deathbeds, people like me will be pawing through your CD collections and slipping it to your twelve-year-old daughters. And you know something? I'm as serious as a spot on a chest X-ray.

Another from dcitron@gate.net:

Your right to smoke is like your right to masturbate. Do it at home with the doors and windows closed, where it won't adversely affect anyone who does not want to voluntarily participate, and you'll be fine. You DON'T have a right to smoke or a right to masturbate in a public place where it will affect others. Kill yourself with cancer—see if we care!

Another from Steve.Jungersen@worldnet.att.net:

As an employer, I don't have a complete ban on hiring smokers but their blatant display of stupidity is a definate [*sic*] consideration when deciding who [*sic*] to hire . . . [I]t's my business and I sure don't want to trust it to someone who doesn't know enough to stop killing himself.

And one more, whose e-mail handle I didn't catch:

The agonizing death in store for most smokers is deserved. Screw you and learn to pay your own medical bills you parasitic bastards.

One might hope that the kind of people who equate smoking with excretion or masturbation are simply uneducated and lacking in taste, not to mention imagination. Yet the address of the third message cited by Dawson suggests that its writer was either a student at or was associated in some way with Cornell University. For another example of the intellectual benefits of higher education, consider the following excerpt from an article written by a lecturer at Massachusetts Institute of Technology.

> I . . . have the misfortune to be a low-ranking academic working in a building named after a highly respected scientist who wanders through the building smoking a pipe. He's twice my age and I feel rather awkward about having to tell him that he stinks. I respect him myself, which makes it that much harder . . .
>
> Walking into an office in which someone has just been smoking is like walking into a room which has just been tear-gassed . . . [I]f an MIT employee were to urinate on the floor of a public area, nobody would suggest that the other people who work in that area be required to bear the burden of negotiating about it. And yet tobacco is both more offensive in smell and more of a health hazard than urine . . .[2]

And this was written in 1985, before the antismokers* started getting *really* mean!

What priggish self-righteousness! Possibly its author is now a professor himself, imparting wisdom to a new generation. Maybe he'll even have a building named after him someday. (Entrance strictly limited to the pure of scent, and that includes pipe smokers like you, Albert Einstein, wherever you are.)

Such extreme, I would even say pathological, hatred of smoking as exhibited above is the product of the increasingly rabid antismoking propaganda of the past couple decades. One never heard such venomous characterizations of smokers before the antis latched onto the "secondhand smoke" issue.

The scatological nature of some of the messages above also suggests to me that there is a parallel between smoking and pornography.

*It is important to make a distinction between antismokers and nonsmokers. Every antismoker is a nonsmoker but not all nonsmokers are antismokers —though the antis are doing their best to change that and, unfortunately, seem to be succeeding.

I mean their histories, not the connection between smoking and sex that I discuss in Chapter 9. That is, some people have always hated either or both. But there is a more interesting "antiparallel." In this country, for most of the 19th and 20th centuries, aversion to pornography was institutionalized in laws ruthlessly suppressing it—not only the *real* stuff, the stuff we "know when we see it," but also borderline material that doesn't raise an eyebrow today. Yet in the past 30 years, although laws against it may remain on the books, hard-core pornography has become readily available to anyone who wants it, while in the same period smoking, which before was freely indulged in almost anywhere by anyone who wanted to indulge in it, has become the object of public condemnation and laws severely restricting it. Strange . . .

Fortunately, the so-called radical right or Christian right is so preoccupied with pornography, along with abortion, homosexuality, school prayer and the teaching of evolution in the schools, that it has been conspicuous by its nonparticipation in the antismoking crusade, yet it has largely escaped criticism for that.

One exception was an article in *Mother Jones* magazine. Even though smoking is (allegedly) responsible for 115,000 miscarriages a year, it noted, groups such as the Christian Coalition who are firmly against abortion rarely say anything about smoking.[3] Another was in a column in *USA Today*. Averring "that smoking kills at least 100 times as many babies every year as 'partial abortions,'" Susan Estrich asked the prolife movement, "How can you be against abortion and not against tobacco?"[4]

The hatred of, or certainly the *dislike* of, tobacco dates as far back as Western civilization's first encounter with that noble plant in the New World. As early as 1604, only a generation after John Rolfe or Drake or Hawkins or other sea captains introduced the leaf to England and men like Sir Walter Raleigh had made it popular, King James I issued his famous *Counterblaste* in which he denounced "the Indian vice" in a much-quoted passage as "a custome lothsome to the eye, hatefull to the nose, harmefull to the braine, daungerous to the Lungs, and in the blacke stinking fume thereof, nearest resembling the horrible Stigian smoke of the pit that is bottomeless."

The king's extravagant language differs from contemporary "flames" only in being more literate and expressive; the intemperance displayed in both are identical. Intemperance? Try paranoia.

How did the venerable use and enjoyment of tobacco fall to its sorry state today in the brief span of three decades, in less than half my own lifetime? As a smoker for those three decades plus nearly two decades before them, I think about my background and life experiences and the reasons why I cannot, despite all the so-called evidence that has persuaded others, share in the universal fear and loathing and condemnation of smoking. And why—perhaps because of the skepticism about all medical authority the smoking issue has engendered in me—I am unable to join the general panic regarding environmental perils of any kind.

My peephole on the world (to appropriate that felicitous conceit of Kurt Vonnegut's) opened in 1927 in the Borough of Avalon, Pennsylvania, a suburb about six miles from downtown Pittsburgh but actually a continuation of it because Avalon is, and always was in this century, solidly connected to the city by homes and buildings: first Pittsburgh, then the North Side (once the independent city of Allegheny), then Bellevue, then Avalon, then other boroughs farther down the Ohio River.

I was the third of four children: a boy, a girl, then two more boys. We lived on the corner of Elizabeth Avenue and the Ohio River Boulevard, overlooking the river of that name. A little-used road when my newly married parents settled there in 1920, the boulevard had during my babyhood been made into a four-lane highway leading directly to Pittsburgh by means of a series of bridges over ravines and was considered to be a triumph of engineering. Traffic to and from Pittsburgh was incessant and heavy even by today's standards. We lived not only with the constant noise of cars and trucks pounding on the brick pavement only a few feet from our house but with exhaust fumes from leaded gasoline and, no doubt, asbestos and rubber particles thrown into the air from brake linings and tires.

Across the boulevard, below a bluff, were four railroad tracks running alongside the river, the frequent trains contributing their own noise as well as coal smoke, which would billow up the bluff in clouds. The river itself was plied by coal-fueled steamboats, adding yet more smoke to the general pollution.

On the other side of the river, directly opposite our house, was Neville Island, an industrial complex where LSTs (landing ships for troops or tanks) were fabricated during World War II. Even before that, despite lessened manufacturing activity during the Depression, Pittsburgh was heavily polluted by smoke and other emissions from its many steel mills, pollution we breathed every day of our lives.

Pittsburgh fully deserved its nickname of "The Smoky City" and its inhabitants knew that it did. I remember a gloomy picture on the front page of *The Pittsburgh Press* sometime in the 1930s taken at high noon on a winter day on Liberty Avenue in the heart of downtown. All the streetlights and car lights were on. It was as if it were midnight.

Everybody heated by coal in those days. I can remember as a child one time kneeling by the big window facing our front porch watching the soot collect on the outside sill (a phenomenon I was not to see again until many years later when I lived for a year on Manhattan Island). We took the dirt and pollution for granted.

A truckload of coal was dumped in our driveway a couple times each winter. After my older brother went off to the Army it was my job, and later that of my younger brother, to shovel the coal through a window into a bin under the front porch. We would periodically have to crawl into the bin to push the coal back from the window with our hands, of necessity breathing in its black dust and getting it all over ourselves. Inside the cellar proper we'd carry the coal from the bin to the furnace in a scuttle. More dirty work.

Near the end of our days in Avalon my father had an "Iron Fireman" installed on the furnace, which automatically fed coal into the fire pit from a hopper by means of an Archimedes screw. This required the use of pebble-size coal called pea coal. It was much easier shoveling pea coal into the bin instead of big lumps, but it was a no less dirty job. You also had to pick out pieces of shale, which could jam the screw, and frequently did.

One advantage of coal was that we never had to worry about negotiating our steep driveway or the hills of Avalon in wintertime; the borough always had plenty of ashes and cinders to spread on the streets when it snowed. The pea coal used by our Iron Fireman, however, did not turn into ashes but into hard, doughnut-shaped "clinkers." We removed the red-hot clinkers with tongs and put them in a bucket to cool —where they must have emitted all kinds of fumes into the household air—then carried them across Elizabeth Avenue to the borough dump. This was a once-beautiful ravine adjoining several acres of woods where we played, until after World War II when what was left of the ravine was filled in and the woods cut down and houses and new streets built on the land.

As I said, we Pittsburghers knew we lived in a filthy environment. One day in hygiene class we were told that the lungs of a native of Pittsburgh were black, while those of someone living in the clean countryside were a pristine pink. I for one took a rather perverse pride in knowing that. I'm not sure if we were shown a picture of a pair of black lungs but I do remember visualizing it in my mind. It didn't occur to me that if coal smoke could turn lungs black, as its dust apparently does with coal miners, it would be on the inside of the lungs, not the outside.

Our teachers never said anything about tobacco smoke that I remember, but today we "know" that it also turns one's lungs black and have the pictures to prove it. For example, the "You Can with Beakman and Jax" feature for kids in the comics pages ran comparison pictures of the lungs of a dead nonsmoker and a dead smoker. The former were "healthy, pink and pretty." The latter, said the author of the strip, were full of "black chunks and clogs of gooey tar."[5]

To say it plainly, this was an outright lie, and those who foist such lies on trusting children should be ashamed. There are no such residues from tobacco smoke in a smoker's lungs, whatever he died from.

In May 1996, a group called the Natural Resources Defense Council, which is active in litigation allegedly on behalf of consumers, claimed that "particulate matter"—soot, dust, gaseous droplets and other fine matter emitted by smokestacks and car exhausts—was causing 64,000 Americans a year to die early of heart and lung maladies, even though the levels were far below what the U.S. Environmental Protection Agency (EPA) considers safe. I'd never heard of this organization, but have since come to know it as only one of a number of similar "public advocacy" groups whose raisons d'être are to scare the pants off people with inflated statistics.

(The NRDC's figure of 64,000 pollution-caused deaths was substantially higher than the one EPA administrator Carol Browner cited the following year at a congressional hearing as justification for tougher standards. According to her, (only) as many as 20,000 elderly people were dying prematurely each year and thousands of other adults and children suffered respiratory ailments because of air pollution.[6])

The NRDC reported that Los Angeles was number one among

the 15 worst cities, with 5,873 deaths. (Not "more than 5,000" or "nearly 6,000" but exactly 5,873.) Atlanta, in whose metro area I now live, was ranked almost at the bottom as 14th (good to know!), with an annual death total of (exactly) 946. My old hometown of Pittsburgh was still up there as eighth, with (exactly) 1,216 deaths.[7]

If 1,216 people died from pollution in modern-day, cleaned-up, rebuilt and beautiful Pittsburgh in 1996, I can only wonder how many thousands were succumbing when I was growing up there in the '30s and '40s. We didn't have a National Resources Defense Council or an Environmental Protection Agency to alarm us back then and I don't remember people dropping like flies in the street, but it stands to reason that the far worse pollution in those days must have affected a lot of people, especially older people, with various respiratory problems.

Yet all my family's relatives seemed, in my child's eyes, to live to fairly ripe ages before their peepholes closed. I don't remember any illnesses at all in my siblings, certainly no major ones. My sister, in fact, never missed a day of school and the only days my older brother missed were from playing hooky. The only health problem I had as a young child was "swollen glands" at the age of 5, followed by a tonsillectomy, a popular surgery in those days which my younger brother (who has been a smoker almost as long as I have) also underwent. And the only really serious disease I ever contracted was pneumonia at the age of 12, which was caused not by pollution but by a bacterium, the same one that carried off my maternal grandmother and many elderly people back then. (Incidentally, the best place to catch pneumonia today is in the hospital, where HAP—Hospital-Acquired Pneumonia—is the leading cause of morbidity and mortality among patients hospitalized for something else.[8])

As if pollution were not enough to kill us all early, my family also indulged in a diet rich in fats (a diet I continue to enjoy today, as much as my wife will let me). Each morning Otto's Dairy would deliver two quarts of milk to our doorstep. They gave you the cream with the milk in those days and the bottles had a bulge at the top where it collected. On cold winter mornings the cream would freeze and expand and pop the paper cap off the bottle. My mother had a special curved spoon that fit into the bulge that she used to retrieve the cream by inserting the spoon into the bottle and turning it upside down. We had whipped cream with dessert nearly every day. Ignorant of the dangers of eating meat, we had that nearly every day too, for my father was one of the fortunate ones who never missed a payday even during the Depression.

We lived and moved and had our beings amid other hazards I've forgotten, but my memories include helping my mother clean clothes with (later banned) carbon tetrachloride at an open basement window but still breathing in a lot of the fumes, helping my father paint the gutters with "red lead" paint (also banned today), riding my bike without a helmet (not yet federally mandated) on the streets of Avalon and shooting off firecrackers on the Fourth of July. No doubt there were many other "risk behaviors" we didn't know about and thus didn't worry about.

My father also smoked, throughout my childhood and that of my brothers and sister—first cigarettes, then, just as I was old enough to wish I could rescue butts from his ashtray, he switched to cigars and pipes, then in his last years to chewing tobacco. I can still see myself sitting next to him at the dining room table as he helped me with some homework and watching the smoke he blew from his pipe at the lamp in the center of the table rise out of the top of the shade.

My mother never smoked but her younger sister, whom I remember as something of a black sheep in the family, did smoke, as well as drink. She had married a former professional Canadian hockey player, who also smoked and who always smelled of alcohol when they came to visit. It was probably from him that my aunt learned these vices. Unfortunately, she died in her 30s from some illness shortly after the birth of a daughter, but she lived longer than two other siblings of my mother's, a sister who died in infancy and a brother who died in early childhood. Death was an all-too-familiar visitor to the nursery when my mother was a girl.

CIGARETTES AND cigarette smoke intrigued me as a youngster, particularly that from the end of a burning cigarette, the so-called "sidestream" smoke which is so terribly dangerous today. I liked to visit the kitchen of the house next door where a playmate of my own age lived and watch his stepmother, an attractive woman, as she smoked Lucky Strike after Lucky Strike. I was fascinated by the way the smoke would rise from the end of a cigarette resting in her ashtray in a smooth, layered, transparent ribbon until it suddenly broke into curling eddies—or as Richard Klein describes it in *Cigarettes Are Sublime*, "the intricate syntax of its swirling articulations."[9] (I wouldn't have understood those words as a child; I'm not sure I understand them now.)

I must have been about seven or eight when I first tried smoking myself. My father still smoked cigarettes at that time and I filched one from an ashtray in the living room and carried it down to the basement. There, sitting next to the washing machine, I lit it. I must have inadvertently inhaled, for I experienced the most delicious dizzy sensation. I guess you would call it a "high" or a nicotine "hit." One or two subsequent puffs from the short butt, however, did not produce the same result, possibly because I didn't inhale—or maybe because one puff had already made me a veteran smoker? In any case, I did not cough uncontrollably or become sickened, as conventional antismoking wisdom proclaims is the invariable reaction of a first-time smoker.

Nor would I then, nor can I now after 53 years of smoking, agree with Klein when he asserts that "[E]very smoker probably intuits the poison [of nicotine] from the instant of experiencing the first violent effects of lighting up, and probably confirms this understanding every day with the first puffs of the first cigarette."[10]

His twice-use of the word "probably" is well-advised for I have never intuited any such thing. Klein writes as a man who loved and still loves cigarettes, or the memory of them, and who is trying to persuade himself that he's glad he doesn't use them anymore. Along with millions of others he has been brainwashed into quitting because, as he says more than once in his book, "Cigarettes are bad for your health." He doesn't say how long he smoked but one assumes cigarettes weren't bad for *his* health, or surely he would have said so.

(Klein has since written a book called *Eat Fat* in which he extols the delights of fat-laden gourmet food but, according to a review of it I read, expresses no concerns about the possible health consequences of such an indulgence.[11])

Strangely enough, enjoyable as that first experience with a cigarette was, I never thought about smoking again for years (nor, alas, was I ever again to get that same "high," even with inhaling). I vaguely remember trying cornsilk one time but don't know whether I attempted to make a cigarette out of it or how I intended to smoke it. In any case I couldn't get it lit. There also were some trees in the neighborhood that had long, thin pods hanging down from the branches that we called Indian stogies. If you held a match to one end of a pod and sucked hard enough on the other end you could sort of "smoke" it. It wasn't until I was in my early teens, however, that I started seriously experimenting with cigarettes. Another boyhood chum, Johnnie Z., had a little shack in his backyard where we would smoke them. Where he or I got them, I don't recall, but they were whole cigarettes, not butts, and unfiltered of course, which left yellow stains on the index and middle fingers. After smoking I would sniff the stains, until they were washed off.

When I was a little older and when nobody was looking (for kids weren't supposed to smoke, even in those unenlightened days), I got my cigarettes from a vending machine in the Colonial, a restaurant/dancehall/bowling alley on the boulevard, where I worked as a pinboy. They were a quarter a pack, with two cents change enclosed in the cellophane wrapper. But I still didn't know how to inhale. A fellow pinboy disdainfully mocked me one time for my prissy manner of smoking. He showed me how it was done.

I loved cigarettes. Either in my friend's shack or upstairs in my third-floor bedroom I loved looking at and handling a package before opening it, then smelling the aroma of fresh tobacco (even tobacco-haters concede it's pleasant), admiring the way the cigarettes themselves were formed, marveling at how they were packed so tightly in the package—two rows of seven, one of six in the middle. I became intimately acquainted with the visage of De Witt Clinton, early 19th-century governor of New York and promoter of the Erie Canal, whose portrait was on the blue federal excise tax strip for some reason. ("20 Class A Cigarettes," it said. I've always wondered if there were other classes. The tax strip was discontinued years ago, I don't know why.) I loved looking at and handling cigarettes almost as much as smoking them, almost as much as blowing out huge clouds of smoke at the open bedroom window, almost as much as watching the ribbon of smoke curl up from the end.

My parents never knew about my smoking at the bedroom window (at least I don't think so), but some years earlier my mother had found a pack of Camels my older brother, who was probably about 14 at the time, had carelessly left in the pocket of a pair of pants due to be washed, and she was rather upset. I was only caught once myself, when I was also about 14. I was on the street with some friends when my father, walking down the hill from the streetcar stop on California Avenue, spotted me with a cigarette in my hand. He said nothing until I got home, and then merely told me he wished I would wait until I was at least 16 and preferably 18, and then if I wanted to smoke it was all right with him. He didn't exact a promise from me, however, nor did I make one.

I tried all the brands available from the vending machine in the bowling alley: Camel, Chesterfield, Lucky Strike, Pall Mall, Phillip Morris, Raleigh, even Kools. I liked Chesterfields because of their elegant name and package design. In fact, it was package design more than anything else that governed my choices. An exception was Pall Malls, which I came to prefer because of their extra length, even though I thought the red package rather garish. Conversely, I disdained Philip Morrises because of their dull tan package. As for Kools, only in desperation would I smoke menthols. Otherwise, all the brands seemed essentially the same. The parents of one of my friends smoked Raleighs exclusively because each pack had a coupon on it redeemable for various items from a catalog—if you accumulated a few thousand or so of them.

I adored cigarettes. While other guys may have fantasized about girls (which I did too) I fantasized about having my own cigarette company. I saw an ad one time for a brand called English Ovals which, as the name indicated, were not round but oval-shaped. I wondered how they made them that way. It would be neat, I thought, to bring out my own brand of cigarettes. Another brand I don't believe I ever tried but which interested me was called Vogue, if memory serves. These came in a variety of pastel colors.

I experimented with rolling my own cigarettes with Bugler tobacco and papers. Not very satisfactory and far inferior to tailor-mades. I never mastered forming them with two hands, much less one-handedly as cowboys could do sitting on their horses, but they were a good-tasting if messy and too-brief smoke. I wished I had a cigarette rolling machine like a friend of my older brother who lived on Elizabeth Avenue had and who I often watched making them.

(That wish was to be granted in the 1970s when Brown & Williamson introduced Laredo. The tobacco came loose in a three-ounce can to be used with paper tubes that had filters on the ends. You made the cigarettes one at a time with a little machine that used a plunger to insert the tobacco into the tubes, a great advance over the Bugler machine that rolled the cigarettes. I later purchased a similar machine and tubes and bulk tobacco from a company in Kentucky. My wife and I both smoked homemade cigarettes for a year or so until the novelty wore off and it became too much bother to make them. Anyway, not only were tailor-mades pretty cheap but you got *double* green stamps on Tuesdays at the cigarette counter at the May Company department store in Cleveland, where we then lived.)

Another teenage memory is of buying a pack of Players during a family trip to Canada to visit my widowered uncle and saving them until we got back home. (The legal age for buying cigarettes in Canada in those benighted days was 15, I believe. Not any more, of course.) They were in a cardboard box instead of a paper package. Sitting in a chair before the third-floor window, my feet up on the radiator, I smoked one each day until they were gone. They were excellent, better than American brands, I thought. Some years later I found a brand called Dunhill that had that Canadian or English taste—$1.75 a carton, plus green stamps!—but they eventually disappeared from the market. The next time I smoked a Canadian cigarette wasn't until 1997, when on a trip to see my cousin I bought a carton of Craven "A" at the duty-free shop at the border. To my disappointment, they didn't have that taste I remembered.

The medical establishment would disagree, but I was not "addicted" to smoking at this stage in my life. It was a sometime, secretive thing, very much associated with budding sexuality, for either smoking made me horny or natural adolescent horniness made me want to smoke. (Don't miss Chapter 9!) Nor was I yet enslaved by nicotine even later when, in 1945, I graduated from high school and spent a year at Carnegie Institute of Technology, now Carnegie Mellon Institute, where I studied music, and smoked daily. We smokers would indulge in this vile behavior freely in the halls of the Fine Arts building and even in the small practice rooms. And no nonsmokers, of whom there were many, ever complained or gave the slightest indication of discomfort or disapproval or suggested they would rather we urinated on the floor instead. But as I said, those were unenlightened times.

(This has nothing to do with smoking, but another memory of those halcyon days at Carnegie Tech is of a heavy wooden table in the second-floor hall of the Fine Arts building next to a huge statue of, I think, Silenus holding the infant Bacchus, or one of those gods. Anyway, someone had discovered—we were music students, after all—

that if several of us would hum a certain low note in unison we could make the huge table vibrate and even jump on the marble floor. Another example of the benefits of higher education.)

It was not until my 19th year, however, on a troopship bound for Japan, that I made the conscious decision to smoke fulltime. Why I did, I don't know; I'd really only been an occasional smoker up until then. There was of course not much else to do during a 21-day voyage on a hellship called the *S.S. General Black* in November 1946. There was also not much to eat. After the first few days, when many of my fellow soldiers were seasick and I could clean up the plates they suddenly abandoned in the mess hall, we virtually starved. There was, however, a flourishing black market in food stolen from the galley by crew members who worked there. I eventually became desperate enough to pay $5 for a few inches of smoked sausage. I lost 21 pounds during that voyage, a pound for each day of it. In any case, I started smoking cigarettes regularly then. Today, more than half a century later, I still do.

UNTIL 1952 I smoked king-size unfiltered brands, mostly Pall Mall. Why I did is another thing I can't explain because filtered cigarettes were available and with unfiltereds I was always annoyed by the bits of tobacco that would get on your tongue and the way the cigarette would stick to your lips. You had to be careful to keep your lips moistened enough to prevent that, but not so moist as to make the end soggy. (Making the end soggy was described by an offensive racist term that cannot be repeated here.) It used to irritate my father when I tapped the end of a cigarette against something to pack the tobacco down. He thought it was pretentious and effete, something actresses did in the movies.

Then in 1952, amid much ballyhoo, Lorillard brought out Kent cigarettes with the "Micronite" filter. I paid no attention to advertising claims regarding the supposed health advantages of this "revolutionary" filter but tried Kents on the recommendation of a friend. I liked them, not knowing that the filters contained a type of asbestos called crocidilite that was used in shipbuilding in World War II and, I have read, is the only form of the mineral that is dangerous, unlike the asbestos once used in brake linings and insulation and fireproofing and which is ubiquitous in the environment.[12] (Nevertheless, despite its relative harmlessness, the more familiar kind of asbestos was to become the object of a vast and costly health scare engineered by the EPA (see Chapter 11). According to the Dana Farber Cancer Research Institute in Boston, 27 out of 33 men employed in making Micronite filters died prematurely from lung cancer or other "asbestos-related" diseases.[13] I smoked nothing but Kents for the four years crocidilite was used in the filter and after that stayed with Kents almost exclusively for another 30 or so years, until the cigarette companies started jacking up the prices of name brands and I switched to cheaper generics. I never developed lung cancer from the crocidilite and so am unable to sue the company as a number of people have done, successfully in at least three cases.[14]

When I started writing this book I decided to try an unfiltered cigarette for the first time in more than 40 years and bought a pack of regular Camels and a whole carton of Pall Malls because I'd received a $2 coupon in the mail. Both packages were the same as they had been since before I was born. I was so used to "lights" that they seemed a little strong to me, although by the time I finished the carton of Pall Malls I was pretty used to them. But again there was that problem of tobacco bits in the mouth and the paper sticking to the lips. I am surprised that some people still smoke such short little things as regular Camels, which are good for only few drags before they burn down. I also decided to try a couple name brands for the first time in 10 years to see if I was missing anything and bought a carton of Marlboro Lites and one pack of Benson & Hedges Lites. They were very smooth, but not so great that I am willing to spend the money they ask for them.

Today, I confess that I don't enjoy smoking as much as I used to. Maybe I've outgrown it, or maybe I'm tired of being lectured by my ex-smoker wife, or maybe because incessant antismoking propaganda has taken a lot of the pleasure out it. Although I smoke constantly while sitting alone at my computer, I smoke very little or not at all at other times. I can't remember the last time I smoked in a social setting. While I have never manifested "typical smoker's cough," honesty compels me to admit that since undertaking this book, smoking heavily at the word processor, I have started bringing up small globs of phlegm occasionally. (Do I hear a chorus of "*A-ha!*s"?) But this just means that the cilia in my tracheobronchial tree are doing their thing, though they supposedly should have been destroyed years ago. As long as they keep on doing what they're designed to do, I won't worry about it.

I might very well have quit smoking some time ago, except that I don't want to do anything to encourage the antismoking establishment—which by the way is a true establishment, battening on taxpayer subsidies, and in California and Massachusetts is supported by money extorted exclusively from smokers. I also want to set an example for younger people.

TO SUM UP, THAT'S where I am "coming from" regarding smoking, as well as environmental pollution and unhealthy habits in general. I am not a doctor, I have only a layman's acquaintance with medicine. All I really know about smoking derives from personal experience and from observing other people, plus whatever common sense I flatter myself as possessing. After 53 years of steady smoking, I remain not merely in good health but in ***robust*** good health. I have known but two people who could reasonably be said to have been injured by smoking—my wife's older sister, who died in her late 60s of what we were told was emphysema, and my wife, who suffered a minor stroke and light heart attack shortly afterward. But in the 23 years I knew my sister-in-law, she was a painfully thin woman with no substance to her. As for my wife, she had been under severe emotional stress during her sister's final days.

Not that I would even attempt to argue with a doctor that factors other than, or in addition to, smoking might possibly have been involved in these cases. The fact remains, however, that everyone else I personally know or have known who has had serious medical problems is or was a lifelong ***nonsmoker***.

Personal experience and observation are limited, of course, and "common sense" can often be dead wrong. Primitive common sense tells us that the earth is flat and that the sun revolves around it; only thanks to verifiable scientific observation do we know what is really going on. (And then the scientific explanation becomes common sense.) Common sense also suggests that drawing the fumes from burning vegetable matter into your lungs hundreds of times a day for years on end cannot be a very healthy thing to do. But because I personally have seen such little evidence of harm to anyone who does it, while observing so many health problems in others who don't do it, the claims of medical science regarding the dangers of smoking simply underwhelm my experience-informed common sense.

(Writer Michael Fumento suggests that the term "common knowledge" is more meaningful than "common sense" because it implies something "known by most people."[15] But common knowledge would be no help to me in writing this book because today the common—indeed, the universal—knowledge is that smoking causes disease and death. It's been conclusively proven, hasn't it? Yet it was also once common knowledge among doctors that bloodletting was good for just about anything that ailed you.)

Any doctor reading this far would consider me either very lucky or willfully ignorant or an idiot or, if not one of those, would assume I must be getting a payoff from the tobacco industry. A psychotherapist would say that I am obviously "in denial" about the dangers of smoking. But the shrinks say that about anybody who disagrees with them. In fact, I'm waiting for the American Psychiatric Association to add smoking to its list of mental "disorders" in its Diagnostic and Statistical Manual (DSM).*

Maybe if I were a doctor or had anything to do with medical care I would think differently. I'm sure doctors could tell me all kinds of stories about the dire effects of smoking in patients they've treated. But these days, any history of smoking in a patient is prima facie evidence that his illness was caused by smoking. Anyway, doctors usually treat only sick people—that's their job; healthy people have no urgent reason to come to them, whether they smoke or not.

My sister's husband, a reformed smoker (the worst kind of ex-smoker), has done voluntary work in a hospital and says, every time he talks to me, "If you could see what I've seen, you'd quit those stupid cigarettes." Yeah, well, what he thinks he's seen in some unfortunate sick persons in the hospital and what actually put them there may be

*Believe it or not, the hundreds of disorders in the DSM—some of which, if diagnosed in a patient by a therapist, can be used to deprive a person of his livelihood, his home, his children and his freedom—are there by virtue of having been *voted* on by panels of psychiatrists, with each disorder subject to revision or deletion in the next edition. For many years, homosexuality, for example, was listed as a psychiatric "disorder" until the gays achieved enough political clout to force it to be removed. Imagine real scientists, physicists, say, deciding on the boiling point of water by means of a ballot.

Today, therapists can keep up to date on changes in the DSM through computer programs such as one called Therascribe™ 3.0. By pointing and clicking with their mouse at a list of problems, they can let the computer come up with appropriate diagnoses and treatment plans for their patients.

two entirely different matters. Again, it's sick people, not healthy people, who check into hospitals, whether they smoke or not.

What about the fact that smokers who get lung cancer or emphysema or any of a host of other diseases outnumber by far nonsmokers so afflicted? All I will say at this point is that those numbers we commonly hear about do not necessarily represent actual people but are extrapolations from epidemiological studies, which are far from unassailable. For a fuller answer I urge the reader to progress further into this book.

But consider lung cancer for a minute, or any other kind of cancer for that matter. A cancer is a cancer and the most experienced oncologist in the world, let alone my brother-in-law, cannot even *guess* what may have caused it without a knowledge of a patient's lifestyle, habits and medical and family history, which can only be obtained from the patient himself or, in many cases, the recollections of other people. And when the doctor does learn these things, his attribution of the cause of the cancer becomes an informed guess, but still a guess. By the same token, the most skilled physician in the world has no way of knowing whether a healthy person who comes in for a routine checkup is or is not a smoker or has ever smoked unless that person tells him.*

It may be a different matter with more detailed examination. When my wife had a chest X-ray at age 78, the radiologist said he saw evidence in her lungs that she had been a smoker, even though she'd quit 15 years before. However, she isn't sure if he said this before or after she told him she used to smoke. Whatever the evidence was, 47 years of heavy smoking had caused no impairment in the *function* of her lungs.

On the other hand, the previous year I had both a regular chest X-ray and a CAT scan of my lungs and nothing was said about any evi- of a smoking history, although that could be because the doctor was already aware that I smoked—which was in fact why he ordered the unnecessary CAT scan in the first place.

*This may not be true in the future. The Food and Drug Administration has approved a new urine test called "NicCheck" which enables a physician to determine whether and how much a person smokes.[16] I would think that it could be defeated simply by a smoker's refraining from smoking for a day or two until the nicotine, or rather its derivative cotinine, cleared his urine. But it raises the possibility that those companies that refuse to employ smokers, even if they only smoke away from the job, could conduct random, unannounced urine tests to ferret out the violators.

To complicate matters, many smokers are becoming increasingly reluctant to tell doctors about their habit, lest they set themselves up for a lecture. That is why the American Medical Association urges doctors to be "aggressive" in identifying patients who smoke. According to the U.S. Agency for Health Care Policy and Research (AHCPR), an arm of the U.S. Department of Health and Human Services, "only about half of current smokers report having ever been asked about their smoking status."[17]

To remedy that situation, the AHCPR has issued guidelines, among which are:

- Ask every patient at every visit if they [*sic*] smoke.
- Write a patient's smoking status in the medical chart under vital signs.
- Motivate patients reluctant to quit.

Note the use of "asked" and "ask." The knowledge that a patient is or was a smoker, which knowledge can only be imparted by the patient himself,* greatly simplifies a doctor's work, for once smoking has been implicated in the etiology of a given disease, no further investigation into other possible factors need be undertaken.

Indeed, by way of making things simpler for medical personnel, the government actually provides "alert" stickers to be put on a patient's hospital chart if he's a smoker. I sent for some from the Centers for Disease Control and Prevention (CDC) in Atlanta and received a sheet of 35 stickers, each an inch-and-a-half-square. Printed on them in dark blue ink are stripes at the top, like the markings on the pavement

*The observant reader will notice that throughout this book I use third-person masculine pronouns—he, him, his, himself—when referring to no one in particular or everyone in general. This should not be construed as a put-down of the female sex or a want of "gender sensitivity" on my part; it is simply that, as I remain unregenerate regarding smoking, so I am when it comes to the politically correct use of language. Some writers, mostly male, probably, give equal time to both sexes: "he and she," "her and him," etc. But this becomes repetitious and only draws attention to itself. Others have thrown in the towel all the way and employ the feminine pronouns exclusively, a practice I find both condescending and distracting and sometimes confusing. ("Is the writer talking about a woman? What woman? Where did she come from?)

of a no-parking area; on the right side is a curling wisp of smoke, and on the bottom the word SMOKER. According to a U.S. Government Printing Office catalog where I learned about them, the stickers are to placed "in a conspicuous location on the outside or inside of the patient chart to remind clinicians and staff of specific ongoing preventive care needs."[18]

Just what is the purpose of this? Is the disease a smoker is suffering from different from the same disease in a nonsmoker? Is the treatment different? Is the patient's doctor helped in any way? I don't think so. Maybe "preventive care" means keeping an eye on a patient to see that he doesn't sneak a smoke out on the balcony or in the bathroom or a closet. But in that case, making him wear a badge or a sign around his neck saying SMOKER would be a more useful "alert" to clinicians and staff than a sticker on a chart. I can't believe any doctor would actually brand a patient in this gratuitously humiliating way. All the doctors I've known have been pretty compassionate people. But the fact that the government makes the stickers available and encourages their use is another indication of the hysteria concerning smoking that infects society today.

Actually, "preventive care" probably means "intervention" (to save smokers from themselves) and the government is not only encouraging it but paying for it. In 1996 three hospitals in Minnesota were the beneficiaries of a $2.5-million grant from the National Heart and Lung Institute of the National Institutes of Health to fund a project to test "methods to promote long-term smoking cessation in hospital patients." Key components of this "intervention" included: (1) organized identification of all smokers as part of the normal admittance procedure; (2) clear labeling of charts of both smokers and nonsmokers—red dot for nonsmokers and black dot for smokers (to match the color of their lungs?); (3) a smoking card clipped to the outside of the chart by office staff at the time of the visit; (4) brief physician counseling about smoking, and (5) follow-up counseling for a year after discharge.[19]

And how can you tell a smoker from a nonsmoker, both of whom are ill enough to be admitted to a hospital? At risk of boring the reader, I have to say it again: only by *asking* them.

On a funnier, but still rather sad, note, there is, or was until somebody stole it, a sign on the wall at the San Francisco Department of

Public Health which said NO SMOKING, and below it repeated the same message—*in Braille.*[20] I'm sure there are some blind smokers, even though a great deal of the enjoyment of smoking is derived from seeing the smoke. But it seems rather unlikely that an unsighted visitor to the department would grope along the wall to find out if smoking was permitted. Possibly the Braille warning was required by the Americans With Disabilites Act, or somebody's interpretation of it. After all, Big Brother is looking out for the welfare of all of us.

(Which reminds me of an evangelist named Herbert W. Armstrong, whom I used to listen to years ago on the radio and who liked to point out that nobody smokes in the dark. He somehow thought this was a good argument against smoking. It was, if he had meant smoking in bed. Otherwise he was wrong, for people do sometimes smoke in the dark, either because they are desperate for a nicotine fix or maybe simply because they like to smoke. It's possible, too, that some people still indulge in the proverbial postcoital cigarette.)

ONE NEED NOT be a hospital patient or cruise alt.smokers to encounter gratuitous slaps at smokers; they pop up all the time on television shows, even if they have nothing to do with the story line, and usually they don't.

For instance, in one episode of "Seinfeld," a man asked Jerry if he minded if he smoked and Jerry replied, "No, I secondhand smoke two packs of cigarettes a day." In another episode, Jerry, George and Elaine were sitting down at their favorite table in Monk's Café and Elaine spotted an ashtray on the table. "Ugh," she said most vehemently, moving the ashtray to another table. "Cigarettes—*I hate them.*" (When I saw this I thought, "Hmm, I wonder what this bit of business is going to lead to." But cigarettes were never mentioned again. In a later episode, smoking was no longer permitted in the restaurant.)

On the other hand, both Jerry and Elaine, as well as Kramer, sometimes smoked cigars. For some reason, though, cigars seem to be exempt from the opprobrium society (excluding the antis who hate tobacco in all forms) heaps on cigarettes. Indeed, there is even a certain cachet attached to cigar-smoking these days and cigar consumption is soaring. Go figure.

On "Cybill," a nun(!) lit a cigarette in Cybill's house and one of her daughters asked her to take it outside, saying, "If you want to kill yourself that's your business, but please don't take us with you."

On "Touched By An Angel," the angels worked to save the soul of a young lawyer defending a cigarette company in a product-liability lawsuit. (The angel named Monica said she was allergic to cigarette smoke, which seems a little odd in a being that can materialize and dematerialize at will.) The company was a real baddie. Not only had it been killing people but it actually tried to bribe the sovereign government of these United States of America not to release the surgeon general's 1964 report linking smoking to lung cancer.

On an episode of "Northern Exposure," that pipsqueak Dr. Joel Whatshisname and some of the other regulars were sitting in the restaurant and for some reason got on the subject of cannibalism. The doctor indicated a couple guys at another table who were smoking and said you wouldn't want to eat *them*, what with their diseased organs.

In the series "The Practice," a small, struggling law firm representing the widower of a woman who smoked herself to death humbled the arrogant attorney for a heartless cigarette company.

At least "Dr. Quinn, Medicine Woman" never had an episode dramatizing the effects of smoking or chewing tobacco, unless I missed it. This is surprising since she was pretty advanced for her time.

Movies, on the other hand, are raising the ire of the antis because of the frequency of smoking in some of them, especially when it is not intrinsic to the character of the actor who is smoking (that is, he's not a villain) and does not serve the plot development of the film (if there is any).* Since the only movies I see are those that eventually turn up on television, I can't comment authoritatively on the prevalence of smoking in the movies. However, in two I have seen, smoking was hardly portrayed as glamorous.

In "Jurassic Park," a technician in the park's computer room constantly had a lighted cigarette between his lips, which he let burn down to the filter. It had nothing to do with the plot or the character and was

*Hollywood, of course, is notorious for planting commercial products or commercial names in movies. In 1983, Sylvester Stallone signed a letter of agreement with Brown & Williamson guaranteeing that he would use B&W products in five of his films for a fee of $500,000.[21] It's not clear whether Stallone got that all that money or even if B&W got anything for it.

quite distracting to me and I couldn't decide whether this was an antismoking message or a subtle prosmoking one.

In the Steven Seagal action film, "The Glimmer Man," a police detective starts to light a cigarette outside the station and another detective pulls it out of his mouth and tosses it on the ground. The first man doesn't protest; he knows that his partner only did it out of concern for his health. Later in the film, Seagal pulls a cigarette (again unlighted) out of the mouth of another character and throws it to the floor. On "Diagnosis Murder," Dick Van Dyke as Dr. Mark Sloan also frequently extracts cigarettes from between people's fingers or lips, but he places them carefully in an ashtray.

Then there is Steve Martin's clever quip: "Do you mind if I smoke? No, do you mind if I fart?" Which takes us back to the antismokers' fixation on the scatological.

Alarmed at surging cigar sales, health officials in San Francisco launched a campaign (paid for by smokers) featuring advertisements likening cigar butts to dog droppings. Posters were put up near popular nightspots reading: "Cigars: They Look Like What They Smell Like. Don't Put Them in Your Mouth!" Ads on several local cable TV stations showed a dog sniffing at a discarded cigar before its owner swept it up with a pooper-scooper.[22]

"We see this as a public health problem," said Alyonik Hrushow, director of San Francisco's Tobacco-Free Project.

Cigars, I'm sure she meant, not dog droppings.

The so-called funny pages of the newspaper are also doing their bit to get the antismoking message across. In "Curtis," for instance, the boy of that name is constantly nagging his father to quit smoking. Garry Trudeau's Mr. Butts puts in frequent appearances in "Doonesbury," but he is such an engaging character that I wonder if Trudeau's satire doesn't sometimes go over the heads of the young people the propaganda is aimed at.

On television, bad news about smoking is a stock in trade. Whenever there is a report about the "latest finding" against smoking, which seems to be every other day, it is invariably accompanied by extreme closeups of unattractive people desperately sucking on cigarettes. In the newspaper, stories about premature wrinkles allegedly caused by smoking are usually illustrated by a photograph of actress Bette Davis in her last years.

Speaking of wrinkles, even in fiction I came across a wholly irrelevant knock against smoking. This was in an anthology of articles and stories dealing with, of all things, dinosaurs. In one story, a woman is having a drink with a doctor in a wine bar:

> His eyes were on her as they settled on the round cushioned stools across from a fake hogshead table, and she took out and lit a cigarette.
>
> "How many of those a day?"
>
> "Five or six." Julia took one puff and laid down the burning cigarette in the ashtray. "Except I'm like every other person who smokes five—a pack lasts me a day and a half."
>
> "You're going to regret it. It's murder on your skin. Another ten years and you'll look like a prune."[23]

Why would a doctor believe that? (Or the author, expressing his own prejudice?) Well, common sense again, which tells us that because nicotine can constrict the tiny blood vessels called capillaries this must have some effect on the skin, and the facial skin is the most obvious part of the body. But again my own experience and observation tell me otherwise. My wife, who smoked heavily from age 16 to 63, has always looked at least 20 years younger than her actual age. But she also always avoided unnecessary exposure to the sun, unlike her younger sister, a never-smoker but a dedicated sun-worshipper who devoped a serious case of skin cancer on her nose and on at least one occasion has been mistaken for my wife's mother. I have been told I look younger than my age. (Unfortunately, the camera doesn't see it that way.) The next-door playmate whose stepmother's cigarette smoke I used to gaze at told me that when she died at 82 there wasn't a wrinkle on her face.

These may be trivial anecdotes to posit against the "common knowledge" of the medical profession regarding smoking and wrinkles, but they are no less valid, and maybe have even more basis in fact, than some of the outlandish claims put forward by the antismokers in this and other areas. It is this kind of personal observation that has led me to view with a jaundiced eye just about everything the experts claim about smoking.

Novels have become another rich source of antismoking propaganda in which tobacco companies are the new villains. For example, in Christopher Buckley's satire, *Thank You For Smoking*, Nick Naylor, a public relations man working for the "Academy of Tobacco Studies," an industry front group, listens as the woman who fields telephone calls "began to cough . . . 'Academy of—*harrg*—Tobacco—*kuhhh*—Studies.' Nick wondered if having a receptionist who couldn't get through 'hello' without having a bronchospasm was a plus."[24]

Buckley's "Academy" is fictional. So is the receptionist. So is her bronchospasm. No matter; the point is made.

In Arthur Freudberg's *GASP!* an embittered wire service editor, told that he is dying of lung cancer, decides to take the tobacco industry down with him and launches a plan to poison hundreds of packages of cigarettes with cyanide crystals and plant them in stores, restaurants, offices, factories and bars across America. Why not? Smokers are going to die anyway, aren't they? Cyanide will be quicker, better than a lingering, painful death.

In John Grisham's *The Runaway Jury*, poison is also used to remove one waffling member of a jury deciding a lawsuit against a tobacco company. Another suspect member of the panel is eliminated by other means. But it's okay; the poison is nonlethal and it's all in a good cause: simply to help justice along by ensuring a well-deserved verdict against the company. After all, the parents of the wife of the man manipulating the jury both died painfully from lung cancer that she *knows* was caused by smoking the cigarettes to which the rotten, conscienceless manufacturer had deliberately addicted them. Right is right.

Unfortunately, not only in fiction but in real life, some people consider the end—the elimination of smoking—so desirable that it justifies any means to bring it about.

IT CAN BE ARGUED that everything I have said in this Introduction questioning the health dangers of smoking, as well as much of what I say throughout the book, is purely "anecdotal" and proves nothing. That is true. But it is also true that much of the evidence against smoking is also anecdotal. I don't mean the cautionary examples of famous people who smoked and died of lung cancer. The fact is that the thousands upon thousands of epidemiological studies reporting the effects of smoking on the human body are themselves based on, or have as their starting point, anecdotal evidence. That is, the researchers who conduct these studies are wholly dependent upon what people tell them about their lifestyles, health histories and their exposure to cigarette smoke, whether firsthand or secondhand—and even sometimes what a third party, perhaps a surviving spouse, recollects about the smoking habits of someone now dead.

To repeat it one more time, researchers have no way of knowing whether a person smokes or has smoked and how much and for how long unless the person *tells* them, and then, of course, if that person has developed some disease, it's obviously "linked" to smoking. This does not necessarily invalidate such studies, of course. The point is that the findings of epidemiological studies are *suggestive* only and thus must be treated with extreme caution. Regrettably, far too often they are not so treated, especially when reporting them to the lay public.

Epidemiology—the study of the sources and causes of infectious diseases—has a long and glorious history. But that was back when it had to do with things like typhoid or tuberculosis or malaria. As Elizabeth M. Whelan, president of the American Council on Science and Health, says, "No longer are we locked in a mammoth struggle with infectious, communicable disease . . . Today, the major preventable killers present themselves in the form of 'lifestyle factors'—specific behaviors that promote premature disease and death."[25]

A sign of this change from the original mission of epidemiology, thanks to medical science's conquest of the "traditional" diseases, is the fact that only one of the seven centers of the Centers for Disease Control and Prevention is still involved with infectious diseases.

But "lifestyles factors" are infinitely complex. They are the "confounders" that plague modern epidemiology. Also today, the terms "disease" and "epidemic," which once pertained only to germ- or virus-caused communicable infections, mean anything antismokers and professional healthists want them to mean. Smoking, for example, is a "global epidemic," according to the World Health Organization.[26]

IN THE MIDDLE AGES, the Church promulgated what were politely called "pious falsehoods"—fabricated stories about miracles wrought by prayers to the saints or by the relics of saints. They were not *really* lies because they had a noble purpose and were simply the means to achieve a worthwhile end: to fortify the faith of the faithful, convert the pagan and confound the unbeliever.

Modern versions of pious falsehoods fuel the antismoking crusade today. They are frequently called by the term "The LaLonde Effect," named after Marc LaLonde, a former Canadian minister of National Health and Welfare, who maintained that antismoking studies, no matter how flawed or unsupported by real scientific evidence, should nevertheless be promoted to the public. Since we already *know* that smoking is deadly, he reasoned, anything that serves to strengthen that knowledge is justified. Again, the end is all-important; that the means to that end may be scientifically or ethically questionable is inconsequential.

Human beings are in many ways still as credulous as they were in the Middle Ages. For that reason I prefer the term "pious falsehoods," and there are a lot of them about smoking in this book.

Notes

1. Joe Dawson, "Essays on the Anti-Smoking Movement." At www. tezcat. com/smokers/issues1.html.
2. Brian Harvey, "Smoking should only be permitted in private." *The Tech*, Volume 105, Number 51, November 22, 1985, p.10.
3. William Saletan, "Sin of Omission." *Mother Jones*, May/June 1996, p. 58. Courtesy of The Advocacy Institute.
4. Susan Estrich, "When Tobacco, Abortion Converge." *USA Today*, April 25, 1996, p. A13. Courtesy of The Advocacy Institute.
5. "You Can." Comics section. *The Atlanta Journal-Constitution*, March 24, 1996.
6. H. Josef Hebert, "EPA chief says stiffer air standards essential to public health." *The Atlanta Journal-Constitution*, February 13, 1997, p. A12. From the Associated Press.
7. Charles Seabrook, "Tiny particles in air kill 900 every year in Atlanta, study says." *The Atlanta Journal-Constitution*, May 5, 1996, p. B1.

8. Jeanmarie Mayer, M.D., G. Douglas Campbell Jr., M.D., "ATS (American Thoracic Society) Recommendations for Treatment of Adults With Hospital-Acquired Pneumonia." *Infect Med* 13(12): 1027-1029, 1033-1036, 1044,1996. From MedPulse at www.medpulse.com/.

9. Richard Klein, *Cigarettes Are Sublime* (Durham: Duke University Press, 1993), p. 7.

10. Ibid., p. 1.

11. Richard Klein, *Eat Fat* (New York: Vintage, 1998). Reviewed by Jacob Sullum in *Reason* magazine, February 1998, p. 52.

12. Dixy Lee Ray, *Environmental Overkill* (New York: HarperCollins paperback edition, 1993) p. 152.

13. Loc. cit.

14. Scott Solomo, "Lorillard to Pay $140,000 to Estate." *Greensboro* (North Carolina) *News & Record*, March 19, 1996, p. B7. Courtesy of The Advocacy Institute. In this case a San Francisco jury found Lorillard liable in the death of a California man who had smoked Kent cigarettes during the 1960s when the asbestos filter was used. According to the same AI report, in September 1994 Lorillard was ordered to pay $1.8 million to another Kent smoker who sued (apparently he was still alive). A September 3, 1995 item in *The Atlanta Journal-Constitution* reported that a Los Angeles jury had awarded $1.3 million to one Milton Horowitz, 70, who claimed he got cancer from asbestos in cigarette filters, presumably Kents. Whether or not the company appealed these decisions or ever paid the damages, I don't know.

15. Michael Fumento, *Science Under Siege: How the Environmental Misinformation Campaign Is Affecting Our Laws, Taxes, and Our Daily Life.* (New York: William Morrow, 1993), pp. 285-286.

16. Amanda Husted, Health Watch. *The Atlanta Journal-Constitution*, January 21, 1997, p. C9.

17. Michael D. Fiore, et al., "The Agency for Health Care Policy and Research Smoking Cessation Clinical Practice Guideline." *Journal of the American Medical Association*, April 24, 1996, p. 1270; Barnaby J. Feder, "U.S. Is Enlisting Doctors in Campaign Against Smoking." *The New York Times*, April 24, 1996, p. A16; Doug Levy, "Health Pros Urged to Help Smokers Quit." *USA Today*, April 4, 1996, p. D1. All sources courtesy of The Advocacy Institute.

18. "Substance Abuse." Subject Bibliography (SB) 163, U.S. Government Printing Office, September 5, 1995, p. 10.

19. "Questionable Promotion of Smoking Cessation in Hospital Patients." Posted on the World Wide Web by FORCES (Fight Ordinances & Restrictions to Control & Eliminate Smoking) at www.forces.org.

20. At www.forces.org.

21. Brown & Williamson Collection at Galen II, The Digital Library of

the University of California San Francisco, at www.library.uscf.edu/tobacco/docs/html/2404.02/2404.02.1.html.

22. "San Francisco's Tobacco Stand." *The Washington Post*, December 28, 1996, p. A9.

23. Charles Sheffield, "The Feynman Saltation," in Byron Preiss and Robert Silverberg, eds., *The Ultimate Dinosaur* (New York: Bantam Books, 1992). p. 39.

24. Christopher Buckley, *Thank You For Smoking* (New York: Random House, 1994), p. 8.

25. Elizabeth M. Whelan, "Seeking Common Ground in Promoting Public Health." From the American Council on Science and Health Website at www.acsh.org/publications/priorities/top-priority.html.

26. E. Loren Buhl, Jr., "Smoking is Causing a Global Epidemic of Death." From Oncolink, the Internet page of the University of Pennsylvania Cancer Center at http://oncolink. upenn.edu/ws/smoke_epidemic.html.

Chapter 1

IN THE BEGINNING WERE THE NUMBERS

Cigarette smoking is a health hazard of sufficient importance in the United States to warrant appropriate remedial action.

— Surgeon General's Report[1]

"You can prove anything by statistics" is a common gibe. Its contrary is more nearly true—you can never prove anything by statistics.

— G. V. Yule[2]

THIS IS HOW "Tobacco Timeline" on the Internet tells the story:

> On a Saturday morning, January 11, 1964, at 9 A.M., 200 reporters were physically locked into the State Department's auditorium to hear a two-hour briefing by surgeon general Dr. Luther L. Terry and a panel of experts. The top-secret measures were felt necessary because of the bold and closely-guarded conclusion reached in the brown paperback book they received titled *Smoking and Health.* When the press conference was over, the reporters ran to the telephones "like flushing ducks off a pond." In 1964, in a country where over 50% of adult males smoked, a multi-billion-dollar industry seemed to hang by the book's astounding verdict: smoking causes cancer.[3]

The Office on Smoking and Health of the Centers for Disease Control and Prevention adds a few more details:

> The circumstances surrounding the release of the first report in 1964 are worth remembering. The date chosen was a Saturday morning to guard against a precipitous reaction on Wall Street. An auditorium in the State Department was selected because its security could be assured—it had been the site for press conferences

> of the late President John F. Kennedy, whose assassination had occurred fewer than two months earlier. The first two copies of the 387-page, brown-covered report were hand delivered to the West Wing of the White House at 7:30 on that Saturday morning. At 9:00, accredited press representatives were admitted to the auditorium and "locked in," without access to telephones. Surgeon General Terry and his Advisory Committee took their seats on the platform. The report was distributed and reporters were allowed 90 minutes to read it. Questions were answered by Dr. Terry and his committee members. Finally, the doors were opened and the news was spread.[4]

As Terry himself recalled 20 years later, "We released [the] report in an explosive manner on a Saturday morning, and it was shocking to much of the public."[5]

There's something in the two accounts above that puzzles me, the first of four curious and surprising things about the famous 1964 report of the surgeon general I encountered when I began researching for this book.

As they record, January 11, 1964 was a Saturday, that day having been selected for the official unveiling of the report because the stock market was closed, thus precluding a "precipitate" selling frenzy by tobacco stock investors. Saturday was also chosen in order to maximize coverage in Sunday's newspapers. But the editorial I wrote about it, which I quoted from in the Preface, is dated January 10, 1964—Friday, the day before that fateful Saturday. How could this be?

Back in the days of "hot type," Newspaper Enterprise Association mailed its clients printed pages of all the various features in that day's package, along with papier-mâché mats from which they cast in lead their own type and engravings. I still have my editorial, which I cut out of the editorial page printout. George DeLong, the colleague who marked up my copy for the pressroom, had given it the title "Puffing in Peril" and the date *printed* on it is "1-10-64." (I always brought my editorials home for my wife to read, then stuck them in large manila envelopes, then, as the number of envelopes grew, put them in a cardboard box, eventually stashing the box in the attic in Ohio, then in an attic in Virginia and finally an attic in Georgia, never dreaming I would ever have reason to dig up this particular editorial again.)

Boyd Lewis, president of the company and a nonsmoker, was in town that week from NEA's New York headquarters on one of his periodic visits to the hinterlands. I distinctly remember encountering him that Friday morning on the stairs leading to the second-floor business offices. He asked me if I'd heard about the surgeon general's report. I said yes I had, and nodded gravely. He knew I was a smoker and looked at me equally gravely and nodded back. It wasn't necessary for him to say that he expected me to write an editorial on the subject, with my usual trenchant comments.

(I was not only NEA's "chief editorial writer," I was its only editorial writer, and one difficulty I labored under was that about half our client editors used my daily musings as their own unsigned editorials while the other half ran them as op-ed columns accompanied by my name and picture. Thus I always had to tread a fine line between being too personally opinionated on the one hand and too bland on the other. However, my editorial on the surgeon general's report expressed my true feelings on the matter. Based on the knowledge I possessed at the time, I wouldn't have written it any other way.)

There also was an editorial staff meeting that afternoon at three o'clock. I'd completely forgotten about it but discovered the minutes of it while rummaging around in another box in the attic. I must have written my editorial about the surgeon general's report that morning because my lead one on the Panama crisis was favorably mentioned. The only reference to the surgeon general's report had to do with an editorial cartoon about smoking, which I don't remember at all.

In the same box I found copies of two letters. The first had been addressed to me by the editor of a newspaper in Redlands, California. Unfortunately, it was made on a chemical copier and most of it had faded away, but I could make out the gist of it. He mentioned "Puffing in Peril" and thanked me for saving him from having to spend a couple hours on a Saturday afternoon writing editorials, and for "writing much better than I would have myself." The date at the bottom was still legible—January 11, 1964. This meant that he had received our Friday mailing on Saturday, the very day the surgeon general's report was supposedly revealed to the public for the first time.

The second letter had been sent to Boyd Lewis by the editor of *The Daily Sun* in Yuma, Arizona, and passed on to me. This copy was in good condition.The editor said he liked the brevity of my editorial on the SG's report but found it "far too mild for the nature of the danger involved." This one was dated January 13, 1964. But if our package had reached California in only one day, on Saturday the 11th, it must have got to Arizona the same day.

It was only when I read that second letter for the second time, after a lapse of more than three decades, that I fully appreciated how immediately and completely the surgeon general's report had been accepted, even by supposedly hard-boiled, cynical newspapermen—or at least by one of them, who thought I had not editorialized strongly enough about "the nature of the danger involved." And it was then, reading between the lines of my own editorial, that I realized that my present reservations about the SG's report actually dated back to the very beginning.

The only source I could have had upon which to base my editorial had to have been the United Press teletype machine, which clattered 24 hours a day a few feet from my desk. If 200 reporters had been locked into an auditorium to prevent premature leaks about the surgeon general's findings, how could UP (later United Press International) have sent out its story a day before the official release (or possibly even Thursday evening, *two days* before it, since I had written my editorial on Friday morning)? Obviously, the closely guarded report had not really been all that closely guarded.

Thirty-three years later I looked up *The New York Times* for January 10, 11 and 12, 1964 on microfilm at the main Cobb County, Georgia, library in Marietta. There was nothing at all about the report on Friday or Saturday but, sure enough, the paper did its usual complete "cleanout," as we used to say, of the event on Sunday, January 12. Jumping from a lead-in article on top of page one were two full pages, 64 and 65, on the story, continuing on page 66 and taking up three-quarters of that page, and another half a page on page 67, all in the *Times*'s customary small type and narrow columns.

There was also an editorial which fully endorsed (or parroted) the report and hit all the bases that were to be hammered on in coming years: "It is now official . . . smoking is harmful to health—and remedial action is necessary . . . [T]he Surgeon General promises that the Public Health Service will recommend further action. The Congress and other concerned Federal agencies cannot evade their responsibilities here . . . The immediate and main thrust of an antismoking campaign should be directed toward the nation's youth."

That last statement put the *Times* well ahead of even the surgeon general. It was to be at least a couple decades before the antismokers realized that despite their best efforts their crusade for the total eradication of smoking was being stymied by a stubborn minority of Americans who persisted in the habit. It was then that they enlisted "the children" to carry the crusade to a smoke-free Jerusalem.

The editorial also stated that the surgeon general's 10-man panel had come to its conclusion after an objective and meticulous study of "many thousands of scientific reports." This was a bit of an overstatement, as we shall see later in this chapter.

(Way down at the lower right-hand corner of page 65 was an item from the Associated Press quoting one scientist who was not convinced there was an association between smoking and lung cancer. "The government has only statistics," said Dr. Harry S. Greene, chairman of Yale University's department of pathology, "and a statistical association has to be interpreted. It might show cause and effect or it might show happenstance. But the results must be subjected to a laboratory test. They've been doing that for 15 years and have come up with absolutely nothing."

(I don't know what kind of laboratory test Dr. Greene had in mind or what previous tests he was referring to, but the tiny size of the item—two and a half inches—and its placement was a sign of how much exposure *The New York Times*, and everybody else in the years to follow, was going to give to dissenting voices. However, the newspaper had done its journalistic duty and reported "both sides" of the issue.)

It is interesting, if only to me, to compare *The New York Time*'s editorial with the one I wrote:

The *Times* called upon both the legislative branch and agencies of the executive branch of the government of the United States of America to lend all assistance to some kind of as yet unspecified "remedial" action against smoking, and for an antismoking campaign especially directed at youth. As for me, the surgeon general's statement about the need for "remedial" action did not even register. As I quoted from myself in the Preface, I wrote simply that people who wanted to smoke would continue to do so despite the report, although they were now officially on notice that they did so at their own risk.

In short, I had actually thought: "That's it for this story; what'll I write about next week?"

In other words, the august *New York Times* called for concerted intervention against smoking on a national scale; I naïvely believed that the decision to smoke or not to smoke was one for each individual to make, guided by the newly revealed facts (or what I then accepted were the facts) about the potential dangers. It was of course the *Times*'s scenario the nation was to embark upon and to enlarge upon and to persist in for the remainder of the century (and will continue into the next), a scenario that has given rise to a myriad of unforeseen and pernicious consequences on American society.

I also checked the almost-as-august *Washington Post* for Saturday, January 11 and Sunday, January 12, 1964 to confirm that it also did not report on the report until the day after its official release. As I expected, its coverage of the story (on Sunday the 12th) was nearly as extensive as that of the *Times* but it was its editorial I was most interested in. It was surprisingly temperate: "The Committee *appears* to have established beyond reasonable challenge that the cigarette is a grave menace to health." [Emphasis added.]

As for the surgeon general's clarion call for "remedial action" to deal with the menace, "What that action should be is not yet clear," said the *Post* in its concluding paragraph, "but it is clear that the report should be read and pondered by every smoker in the land. A national habit which the Committee attributes largely to psychological and social drives entails an appalling drain on our national health and vigor. It can no longer be ignored as a harmless addiction."

I'm sure that a search of the archives of every newspaper in the land (other than a few hundred NEA clients who received our mailing the next day) would further confirm that Saturday, January 11, 1994 was the day the surgeon general's findings were revealed to the public. So how I could have written about it on Friday the 10th remains a mystery.

Unfortunately, Newspaper Enterprise Association did not wield the prestige of a *New York Times* or a *Washington Post*, nor did any of its subscribers, most of which were small-to-medium newspapers in small-to-medium cities. So anything written by me about the surgeon general's report counted for very little in the scope of things.

THE SECOND CURIOUS and surprising thing I learned about the report was that it seemed to have virtually disappeared into some sort of void. At least, it wasn't available anywhere the ordinary person could readily gain access to it.

Even before I began this writing, I knew that I had to obtain a copy of the all-important *Smoking and Health*. After all, it was what started everything this book is about. How could I write about the profound societal changes of the past three decades that this historic report set into motion on January 11, 1964 without seeing with my own eyes what the SG's advisory committee had actually said? How could I (fond thought) even contemplate making an analysis of the committee's conclusions without knowing something about how they had been arrived at? To my knowledge, no one had ever done such an analysis, certainly no layman like me. Like some kind of scripture, the surgeon general's landmark report was still venerated by believers three decades after it was handed down from the mountain but nobody consulted it any more, if anybody ever had.

But *Smoking and Health* was not in the Cobb County, Georgia, library system or in the main Fulton County library in downtown Atlanta. It didn't matter, however, because I had just acquired a computer with the capability of accessing the Internet and World Wide Web. On one of the few prosmoking—or, more accurately, anti-antismoking—sites on the Web I came across the name of one Lauren A. Colby, Esq., an attorney in Frederick, Maryland, who had written and self-published a small book called *In Defense of Smokers*, one chapter of which deals with the report. At that time he would send the book free to anybody who asked for it. (It is now available only by downloading from the Internet[6] but still at no charge.) I sent for a copy, read it, then wrote a letter to Mr. Colby. I told him of my inability to obtain the famous report. I asked him if he knew if it was available from the U.S. Government Printing Office and if I should write them. He said that he had had the same problem and that I would be wasting the postage.

> When I was trying to get the 1964 Report [he e-mailed me], I happened to be traveling a great deal, in connection with some hearings. Every time I visited a different city, I'd drop into the local library and asked whether they had the report. The answer was always "no." Plus, I made dozens of phone calls to libraries all over the U.S., with negative results.
>
> There is an office within the office of the Surgeon General, called "The Office on Smoking *and* Health," which works closely with a semiprivate organization called the "Office on Smoking *or* Health" (I'm not exactly sure how the two are related, but they are as "thick as thieves." I placed a call to the "and" office in D.C., and

> was told they couldn't help me. However, the lady suggested that I call a number in Atlanta (I'm not sure whether Atlanta was "and" or "or").*
>
> I called Atlanta, but got voice mail. Left a message. Weeks later, a lady called me and said that her organization had just one dog-eared copy of the report. She didn't know of any other place that I could get a copy, but she *did* know about a place in Alexandria [Virginia] which had the microfiche. That's how I got my copy.

(The Library of Congress has the report, of course, as I found out later by browsing the library's Internet catalog. It is listed under Call Number RA1242.T6U5, with the notation that it is for sale by the U.S. Government Printing Office. It may have been once but it isn't anymore. The LOC catalog also listed an edition published by D. Van Nostrand. In early 1998, still curious, I put in a belated request through my local library to the Interlibrary Loan System. They located a copy of the D. Van Nostrand hardcover edition in the library of Kennesaw Junior College. The elusive report had been available only a few miles away all the time! It is still strange, however, that such an important work should have required so much effort to find.)

Because he's a nice guy, and willing to help anybody who's trying to expose the pious falsehoods that have been spread, and continue to be spread, about smoking, Colby graciously offered to make a photocopy of his photocopy for me. (I'm also indebted to him for providing me with a copy of an obscure review of *Smoking and Health* by a professor of statistics named K. A. Brownlee, which I discuss below.)

One spring day in 1996 the heavy package arrived from Frederick. At long last I held the actual sacred text itself, or a reasonable facsimile thereof, in my trembling hands, all 387 pages of it.

I quickly discovered a third curious thing: there was no date on the title page. Only on the very last page, at the bottom in small type, was "U.S. Government Printing Office: 1964 O—714-422." I remarked

*Colby has since agreed with me that he was probably thinking of the Coalition on Smoking OR Health (it capitalizes the "OR"), composed of the American Heart Association, The American Lung Association and the American Cancer Society. The Office on Smoking and Health is part of the Centers for Disease Control and Prevention (CDC) in Atlanta, Georgia. There is also a private organization called Action on Smoking and Health (ASH), about which much, much more later in this book.

on this to Larry (we were now electronically corresponding regularly).

"Yeah, this is definitely Orwellian!" he replied. "However, the fact that there was no date on the Report kinda shows that it was never intended as a serious scientific document. Maybe that's why medical and other libraries didn't keep it."

You've got to be kidding, Larry. Whether or not it was truly scientific, the report was certainly taken seriously (what an understatement!), both by the medical community and the community at large, as few such documents in history have been. Still, the absence of a date on its title page and its nonexistence in public libraries remain as curious puzzles, again if only to me. Just to prove something to myself, I did write to the Government Printing Office to order a copy of the report. Larry was right: it was a waste of postage. All I got was a list of other publications by the Public Health Service. Not a word about *The Report.*

BACK TO JANUARY 11, 1964 and those 200 reporters locked in the State Department auditorium and holding the thick report in their hands, and no doubt itching to rush to the telephones or to their typewriters.

Even if they were given an hour and a half to read it, I doubt if many of them did more than flip through its 387 pages. Or if some of them did try to examine it closely, I doubt if they understood much of what they were reading. Indeed, I doubt if all the members of the advisory committee itself understood everything; only one of them was an epidemiologst and only one a statistician, and the report is full of tables in tiny type, molecular diagrams, logarithmic graphs and arcane and highly technical passages.

One of the best examples is Appendix II to Chapter 8 of Part II, which I've reproduced on the following three pages to illustrate what I'm talking about. (Totaling 182 pages, Chapters 8 and 9 of Part II, which bears the title, "Evidence of the Relationship of Smoking to Health," constitute both the bulk and the core of the entire report.)

APPENDIX II

Stability of Mortality Ratios

In computing the mortality ratio of a group of smokers to a group of non-smokers, each group is subdivided into age-classes (usually 5-year). For the ith age-class let y_i denote the number of smoker deaths and x_i the number of non-smoker deaths. The "expected" number of smoker deaths in the ith class (expected on the assumption that smokers have the same age-specific death rates as non-smokers) is

$$\frac{(\text{Person-years for smokers in class i})}{(\text{Person-years for non-smokers in class i})} x_i = \lambda_i x_i \qquad \text{(say)}$$

The estimated mortality ratio $\hat{R}$ is defined as

$$\hat{R} = \frac{\Sigma y_i}{\Sigma \lambda_i x_i} \qquad (1)$$

summed over the age-classes.

In the interpretation of the values of R found in the seven studies, much weight has been given to the consistency of the values from one study to another, on the grounds that if the values of R for a particular cause of death are high in all seven studies, this evidence is more impressive than R values that are high in say, three studies but show no elevation in the remaining four studies. As a consequence, the question whether the value of $\hat{R}$ in an individual study is significantly above unity, in the technical sense of this term, becomes less important. Nevertheless, an answer to this question is occasionally useful in the analysis. Moreover, for some causes of death the total numbers of deaths, even when all seven studies are combined, are small enough so that a measure of the stability of the combined $\hat{R}$ is needed.

Assumptions

In attempting to get some idea of the stability of $\hat{R}$ without too much complexity, the following assumptions will be made.

1. The numbers of deaths y_i and x_i are distributed as Poisson variables. As Chiang (3) has shown, a more accurate assumption is to regard y_i and x_i as binomial numbers of successes. But with causes of death for which the probability of dying in a 5-year age span is very small the Poisson assumption, which is slightly conservative, is reasonable.

2. The quantities λ_i can be regarded as known constants. This is not quite correct. Initially, the λ_i are the ratios of the numbers of smokers to non-smokers in the age-classes, which can reasonably be regarded as given. In subsequent years, however, the numbers are depleted by deaths, and the number of deaths is a random variable. When death rates are small, however, this assumption should introduce little error.

3. The variates y_i and y_j are uncorrelated. An error in the age assigned to a death, putting it in the wrong age-class, induces a negative correlation between y_i and y_j. The existence of such errors should have no effect on

the variance ascribed to Σy_i on the assumption of independence. The same remarks apply to the assumption that x_i and x_j are uncorrelated.

4. The variates x_i and y_i are uncorrelated. An error in assigning a death to the correct smoking category would induce a negative correlation between x_i and y_i. Such errors should of course not be allowed to happen, since they vitiate the comparison of the death rates that is the main point of the study, but occasional errors of this type may have occurred.

With these assumptions the numerator Σy_i of $\hat{R}$ follows a Poisson distribution. The denominator $\Sigma \lambda_i x_i$ is a linear function of independent Poisson variates, and numerator and denominator are independent of one another. The exact distribution of a ratio of this type has not been worked out. Two approximate methods of obtaining confidence limits for the true mortality ratio $\hat{R}$ will be given. Confidence limits are presented rather than the standard error of $\hat{R}$ because the distribution of $\hat{R}$ is skew when the numbers of deaths are moderate or small, so that the standard error is harder to interpret.

The Binomial Approximation

If the λ_i can be regarded as approximately constant ($=\lambda$, say) then $\hat{R}$ becomes of the form $y/\lambda x$, where y and x are independent Poisson variates. Since λx then represents the expected number of deaths of the smokers, the quantity λ is estimated as the ratio of the expected number of smoker deaths to the number of non-smoker deaths.

By a well-known result it follows that $x/(y+x)$, the ratio of non-smoker deaths to smoker plus non-smoker deaths, is distributed as a binomial proportion with

$$n = \text{number of trials} = y + x$$
$$p = \text{probability of success} = 1/(1+\lambda R)$$

where R is the true mortality ratio. Confidence limits for R are found from those for p.

Example. For the study of men in 25 States, the figures for lung cancer for cigar and pipe smokers are as follows:

	Non-smokers	Smokers	
	Observed	Observed	Expected
Number of deaths	16(x)	15(y)	9.71(λx)

Hence, $\lambda = 9.71/16 = 0.607$ and the binomial ratio is $16/31 = 0.516$. Hald's (9) table of the 95 percent two-tailed confidence limits of the binomial distribution gives 0.331 and 0.698 as the confidence limits for p. Those for R are given by the relation

$$R = (1-p)/\lambda p$$

This yields 0.7 and 3.3 as the 95 percent limits for R. Since the lower limit, 0.7, is less than unity, the estimated $\hat{R}$, 1.5, is not significantly above unity.

Unfortunately the assumption that λ_i is constant is not true in these studies. For instance, in the study of men in 25 States λ_i has the value 3.85 for cigarette smokers aged 45–49 and declines steadily with increasing age to a value of 0.96 for men aged 75–79. For cigar and pipe smokers the fluctuation in γ_i with age is less drastic but is still noticeable.

The Normal Approximation

This approach avoids the assumption that the λ_i are constant, but makes other assumptions that are shaky with small numbers of deaths. If R is the true mortality ratio, the quantity

$$y - Re$$

where $e = \Sigma\lambda_i x_i$ is the expected number of smoker deaths, will follow a distribution that has mean zero. If μ_i, m_i denote the true means of y_i and x_i, respectively, the variance of $(y - Re)$ is

$$\Sigma(\mu_i + R^2\lambda_i^2 m_i)$$

The basis of this approximation is to regard the quantity

$$\frac{y - Re}{\sqrt{\Sigma(\mu_i + R^2\lambda_i^2 m_i)}} \qquad (2)$$

as normally distributed with zero mean, since y_i and x_i are regarded, as previously, as independent Poisson variates. The 95 percent confidence limits for R are then obtained, by a standard device, by setting the absolute value of this quantity equal to 1.96 and solving the resulting quadratic equation for R.

Since the μ_i and the m_i are unknown, a further approximation is to substitute y as an estimate of $\Sigma\mu_i$ and $\Sigma\lambda_i^2 x_i$ as an estimate of $\Sigma\lambda_i^2 m_i$.

Example. For the example previously discussed the data are as follows:

$$y = 15 : e = 9.71 : \Sigma\lambda_i^2 x_i = 6.059$$

On squaring (2), the quadratic equation becomes

$$(15 - 9.71R)^2 = 3.84(15 + 6.059R^2)$$

The roots are found to be 0.7 and 3.4, in good agreement with the limits 0.7 and 3.3 given by the binomial approximation. This agreement is better than will usually be found with small numbers of deaths.

The following are 4 comparisons of the confidence limits for cigarette smokers in the same study.

Cause of death	Number of deaths			Mortality ratio	95 percent limits	
	Non-smokers observed	Cigarette smokers			Binomial	Normal
		Observed	Expected			
Cancer of lung	16	399	41.20	9.7	(5.0, 14.5)	(5.0, 21.4)
Emphysema	7	115	15.31	7.5	(3.5, 18.1)	(4.0, 40.0)
Cancer of rectum	16	64	38.42	1.7	(1.0, 3.3)	(1.0, 3.6)
Influenza and pneumonia	29	97	58.01	1.7	(1.1, 2.6)	(1.1, 2.9)

And I thought I was going to "analyze" the advisory committee's conclusions! I'm still wondering what the difference is between "R" with the ^ on top and plain old "R" or between "y_1" and "y_i"? Are we talking about real people here?

And why go into such detail about a study of pipe and cigar smokers and not cigarette smokers when it was cigarette smoking the committee was to indict while finding pipe and cigar smoking more or less harmless?

Fortunately for those 200 reporters, they didn't have to read or understand the report. Everything was laid out by the Public Health Service in a release that was distributed at the January 11 press conference.

To digress for a moment, a couple of interesting historical notes are contained in a story by Marjorie Hunter, headed "Smoking banned at news parley," in the January 12, 1964 *New York Times*:

> There was not a whiff of tobacco smoke in the State Department auditorium today when the report on smoking and health was released.
>
> Nine "no smoking" signs were fastened to the walls.
>
> But in the lobby and corridors outside, a few newsmen and Government and tobacco industry spokesmen puffed self-consciously on cigarettes.
>
> Some looked sheepish. Some slipped into vacant rooms along the corridors. Some puffed determinately, as if trying to convince themselves that they were not a bit worried about the report's conclusion that cigarette smoking enhances the death rate.

Already, the "guilt factor," without which the coming antismoking crusade would never have gotten off the ground, was in full operation among smokers.

Ms. Hunter further wrote that:

> One of the heaviest smokers this morning was J. Stewart Hunter, the Surgeon General's assistant for information. "I must have smoked 15 cigarettes," he confided. "I was nervous. We were scared we'd be stormed by 5,000 folks, all clamoring to get in here." Instead, only 200 persons showed up. Most were newsmen. Others represented the tobacco industry and various health organizations and departments of Government. Far more people used to show up for President Kennedy's news conferences in the same auditorium.

So only "most" of the 200 attendees were reporters. While the surgeon general's report proved to be, indeed, a watershed event, the hard-bitten, heavy-smoking practitioners of the journalistic profession at the time were not universally in attendance at its birth and were perhaps not all that concerned with the subject. Antismokers were going to have to do a heck of a lot more to rally the national media behind the call for "remedial action"—and their successful doing of it is, of course, the reason for this book.

I HATE TO THINK what the statistical gobbledygook I reproduced on pages 40-42 would have been like if the "Assumptions" in Appendix II had not avoided "too much complexity"! There is a lot of such padding in the report. I do not use the word in any derogatory sense. Such elaborate detail was not "padding" by the advisory committee but the result of its determination to examine the question of smoking and health from all possible angles and approaches and provide the completest possible documentation for its conclusions. Overall, the report is an impressive collection of just about everything that was known or suspected or alleged about tobacco and its uses and effects at the time it was written.

Ignoring the mathematical symbols, the table for the study of men in 25 states in the "Binomial Approximation" does seem on its surface to be pretty straightforward. The figures indicate that there was one more death from lung cancer among nonsmokers than among pipe and cigar smokers. But could any meaningful conclusion be derived from such a small number of deaths—a total of only 31? It could hardly have meant that nonsmokers ought to take up pipe or cigar smoking! Appendix II in fact states that the "Normal Approximation" involves "shaky" assumptions. Or do the numbers 15 and 16 mean something other than the actual, counted number of deaths? As we will see below, the 25-state study involved no fewer than 448,000 men and lasted for more than three years. Were there really only 15 deaths among pipe and cigar smokers? Also of interest, even though the number of smoker deaths exceeded the "expected" number, so did nonsmoker deaths.

A statistician could explain it all and would probably consider it ridiculously elementary. In fact, by dint of plowing through a couple beginner texts on statistics, I can appreciate now that the formulas in Appendix II really are fairly basic, especially compared to some statistical exercises that require the use of special computer software programs to do the calculations. The "Poisson distribution" is a standard formula in statistics. But again I doubt that questions like those posed above were running through the minds of those restless reporters (how many, if any, where versed in statistics?) and I have reproduced Appendix II only to illustrate the difficulties facing any nonscientist who would have attempted to "analyze" the report. Anyway, in his briefing, the surgeon general may have noted in passing that lung cancer among pipe and cigar smokers was not found to be of any great danger, so the reporters didn't have to try to understand the convoluted mathematics of those tables. The main conclusion of the report—the one the SG certainly concentrated on, the one the reporters had their ears tuned for, the one that flushed them like "ducks off a pond" to the telephones— was the connection between lung cancer and *cigarette* smoking. And that connection was clear and unmistakable, as shown by another table from the same 25-state study at the bottom of page 119. To summarize it:

- For cancer of the lung, 16 deaths were again observed among nonsmokers, but 399 deaths were observed among cigarette smokers.

- For emphysema, the observed number of nonsmokers deaths was 7, but was 115 among cigarette smokers.

- For cancer of the rectum, the observed number of nonsmoker deaths was again 16, but was 64 among cigarette smokers.

- For influenza and pneumonia, the observed number of nonsmoker deaths was 29, and of cigarette smokers it was 97.

This was a total of 68 nonsmoker deaths and 675 smoker deaths from these diseases, or approximately 10 smoker deaths for every nonsmoker death. This is very impressive on the face of it. Yet not only does a total of 743 deaths out of nearly half a million subjects over three years seem rather few on which to base a sweeping verdict but, if my arithmetic is correct, those 675 smoker deaths amounted to only about 1.5 thousandths of that half million. Moreover, as I will explain in the next chapter, when you compare smoker vs. nonsmoker deaths on the basis of their death rates per 100,000 people, you find—believe it or not—that a smoker in this study had 99.9 percent of the chance that a nonsmoker had of *not* contracting these diseases!

As for the "confidence limits" (more usually expressed as the "confidence interval") from which the surgeon general derived the "mortality ratios" in this table (more usually expressed as the "relative risk"), in the course of writing this book I have of necessity learned a little bit about epidemiology. (Just enough to be dangerous, some might say, but the same could also be said of many of the researchers who conduct smoking studies.) A 95-percent confidence interval, which is considered to be the gold standard in epidemiology, means that the authors of a particular study are 95 percent confident that their findings are not due to pure chance or to certain "variables" or "confounding" factors not taken into consideration—diet, alcohol use, family health history, etc.

To put it another way, there is only a five percent possibility that the "relative risk" is due to chance. Relative risk, or RR, is the estimated excess risk that people who do something, like smoking, or are exposed to something, like radon or asbestos, have of acquiring a particular disease or illness compared to people who don't do that something or aren't exposed to that something.

To be even more specific, a 95-percent confidence interval means that there is a two and one-half percent chance that the risk is actually somewhat higher and a two and one-half chance that it is actually somewhat lower than the figure they hand out to the newspapers. The essential thing is that the RR must be at least above unity, or 1.0, and preferably above 2.0, for the RR to be considered "statistically significant." *

But even if a risk found in an epidemiological study is statistically significant, and especially if it is just barely so, it does not mean it has anything to do with real life in the sense that it enables anyone to predict that any given human being will or will not acquire the disease being studied.

Since the lower limit of the confidence intervals the surgeon general reported for cancer of the rectum and for influenza and pneu-

*"In epidemiology, relative risks of less than 2 are considered small and are usually difficult to interpret. Such increases may be due to chance, statistical bias, or effects of confounding factors that are sometimes not evident . . . Lynn Rosenberg, Sc.D., Boston University School of Medicine, points out that a 'difference in risk of 50 percent (relative risk of 1.5) is small in epidemiological terms, and severely challenges our ability to distinguish whether it reflects cause and effect or whether it simply reflects bias.'"[7]

monia are either at unity (1.0) or just above, the risk to cigarette smokers of contracting these diseases because they smoke cigarettes really amounted to no risk at all.

Ah, but for lung cancer and emphysema, the confidence intervals, which range in the first case from 5.0 to 21.4 and, in the second case, from 3.5 to 40.0, are significant indeed, at least epidemiologically speaking. The only question is: how valid were the studies themselves in terms of accounting for and eliminating all possible confounding factors before they arrived at these figures? We'll see below how well they did on that score.

THE 25-STATE STUDY was one of a mere seven studies that the advisory committee used as the basis for its conclusion regarding cigarette smoking and lung cancer. But before looking at those studies, a little background may be in order. (Much of it cribbed from Gene Borio's "Tobacco Timeline" [see Note 3 for this chapter] and "A Capsule History of Tobacco" on the Internet. Borio's "Tobacco BBS" or bulletin board at www.tobacco.org is also an excellent source of current news and commentary in the never-ending crusade against smoking.)

Tobacco has been hated and preached against ever since the weed was introduced into Europe from the New World in the 16th century. Its use nevertheless spread rapidly to every part of the globe, despite such severe penalties as cutting off the noses of smokers in Russia and even executing them in Turkey. But this hatred was based on little but pure prejudice. This inexplicable prejudice still operates today and seems to be so fundamental to the worldview of a certain portion of the human race that it would continue to exist even were it somehow proved that tobacco promotes health and long life.

And although antitobacco "authorities" frequently claimed that smoking was a cause of any number of diseases or disabilities, especially after the advent of the cheap, convenient and ubiquitous cigarette in the late 19th century, it was not until near the middle of the 20th century that doctors began reporting a worrisome increase in the incidence of lung cancer, up until then a rare disease, with the victims overwhelmingly found to be cigarette smokers. Credible scientific support for the suspected smoking-lung cancer connection soon began to appear.

In 1950, for example, Dr. Morton Levin published the results of a

10-year epidemiological survey of Buffalo, New York, patients in the prestigious *Journal of the American Medical Association* (JAMA). His startling finding was that smokers were statistically twice as likely as nonsmokers to develop lung cancer. (Startling, that is, until you remember that "statistically twice as likely" meant that the relative risk he found must have been around 2.0, or only marginally significant.) But this was the heyday of cigarette smoking and few people outside or even inside the medical establishment paid much attention.

In 1952, however, *Reader's Digest*, which was a pioneer in and still is a leading fount of antismoking propaganda for the millions, published an article titled "Cancer by the Carton," based on the findings of Levin and others. This helped set off a "tar derby" among the companies and the introduction of cigarettes with lowered tar and nicotine levels and improved filters.* The *Digest* later published another article comparing filtered cigarettes in which it gave Kents high marks. I vaguely remember the article. Whether or not I read it or only heard about it, it may have been a factor that prompted me to start smoking Kents with their "revolutionary" new Micronite filter that was later claimed to have been so deadly because it contained asbestos. The "tar derby" continued in pace with the public's increasing awareness of the smoking-and-health issue. In point of fact, by the early 1960s, even before the surgeon general's advisory committee set about its work, the number of cigarette brands had expanded from the original "big five"—Camel, Lucky Strike, Chesterfield, Old Gold and Philip Morris—to no less than 17 major brands, with all of the newcomers filtered.

(Now that I think back to the 1950s, I can recall a few people, maybe parents of a friend of mine or acquaintances of my own parents, who had once been cigarette smokers and had simply quit—entirely unaware that they had kicked a habit we are now told is as bad as shooting heroin and even more addictive. Whether they did so out of health concerns or other personal reasons, I don't know, any any more than I know why my father switched from cigarettes to pipes and cigars in the 1930s.

*According to C. Harcourt Kitchin, the chief reason the companies introduced filtered brands, at least in Britain, was not for health reasons but because only the tobacco content of cigarettes was taxed. I would guess also that since filtereds used less tobacco than unfiltereds, they probably could get more of them out of a given quantity of tobacco.[8]

(It was also around this time that I read an article somewhere by a well-known writer of that day, Quentin Reynolds, whose doctor advised him to stop smoking because his throat "looked like a piece of raw meat." What should it look like? I thought. Cooked meat? Of course, the doctor meant that the throat was inflamed and, naturally, the inflammation could *only* have been caused by smoking. I seem to remember a certain tone of bitterness in Reynolds's account as he suddenly recognized the power he had allowed cigarettes to attain over him, and a sense of having been "betrayed" by those little white cylinders he had once enjoyed setting fire to. Or maybe I am projecting this thought into the past because I have heard that kind of feeling expressed by contemporary ex-smokers.)

One of the most notable studies was published in JAMA in 1953. Drs. Graham and Wynder reported that tobacco tar condensates from tobacco smoke painted on the skins of mice caused tumors which, by logical extension, implicated tobacco smoke with lung cancer in humans. This study was alarming enough to the industry that it hired the public relations firm of Hill & Knowlton* to deal with the smoking "health scare" and to form the Tobacco Industry Research Committee (later the Tobacco Research Council), with the purported purpose of encouraging research on smoking and health. In charge would be a scientist "of unimpeachable integrity and national repute" overseeing an Advisory Board composed of "distinguished men from medicine, science, and education." In January 1954 The TIRC ran a full-page "A Frank Statement to Smokers" in more than 400 newspapers:

> Recent reports on experiments with mice have given wide publicity to a theory that cigarette smoking is in some way linked with lung cancer in human beings.

*This is something else I didn't know until I started researching for this book. In 1964, when I lived in New York, a Hill & Knowlton account executive named Ben Schechter took me out to lunch at least once a month, during which he would pitch a "hook" upon which to hang a column mentioning one of his clients. Not once was it suggested I write something about the smoking controversy, even though Ben and other H&K executives I met knew that I smoked and would be favorably inclined to the industry. In fact, in 21 years of writing editorials after 1964, not once was I approached by *anybody* to write about smoking. It makes me feel kind of slighted.

> Although conducted by doctors of professional standing, these experiments are not regarded as conclusive in the field of cancer research. However, we do not believe that any serious medical research, even though its results are inconclusive, should be disregarded or lightly dismissed. At the same time we feel it is in the public interest to call attention to the fact that eminent doctors and research scientists have publicly questioned the claimed significance of these experiments.
>
> . . . We accept an interest in people's health as a basic responsibility, paramount to every other consideration in our business. We believe the products we make are not injurious to health. We always have and always will cooperate with those whose task it is to safeguard the public health . . .

This was damage control, or what today we call "spin-doctoring." But even a cynic would agree that one sentence in the industry's statement was sincere and came straight from the heart:

> [T]he fact that cigarette smoking today should even be suspected as a cause of a serious disease is a matter of deep concern to us.

Regarding the mice experiment, it is a fact that just about anything causes cancer in laboratory mice or rats. Indeed, they're specifically bred for susceptibility to carcinogenic substances. They also have to be subjected to massive doses of a substance, vastly exceeding anything people encounter in the real world, in order to achieve a result within their short lifetimes. It is another fact that people don't paint the inside of their lungs with concentrated tobacco "tar" (smoke condensates) mixed with acetone, where it is left to fester for weeks, as was done on the skins of the mice in Wynder's and Graham's "bioassay" and later on rabbits' ears in a second experiment by Graham in 1956. It is a further fact that no one has ever induced *lung* cancer from tobacco smoke itself in an animal.

This in no way proves that tobacco smoke does not cause lung cancer in humans. But researchers tend to extrapolate findings from animal experiments to humans when it supports whatever they are trying to prove. When the experiments don't result in anything except a lot of dissected animals, they tend to keep quiet about it or, more usually, call for "more studies," which translates into "more money."

In any case, by the end of the 1950s, a fierce debate was raging within the medical community over the dangers of smoking. Or that was the impression the TIRC labored to create—that physicians were divided over the issue. Indeed, some were; in editorials in its *Journal*, none other than the American Medical Association downplayed the significance of the mounting evidence against smoking. But that, it was charged, was because the docs were more worried about the specter of socialized medicine than about smoking. According to one source, the AMA later struck a deal with southern tobacco state congressmen. In return for the AMA's issuing a statement contradicting the surgeon general's 1964 report, the congressmen threw their votes against Medicare, which eventually came anyway.[9]

With or without the wholehearted support of the AMA, however, a tidal movement against smoking was building. From the section "Historical Notes and Chronology" in Chapter I of the 1964 *Smoking and Health*, pages 6 and 7:

> The U.S. Public Health Service first became officially engaged in an appraisal of the available data on smoking and health in June, 1956, when under the instigation of the Surgeon General, a scientific Study Group on the subject was established by the National Cancer Institute, the National Heart Institute, the American Cancer Society, and the American Heart Association. After appraising 16 independent studies carried on in five countries over a period of 18 years, this group concluded that there is a causal relationship between excessive smoking of cigarettes and lung cancer.
>
> Impressed by the report of the Study Committee and by other new evidence, Surgeon General Leroy E. Burney issued a statement on July 12, 1957, reviewing the matter and declaring that: "The Public Health Service feels the weight of the evidence is increasingly pointing in one direction; that excessive smoking is one of the causative factors in lung cancer."
>
> Again, in a special article titled "Smoking and Lung Cancer—A Statement of the Public Health Service," published in the Journal of the American Medical Association on November 28, 1959, Surgeon General Burney referred to his statement issued in 1957 and reiterated the belief of the Public Health Service that: "The weight of evidence at present implicates smoking as the principal factor in the increased incidence of lung cancer," and that: "Cigarette smoking particularly is associated with an increased chance of developing lung cancer."

Somewhere between 1956 and 1959, it seems that the "weight of evidence" was no longer indicting just "excessive" smoking of cigarettes but any kind of cigarette smoking.

Even so, it took increasing pressure from the old-line public health organizations over the next two years to motivate the government to "do something." In the summer of 1961 the American Cancer Society, the American Heart Association, the National Tuberculosis Association and the American Public Health Association petitioned President Kennedy to appoint a national commission to study "the widespread implications of the tobacco problem"[10] by investigating the accumulating studies (by this time more than 7,000[11]) implicating smoking with lung cancer as well as other diseases, and, it was hoped, come up with a definitive and authoritative conclusion.

The new president had more pressing matters on his mind and it was nearly another year before Surgeon General Luther L. Terry, now under pressure from some members of Congress, formally proposed to Secretary of Health, Education and Welfare Abraham Ribicoff the formation of an advisory committee composed of "outstanding experts who would assess available knowledge in this area (smoking vs. health) and make appropriate recommendations."[12]

In July 1962 the SG met with representatives from the American Cancer Society, the American College of Chest Surgeons, the American Heart Association, the American Medical Association, the Food and Drug Administration, the National Tuberculosis Association, the Federal Trade Commission and the President's Office of Science and Technology, plus the industry's six-year-old Tobacco Institute, to compile a list of more than 150 scientists and physicians "working in the fields of biology and medicine, with interests and competence in the broad range of medical sciences and with capacity to evaluate the elements and factors in the complex relationship between smoking and health."[13] Any of the organizations, including the Tobacco Institute, had right of veto over any name, no questions asked. From that list Terry appointed a 10-member advisory committee.

Wrote Elizabeth Drew later in *The Atlantic*, "The cigarette industry, it was widely assumed, had been boxed in."[14]

The report's "Historical Notes and Chronology" cites seven "significant developments" since Burney's statement in 1959 on the position of the Public Health Service as the reasons for the advisory committee's undertaking:

1. New studies indicating that smoking has major adverse health effects.

2. Representations from national voluntary health agencies for action on the part of the Service.

3. The recent study and report of the Royal College of Physicians and Surgeons of London (which had reported early in 1962 that cigarette smoking was a cause of lung cancer and bronchitis, probably contributed to the development of coronary heart disease and various less common diseases, and delayed healing of gastric and duodenal ulcers).

4. Action of the Italian government to forbid cigarette and tobacco advertising; the voluntary curtailing of cigarette advertising by Britain's major tobacco companies on TV, and a similar decision on the part of the Danish tobacco industry.

5. A proposal by Senator Maurine Neuberger that Congress create a commission to investigate the health effects of smoking.

6. A request for technical guidance by the Public Health Service from the Federal Trade Commission on labeling and advertising of tobacco products.

7. Evidence that medical opinion has shifted significantly against smoking.

Needless to say, all of this history, from the first reports of smoking-caused lung cancer to the appointment of an official government commission, passed completely over my head as I smoked blithely and happily away, preoccupied with living my so-called life.

In November 1962, the 10 members of the advisory panel and their staff assistants convened for the first time in the basement of the National Library of Medicine at the National Institutes of Health in Bethesda, Maryland, and, assisted by some 189 outside "contributors," set about the gargantuan task of sifting through more than 6,000 articles from 1,200 journals up to 1959 (evidently the origin of *The New York Time*'s "many thousands"), supplemented by an additional 1,100 titles provided by the National Library of Medicine . Over the next 13 months their work continued, enveloped in an aura of secrecy reminiscent of that in which Enrico Fermi and his team of nuclear scientists had achieved the first atomic chain reaction under Stagg Field at the University of Chicago 22 years before.

The analogy is not inapt. The surgeon general's 1964 report was to set off a chain reaction in American society—and indeed around the world—as significant and far-reaching in its way as the one in Chicago in 1942. But while the resulting atomic bomb changed the world forever in an instant, we have yet to witness the final consequences of the bomb the Advisory Committee to the Surgeon General of the Public Health Service exploded on January 11, 1964.

Looking back now—considering the centuries-old prejudice against tobacco (even if it may not have been shared by every or even any member of the surgeon general's advisory committee or staff, about half of whom were smokers); considering the thousands of studies condemning it; considering Surgeon General Burney's prior public statements on behalf of the Public Health Service; considering the secrecy in which the advisory committee labored (they were fully aware that they were in the process of fashioning a document that would have profound social ramifications)—considering all this, it is clear to me that the entire investigation was really an exercise in validating what many medical authorities already believed. In short, the historic verdict on page 232 of the report that "Cigarette smoking is causally related to lung cancer in men" and "The data for women, though less extensive, point in the same direction" was nothing less than foreordained.

As NOTED ABOVE, the advisory committee relied chiefly upon seven studies. It wasn't until Chapter 8 and page 81 of the report—after explaining how the investigation was conducted and what criteria* were used for judgment and after presenting a summary of its conclusions, followed by tables on the consumption of cigarettes in the United States and diagrams of the chemical and physical characteristics of tobacco and tobacco smoke and the pharmacology and toxicology of

*"Statistical methods *cannot establish proof of a causal relationship* in an association. The causal significance of an association *is a matter of judgment* which goes beyond any statement of statistical probability," said the report [emphases added]. To guide them in making the leap from a statistical association to the judgment of a causal relationship between smoking and disease, the advisory committee relied on five criteria: the consistency of the association, the strength of the association, the specificity of the association, the temporal relationship of the association and the coherence of the association.[15]

As for nicotine, the committee held that it was a habit-forming but not a physically addictive drug. That verdict was not to be long tolerated by the antismoking community (see Chapter 4).

nicotine—that the report got around to the actual studies on which it based its conclusions. (How many of those reporters in the State Department auditorium read that far?)

These were seven large "prospective" studies of American and Canadian males. The text explains that in a prospective study, information about current and past smoking habits is first obtained from the members of the group to be studied, along with supplementary information such as age. "Provisions are also made to obtain death certificates for all members of the group who die in subsequent years. From these data, overall death rate and death rates by cause are computed for the different types of smokers, usually in five-year classes." In brief, the job is to follow a number of people over a number of months or years and record who dies and what from, and whether they were smokers or nonsmokers.

The earliest study was begun in October 1951, the latest in October 1959. They were (with the names of the researchers and duration of the study in parentheses):

(1) 34,000 British doctors responding to a questionnaire sent to all members of the medical profession in the United Kingdom. (Doll and Hill, from October 1951 to 1956.)

(2) 188,000 white American men in nine states between the ages of 50 and 69 enrolled by American Cancer society volunteers. (Hammond and Horn, from January-March 1952 to 1958.)

(3) 248,000 holders of U.S. Government Life Insurance policies, available to veterans who served in the armed forces between 1917 and 1940. (Dorn, from January 1954 and January 1957 to 1958.)

(4) 67,000 men aged 35-64 in nine occupations in California who were suspected of being subject to higher than usual occupational risk of developing lung cancer. (Dunn, Linden and Breslow, November 1953 and May 1957 to 1960.)

(5) 60,000 California members of the American Legion and their wives. (Dunn, Buell and Breslow, from May-November 1957 to end date not given.)

(6) 78,000 pensioners of the Canadian Department of Veterans Affairs who served in World Wars I and II and the Korean War. (Best, Josie and Walker, from September 1955 and July 1956 to 1961.)

(7) 448,000 men in 25 states enrolled by American Cancer Society volunteers. (Hammond, October 1959 and February 1960 to 1963.)

Because these seven studies were culled from some 7,100 other studies or articles or reports on smoking from at least 1,200 journals, it is reasonable to assume that they must have been the best-conducted and most probative the advisory committee could find in the whole bunch. (The first three had already been used in the report of the Royal College of Physicians and Surgeons two years before. The surgeon general's 1964 report not only adopted the same title as the British report—*Smoking and Health*—but borrowed heavily from it.)

But before looking at their findings I'll quote from the surgeon general's report some of the advisory committee's own caveats regarding them, lest I be accused later of having the temerity to try to second-guess these experts. (I don't know if these reservations about the reliability of the studies were included in the Public Health Service's press release. Even if they were, I doubt very much that they were dwelled on during the presentation to reporters on January 11, 1964.)

From pages 84 and 85 (all emphases in what follows are mine):

> Smokers and nonsmokers may differ with regard to variables other than age that are known or suspected to influence death rates, such as economic level, residence, hereditary factors, exposure to occupational hazards, weight, marital status, and eating and drinking habits. [The "confounding" factors—D.O.] In the summary results to be presented in subsequent sections, as in most results previously published, the death rates of smokers and non-smokers *have not been adjusted so as to equalize the effects of these disturbing variables . . .*
>
> A further complexity in interpreting the results comes from interrelationships among the variables that describe the habit of smoking. As will be seen, the death rates of a group of cigarette smokers vary with the amount smoked, the age at which smoking was started, the duration of smoking, and the amount of inhalation. In trying to measure the "net" effect of these variables, such as the number of cigarettes smoked per day, we should make adjustments so that the different groups of smokers being compared are equalized on all other relevant aspects of the practice. *This can be done at best only partially. Most studies measured only some of the variables on which adjustment is desirable.* When the data are subclassified in order to make the adjustments, the number of deaths per subclass are small, with the consequence that *the adjusted death rates are somewhat unstable.*
>
> Consequently, like previous reporters on these studies, we have

used our judgment as to the amount of subclassification and adjustment to present. *The possibility that part of the differences in death rates may be associated with smoking variables other than the one under discussion cannot be excluded.*

Pages 94 and 95:

None of the [seven study] populations was designed, in particular, to be representative of the U.S. male population. Any answer to the question "to what general population of men can the results be applied?", *must involve an element of unverifiable judgment.* However . . . taken as a whole, the seven populations offer a substantial breadth of sampling of the type of men and environmental exposures to be found in North America and Britain . . .

The seven studies differ considerably in size. They vary also in the extent to which they are free from methodological weakness. The studies of men in nine states [*sic*] and men in 25 States [*sic*], for instance, suffer from the difficulties that the populations studied are hard to define, that the smokers and nonsmokers were recruited by a large number of volunteer workers, and that completeness in the reporting of deaths was hard to achieve, since this depends on reports from the volunteers. On the other hand these studies have the advantage of being large [they were the two largest—D.O.] and of having a broad geographic representation of the U.S. male population . . .

Pages 95-98:

In all studies the death rates for non-smokers are *markedly below* those of U.S. white males in 1960. Even the smokers of one pack of cigarettes or more daily have death rates that average slightly *below* the U.S. white male figure. To some extent this is to be expected, since hospitalized and other seriously ill persons are not recruited in such studies. The sizes of the differences appear, however, surprising for the studies with United States populations . . .

It is clear that the seven prospective studies involve populations which are healthier than U.S. males as a whole. Secondly, the low death rates for non-smokers suggest the possibility that the studies recruited *unusually healthy groups of non-smokers* . . .

In all five studies that had a clearly defined target population, *sizeable proportions of the population were omitted.* The major reason was failure to answer the questionnaire . . . The possible effects of these amounts of non-response on the mortality ratios *have received little discussion* . . .

But even after adjusting for possible overestimation of mortality ratios because of nonresponse, the committee stated that:

> [U]nder *assumptions that are rather extreme*, although consistent with the available data, the mortality ratio of cigarette smokers would still remain substantially higher than unity [1.0] for these amounts of over-estimation . . . On balance we are inclined to agree with the opinion expressed by the authors of several of the studies to the effect that the general result of errors in reporting smoking history is to depress the mortality ratio of smokers relative to non-smokers, so that reported ratios will tend to be underestimates so far as this source of error is concerned.

In other words, both the study authors and the advisory committee were making informed guesses here. Or when in doubt, assume the worst.

In the British doctors study, for example, 32 percent of the doctors the questionnaire was sent to didn't send it back. Nevertheless, Doll reported that the death rate of the nonrespondents was higher than that of the respondents and that there were relatively more smokers among the nonrespondents than among the respondents. How he ascertained this if the nonrespondents didn't respond was not explained.

> In the 25-state study, *over 20 other variables* that may be associated with death rates were recorded. (Page 99)

> [I]t is not unreasonable to speculate that the kind of men who become regular cigarette smokers are, to a moderate degree, less inherently able to survive to a ripe old age than non-smokers. *We know of no way* to make a quantitative estimate of the difference in death rates that might be attributable to such constitutional and genetic factors. (Page 104)

(In the last chapter in the report, Chapter 15, the committee also considered the possibility that there are morphological differences between smokers and nonsmokers. In 1963, C. C. Seltzer had published in the *Journal of the American Medical Association* the results of a study of 922 Harvard graduates. He found that cigarette smokers were larger than nonsmokers, averaging 4.37 pounds heavier, pipe smokers larger still and cigar smokers the largest. The committee decided, however, that the data were "too meager to permit a conclusion." I think they were right. In my experience, smokers come in all shapes and sizes.)

> [P]art of the difference [between smokers and nonsmokers] may represent *a general debilitating effect of cigarette smoking* in addition to marked effects on a few diseases . . . though there are difficulties in making this hypothesis precise enough to be subject to medical investigation. (Page 105)

This was not even informed guesswork. On page 113 the report again suggests "the possibility that cigarette smoking has some general debilitating effect, although no medical evidence that clearly supports this hypothesis can be cited." My uninformed guess is that they decided, "Doesn't matter. We'll throw it in anyway."

With the above reservations in mind, what *did* those seven studies say?

1. For males who smoked cigarettes only, the overall death rate, expressed as the "mortality ratio," was higher than that for nonsmokers in all the studies. The increases ranged from 44 percent for the British doctors (Doll and Hill) to 83 percent for men in 25 states (Hammond).

2. For smokers of other forms of tobacco as well as cigarettes, the increases in death rates were in all cases lower than for smokers of cigarettes alone.

3. For smokers of cigars or of pipes only, three of the studies showed small increases in overall death rates, ranging from 5 to 11 percent. However, the British study and the study of men in 25 states found slight *decreases* in death rates for pipe and cigar smokers compared to nonsmokers!

It's not clear to me what the difference, if any, is between a "morality ratio" and a "relative risk." The "relative risk" is what researchers have usually reported in the multitudes of smoking studies that have been conducted, and continue to be conducted, since 1964. So I am assuming that these terms are interchangeable.

The only place in the 387 pages of the report where I found the term "relative risk" used was in the heading of a section in Chapter 9 on page 160: "Relative Risk Ratios From Retrospective Studies." There it was stated (with bracketed words added) that:

> Retrospective studies are usually designed to establish the probability of an association of an attribute A [say smoking] with disease X [say lung cancer]. Procedurally, one compares a supposedly representative group of patients with disease X, with another group as controls, in regard to the percentages of individuals with and without the attribute A.

Evidently "the probability of an association" is also another term for "relative risk."

As for the difference between a prospective study and a retrospective study, in the first kind the researchers wait to see how many of those who have attribute A (say smoking) develop and/or die from disease X (say lung cancer) over a period of months or years, while in the second kind the researchers look at those who already have disease X, or have died from it, and try to determine whether they also have or had attribute A (they are or were smokers).

The advisory committee did in fact examine 29 retrospective studies, and in each of those that investigated male lung cancer, the degree of association with smoking increased as the amount of smoking increased. However, the committee did not rely on them in reaching its historical conclusion because of well-known problems with retrospective studies, especially "recall bias." In such studies researchers depend upon the personal testimony of people as to how much they smoke or, if they no longer smoke, their recollection of how much they used to smoke. If the subjects are deceased, next best (or worst) are the recollections of their survivors or someone who knew them. While death certificates are used when available, these are also notoriously unreliable.

It was because of such deficiencies in retrospective studies, the committee noted on page 160, that several "courageous" investigators were led to undertake the protracted, expensive and difficult prospective approach. Among the first to do so were Doll and Hill, whose pioneer study of British physicians was initiated in October 1951.

(We have come full circle. In the field of smoking, the courageous investigators today are those who resist the temptation to apply for some of the abundant antismoking grant money that is available—much of it extorted from smokers—and to make a name for themselves by conducting yet another study into some aspect of smoking and health or, quite frequently, simply publish a rehash of previous studies.)

Other than in this section heading, the report doesn't use the term "relative risk" again. Thus one must assume that in a table on page 164 of ratios for lung cancer by smoking status, even though they are called "mortality ratios," the ratios given are relative risks. And for the seven studies they range from a ratio of 6.0 in the Dorn study to 25.2 in the Best, Josie and Walker study, for all smokers.

Recalling what Dr. Rosenberg was quoted as saying in the footnote on page 46, a relative risk of 1.5 is a 50-percent risk. That would mean that a relative risk of 2.0 would be a 100-percent risk, a relative risk of 3.0 a 200-percent risk, and so on up to that 25.2 relative risk in the Dorn study, which would be—what?—a *2,420-percent* risk?!

It is here that my headlong plunge into epidemiology began to arouse in me a profound skepticism. In ordinary, everyday language, 100 percent means a sure thing. If the weatherman predicts a 100-percent chance of rain, it means he's absolutely sure it's going to rain—*he couldn't be any more sure.* If someone jumps off a 10-story building, we can also be pretty darn close to 100-percent sure that he will kill himself (although there have been miraculous survivals from a fall that far or even farther). If he jumps off a 20-story building and falls twice as far, the risk of death would still be 100 percent, not 200 percent. A dead (no pun intended) certainty can't be greater than 100 percent, can it?

It is in fact because of this commonsensical understanding that 100 percent of anything is as high as you can go that antismoking researchers like to present their findings in terms of percentages—as, for example, a study I discuss in the next chapter that claimed that nonsmoking nurses married to smoking spouses had a 91-percent greater chance of lung cancer than nurses married to nonsmoking spouses.

Wow—91 percent! That's awfully close to the 100-percent-sure death-inviting risk of jumping off a tall building. And that was precisely the purpose of it—to convey to the ordinary person the idea that not only do almost *all* nurses married to smokers get lung cancer but so does nearly *everybody* married to a smoker. They can get away with it because not many people know that in epidemiology, a "91-percent risk" is a relative risk of 1.91, which is so small, so close to what epidemiologists call the "noise" or background level, that it is meaningless. Nevertheless, the American Heart Association had no compunctions about issuing a press release announcing this finding. It was heralded on an Atlanta TV news program as "new evidence of the danger of secondhand smoke."

Another source of skepticism for me was reading about "the latest study" showing that people who smoke are X number of times "as likely" or "more likely" to develop this or that disease than nonsmokers. For lung cancer, it has been put at from 10 to 20 times "as likely" for a smoker.

I wrote to Marilyn vos Savant's "Ask Marilyn" column in *Parade* magazine and asked her to explain this "times as likely" business, but the question was never used. Either it would have required too long an answer or it was simply too stupid to consider.

Eventually it dawned on me that my problem was that these "times as likely" figures are seldom related to any kind of baseline. That is, how many people do they actually refer to? For example, in Chapter 10 I cite a study which claimed that teenagers who smoke are "18 times as likely" to attempt suicide as teenagers who don't smoke. Does that mean that for every nonsmoking teen who attempts suicide, 18 smoking teens do? But *how many* teens attempt suicide? For that matter, how many succeed, and how are they broken down between smokers and non-smokers?

You have to have a very significant relative risk to come up with a "times as likely" number that high, and it usually only happens with lung cancer. That is why, for most "smoking-related" diseases or behaviors, researchers like to present the risk as a percentage; it sounds so much more impressive that way.

To sum up my amateur's "analysis" of the surgeon general's report, I believe that there probably is a dose-response or dose-effect factor involved with smoking because it makes sense to me that anyone who chain-smokes two, three or four packs of cigarettes a day (though not necessarily how many years he does so) is courting injury to his health in some way. Too much of anything, including pure drinking water, is not good for you. It is an old axiom of medicine that "the dose makes the poison." That many cigarettes a day could overwhelm the body's constantly operating recuperative powers, which is why, contrary to medical authority, I think the number per day is more important than the number of years.

(Incidentally, as for true chain-smoking—lighting each cigarette from the butt of the proceeding one—my "personal best" is 18 consecutive cigarettes. But that was an exception and a long time ago and they were only king-size cigarettes, not the 100s I smoke today. My normal consumption has always been around a pack a day.)

Otherwise, however—as a layman, as an ordinary shnook like those 200, or how many there were, reporters locked in the State Department auditorium on January 11, 1964, like the editors of their newspapers and magazines and wire services, and especially like the millions of readers and viewers of and listeners to the news media—I am forced in the end to accept on faith alone the conclusion of the surgeon general's advisory committee that smoking *may* cause or otherwise be implicated in lung cancer, at least in some cases.

But that smoking *will* cause lung cancer or some other dire disease—inevitably and universally, as most people have been taught to believe—or even that it may only *probably* cause lung cancer or some other disease, a lifetime's observation of people who smoke and people who don't smoke, plus my own half-century of smoking in good health, plus what I have learned about epidemiology, plus critiques by knowledgeable people of smoking studies conducted subsequent to the surgeon general's 1964 report, keep telling me: *it just ain't so.*

As the report itself states, epidemiology does not, and indeed cannot, show causation between attribute A and disease X but only a statistical association or correlation. The association between smoking and lung cancer is, and always will be, at its basis, statistical. This is why, to buttress its case against smoking, the advisory committee was forced to go beyond the raw numbers into the realm of subjective judgment. (Was the association consistent among the studies? Was the association strong? Was it coherent? That is, did it make sense?)

That "it's only statistical" is of course the frail reed that the cigarette makers have always clung to, or did cling to from 1964 to 1997, until sheer brute, extortionate force exerted by 40 *mafiosi*, a.k.a. the attorneys general of that many states (see Chapter 12), forced them to confess otherwise. (One wonders: if the "merchants of death" are nothing but a bunch of liars, what value is their confession? Are they saying under their breaths, in paraphrase of Galileo before the Inquisition, "Nevertheless, it's still only statistical."?)

Medical science is still searching for causation; i.e., how *exactly* does smoking cause lung cancer? One of the possible culprits the SG's 1964 report looked at was benzo(a)pyrene, which it called the most carcinogenic of all the many suspected carcinogenic substances in tobacco smoke. It's still being looked at. In 1996 some researchers in Texas claimed to have discovered *exactly* how the benzo(a)pyrene in cigarette smoke initiates lung cancer (see Chapter 2).

This "discovery" was, of course, widely reported in the media and has become part of "common knowledge," even though it was pure malarkey. Unfortunately for the researchers, this compound is present everywhere in the environment and in greater amounts than in tobacco smoke.*

But what about those statistics in the 1964 report? At least one statistician at the time was less than impressed: K. Alexander Brownlee, associate professor of statistics at the University of Chicago and a member of the Royal Statistical Society of London, whose review of *Smoking and Health* was published in the *Journal of the American Statistical Association.*[18] In the second paragraph of his review, Brownlee wrote:

> I have observed amongst some statisticians a wistfulness that statistics has not so far played a larger part in science generally. Since this association between smoking and lung cancer, interpreted by many as one of causation, is of prime importance, one might have expected it to be greeted with enthusiasm and loud admiration. On the contrary, the comments and reactions of the statistical profession have been very restrained. By and large, in fact, the silence has been deafening.

(By and large, in fact, in the course of researching for this book I have noticed that the scientists who are usually most skeptical of studies purporting to show statistical associations between smoking and disease are . . . *statisticians.*)

As I had, Brownlee noted the absence of a publication date to the report, as well as the lack of an index, which made it difficult to look up subjects. He also observed that the list of organizations that met with the surgeon general on July 24, 1962 to suggest candidates for an advisory committee "appears to be heavily weighted towards government agencies and organizations large, general, and active in public relations, and to have low representation of societies with specifically scientific outlooks." No statistical society was represented, he commented.

To cut to the chase, in Brownlee's opinion a key factor in determining whether or not one accepted the report's conclusions was

*Benzo[a]pyrene (B[a]P) is one of the polycyclic aromatic hydrocarbon PAH compounds. Because it is formed when gasoline, garbage, or any animal or plan material burns, it is usually found in soot. The chemical combines with dust particles in the air and is carried into water and soil and onto crops . . . People may be exposed to B[a]P from environmental sources such as air, water, and soil and from cigarette smoke and cooked food . . ."[16] According to Joe Dawson, "A ten-pound bag of charcoal produces as much smoke (and harmful chemicals) as 160 packs of cigarettes."[17]

how one interpreted Table 26 on pages 109-110. This was a compilation of the smoker-nonsmoker mortality ratios for 24 diseases and one other category (accidents, suicides, violence) from the seven studies, listed in order of mortality ratios, from highest to lowest. They were:

Cancer of lung; bronchitis, emphysema; cancer of larynx; cancer of oral cavity; cancer of esophagus; stomach and duodenal ulcers; other circulatory diseases; cirrhosis of liver; cancer of bladder; coronary artery disease; other heart diseases; hypertensive heart disease; general arteriosclerosis; cancer of kidney; all other cancer; cancer of stomach; influenza, pneumonia; all other causes; cerebral vascular lesions; cancer of prostate; accidents, suicides, violence; nephritis; rheumatic heart disease; cancer of rectum; cancer of intestines.

The mortality ratios (relative risks?) ranged from 10.8 for cancer of the lung down to 0.9 for cancer of the intestines, with all but eight below 2.0.

> If one believes [Brownlee wrote] that the observed association between smoking and lung cancer is substantially real, and not an artefact of biased sampling, then one would seem required also to accept the observed association between smoking and almost all causes of death as substantially real.
>
> If one believes that the observed association between cigarette smoking and virtually all causes of death is substantially real, then one must take one of the following positions:
>
> (a) All the associations are due to causation.
>
> (b) Some of the associations are due to causation and others to correlations, concealed or otherwise.
>
> (c) All of the associations are due to correlations, concealed or otherwise . . .
>
> If one adopts position (a), then one is under some obligation to provide hypotheses as to possible mechanisms, or to hold out hope that future research will provide these hypotheses. The difficulty with the smoking hypothesis is that it has not really got to first base on even lung cancer, let alone the other 24 causes of death, even though the matter has been under intensive investigation for ten years or more.

(And, as noted above, more than three decades after the report was published to the world, the search for a possible "mechanism" by which smoking causes lung cancer continues.)

But if one adopted position (b), averred Brownlee, one was then placed in the unenviable position of admitting that concealed correlations account for some diseases but not for others. And once one admits that concealed correlations account for a substantial number of the observed associations, "then one has to work very hard to disprove the hypothesis that they may account for all the observed correlations [position (c)]."

For lung cancer, one correlation emphasized in the report was that between the observed rise in lung cancer incidence in the 20th century and the per capita increase in cigarette consumption during the same period. But, said Brownlee:

> All statisticians know that the presence of a positive, zero, or negative correlation between two variables observed over time has been the basis for more ludicrous nonsense than any other statistical procedure. For example, the incidence of cancer of the stomach has been declining for many years . . . but only a madman would infer that the increased smoking has caused the decreased stomach cancer.

Actually, it's not such a mad idea today. Some modern studies have "suggested" (a cautious word researchers always use) that smoking may have a protective effect against stomach and colorectal cancer (see Chapter 3). In fact, on page 229 of the report the advisory committee stated that "the mean gastric cancer ratio for cigarette smokers [given as 1.4 in Table 26] is below the mean total mortality ratio" and concluded that *"No relationship has been established between tobacco use and stomach cancer."* [Emphasis mine.]

Yet it placed stomach cancer as 16th in the list of 25 smoking-related causes of death in Table 26. One asks why, if there was no relationship between this disease and tobacco use.

In my personal opinion, Brownlee's position (b) is the only logical one. It would go against all common sense to believe that smoking "causes" accidents, suicides and violence, which are listed as number 21 among the 25 alleged causes of deaths among smokers. There must be a multitude of other factors involved. But if there are hidden correlations in this category, then, as Brownlee said, you have the job of showing that there are no hidden correlations involved with all the other categories.

Table 26 really proved too much, and thus proved nothing. By associating smoking with so many named diseases and "other" or "all other" diseases and causes and happenstances, the advisory committee not only violated but made rather a mockery of one of its own criteria: "the specificity of the association."

As for the correlation between the historical increase in lung cancer and the increase in cigarette smoking, Brownlee suggested a possible explanation:

> The generation born in 1880 reached the age of 20 in 1900, and a substantial fraction, 24 percent, had died by this time, presumably largely due to the traditional infectious diseases of childhood. The generation born in 1900 reached the age of 20 in 1920, and a lesser fraction of this generation had died by this age, namely 15 percent. Therefore, the 1900 cohort at the age of 50 represents quite a different stratum from the 1880 cohort at the same age of 50, since the former includes the "weaklings" who were eliminated from the latter.
>
> The relatively large number of cases of lung cancer observed in the 1900 cohort can merely be largely those who would not have survived to run the risk of lung cancer if they had been born 20 years earlier. On this model the alleged historical increase in rate of lung cancer can be readily accounted for.

It was an interesting theory at the time. But now almost all the people born in 1900 are gone, and because the case against cigarette smoking is settled as far as everybody except a few people like me is concerned, no one is going to waste time speculating about possible significant differences between that generation and the one that preceded it, even though—and I think this is important—it was chiefly individuals who were born in the early years of the century who were the subjects of the seven studies cited in the surgeon general's report. It is also possible that another of Brownlee's suggestions is still valid: that in the early days many cases of lung cancer may have been misdiagnosed as tuberculosis.

Brownlee also discussed benzo(a)pyrene and noted that cigar smoke has almost four times as much and pipe smoke about 10 times as much as cigarette smoke, "yet pipes and cigars are pretty well innocent of the charge of association with lung cancer."

(The advisory committee did conclude, however, that pipe smoking was causally related to cancer of the lip. But how pipe smoking could cause cancer of the lip when the tobacco doesn't touch the pipe smoker's lips, the committee didn't say. I would think that cigars, which do touch the lips, would be more likely to cause cancer of that site, but apparently they don't. Maybe pipe stems are the culprit.)

The difference between cigarettes and cigars and pipes "is a puzzling feature of the indictment of tobacco," Brownleee wrote, and then speculated:

> It could be, of course, that the variety of tobacco used differs significantly, that cigars and pipes do not use cigarette paper, that possibly cigars and pipes burn at lower temperatures, or that many cigarette smokers inhale whereas few pipe or cigar smokers do. But if inhalation is the crucial item, then it should show up strongly when cigarette smokers are analyzed into inhalers and non-inhalers, and as reported above, the present evidence is not clear.

Brownlee was here referring to page 188 of the report where "contradictory information" about inhalation is discussed. Several retrospective studies in which inhalation and the amount of smoking were considered came up with "the provocative finding that with increase in daily amounts of cigarettes smoked the differences in risks between inhalers and noninhalers *diminished* [emphasis added]. There is no immediate explanation for this apparent discrepancy."

It was more than provocative. It was astonishing. In one of their first studies, a retrospective study, Doll and Hill had asked lung cancer patients if they inhaled. When the results came back showing that fewer lung cancer patients inhaled than did smokers without lung cancer, they were at such a loss for an explanation that they simply stopped asking subjects if they inhaled.[19]

This also goes against common sense—that the more you inhale, the less risk you take compared to a smoker who doesn't inhale. Nor does it square with the dose-response relationship the seven prospective and 29 retrospective studies found: that the more you smoke and the more years you smoke, the greater the chance of lung cancer. My explanation is, well, there are studies and then there are studies and one is always free to pick and choose among them, depending upon what one wishes to prove. Also, the medical research community had barely begun marshaling its forces against smoking back then. Today those retrospective studies that found an inverse relationship between the amount of cigarette smoke inhaled and the risk of disease would either be laughed out of court or never published at all.

In any case, cigar smokers were to be allowed pretty much of a free ride over the ensuing years while the tobacco haters concentrated on cigarettes. That is changing, thanks to the recent upsurge in the popularity of cigars. For sure, we will sooner or later be seeing all kinds of "latest studies" reporting that cigar smoking is every bit as dangerous as cigarette smoking and demands that the Food and Drug Administration regulate the nicotine content in cigars as well as in cigarettes, and eventually eliminate it entirely in both.

That raises an interesting question in my mind. Since the typical cigar smoker doesn't inhale but derives his pleasure from the taste of the tobacco, the feel of the cigar in his mouth, the holding of it in his hand, the sight of the growing ash on the end and the blue smoke he blows into the air, would it make any difference to him if it were nicotine-free? If it didn't, that would drive the antismokers nuts. It isn't nicotine they hate, it's smoking.

I am acquainted with only one cigar smoker, Lauren Colby, who does inhale the smoke and has been doing it for more than 40 years at the rate of six or seven cigars a day, plus a few pipes. He writes in *In Defense of Smokers*:

> The fact remains that inheritance seems to play a major role in cancer. Pancreatic cancer is very rare, but former President Jimmy Carter has seen it in at least four members of his family: his two sisters, his brother and his father. His mother died from breast cancer which metastasized to her pancreas.*
>
> Diabetes is the scourge of my family. Three of my four grandparents died from the disease. All were obese and consumed a diet rich in starches and sugars. As a young man, I was obese and ate a lot of starches and sugars. I chose to go on a life-long diet, in which I refrained from eating starches and sugars. Simply avoiding starches and sugars is enough to control my weight (I weighed 240 lbs. when I first went on the diet at the age of 38; now, I weigh 162 lbs.) I consider this a sensible precaution. If I had a history of cancer in my family, especially lung cancer, I might choose not to smoke. However, I have no such history, so I puff away.[20]

Speaking of cigars has made me realize that even a veteran ciga-

*Another curiosity: on the "Regis and Cathy" television show on December 26, 1996, Mr. Carter said that the reason he never started smoking was because he saw his brother and sister die of lung cancer from cigarettes. Since even the medical profession agrees that it takes a number of decades for smoking to cause lung cancer, this means that he waited around for at least 20 or 30 years to see how smoking affected his relations before making the decision not to smoke. *Come on, Jimmy . . .*

rette smoker like myself, as anti-antismoking as I can be, has been subtly influenced by decades of antismoking propaganda. When I see a picture of Arnold Schwarzenegger smoking a cigar it seems like a perfectly normal thing to do. The same with the handsome young officer who used to smoke cigars on the TV series "JAG" (until antismoking propaganda or something got to him and he gave them up.) The officer even shared one with his lovely sidekick. But if he had lit up a cigarette I would have been shocked. If she had smoked a cigarette, I would have been even more shocked (but pleased).

There's something about cigars—I don't know what: an impression of masculinity (though they look good on women too), of success, of self-confidence and satisfaction with one's status in life. They're also a prop or an emblem one can flourish. Cigarette smoking, which is now déclassé thanks to the antis, seems almost a furtive and sneaky and aberrant behavior.

Again we've come full circle. Tobacco men in the later part of the 19th century were quite as contemptuous of the new fad of cigarettes as any modern antismoker, as illustrated by a passage from the 1948 novel, *Bright Leaf.* In an early scene, the president of a tobacco company, Major James Singleton, has been approached by the inventor of a revolutionary cigarette-making machine capable of cranking out tens of thousands more cigarettes a day than the hand-rolling method then used. The major explains why he is not interested:

> "Believe me, I'm sorry, Mr. Barton. No hard feelings to you and your machine, understand . . . My family has been in tobacco, one way or another, for the last hundred years or so. We started raising it in Virginia way back before the Revolution . . . All that time we have been talking, eating, thinking, chewing, smoking, admiring tobacco to a man—why, it's been the very breath of our lives! That kind of association with and feeling for a thing makes for a pretty steady tradition, Mr. Barton. This tradition is built on everything that has to do with tobacco: its cultivation, its marketing, its proper function in the society of man. It's the sort of tradition that is respected in this part of the country and any place where tobacco is understood or admired . . .
>
> "And—again without meaning any offense, sir!—I simply can't agree with you about cigarettes . . . I've never been able to see them myself. In fact, I have always regarded their entrance into the business as a distinct step downward toward degeneracy and degradation in the use of a noble plant. A little paper wrapped around

> some low-grade sweepings and stuck into the mouths of grown men! It turns my stomach every time I have occasion to witness it. So you can see, Mr. Barton, I could not in all honesty encourage something that might help promote a condition that I not only deplore, but which is entirely opposed to my way of thinking about tobacco."[21]

Today, alas, the thousands of tobacco farmers for whom the cultivation of the "noble plant" is, as it was for the major, a proud tradition going back generations, are the indirect casualties of the crusade against smoking. Many make a living growing tobacco on small plots that are not suitable for anything else. The antis have shed crocodile tears over what will happen to them when, as they intend, the use of tobacco in all its forms disappears.

I don't know whether Brownlee was a smoker whose criticisms of the surgeon general's report were partially motivated, perhaps unconsciously, by a wish to defend the habit, or whether he was an entirely disinterested observer whose sole concern was to uphold the standards of the statistics profession. I believe it was the latter. In any event, there is no point in quoting further from his paper, nor even in further examination of the report itself. The questions Brownlee raised were either ignored or were soon forgotten in the epidemiological frenzy against smoking that followed after 1964. Indeed, the seven studies on which the report was based are no longer of any interest to anyone. Few scientists today, including epidemiologists, could even tell you what they were.

THIS IS ALL VERY well, you may say. But even if the original seven studies weren't absolutely conclusive, there have been gazillions of new studies since then that have confirmed their findings. Haven't there?

That's what I used to think. Now we come to the fourth surprising thing I learned about the 1964 report, perhaps the most significant thing of all—a major shortcoming in the evidence on which the advisory committee based its conclusions about cigarette smoking, a shortcoming which most people have never heard about. It may in fact lend additional validity to Brownlee's theory about the generation born in 1900, a cohort that grew up smoking strong, unfiltered cigarettes. For this I quote from the encyclopedic and much-acclaimed history of the tobacco industry, *Ashes to Ashes*, by Richard Kluger, who is by no means a partisan of smoking:

> [T]he careful, temperate, and comprehensive report of the Surgeon General's panel had but one glaring fault—an omission that was never admitted or subsequently corrected . . . The elevated mortality rates of smokers, so neatly corresponding to dose-response measurements, were entirely or largely based upon the use of pre-filter cigarettes. During the five years prior to the report, the industry had reduced the tar and nicotine yields of the filter brands by an average of 40 percent; half the smoking population, moreover, was now using filter brands . . . Cigarettes with a filter that was more than cosmetic simply had not been on the market long enough for epidemiologists to conduct a meaningful population study—and the better part of another generation would be required before the mortality rates of those who smoked high-filtration brands exclusively could be calculated.

And here is the kicker (the emphasis is mine):

> *In fact, such a study has never been made in the three generations* [sic] *since the original report to the Surgeon General, doubtless because the public-health community has long since considered the case against cigarettes conclusively proven.*[22]

That statement is puzzling to me, for there have been plenty of studies since 1964 and they must have involved filtered cigarettes because that is the kind most smokers have been smoking for the past three decades. (One such study is cited in Chapter 3.) Kluger's central point remains valid, however: the surgeon general's report was based on outdated studies involving a product no longer universally used. Combine this "glaring fault" with the advisory committee's own reservations that I listed above about those very studies and there would seem to be very good grounds for stating that the case against cigarettes was anything but "conclusively proven" in 1964.

Why didn't the tobacco industry jump all over this "glaring fault"? Well, it did protest meekly, Kluger records, but "a more vigorous denunciation would likely have been taken as the companies' tacit acceptance of the [advisory committee's] findings with regards to unfiltered cigarettes, as well as an undemonstrable health claim for the filter brands that might have invited the Federal Trade Commission's wrath."

I doubt if the cigarette companies were particularly worried about the FTC. After all, they'd been making thinly disguised health claims about their product for years, even using models dressed like doctors in their advertisements, and had often been slapped for it.

Kluger is right about the first point, though. What really made the cigarette manufacturers hold their tongues was that the slightest hint of an admission that there just might possibly be health hazards associated with smoking cigarettes, even if only with pre-1960s unfiltered ones, would have laid them open to even more lawsuits than they were to be faced with in the coming years. The same with any acknowledgment that they were working on developing less harmful cigarettes. They may also have simply hoped that the surgeon general's report would fade from the public's consciousness in time. They could not have foreseen, any more than anybody else could have foreseen in 1964, the antismoking firestorm to come.

In any event, for all the vaunted power and influence of the tobacco industry, its behavior in the years following 1964 was to be characterized by high ineptitude and low courage. The consequence is that nothing the industry says in its own defense, even if true, is believed. The consequence is that anything anybody else says in defense of smoking is taken as proof that he is "in the pay of Big Tobacco."

Yet how else could it have been? Had the industry been open and aboveboard in 1964 and conceded that the surgeon general's report had validity, the ever-hungry vultures among us—the product-liability lawyers—would have had a field day. To paraphrase the wisecrack, no good deed by the tobacco industry would have gone unpunished.

Even if the surgeon general had held out a hand to the industry, inviting its cooperation and participation in further investigations into the harmful effects of smoking and how they might be ameliorated—which he did not do—and suggesting that the companies be offered some protection from retaliation for that cooperation—which of course he would have had no authority to do—a litigious society would not have countenanced it for an instant.

But there was to be no cooperation with the merchants of disease and death, much less any kind of "compromise." The surgeon general was not interested in promoting healthy, or even less dangerous, smoking. War had been declared, and in the coming years each retreat by the industry would only enourage demands by the emergent antismoking movement for ever more forceful onslaughts against smoking.

That the industry was indeed aware of possible health hazards associated with smoking—was in fact even *more* aware than was the surgeon general's advisory committee when the committee began its investigation—seems pretty well demonstrated in *The Cigarette Papers*, published by Stanton Glantz and colleagues at the University of California, a compilation of documents stolen from the files of the Brown & Williamson Tobacco Company and its parent, the British American Tobacco Company (BAT).[23]

However, far from proving the reprehensibility of the industry for allegedly hiding what it knew because it didn't give a damn what its products might do to people, these documents show that B&W at least was deeply concerned about these hazards and that it expended considerable efforts in trying to come up with a cigarette that minimized them. Unfortunately, such efforts were unsuccessful. (To my mind, the most amazing "revelation" in *The Cigarette Papers* is how impressed the company was by those essentially meaningless experiments in which tobacco "tar" was painted on the skins of mice and how much it worried about them.)

But even if the tobacco companies did suppress (or, if you will, lie about) what they knew about smoking and its health dangers, as a legion of industry whistleblowers has claimed, for people to be angry about that is to suggest that they believed the companies all these years and did *not* believe the surgeon general. That is patently not true. (Except, of course, for those people who were to file liability suits based on the premise that they didn't know that smoking was bad for their health because the cigarette makers never told them it was and thus, by implication, told them it wasn't.)

For people to be angry that the cigarette companies lied to them is further to suggest that even though Americans have known the "official" truth about smoking since 1964, they *couldn't know for absolutely sure* because the industry had never confirmed it. That was part of the motivation behind the disgusting inquisition of seven tobacco CEOs by Rep. Henry Waxman in 1994 (see Chapter 12)—to put them under oath in hopes of forcing them to admit what everyone had known since 1964, and when they refused to admit it, to accuse them of perjury. That is the reason for the antismokers' feeling of smug satisfaction when a plaintiffs' attorney in the 1997 flight attendants' suit in Florida cleverly led one industry executive to concede that secondhand smoke "might have" caused thousands of lung cancer deaths (see Chapter 3).

Americans really must place great trust in and have great respect for the scientific knowledgeability of the tobacco industry after all.

AT THAT HISTORIC meeting on July 24, 1962 between Surgeon General Terry and the representatives of the various private health organizations and government agencies, it was agreed upon that the investigation into smoking and health would be undertaken in two consecutive phases:

"Phase I—An objective assessment of the nature and magnitude of the health hazard, to be made by an expert scientific advisory committee which would review critically all available data but *would not conduct original research* [emphasis added]. This committee would produce and submit to the Surgeon General a technical report containing evaluations and conclusions."

(Phase I resulted in, of course, *The Report.*)

"Phase II—Recommendations for actions were not to be a part of the Phase I committee's responsibility. No decisions on how Phase II would be conducted were to be made until the Phase I report was available. It was recognized that different competencies would be needed in the second phase and that many possible recommendations for action would extend beyond the health field and into the purview and competence of other Federal agencies."

What this tells me is that even before Phase I (the investigation) was initiated and even longer before its conclusion (the report) was available, the surgeon general already envisioned the necessity of "action" against smoking. This further fortifies my assertion that the condemnation of smoking was foreordained.

That conclusion, the most significant and oft-quoted statement in the entire report, was:

"Cigarette smoking is a health hazard of sufficient importance in the United States to warrant appropriate remedial action."

The Phase II strictures notwithstanding, what else was this but a "recommendation for action" against smoking of the most sweeping nature? And what "action," and "actions," this simple statement has inspired, actions that have indeed gone "beyond the health field and into the purview and competence of other Federal agencies"! Americans have been "remediated" up the wazoo.

I wonder . . .

Had the members of the advisory committee been able to foresee what was to flow from their work—the ostracizing of smokers from respectable society; the loss of or denial of employment to smokers (Chapter 8); the general hysteria over secondhand smoke with its consequent bans on smoking in workplaces and other public places (Chapters 6, 7 and 8); an antismoking lobby feeding on money extorted from smokers in the form of higher and higher taxes and fomenting discord, acrimony and fear among Americans; the denial of child custodial rights to smokers (Chapter 7), the corruption of science and the manufacture of statistics in the cause of a "smoke-free" society (almost all the chapters but especially Chapter 6); in short, the whole sorry mess—I wonder, had they been able to foresee all this, would they have approved of it? Or might they have been appalled and said to themselves, *"My God! What are we starting here?"* Might they then have recommended something different? Might they have said something like:

"We believe that we have established with reasonable certainty the existence of a number of possible health risks associated with smoking, that of lung cancer and cigarette smoking in particular. Although further confirmatory studies in this area are needed and encouraged, we believe that cigarette smoking is an overall health hazard of sufficient magnitude in the United States that the public should be made aware of it. Having accomplished that, our task is finished. Further actions, if any, lie within the realm of the individual responsibility of the ordinary citizens of this country. Those who smoke, as well as those who may be thinking of taking up smoking, must now decide for themselves whether the perceived benefits they derive from the use of tobacco outweigh what, in our best scientific judgment, are risks to their well-being and their very lives. Those decisions, however, are each individual's, and his alone, to make."

But they couldn't foresee, and of course weren't about to suggest that the product of their 13 months' labor was something people should merely think about, much less admit that Terry's "explosive" report was, in epidemiological terms, actually more like a firecracker in a barrel than a real bomb. So they called for "appropriate remedial action"—by "different competencies . . . and other Federal agencies."

That ever-so-innocent-sounding phrase, "appropriate remedial action," echoes through American society today with all the sinister overtones of some kind of "final solution."

THE SURGEON GENERAL'S 1964 report taught us more than about smoking and health. In fact, in retrospect, that is probably the least important thing it taught us. The most important thing it taught us is that our bodies do not belong to ourselves but to society at large and thus that the healthy maintenance of those bodies falls under the rightful purview of the governing authority of that society—the state and its "competency" (i.e., power). If we don't have enough sense to do the right thing healthwise for ourselves after we have been thoroughly warned about the consequences of our personal behavior, the state will take whatever "appropriate" measures it deems necessary to do it for us. After all, it's for the general welfare as well as our own. (Ask not what smoking does to you. Ask what it does to your country.)

This is a disturbing echo of the concept of *Pflicht zur Gesundheit*— "the duty to be healthy"—of Hitler and his National Socialists.[24]

The surgeon general's 1964 report also created lifetime employment opportunities for many people. As famed epidemiologist Ernst Wynder, whose work was cited 21 times in Chapter 9 alone in the report, recently wrote: "[I]f, in the late 1940s, my idea had been to study the relevance of electromagnetic fields to brain cancer rather than whether cigarette smoking caused lung cancer, my career might well have taken a very different turn."[24]

And if, in the mid-1960s, the surgeon general's report had not been written, American society also might well have take a very different and, I believe, a far happier, turn in the years that followed.

Truly can it be said that seldom in the annals of scientific endeavor has a single field of research been so rewarding to so many for so long as that devoted to finding out more and more bad things about tobacco and smoking.

And as another legacy of the surgeon general's 1964 report, sadly can it be said that because of the present atmosphere of political correctness in which this field of science operates, the few dissident scientists who dare to question some of those findings do so at risk, at best, of being accused of shilling for the tobacco industry and, at worst, of placing their professional reputations, if not their careers, in jeopardy.

In the chapters that follow I will attempt to give some small voice to the conscientious objectors in the crusade against smoking and will refer again to the 1964 Report of the Advisory Committee to the Surgeon General of the Public Health Service, which, as if it needed to be repeated, started the whole sorry mess.

Notes

1. *Smoking and Health*. Report of the Advisory Committee to the Surgeon General of the Public Health Service, U.S. Department of Health, Education and Welfare, Public Health Service Publication No. 1103, p. 33.

2. G. V. Yule, "The function of the scientific method in scientific investigation." Industrial Fatigue Research Board Report, 1924. Quoted in J. O. Irwin, "The place of mathematics in medical and biological statistics." *Journal of the Royal Statistical Society*, Series A, 1963. Requoted in Brownlee, p. 733 (see Note 18 infra). Yule was an early 20th-century pioneer in the science of statistics.

3. Gene Borio, "Tobacco Timeline." At www.tobacco.org/History/Tobacco_History.html#aal.

4. "History of the 1964 Surgeon General's Report." Office on Smoking and Health, National Center for Chronic Disease Prevention and Health Promotion, Centers for Disease Control and Prevention (CDC). Posted on the CDC's Tobacco Information & Prevention Sourcepage at www.cdc.gov/needphp/osh/30yrsgen.htm.

5. Quoted by CNN correspondent Dan Ronan in "Tobacco war smoldered for decades." Posted on the World Wide Web June 20, 1997.

6. At www.lcolby.com/.

7. "Abortion and Possible Risk for Breast Cancer: Analysis and Inconsistencies," National Cancer Institute CancerNet. From University of Pennsylvania Internet page at www.oncolink.upenn.edu/pdq600342.html.

8. C. Harcourt Kitchen, *You* MAY *Smoke* (New York: Award Books, 1966), p. 23.

9. Q&A in "Walter Scott's Personality Parade." *Parade*, October 27, 1996, p. 2.

10. *Smoking and Health*, p. 7.

11. "History of the 1964 Surgeon General's Report."

12. *Smoking and Health*, p. 7.

13. Loc. cit.

14. Elizabeth Brenner Drew, "The Quiet Victory of the Cigarette Lobby: How It Found the Best Filter Yet—Congress." *The Atlantic*, September 1965. From "The Atlantic Unbound" at www.theatlantic.com.

15. *Smoking and Health*, p. 17.

16. ATSDR (Agency for Toxic Substances and Disease Registry) of the Centers for Disease Control and Prevention, Public Health Statement, May 1990. At www.atsdr.cdc.gov:8080/ToxProfiles/phs8805.html.

17. Joe Dawson, "Essays on the Anti-Smoking Movement." At www.tezcat. com/smokers/issues1.html.

18. K. A. Brownlee, "A Review of 'Smoking and Health.'" *Journal of the American Statistical Association*, 60, 1964, pps. 722-739.

19. Kitchin, p. 61.

20. Lauren A. Colby, *In Defense of Smokers*. Self-published 1995, p. 42.

21. Foster Fitz-Simons, *Bright Leaf* (New York: Rinehart & Co., 1948).

22. Richard Kluger, *Ashes to Ashes: America's Hundred-Year Cigarette War, the Public Health, and the Unabashed Triumph of Philip Morris* (New York: Alfred A. Knopf, 1996), pp. 260-261.

23. Stanton A. Glantz et al., *The Cigarette Papers* (Berkely: University of California Press, 1996).

24. Robert Proctor, *Racial Hygiene: Medicine Under the Nazis* (Harvard University Press, 1998), p. 248. Cited in Sean Gabb, "Smoking and Its Enemies: A Short History of 500 Years of the Use and Prohibition of Tobacco." From FORCES Canada at www.forces-cdn.com/forest01.htm.

25. Ernst Wynder, *American Journal of Epidemiology* 1996; 143;747-749. Quoted by Steven Milloy on his "Junk Science" page at www.junkscience. com/ news/wynder.html.

Chapter 2

AND THE NUMBERS WERE FRUITFUL AND MULTIPLIED

Epidemiology is a crude and inexact science. Eighty percent of cases are almost all hypotheses. We tend to overstate findings either because we want attention or more grant money.

— Charles Hennekens[1]

One might say that giving computers to analysts was akin to giving aerosol paints to graffiti artists.

— John H. Fennick[2]

Eat less fat, don't smoke, exercise regularly, drink alcohol only in small quantities, practice safe sex, use seatbelts, avoid lawyers and doctors unless absolutely necessary, and choose your parents carefully . . . In spite of the most prudent behavior, however, our epitaphs may still be: "Stopped smoking 1968. Stopped drinking 1973. Stopped eating meat 1981. Died anyway 1993."

— Peter H. Gott, M.D.[3]

IN MIDSUMMER 1997, the USA cable channel ran back-to-back versions of the same movie, "Twelve Angry Men"—the original film that was released in 1957, followed by a modern remake for television.

I'd seen the first one and remembered that it had starred Henry Fonda as a lone juror in a murder trial stubbornly holding out against a snap verdict of guilty that every other juror favored. I was curious to compare it with the remake to see what difference 40 years might have made, not in the story but in the environment of the jury room.

The 1997 version was virtually a scene-for-scene and word-for-word replay of the original. What differences there were were minor. For instance, the jury was still all male but no longer all white. There was a nonworking electric fan in the 1957 jury room; in 1997 it was a nonworking air-conditioner. This time Jack Lemmon played the Fonda character. In 1957, the juror most vociferously demanding that the accused be found guilty was played by Lee. J. Cobb; in 1997, George C. Scott was the "bad guy."

But here is where 40 years of intervening history come in: in 1957 there were no fewer than five ashtrays on the long table the 12 men sat around and several of them smoked during deliberations, mostly cigarettes but also one pipe. In keeping with what has been true throughout history, the majority did not smoke.

(If it means anything, one member of the 1957 cast was Jack Klugman, who later attributed severe damage to his vocal cords to his cigarette smoking. Yet, curiously, he was one of the jurors who didn't smoke in the film.)

I don't remember if there was a "No Smoking" sign in the 1997 jury room; there wasn't, of course, in 1957. In any case, Scott was the *only* juror who smoked in 1997, and he did it in the washroom.

One point of this exercise is that in 1957, those jurors who smoked did so freely and naturally, as Americans did most everywhere back then, and none of the nonsmokers objected, or even thought about objecting. But one can be sure that if Scott had lit up in the 1997 jury room, there would have been all kinds of exclamations of distress and moralistic lectures from his nonsmoking fellows.

There was, however, one incident having to do with smoking in the 1957 movie. The foreman, Martin Balsam, is standing at the head of the table trying to say something and smoke from the cigarette of a nearby member of the jury keeps drifting into his face. He waves at it irritatedly and says to the man, "Would you mind?" To which the other replies, "Oh . . . sorry."

But this was hardly some kind of early antismoking statement; Balsam himself smoked in the movie. It was simply a bit of naturalistic byplay. Scott's apparently voluntary banishment to the lavatory was likewise quite naturalistic in 1997. Only a nut like me would even notice it. (It was a little strange, though, that none of the men complained about his fouling the air in that small room.)

Half of all present-day Americans weren't alive 40 years ago and many others were too young to have memories of what it was like in 1957, when smoking was simply something some people indulged in and others didn't, when it was not the divisive issue it is today and when certainly nobody regarded it as a social offense on a galactic federation scale. Yet even many who were in adulthood four decades ago, and who smoked, have undergone a fundamental "attitude adjustment" toward smoking since then.

The example closest to home for me is that of my wife, who was a heavy smoker of cigarettes from age 16 to 63 (but is nevertheless still alive and healthy in her 80s and looks to be in her 50s) and who is an otherwise tolerant and nonjudgmental person. Every time we watch an old film on American Movie Classics, she remarks, in a disapproving tone, something on the order of, "They're doing an awful lot of smoking in this movie"—having completely forgotten that the smoking was a reflection of the times and not, as antismokers allege about smoking in current movies, an insidious scheme by the cigarette companies to seduce impressionable youth.

Some years ago, in Venice, Florida, I went to a restaurant with my wife's sister's husband and five or six of his friends. They were all several years older than me and all of them, I believe, were veterans of World War II. When the host asked, "Smoking or nonsmoking?", they all laughed and chuckled, as if to say: What a silly question. Do we look like we're stupid enough to smoke? No one asked me and I didn't say anything.

I don't know how many of those guys were former smokers, but would bet most of them were. Their old comrade the cigarette was now their enemy. My brother-in-law, however, who had been a tail gunner on a B-24 in the Pacific theater, never smoked or drank a day in his life, yet his last 10 years were spent in and out of hospital, either in his hometown of Framingham, Massachusetts, or in Sarasota, Florida, as he went through one health crisis after another. He always recovered, so strong was his constitution. We used to say he would outlive all of us because the doctors monitored him so closely. It was only after his kidneys failed and he went on dialysis and after two heart bypass operations that a massive stroke felled him at the age of 75.

My wife and I visited him in the hospital in Sarasota after the second operation. Three doctors came into the room to talk to him. They had given him a 20 percent chance to survive the operation and I heard them tell him that if he had been a smoker, he wouldn't have had any chance at all.

Thus smoking was adjudged guilty even though it wasn't anywhere near the scene of the crime in this case.

The change in the way the overwhelming majority of Americans view smoking today is the major accomplishment of the surgeon general's 1964 report on *Smoking and Health.* Which brings me to a second reason for dwelling on "Twelve Angry Men." In both the 1957 and 1997 versions, the Fonda/Lemmon character gradually persuades the 11 other jurors, who are chafing to discharge their duty and get back to their lives, to overcome their prejudices against the defendant and take a close, analytical look at the evidence. They do so and eventually find him not guilty.

That was what I attempted to do in Chapter 1 regarding the surgeon general's indictment of smoking—to take a look at the original evidence and try to arrive at some verdict about its validity. It was, when I first started out, an endeavor wholly out of range of my competence as a lay person untrained in medicine, epidemiology or statistics. But the jurors in both versions of "Twelve Angry Men" are also ordinary people, unskilled in forensics. It is their collective, native common sense and the use of logic that eventually leads them to agree that the evidence against the defendant simply does not hold water.

That is how our justice system should work and does work (one hopes) more often than not. To paraphrase Winston Churchill's definition of democracy, it's probably the worst system we could use for arriving at the guilt or innocence of an accused person—except for every other system. Or to paraphrase another saying about war and generals, the administration of the law is too important to be left to the lawyers. But when it comes to the medical establishment and its unanimous indictment of smoking, anyone without medical expertise who attempts to judge the evidence armed only with common sense and personal experience and observation is undertaking a hopeless and, many would say, a foolish if not downright suspicious task. People's health is too important to be left to any but the health experts.

Maybe so, but when medical findings (or beliefs or assumptions) are translated into laws or ordinances affecting people's personal lives and behavior; when they divide the citizenry into the favored and disfavored, with the taking away of certain rights from the latter (even such a basic one as the right to earn a living) and the giving of more rights to the former; when they promote and justify all manner of discrimination against and disparagement of the minority in however "good" a cause—when this happens, as it has in the case of smoking, even the medically untutored citizen retains the right to say: *"Wait a minute. Is all this evidence really true? Even if it is true, is what we are doing on the basis of it wise and necessary?"*

So just for the sake of curiosity, let's delve a little more into epidemiology and statistics and in this and following chapters look at some of the important evidence against smoking that has been presented since the surgeon general's 1964 report.

Above all, let's exercise our common sense.

MY ATTEMPTS TO become at least minimally conversant with statistics and its uses have come a long way since I undertook this book, but it is a monumentally daunting field to the layman, especially one not especially skilled in mathematics. Even before I wrote Chapter 1, I'd already encountered "one-tailed" and "two-tailed" distributions and "standard deviations" and "logistic regression analyses" in epidemiological studies, but that was merely the tip of the iceberg. A catalog I received from John Wiley & Sons, a publisher of books on statistics, listed volumes on such topics as:

"Discrete Multivariate Distributions," which include such "families of distributions" as "multinominal, binomial, negative binomial, Poisson, power series, hypergeometric, Pólya-Eggenberger, Ewens and order *s*."

If you wanted to get into "Continuous Univariate Distributions," you'd be dealing with "extreme value, logistic, Laplace, beta, uniform, slash, *F*, *T*, noncentral *t*" and still other distributions such as "Pearson family, Johnson family, lognormal, gamma, loggamma, generalized gamma, Cauchy, exponential, Pareto, Rayleigh, chi-squared, inverse Gaussian and Weibull."

Then there are your "Univariate Discrete Distributions" which, according to the catalog, would introduce you to "extensive new work on mixtures, including generalized hypergeometric families; the increasing relevance of Bayesian inference to discrete distribution theory; the rapidly growing field of computer-generated, discrete random pseudo-random variates, and much more."

"Bayesian theory" is a whole field in itself, involving "single equation nonlinear models," "time series models" and "multivariate regression models." Not to be overlooked is "discrete stochastic dynamic programming," which has something to do with "discrete-time Markov decision processes."

But we're interested in how statistics is applied to the study of human health and things like smoking that affect it, and that gets us into the field of biometrics and such areas as "empirical Bayes and hierarchical Bayes procedures in simultaneous estimation of parameters and computer-intensive statistical methods" as well as "multivariate and multidimensional analysis" and "Bayesian analysis of sequential trials," without which we cannot hope to make meaningful "risk assessments."

Fortunately for today's medical researchers, it isn't necessary to have much more knowledge of statistics than I have. The early statisticians did the drudge work of solving equations and devising tables and formulas and so on, either by hand or with primitive mechanical calculators. Today it's all contained in computer software programs, and just as anybody with a can of spray paint can be a graffiti artist, anybody with a computer and one of these programs can come up with the "latest study." By tweaking a "parameter" here or fine-tuning a "parameter" there or "adjusting" for this or that "variable," you can arrive at just about any "finding" you want to, especially when dealing with "relative risks" that are, in most studies having to do with smoking and health, so close to pure chance that they could easily go one way or the other.

Statistics is a valuable means of telling us about probabilities—if, like any tool, it is properly used. In his 1964 report, the surgeon general illustrated a typical use of the "Poisson distribution" (see pages 40-42 of this book). Invented by French mathematician Siméon Denis Poisson in the 19th century, one of this formula's earliest applications was to calculate the probable number of annual deaths from horse kicks in the 14 cavalry corps of the German army between 1875 and 1894.[4]

More modern examples include using the Poisson distribution to help a grocery store manager determine the probability that he will sell X number of cans of, say, artichoke hearts in one week or half a week or two weeks or any period of time, based on the past average of cans sold per week. Or the formula could tell the manager of a busy airport the probability that any particular plane will be on the runway at any particular moment.

In these kinds of cases, the variables and confounding factors associated with them are few, if any, and can be pretty well defined and controlled for. Not so with living things like laboratory mice or rats or other animals, however, and even less so with human beings, when we are dealing with diseases and their causes.

Say that researchers want to estimate the probability that a new artificial sweetener might cause cancer in humans. It would be wholly impractical, as well as unethical, to test it directly on people. You'd have to enroll one group—perhaps consisting of hundreds if not thousands of volunteers—who would consume the chemical, say in a soft drink, and another "control group," similar in number and every other way to the first group, who would consume the same beverage sans the chemical under investigation. Both groups would have to be young, because you would have to follow the subjects for at least 20 years since it would take that long for cancer to develop in people.

Much, much easier and quicker to do a "bioassay" with laboratory mice. Here you can feed massive quantities of the chemical to a couple hundred of the unfortunate animals—quantities equivalent to a person's drinking thousands of cans of soda pop a day—and simply count how many of the mice had developed tumors at the end of a couple years, which is the average lifespan of the animals. Then you could report that yes, indeed, this chemical can cause cancer in people. One scientist calls this the "stuff and snuff" method.[5]

Unfortunately, some of the problems with this approach—ignoring the big one that a human would die of sheer bloat before he could drink anything remotely approaching thousands of cans of anything a day—are that different species or strains of laboratory animals are prone to different kinds of cancers, not all of which occur in humans. In some strains of mice "genetic drift" has increased the rate at which they develop spontaneous tumors. There may be factors the researchers are not even aware of. An example of this was the discovery by Italian scientists that the element manganese, which is present in most standard rodent diet formulations, was sometimes at levels up to nine times higher in the food the rodents were fed than the amount of manganese that was found to cause cancer in bioassays testing the element.[6] Obviously, overlooking a confounding factor like this could seriously "skew" (translation: screw up) the results of a study.

Sometimes just plain human fallibility can produce a misleading result. In September 1996, researchers at the University of North Carolina reported a study in *The New England Journal of Medicine** showing

*Or as one statistician heard a colleague say, "*The New England Journal of Medicine*? Oh, the *National Enquirer* of the medical world."[7]

that poor blacks 30 years ago ate healthier food than well-off whites. A year later they discovered that—oops—"an error in the computer program used to analyze their data" had given them a result 180 degrees wrong. In reality there was little difference in the healthfulness of whites' and blacks' diets in the 1960s.[8]

As Emily Litella, the comedic parody character on the television program "Saturday Night Live," would have said, "Never mind."

As fraught with complications as animal studies are, consider the statistical gymnastics a team of researchers went through after following a total of 20,551 U.S. male physicians aged 40 to 84 for up to11 years in attempt to find out if the eating of fish helped prevent heart attacks:

> Relative risks were computed using Cox proportional hazards models, controlling for age and randomized aspirin and beta carotene assignment. A multivariate Cox proportional hazards model was used to control for potential confounders, including prior cardiovascular disease, body mass index, smoking status, history of diabetes, history of hypertension, history of hypercholesterolemia, alcohol consumption, vigorous exercise, and use of vitamin E, vitamin C, and multivitamins. Other dietary factors (red meat, vegetables, fruits, dairy, chicken or turkey, and fried foods) were tested individually for associations with sudden cardiac death in separate Cox models, and each was entered into the multivariate model to test for confounding. Tests for trend were performed by assigning an ordinal variable for each level of consumption and modeling this as a continuous variable in separate Cox proportional hazards models. For each RR [relative risk], 2-sided *P* values and 95% confidence intervals (CIs) were calculated. The relationships between both fish intake and n-3 fatty acid intake and risk of sudden death were explored further using spline regression modeling. Restricted cubic spline models with 4 or 5 knots were used to flexibly model these relationships using measured values of fish or n-3 fatty acid intake and avoiding the need for prior specification of the RR function or the location of a threshold exposure value.[9]

After all that, their conclusion:

"The existing evidence *suggests* that consumption of fish once a week will help prevent coronary heart disease and therefore should be a component of a healthy diet." [Emphasis added.]

No one ever knew that eating fish was good for you before.

(Funny thing: Americans are awed by epidemiological statistics, especially regarding smoking, yet don't trust the use of statistical sampling in the 2000 census—the Republicans in Congress don't, that is.)

Even if a study is well-structured and the controls and adjustments for variables and confounding factors and the resulting statistics are impeccable, what a researcher *doesn't* tell us because of the way in which he presents his findings can be as revealing as what he *does* tell us.

Consider that pioneer 1956 study by famed researchers Richard Doll* and Austin Bradford Hill[10] that was ranked first among the seven studies upon which the surgeon general based his landmark 1964 report (see page 55 of this book). By extrapolating from the actual smoker and nonsmoker deaths they recorded among British doctors, Doll and Hill calculated that the death rates for lung cancer in the general population were 166 per 100,000 for smokers of 25 or more grams of tobacco a day, or a pack or more, compared with only seven deaths per 100,000 for nonsmokers. Thus smoking was associated with an almost 24-fold increase in the risk of death from lung cancer (166 divided by seven=23.7).

But look at the figures from another angle. What Doll and Hill reported was that 99,993 nonsmokers out of every 100,000 people escape death from lung cancer as opposed to 99,834 smokers per 100,000 who are so lucky (subtracting seven nonsmoker deaths and 166 smoker deaths from 100,000 respectively). When we divide the smaller number by the larger number, we get a smoking vs. nonsmoking "survival factor" of appoximately 0.998.

What this means is that, while a person who smokes may indeed incur a 24 times greater risk of dying from lung cancer than a person who doesn't smoke, the smoker also has 99.8 percent of the nonsmoker's chance of *not* dying from lung cancer. But only the "24 times as likely" risk was considered by the surgeon general. Why?

There would seem to be but two explanations: either Luther L. Terry and his advisory committee were unaware that epidemiological findings can be presented in more than one way, which would not speak well of their scientific competence, or they opted for the version they

*Subsequently knighted Sir Richard for his work in alerting the world to the scourge of tobacco. Maybe I am hopelessly prejudiced, but I have trouble placing a great deal of confidence in a physician who deliberately misuses, as Doll does, the term "epidemic" in regard to smoking.

knew would resonate most deeply among Americans, which would speak better of their public relations acumen than their scientific integrity and impartiality.

If the calculation above seems like some sort of statistical sleight of hand, it is easily verified with a hand calculator by multiplying 100,000 by 0.998. The result is 98,800, which is reasonably close to the extrapolated number of smokers per 100,000 the Doll and Hill study calculated do not die of lung cancer. (Multiplying the full factor of 0.99841 against 100,000 gives an even closer result: 99,841.)

To put it the other way around, the nonsmoker's chance of not dying from lung cancer is a mere one two-thousandth of a percent better than the smoker's (subtracting 0.998 from 1.000, which is "unity" or equal chance). Not exactly an impressive margin.

The first two calculations are from an article by Peter Finch, a professor of mathematical statistics in Australia, published on the Internet by the British organization FOREST (Freedom Organisation for the Right to Enjoy Smoking Tobacco).[11] The third bit of elementary arithmetic is my own.

Finch applied the same method to another study,[12] this one of ischemic heart disease, or IHD (a term synonymous with coronary heart disease, or CHD). Among other things, this study reported the estimate that, for males below age 45 who smoke 25 or more cigarettes a day, the death rate from IHD is 104 per 100,000 and for like-aged nonsmokers is only seven per 100,000, the same as Doll and Hill's figure for lung cancer deaths among nonsmokers. Since 104 divided by seven is 14.8, that meant that male smokers, in this age group and in this study, ran nearly 15 times the risk of nonsmokers of dying from coronary heart disease, and the researchers duly informed the scientific community of that, and no doubt the newspapers as well.

"This way of telling it is a very effective way of highlighting the message that 'smoking kills,'" comments Finch.

("Smoking Kills" is one of six rotating warnings on cigarette packages in Australia. In Ireland, I'm told, it's "SMOKING KILLS!" As actress Brooke Shields is reported to have said, "Smoking kills. If you're killed you've lost a very important part of your life.")

But what is the smoker's chance of *not* dying from coronary heart disease? When we answer that question, things once again appear in a different light.

To answer it, Finch says, again note that 99,993 per 100,000 nonsmokers escape death from IHD whereas 99,896 smokers do (seven and 104 subtracted from 100,000 respectively). Dividing 99,896 by 99,993, this time we get a smoker vs. nonsmoker "survival factor" of 0.999. (To prove it again, multiplying 0.999 against 100,000 gives the figure of 99,900—almost exactly the same as the 99,896 smokers that this study estimated do not die of IHD.)

In other words, while the data tell us that smoking is associated with a 15-fold increase in risk of death from IHD, it also tells us that the smoker nevertheless has 99.9 percent of the chance of a nonsmoker of escaping death from IHD—*or virtually the identical chance.*

And this time the nonsmoker's chance of not dying from IHD is only about a thousandth of percent better than the smoker's.

(Incidentally, it is a curious fact, if it is a fact, that while heart disease is the leading cause of death among the general population, neither it nor lung cancer is the leading cause of death among smokers. That is, according to one source, "smoking results in about as many deaths from heart disease among smokers as it does lung cancer deaths."[13] If it is true, as we are told, that lung cancer takes one of every 10 smokers, then heart disease must take another tenth, which means that eight out of 10 smokers die from something other than lung cancer or heart disease. Furthermore, according to the Centers for Disease Control and Prevention, smokers who stop smoking cut their risk of heart disease in half after one year.[14] Maybe nonsmokers worried about their hearts ought to take up the habit for a while and then quit!)

I tested Finch's method of looking at statistics with a claim I found in a book called *Cigarettes: What the Warning Label Doesn't Tell You* (about which more below). The authors cite one study which found that the death rate for people with asthma who had never smoked was 3.7 per 100,000, whereas among current and former smokers it was 8.3 per 100,000. Smokers were thus more than twice as likely to die from asthma than never-smokers.[15]

So as not to give smoking even the slightest statistical edge, let's say that nonsmokers' death rate from asthma is only three per 100,000 and that of smokers is nine—a full three times greater. Even minimizng the one death rate and maximizing the other, the chance a smoker has of not dying from asthma is 99.9 percent of that of the never-smoker (99,991 divided by 99,997). Again almost the identical chance.

How can all this be? If smoking is, allegedly, a proven health risk for an array of diseases, and especially for lung cancer and heart disease, how can the smoker's chances of not dying from those diseases be so close to the nonsmoker's chances?

The explanation simply is that in studies of these diseases we are dealing with very small numbers of deaths (of some of the subjects in the studies themselves) projected to a very large population. It is by multiplying the small X-per-100,000 death rate by the number of 100,000s in a total population that we come up with impressive numbers.

Here the unconvinced reader (is there any other kind?) may interpose an objection: If smokers' and nonsmokers' chances of not dying from lung cancer or heart disease are practically the same, why is it that in *every* study of these diseases smoker deaths *always* outnumber nonsmoker deaths?

That's a very good question, even if I raised it myself—although it should be clarified to say: every smoking study that we are *told* about. Studies that fail to come up with the results the researchers are looking for are seldom reported. Anyway, the question actually states that in every epidemiological study, a certain number of people turn up dead. This is because in any random population observed over a period of years, some people are inevitably going to die.

The fact that, in studies of smoking, dead smokers outnumber dead nonsmokers is certainly presumptive evidence that smoking may have been a causative factor in the smokers' deaths. But we are not talking about how many smokers vs. nonsmokers die in a particular study but about the comparative chances that *everybody* in the population at large has of not dying from the disease in question.

As one commentator wrote in *Fortune* magazine a decade ago:

> Although the Public Health Service has been reticent about publishing the fact, every study cited in support of the statement that "cigarette smoking causes cancer" reveals that a smoker is unlikely to get cancer—only that he is statistically more likely to get it than a non-smoker. No one can say how much more likely. This is true of all supposed carcinogens.[16]

No epidemiological study, even one that involved a truly random population in which subjects and controls were perfectly matched—which is impossible and is why researchers must "control" and "adjust" for all kinds of variables—can predict what will happen to any individual. Epidemiological studies only tell us what did happen to a certain number of people in the study itself. The big numbers we get when we extrapolate that number to the general population do not represent any actual dead people who have been counted, or even could be counted. They are an abstraction. No matter how many studies come up with more dead smokers than nonsmokers, it is the *chance* that any actual, real person has of dying or not dying from smoking that is the important thing.

Of course, whether or not anyone should decide to continue to smoke or to take up smoking based on that chance is also the important thing. I repeat Prof. Finch's discussion of that below.

FORGETTING THE "comparative chances" aspect for a minute, is Doll and Hill's smoker lung cancer death rate estimate even remotely valid today, assuming it ever was valid?

According to the Census Bureau's Statistical Abstract of the United States, the death rate from all causes was 880 per 100,000 in 1995 when the U.S. population was approximately 263 million.[17] (This was the latest year listed on the bureau's Website at the time of this writing.) Multiplying 880 times the number of hundred thousands (2,630) gives us a figure of 2,314,400 total deaths from all causes in 1995.*

Lauren Colby tells me that it is estimated that about six percent of all deaths in any given year are due to lung cancer (which is another way of saying that 94 percent of all deaths are *not* due to lung cancer). If this estimate is correct, it means that nearly 139,000 Americans must have died from that disease in 1995. Medical authorities also generally agree that at least 80 per cent of lung cancer deaths are "caused by smoking," which means that slightly over 111,000 smokers paid the ultimate price for their habit and perished from lung cancer in 1995. This works out to about 4.8 percent of all deaths.

Yet according to figures fed to Ann Landers on the occasion of "The Great American Smokeout" in 1995 and reported in her column, the American Cancer Society predicted that more than 157,000 smokers would die from lung cancer that year (see Chapter 5). That's 46,000 more deaths than the 111,000 estimate.

*Of course, the bureau had to do it the other way around first. That is, count the total number of deaths, then calculate the rate per 100,000.

In its 1995 "Cancer Risk Report" which I found on the Internet, however, the society estimated that there would be a *total* of 157,400 lung cancer deaths that year and further stated that "About 30 percent of all cancer deaths can be attributed to smoking."[18] Thirty percent of 157,400 is only 42,200. Thus on the one hand the society was telling Ann that *all* lung cancer deaths are attributable to smoking and on the other hand was suggesting that 70 percent of lung cancer deaths occur among nonsmokers!

The ACS wasn't suggesting any such thing, of course, for elsewhere it has claimed that not 80 but 90 percent of lung cancer deaths are "caused by smoking." But even applying 90 percent to the 139,000 figure from the previous page, that comes to some 125,000 smoker lung cancer deaths in 1995, which is still 32,400 fewer deaths than the society's prediction of 157,400.

I am not deliberately trying to confuse anyone; it's only that I myself am confused. Unfortunately, things become even more confusing when we consider that, according to the Census Bureau, the death rate from *all* cancers was 200 per 100,000 in 1995, or a total of 526,000.* Six percent of that (the percentage of lung cancer deaths among all deaths) is 31,560, and 80 percent of that (the conservative percentage of lung cancer deaths "caused by smoking") is 25,248—which is nearly 132,000 fewer smoker lung cancer deaths than the Cancer Society's prediction. And even using the society's 90 percent figure gives a difference of more than 128,000.

It's also nearly 86,000 fewer lung cancer deaths "caused by smoking" than the figure we get when we multiply 4.8 percent times total deaths in 1995.

It's also some 302,000 fewer lung cancer deaths "caused by smoking" than we get when we apply Doll and Hill's rate of 166 per 100,000 to the 75 percent of the U.S. population that was over the age of 18 in 1995.

What if the estimate that 4.8 percent of all deaths in a given year are smoker lung cancer deaths is way off base? What if it were higher?

*Could this be where the Cancer Society arrived at its figure of 157,000-plus smoker lung cancer deaths? Thirty percent (the percentage of all cancer deaths it says are attributable to smoking) of 526,000 is 157,800. But in this case then, the society would be saying that *all* cancer deaths among smokers are lung cancer deaths!

It's certainly possible, but to get the cancer society's number of 157,400 smoker lung cancer deaths it would have to be quite a bit higher—not 4.8 percent but 6.8 percent of deaths from *all* causes in 1995.

How many people really die from lung cancer every year because they smoke? Doll and Hill didn't know. The Census Bureau doesn't know. The American Cancer Society doesn't know. I sure as heck don't know. Nobody knows.

WELL, I'VE OFTEN been asked (more usually, challenged), what about all those famous actors and actresses and other prominent people who smoked and died of lung cancer—Edward R. Murrow, Gary Cooper, John Wayne, Yul Brynner, Audrey Meadows? The list is endless.

This is what is called anecdotal evidence, and all I can say is, my anecdotal evidence is as good as your anecdotal evidence. For instance, Hal Roach, the producer of the original "Our Gang" movies, is said to have smoked four packs of cigarettes a day, and he lived to 102. We all remember that George Burns was never without a cigar in his hand, and he just missed the 100 mark. (Of course, he may not have inhaled cigar smoke directly but he breathed the fumes for many, many years, and we "know" how deadly secondhand smoke is, not to mention the danger of oral cancer from cigars.) And top this—the amazing Jeanne Calment of France, who lived till 122 and only stopped smoking cigarettes at 120 because she could not longer see to light the things.

When my nonsmoking son read the above paragraph in an early draft of this book, he remarked that it was really a pretty weak argument. After all, he said, how many Hal Roachs or Jeanne Calments are there? And true enough, if we were to get into a numbers game that pitted smoking anecdote against smoking anecdote, skeptics like me would lose. But would that prove anything, or would it only be a reflection of the fact that we keep a count of those smokers who die of lung cancer or some other "smoking-related" disease but not of those who don't die. Anyway, as another person reminded me, "The plural of anecdote is not fact"—and that should work both ways, shouldn't it?

If we were to put the existence of UFOs up to a popular vote, the nonbelievers would again be overwhelmed. But what would be proved? If the government were ever to admit that it had been covering up the truth about visitations by UFOs for 50 years and had even recovered dead aliens from UFO crashes, we would immediately witness an explosion of UFO sightings and people would quite sincerely and truthfully swear to their factuality.

In a similar way, the fact that the government told us in 1964 that "smoking kills" goes a long way toward explaining many of the subsequent "sightings" of smoking-caused deaths.

It's in the genes, I'm increasingly coming to believe. Maybe John Wayne et al. were constitutionally susceptible to lung cancer. Maybe there was also something in their genes that predisposed them to go into show business. Or maybe the simple fact is that smoking, and smoking alone, did indeed kill them. But again, it's only those smokers who die of lung cancer that we hear about, not those who don't die.

THIS IS PROBABLY as good a place as any to insert an unfortunately necessary disclaimer: This book is written from the viewpoint of an ordinary layperson who decided to try to pierce the statistical smokescreen (forgive me) generated by the antismoking movement in hopes of finding out what really are the health dangers of smoking and whether they are of sufficient magnitude to justify the extreme "remedial actions" that have been imposed, and continue to be imposed, on American society.

I have never received any money from any cigarette company, and I would decline it were it offered. I must confess that I have gotten a number of free cartons of Doral from R. J. Reynolds for sending in tabs from cigarette packages, and my wife and I were both given a souvenir pen and complimentary pack of cigarettes one time when we toured the Philip Morris plant in Richmond, Virginia. (The company used to conduct daily tours, open to anyone, but for some reason discontinued them several years ago.) I also occasionally receive coupons in the mail for a few dollars off a carton from some of the companies. But that's the extent of it.

Furthermore, I have never knowingly owned stock in any cigarette company, or even had any communication whatsoever with any cigarette company before or during the writing of this book. Maybe I'll receive a letter from one of them saying, "Good job trashing the antismokers, Mr. Oakley. Please accept this check as a token of our appreciation." I won't, but I hereby give advance notice anyway that I will return it.

Not only do I not now have, nor have I ever had, anything to do with any cigarette company or anyone associated with the tobacco industry, I have no trust in, no respect for and vanishing sympathy for the whole bunch of them. They have shown themselves to be quite willing to sell their only friends—the consumers of their products—down the river. But that's something I get into in Chapter 12.

Incidentally, speaking of the tobacco industry's "friends," in his book, *Thank You For Smoking,* Christopher Buckley ridicules the kind of people who constitute the membership of the "prosmoking" or "smokers' rights" groups I mention in this book. He portrays them as a rather pathetic crew, both in they way they are hooked on smoking and how they are used as pawns by an industry that itself views them with amused contempt.

The only thing I disagree with is the characterization of smokers' advocates as pathetic. Betrayed, yes. Pathetic, no. The pathetic smokers are those who have not rallied to support the few and small smokers' advocates groups but instead stand by silently and submissively as the antismokers push them farther and farther to the margins of decent society—even while picking their pockets with higher and higher taxes.

Finally, the statistics in the examples above are those reported by respected researchers and institutions. If following the numbers to their logical conclusions leads us to a different picture of the risks of smoking than is officially reported, shouldn't people know about it?

Not that most people will believe anything I say in this book. But it's possible that a few readers will be encouraged to reexamine what they know, or think they know, about smoking and, more important, what they think this nation should do about smoking.

It may be a vain hope. I recently came across a book titled *You* MAY *Smoke* by a Briton named H. Harcourt Kitchin, a layman like myself, who attempted to stem the rising antismoking tide. This slim volume, published in 1966, examined the flaws in both the 1962 report of the Royal Society of Physicians and Surgeons and the 1964 report by the U.S. surgeon general. Although Kitchin's arguments remain valid today, it goes without saying that his effort went for naught.

Maybe it was because the book was premature; the antismoking crusade was barely getting under way in 1966. In any case, I'd never heard of the book or seen any reference to it, even on a "prosmoking" Internet site, but my local library was able to borrow a frayed and yellowed copy of it from, of all places, Jerry Falwell's Liberty Baptist

College in Lynchburg, Virginia, and I quoted it from it in Chapter 1.

I'm indebted to Stanton Glantz's *The Cigarette Papers* (also cited in Chapter 1) for alerting me to *You* MAY *Smoke*. That was hardly the intention of this prominent antismoking activist, of course. He'd come across references to it in one of those stolen Brown & Williamson Company documents and discovered—oh, the perfidy!—that a British cigarette company, Carreras Tobacco, had purchased 7,000 copies of the book and that an American public relations firm working for B&W had approached and assisted Kitchin in publishing a U.S. edition.

Just one more pebble to be added to the mountain of evidence showing the utter lack of conscience on the part of the tobacco industry and just how low it will stoop to defend itself.

TO GET BACK TO Prof. Finch, his calculations don't mean that smokers can continue on their merry way without a worry that they might be inviting a health problem sometime in the future. As he writes:

> These relatively high percentage chances of escaping the disease in question do not by themselves establish that smoking is harmless. For one thing, they ignore death from other causes and refer only to one disease at a time rather than to the spectrum of diseases with which smoking has been associated . . .
>
> The point here is not that the second calculation [comparing the numbers of smokers and nonsmokers who don't die from the disease] exonerates smoking but that presenting only the result of the first calculation [the "times as likely" figure for smokers] suppresses an aspect of the data that could lessen the force of the message that "smoking kills." For telling a 40-year-old male heavy smoker that his chance of not dying from IHD is about 99.9 percent of that of a comparable non-smoker is much less likely to persuade him to abandon smoking than telling him that his chance of dying from IHD is almost 15 times that of a comparable non-smoker.

This of course is why studies never mention the more favorable chance. Doctors don't want to be perceived as encouraging anybody to smoke, and as Finch himself acknowledges, there is some degree of risk associated with smoking.

"Nevertheless," he says, "even if one accepts the edited versions of the facts presented by health promoters, then their message should perhaps more accurately be: *smoking kills relatively infrequently*." [Emphasis mine.] He goes on:

> The fact that a smoker has almost as much chance as a comparable non-smoker of escaping a disease does not itself make that a chance worth taking. One can best see this in an unemotional context that has nothing to do with smoking and the diseases that have been associated with it. Early work on the vaccination of children against polio showed that polio was contracted by 57 in 100,000 unvaccinated children, but only 16 in every 100,000 vaccinated children. This meant that an unvaccinated child was about 3.6 times more likely to contract polio than a vaccinated child. On the other hand, an unvaccinated child had 99.96 per cent of the chance of a vaccinated child of escaping polio. Nevertheless most people did not see this as a chance worth taking.
>
> This does not mean that vaccination is pointless. It is mentioned here only because it has been argued that the logic that sees polio vaccination as worthwhile should also suggest that smoking be abandoned. However, this argument ignores what the smoker sees as the benefits of smoking. Thus, in the case of smoking, as opposed to refusing to be vaccinated, some people do see a benefit in it and may value that benefit so highly that they see 99.9 per cent of the chance that a non-smoker has of escaping death from IHD as worth taking. A person's decisions about what risk factors to avoid involve balancing what he or she perceives as their benefits against the chance of falling to what some say might be their consequences.

And there in a nutshell is what bugs antismokers—the idea that any sensible person would weigh some perceived benefits of smoking against the possible—if not probable, if not inevitable—consequences and deliberately and freely c*hoose* to smoke.

This attitude was reflected in a letter sent to *Reason* magazine by Elizabeth M. Whelan, Sc.D., president of the American Council on Science and Health, in response to an article by senior editor Jacob Sullum. Sullum had written about how, with the traditional infectious diseases largely conquered, the public health field had switched to combating "metaphorical epidemics" like smoking and other health-threatening habits or lifestyles, and speculated about how this new emphasis could affect individual freedom.

Whelan observed:

"People tend to succumb to social pressure and impulse in adopting health-compromising lifestyles and then justify their actions by rationalizing about them . . . Choices made by neglecting likely negative consequences may give some people a sense of 'freedom,' but how free can someone be who chooses chronic self-destruction?"[19]

To which Sullum responded that this notion of freedom "gives me the willies."

He wrote:

> Personally, I do not perceive enough benefit in smoking to justify the risk. But I'm sure a lot of smokers would have a hard time understanding why I enjoy bungee jumping. By saying that individuals who defend their "health-compromising" lifestyles are simply "rationalizing". . . Ms. Whelan impl[ies] that such choices are inherently irrational and that people who make them must be ignorant, stupid, or crazy. . . If people are free only to make careful, reasonable, fully considered choices that they will never regret, they are not free at all.

Here, however, I would disagree slightly with both Prof. Finch and Mr. Sullum. I really don't think that many smokers have made a decision, freely or otherwise, rational or otherwise, to smoke. Most smokers I know fully believe all the warnings about the health risks of smoking, yet they smoke anyway—not because of "addiction" or a weighing of perceived benefits vs. the risks or because of a what-the-hell-you're-gonna-die-eventually-whatever-you-do attitude but because, unconsciously, they sense that the risks to them personally are remote, even though, consciously, they may accept that for the entire class of smokers the risks are real and substantial.

To this it can be countered that the damage done by smoking accumulates by such slow and imperceptible degrees over many years that the smoker may not become aware of the damage until too late. I can only speak for myself, and it's been more than half a century since I started smoking. I'm now in my 70s and normal aging alone ensures that someday I will develop some kind of health problem or problems, one of them eventually terminal. Will I have croaked because I smoked, or because we all wear out sooner or later?

It should also be remembered that the main case the antis make against smoking is that it causes *premature* death, and that is a flexible term. As average expected lifespan has advanced over the past 100 years, from the 40s or 50s at the turn of the century to the 70s today, so has the age advanced at which we consider a death to be premature. But to the antis, no matter at what age a smoker dies, it is always "premature."

In all the years between 1964 and 1994, between Surgeon General Terry's report and my starting research for this book, I had no reason to suspect that this landmark document was not all it was cracked up to be. If anyone had asked me, I would have said I believed it, more or less, although I continued to smoke. When I was with Scripps Howard News Service from the late '70s to the mid-'80s, where I was one of three editorial writers, I somehow always got stuck with writing an editorial on Surgeon General C. Everett Koop's latest annual blast against smoking. But I never did actually editorialize; I merely, dutifully and reluctantly, wrote a column repeating his words without comment. I realize now that I was not only getting sick and tired of the endless assaults on smoking issuing from the surgeon general's office and everywhere else but that, intuitively, I had known all along that they were so much hokum.

DR. WHELAN'S LETTER to *Reason* brings me to the book I mentioned above, *Cigarettes: What the Warning Label Doesn't Tell You.* The book was compiled under the auspices of her American Council on Science and Health (ACSH) and is a compendium (in fewer than 200 pages) of everything that is known, suspected, alleged or assumed about the role of smoking in just about every human disease, affliction, ailment and condition under the sun.

The Preface gives a roster of 20 "selected established and suspected health effects of cigarette smoking" that are discussed in the book's 20 chapters. They are:

Lung Disease: Lung cancer. Chronic obstructive lung disease. Increased severity of asthma. Increased risk of developing various respiratory infections.

Cancer: Esophageal, laryngeal, oral, bladder, kidney, stomach, pancreatic, vulvular, cervical and colorectal cancers.

Heart Disease: Coronary heart disease. Angina pectoris. Heart attack. Arrhythmia. Aortic aneurysm. Cardiomyopathy.

Peripheral Vascular Disease: Peripheral vascular disease. Thromboangiitis obliterans.

The Skin: Wrinkling. Fingernail discoloration. Psoriasis. Palmoplantar pustulosis.

Surgery: Need for more anesthesia during surgery. Increased risk of postsurgical respiratory infection. Increased need for supplemental oxygen following surgery. Delayed wound healing.

Orthopedic Problems: Spinal disc degeneration. Less successful back surgery. Musculoskeletal injury. Delayed fracture healing.

Rheumatological Conditions: Osteoporosis and osteoarthritis.

Environmental Tobacco Smoke and Pediatric Illnesses: Infections of the lower respiratory tract. More severe asthma. Middle ear infections. Crohn's Disease and ulcerative colitis. Sudden Infant Death Syndrome. Impaired delivery of oxygen to body tissues.

Complications in Obstetrics and Gynecology: Infertility. Miscarriages. Fetal growth retardation. Prematurity. Stillbirth. Premature "water breaking." Transmission of HIV to the fetus. Birth defects. Intellectual impairment of offspring. Sudden Infant Death Syndrome. Earlier menopause.

Male Infertility and Sexuality Dysfunctions: Decreased sperm motility. Decreased sperm density. Impotence.

Neurological Disorders: Transient ischemic attack. Stroke. Worsened multiple sclerosis.

The Brain and Behavior: Depression.

Abnormalities of the Ears, Nose and Throat: Snoring and hearing loss.

The Eyes: Cataracts. Complications from Grave's disease. Macular degeneration. Optic neuropathy.

Oral Health: Periodontal disease.

The Endocrine System: Increased metabolic rate. Blood sugar abnormalities. Increased waist-to-hip ratio (redistribution of body fat).

Gastrointestinal Disease: Stomach and duodenal ulcers. Crohn's Disease.

The Immune System: Impaired humoral and cell-mediated immunity.

Emergency Medicine: Injuries from fires. Occupational injuries.

Holy, uh, smoke! What a list! If we could only eliminate smoking, doctors could play golf all day long.

I look at the most important of these diseases or disorders in this book and the evidence that smoking is a causative factor of or is "associated" with them. (One I don't look at is palmoplantar pustulosis, which I never heard of but believe is a form of psoriasis.) But I must say something here about Crohn's Disease, which is actually a group of inflammatory diseases that can occur anywhere in the gastrointestinal tract, and ulcerative colitis, an inflammatory disease of the colon.

According to the highly respected *Merck Manual of Diagnosis and Therapy*, the cause or causes of both these diseases is unknown. Although numerous hypotheses have been put forward, ranging from bacteria and viruses to environmental chemicals to poor diet, none has been proven. They may strike both sexes at any age, although Crohn's Disease is more common among Jewish people and seems to run in families.[20]

Nowhere does the manual suggest smoking as a possible factor, let alone "environmental" tobacco smoke. Ditto for Grave's Disease (hyperthyroidism/goiter). For the ACSH to implicate smoking in these diseases is more than a wild stretch; it is an irresponsible one.

Of all the maladies listed above, the only one I have personal experience with is periodontal disease.

The first time I had my teeth deep-cleaned (at age 68), the periodontist asked me if I smoked. To avoid a possible lecture, I told a half-lie and said I used to. My gums were fibrous, he said, and that was caused by smoking. I asked him how he knew. "How do I know? Why, 15 years of practice and hundreds of papers." I didn't ask him if his personal observation had come first and was later confirmed by articles in dental journals, or whether he first learned about this cause of fibrous gums from his reading and then began observing it in his patients who smoked.

Was smoking the cause of my periodontal disease? Don't nonsmokers ever get it? Or was it because I inherited bad teeth and the water wasn't fluoridated when I was growing up in Pittsburgh and my mother let me indulge in sweets and didn't make me brush immediately afterward and we never heard of flossing and all that? I still smoke, but my gums are improving and my teeth (those I have left) are more sound than they have ever been, thanks to conscientious brushing and flossing and regular cleanings by the periodontist.

More personal experience:

Twice, when I have had a tooth extracted by other dentists, I have been advised not to smoke because that would cause "dry pockets." I smoked anyway, and my "pockets" stayed wet.

A few years ago in Georgia I cracked a rib when I tripped and fell against a low retaining wall in my backyard (which figures since according to *Cigarettes* smokers are more likely than nonsmokers to have accidents). The doctor at the emergency clinic advised me not to smoke for a couple weeks because that could invite pneumonia. I smoked anyway and didn't get pneumonia and, despite the "delayed fracture healing" the American Council on Science and Health says smoking causes, the fracture healed in the same amount of time the medic said these things normally took to heal.

I'd cracked a rib once before, when after my retirement from Scripps Howard I became a school bus driver in Fairfax County, Virginia. I was standing on the bus's bumper one morning checking under the hood and slipped off the bumper. My chest hit hard against the edge of the radiator. At the clinic they gave me a big elastic bandage to wear around my chest. When I asked the doctor in my second rib-cracking episode about that, he told me that was the worst thing you could do.

I don't pay a whole lot of attention to doctors.

As if anticipating my immediate knee-jerk argument against *Cigarettes*, in the Introduction, one Kristine Napier, who is not identified in the Acknowledgments, writes that "[E]veryone knows at least one smoker 'who has smoked for 40 years and is healthy as a horse.'"

But consider an analogy of two soldiers, she suggests, each of whom must traverse a field. Soldier A has to cross a field laden with land mines, and soldier B a field relatively free of such deadly traps. Even though each soldier may cross his field safely, the odds definitely favor soldier B. Soldier A may avoid many, perhaps even most, of the land mines, but he is highly unlikely to avoid all of them.

According to the American Council on Science and Health (and everybody else), the odds are heavily against the smoker. If he doesn't trip the lung cancer land mine, he may fall afoul of the esophageal cancer land mine. Or if he misses that one, there are the peripheral vascular or the osteoporosis or the psoriasis, etc., etc., land mines. So pay no attention to all those healthy smokers "everybody knows." Above all, don't ask how realistic the odds are.*

*I remember as a boy hearing that the expected lifespan of a Royal Air Force pilot in the Battle of Britain in 1940 was something like two weeks. But I later read in a book I have unfortunately lost that, despite the odds, the overwhelming number of pilots who survived those two weeks went on to survive the entire six-months-long battle.

This is a vivid analogy, but a little misleading. In real life, both soldiers (representing all of us) cross the same minefield and face the same deadly traps of disease and accident. Leaving aside the role genetics may play* in endowing some of us with greater or lesser protection from one or another of those traps and others of us with more or less vulnerability to them, the difference between soldier A and soldier B is the former's lack of caution. He just plows on ahead, ignoring warnings from such as Whelan et al. that his recklessness—his smoking—is "highly likely" to get him blown up or seriously injured.

But smoking is not the only so-called risk factor in life, although in the view of ACSH it apparently outweighs all others. Many people have unhealthy diets. Many work in high-risk occupations. Many engage in dangerous sports. Nor is there only one single risk factor associated with the major diseases. Consider heart disease, or the family of diseases we lump under that term, which kills more Americans every year than any other disease. Heart attacks from coronary artery disease (CAD) alone took away some 487,000 of us in 1994.[22] The term CAD embraces arteriosclerosis (degenerative changes in the arteries) and atherosclerosis (fatty deposits, or plaque, on the arterial walls).

According to my source for this figure, the famous Framingham Heart Study, now in its 50th year, has to date identified over 100 potential risk factors for atherosclerosis.

This isn't a typo. The researchers believe there may be *100* potential risk factors for atherosclerosis. The major "modifiable" ones that individuals can do something about by way of helping them tread more safely through life's minefield include smoking, obesity, high blood pressure, physical inactivity, diabetes and cholesterol. The "unmodifiable" risks, those you can't change, include age (45 percent of the deaths in 1994 were of people over 65), gender and family history (genetics again).[23]

But an earlier source reported that the dedicated researchers in

*Which is leaving aside a heck of a lot. Some hereditary diseases which have been traced to defects in specific genes include: Alzheimer's, neurofibromatosis, cystic fibrosis, muscular dystrophy, retinoblastoma (tumor of the retina), Wilm's tumor (childhood kidney cancer), hemophilia, Hodgkin's disease, amyotrophic lateral sclerosis (Lou Gehrig's disease), colon cancer and, yes, lung cancer.[21]

Framingham had identified some *200*(!) risk factors for heart disease, which I guess must include CAD and IHD and CHD and everything else that can affect the heart.[24]

(Although my brother-in-law lived in Framingham he wasn't a participant in the study, which is a good thing for them because his health history would have seriously confounded their statistics. Incidentally, while he never smoked or drank, he refused to wear a seat belt in a car. That was a modifiable risk factor for personal injury that he voluntarily assumed.)

It really doesn't matter whether it's 100 or 200 risk factors or some other ridiculously outlandish number, for how could people possibly avoid all of them, even if they knew what they were? How many more will the Framingham study "identify" in its second half-century, and what value will its findings be? You might as well say that being alive is a major risk factor for death from a heart attack. Indeed, simply having been born is the one constant factor in deaths from every cause.

According to cardiologist William Castelli, director of the Framingham study, while smokers have a 70 percent chance of dying of a heart attack, and while high blood pressure increases the risk of heart attack and stroke by up to five times, high total cholesterol and low HDL (high-density lipoprotein cholesterol, the "good" kind) are among the strongest predictors of heart disease. And for him personally, high cholesterol is the Number One risk factor.

"I'm living proof that you can beat the odds of heart disease—even if it runs in your family," he says. He is the first male among his kin ever to reach the age of 50 without having a heart attack.[25]

(The first male? That suggests that gender might be a greater heart attack risk factor for him than high cholesterol.)

Dr. Castelli did it by bringing his total cholesterol down from somewhere in the 270s to 190 and raising his HDL to 63 from a former 49, and he accomplished that by starting, in his 30s, to jog every day and to cut down on dietary fat.

"When you see the Golden Arches," Castelli told an audience of elderly residents of Framingham and next-door Natick at a health fair in 1997, "you are probably on the road to the Pearly Gates."[26]

Probably? For everyone? I've eaten hamburgers and french fries all my life and smoked for most of it, and if I'd never taken a bite out of one of those fatty things or sucked on a single "cancer stick," I couldn't be any healthier than I am (knock on my wooden head). Even if smokers have a 70 percent chance of dying from a heart attack (70 percent of what—a 100 percent chance?), I humbly submit that there is probably just as much, if not more, of a chance that other important factors are also involved, chief of which is a natural proneness toward high cholesterol, a condition my wife has but I don't, thanks to my wise choice of forebears.

According to the National Center for Health Statistics, a branch of the Centers for Disease Control and Prevention, 738,731 Americans died of diseases of the heart in 1995.[27] The American Council on Science and Health says that "Each year, cigarette smoking accounts for nearly 200,000, or one fifth, of all deaths from heart disease in the United States."[28] That would mean there are nearly a *million* heart disease deaths each year. Again never mind; the ACHS is grinding its ax.

Let's assume that a fifth of annual heart disease deaths are caused by smoking. That means that four-fifths of annual heart disease deaths are *not* caused by smoking but by something else, and the most likely something else is a high-fat diet.

Or so I believed until recently. A common airborne bug called *Chlamydia pneumoniae*, which is responsible for 10 percent of the respiratory illnesses people usually call flu, is being increasingly scrutinized as a cause—possibly even the most important cause—of heart disease. Or if not exactly a cause per se, certainly an important trigger for a heart attack. A cousin of *Chlamydia trachomatis,* which according to the Merck Manual is now the most common cause of sexually transmitted diseases in the United States, *Chlamydia pneumoniae* was discovered in the 1960s by Dr. Thomas Grayston of the University of Washington, but only in the past few years did researchers begin detecting telltale signs of the bacterium in plaque taken from the clogged arteries of heart patients.

According to Grayston, the "scenario" may go something like this:

> An unfortunate soul inhales *C. pneumoniae.* To fight off the bacteria, the immune system sends macrophages—cells that are supposed to destroy invaders—to the lungs. Lab tests have shown, though, that the microbe can survive being gobbled up by the immune cells. Now the macrophages carry the wily bugs throughout the body. Everywhere they go, they assail the arterial walls, entering cells to reproduce.

> Because macrophages seek out trouble spots, *C. pneumoniae* are often carried to places where there's already an arterial injury—say, from a deposit of bad cholesterol. As the bacteria damage or kill cells in the coronary arteries, more macrophages arrive to repair the injury, but they only bring more of the intruder. A pile of macrophages, reproducing bacteria, and other detritus forms in the arterial wall. As it grows it bulges into the bloodstream and narrows the artery, setting the stage for a clot to choke off blood flow.[29]

Confirmation of this scenario could help solve two medical mysteries: 1) why half of all heart attacks happen to people with normal levels of cholesterol, and 2) why the incidence of heart disease, which began rising in the 1920s (as did lung cancer), has been falling (as has cancer of all kinds, including lung cancer), even though Americans are living as high on the fatty dietary hog as ever. It would also raise the possibility that heart attacks could be treated, or even prevented, with ordinary antibiotics. In fact, the decline in heart disease could be due to the introduction of antibiotics, which have inadvertently been killing *C. pneumoniae* while being administered for other purposes.

If so, the *Chlamydia pneumoniae* story would repeat that of another common bacterium, *Helicobacter pylori*, which doctors now know causes most stomach ulcers and can be eradicated with antibiotics. These discoveries have inspired scientists to start pursuing other bacteria and viruses as possible culprits in a number of debilitating diseases, including cancer. Maybe even lung cancer?

In the meantime, universal medical opinion holds that a diet high in fats is the best way to set oneself up for heart disease. So how come the states aren't suing the fast-food industry to the tune of a few hundred billion dollars as reimbursement for the medical costs it has inflicted on society by enticing unsuspecting people through seductive advertising—*much of it aimed at hooking little children!*—to scarf down those fatally fatty hamburgers, french fries and chocolate shakes? Why hasn't the victim of a heart attack caused by clogged arteries sued one of the hamburger chains?* Surely hamburger lovers are no more re-

*It's already happened to the dairy industry. In Washington State, one Norman Mayo filed suit against Safeway stores and the Dairy Farmers of Washington, claiming that a lifetime of drinking milk contributed to his clogged arteries and a minor stroke he suffered. In addition to monetary balm, he

sponsible for their personal choices than those hopelessly "addicted" smokers who have sued the cigarette companies. What kind of secret research is this industry hiding from us? How come employers aren't refusing to hire people who are "addicted" to Big Macs, or aren't firing people caught chewing on one during lunch break, as many companies have done to smokers (see Chapter 8)?

Never fear. Once they've eradicated smoking, the healthists, the lifestyle monitors, those who know what's best for everyone, will get around to hamburgers. Indeed, some of them have already demanded that the federal government "do something" about our reckless eating habits (see Chapter 5).

All we need is a book called *Fast Food, Slow Death: What Ronald McDonald Doesn't Tell You.*

THE LONG LIST OF hazards the American Council on Science and Health says the smoker flirts with reminds me of the comic strip "Shoe." In one strip the character Cosmo takes his antique and ever-malfunctioning automobile into the shop. After the mechanic stares at the engine for a while, Cosmo asks, "What do you think it is?" "It could be anything," opines the mechanic. "That's what *I* thought," says Cosmo.

Imagine going to a doctor to find out why you're feeling so poorly lately, and even before examining you his saying, "It could be some respiratory infection. It could be an ulcer. It could be heart disease. It could be your blood sugar is up. It could be your metabolism. It could be anything."

Indeed, so many are the health hazards the smoker courts that, writes Napier in *Cigarettes*, "the full spectrum of diseases causally linked with smoking can be described collectively as 'tobaccosis.'" The term is again defined in an Afterword as "denot[ing], collectively, all those diseases resulting from the smoking, chewing and snuffing of tobacco and the breathing of tobacco smoke."

Medieval alchemists searched in vain for a "universal solvent" and an elixir that would both transmute base metals into gold and prolong

---

also wanted a warning label on milk. "It's my opinion that the dairy industry is to blame," he said. "They push their dairy products without warning you of the hazards."[30]

life. We moderns have succeeded in discovering the "universal agent" of disease—"tobaccosis"—and the elixir of life is simply to avoid tobacco.

Wonderful. Now all the doctor has to do is ask you if you smoke and he can then proclaim, "Why, it's obvious what your problem is. You're suffering from tobaccosis."

Doctors, thank goodness, delve a little more deeply than that. A shoot-from-the-hip diagnosis of "tobaccosis" would be of no more value to them or to their patients than was the diagnosis of "neurasthenia" that 19th-century physicians often fell back on when they could find no obvious cause of an ailment.

Is the American Council on Science and Health seriously suggesting that medical science adopt the term "tobaccosis"? Apparently it is. It's needed, says the Afterword, because "few [people] are yet aware of the bodywide range and nature of the total spectrum of diseases caused by tobacco . . . because such diseases are treated disparately by clinical specialists and assigned numerous anatomic diagnoses devoid of the unifying term tobaccosis. Hence the basic causative role of tobacco is often missed and disregarded."[31]

(Here the attentive reader may point out that Prof. Finch also spoke of "the spectrum of diseases with which smoking has been associated." But I doubt very much that he would agree that such a varied group of diseases warranted the all-embracing suffix "osis.")

In the next paragraph the ACSH further justifies the term by noting that in the case of tuberculosis, "the records all patients with any manifestation of tubercle bacillus infection are ordinarily labeled tuberculosis. The same is true for histoplasmosis, asbestosis, silicosis, syphilis and AIDS."

There is one problem with this. Tuberculosis is not a "spectrum" of a score of different and unrelated diseases. It is a single disease caused by *Mycobacterium tuberculosis* and related organisms, and by those organisms alone. The same with the other "osises." With the possible exception of AIDS, they also are single diseases, each caused by an identifiable germ, virus or environmental agent uniquely associated with that disease. This misuse of the suffix "osis" suggests to me that the authors of *Cigarettes* are infected with a bad case of "antitobaccosis," which in their case is indeed a spectrum—of biases, prejudices and selective interpretations of clinical evidence.

As for the book's subtitle, *What the Warning Label Doesn't Tell You,*

I trust that the council isn't advocating that the tobacco companies be required to list all the diseases, etc., allegedly caused by tobacco and smoking on their cigarette packages. The type would have to be so small you'd need a magnifying glass to read it. Anyway, smokers don't read the warning labels that are already there and nonsmokers don't need to be warned. So who would be served? Teenagers, maybe? But there's good reason to believe that the more the antismokers have tried to scare teenagers away from smoking, the more attractive they have made it to them (see Chapter 10).

Yet while doctors don't jump to a diagnosis before actually examining a patient, some of the first questions they do ask of every patient today are, "Do you smoke?" "How long have you smoked?" "How many cigarettes a day do you smoke?" "Have you ever smoked?" "How long and how much did you smoke?" Questions like that have been on every questionnaire I've filled out during a first-time visit to a doctor in recent years.

Luckily so far, in my own crossing of life's minefield, those visits have been infrequent and, except for my two rib accidents, have been for general checkups—just to make sure; after all, you know what they say about smoking.

The first such examination I'd had in many years was in 1992. I confessed my sin of smoking to the M.D., but try as he might he couldn't find anything wrong with me. Lung X-ray—clear. Sphirometer test—I blew it off the dial. Blood pressure and everything they test for in the blood—normal. Prostate gland—ditto. Cholesterol—only about 140. Muscle tone and joint articulation and reflexes—fine.

He pronounced me in good health—"at this time"—but advised me to stop smoking. Certainly I was aware, wasn't I, of all the studies showing the risks of smoking. What did I think about them?

I mumbled something to the effect that I thought a lot of studies proved what the people doing them wanted to prove. He kind of scoffed gently at that.

My heart was also okay, as far as he could tell. But he recommended I see a cardiologist for a stress test and he arranged an appointment. Once again I failed miserably to exhibit any problems, from smoking or anything else.

The first doctor also recommended I have a sigmoidoscopic examination and here, at last, they found something warranting "remedial action." Like President Reagan, I had polyps, which can turn cancerous, growing on the walls of my colon. So I had a polypectomy. It's a fairly routine, outpatient operation which doesn't require general anesthesia, only something to put you in a kind of twilight zone. Thus I didn't need the extra anesthesia and postsurgical oxygen Whelan et al. say smokers have to have. Since then I've had a second polypectomy because the polyps started to grow again, as they did with President Reagan, but as far as I know smoking has never been blamed for this condition, even by Whelan et al.

(A sad side note is that the surgeon who performed the first operation was forced to retire in the prime of his career because of unusually severe tinnitus, a ringing, or in his case a roaring, in his ears that rendered him unable to practice any longer. I myself have mild tinnitus, but this is quite common, especially among the elderly, and also isn't blamed—yet—on smoking.)

Four years later, I visited an osteopath because of "jumpy legs" which bothered me periodically. He gave me the same complete examination as the first doctor, and the only problem he could find was a buildup of wax in my ears. But I had also confessed my irrational, self-destructive lifestyle choice of smoking and he was of course aware of all those studies in scientific journals. He thought he saw a suspicious spot on my lung X-ray and had me undergo a CAT scan at the clinic next door. When the result came back negative, he expressed amazement that I could have smoked for so many years and be so healthy. In fact, he said it twice: "I'm amazed." Doctors have been snow-jobbed along with the rest of us by the antismokers.

There's a disease of the blood vessels of the lower limbs called Buerger's disease (the "thromboangiitis obliterans" in the list above from *Cigarettes*). Seventy years ago doctors, including Dr. Leo Buerger himself, believed it was almost exclusively a "Jewish disease."[32] Today doctors believe it is almost exclusively a smoker's disease. But they can't find anything wrong with my circulation, and although Buerger's disease does apparently occur most commonly in smokers and the symptoms often disappear if they stop smoking, it sometimes afflicts nonsmokers too.

Could be that other notorious drug, caffeine, is the culprit. I drink seven or eight big cups of coffee a day. Or it could be the two shots of booze I reward myself with every afternoon after a hard day at the word processor.

Now that I think about it, "it could be anything."

What I really wonder about is whether the $450 (or whatever it was; I forget the exact amount) that Medicare coughed up as its share of the cost of my CAT scan, as well as for my previous stress test, whatever it cost, went on the books as "smoking-related" expenditures. Would that be fair, just because the doctors only ordered them because I was a smoker? Do doctors report it to the government if a patient smokes? Were my brother-in-law's years of kidney dialysis (wholly paid for by Medicare) and his other illnesses recorded as nonsmoking-re lated? Who records this stuff anyway? Who determines which person's medical costs are "smoking-related" and which person's aren't? How do all those states claiming reimbursement from the cigarette companies for the billions of dollars of excess Medicaid costs they allegedly foist on nonsmoking taxpayers—which really means extorting money from smokers because it will ultimately come from them in the form of higher prices for cigarettes—how do they know down to the decimal point which costs are "smoking-related" and which are not?

Well, they don't know and they don't *have* to know. It's "common knowledge" that if a smoker gets sick, it's because he smokes. (Nonsmokers never get sick, or hardly ever. Even if they do get sick, their treatment doesn't cost the healthcare system anything.) And thanks to the tobacco companies' running away with their tails between their legs, the con artists will never have to prove their claims in a court of law.

Speaking of Medicare and making people pay for other people's medical costs brings me to my most recent physical examination, in 1997, when I joined Kaiser Permanente's "Senior Advantage" program. And what an advantage it is for old geezers like me, who pay nothing for their medical and hospital insurance (except for a small amount deducted from their social security checks that they never miss), because this and similar programs for seniors are subsidized by raiding the paychecks of all those sappy baby boomers and members of the "X" generation.

This time, fed up with feeling apologetic about smoking, I straight-out lied and told the doctor I had never smoked. I had debated about it with myself, and decided that omitting this information would not compromise the doctor's ability to establish the state of my health; to the contrary, eliminating the extraneous issue of smoking would aid him. Too late, it afterwards occurred to me that I might also have inadvertently confirmed any belief he might have that only nonsmokers are healthy. Oh, well.

"No history of smoking," he said as he wrote that down. Because of that (I'm guessing) he didn't even have my lungs X-rayed. At least that's one cost to Medicare they couldn't record as "smoking-related." I consider this as both a personal act of revenge against the states' attorneys general and a small way of thanking the boomers and X-ers, who are maintaining me and all seniors in a style of living no previous older generation in history ever enjoyed.

Anyway, once again I was pronounced in fine fettle—except my cholesterol was up to 148.

Finally, in early 1998 I had an operation to remove a hydrocele, a fluid-filled sac, from a personal area of my body. I'd had it for years and every doctor said not to worry about it, hydroceles never turned cancerous. But it had grown quite large and uncomfortable. When the Kaiser urologist said he preferred to do the surgery under general anesthesia (the patient under it, that is, not him), I felt a little trepidation. I hadn't had general anesthesia since my tonsillectomy at age 5. They didn't know I was a smoker. What if they didn't give me enough anesthetic or enough oxygen? What if I choked on phlegm? What if Whelan et al. were right?

But all went well. I was no sooner put under than it seemed that they were bringing me out of it. I asked the anesthesiologist how I'd done. Just fine, she said. How was my oxygen level? Also fine. I then told her that I'd been smoking cigarettes for 52 years. She expressed no astonishment at, or even much interest in, that revelation. Which confirmed my belief that it is the antismoking zealots who manufacture these scares about smoking, not your workaday physicians.

Yet for all my familiarity with the tactics of the zealots, I'd let them sucker me in by planting unnecessary fear in my mind.

All of which personal history is again purely anecdotal and proves absolutely nothing, though I'm sure it has been intensely fascinating to the reader.

WHERE WAS I? Oh, yes, Dr. Whelan. I had lunch with her one day in 1975 when she was in Cleveland promoting her first book, *Panic in the Pantry* (co-authored with Frederick J. Stare, M.D., chairman of the department of nutrition at Harvard School of Public Health, and with her a founder of the American Council on Science and Health). I was happy to help publicize her book with an editorial mentioning it because it presented a nonalarmist view of and effectively debunked a flurry of scares at that time about the dangers of additives and pesticides and other suspect stuff in the food we ate.

I don't remember if I smoked in the restaurant, but if I did she said nothing about it. I do know that smoking was not discussed during our lunch. But this was before secondhand smoke hysteria started and before smoking became a social offense as bad as urinating on the floor, so I may have smoked. If I did, and if she was as vehemently antismoking then as she is today, she exhibited considerable politeness and self-restraint in not lecturing me. Her favorite terms for the cigarette companies are "merchants of death" and "purveyors of poison" and she has written at least one other antismoking book, which I haven't read, *A Smoking Gun: How the Tobacco Industry Gets Away With Murder.*

It saddens me that a person who demonstrated, and still does demonstrate, so much common sense when it comes to exaggerated environmental dangers can not only so sincerely believe that smoking is either implicated in or is *the* cause of a multitude of health problems but can so earnestly promote that belief—and the fears it engenders—to the general public.

Not that she or the specialists who reviewed each chapter in *Cigarettes* are, as Dave Barry would say, making anything up. They cite study after study. They are also reasonably honest; if there are conflicting studies, with one indicting smoking in this or that disease and another finding no evidence against smoking, they tell the reader. But then they take it back.

For instance, on page 19 they note that there is an abundance of literature on smoking and prostate cancer and that most of it does not support an association. However, this is followed by a sentence, which I quote in full below, to the effect that smoking increases the severity of this cancer.

On page 106 they note that the risk of Alzheimer's disease appears to decrease the more cigarettes are smoked per day and the more years they are smoked, possibly because smoking boosts the function of the neurotransmitter acetycholine. But then they say that other researchers postulate (I think they mean "suggest") that it is actually a difference of genes in smokers and nonsmokers that accounts for this "paradox" rather than any protective effect of smoking. A difference in genes is never "postulated" in regard to any other disease, however.

On page 147 they note that a bacterium, *Helicobacter pylori*, is associated with an increased risk of developing ulcers, which occur in smokers and nonsmokers alike. (This bacterium is far more than merely "associated" with ulcers, as I mentioned above.) But smoking decreases immunity, they say, thus lowering resistance to infection by this organism.

I also find it significant that throughout the book it is stated that "one study" has estimated this or "one study" has found that.

Some examples from just the first chapter:

"One study has estimated more than a doubling of penile cancer among men who smoke more than 10 cigarettes a day compared with nonsmokers. Another study has estimated more than a tripling of risk for people with a history of more than 45 pack-years." (Page 17)

"One study has estimated that the risk of anal cancer is elevated by almost eight times for heterosexual men who smoke and by more than nine times for women who smoke." (Page 18)

"One study found that smokers had a higher incidence of more invasive and high-grade prostate cancer than did nonsmokers." (Page 19)

Such statements are always followed by a reference number, with the study identified at the end of the chapter. This certainly doesn't mean that the authors could not have cited more than the one study regarding a particular disease or disorder or condition, etc. Frequently they do in fact reference several studies in support of a statement. But the book is aimed at a general audience, not a scientific one, so the multitude of references that typically buttress an article in a scientific journal isn't necessary here.

Yet allowing for that, the fact that *Cigarettes* relies so often on single studies suggests to me that the book ought to carry a warning label of its own, perhaps borrowing the caution of one statistician:

> [M]aking one study is about the same as throwing a pair of dice, once, observing that the result is, say, ten, and proclaiming "When you throw dice, the number ten comes up" . . . Never read anything, or listen to anyone, if the opening statement resembles "According to one study . . . "[33] [Second ellipsis in original.]

To wind up this chapter, let's look at two examples of "one study," each of which was conducted on a different battlefront in the crusade against smoking and both of which were ballyhooed as having broken new ground in confirming the health dangers of cigarettes.

The first was not an epidemiological study that observed living persons but a laboratory study which, its authors claimed, led them to the holy grail of the antismoking movement—the elusive, long sought-after "smoking gun," the exact biological mechanism by which smoking causes lung cancer, or, as *The Wall Street Journal* put it, "the final link in the chain of evidence.[34]

This study involved a gene called the "p53" gene. In the late 1980s, according to the *Journal*, researchers at Johns Hopkins in Baltimore had discovered that p53 is a tumor suppressor that regulates cell division and keeps cells from going out of control and turning cancerous. Because it performed that function, it was called "the guardian angel" gene. It was "suggested" that damage to that gene by cigarette smoke "could" cause lung cancer.

Here already I get a little confused because in April 1996, cancer researchers at the Kimmel Cancer Center at Thomas Jefferson University in Philadelphia reported in the scientific journal *Cell* that they had found a gene they called FHIT (fragile histidine triad) which functioned as a shield to block the growth of cancerous tumors and that, when damaged by cigarette smoke, played "a critical role in the development of lung cancer."[35]

Whether FHIT is another name for p53 or is a different gene entirely, the big news came a few months later when, in October, a team of cancer researchers at the M.D. Anderson Cancer Center in Houston announced that they had found a "direct link" between cigarette smoke and damaged p53. The discovery was reported in *Science*, the journal of the American Association for the Advancement of Science, in an article titled "Preferential Formation of Benzo(a)pyrene Adducts at Lung Cancer Mutational Hotspots in *P53*,"[36] authored by biochemist Moon-Shon Tang and colleagues.

(The print and television news media were also informed, of course. But while ABC's Peter Jennings and NBC's Tom Brokaw merely told viewers about it, CBS's Dan Rather played it up big as usual by running video footage of Tang making the historic announcement at a press conference in Houston.)

Benzo(a)pyrene, or BAP, had been a leading carcinogenic, or cancer-causing, suspect in cigarette smoke even before the 1964 surgeon general's report. According to Tang et al., however, it isn't BAP but a metabolite of BAP, benzo(a)pyrene diol epoxide, or BAPDE, that is the nemesis of the p53 gene. (A metabolite is a substance produced by an organism's natural process of metabolism. Metabolites flow into the bloodstream where they are carried throughout the body, including of course the lungs.)

Tang et al. stated that in about 60 percent of lung cancer cases, there is mutational damage to the p53 gene. The Philadelphia researchers had stated that the FHIT gene was mutated in 80 percent of the lung tumors they tested. In either case, it is the same as saying that in 20 to 40 percent of lung cancer cases there is *no* damage to the genes. Thus whichever the gene and whatever the percentage, a logical conclusion is that people can get lung cancer even if their genes are in perfect, unmutated condition.

This is only one obstacle in the way of accepting Tang et al.'s finding. In a critique of their experiments, Lauren Colby, who seems to be one of the few commentators who actually read the *Science* article, points out that the researchers did not study any actual human lung cancers. Rather, they studied cultured human cells, which they exposed to BAPDE and then tested for mutational damage. He writes:

> Not having any humans to work with, the authors of the study compared the mutations which they had induced with specimens of DNA taken from a gene data base, compiled by others. Now, if the goal of the study was to prove that BAP from smoking causes lung cancer (and that was, indeed, the goal), it would seem to be scientifically necessary to compare the genes of smokers who fall victim to lung cancer with those of non-smokers who fall victim to the disease. Such a comparison would show whether lung cancer in smokers has a different etiology (cause) than in non-smokers.
>
> The authors of the study, however, deliberately excluded from the study any DNA samples obtained from non-smokers or from "radon associated cancers." They did not say how they knew whether any particular samples came from non-smokers or were "radon associated"; apparently they took the word of the people who compiled the data base. The point is, however, that while all experiments should always be controlled, these authors deliberately threw out the controls![37]

In my own opinion, the first and biggest obstacle to pinning the blame for lung cancer on the BAP in cigarette smoke is, as I noted in

Chapter 1, that BAP is a ubiquitous substance in the environment. It is produced by the combustion of vegetation and fossil fuels as well as the cooking of food. In fact, better than 90 percent of the BAP consumed by humans, including smokers, comes from food.

Colby continues:

> The authors of the study apparently concede that BAP, in and of itself is not terribly carcinogenic (although, like any irritating substance, it will produce skin cancers in specially bred "nude mice"); it must be converted to BAPDE. There is no evidence that the lungs, themselves, can metabolize BAP into BAPDE. Even if they could, the amount of BAP reaching the lungs from cigarette smoke is dwarfed by the amount reaching the lungs in the blood supply (and already metabolized into BAPDE) from consumption of burnt food. Thus, at the outset, the study appears flawed. However, it gets worse!
>
> The authors make the astonishing statement that "This study provides a direct link between a defined cigarette smoke carcinogen and human cancer mutations." I say "astonishing," because the study dealt with BAPDE, not BAP, and there is no BAPDE in cigarette smoke. Thus, at best, the study could claim only an "indirect link." But, because of the failure to take into account the BAP consumed in food, it isn't possible to claim even an "indirect link." The study could just as well be said to prove an indirect link between the consumption of burnt food and lung cancer. However, it doesn't prove even that, because (a) it does not explain lung cancer in the 40% of victims who have no p53 gene damage and (b) the authors compared their results with DNA samples which they selectively picked and chose, throwing out those which they deemed to be "radon associated" or from non-smokers (free translation: throwing out those that would not have validated their conclusions).

This is a devastating analysis—and why was it left for a nonscientist to make it? To my knowledge, no scientist has pointed out the fatal deficiencies in the Tang study. At the same time no researcher has even bothered to try to replicate it, which is the way things are supposed to be done in science. We haven't heard anything more about this "smoking gun" since October 1996. The p53 gene seems to have gone . . . *fhit.* Yet as far as the general public is aware, science now "knows" exactly how smoking causes lung cancer.

This p53 gene business only deepens the mystery for me. Whether it is BAPDE or some other metabolite in the blood that sets off lung cancer, or whether it's something in cigarette smoke acting directly on lung tissues, why should it take 20 or 30 or 40 or more years for a tumor to appear?

I can understand how microscopic particles of asbestos or coal dust can reside in the deep recesses of the lungs for many years before they cause mesothelioma or black lung disease. That is, I can visualize some sort of "festering" process. But a pathologist dissecting the lungs of someone who died of lung cancer has no way of knowing whether the victim smoked or did not smoke. There are no residues of anything from cigarette smoke in the lungs and no histological (tissue) differences between a smoker's tumor and a nonsmoker's. In fact, the pathologist cannot tell whether the cancer originated in the lungs or whether it metastasized from some other organ. The only way he can "know" that smoking caused the cancer is if the victim's medical record shows a history of smoking during some period in his life.

Actually, the search for the biological mechanism by which smoking causes (or may cause) lung cancer always was a fruitless and unnecessary quest—and not just because everybody, laymen and doctors alike, everybody with half a brain, already "knows" that it does. There are any number of diseases or conditions whose causative agents have been identified but medical science doesn't fully understand the exact mechanism by which they affect the body, yet nevertheless has ways to treat them. For example, in the 1960s doctors in Europe became aware that women who had taken the new sedative thalidomide in early pregnancy were giving birth to babies with undeveloped limbs. Even though they didn't know exactly how the drug worked its mischief on the fetus, they didn't *need* to know in order to remedy the situation.

However, there is an important difference between knowing from sad experience that thalidomide causes birth defects and that the "cure" is simply to prevent pregnant women from taking the drug, and "knowing" from epidemiological studies that cigarette smoking causes lung cancer and attempting to frighten or force people to give up the habit.

If some madman were to administer thalidomide to a group of women at the right stage of pregnancy, he could predict with certainty that all, or certainly most, of them would deliver defective babies. But not only does a mere one out of 10 smokers ever develop lung cancer (we're told), no one can possibly predict which one. Our knowledge of thalidomide is the result of the direct observation of its effect on real people; our "knowledge" about cigarette smoke is a statistical abstraction from epidemiological studies. No matter how many people we can cite who smoked and died of lung cancer, this evidence remains at bottom purely anecdotal. It may be highly suggestive, even persuasive, evidence, but so is my anecdotal evidence in the other direction.

We're back again to Prof. Finch and the question of chances. With something like thalidomide, the chance of harm is virtually certain. With smoking, it is, to paraphrase him, relatively infrequent.

In the meantime, although we also "know" that secondhand smoke kills, dedicated researchers continue to pile up what they would have the public believe is convincing evidence in that area. The second "one study" is perhaps even more important than the first, both because it is one of the most recent in this field and because of its social ramifications. It was announced by the American Heart Association on May 20, 1997:

> DALLAS, May 20—Constant exposure to second-hand smoke—in the workplace or at home—nearly doubles the risk of having a heart attack, a landmark study of more than 32,000 women suggests. Results of the research appear in today's American Heart Association journal *Circulation*.[38]
>
> Boston scientists say their 10-year investigation involving female nurses found a higher level of risk from passive smoking than has been seen before and provides the strongest evidence yet that exposure to smoke in the workplace is as dangerous as exposure at home.
>
> Healthy, non-smoking nurses who said they were regularly exposed to "passive" smoking by their co-workers or home companions had a 91 percent higher relative risk of a heart attack or death, compared to nurses who were not subjected to smoke, the researchers at Brigham and Women's Hospital and Harvard Medical School report. For nurses who reported only occasional exposure to smoking in work or home environments, heart disease risk was 58 percent greater.
>
> "Those are larger risks than have been previously reported," says Ichiro Kawachi, M.D., the study's lead author . . .[39]

Reaction of the media was predictable. A few examples:

The Washington Post: ". . . the largest study ever conducted on the issue . . . provides strong new evidence . . . " (John Schwartz, staff writer.)

The Los Angeles Times: ". . . the largest study of its kind ever conducted . . . one more powerful scientifically based argument for banning all smoking in the workplace . . . " (Commentary.)

Associated Press: "The findings . . . could help advocates of a nationwide ban on smoking in workplaces . . . " (Melissa Williams, AP writer)

USA Today: " . . . Passive smoking is deadly . . . The U.S. Occupational Safety and Health Administration has dallied since 1994 over a workplace smoking ban, trying to accommodate smoking interests. It's time it saved some lives instead." (Editorial, "Bring on the Ban".)

No newspaper informed its readers that a "91 percent greater risk" meant that the researchers had established a relative risk of a mere 1.91, which it may be remembered from Chapter 1 is barely significant, if it is significant at all. A "58 percent greater risk," or a relative risk of 1.58, is even less significant. Yet that 91 percent risk was represented by the American Heart Association as nearly a doubling of the risk of a heart attack.

Not that there is anything new about this. Researchers and institutions have always reported statistics in ways that are most easily understood (actually, misunderstood) by the general public and that make their "findings" look important—although the antismoking movement has raised this technique to a high state of perfection. As one student of the subject wrote a full decade before the crusade against smoking was launched, "The secret language of statistics, so appealing in a fact-minded culture, is employed to sensationalize, inflate, confuse, and oversimplify."[40]

Some of the other findings of the Brigham and Women's/Harvard study the newspapers did not report:

- "Among women exposed only at work, the multivariate relative risks of total CHD [coronary heart disease] were 1.49 (95% CI [confidence interval], 0.71 to 3.14) among those occasionally exposed and 1.92 (95% CI, 0.88 to 4.18) among those regularly exposed to second-hand smoke." (Page 2376 of *Circulation.*)

(Another reminder: when the lower boundary of a confidence interval range is below one, the result of that calculation is considered to be statistically insignificant by every authority on epidemiology.)

- "The multivariate relative risks of total CHD were 1.81 (95% CI, 1.08 to 3.02) in women exposed at home or work and 1.36 (95% CI, 0.72 to 2.54) in women exposed in both settings. However, the data on women exposed in both settings was based on a small number of cases (n=24)." (Page 2376.) [Which is rather a long way from 32,000!—D.O.]

• "There was no relation apparent between duration of living with a smoker and risk of CHD." (Page 2374.)

• "Unknown confounding factors may have contributed to the observed excess risk . . ." (Page 2377.)

• "A limitation of the present study was its reliance on self-reported assessments [anecdotal evidence—D.O.] of exposure to passive smoking." (Page 2377.)

• "A further limitation of this study is that exposure to passive smoking was ascertained only at baseline." (Page 2378.)

What that last sentence refers to is that only at the beginning of the study (1982) were the nurses asked how much cigarette smoke they "thought" they were exposed to. They were never asked again in the 10-year duration of the study.

The above passages from the study were published on the World Wide Web by the National Smokers Alliance, a smokers' advocate group partially supported by the tobacco industry.[41] The following critique by Martha Perske was also published by the NSA (but who else would publish it, certainly not the unbiased mainstream media). Ms. Perske is, like me, a private citizen with no medical credentials. She is an award-winning artist and stamp designer. However, she possesses common sense and uses it in a new vocation dedicated to exposing the exaggerated claims, if not outright fraudulent "science," of the antismoking movement. She writes (with underlining and other emphases hers):

> The Harvard study—supported by public funds from the National Institutes of Health—seems to have been presented to the media in a disingenuous way, apparently in an attempt to rouse public resentment and promote smoking bans.
>
> For example, not mentioned in the Harvard press release or the American Heart Association's website release is the fact that this study found no statistically significant increased risk from exposure to secondhand smoke in the workplace. Instead, the American Heart Association's release states, "The finding of high risk associated with workplace smoke is a very important one, Kawachi emphasizes." *What high risk?* The finding wasn't even statistically significant!
>
> In the Harvard press release, Kawachi says that the "strong association" suggests that secondhand smoke is responsible for up

to 60,000 deaths each year from coronary heart disease, and *"From the standpoint of alleviating risk, the good news is that certainly smoke-free building policies would go a long way to changing this picture."*

By presenting their results according to exposure at home OR work, the Harvard researchers were able to make it appear there was risk from workplace exposure (and thus a need for smoking bans), when in fact there was no statistically significant increased risk at all from workplace exposure alone. All significant findings reported by the Harvard researchers involved exposure in the home, and even those are questionable . . .

[V]irtually all of the relative risks reported in the Harvard study are below 2.00, and according to the National Cancer Institute, relative risks below 2.00 are considered "small" and could be due to statistical bias, confounding factors, or chance. Not exactly the "high risk" claimed by Kawachi.

Perske also calls attention to these shortcomings:

1. The study—while erroneously touted in the press as the largest ever done—was based on only 152 coronary heart disease cases, 25 of which were fatal. The largest studies ever done were based on data from the American Cancer Society and reported no increased CHD risk from workplace exposure and no statistically significant increased risk for women married to smokers.

2. There were no measurements of actual exposure to secondhand smoke. Study subjects were asked if they were "occasionally" or "regularly" exposed to secondhand smoke, and they were asked this question only once, at the beginning of the 10-year study. Follow-up questionnaires were mailed to study subjects every 2 years to update information on cardiovascular risk factors, etc., but no attempt was made to update self-reported information on secondhand smoke exposure.

3. Study subjects were all female nurses, not representative of the U.S. female population. Nurses often work under stressful conditions, yet the Harvard team did not consider or adjust for "stress."[42]

Alas, she concludes, "This is yet another secondhand smoke study that has been overblown in the media. Unfortunately, after it's been sensationalized in neon lights, it's next to impossible to get the media to take a second look, let alone investigate the possibility that the public (whose money was used to fund the study) was knowingly misinformed in order to advance the anti-smoking agenda."

And once again it was left to a layperson to expose the fallacies in an antismoking study, while the scientific community remained silent.

I don't know who financed the p53 gene experiment, but would it be altogether too cynical of me to suggest that both it and the nurses' study (not to mention many other such studies) were conducted because there is a great deal of grant money—much of it lifted from the pockets of smokers—available from the government and private health associations for just about anyone with minimal scientific credentials and a half-baked theory who wants to cash in on the antismoking crusade? It's the best way for a researcher to get his name in print and enhance his career these days.

Speaking of nurses and stress and half-baked theories, Dr. Kawachi headed another team of researchers who studied another bunch of nurses—86,626 of them no less—from 1980 to 1990 and "discovered" that coffee drinkers are less likely to commit suicide than those who don't imbibe. (Note carefully the tense: "coffee drinkers *are* . . ," not "coffee drinkers *were* . . ." Researchers try to avoid using the past tense, for that might suggest to the public that the findings of their studies had limited import, applying only to the actual participants in the studies at the time of the studies and not to everyone in the world for all eternity.)

Specifically, out of those 86,626 nurses the study recorded 11 suicides among those who drank two cups of coffee per day, compared with 21 suicides among those who said they almost never drank coffee. To give it a number, drinking two or three cups of coffee a day reduced the risk of suicide by 66 percent. Kawachi cautioned, however, that the results may not be significant because doctors might have told nurses who were depressed (for any number of reasons) not to drink coffee.[43]

In any case, one presumes that the nurses who committed suicide had told the researchers about their rate of coffee drinking *before* they killed themselves. Somehow, even though I'm a coffee drinker, reading about that study left me very depressed.

I don't know if this coffee-drinking group of nurses included any of the 32,000 secondhand-smoke-inhaling nurses in Kawachi's other study that was going on at the about the same time, but obviously the doctor was a busy man. He is also a prime example of a researcher who has found rewarding lifetime employment thanks to the antismoking movement and Americans' general hypochondria.

As for why reputable journals publish studies like these in the first place, that is another question entirely. Where is the peer review that is supposed to weed out this kind of junk science?

In the next chapter I'll examine some even more egregious examples of junk science conducted in the cause of a "smoke-free society."

Notes

1. Quoted in *The New York Times*, October 11, 1995, and cited in "Secondhand Smoke-and-Mirrors (How the Pros Tamper with Jury Pools)." Posted on Steven Milloy's Junk Science page at www.junkscience.com/news/mirrors.htm. Hennekens was one of seven authors of the notorious secondhand smoke study of nurses published in *Circulation* (see Note 38 infra).

"[T]he whole apparatus of grants-and-research projects . . . discourages candid acknowledgement that one may work for years at what turns out to be a dead end, and constitutes a standing encouragement to exaggeration, half-truth and outright dishonesty about what one has achieved."—Susan Haack, professor of philosophy at the University of Miami. *Skeptical Inquirer*, November/December 1997, p. 38.

2. John H. Fennick, *Studies Show: A Popular Guide to Understanding Scientific Studies* (Amherst, N.Y.: Prometheus Books, 1997), p. 69.

3. Peter H. Gott, M.D., "Health Warnings: Enough Is Enough." Column distributed by Newspaper Enterprise Association, December 5, 1993.

4. Martin Feinstein, Ph.D., *Statistics*, in Barron's EZ-101 Study Keys (Hauppage, N.Y.: Barron's Educational Services, 1994), pp. 49 and 50.

5. Unattributed quote in Laurie McGinley, "Of Mice and Men: How Ex-Lax, Trusted for Nearly a Century Became a Cancer Risk." *The Wall Street Journal*, September 26, 1997. At www.junkscience.com/news.exlax.htm.

6. "Manganese Mangles Mice Experiments." At www.junkscience.com/news/manganes.html.

7. Quoted in Fennick, p. 10.

8. "Study Was Wrong." News & Notes. *The Atlanta Journal-Constitution*, December 18, 1997, p. E3.

9. Christine M. Albert, M.D. et al, "Fish Consumption and Risk of Sudden Cardiac Death." *Journal of the American Medical Association*, 1998;279:23-28 (January 7, 1997). At www.junkscience.com/news/eatfish1.htm.

10. Doll, R. and Bradford Hill, A., "Lung Cancer and Other Causes of Death in Relation to Smoking." *British Medical Journal*, November 10, 1956, pp. 1072-81.

11. Peter D. Finch, "A Closer Look At Statistics on Smoking and Health." From ftp://demon.co/uk/doc/liberty/FOREST/.

12. Breslow, N. and Day, N., "Statistical Methods in Cancer Research." IARC (International Agency for Research on Cancer) Scientific Publications No. 32 (1980), Lyon, Table 2.1, p. 68.

13. Gary T. Schwartz, "Tobacco Liability in the Courts," in Robert L. Rabin and Stephen D. Sugarman, eds., *Smoking Policy: Law, Politics, and Culture* (New York: Oxford University Press, 1993), p. 133.

14. "They can't kick the habit: Smokers' ranks decline little." *The Atlanta Journal-Constitution*, December 26, 1997, p. C5. From the Associated Press.

15. American Council on Science and Health, *Cigarettes: What the Warning Label Doesn't Tell You* (Amherst, N.Y.: Prometheus Books, 1997), p. 10.

16. B. Bruce-Biggs, "The Health Police Are Blowing Smoke." *Fortune*, April 25, 1988. Quoted in David Pietrusza, *Smoking* (San Diego: Lucent Books, 1997), p. 31. Pietrusza didn't identify Bruce-Biggs so I looked up the *Fortune* article and found that he is, or was, an independent policy analyst with no connection with the tobacco industry and a smoker of 30 years' standing. I don't know if he's still standing.

17. "USA Statistics in Brief." From http://ftp.census.gov/stat_abstract/brief.html.

18. American Cancer Society, "Cancer Risk Report, 1995." At www.cancer.org/crrtobac.htm.

19. Letters. *Reason*, April 1996, p. 10.

20. *The Merck Manual of Diagnosis and Therapy*, Sixteenth Edition (Rahway, N.J.: Merck Research Laboratories, 1992), pp. 830, 834.

21. "Inherited genetic disorders." *The Atlanta Journal-Constitution*, March 24, 1993, p. B3.

22. "Coronary Artery Disease, Risk Factors and Detection." North Fulton (Georgia) Regional Hospital *Health Focus*, Winter 1997-1998, p. 7.

23. Ibid.

24. Ilene Springer, "Castelli speaks from the heart." *AARP Bulletin*, May 1992, p. 16.

25. Loc. cit.

26. David Guarino, "The heart of health for seniors; Cardiologist Castelli tells forum goers they must watch diet." *Middlesex News*, November 13, 1997, p. 1A.

27. "Deaths and death rates for the 10 leading causes of death in specified age groups: United States, preliminary 1995." At www.cdc.gov/nchswww/datawh/statab/pubd/453s216h.htm.

28. *Cigarettes*, p. 26.

29. Michael Mason, "Are Heart Attacks Contagious?" *Hippocrates* 1997; 11(12):42-45. At www.medscape.com/time/hippocrates/1997/v11.n.12/h1112.01.maso.html#Beyond.

30. "Brickbats." *Reason*, October 1997, p. 20; *The Atlanta Journal-Constitution*, January 1, 1997, p. A17; R. Cort Kirkwood, "Warning: Idiots may be hazardous to their health." *The Ottawa Sun*, June 11, 1997. At www.canoe.ca/OttawaSun/home.html.

31. *Cigarettes*, p. 169.

32. Bergen Evans, *The Natural History of Nonsense* (New York: Vintage Books, 1946), p. 216 in 1958 paperback reprint.

But even while this renowned rationalist was puncturing many of the fables and myths men live by, he uncritically passed on this piece of nonsense: "Irritability, restlessness, impaired memory, depression of spirits, insomnia, headaches, and fatigue have all been demonstrated to be the physical consequences of excessive smoking. Even two cigarettes can produce measurable dulling of sensitivity and increase of tremor." (Ibid. pp. 160,161.) Evans obviously was a nonsmoker with no firsthand acquaintance either with cigarettes or with people who used them.

33. Fennick, pp. 225-226.

34. "Researchers Show How Smoking Causes Cancer." *The Wall Street Journal*, October 18, 1996, p.1.

35. Associated Press, "Damaged Gene May Open Pathway to Lung Cancer." *The Washington Post*, April 7, 1996, p. A13; Associated Press, "Damaged Gene is Linked to Lung Cancer." *The New York Times*, April 6, 1996, p. A24. Sources courtesy of The Advocacy Institute Also CNN correspondent Andrew Holtz, "Genetic breakdown linked to lung cancer." Cited on the University of Arizona's Internet site at http://hinet.medlib.arizona.edu/~pubhlth/04099601.htm.

36. *Science* 1996;274:430-432.

37. At www.lcolby.com/addendum.

38. *Circulation* 1997;95:2374-2379.

39. "Steady exposure to 'passive' smoke nearly doubles risk of heart attack death for women, study shows." At www.amhrt.org/news/974531.html.

40. Darell Huff, *How to Lie With Statistics* (New York: W. W. Norton, 1954), Norton paperback reissue 1993, p. 8.

41. At www.speakup.org/harvrel.html.

42. Martha Perske, "Alarmist Media Reports Regarding The Harvard Study by Kawachi, et al." At www.speakup.org/harvprsk.html.

43. Ichiro Kawachi et al., *Arch Intern Med* 1996;156:521-525. At www.junkscience.com/news/coffee-suicide.html. Also the Nashville *Tennessean*, April 17, 1996, p. D-1; Bill Hendrick and Amanda Husted, "Women and coffee." *The Atlanta Journal-Constitution*, March 11, 1996. p C2.

Chapter 3

STUDIES, WE'VE GOT STUDIES

I don't get it. I did everything right to take care of myself and look what happened. Why in the world did I do all those push-ups?

— Jacqueline Kennedy Onassis[1]

The evidence linking tobacco to human disease is so overpowering that we should never have to do another study.

— Richard Bordow, M.D.[2]

There's a hell of a lot of junk coming out under the guise of epidemiology.

— Epidemiologist Richard Peto[3]

BACK IN 1958, Charles McArthur and colleagues at Harvard University found that, among a group of 252 Harvard men they had followed for about 15 years, the ability of smokers to stop smoking was directly related to how long they had been breast-fed as babies. The longer they had been breast-fed, the more likely it was that they would be able to quit. Conversely, the earlier they had been removed from the maternal nipple, the less likely they would be able to quit.

For example, light smokers who could stop smoking had been weaned at an average of eight months; heavy smokers who could stop had been weaned at 6.8 months, and those smokers (mostly heavy) who tried to stop but couldn't had been weaned at the early age of 4.7 months.[4]

The obvious lesson of this stunning discovery was that smokers, especially those who couldn't quit the habit, were suffering from oral needs that were not satisfied when they were infants, and hence as adults were hooked on a surrogate teat in the form of a cigarette. (One can only speculate about men who were never breast-fed at all; they evidently were not surveyed. I also wonder what the explanation is for chewing gum chewers.)

But wait a minute. Did anybody really look at those figures? Consider just the last group of men who were weaned at 4.7 months. What is seven-tenths of a month? In a month of 31 days, it's 21.7 days. What is seven-tenths of a day? It's 16.8 hours. What is eight-tenths of an hour? It's 48 minutes.

At first glance, it would seem that 252 adult males not only knew that they had been breast-fed but could tell you down to the very minute when, with what must have been great psychological trauma, they were rudely and abruptly taken off the breast!

Well, they couldn't know, of course; it was "purely statistical" (just as no family has 2.3 children, although that is said to be the "average" family size in the United States). But such finely tuned statistical precision is typical of studies about smoking and is what impresses people and makes them believe anything the researchers come up with.

Another example of impressive-sounding statistical precision was reported by the Academy of General Dentistry. It concerned two separate studies, one of 495 healthy men and the other of 583 healthy postmenopausal women, each extending over 30 years. The studies found that males who start smoking at age 18 lose their teeth at the rate of 2.9 teeth every 10 years and that female smokers lose 1.5 teeth every 10 years. Both male and female smokers were twice as likely to lose teeth as nonsmokers.[5]

I would think that if you've lost nine-tenths of a tooth, or even half a tooth, you've pretty much lost a whole tooth. Again the point is that those fractions of teeth were mathematical artifacts derived from statistical analysis of the studies. But note the use of the present tense above. The researchers leaped to the conclusion, or at least conveyed the idea to the public, that because people in their studies with a smoking history *had lost* teeth at a certain rate, *all* smokers *are losing* their teeth at the same rate. This kind of generalization is also typical of smoking studies.

Even if the men in the McArthur study had known when they were weaned, they could only have obtained that knowledge from their mothers. (This is called anecdotal evidence, which is valid only when it goes against smoking, unlike my anecdotal evidence, which the antismoking community of course rejects out of hand. In this case, however, it was not just anecdotal evidence but secondhand anecdotal evidence.) I doubt if my mother, who nursed me and three siblings, could have told any of us, had we been so curious as to ask her, what year, let alone what month, she had put us on the bottle or solid food.

But "Interestingly," adds my source, "McArthur found no clear-cut difference between smokers and lifelong nonsmokers as to how long they had been breast-fed."

The entire study really proved nothing? Fifteen years down the drain? Another "never mind"? Well, at least this was one smoking study smokers didn't have to pay for since it was completed in 1958.

It's easy to make fun of this study because, even if it had revealed some truth we never knew before, that knowledge would be something less than momentous. It usually takes a little more effort—though not a whole lot—to perceive the flaws in modern studies used as weapons in the antismoking crusade and to realize that they too, more often than not, prove nothing, unless it's the researchers' bias.

MOTHERS HAVE BEEN getting a bad rap since at least 1942, when author Philip Wylie in his book, *A Generation of Vipers*, coined the term "momism" to describe what he saw as too much adulation of mothers in American society and too much maternal overprotectiveness of offspring, particularly male offspring, to the detriment of their independence and self-reliance as adults.

Although "momism" had nothing to do with smoking and has long since joined the lexicon of forgotten terms, today's mothers are not only guilty of bringing smokers into the world by weaning them too soon but, through their own smoking, are responsible for disabling their offspring in countless other ways. Let us count a few of them:

"Women who smoke during pregnancy are increasing their chances of giving birth to a future juvenile delinquent, a new study suggests." (Note those last four words; they constitute the most common phrase in all health reports.)

That was the lead sentence of a July 1997 Internet flash from Action on Smoking and Health (ASH),[6] which is ever-eager to trumpet how smoking parents are harming their children. (For how eager they are, even to the extent of encouraging the break-up of families, see Chapter 7.)

The study, reported in *Archives of General Psychiatry*, was conducted by Dr. Lauren Wakschlag and a team of researchers from the University of Chicago Medical School and the University of Pittsburgh.

The researchers studied 177 boys aged 7 to 12 who had been referred to outpatient clinics in Pennsylvania and Georgia for possible "conduct disorder." Conduct disorder, ASH explained in a follow-up release,[7] is a persistent pattern of "lying, setting fires, vandalism, physical cruelty, forcible sexual activity and/or stealing." Three of these behaviors exhibited for six months earned a boy the conduct disorder label, and 105 of the boys were so diagnosed.

The mothers of all 177 were then asked if and how much they had smoked during pregnancy. Forty-two said they had smoked more than half a pack a day, while 23 said they had smoked up to half a pack a day. The other 112 mothers said they hadn't smoked at all. (Note the word "said." Anecdotal evidence again.)

When this data was put through the statistical mill, out came the finding that 80 percent of the sons of the heavier smokers and 70 percent of the sons of the lighter smokers had conduct disorder. For nonsmoking mothers, only 50 percent of their sons exhibited the disorder.

Dr. Wakschlag acknowledged that "smoking during pregnancy was found to be associated with a number of other risk factors for conduct disorder, including having less affluent and less well-educated parents, larger family size, maternal use of alcohol and other drugs during pregnancy, having a biological father who met diagnostic criteria for antisocial personality and/or substance abuse disorders and maladative parenting."

But after using "statistical methods" to eliminate the effects of these other variables, the researchers found that mothers who smoked more than half a pack of cigarettes a day during pregnancy were more than four times as likely to have a child with conduct disorder than mothers who did not smoke during pregnancy.

One can be sure that if the researchers had been trying to make a case against something other than smoking, say maternal TV watching, "statistical methods" would also have yielded the desired result.

Come on. Smoking during pregnancy overrides every other influence as a cause of a child's conduct disorder—even having low-income, poorly educated, alcohol-using, drug-taking, antisocial and all-around lousy parents? Even gullible nonsmokers have to shake their heads at that. Were any children of high-income, high-education and well-adapted parents, smoking and nonsmoking, studied as a control group? Apparently not. That might have "confounded" their finding.

Nonsmoking women can take little comfort in this study, however, for their chance of bringing a sadistic, violent, pathological liar of a child into the world is 50-50 if they have a son. But there's one bright side: since about half of all newborns are girls, nonsmoking women's chance of giving birth to a moral monster drops to a mere 25 percent. That should be quite reassuring to all nonsmoking expectant moms.

Even if her child doesn't turn out to be a delinquent, a mother who smokes during pregnancy is bequeathing him, or her, a "significantly lower" IQ than the mother who doesn't smoke during pregnancy, and the more cigarettes smoked, the lower the IQ.

That disturbing information was reported in *Science News* in February 1994 and was the finding of a Cornell University/University of Rochester study published in the journal *Pediatrics*.[8] Specifically, 3- and 4-year-old children whose mothers smoked 10 or more cigarettes a day during pregnancy scored an average of nine points lower on IQ tests than the children of nonsmokers. Even after "controlling" for other factors the deficit was still more than four points.

Again, fortunately, there's a bright side. The researchers also found that a comprehensive program of nurse home visitation during pregnancy largely eliminated the potential IQ deficits of children born to smoking women, in part, they think, by reducing the number of cigarettes smoked (with nagging, warning, frightening?) and by improving the diets of the women. (And I'll give you one guess which they would say was more important, a healthier diet or less smoking.) When smokers were visited by nurses throughout their pregnancies, their 3- and 4-year-old children had average IQ scores five points higher than the children of smokers who were not visited.

Interestingly enough, no significant differences were found among children younger than 3 and no independent effects were found at any age from exposure to secondhand smoke. The researchers also stated that no mental deficits from prenatal smoking have been shown to exist in children older than 4. Does that mean that children start getting smarter on their own after age 4, even if their mothers smoked during pregnancy? Could it be because kids go into kindergarten or preschool after that age and receive more intellectual stimulation than they may have gotten at home? Your guess is as good as mine.

Alas, once again mothers who don't smoke shouldn't necessarily be congratulating themselves. They too may be harming their children.

For instance, other researchers have found that mothers who criticize their children too severely "could "(another word to note) be reducing their children's IQ scores. So reported Drs. Mary Gauvain and Beverly Fagot in the journal *Developmental Psychology*.[9]

They followed 93 children and their mothers and found that disapproving behavior by the mother increased a child's likelihood of developing learning problems by age 5. Specifically, children whose mothers gave them disapproving looks and criticized them had lower verbal and math scores on IQ tests at that age.

Which gives even deeper meaning to the phrase, "Looks can kill."

Is it possible that the parents of some of these low IQ kids just aren't feeding them right (though that surely must have been one of the variables "controlled for" in the Cornell/Rochester study)? Another study in *Pediatrics* found that heavy smokers "may" (another word to note) be providing their children with less nutritious food than nonsmoking parents. Children of low-income families whose parents each smoked more than 20 cigarettes a day consumed diets higher in fat, salt, cholesterol and total calories and lower in fiber and vitamin A than children whose parents didn't smoke.[10] For this reason the researchers suggest that smoking cessation interventions should specifically target low-income parents.

This study didn't investigate the effects of poor diet on children's intelligence, but I wonder again if the researchers compared the study group to a control group of high-income parents. High income usually goes with better education, and better educated parents, smokers or nonsmokers, are more likely to see that their children eat well. But it wasn't income or educational levels these researchers were interested in. It was smoking.

Incidentally, the title of the *Pediatrics* article was "Tobacco May Compete With Other Food Dollars." With higher and higher taxes being placed on cigarettes, thanks to antismoking agitation (and the companies adding their own price increases, thanks to their greed), and because low-income, less educated people constitute the majority of smokers today, and because we *know* that smokers are hopelessly addicted to the weed, the antismokers may actually be ensuring that the children of low-income families will enjoy even poorer diets in the future.

* * *

ALL OF THE ABOVE handicaps inflicted upon children by their smoking mothers depends of course on whether their mothers didn't kill them outright in the womb with their smoking.

According to an article in the April 1995 *Journal of Family Practice*,[11] between 20 and 62 percent of all pregnancies end in spontaneous abortion, and as many as 7.5 percent of these miscarriages "may" be caused by smoking. This "is a poignant reminder that use of tobacco products affects many innocent individuals who have not chosen to assume the risks involved," said one or the authors of the study, Dr. Joseph R. DiFranza, a doctor in the Fitchburg Family Practice Residency Program at the University of Massachusetts and another individual who has found a career in antismoking research. (Make that "research.")

The study was not based on any original research, however, but rather on a "meta-analysis" of some 100 studies of the relation between smoking and prenatal and neonatal (newborn) health. Meta-analyses, which are combinations of different studies from which researchers pick out what is useful to them and discard the rest, are notoriously slippery (see Chapter 6). But based on theirs, the researchers came up with a "best case" *estimate* (note that word too) of 19,000 tobacco-induced miscarriages a year. This in turn was based on the lowest *estimate* of the proportion of pregnant women who smoke and included only those pregnancies and miscarriages that were recognized by the women and their doctors.

Their "worst case" *estimate* was 141,000 tobacco-induced miscarriages. This figure was based on the highest *estimate* of smoking prevalence among pregnant women and included miscarriages that occurred before the women realized they were pregnant.

The best way to reduce this toll, the study concluded, would be to "focus on preventing nicotine addiction among teenage girls."

The researchers also found "evidence" from many of the 100 studies that smoking elevated the risk of stillbirths, neonatal deaths and SIDS (Sudden Infant Death Syndrome). Indeed, "The most dramatic effect of maternal smoking is on the risk of SIDS, which is tripled" when mothers smoke, they reported. In fact, two-thirds of SIDS deaths among children of women who smoke during pregnancy can be attributed to smoking, they said.

Rather than attempting to challenge these 100 studies, which I haven't seen, I will refer the reader to the studies in the bibliography near the end of this chapter that tell a much different story about the smoking/miscarriage/stillbirth/neonatal death connection. However, the idea that parental smoking is largely, or even partly, responsible for SIDS is vigorously questioned—not by me, not by any prosmoking organization, not by the tobacco industry, but by the Sudden Infant Death Syndrome Foundation itself (see Chapter 8). Because the smoking/SIDS allegation has been pretty much blown out of the water, I respectfully suggest at least a modicum of skepticism regarding the other DiFranzi et al. claims.

If smoking mothers have a lot to answer for, yet again those who don't smoke aren't going to be let off the hook, especially if they work outside the home.

Long hours and high stress on the job "may" increase the risk of miscarriage early in pregnancy, according to a study of female lawyers. The study, published in the *Journal of Occupational and Environmental Medicine*, looked at 584 women who graduated from the University of California-Davis law school between 1969 and 1985.[12]

Women who "said" that they worked more than 45 hours a week were both five times more likely to characterize their jobs as "high stress" and three times more likely to have a miscarriage early in pregnancy than those who worked less than 35 hours.

Unfortunately, even stay-at-home moms who aren't stressed at work but who are depressed (maybe because they're stuck in the house all day?) can cause their children to have behavioral problems.

Geraldine Dawson, a University of Washington psychology professor, studied the brain activity of 117 children, 54 with mothers who had been diagnosed as depressed when their infants were 14 months old and 63 children whose mothers were not depressed. She found that nearly 39 percent of the children with depressed mothers exhibited reduced brain activity.[13] This was true both at 14 months and at 3 and a half years.

These children, she said, "may" be vulnerable to their own depression and other emotional problems in later childhood.

Maybe stressed or depressed women should get away from both home and job occasionally and take up some activity, perhaps join an exercise club. Surely this would be good for their mental as well as their physical health.

Then again, maybe not. From Australia comes the warning that pregnant women who exercise "could" affect the birthweight of their babies as badly as smoking. Dr. Robyn Bell, an epidemiologist at Melbourne's Royal Women's Hospital found that women who exercised at least five times a week gave birth to more premature and low birth weight babies.[14] A low birthweight baby was defined as one weighing less than 2.5 kilograms (about five and a half pounds).

Some of the heavy exercising women in her study gave birth to babies near two kilograms (about 4.4 pounds) and one gave birth eight weeks early. On the basis of these few examples, she concluded that overexercise was "probably (yet another word to note) equivalent to smoking a packet of cigarettes a day" and "may produce an effect on the same order as smoking in terms of public health."

On the other hand, a young woman's risk of developing breast cancer is "dramatically" reduced if she engages in regular physical exercise, according to a study published in the *Journal of the National Cancer Institute* and based on a survey of 545 breast cancer patients and 545 other women without the disease.[15]

Each woman estimated (anecdotal evidence) how much time she had spent on such activities as team sports, swimming, running and jogging, gymnastics and dance or exercise classes. This info was fed into the computer and "adjusted" for such differences as the age of first menstruation, age at first full-term pregnancy, number of full-term pregnancies, use of oral contraceptives and family history of breast cancer (also anecdotal evidence). Out popped the finding that, despite these differences one might think were rather important, the more a woman had exercised, the lower her risk of breast cancer.

Unfortunately, as we have seen, too much exercise by a pregnant woman is "probably" equivalent to smoking a pack of cigarettes a day and can result in an underweight or premature baby. We have also seen that smoking can cause a spontaneous abortion when a woman may not have been aware that she was pregnant, so presumably its equivalent in exercising could too.

Thus women who are pregnant as well as those who could be pregnant and not know it face a dilemma: in the first case, whether *not* to exercise and avoid having an underweight or premature baby but risk breast cancer or, in the second case, whether *to* exercise and avoid breast cancer but risk having a miscarriage.

My advice to all of them: avoid health studies.

Finally, even if a mother who smokes during pregnancy doesn't bring a tobacco-induced miscarriage upon herself, even if she doesn't give birth to an intellectually retarded child or a sociopathic son, and even if she has a daughter who is lucky enough to escape being among the 25 percent of girls who develop conduct disorder, her smoking may affect her daughter in another way.

"A new study shows (another oft-used phrase)," said my source, that the daughters of women who smoke cigarettes during pregnancy are more likely themselves to smoke during adolescence. This study was reported in the *American Journal of Public Health.*[16]

Dr. Denise Kandel of Columbia University studied some 1,000 adolescent girls and found that they were four times as likely to smoke if their mothers had smoked during pregnancy. (Another instance of secondhand anecdotal evidence; she could only have gotten this information from the girls, who could only have gotten it from their mothers.) The finding held true even after taking into account (another way of saying "controlling" or "adjusting" for) environmental and social factors such as education and whether the mother or other household members smoked while the girls were growing up.

As for why maternal smoking during pregnancy didn't seem to be a factor in boys' smoking in adolescence, Dr. Kandel speculated that male sex hormones "could" provide protection against nicotine's stimulatory effects.

Well, if that's so, you may ask, why don't the hormones of sons of smoking mothers protect them against becoming delinquents? That's not a fair question because that study was done after Dr. Kandel's and she probably wouldn't have been aware of it anyway. Why confuse her?

In any event, she suggested that prevention programs should target daughters whose mothers smoked during pregnancy.

With all this antismoking "prevention" and "intervention" and "targeting" going on, medical researchers may reach the point where they won't have the time to conduct studies. One can dream.

So much for mothers and other women. Whatever consolation it may be to them, smoking fathers too are doing terrible things to their children. I'll cite just one study, both to keep this chapter within reasonable bounds and because it is one of the most outrageous examples in recent years of how antismoking bias can pollute medical research.

The study, which was published in the December 1997 *British Journal of Cancer*, found that the children of fathers who smoke 20 cigarettes a day have a 30-percent higher risk of developing cancer than the children of nonsmoking fathers. For children whose fathers smoked 40 or more cigarettes a day, the risk was 60 percent higher.

About 1,500 children under 16 are diagnosed with cancer or leukemia each year in the United Kingdom. The study "suggested" that 150 of those cases "may" be associated with fathers' smoking. "[I]n Europe alone, there would be around 1,000 fewer cases of childhood cancer each year if fathers didn't smoke," said Dr. Tom Sorahan, leader of a team of researchers from the University of Birmingham, demonstrating his intellecual ahtleticism by leaping from a shaky surmise to a distant conclusion.[17]

The study was based on interviews (anecdotal evidence) with the parents of 2,567 children who died of cancer in Great Britain between 1971 and 1976 and interviews (also anecdotal) with the same number of parents of healthy children. (At least this time there was a control group.) Once again, the findings could not be explained by social class, family size or age of parents.

The researchers also reasoned that secondhand smoke wasn't responsible for these cancers because mothers' smoking would be expected to be at least as important as fathers' smoking, and it wasn't. So what was the explanation?

"Damaged sperm is the likeliest culprit," said Sorahan, winging back in from way out in left field.

Carol Thompson, president of the Smokers' Rights Action Group, who writes for FORCES Canada and is not known for excessive reserve when debunking the antismokers, shot a rather large hole in that theory.

"In the first place," she writes, "it is nothing but sheer, empty speculation to claim that 'damaged sperm' causes any kind of cancer. There is not a single type of cancer that has been shown to be caused by 'damaged sperm.'

"Furthermore, hot baths are known to damage sperm. And the only known effect of damaged sperm is failure to conceive, not cancer or even birth defects.

"Furthermore, different cancers are known to have different

causes—cancer is not a single disease—and it is sheer scientific nonsense to lump all forms of cancer together and simply call them 'cancer,' as in this article.

"Plus, the leukemias have been increasingly linked to infection or other factors which [the researchers] did not investigate. These quacks did nothing but cobble together some circumstantial evidence with a flimsy glue of speculation and spew it into the public's faces with an act of bravado."[18]

I will only add two comments.

1. The risks of 30 percent and 60 percent meant that the researchers, after "controlling" for family social class, etc., could only come up with a relative risk of 1.3 for moderate smoking and a relative risk of 1.6 for heavy smoking, both of which are well below the 2.0 relative risk which is considered the very minimum for a study to be considered statistically significant.

2. It is a sad thing when parents in the midst of terrible grief are encouraged to believe that it was something they did that caused the death of their child. But that too is a typical tactic of antismokers (again see Chapter 8). Anything goes in the cause of a "smoke-free society."

THE MENTION OF leukemia forces me to digress briefly to two other studies, which have nothing to do with smoking but give some insight into what it means to "adjust" and "control" for various factors in an epidemiological study and how much trust we should place in this procedure. The first one has few rivals as an example of how even the most ludicrous "finding" can be published in the scientific literature—because the computer said it was so.

I crib what follows from Steven Milloy's *Science Without Sense*, a humorous and all-too-brief but eminently readable "handbook" on how to win fame, if not fortune, in the field of public health research. Milloy is a biostatician who, as "the Junkman," maintains the Junk Science page on the World Wide Web (www.junkscience.com) which I cite in almost every chapter in this book.

Seems some researchers decided to do a case-control, or retrospective, study of the possible risk factors in childhood leukemia. Looked at were such things as children's exposure to environmental chemicals, electric and magnetic fields, past medical history, parental smoking and drug use and the dietary intake of nine different foods. These included breakfast meats, hot dogs, luncheon meats, hamburgers and several fruit beverages.

This is called "data dredging," says Milloy. "You have to analyze your data forwards and backwards, from the top, bottom, and sides, from the inside out, and from the outside in. You slice it, dice it, and pick it apart any way you can to find an artifact (I mean risk) worth all this trouble."

In examining the myriad of possible statistical associations with childhood leukemia, the study identified breast-feeding, indoor pesticides, children's use of hair dryers, black and white television sets, incense, mother's exposure to spray paints during pregnancy, and so on.

It was obvious right from the start, he says, that the researchers had no idea what they were looking for; they were simply on a fishing expedition. "Amazingly, they caught a big one!"

The one association that stood out was that between eating more than 12 hot dogs a month and leukemia. For this association, the researchers came up with a whopper of a relative risk—9.5—nearly eight times greater than the mere 1.19 risk of getting lung cancer from secondhand smoke the Environmental Protection Agency came up with in what Milloy calls "the Mona Lisa of all meta-analyses" and which has been used to brand smokers as Public Enemy No.1 (see Chapter 6).

In other words, children who ate more than 12 hot dogs a month were nine and a half times more likely to develop leukemia than children who ate few or no hot dogs. The association was biologically plausible, the researchers said, because hot dogs contain nitrites, which have been associated, or "linked," to leukemia in rats and mice.

"A great result from a fishing expedition," says Milloy. The press was informed, of course. I remember reading about it in my local newspaper, but either lost or failed to save the clipping.

Unfortunately, the researchers made a serious error that called into question the validity of their "finding": they admitted that they were unable to come up with an association between leukemia and other types of processed meats, including ham, bacon, sausage and luncheon meats, all of which also contain nitrites. They should have omitted this information from their report, Milloy says.[19]

Is it possible that the authors of at least some of the hundreds of studies "linking" smoking with name-your-disease *did* take care to avoid this kind of error and *did* omit "inconvenient" information because it would have contradicted their findings and only have confused people and "sent the wrong message" about smoking?

The second example of a statistical fishing expedition actually has to do with a sport—hunting. This study found that children who live in Michigan are nearly three times as likely to be neglected and are twice as likely to be physically abused or sexually assaulted if they live in a county with an above average number of hunters.

The researchers compared Michigan and New York state. There were 235.2 identified victims of child abuse per 100,000 Michigan residents, but just 30.2 victims per 100,000 residents of upstate New York. There are also 25.4 child victims of sexual assault per 100,000 Michigan residents, but only 13.2 per 100,000 in upstate New York. (New York City was conveniently excluded from both calculations.)

Now here's the kicker: Michigan sells 16,430 hunting licenses per 100,000 population; New York, with almost identical licensing requirements, sells 8,627. Only seven percent of upstate New York residents hunt, while 9.6 percent of Michigan residents do.

Even when other factors associated with child abuse were considered, such as below average family income and population density, hunting participation was in first place. The association of hunting with child abuse may be even stronger, the authors of the study said, because most experts "believe" that child abuse tends to be underreported in rural areas where witnesses are few.

They did not go so far as to allege that hunting "causes" child abuse, but the data "support a *hypothesis* that both hunting and child abuse reflect the degree to which a social characteristic called dominionism prevails in a particular community" and "the coincidence of high hunting population with both poverty and child abuse is in itself indicative that hunting *may* be symptomatic of a poor social environment." [Emphases added.]

It may also be indicative of something else that the study was reported in an animal rights magazine.[20]

ALTHOUGH THE following studies also don't necessarily have a connection with smoking, they illustrate the kinds of speculation, guesswork and leaps of (il)logic that characterize smoking studies. They show that there is another way fathers may be harming their children—by dying early and thus depriving them of half of the nurture, guidance and role models growing children need, as well as probably the greater part of a family's income.

For example, men who have high levels of anxiety (perhaps worried about what their secondhand smoke is doing to their children?) "may" be at an increased risk of sudden death from heart attack. So concluded a 32-year study of 2,280 men aged 21 to 80 by researchers at the Harvard School of Public Health.[21]

The subjects were asked five questions and their answers were rated on an "anxiety scale": Do strange people or places make you afraid? Are you considered a nervous person? Are you constantly keyed up and jittery? Do you often become suddenly scared for no reason? Do you often break out in a cold sweat?

This was worse than ordinary anecdotal evidence; it was highly *subjective* anecdotal evidence.

Anyway, men who scored highest on the "anxiety scale" by answering "yes" to the most questions were four to six times more likely than men who scored lowest to suffer fatal heart arrhythmias. During the study, 26 men had sudden cardiac deaths.

Only 26 deaths out of 2,280 men in a period of 32 years? That's just a fraction more than one percent of the study group. Seems a pretty small number for that many men for that many years. How old were those who died? That would seem rather important, but my source doesn't say.

Depression is another thing that takes a toll of men in the prime of life. Men who felt hopeless or thought of themselves as failures and expressed high levels of despair (subjective anecdotal evidence again) had a 20 percent greater increase in atherosclerosis, or narrowing of the arteries, which can lead to heart attacks and strokes, according to a report in the August 1997 issue of the American Heart Association journal *Arteriosclerosis, Thrombosis and Vascular Biology*.[22]

"This is the same magnitude of increased risk that one sees in comparing a pack-a-day smoker to a nonsmoker," said Susan Everson, an associate research scientist at the Human Population Laboratory of the Public Health Institute in Berkeley, California, and lead author of the report.

Sleeplessness is also related to anxiety and depression and its incidence among America's workers "could" be costing employers more than $18 billion a year in lost productivity.

An *estimated* 47 percent of U.S. workers *say* they suffer from sleeplessness, and at least 36 million Americans *think* this negatively affects their job performance, according to a survey by the Louis Harris organization that was sponsored by McNeil Consumer Products Company, which just happens to be a maker of pain reliever and sleep aid products.[23]

Good to know that something other than smoking is at least partly responsible for America's lost productivity.

If a man has never finished high school, he may also not live to see his children grow up. Dr. Murray Mittleman and colleagues of Harvard Medical School interviewed 1,623 patients who had suffered heart attacks and found a direct "link" (yet one more word to note) between anger and heart attacks and between anger and whether or not the subjects had finished high school.[24]

Nearly four percent of patients with less than a high school diploma "said" they felt "very angry, furious or enraged" two hours before their heart attacks, compared with only 2.2 percent who had finished high school and 1.7 percent of those with college experience.

Four percent, 2.2 percent and 1.7 percent equal approximately 65, 36 and 28 men respectively out of a total of 1,623 men (I can do statistics too). Again pretty sparse evidence on which to hang a theory, but enough to get your name and your study in a scientific journal, even if it's not about smoking.

Unfortunately, even if a man doesn't suffer from anxiety or despair or anger but becomes an outstanding success in life, he may be cutting that life short, especially if he succeeds too soon.

A study by Dr. Steward McCann of the University of Cape Breton in Nova Scotia looked at 162 leaders in America, Canada, Britain, France and New Zealand, including vice presidents, Supreme Court justices, British monarchs, popes, signers of the Declaration of Independence and first-time Oscar winners, and found that the younger the leaders were when they reached the top, the more likely they were to die before their time.[25]

You're not anxiety-ridden or depressed and you are a high school graduate but not a young national leader and you sleep well, you say. Even so, if you're the pushy "Type A" type you're 60 percent more likely than mild-mannered guys (such as myself) to die from a heart attack or stroke or suffer from other conditions such as high blood pressure.

That information is from a 20-year study involving 750 middle-class white men, conducted by Dr. Michael Babyak of Duke University Medical Center and published in the *Journal of the American Psychosomatic Society*. It was the first study to "link" long-term health risks with "social dominance" in Type A men, Dr. Babyak said.[26]

The exact reason Type As "may" be at greater risk of heart attack—about 50 percent "more likely" than easy-going Type Bs—was "suggested" by a study conducted nearly five years before Babyak's: it's because their bodies make unusually small amounts of good cholesterol, or HDL (high-density lipoprotein).

"Type As have substantially lower HDL. That seems to explain their greater risk of heart attacks," said JoAnn Manson of Brigham and Women's Hospital in Boston.[27]

We'll take her word for that as we add "seems" to our list of weasel words to watch out for.

If further research confirms this "link," she said, it would provide more support for the belief that reducing stress is good for the heart.

I'm willing to believe it. Just look at that high-pressure cooker called Wall Street—"the heart attack capital of New York," in the words of Ellen Karasik, an assistant vice president at NYU Downtown Hospital in Manhattan.[28]

The heart attack death rate during business hours for the 5,000 people who work at the stock exchange is 60 percent higher than the national rate for men between 18 and 65, according to the National Center for Health Statistics, and may be 10 times higher than that of the general public, according to Dr. Ira Schulman, directory of cardiology at the same hospital.[29]

On the other hand, maybe stress *isn't* a factor in heart disease after all. A four-year study of 1,489 men conducted at Duke University Medical Center between 1986 and 1990 found that coronary heart disease was just as common in patients with little on-the-job stress as among those with high-stress jobs.[30]

I'll let the researchers fight that out among themselves. In the meantime, the good news is that men who drink milk have a lower incidence of stroke. Scientists who tracked 3,150 men for 22 years reported in the American Heart Association journal *Stroke* that those who didn't drink milk were twice as likely to have a stroke as men who drank at least 16 ounces of milk a day.[31] (Tell that to the guy who sued the Washington state dairy industry. See footnote on page 107.)

Unfortunately, the researchers don't know if it's the milk that protects against stroke or if it's an overall healthier lifestyle. I've just thrown this study in as an example of how apparent correlations between all sorts of things and all sorts of other things occupy the energies of medical researchers. At least it keeps them off the streets.

To repeat the statement by statistician K.A. Brownlee from Chapter 1, ". . . the presence of a positive, zero, or negative correlation between two variables observed over time has been the basis for more ludicrous nonsense than any other statistical procedure."

Speaking of correlations, there's even better news for men: the more sex you have, the healthier you'll be. Epidemiologist Stephen Frankel and colleagues at the University of Bristol, England, followed 918 men from the Welsh town of Caerphilly and five nearby villages for 10 years. During the study, 150 of the men died, 67 of them from heart disease. When they crunched their numbers in the computer, Frankel et al. found that the risk of death from all causes was halved in men who reported the highest frequency of orgasm, compared to men with the least sexual activity.[32] (One must assume the researchers were confident that the first group didn't fudge the truth just a little.)

Again, they don't know which is cause and which is effect. It may be that sexual activity protects a man simply by giving him a cardiovascular workout. On the other hand, it may simply be that men with a good sex life lead happier, less stressful lives. The findings need to be confirmed by other research groups, says Frankel. (I'm sure he won't lack for volunteers. The only problem will be to get wives and girlfriends to cooperate.)

One thing everyone can agree on is that, with or without sex, a cardiovascular workout is good for you, and luckily for men they don't have to worry about the complications of pregnancy.

"Every American adult should accumulate 30 minutes or more of moderate intensity physical activity a week," recommended Dr. Steven N. Blair, director of epidemiology at the Cooper Institute for Aerobics Research in Dallas.[33] It need not be strenuous exercise. "We're talking about walking three to four miles an hour, 15 to 20 minutes per mile."

He pointed to a study of 10,269 middle-aged Harvard University alumni (where would researchers be without Harvard alumni?) that found that those who started exercising reduced their risk of death just as much as those who quit smoking cigarettes.

Hmm . . . Moderate exercise is as beneficial as quitting smoking. But too much exercise is the same as smoking a pack of cigarettes a day. Depression is also as bad for the arteries as a pack of cigarettes a day. But anxiety is a greater risk for sudden heart attack death than smoking.

Smoking, it would seem, has become the modern benchmark against which health researchers measure the results of their studies. There's a use for the weed after all!

They never express it the other way around, of course, as in, perhaps: Smoking a pack of cigarettes a day is no worse for your health than overdoing it at the exercise club. Or being down in the dumps or possessed by worries.

ONE OF THE MOST bald-faced and brazen pieces of antismoking propaganda I have ever seen was an article in *Reader's Digest* titled "How Smoking Clouds Your Brain," which purported to prove that smokers' perception that cigarettes make them feel more alert, clearheaded and able to focus on work "is mostly an illusion."[34]

It reported an experiment conducted by psychologist George Spilich and colleagues at Washington College in Chestertown, Maryland, in which three groups of young people—nonsmokers, active smokers and smokers deprived of cigarettes—were put through a series of five tests of increasing complexity.

The tests began with each subject sitting in front of a computer screen and pressing the space bar as soon as he or she recognized a target letter among an array of 96. The next test required them to scan sequences of 20 identical letters and respond the instant one of the letters transformed into a different one. A third test required them to remember a sequence of letters or numbers and respond when that sequence appeared amid flashed groupings on the screen. The fourth test required them to read a message, then answer questions about it. Finally, the subjects were tested with a computer-generated driving simulator, similar to a quick-paced video arcade game, where they had to operate a steering wheel, gearshift and gas pedal and "cope with unexpected challenges such as twisting roads, the sudden appearance of cars and oil slicks."

"As our tests became more complex," Spilich et al. found, "nonsmokers outperformed smokers by wider and wider amounts."

By the end of the last test, the cigarette-deprived smokers were involved in roughly 67 percent more rear-end collisions than nonsmokers. And smokers who had just had a cigarette did even worse: they were involved in significantly more simulated accidents and three and a half times more rear-end collisions than were nonsmokers.

On the basis of these tests, Spilich et al. speculated that "a smoker might perform adequately at many jobs—until they got complicated. He could drive a car satisfactorily so long as everything remained routine, but if a tire blew out at high speed he might not handle the emergency as well as a nonsmoker. A smoking airline pilot could fly adequately if no problems arose, but if something went wrong, smoking might impair his mental capacity. If lack of sleep were also a problem, smoking could leave such a pilot relatively impaired—with dangerous consequences."

I have no comment about the validity of these findings but will again only refer the reader to the bibliography below, as well as to the next chapter where I cite a number of tests that demonstrated exactly the opposite—that smoking enhances mental alertness.

Regarding smoking airline pilots, however, the article stated that in 1978, the Federal Aviation Administration decided to let them smoke while flying, even as it was being forbidden for their passengers. "According to Dr. Andrew Horne, formerly with the agency's Office of Aviation Medicine," said the article, "the Federal Aviation Administration maintains this policy not because smoking makes pilots more alert, but because prohibiting cigarettes to chronic smokers might plunge them into mental impairment while flying an airliner."

This is absolutely reprehensible. It is one of the worst examples I have seen of how far the antismokers will go in an attempt to instill the fear of smoking in the public mind, and both the author and *Reader's Digest* should be ashamed of themselves. But, more's the pity, I'm sure they sincerely believe they are serving a good cause, and if it requires pious falsehoods (a.k.a. lies) to forward that cause, so be it.

Even if what Dr. Horne said is true, and I have no evidence that it is not, one could just as well suggest that the FAA allows pilots to smoke, not to keep them from crashing and killing everyone aboard, but because it sharpens their flying skills.

The FAA also knows that a lot of airline pilots drink. Some in fact have been known to be alcoholics. The agency does not permit pilots to fly until, I believe, at least eight hours after their last drink, even at the risk that this deprivation "might plunge them into mental impairment."

I wonder which kind of pilot your average airline passenger would prefer to have at the controls—an alcohol-deprived one or a nicotine-deprived one.

I don't know how many fighter pilots in World War II smoked, but I'm sure a lot of them did and doubt if many of them were shot down because they tangled with nonsmoking enemy pilots. I know that Eddie Rickenbacker smoked cigarettes while he was becoming America's Ace of Aces in World War I. I've seen group photographs of members of the Lafayette Escadrille, and in every one almost all the pilots are standing around with cigarettes in their hands. I also don't know how many fighter pilots today are smokers. Maybe none is. But all that would prove is that if you train hard and stay alert, even a nonsmoker can fly as well as a smoker.

"How Smoking Clouds Your Brain" also makes a big deal of the fact that cigarette smoke contains carbon monoxide (CO), a gas that bonds to the blood's hemoglobin "at least 200 times more tightly than oxygen does . . . If a significant percentage of your hemoglobin were thus made useless by carbon monoxide, you would almost certainly die." Indeed so. If the body is given the choice, it will take carbon monoxide over oxygen any day.

The implication is that smokers are absorbing a deadly gas that, in sufficient amount, would kill them. (Never mind that a person walking along a busy city street inhales more CO than he could get from smoking hundreds of cigarettes.) If I were ever to decide to slip this mortal coil ahead of time, it would be in a closed garage with a car engine running, not by chain-smoking cigarettes.

"Each cigarettes pumps ten to 20 milligrams of carbon monoxide into your lungs," the article goes on. "People typically lose three to nine percent of their oxygen-carrying capacity while smoking. During periods of intense smoking, this loss can reach over ten percent, which may slow reaction time and reduce mental awareness."

So not only is a cigarette-deprived pilot a menace, so is an actively smoking one! Is the FAA aware of this?

I hate to weary the reader with my personal experiences but anti-smoking propaganda like this forces me to. It was because I used to be a private pilot that this *Reader's Digest* article rankled me more than any other antismoking bullhockey it has published.

In 1956, with about 200 hours in my logbook, I flew a 65-horsepower Luscombe (what a great plane!) from Cleveland, Ohio, to pre-Castro Cuba and back, smoking all the way. After that adventure I sold the Luscombe and took up sailplaning, going as far as to win one leg of the "Silver C" badge—a five-hour duration flight—at the soaring capital of America in Elmira, New York, even though cigarette-deprived. (There was no lighter or ashtray in the Schweitzer 1-26 and I didn't think about smoking anyway.)

Then marriage and all sorts of other stuff (like earning a living) intervened and I gave up flying. In 1992, however, I decided to reactivate my license just to see if I could still cut the mustard. Somehow, despite having smoked for some 46 years up till then, I passed the third-class pilot's physical.

During my retraining I obtained an FAA pamphlet titled "Medical Facts for Pilots" (FAA-P-8740-41) which informed me that "Smoking several cigarettes can result in carbon monoxide saturation sufficient to effect visual sensitivity equal to an increase of 8,000 feet altitude."

Because I had flown at an average altitude of 6,000 feet during my Cuban trip, that meant I had actually been at 14,000 feet most of the way, and either a pressurized cabin or supplemental oxygen are advisable beginning at about 10,000 feet. I was too dumb to know it and, thus protected either by ignorance or the favor of the gods, made the flight without mishap. (Or did the FAA pamphlet possibly exaggerate slightly?)

Another personal anecdote, not mine but that of Lauren Colby, who is also both a smoker and a pilot:

> About six months ago [he told me via e-mail in 1996], I was flying a single engine airplane, a 1979 Cessna P210, over Ohio when a cylinder head blew. Climbing out of Toledo, the engine got dangerously hot and all of a sudden there was a loud noise and it quit. It had physically broken the bolts that hold a cylinder head to the block, and was throwing oil all over everything. I was at 6,000 feet [equivalent to 14,000 feet for a smoker, remember —D.O], sinking a thousand feet a minute, so I had six minutes to find an airport and make an emergency landing. I used 15 seconds to grab and light a cigar! After that, finding the airport and making the emergency landing was easy!!!"

Fortunately for Colby there was an airport nearby, in Fremont, Ohio. But "it could have been a real tragedy," he added. "The airport could have been non-smoking!!!"

THE FOREGOING ENABLES me to segue into a related subject—the class-action suit by 60,000 flight attendants demanding compensation from the tobacco industry for harm done to them by the secondhand smoke of airline passengers (*Broin v. Philip Morris, Inc., R.J. Reynolds Tobacco Co., Brown & Williamson Tobacco Corp., and the Lorillard Tobacco Co.*) and a government study that made hash of their claims—or might have if the cigarette companies had not copped out before the jury hearing the case in Miami in 1997 had a chance to deliberate on a verdict.

For nearly two decades Americans have been bombarded with study after study condemning secondhand smoke, or ETS. Rarely have they been told about studies exonerating it. One you probably never heard of was titled "Airliner Cabin Environment Contaminant Measurements, Health Risks and Mitigation Options," conducted in 1989 by the U.S. Department of Transportation in hopes of obtaining data to support a worldwide ban on smoking in airliners. Because smoking was already banned on many domestic flights, no-smoking planes were readily available for comparison with test planes in which the effects of smoking on cabin air were monitored.

To DOT's surprise, it was discovered that levels of respirable suspended particulates, nicotine and carbon monoxide were actually *the same or higher* in nonsmoking flights than in the nonsmoking sections of smoking flights. It also estimated that for business passengers flying 480 hours a year starting at age 35, the lifetime risk of premature cancer deaths from environmental tobacco smoke (ETS) was .27 deaths per 100,000 cabin occupants. (That's *point* 27.) For cosmic radiation, it was 504 deaths—some 1,867 times higher than the Environmental Protection Agency's alleged risk from ETS.[35]

Did that give the department pause? Maybe for a milliscecond. DOT still declared that smoking should be totally extinguished from the skies because it would be too expensive to improve the ventilation and filtration of airliner cabin air. How expensive? According to Sara Mahler-Vossler: 36 cents per smoker on a Boeing 747, 93 cents on a 727.[36]

The real reason it would be too expensive (though DOT didn't say so) was that, thanks to the smoking bans on domestic flights, the airlines had stopped ventilating cabins by blowing out stale air and replacing it with fresh air, which consumed a lot of jet fuel, and were using the cheaper method of mixing recirculated stale air with fresh air.

The airlines were in fact saving fuel worth $100 million a year this way, according to a witness for the cigarette makers at the flight attendants' trial, engineer and aviation consultant Martin Godley.[37] In many ways, airliner cabin air is actually worse today than it was before smoking was banned—and everybody thinks this was a great victory for the health, comfort and well-being of America's commercial airline travelers.

Judge Robert Kaye of Dade County Circuit Court allowed only limited testimony about cosmic radiation, as well as about ozone, a naturally occurring carcinogen that can enter jets at high altitude, and another study on airliner cabin air by occupational safety expert Yolanda Janczenski, who had found no meaningful difference in cabin air pollutants before and after smoking was banned.[38] The point at issue, the judge said, was whether secondhand smoke caused the diseases alleged by the flight attendants, not whether something else might also have caused them.

That issue was never determined. However, as for firsthand smoking, even though it wasn't at issue in the trial, a plaintiffs' attorney exacted a truly staggering, earthshaking, mind-boggling and frightening admission from one tobacco company executive.

After being on the stand for some two hours, Philip Morris CEO Geoffrey Bible was asked by Ron Motley, a private attorney representing the state of Florida: "Would Philip Morris agree that a single American citizen who smokes their products for 30 or more years, a single one, has ever died of a disease caused in part by smoking cigarettes?"

"I think there's a fair chance that one would have, might have," Bible responded, stepping neatly into the trap.

Well, how about 1,000? Motley asked. "Might have," Bible answered. How about 100,000? "Might have." And newspaper headlines were born.[39]

Oh, the perfidy of those tobacco people, keeping that knowledge from us all these years!

Naturally, Motley did not ask Bible if he thought it possible that an airline passenger might ever have been harmed by cosmic radiation, which even the U.S. Department of Transportation estimates is nearly 2,000 times more dangerous than secondhand smoke. Attorneys suing tobacco companies aren't stupid; only those representing tobacco companies are.

Not that it mattered, because the defense abruptly settled the ***Broin*** suit. The reason, given in a Brown & Williamson statement, was solely in the interest of "keeping the proposed federal legislation on track."[40] This was a reference to the so-called "global" tobacco settlement that had been reached between the industry and 40 state attorneys general, America's most successful and admired legal thieves (see Chapter 12). It was not, said B&W, an admission that ETS causes disease.

The settling defendants agreed to pay $300 million to establish a foundation for scientific research in diseases associated with cigarette smoking and to support the enactment of federal legislation prohibiting smoking on international flights originating in or terminating in the United States. (DOT would like to ban it on all flights all over the world, but there's some silly inconvenience called national sovereignty that interferes.)

Susan and Stanley Rosenblatt, the attorneys representing the flight attendants, were to receive a cool $46 million in legal fees, but that was only half of the $93 million they said they deserved for the billable hours they put in over six years of virtually fulltime work in preparing for the suit. Anyway, 25 percent of their take would be donated to charity, said Susan Rosenblatt.[41]

That sure makes me feel a lot better about this deal since I and other smokers, not the cigarette companies, will be paying for it. Incidentally, I haven't flown in an airliner since 1985, so I don't know how many flight attendants I may have injured.

As for the flight attendants themselves, they received zero, zilch, not one penny. As part of the settlement, however, they were given the right to sue the cigarette companies as individuals and, in a complete reversal of traditional American law that says a defendant is considered innocent until proven guilty, the companies agreed that in any such suit the burden of proof would be on them to prove that secondhand smoke *did not* cause his or, more usually, her disease, whatever it might be alleged to be.

These cigarette company guys are simply much too clever for the likes of me to understand.

* * *

STUDIES THAT HAVE associated smoking with a multitude of diseases far outnumber those that have found no such association, or even that in some cases smoking may have a beneficial health effect. But there are still more than just a few of the latter. Unfortunately, they have seldom been reported in the popular media and many doctors themselves may never have heard of them—even though everyone knows it's only the tobacco industry that suppresses studies about smoking.

The following are among 37 such studies culled from the Centers for Disease Control and Prevention's "Bibliography of Continuing Smoking Studies, 1984-85" by Wanda Hamilton, vice-president of the Florida Smokers' Rights Association and an information specialist for Smoker's United Network, a network of smokers' rights activists around the country. She was kind enough to provide me with a copy of her bibliography, which I in turn have culled for those studies I think are the most interesting and provocative.

She deliberately excluded any study listed by the CDC as having been funded in full or part by the tobacco industry. All the abstracts quoted were written and submitted by the principal investigators of the study, but for the sake of economy she included only a summary or salient quotations (which I have italicized) from the original abstract, and for ease of reference categorized them under various headings. The numbers at the left of each citation are the index numbers assigned by the CDC. (Some of the studies were not indexed in the bibliography, nor was the source of funding given for all of them.) The introductory comments in quotes in the block paragraphs under four of the category headings and the Appendix are Hamilton's.

<u>Smoking and Lung Cancer</u>

"Though there can be no doubt about the well-established correlation between smoking and lung cancer, smoking is by no means the only risk factor for lung cancer, and in some occupations cigarette smoking appears actually to help protect against getting the disease . . . [L]ung cancer among nonsmokers seems to be increasing, while the rate of lung cancer among smokers is decreasing, thanks to the advent of filtered cigarettes, which nearly every study has shown decreases risk anywhere from 20 percent to 30 percent (only one such study is listed here)."

In general filter-tipped cigarette smokers appear to be [at] *20% lower risk of squamous cell lung cancer than nonfilter cigarette smokers.*
— 1216. American Health Foundation. Wynder, E.L.; Goodman, M.T.; Kabat, G.C. et al. "Studies in Tobacco-Related Cancers." June 1982-June 1985. Funding: National Cancer Institute (of the Department of Health and Human Services).

Rising lung cancer mortality rates during 1953-1982 were similar for both sexes in all parts of Oregon . . . Occupational risk differences among both sexes far exceeded those noted with other risk factors [including smoking—D.O.], *suggesting that occupational differences deserve primary emphasis in future efforts at lung cancer control.*
— 1375. University of Oregon School of Medicine. Morton, W.E. "Epidemiology of Lung Cancer in Oregon."

A possible flattening in the dose-response was found and a low relative risk in an area of the world with one of the highest recorded incidences of lung cancer. The flattening of the dose-response curve occurred with an above-average consumption of 20 cigarettes/day. [That is, the more cigarettes smoked, the lower the risk of lung cancer!—D.O.)
— 0590. West of Scotland Cancer Surveillance Unit (Glasgow) and University of Michigan School of Public Health. Gillis, C.R.; Hole, D.J.; Hawthorne, V.M. et al. "Retrospective Case Control Study of Smoking Habits and Lung Cancer in the West of Scotland." Funding: National Institutes of Health (NO1-CP-05646).

Excess risks of lung cancer found in miners and foundry workers could not be fully explained by the high prevalence of smoking among these occupations.
— 0495. University of Zurich Institute of Pathology. Schuler, G. "Epidemiology of Lung Cancer in Switzerland."

Smoking has a protective effect on immunological abnormalities in asbestos workers.
— 0429. Institute of Immunology and Experimental Therapy (Poland). Lange, A. "Effect of Smoking on Immunological Abnormalities in Asbestos Workers."

Relative risk of lung cancer for asbestos workers was highest for those who had never smoked, lowest for current smokers, and intermediate for ex-smokers. The trend was statistically significant. There was no significant association between smoking and deaths from mesothelioma.
— 0565. University of London School of Hygiene and Tropical Medicine. "Cancer of the Lung Among Asbestos Factory Workers."*

Over the 22 years of followup, exposed workers have had a very high risk of respiratory cancer, mostly of the lung. The risk has been dose related and has been much higher in nonsmokers and ex-smokers than in current smokers. The epidemic began to subside shortly after exposure to chloromethyl ethers ceased.
— 1388. Hahnemann Medical College and Hospital (Philadelphia). Weiss, W. "Lung Cancer Due to Chloromethyl Ethers."

Presence of chronic respiratory symptoms at baseline [beginning of study] *was inversely related to cessation of smoking. Respiratory impairment was positively associated with smoking cessation, but failed to reach statistical significance.*
— 1544. Department of Health and Human Services, Public Health Service, National Institute of Occupational Safety and Health. Ames, R.G. "Respiratory Effects of Exposure to Diesel Emissions in Underground Coal Miners." Funding: NIOSH.

Lung volume parameters were found to decrease with age, but there was no significant modification related to tobacco consumption.
— 0241. Institut d'Etudes et Recherches Pneumophtisiologiques (Institute of Studies on Tuberculosis, France). Kleisbauer, J.P. "Longitudinal Study of the Methods of Early Detection of Respiratory Diseases in a Population of Cab Drivers."

*In September 1997, Raymark Industries, Inc. of Bountiful, Utah, which used to make asbestos products and has paid more than $400 million to settle asbestos-related health claims, filed suit against the tobacco industry to try to get some of that money back. "Raymark has always disputed, and continues to dispute, that asbestos is a pure carcinogen, and contends that cigarette smoke inhaled by the asbestos claimants caused the cancers complained of," the lawsuit stated. A dozen other current or former asbestos manufacturers indicated they would join the Raymark suit. As of this writing it remained to be seen whether the tobacco industry would defend itself by citing exonerating studies such as the two above or whether it would play stupid again and shell out more millions from the pockets of smokers.[42]

Neither smokers nor nonsmokers showed any changes in bronchial responsiveness after smoking cigarettes.
— 0391. Yokohama City University School of Medicine (Japan). Okubo,T; Suzuki, S.; Sano, F. "Acute Effect of Smoking on Bronchial Responsiveness."

Smoking and Heart Disease

"The connection between smoking and heart disease is far more tenuous than that between smoking and lung disease. Though the medical establishment considers smoking to be a risk factor—among many risk factors—for heart disease, the fact remains that anywhere from 30 to 50 percent of those admitted to hospitals for coronary problems exhibit none of the known risk factors (including smoking) and that the research is by no means either consistent or conclusive in linking smoking to this disease. It is true that deaths from heart disease, which is still the number one cause of death, are declining, but most researchers attribute this to better surgical and medical techniques, not to a decline in smoking rates, since deaths from heart disease are declining worldwide, even in countries with high smoking rates."

No statistically significant association was found in either community between smoking and coronary heart disease, hypertension or somatic complaints.
—1477. University of Texas, School of Allied Health Sciences. Philips, B.U. Jr.; Bruhn, J.G. "Smoking Habits and Reported Illnesses in Two Communities With Different Systems of Social Support." Funding: University of Texas, National Institute of Mental Health. 1981-83.

Preliminary data indicate greater frequency of anterior infarctions among nonsmokers . . . Among patients with unstable angina, smoking was associated with less persistent rest pain and a lower proportion of smokers had chronic angina of effort prior to hospital admission. Preliminary analysis suggests a marginally lower in-hospital mortality rate among smokers after controlling for age and other prognostic factors.
— 0298. St. Vincent's Hospital, Department of Preventive Cardiology (Dublin, Ireland). December 1980-January 1986.

Preliminary data indicate a high prevalence of IHD [ischemic heart disease] *in South Wales. A significant association between white cell count and IHD*

defined cross-sectionally is not explained by smoking habits. Prevalent IHD is not explained by smoking habits.
—0598. Medical Research Council, Epidemiology Unit (Wales). Yarnell, J.W.G.; Elwood, P.D.; Sweetham, P.M. "Caerphilly Prospective Study of Ischemic Heart Disease."

Recent secular trends in sex and age specific mortality from ischemic heart disease both in the United Kingdom and in the United States appear to be independent of changes in cigarette consumption.
— 0564. University of Leeds, Department of Medical Physics (England). Burch, P.R..J. "Tests of Causal, Constitutional, and Mixed Hypotheses of Associations Between Smoking and Disease in Man." 1972 and continuing. Funding: University of Leeds.

No significant differences were observed between smoking and nonsmoking women with respect to myocardial infarction and death during the 12-year followup.
— 0464. Sahlgrenska Hospital, Medical Department. Bengtsson, C.; Lapidus, L.; Hallstrom, T. "The Population Study of Women in Gothenburg, Sweden."

In asymtomatic male aviators (aged 30 to 60), age and ratio of total cholesterol to high density lipoprotein cholesterol are most highly correlated with degree of coronary artery disease found on angiography. After removing the effect of age and this ratio, no statistically significant variance is explained by other risk factors [including smoking — W.H].
— 1465. Department of Defense, Department of Air Force School of Medicine (Brooks Air Force Base, Texas). Tolan, G.D.; Honch, P.; Hickman, R. et al. "Multivariate Approaches to the Detection of Asymptomatic Coronary Artery Disease." Funded by U.S.A.F. 1971 continuing.

Pipe smokers have a higher intake of nicotine than cigarette smokers (as measured by serum and urinary cotinine levels). Since pipe smokers have little excess of CHD [coronary heart disease], *higher chronic nicotine exposure is unlikely to be the cause of the excess seen in cigarette smokers.*
— 0534. Medical College of St. Bartholomew's Hospital, Department of Environmental and Preventative Medicine (England). Wald, M.J.; Bailey, A. "Nicotine and Heart Disease."

ETS (Environmental Tobacco Smoke) and Heart Disease

No difference in prevalence of cardiovascular symptoms was found between those living with smokers and those not.
— 0591. West of Scotland Cancer Surveillance Unit, Ruchill Hospital. Gillis, C.R.; Hole, D.J.; Hawthorne, V.M. "Health Effects of Exposure to ETS in the West of Scotland."

Smoking and "Throat" Cancer

All countries experienced a sharp increase in lung cancer mortality; laryngeal and oral cavity cancers showed divergent trends (10 countries had steady or decreasing rates). Results suggest that tobacco may not be the major causative factor for laryngeal and oral cavity cancers.
— 0244. Institut National de Recherche et de Securite (France). Moulin, J.J.; Mur, J.M.; Cavelier, C. "Comparative Epidemiology, in Europe, of Tobacco-Related Cancers (Lung, Larynx, Pharynx, Buccal Cavity)." Data from the World Health Organization, 1950-1977.

Secular trends in mortality from esophageal cancer in the United Kingdom are independent of secular changes in cigarette consumption, but well correlated with secular changes in alcohol consumption . . . alcohol acts as an indirect causal agent. The proximal causal agent is likely to be a precipitator, such as a microorganism. Genetic disposition is also indicated.
— 0564. University of Leeds, Department of Medical Physics (England). Burch, P.R.J. "Tests of Causal, Constitutional and Mixed Hypotheses of Associations Between Smoking and Disease in Man." Funding: University of Leeds. 1972 and continuing.

. . . alcohol consumption was the dominant risk factor for esophageal cancer.
— National Cancer Institute. Blot, W.J.; Brown, L.M.; Ershow, A. et al. "Epidemiological Studies of Tobacco Use and Risk of Cancer."

Smoking and Renal (Kidney) Cancer

Preliminary results implicate relative weight in both men and women as a principal risk factor in renal cell carcinoma. Comparison with population controls failed to implicate smoking or beverage use as risk factors.
— 1363. University of Oklahoma, Health Sciences Center. Asal, N.R.;

Geyer, J. "Risk Factors in Kidney Cancer." October 1981-February 1985. Funding: National Cancer Institute.

A weak positive association with cigarette smoking has been found, but only after controlling for selection biases . . . Findings appear to confirm previously observed associations with obesity, northeastern European ancestry, renal calculi [kidney stones], *and use of phenacetin-containing analgesics.*
— 1060. Harvard University, School of Public Health, Department of Epidemiology. MacMahon, B.; Maclure, K.M. "A Case Control Study of Renal Adenocarcinoma." Funding: Harvard School of Public Health, National Cancer Institute.

ETS and Bladder Cancer

No association was found for exposure to sidestream smoke, coffee drinking, or artificial sweetener use. The association of several occupations with bladder cancer has been found in males.
— 1216. American Health Foundation. Wynder, E.L.; Goodman, M.T..; Kabat, G.C. et al. "Studies in Tobacco-Related Cancers." Funding: National Cancer Institute.

Smoking and Endometrial, Ovarian and Breast Cancer

Overall, smoking was not found to be associated with any of the cancers studied.
— Centers for Disease Control and Prevention, Epidemiologic Studies Branch, Division of Reproductive Health. Rubin, G.; Franks, A.L.; Stroup, M. "Smoking and Endometrial, Ovarian, and Breast Cancer." Funding: National Institute of Child Health and Human Development.

The risk of breast cancer does not appear to be influenced by cigarette smoking.
— 1039. Boston University Medical Center, Drug Epidemiology Unit. Shapiro, S.; Rosenberg, L.; Kaufman, D. "Multiple Case-Control Study of the Long Term Effects of Drug Use in the Treatment of Chronic Disease." Funding: Food and Drug Administration and National Institute of Child Health and Human Development.

Smoking and Cervical Cancer

Sexual behavior and socioeconomic indicators predict cervical cancer incidence, as has been demonstrated in numerous other studies.

— University of Utah, School of Medicine. Lyon, J.L. "Epidemiological Investigation of Cervical Cancer in an Area of Low Incidence." Funding: National Cancer Institute.

Smoking and Pregnancy

"Some studies have found a correlation between maternal smoking during pregnancy and lower birthweight in babies. However, there are many factors which correlate with low birthweight, and the dominant risk factors seem to be the mother's age and the mother's socioeconomic class. Even those studies which show a correlation between maternal smoking and low birthweight speak of weight differences in grams, not ounces, and one ounce=28.35 grams."

Risk factors associated with low birthweight (in rank order):
1. *Mother's age (too young or too old)*
2. *First pregnancy*
3. *More than two previous stillbirths*
4. *Lower birthweight of older siblings*
5. *Small stature and weight of mother*
6. *Fewer examinations during pregnancy*
7. *Smoking by mother or father*

— 0360. Department of Public Health, Jichi Medical School (Japan). Nagai, M.; Yanagawa, H.; Kawaguchi, T. et al. "A Study of the Factors Associated With Low Birth Weight. A Case-Control Study in Tochigi Prefecture." April 1982-December 1984.

Women who smoke during pregnancy have full-term babies which, on the average, are 5-6 grams [about a fifth of an ounce—D.O.] *smaller than full-term babies born to nonsmoking mothers.*

— 0755. University of Colorado, Health Sciences Center. Moore, L.C. "Maternal O_2 [dioxide] Transport During Pregnancy at High Altitude."

Birthweight lower in the smoking group, but the incidence of smoking was higher in young, unmarried women of lower socioeconomic status. Perinatal death was also higher among young, unmarried low income women . . . No differences in antepartum hemorrhage or congenital abnormalities between the groups . . . Hypertension and postpartum hemorrhage were lower in smokers.

— 0045. University of Tasmania, Queen Alexandra Hospital, Department of Obstetrics and Gynecology. Correy, J.; Newman, N.; Curran, J. "An Assessment of Smoking in Pregnancy."

The proportion of complications of pregnancy and delivery were similar in smokers and nonsmokers.
— University of Oslo (Norway). Dalaher, K.; Grunfeld, B.; Jansen, A.

Data do not confirm the suggestion that changes in cord blood vessels similar to those of atherosclerosis are brought about by maternal smoking during pregnancy. Pathological changes in the cord at term may be found in infants of healthy, nonsmoking mothers.
— 0184. Universität Freiburg, Anatomisches Insitut (Germany). Staubesand, J.; Seydewitz, V.; Hugod, C. et al. "Effects of Maternal Smoking on the Neonatal Umbilical Cord."

Parental Smoking, ETS and Children

No convincing differences for viral infection or respiratory illness were seen with parental smoking as an isolated factor.
— 1462. Baylor College of Medicine, Influenza Research Center (Texas). Gardner, G.C.; Frank, A.L.; Taber, L.H. "Effects of Social and Family Factors on Viral Respiratory Infection and Illness in the First Year of Life." A longitudinal study, 1975-80.

The correlation matrix revealed that maternal education was the variable most significantly inversely correlated with infection . . . Its statistical significance persisted in the presence of other added factors . . . Maternal education appeared to have played a highly significant role in the health of the children studied.
— 0878. University of Kansas, College of Health Sciences. Homes, G.E.; Hassanein, K.M.; Miller, H.D. "Factors Associated with Morbidity Among Breast Fed and Formula Fed Babies."

Nicotine and Smoking: Benefits

"Though the risks of smoking are highly publicized (and highly exaggerated), the medical benefits of smoking are rarely mentioned. The greatest risks of smoking come from the tars released during the combustion of tobacco, and these tars are implicated in lung cancer and other breathing disorders, though even the tar apparently has some beneficial effects in protecting the lungs from some noxious particulate matter (e.g. asbestos). According to most studies, the chief medical benefits of smoking are from the nicotine, which occurs naturally in tobacco as well as in certain vegetables such as tomatoes, potatoes and red peppers, though in much smaller amounts. Interestingly, these three plants originated in the Americas, so nicotine was essentially a 'New World' substance. Native Americans were well aware of the curative properties of tobacco, and used it both medicinally and ceremonially."

1. *Smoking improves human information processing*
2. *Higher nicotine cigarettes produce greater improvements than low-nicotine cigarettes*
3. *Nicotine tablets produce similar effects*
4. *Nicotine can reverse the detrimental effects of scopalamine on performance*
5. *Smoking effects are accompanied by increases in EEG* [electroencephalograph] *arousal*

— 0574. University of Reading, Department of Psychology (England). Warburton, D.M.; Wesnes, K. "The Effects of Cigarette Smoking on Human Information Processing and the Role of Nicotine in These Effects."

In general, motor performance in all groups improved after smoking.
— 0530. London University, Institute of Psychiatry. O'Connor, K.P. "Individual Differences in Psychophysiology of Smoking and Smoking Behavior."

Smokers in general are thinner than nonsmokers, even when they ingest more calories.
— 0885. Kentucky State University. Lee, C.J.; Panemangalore, M. "Obesity Among Selected Elderly Females in Central Kentucky." Funding: U.S. Department of Agriculture.

[S]mokers had less plaque, gingival inflammation and tooth mobility than nonsmokers and similar periodontal pocket depth.
— Veterans Administration Outpatient Clinic (Boston). Chauncey, H.H.; Kapur, K.K.; Feldman, R.S. "The Longitudinal and Cross-Sectional Study of Oral Health in Healthy Veterans (Dental Longitudinal Study)."

Smokers have lower incidence of postoperative deep vein thrombosis than nonsmokers.

— Guy's Hospital Medical School (England). Jones, R.M. "Influence of Smoking on Peri-operative Morbidity."

Hypertension is less common among smokers. Hypertension prevalence rate among smokers was 3.94 percent; among nonsmokers the rate was 4.90 percent.
— 0146. Shanghai Institute of Cardiovascular Diseases. (China) Chen, H.Z.; Pan, X.W.; Guo, G. et al. "Relation Between Cigarette Smoking and Epidemiology of Hypertension."

RBCs [red blood cells] *from cigarette smokers contain more gluahione and catalase and protect lung endothelial cells against O_2* [dioxide] *metabolites better than RBCs from nonsmokers.*
— 0759. University of Colorado. Refine, J.D.; Berger, E.M.; Beehler, C.J. et al. "Role of RBC Antioxidants in Cigarette Smoke Related Diseases." January 1980 and continuing.

Appendix

"Following are studies listed in the Centers for Disease Control's 'Bibliography on Smoking and Health, 1991.' Many newer studies appear in this more recent CDC bibliography which support the earlier studies listed in the foregoing selected bibliography, including a lower risk of breast cancer, lower risk of endometrial cancer in smoking women, the improvement of fine motor control for smokers, lower incidence of overweight in smokers, lower incidence of high blood pressure among smokers. Below are selected studies which demonstrate the protective effect of smoking on Parkinson's Disease* and ulcerative colitis."

Several epidemiological studies have indicated that there may be an inverse relationship between smoking and Parkinson's Disease. There is an apparent protective effect of cigarette smoke.
— 1102. Carr, L.A.; Rowell, P.P. "Attenuation of Methyl-4-phenyl-1,2,3,6-tetrahydophyridine-induced neurotoxicity by tobacco smoke." Published in *Neuropharmacology* 29(3):311-4, March 1990.

These results indicate that in sufficient doses chronic treatment with nicotine may be considered in the pharmacological treatment of Parkinson's disease. It re-

*See also Chapter 4 in this book for more studies regarding the possible protective effects of smoking on Parkinson's Disease, as well as Alzheimer's.

mains to be demonstrated whether these protective actions can be extended to include also other injured neurons.
— 1190. Janson, A.M.; Fuxe, K.; Agnati, L.F.; Jansson, A. et al. "Protective Effects of chronic nicotine treatment on lesioned nigrostriatal dopamine neurons in the male rat." Published in *Progress in Brain Research* 79:257-65, 1989.

Several studies have reported an apparent protective effect of cigarette smoking for the risk of idiopathic Parkinson's disease (IPD). These observations are supported by neurochemical studies . . . These findings suggest that the inverse association between smoking and IPD may apply to NIP [neuroleptic-induced parkinsonism].
— 4014. Decina, P.; Caracci, G.; Sandik, R.; Berman, W. et al. "Cigarette smoking and neuroleptic-induced parkinsonism." Published in *Biological Psychiatry* 28(6):502-8, September 15, 1990.

There is a low prevalence of smoking in ulcerative colitis. The disease often starts or relapses after stopping smoking.
— 4101. Prytz, H.; Benoni, C.; Tagesson, C. "Does smoking tighten the gut?" Published in *Scandinavian Journal of Gastroenterology* 24(9):1084-8, November 1989.

These results indicate that nonsmokers and especially ex-smokers of cigarettes have a greater risk of UC [ulcerative colitis] *and thus confirm the results of other studies.*
— 4134. Lorusso, D.; Leo, S.; Misciagna, G.; Guerra, V. "Cigarette smoking and ulcerative colitis. A case control study." Published in *Hepato-Gastronenterology* 36(4):202-4, August 1989.

Ms. Hamilton has also provided me with references to a number of other studies having to do with maternal smoking, which evidently eluded Dr. DiFranza (page 134). Some of them:

We recently found no significant association between maternal smoking and either stillbirths or neonatal deaths when information about the underlying disorders, obtained from placental examinations, was incorporated into the analysis. Similar analyses found no correlation between maternal smoking and preterm birth. The most frequent initiating causes of preterm birth, stillbirth, and neonatal death are acute chorioamnionitis, disorders that produce chronic low blood flow from the uterus

to the placenta, and major congenital malformations. There is no credible evidence that cigarette smoking has a role in the genesis of any of these disorders.
— R.L. Naeye, "Disorders of the placenta, fetus, and neonate, diagnosis and clinical significance." (New York: C.V. Mosby Co., 1992). [Naeye's work is highly significant because it depended on actual examination of a study population of ca.56,000 pregnancies in the Collaborative Perinatal Study—W.H.]

[T]he increase of SGA [small for gestational age] *infants in women whose pregnancies are complicated by abruption is not explained by maternal smoking . . . The association with SGA status was identical for smokers and non-smokers.*
— Voigt, L.F.; Hollenbach, K.A. et al. "The relationship of abruptio placentae with maternal smoking and small for gestational age infants." *Obstetrics and Gynecology* 75(5):771-4, May 1990.

No significant effect of smoking on the miscarriage risk was seen.
— Sandahl, B. "Smoking habits and spontaneous abortion." *European Journal of Obstetrics, Gynecology and Reproductive Biology*: 31(1):23-31, April 1989.

There was no evidence of an association between any congenital defect and smoking.
— McDonald, A.D.; Armstrong, B.G.; Sloan, M. "Cigarette, alcohol, and coffee consumption and congenital defects." *American Journal of Public Health*, 82(1):91-3, January 1992.

Smoking was not associated with the risk of ectopic pregnancy after adjustment for potential confounding factors (including history of pelvic inflammatory disease).
— Parazzini, F.; Tozzi, L. et al. "Risk factors for ectopic pregnancy: an Italian case-control study." *Obstetrics and Gynecology.* 80(5):821-6, November 1992.

The overall relative risk for cancer in children with mothers reporting smoking during pregnancy was 0.99. [A relative risk of less than 1.0 means that mothers who smoked during pregnancy had slightly FEWER children who developed childhood cancer than non-smoking mothers, but the difference is so small that in reality one should say that there is no difference—W.H.]

— Pershagen, G.; Ericson, A. et al. "Maternal smoking in pregnancy: does it increase the risk of childhood cancer?" *International Journal of Epidemiology*. 21(1):1-5, February 1992.

[T]here was no indication of any SA [spontaneous abortion] *effect resulting from active smoking.*
— Mantel, N. "Re: Tobacco smoke exposure and pregnancy outcome among working women." *American Journal of Epidemiology* 135(7):837-8, April 1, 1992 (letter).

. . . found no increased risk [of congenital malformations] *for infants of smokers.*
— Malloy, M.H.; Kleinman, J.C., et al. "Maternal smoking during pregnancy: no association with congenital malformations in Missouri 1980-83." *American Journal of Public Health*, 79(9):1243-6; September 1989.

The protective effect of smoking on preeclampsia [a form of toxemia] *was stronger for women who continued to smoke after 20 weeks of pregnancy. While smoking tended to reduce the risk of gestational hypertension, this effect was less evident than that for preeclampsia.*
— Marcoux, S.; Brisson, J.; Fabia, J. "The effect of cigarette smoking on the risk of preeclampsia and gestational hypertension." *American Journal of Epidemiology*, 130(5):950-7, November 1989.

In an accompanying e-mail to me, Hamilton wrote:

> What one finds in looking at the research is that it's often contradictory. The problem seems to be that there are so MANY variables, and actually whatever negative influence researchers do find about smoking and pregnancy is so small that it's barely significant. Quite a few studies have found that maternal smoking is ONE among many risk factors for low birthweight in babies, but in none of them is it among the greatest risk factors and in fact may not exist at all once economic class or placental infection are taken into account . . . The great preponderance of the research has found NO connection between smoking and congenital abnormalities, and that in fact smoking mothers seem to produce slightly fewer neonates with congenital abnormalities.

She also added an interesting statistic:

> In 1986 there were 12 nations with lower infant death rates than the U.S.; now there are 28, even though the U.S. has a lower smoking rate than all those other countries.

* * *

JUST IN CASE the studies cited above cause any smokers to feel smug about their disgusting addiction, the fact is that all of us—whether we smoke or don't smoke—are at daily risk of contracting serious diseases from a multitude of carcinogenic (cancer-causing) chemicals surrounding us—*some manufactured by our own bodies.*

That is the seemingly frightening finding of numerous studies conducted both by federal agencies and by researchers in the private sector. In her book, *The Apocalyptics,*[43] an epic exposé of the health and environmental scare artists, Edith Effron listed the following examples she found in a search of the scientific literature:

Cholesterol, found in the human brain, spinal cord, and fat, is carcinogenic and a carcinogen promoter. (Wogan, 1974; International Agency for Research in Cancer (IARC), Vol 10. 1976; National Institute of Occupational Health and Safety (NIOSH), 1976.)

The digestion of sugars produces acetaldehyde in the blood; acetaldehyde is reported to be mutagenic. (Environmental Protection Agency, *Potential Industrial*, 1977.)

The metabolism of carbohydrates requires insulin, which is reported to be carcinogenic. (NIOSH, 1976.)

Saliva contains bacteria which convert nitrate to nitrite, which may form carcinogenic nitrosamines. (Tannenbaum, Archer et al., 1978; Tannenbaum et al., 1974.)

The stomach contains bacteria which are reported to produce carcinogenic nitrosamines. (Sander, 1973.)

Trace amounts of nitrosamines are normally present in human blood following consumption of conventional foodstuffs. (Fine, et al. 1977.)

Intestinal bacteria are reported to produce carcinogenic nitrosamines (Tannenbaum, Fett et al., 1978); *to metabolize sterols to carcinogenesis* (Moore et al., 1979) *and to form co-carcinogens from bile acid to produce a carcinogenic metabolite, ethionine.* (Lewis et al., 1977.) E.coli *incubated in a sterile medium produced the reported carcinogen benzo(a)pyrene* (J. Miller, 1973.)

Mutagens, identified as N-nitroso compounds or volatile nitrosamines, have been found in the feces of healthy people. (Bruce et al., 1977; Varghese et al., 1978; Wang, 1978.)

Natural human sex hormones—estradiol, estrone, estriol, progesterone, and testosterone—are reported to be carcinogenic. (Clement Associates, 1978; IARC, Vol. 6, 1974).

Steroid hormones may precipitate or promote cancer; the synthetic steroids are reported to be metabolized in the human body by the same mechanisms as those of the natural hormones. (IARC, Vol. 6, 1974.)

Smegma [a cheeselike sebaceous secretion that collects beneath the foreskin or around the clitoris] *is a reported carcinogen; horse smegma is carcinogenic in mice. It is recommended by some scientists that the carcinogenicity of smegma be studied further in connection with penis cancer.* (Muir et al., 1979.)

Sperm may cause testicle and prostate cancer. In rats, the penetration of sperm into the cells and tissues of testicles and prostate caused cancer of those tissues. (Stein-Werblowski, 1978.)

Mother's milk contains lactose—milk sugar. It is reported to be carcinogenic. (NIOSH, 1976.)

Radioactive substances of natural origin are in the air we breathe and the food we eat. These radioactive elements become incorporated into our tissues to such an extent that, on average, the atoms of which our bodies consist are disintegrating at a rate of about 500,000 every minute, due to the presence of naturally radioactive species of carbon, potassium, and other elements. (Eisenbud, 1978.)

Comments Effron:

> These data, exclusively natural, suggest that by virtue of the nature of reality itself, there is nothing we can breathe, eat, or drink without encountering carcinogens . . . We see that carcinogens are reported to be every kind of thing: they are animate, inanimate; chemical, physical; animal, vegetable, and mineral . . They are everywhere: they rain down upon us from the skies, they radiate upward from crevices beneath the sea, from the rocks and soil, they flow through the veins of plants and trees, they gush out in torrents from forests. They are alive: They grow, they crawl, they bloom, they blossom. And they are inside us: They are part of our vital physiologi-

> cal processes; they course through our bloodstream, through our hormones; they are in our saliva, in our digestive tracts. We inhale them, we drink them, and we feed on them ceaselessly, and in the act of absorbing them, we renew the needed supply in our bodies, for we cannot live without them . . .[44]

Effron is seconded by Roger Bate, an environmental economist at England's Cambridge University in an interview by *The* (London) *Daily Telegraph*. Every time we eat, every time we breathe in, we play a giant game of Russian roulette with nature, he says. "There are at least 1,000 chemicals in coffee, and 19 of the 27 that have been tested are carcinogens . . . Peanut butter, lettuce, orange juice, black pepper, nutmeg, broccoli, they are all carcinogens."

If you want to suck in some serious benzo(a)pyrene, stand anywhere near a grilling hamburger, he adds. The cooking of bacon gives rise to the carcinogen n-nitro pyrrolidine, more than you could expect from passive smoking, and environmental tobacco smoke is peanuts next to the potentially deadly vapor of the frankfurter.

Finally, you also have more chance of contracting cancer from eating commercially grown mushrooms, which contain a potent genotoxic carcinogenic hydrazine derivative called agaritine, than from passive smoking.

But how big a chance is the question. And the answer is, vanishingly small to nonexistent. (Except, of course, in the eyes of those whose careers are devoted to scaring the hell out of everybody.)

"So why do we panic?" asks the *Telegraph*. "It is our modern failure to understand the dictum of Paracelsus, that the dose makes the poison. These days we are slow to see how something may be dangerous, but trivially dangerous. The public's mind works in binary: yes, no, black, white. Politicians and journalists tend to demand one-armed scientists, with no 'on the one hand, on the other.'"[45]

Does anybody think that if we could just eliminate smoking, the world would be Eden again?

By way of making all of us feel better and to conclude this chapter, the latest data from the National Center for Health Statistics and the Census Bureau show that the infant mortality rate in the United States has fallen to an all-time low (although still higher than many other countries) and life expectancy at birth has reached an all-time high of 76.1 years.[46]

For those of us who arrived on the scene too soon to share in this promising future for today's newborns, there is some slight solace. According to Harvard's Center for Risk Analysis in Boston, most of the people who die from cancer and heart disease tend to be near the end of their normal lifespan. Even if cancer or heart disease were conquered, other factors in the aging process would bring those lives to a natural end.[47]

Notes

1. To a friend shortly before her death from cancer, quoted in *Vogue*. *The Atlanta Journal-Constitution,* August 3, 1994, p. A7.

2. Quoted in Dennis L. Breo, "Kicking Butts—AMA, Joe Camel and the 'Black Flag' War on Tobacco." *Journal of the American Medical Association*, October 27, 1993, p. 1978. Courtesy the Advocacy Institute.

3. Quoted in Robert Matthews, "Cancer Reports Are Junk." *The Sunday Correspondent*, October 5, 1989. At www.forces-cdn.com/scares.htm.

4. Charles McArthur et al., "The Psychology of Smoking." *Journal of Abnormal and Social Psychology* 56 (1958), pp. 272-273. Cited in David Krogh, *Smoking: The Artificial Passion* (New York: W. H. Freeman, 1991), pp. 16-17.

5. Health Watch. *The Atlanta Journal-Constitution*, December 6, 1996, p. F2.

6. At www.ash.org/july97/7-97-3.html, citing *Archives of General Psychiatry* (1997);54:670-676.

7. At www.ash.org/97/august/8-19-97-1.html.

8. K. A. Fackelmann, "Mother's smoking linked to child's IQ drop." *Science News*, February 12, 1994, p. 101.

9. News & Notes. *The Atlanta Journal-Constitution*, May 13, 1997, p. B3.

10. "Tobacco May Compete With Other Food Dollars." *Pediatrics*, March 12, 1996; Sandra Boodman, "Smoking Parents Linked to Children's Poor Diet." *The Washington Post*, March 26, 1996, Health Section, p. 5. Sources courtesy of The Advocacy Institute.

11. *Journal of Family Practice*, (April 1995);40:385-394..

12. Health Watch. *The Atlanta Journal-Constitution*, May 13, 1997, p. C3, and reported again in the AJC, September 10, 1997, p. B3.

13. Bill Hendrick and Amanda Husted, "Maternal depression can affect baby, research suggests." *The Atlanta Journal-Constitution*, July 22, 1996, p. E2.

14. From FORCES USA Weekly Tobacco News, October, 1996, at www.forces.org.

15. Jeff Nesmith, "Exercise cuts breast cancer risk." *The Atlanta Journal-Constitution*, September 21, 1994, p. A4.

16. Anne Rochell, "Smoking: Like mother, like daughter." *The Atlanta Journal-Constitution*, October 4, 1994, p. A14.

17. From the Tobacco Bulletin Board, at www.tobacco.org/News/fathersmoking.html. Also *The Washington Post*, November 19, 1997, p. AO7. From http.yahoo.com/headlines/971117/news/stories/smoking_1.html.

18. Carol Thompson, "Counterpoint—Talking Back to the Media." FORCES Canada at www.forces-cdn. com/counterp.smo-dads.htm.

19. Steven Milloy, *Science Without Sense* (Washington: Cato Institute, 1995), pp. 26-28.

20. "Michigan Stats Confirm Hunting, Child Abuse Link." *Animal People*, October 1995. At www.junkscience.com/news/michigan.htm.

21. Amada Husted, "32-year study links anxiety, sudden heart attacks in men." *The Atlanta Journal-Constitution*, November 14, 1994, p. C4.

22. "Depression takes toll on heart." *The Atlanta Journal-Constitution*, August 26, 1997, p. B3. From the Associated Press.

23. Kia Morgan Allen, "Survey suggests sleep problems present nightmare for business." *The Atlanta Journal-Constitution*, March 28, 1997, p. H12.

24. Bill Hendrick, "Anger, education levels linked to heart attacks." *The Atlanta Journal-Constitution*, April 14, 1997, p. C3.

25. Bill Hendrick and Amanda Husted, "Success at an early age could mean shorter life." *The Atlanta Journal-Constitution*, August 12, 1996, p. D8.

26. Bill Hendrick, "Pushy men flirt with death, study says." *The Atlanta Journal-Constitution*, May 28, 1997, p. D3.

27. "New heart attack theory for Type A's." *The Atlanta Journal-Constitution*, November 18, 1992, p. E12. From the Associated Press.

28. "Wall Street tries to arrest frequent heart attack deaths." *The Atlanta Journal-Constitution*, December 31, 1997, p. C7. From Bloomberg News.

29. Ibid.

30. "Job stress not a factor in heart disease, study finds." *The Atlanta Journal-Constitution*, August 5, 1995, p. E7. From *The Boston Globe*.

31. Amanda Husted, "Milk and strokes." *The Atlanta Journal-Constitution*, May 7, 1996, p. D5.

32. Smith, G. D., Frankel, S, and Yarnell, J. "Sex and death: Are they related? Findings from the Caerphilly cohort study." *British Medical Journal* 337 315 (December 20 & 27, 1997). Cited in Kathleen Fackelmann, "Valu-

able Vices." Science News Online, February 18, 1998. At www.sciencenews.org/sn_arc98/2_28_98/bob1.htm.

33. "A walk is as good as a workout." *The Atlanta Journal-Constitution*, July 30, 1993, p. E1. From the Associated Press.

34. Lowell Ponte, "How Cigarettes Cloud Your Brain." *Reader's Digest*, March 1995, p. 127.

35. "Alt.smokers.faq (frequently asked questions) v1.5." At www. cris.com/~trieger/smokers-faq.html.

36. Sara Mahler-Vossler, "Should Americans Be Concerned About the Toxicity of Second-Hand Smoke?" At www.forces.org/pages/sar-art3.htm.

37. Michael Connor, "Airlines saved millions cutting fresh air on jets." Reuters Security News at http://biz.yahoo.com80/finance/97/09/22/amb_bgl_htm.

38. Ibid.

39. Mike Williams, "Exec admits possible health risks." *The Atlanta Journal-Constitution*, August 22, 1997, p. A21.

40. "Brown & Williamson's Statement Regarding Broin Settlement." PR Newswire at http://biz.yahoo.com/prnews//97/10/10/yo0015-yo-4.html.

41. Jim Loney, "Tobacco deal talks got serious when defense began." From Reuters at http://biz.yahoo.com/finance/97/10/10/bgi_g_9/html.

42. Brendan Murray, "Asbestos firm sues tobacco giants." *Atlanta Business Chronicle*, September 22, 1997. At www.amcity.com:80/atlanta/stories/092297/story.html. Also CNN, "Tobacco faces a new foe." At www.cnnfn.com/hotstories/companies/9709/24/asbestos_pkg1. Sept. 24, 1997.

43. Edith Effron, *The Apocalyptics: Cancer and the Big Lie: How the Environmental Movement Controls What We Know About Cancer* (New York: Simon and Schuster, 1984), pp. 175-176.

44. Ibid, p. 177.

45. *The* (London) *Daily Telegraph*, September 27, 1997. From Infoseek News Center Article at www. infoseek.com.

46. "Infant mortality rate falls to record low, report says." *The Atlanta Journal-Constitution*, December 2, 1997, p. D3. From the Associated Press.

47. Michael Ryan, "What's *Really* Risky?" *Parade*, June 15, 1997, p. 12.

Chapter 4

ADDICTED TO 'ADDICTION'

I was a slave to cigarettes.

— George Autry[1]

Several pharmaceutical companies and many medical programs now make use of the idea that smoking is an addiction to warn smokers that they can never possibly quit without medical help since smoking—like drug addiction—involves physical dependence on a drug . . . The smoking industry is too vast and the number of smokers wishing to quit too lucrative for smoking to be overlooked as a medical problem.

— Stanton Peele[2]

IN A LIVING LANGUAGE like English, words are constantly subject to disuse, misuse and overuse, as well as redefinition. But in recent years few words have been more bent out of shape than has the term "addiction." So popular has this label become that it is applied not only to behaviors that people (some people) seem *compelled* to practice, such as drinking alcohol to excess, but also to things people merely *like* to do, such as eating chocolate or having sex or even communicating with others via the Internet.[3] When it is applied to smokers by antismokers, especially in the adjectival form, it is more often as an epithet or invective than as a medically justified description or explanation of the smoker's behavior.

My oldest dictionary (Webster's International Unabridged, Second Edition) defines the noun as: "State of being addicted; indulged inclination; also habituation, esp. to drugs." The adjective, "addicted," is defined simply as: "Given up or over (to); devoted (to)."

My newest dictionary (The Random House Dictionary of the English Language, Second Edition-Unabridged) defines the noun as: "the state of being enslaved to a habit or practice or to something that is psychologically or physically habit-forming, as narcotics, to such an extent that its cessation causes severe trauma." It also goes further than Webster's in its definition of the adjective as: "given up or devoted to a practice or habit or to something psychologically or physically habit-forming."

The first dictionary was originally published in 1933 and revised in 1948, the second was published in 1987. Thus in 39 years, addiction went from "indulged inclination" all the way to "the state of being enslaved." Paradoxically, we seem to cling to both definitions, both the mild and the severe, depending upon our prejudices and whom we're applying the label to, and that causes no end of confusion and misunderstanding.

We're using the first definition when, in a playful, nonpejorative sense, we speak of someone as a "chocoholic" or a soap-opera junkie or a caffeine addict. When it comes to smoking, however, everybody knows the smoker is truly addicted—that is, "enslaved"—whether or not he is a light smoker or a chain-smoker, whether or not he wishes he could quit or simply doesn't want to. When it comes to smoking, moderating words used in both dictionaries—"habituation" in the first, "habit-forming" and "practice or habit" in the second—have been deemed, as they would have said in Watergate days, "inoperative."

It was not always so. In Surgeon General Luther L. Terry's 1964 report on *Smoking and Health*, from which all else discussed in this book has flowed, Chapter 13 was titled: "Characterization of the Tobacco Habit." In the section, "Distinction Between Drug Addiction and Drug Habituation," it was stated:

> Smokers and users of tobacco in other forms usually develop some degree of dependence upon the practice, some to the point where significant emotional disturbances occur if they are deprived of its use. The evidence indicates this dependence to be psychogenic in origin. In medical and scientific terminology the practice should be labeled *habituation* to distinguish it clearly from *addiction*, since the biological effects of tobacco, like coffee and other caffeine-containing beverages, betel morsel chewing and the like, are not

> comparable to those produced by morphine, alcohol, barbiturates and many other potent addicting drugs.[4] [Emphases in original.]

In another section, "Relationship of Smoking to Use of Addicting Drugs":

> Undoubtedly, the smoking habit becomes compulsive in some heavy smokers but the drive to compulsion appears to be solely psychogenic since physical dependence does not develop to nicotine or to other constituents of tobacco, nor does tobacco, either during its use or following withdrawal, create psychotoxic effects which lead to antisocial behavior . . . In contrast to drugs of addiction, withdrawal from tobacco never constitutes a threat to life. These facts indicate clearly the absence of physical dependence."[5]

According to Richard Kluger in his voluminous work, *Ashes to Ashes*, all this was essentially the personal view of Maurice H. Seevers, the author of Chapter 13 in the surgeon general's report, whom he describes as an expert on habit-forming drugs but also "an egregious protector of the [tobacco] industry's interests." Seevers was one of two members of the SG's 10-member advisory committee recommended by the tobacco manufacturers. The other was Harvard's Louis Fieser, "a towering figure in organic chemistry," but "ten years past his prime," according to Kluger.[6]

None of the other "uneasy" members of the panel possessed the credentials to challenge Seevers, says Kluger. "Thus smoking was decreed a habit, not an addiction, and the tobacco industry was rewarded for its championing of Seevers . . ."[7]

Kluger apparently knows everything about everybody who has ever even remotely been involved with tobacco, cigarettes and smoking in the past 100 years, so I can't contradict his implication that Seevers foisted his own opinion on the committee. But who foisted it on the World Health Organization? The SG's report adopted, or at least repeated, the definitions created in 1957 by WHO's Expert Committee on Drugs Liable to Produce Addiction, which the committee (or Seevers?) noted "are accepted throughout the world as the basis for control of potentially dangerous drugs."[8]

Those definitions were:

Drug Addiction	Drug Habituation
Drug addiction is a state of periodic or chronic intoxication produced by the repeated consumption of a drug (natural or synthetic). Its characteristics include:	Drug habituation (habit) is a condition resulting from the repeated consumption of a drug. Its charateristics include:
1) An overpowering desire or need (compulsion) to continue taking the drug and to obtain it by any means;	1) A desire (but not a compulsion) to continue taking the drug for the sense of improved well-being it engenders;
2) A tendency to increase the dose;	(2) Little or no tendency to increase the dose;
3) A psychic (psychological) and generally a physical dependence on the effects of the drug;	(3) Some degree of psychic dependence on the effect of the drug, but absence of physical dependence and hence of an abstinence syndrome;
(4) Detrimental effect on the individual and on society.	(4) Detrimental effects, if any, primarily on the individual.

The foregoing is purely of historical interest today. Not long after the SG's report, the World Health Organization dropped this distinction between addiction and habituation, as well as eventually going all the way off the deep end regarding the "global epidemic" of smoking-caused diseases as the antismokers, most of whom were and are Americans, began exerting overweening influence in the organization. However, it was to be another 24 years before one of Terry's successors effectively put the kibosh on the notion that smoking is merely a habit.

But one statement from Chapter 13, innocent at the time, now appears to have been more frighteningly prophetic than Dr. Seevers could have imagined (assuming he wrote it):

> Even the most energetic and emotional campaigner against smoking and nicotine could find little support for the view that all those who use tobacco, coffee, tea, and cocoa are in need of mental care even though it may *at sometime in the future* be shown that smokers and non-smokers have different psychologic characteristics.[9] [Emphasis mine.]

The future has arrived. Today we ***know*** that the chief psychological characteristic differentiating the smoker from the nonsmoker is that the former is sick in the head. Anyway, that's what I hear from a doctor named William Van Horn, an M.D. who "specializes in the brain" and conducts a daily call-in program on an Atlanta radio station. Anybody who smokes, he says, has some kind of underlying emotional problem.

(I also can't resist quoting one other, curious, sentence from Chapter 13, from a paragraph on organ tolerance to nicotine: "Animal studies indicate considerable tolerance to small [doses of nicotine] but little if any to convulsant or lethal doses."[10]

(Although I am not a physiologist, I would state without reservation that a dose of nicotine high enough to cause an animal to go into convulsions or to kill it outright is an unambiguous indication of *zero* tolerance to that amount of nicotine.)

IT WAS IN SURGEON General C. Everett Koop's 1988 Report, *The Health Consequences of Smoking*, the seventh to be issued during his unfortunate incumbency, that the 1964 report's distinction between addiction and habituation was officially repealed.[11] (I almost typed "Surgeon General Kook" but I stifled myself.)

The 1988 report's major conclusions:

1. Cigarettes and other forms of tobacco are addicting.
2. Nicotine is the drug in tobacco that causes addiction.
3. The pharmacological and behavioral processes that determine tobacco addiction are similar to those that determine addiction to drugs such as heroin and cocaine.[12]

So what is our modern, up-to-date definition of addiction? According to a 1995 pamphlet from the Centers for Disease Control and Prevention's Office on Smoking and Health in Atlanta, the indicators are:

- The drug-seeking or -taking behavior is driven by strong, persistent and often irresistible urges.
- The substance is mood-altering and enters the brain through the blood stream.
- The drug is reinforcing—that is, the effects of the drug are so rewarding that the user continues to take it.
- There are regular patterns of use, continued use despite

harmful effects, relapse following an abstinent period, and recurrent cravings for the drug.
- Dependence-producing drugs often create a tolerance, physical dependence and pleasant effects.

For "substance" or "drug," substitute "activity" or "hobby" and these criteria could apply to any number of things. Consider for only one example the "runner's high" experienced by the dedicated jogger, who may continue to run despite the pain of shin splints and the possibility of permanently disabling injury if he doesn't stop.

But nicotine is even worse than illicit drugs, according to the CDC pamphlet. It notes that:

- Eighty-three percent of cigarette smokers smoke every day, but only 10 percent of drug users are daily users.
- Eighty-five percent of people who have ever tried an illicit drug have quit using that drug, but only 63 percent of people who have ever tried a cigarette have quit smoking.

This is transparently naïve, if not deliberately deceptive. Cigarettes are a legal and easily obtainable product (though who knows for how long?) while the procurement of a hard drug can require driving into a dangerous area of town in the dark of night to deal with a type of person you wouldn't want to invite into your home. Illicit drugs are also a lot more expensive than cigarettes. Moreover, you can smoke a cigarette while going about everyday activities—talking on the telephone or working at your desk (if smoking isn't banned), strolling through the park (if smoking isn't banned), after a good meal (if smoking isn't banned), etc., etc.—and smoking doesn't interfere with the performance and enjoyment of those activities (unless it's banned). Can the same be said of hard drugs? The fact that 83 percent of cigarette smokers smoke every day testifies not only to the easy availability of cigarettes but to the absence of anything comparable to the mental and physical consequences of using narcotics. In fact, it proves the absolute harmlessness of nicotine in this respect. And what about the 17 percent of smokers who don't smoke every day? Aren't they addicted to nicotine? If not, why not?

The consequences of narcotic drug use on one's health and personality and ability to function in the world are so much more profound than the consequences of smoking that I am simply amazed that anyone could seriously equate the two. Yet that is what Dr. Koop did and in so doing actually trivialized the problem of hard drugs. The only word for this is—*insanity*.

Amazingly, however, in the face of all the evidence to the contrary, many people go beyond Koop and believe that smoking is even *more* addicting than hard drugs. Psychologist and addiction expert Stanton Peele says that whenever he speaks before groups of addiction counselors and other audiences, he always asks them which is the most difficult addiction to quit.

> The response is overwhelmingly "Smoking." I then ask how many people have quit smoking—usually from a third to half of the audience respond affirmatively. I then ask how many of these quit because of Smokenders or any other treatment program. The greatest percentage I ever got was 10 percent once; more often, *no one* had quit through treatment, even in audiences with 50 or more ex-smokers.[13] [Emphasis in original.]

This confirms once again that most people who quit smoking do so on their own without clinical assistance. It also tells me that the audiences Peele speaks to have never used hard drugs, thus the only "addictive" drug they are familiar with is nicotine. Only when tobacco is put on a par with hard drugs—that is, outlawed—will we be able to make fair comparisons between the two. Incidentally, it may surprise many people to learn that the label "drug addiction" is no longer generally used by the experts. Dr. Koop explained:

> The terms "drug addiction" and "drug dependence" are scientifically equivalent: Both terms refer to the behavior of repetitively ingesting mood-altering substances by individuals. The term "drug dependence" has been increasingly adopted in the scientific and medical literature as a more technical term, whereas the term "drug addiction" continues to be used by NIDA [National Institutes on Drug Abuse] and other organizations when it is important to provide information at a more general level.[14]

When it is important to provide information at a more general level?! Maybe I am overskeptical, but what this says to me is that when the experts talk (down?) to us peasants about drugs, including and probably especially nicotine, they don't use the term "dependence" because that sounds a tad soft. They use the stronger term "addiction" because it carries a lot more semantic freight for the ordinary person. Imagine the furor if some politician were to charge that everyone dependent upon public assistance was welfare-addicted.

What about all those millions of former smokers who have successfully quit smoking, whom Bob Dole was referring to when he made the statement during the 1996 presidential campaign—for which he was thoroughly raked over the coals—that he thought tobacco might be an addiction for some people but not for everyone (and, in my opinion, was simply voicing the commonsensical obvious)?

Dr. Koop acknowledged them in his 1988 Report:

> Many smokers have quit on their own ("spontaneous remission") and some smokers smoke only occasionally. However, spontaneous remission and occasional use also occur with the illicit drugs of addiction, and in no way disqualify a drug from being classified as addicting.[15] [Parentheses and quotation marks in original.]

This is the only time I have ever seen the term "spontaneous remission" used in this sense. Most people, I think, understand it to mean the sudden, and usually temporary, disappearance of disease symptoms in a patient which the doctors can neither predict nor explain. To use it as Koop did is to imply that people don't stop smoking, or limit their smoking, as a matter of choice or will power but that it is something that "just happens."

To members of a group called "Nicotine Anonymous," kicking the smoking habit doesn't "just happen" but requires the assistance of a "Higher Power." Like many other self-help groups, NicAnon, formed in Phoenix, Arizona in 1990, follows a quasi-religious 12-step program modeled after that of Alcoholics Anonymous (emphases below are theirs):

1. We admitted we were powerless over nicotine—that our lives had become unmanageable.
2. Came to believe that a Power greater than ourselves could restore us to sanity.
3. Made a decision to turn our will and our lives over to the care of God *as we understood Him.*
4. Made a searching and fearless moral inventory of ourselves.

5. Admitted to God, to ourselves, and to another human being the exact nature of our wrongs.
6. Were entirely ready to have God remove all these defects of character.
7. Humbly asked him to remove our shortcomings.
8. Made a list of all persons we had harmed, and became willing to make amends to them all.
9. Made direct amends to such people wherever possible, except when to do so would injure them or others.
10. Continued to take personal inventory and when we were wrong promptly admitted it.
11. Sought through prayer and meditation to improve our conscious contact with God *as we understood Him*, praying only for knowledge of His will for us and the power to carry that out.
12. Having had a spiritual awakening as the result of these steps, we tried to carry this message to nicotine users and to practice these principles in our affairs.[16]

How the members of Nicotine Anonymous identify those they have harmed (with secondhand smoke?), or how they make amends to them, or how making amends to them might injure them, is not clear. No doubt they also believe that if they ever took one puff from a cigarette again they would be sent back down the road to ruin, even as AA teaches alcoholics that they will be alcoholics for the rest of their lives.

"It is an odd program in self-esteem that rewards people for calling themselves helpless, childish, addicted and diseased and punishes them for claiming to be healthy," says Wendy Kaminer in her book *I'm Dysfunctional, You're Dysfunctional*, a critique of 12-step programs and the self-help movement.[17]

Peele calls it the "disease theory" of addiction:

> Disease theories of life have struck on a fundamental truth: everything that humans do—eating, drinking, sleeping, drug taking, loving, raising children, learning, having sex, having periods, feeling, thinking about oneself—has a healthy and unhealthy side, sometimes both at the same time or often alternating one with another. By elevating the unhealthy side of normal functioning to the status of disease state, therapists and others who claim the mantle of science now *guarantee* the preeminence, pervasiveness, and persistence of sickness in everyday life.[18] [Emphasis in original.]

Antismokers also point to certain "withdrawal symptoms" many people experience when they quit smoking—nervousness, headaches, vague aches and pains and, yes, the craving for a cigarette that for some may never go away—as proof that nicotine is as addictive as any hard drug. But consider one doctor's description of what a true drug addict goes through when he doesn't get his fix:

> Symptoms include insomnia, marked anorexia, violent yawning, severe sneezing, weakness and depression, nausea and vomiting, intestinal spasm and diarrhea. Heart rate and blood pressure are elevated; there is a marked chilliness, alternating with flushing and excessive sweating. The addict experiences waves of gooseflesh, his skin resembling that of a plucked turkey, which is the basis of the expression "cold turkey." Abdominal cramps and pains in the bones and muscles of the back and extremities are characteristic, as are muscle spasms and kicking movements that may be the basis for the expression "kicking the habit." Other signs include ejaculations in men and orgasm in women. The failure to take foods and fluids, combined with vomiting, sweating and diarrhea, results in marked weight loss and dehydration. Occasionally, there is cardiovascular collapse.[19]

Not only do smokers who stop smoking ***never*** experience anything ***remotely*** approaching this, not only do they ***never*** check into detox facilities, but the American Heart Association reports that 85 percent or better of them break the habit completely on their own.[20] And interestingly enough, those who have smoked the longest and the heaviest have the easiest time quitting, at least according to a study of 4,000 smokers by the Addiction Research Foundation in Canada. It found that people age 44 and older who smoked 25 or more cigarettes a day had a better chance of quitting than younger people who smoked fewer cigarettes.[21*] Yet we are told and told and told yet again that "nicotine is every bit as addictive as heroin, etc."

THE PERSON MOST vigorously pushing the nicotine-addiction connec-

*The same may also be true for many so-called alcoholics. Another Canadian study, based on two surveys involving 12,000 people, found that 77 percent who had recovered from an alcohol problem for a year or more had done so without formal help or treatment and that 38 percent in one survey and 63 percent in the other had resumed moderate social drinking.[22]

tion in recent years was former Food and Drug Administration Commissioner David A. Kessler. In a statement before the U.S. House of Representatives Subcommittee on Health and the Environment on March 25, 1994, he presented another indication of addiction to tobacco:

"When a smoker sleeps, blood levels of nicotine decrease significantly . . . Experts in the field tell us that smoking the first cigarette of the day within thirty minutes of waking is a meaningful measure of addiction."[23]

I'm glad to know that, by this measure at least, I am not a nicotine addict and never have been. Since beginning to smoke 53 years ago, I never have had a cigarette until at least an hour or two after waking; I simply don't want one earlier. I also seldom smoke in the evening because I spend that time with my wife reading or watching TV and she objects. (To my smoking, not to me. I think.) This is no hardship for me. After a day of heavy smoking at the computer, I have no desire to smoke in the evening.

She on the other hand "had to have" a cigarette immediately upon arising, even before she dressed. Yet I fully believe that her onetime need for that first cigarette was purely psychogenic, just as Dr. Seevers maintained, for she quit cold turkey on the day of her heart attack. Not that her 47 years of smoking were ended just like that; for a long time she would carry a pencil around in her fingers in place of a cigarette. That strong tactile association with cigarettes was surely not unusual, as witnessed by another successful quitter: "What surprised me was that the addiction was not as difficult to overcome as the habit of having something in your hand."[24]

There is no end to the misinformation published about the nicotine-addiction connection. Philip J. Hilts wrote in *The New York Times* that "They [cigarettes] not only create dependence among users but also elicit a high degree of tolerance, *the need for more and more of the drug* to satisfy a craving.[25] [Emphasis added.]

This is another attempt to equate nicotine with hard drugs and is simply not true. Yes, smokers do develop a tolerance (or a need, if you insist) for nicotine, and it can be a high degree or a low degree. But unlike the craving for cocaine or heroin it reaches a certain level and stays there. Dr. Kessler himself illustrated that in his testimony before the House subcommittee when he quoted from a document from an unspecified tobacco company which tested a group of European smokers with cigarettes having different levels of nicotine content or "impact":

> It is clear that consumers are less tolerant of decreases than they are of increases in nicotine delivery. By the time nicotine level falls to approximately 0.34 milligrams,* fifty percent of consumers will be saying that the level of impact is so low they would reject the product. To reach the equivalent state of fifty percent of consumers rejecting the product as having too high an impact level, a nicotine level of approximately 5.0 milligrams would be required. Again, it is important to note that *there is a clear upper as well as lower rejection limit* for nicotine in smoke.[26] [Emphasis mine.]

Maybe the unidentified company was Philip Morris. According to former Philip Morris scientist turned whistleblower Ian L. Udess, in a sworn affidavit before the FDA, "Nicotine levels were routinely targeted and adjusted . . . Knowledge about the optimum range for nicotine in a cigarette was developed as a result of a great many years of investigation . . . Philip Morris clearly understood . . . [that] they would have trouble sustaining the sales of a good-tasting product that was too low in nicotine."[27]

Well, shame on Philip Morris. Obviously, if it had a speck of civic-mindedness it would have used its "secret" knowledge to market such a product anyway, even if nobody wanted it.

That smokers become accustomed to a certain level of nicotine is also shown by experience with so-called low-tar/low-nicotine cigarettes. According to Dr. Jack E. Henningfield, chief of clinical pharmacology at the National Institutes on Drug Abuse, the smoking machines used to arrive at the figures for particular brands are meaningless because the tests don't take into account a smoker's compensating behavior, such as covering up the tiny air holes around the filter with his fingers, taking deeper puffs and holding them longer and, perhaps most important of all from a health standpoint, smoking more cigarettes in order to get his accustomed level of nicotine.[28]

Incidentally, Dr. Henningfield is not impressed that more than 40 million people have quit smoking over the past 30 years. "That amounts

*A milligram is one one-thousandth of a gram, or about one twenty-eight-thousandth of an ounce.

to a lot of lives saved," he granted on the Public Broadcasting Service television program "Frontline." "The bad news is that that only amounts to about 2.5 percent—2.5 percent only that have been able to quit smoking per year, on average. That is a lousy rate of quitting by oneself, when we compare that to what we know about heroin addiction, cocaine addiction and alcoholism."[29]

Either Dr. Henningfield didn't explain "what we know" about hard drug addiction or alcoholism or it was left on the cutting room floor. But 40 million ex-smokers doesn't prove anything, evidently; we need more aggressive "intervention" (name your favorite method) against smoking. Two years later, Dr. Henningfield was again shown on television saying that nicotine addiction is "ten times worse" than heroin or cocaine addiction.[30]

Commissioner Kessler also put in a cameo appearance on the same "Frontline" program. In an audio segment from National Public Radio's "Talk of the Nation" he fielded a telephone call from a listener.

> **1st Caller:** Hi. Many years ago, I was addicted to cocaine for about two or three years. When I realized what I was doing to myself, I stopped and I stopped cold turkey. I'm still smoking. I've been smoking since I'm 16. I'm 52 years old and I can't stop smoking. I smoke about a pack, a pack and a half of cigarettes a day.
>
> **Kessler:** And it was harder to stop—it's harder to stop smoking?
>
> **1st Caller:** Yes.
>
> **Kessler:** I mean, ask smokers whether the nicotine is addictive in cigarettes. And I think—just listening to smokers—I mean, they tell you unequivocably [*sic*] how addictive it is.

Maybe I am just too cynical (or maybe it's my "addiction" to cigarettes talking) but I tend to wonder if people like "1st caller" don't sometimes tell people like the commissioner what they think he wants to hear, or what they themselves want to believe. I still maintain that it is less a matter of addiction to a hard drug versus alleged addiction to nicotine than a matter of cost and availability and convenience. For a trivial example (but the best I can do), I find it much easier to quit eating cashews, which I love, than to quit eating peanuts. The reason is that peanuts are a lot cheaper than cashews and I'm a tightwad. (Make that "frugal.") I don't know what I will do when the antis succeed in raising the price of a carton even of generic cigarettes to 30 or 40 dollars, payable either to federal and state tax collectors or, more probably, to reinvigorated organized crime. I may have to switch to marijuana, which, paradoxically, seems to be on the way to being legalized even as tobacco heads for outright prohibition (see Chapter 12).

On the other hand, "1st caller" may have truly believed what he told the commissioner. As Richard J. De Grandpre wrote in *Reason* magazine:

> As any former smoker could tell you, ex-smokers crave cigarettes at certain times and in certain situations for months, even years, after quitting. In these cases, the desire to smoke is triggered by environmental cues, not by withdrawal symptoms. This is one reason why people who overcome addiction to illicit substances such as heroin or cocaine say they had more difficulty breaking the cigarette habit. Because regular tobacco users smoke in a wide array of circumstances (when bored, after eating, when driving) and settings (home, work, car), the cues that elicit the urge are more ubiquitous than for illicit drug use.[31]

Because of smokers' compensating behavior with low-nicotine cigarettes, at least one scheme for gradually eliminating smoking would be doomed to failure. Dr. Neal Benowitz, professor of medicine at the University of California-San Francisco, has proposed that the Food and Drug Administration dictate the maximum allowable level of nicotine in cigarettes and then lower this level every year. The idea is that smokers would be gradually weaned off nicotine until eventually there would be no more addicts.[32]

If the FDA ever did put such a scheme into practice with the hope of saving smokers from themselves, it would be placing itself in the curious position of forcing them to *increase* their consumption of cigarettes in order to obtain the same amount of nicotine. The cigarette manufacturers would love that. And, of course, smoking more cigarettes would expose smokers to more of the suspected carcinogenic chemicals contained therein. In short, ultra low-nicotine cigarettes might end up killing *more* smokers than current brands allegedly do.

Somehow this simple fact seems to escape those urging a crackdown on nicotine. For example, my favorite source of (mis)information about smoking, *The Atlanta Journal-Constitution*, echoed Dr. Benowitz in calling for the FDA to ban high-nicotine cigarettes and "gradually force the industry to lower nicotine levels. In the next century, only nicotine-free cigarettes ought to be sold."[33]

If this didn't kill more smokers it would certainly result in a thriving black market in "real" cigarettes and demands that Congress appropriate more funds to a beefed-up Bureau of Alcohol, Tobacco and Firearms. As for zero-nicotine cigarettes, Philip Morris tried to market one, a brand called "Next." Nobody bought it. I also remember that years ago somebody brought out a cigarette made of lettuce leaves that was even less satisfactory than the time-honored cornsilk.*

Dr. Benowitz is mistaken on another count. He told "Frontline" that "About six to 12 milligrams of nicotine are contained within most commercial cigarettes."[35] The actual figures range from 0.1 milligrams in a Carlton cigarette to 1.5 milligrams in Winston and Camel unfiltereds, with the average (in 1994) at 0.8 milligrams per cigarette, compared to 2 milligrams per cigarette in the 1950s.[36] Of course, as we have seen, the determined smoker can magnify the amount of nicotine he gets from his favorite brand by his compensating behavior.

(In the interest of thorough research for this chapter, I bought a carton of Carltons. They reminded me of those "Indian stogies" I tried to smoke as a boy, they were so hard to draw on. My "compensating behavior" was to snip off the bottom half of the filter at the line of little air holes. Then they were a decent smoke, although they were so loosely packed they burned down very quickly. My experience with Carltons suggests to me that it is not just more *nicotine* that people are trying to get when they use various methods to increase the output from such low-tar, low-nicotine cigarettes but also simply more *smoke*.)

Perhaps what Dr. Henningfield was thinking of when he alluded to "what we know" about heroin, cocaine and alcohol is a scale he and Dr. Benowitz came up with that ranks the addictive qualities of these drugs, along with nicotine, caffeine and marijuana, according to five

*Shortly after I wrote this, a pharmaceutical chemist named Puzant Torigian started marketing a cigarette made of lettuce leaves called Bravo. Torigian said his goal is to help those addicted to tobacco smoking kick the habit by giving them a nicotine-free alternative that looks and burns like a cigarette, even though the taste, he admitted, is not exactly the same.[34]

criteria. On his Internet page, "Essays on the Anti-Smoking Movement," Joe Dawson lists these criteria with his explanation of what they mean:[37]

1. Withdrawal: refers to the severity of symptoms experienced upon ceasing the use of the drug.
2. Reinforcement: refers to the tendency to self-administer the drug, as observed in laboratory rats.
3. Tolerance: refers to an increase in the amount of a drug necessary to experience the same effect.
4. Dependency: not rigorously defined but appears to refer to the determination of the subject to continue using the substance in question, or perhaps simply to the pleasure experienced.
5. Intoxication: refers to the degree to which (mental) functionality is impaired.

On only one of these criteria—Dependency—did Henningfield and Benowitz place nicotine higher, i.e., worse, than the other drugs. On every other criterion they ranked nicotine either much lower than most of the others or at the bottom. But since, as we have learned from Dr. Koop, scientists now consider the term drug dependence to be the equivalent of the term drug addiction, on that one criterion alone nicotine is alleged to be as "addictive" as heroin or cocaine.

However, prior to this report, says Dawson, addictiveness had been assessed solely upon the first three and the fifth criteria. While those four can be quantified to some extent, "Dependence" is a new criterion that is purely subjective and based upon the doctors' personal opinions and experience. The fact is that people are "dependent" upon smoking for a number of reasons other than merely to obtain nicotine and I'll quote from Dawson again in that regard later in this chapter.

Thus the very definitions of "addiction" and "addict" have been changed, he says, not only in order to apply it to nicotine but to characterize it as one of the most addictive drugs of all. Dawson's new definitions, which a latter-day Ambrose Bierce might well put in an updated *Devil's Dictionary*, are:

Addiction — a condition entitling those not affected by it control those who are.

Addict — one expected to surrender to the ministrations of those who despise him.

* * *

BUT LET'S LEAVE THE subject of addiction for a moment. What about nicotine itself, that powerful, mysterious drug so pervasive in our culture for the past 400 years? Is it as harmful as it is claimed to be? Or is it possible it may even have some benefits?

Antismokers like to point out that nicotine is a poison, powerful enough to be used in pesticides. (But any substance can kill you, even pure water, if ingested in sufficient quantity.) According to Action on Smoking and Health (ASH), "one-fortieth of a gram of nicotine usually gives rise to toxic symptoms in a nonsmoker."[38]

No doubt it does. That much nicotine could make even a chain-smoker of unfiltered Camels queasy, to say the least. One-fortieth of a gram is 25 milligrams—twice as high as even the inflated upper level of nicotine Dr. Benowitz said is contained in most commercial cigarettes.

Nicotine is named in honor(?) of Jean Nicot, the French ambassador to Portugal, who sent seeds of the newly discovered tobacco plant to the Queen Mother, Catherine de Medici, in 1561 or thereabouts and who extolled its medicinal benefits. For the next couple centuries after its introduction to the West, tobacco was claimed to be a cure or preventative for every disease then known, with as little scientific basis for such claims as for later ones blaming it for every disease.

The scientific name of the plant itself is *nicotiana*, given to it in the 18th century by the great Swedish botanist Karl von Linné, better known by his Latinized name, Carolus Linneaus, who identified two species: *nicotiana rustica* (a wild-growing, nicotine-rich form) and *nicotiana tabacum* (the stuff causing all the trouble today). Nicotine, the pharmacologically active ingredient in *nicotiana*, has been known to chemists as an alkaloid $C_{10}H_{14}N_2$ since 1828, when two Heidelberg medical students, Ludwig Reimann and Wilhelm Posselt, announced its chemical composition and called it a dangerous poison. (Interestingly enough, nicotine is also naturally present in some vegetables, such as eggplant, potatoes and tomatoes, although in far lesser amounts than in tobacco.)

But even as early as Columbus's time, long before nicotine was identified, the habit-forming (or, if you insist, the addictive) quality of the tobacco plant was recognized, at least anecdotally. Writing in *The New Republic*, Thomas W. Laquer recounts the testimony of Bartoleme de las Casas, who accompanied Columbus on his first voyage to the

New World. When the good friar admonished some sailors for smoking rolled up leaves of tobacco, they replied that "they were not able to stop taking them."[39]

This could have meant simply that the guys *liked* the weed, but let it go. The first health warnings about tobacco date back at least to the 18th century. In 1701, one Nicholas Andryde Boisregard reported that excessive tobacco use by young people caused them to have trembling hands, staggering feet and to suffer a withering of "their noble parts." In 1761, John Hill of England warned snuff users that they risked cancer of the nose.[40]

On the first page of his *Primer of Physiology and Hygiene*, published in 1895, William Thayer Smith, M.D., claimed that the cigarette "so seriously undermines the power of self-control that persons once addicted to its use very often find it impossible to break up and abandon the habit." Garry Trudeau, that indefatigable antismoking satirist, had his Mr. Butts displaying a reproduction of that page in a Sunday "Doonesbury" cartoon strip for "kids" to show "next time someone tries to 'educate' you with the latest research. Just say, 'Hey, get a life—that's ancient history!'"[41]

Trudeau's satirical sword has two edges, however. His discovery of this old medical manual would seem to undermine claims that the cigarette companies have been "hiding the truth" about nicotine from the medical community for all these many years.

Indeed, the effects of nicotine on the brain were described more than 100 years ago by British scientists. By the 1930s many authorities accepted tobacco use as habitual or addictive. In 1942, researcher L. M. Johnston successfully substituted nicotine injections for smoking.

"The publication of this historic experiment wasn't suppressed by Philip Morris; it was reported in *The Lancet*, an internationally renowned British medical journal," writes Brad Rodu, chairman of the oral pathology department at the University of Alabama (and no friend of smoking).[42]

Conducting a search using "Medline," the National Library of Medicine's computerized data base, Rodu found that nicotine was the focus of 1,500 medical research articles between 1976 and 1984, with Philip Morris alone publishing 250 of them. Almost 4,000 additional studies were published in the following decade.[43]

For good reason did Laquer comment in his *New Republic* article:

"That tobacco contains a drug, or is a drug, is without doubt the most ludicrous 'discovery' of our day . . . Our own FDA's sudden 'discovery' that tobacco is addictive is another anticlimax."[44]

But amazingly no one seems to have paid any attention to these thousands of studies. Otherwise the antis wouldn't be continually coming up with tobacco company whistleblowers bearing revelations of "secret" and "suppressed" industry research into nicotine. Would they?

Even the American Medical Association never heard about them. Otherwise, it wouldn't have announced in July 1995 that it planned to publish in its *Journal* summaries of certain papers that had been anonymously sent to antismoking activist Stanton Glantz describing activities of the Brown & Williamson Tobacco Company and its parent, British American Tobacco Company (BAT), which papers "suggest that these companies recognized the harmful and addictive properties of cigarettes as much as 30 years ago."[45] Would it?

Otherwise, an FDA advisory panel wouldn't have announced in August 1994 its discovery that nicotine is an addictive substance, would it? And Commissioner Kessler wouldn't have called it "a very significant finding." Would he?[46]

All that aside, the important fact is that no one has ever demonstrated that nicotine is physically harmful in the amounts smokers are accustomed to. A drug—yes. Habit-forming—yes. Zapping into the brain within seconds of the first puff—definitely. Producing typical and measurable physiological effects on heart rate and psychological effects on mood—undeniably. But in and of itself injurious to the body in the amounts smokers obtain—no. The fact that the Food and Drug Administration has okayed the over-the-counter sale of nicotine in the form of chewing gum and skin patches is proof of that. (The patch delivers 15 milligrams of nicotine per day through the skin, or about the same amount a smoker takes in from 15 cigarettes.[47])

(As I was writing this, TV ads for nicotine patches and gum were starting to rival automobile ads in frequency. In one commercial, actor James Garner exclaimed that after 50 years of smoking he was finally able to kick the habit in only six weeks, thanks to Nicotrol skin patches. The harm that 50 years of smoking had done to his health was not apparent on the screen, not did he mention any.

(Nicotine gum was treated humorously in a comic strip called "Rhymes With Orange." In the first panel were the words: "The Changing Face of Romantic Literature." The next panel showed a man and woman on a porch looking off into the distance. The words, in typewriter-style print, read: "Chapter One—Sunset, after a fabulous meal. We sit out on the front porch, stuffed and happy. My love leans down to pass me a piece of nicotine gum, and we chew in silence as the liquid orange ball disappears behind the horizon."[48] And if the couple later had sex, no doubt another stick of nicotine gum would be in order in the afterglow.)

Around the same time the FDA approved sale of gum and patches over the counter it approved the prescription-only use of a nicotine-containing nasal spray, which it said was more effective than either gum or patches, although the spray only helped about 25 percent of those trying to quit. The agency also cautioned that the spray might have side effects, such as causing nasal sores, and that smokers could become as addicted to that form of nicotine delivery as they are to cigarettes. It suggested that the spray was best used for only three months and should never be used for more than six months.[49]

It is interesting that the violently antismoking group, Action on Smoking and Health, approves the use of these sources of nicotine for smokers trying to quit, yet when R. J. Reynolds announced plans to test-market Eclipse, a low-nicotine and virtually smokeless cigarette (in which the tobacco is not burned but is heated by a glowing carbon tip) ASH immediately petitioned the FDA to prevent its being marketed in the United States. Their grounds: Eclipse was not a real cigarette but a "drug-delivery device."[50] But what are nicotine patches and gums if not drug-delivery devices that the FDA has approved for nonprescription over-the-counter sale?

That raises a question: if obtaining nicotine from a spray or a patch or chewing gum can help a smoker stop smoking, why wouldn't obtaining nicotine from a cigarette help a smoker stop smoking? Well, it probably would—if the smoker set a definite stop-smoking date and had enough determination to gradually diminish his daily consumption of cigarettes down to the vanishing point over that period of time. The trouble is, it is not only a matter of weaning oneself from nicotine but also from all the other pleasurable little habits that accompany smoking—and these, in truth, are the hardest to give up.

Kaiser Permanente in Atlanta uses a weaning approach in its six-week "Be Smoke Free" class. "For the first three weeks, each week, [the class enrollees] change brands to a lower nicotine level," explains Malbea Britton, the class instructor. "By the third week, everyone's smoking an extra-light brand. Finally comes quit day. "That's when they go cold turkey."[51]

But even assuming that the step-down brands the participants gradually switch to actually do contain less nicotine than the brands they start with, we've seen that smokers have a way of maintaining their accustomed nicotine intake no matter what brand they smoke. Moreover, the body's "need" for nicotine is far from the only factor involved in smoking. (As Ms. Britton is aware: "Most people find it's sheer habit—that it goes with talking on the telephone, drinking coffee, or driving.") Smoking is accompanied by a whole host of deeper, psychological satisfactions that spray or gum or patches can't replace, which is why there is a high relapse rate among smokers trying these nicotine substitutes and why the most successful quitters are those who one day simply stop cold turkey—which, as Ms. Britton says, is what the Kaiser Permanente patients finally do, after psyching themselves up for it over a period of weeks.*

If the Coalition on Smoking OR Health, composed of the American Heart Association, American Lung Association and American Cancer Society, had its way, smokers wouldn't even be able to obtain low-tar or low-nicotine cigarettes—not without the government's permission or a doctor's prescription. In 1992 the coalition petitioned both the FDA and the Federal Trade Commission to classify low-tar or low-nicotine cigarettes as drugs and to control their sales on the ground that such cigarettes carried an implied claim that they were safer or less addictive than regular cigarettes.[53] What would be the purpose of this? Well, one thing it would do would be to give Those Who Know Best another way to control the behavior of those of us who don't know what's best for ourselves or refuse to do what's best.

*The poor success rate of most smoking cessation programs pleases John Banzhaf, executive director of Action on Smoking and Health. He cites a $45-million National Cancer Institute program which produced no significant declines in smoking rates, especially among heavy smokers. The reason: "the tremendous strength of the addiction to nicotine." "Ironically," he says, "the NCI's failure among heavy smokers may help plaintiffs to win in class-action suits now being brought on behalf of smokers. Nicotine addiction is a key issue both offensively and defensively."[52] That's why he's pleased.

No, it isn't nicotine that is the problem from a health standpoint; it's all those other nasty chemicals, or some unknown one or several of them, that unfortunately accompany nicotine in tobacco smoke. Yet it is nicotine and the industry's alleged "manipulation" of it in cigarettes that consumes the FDA and is the subject of virtually every antismoking article printed.

This is another example of how the failure to define a term precisely causes confusion and misunderstanding. *Of course* the tobacco companies "manipulate" the content of nicotine in their products. So do dairy companies "manipulate" the fat content of the milk or cottage cheese they sell. Does anyone think the cigarette manufacturers simply take a bunch of tobacco leaves and indiscriminately throw them into a hopper and whatever comes out comes out? How can one brand of cigarettes contain more or less nicotine than another brand if somewhere along the line the nicotine content is not "manipulated"?

(For that matter, I assume that the makers of nicotine gum, patches and sprays get their nicotine from tobacco. How do they put precise doses of nicotine in their gum, patches and sprays unless they "manipulate" it?)

There is nothing sinister or nefarious about it. Different varieties of tobacco, and even different parts of the same plant, contain different levels of nicotine, as well as "tar." Burley is higher in nicotine than flue-cured tobacco. The companies create a blend using these different plants and parts of plants, along with what is called "reconstituted" tobacco, or tobacco sheet, made from bits and pieces of leaf and stalk and stems (and for all I know, sweepings off the floor). Because some nicotine is lost in the process of making the sheet, nicotine extract is added to it. (If "tar" is the real culprit, there are methods for reducing it in the final product, but fortunately these methods also reduce the levels of nicotine. Apparently you can't have one without the other.)

In any case, the companies do not artificially increase the nicotine content above naturally occurring levels. In fact, according to Tobacco Institute spokeswoman Brennan Dawson, "There is less nicotine in every finished cigarette in America than in the leaf you start off with."[54] Unfortunately, the antis either have no independent means of verifying that or they don't want to verify it. The FDA knows this is true, yet it encourages the public to conceive the image of glazed-eyed tobacco company executives standing over vats of tobacco and pouring nicotine into them. Actually, according to one writer, "The FDA's position . . . does not turn on the issue of adding extra nicotine to tobacco. Since tobacco companies have technology available to take nicotine out of tobacco, FDA officials have said, the inclusion of any significant amount of nicotine in the final product *could be interpreted* as manipulation."[55] [My emphasis.]

In other words, the tobacco companies can't win for losing.

There is certainly *no more* nicotine than what you start off with, as the ABC television network was forced to concede when, after Philip Morris and R. J. Reynolds sued it for $10 billion for claiming on its "Day One" program that the cigarette manufacturers "spike" their cigarettes with nicotine, ABC issued a retraction and apology.[56]

It was an ignominious retreat by the network, and it caught a lot of flack for it. "Not since NBC apologized to General Motors for a 1992 program featuring a staged truck explosion has a television network backed down in such a public way in the face of a corporate lawsuit," said a column in *The Atlanta Journal-Constitution*.[57]

At the very least, this would suggest that PM and RJR must have had the facts on their side. Yet tobacco industry critics seldom allow facts to color their opinions. Harvard law professor Laurence Tribe called it "a disgraceful settlement." Mike Wallace, CBS correspondent, ex-smoker and onetime star in television cigarette commercials, was "utterly bewildered as to why they settled."[58]

New York Times reporter Philip Hilts, who is also a fellow at Harvard University's School of Public Health, wasn't bewildered: "ABC went out and did a report, and they got a $10-billion lawsuit, which the lawyers felt they were doing rather well on, they got good discovery [documents from plaintiffs PM and RJR] and so on, but then, as a corporate decision, when ABC merged with Disney, they decided they didn't need this on board and jettisoned the suit and settled it."[59]

For once Hilts may not be entirely off the mark. The sudden multibillion-billion-dollar merger between ABC and Disney apparently was a precipitating factor in the network's capitulation. (We know it certainly couldn't have been from want of moral conviction on ABC/ Disney's part; only the tobacco industry lacks integrity.)

From the transcript of another "Frontline" program, anchored by reporter Daniel Schorr:[60]

Schorr: . . . ABC was marshaling its legal forces to contest the $10-billion libel suit that Philip Morris had filed over the original "Day One" reports about the manipulation of nicotine content . . . But ABC was worried about trying the case before a judge and jury in Richmond, Virginia, where tobacco means jobs, so they came to test their case here in Raleigh, North Carolina, a tobacco town like Richmond. Two mock juries were assembled to hear the arguments for Philip Morris and for ABC and the proceedings were videotaped . . . The results were encouraging . . . Juror Carlos Ector:

Ector: Most of the people voted for ABC. Even some of the people [who] were die-hard smokers, they said even though they smoked, they still believed that what the tobacco industry was doing was wrong. They were not going to stop smoking, but they still believed they were wrong.

Schorr: After 16 months of preparation, ABC's lawyers moved to dismiss the case, claiming that documents in their possession—quote—"eliminated any factual dispute as to whether Philip Morris adds significant amounts of extraneous nicotine during the production of reconstituted tobacco. It does."

But still preparing for trial, ABC attorneys asked the former surgeon general, Dr. C. Everett Koop, to be their lead-off witness. Their letter said, "We are as confident of victory as any prudent trial lawyers should be."

Then, just six days later, a bombshell.

Diane Sawyer: [Clip from ABC "World News Tonight," August 21, 1995] The $10-billion lawsuit filed against ABC News by Philip Morris and R.J. Reynolds was settled this evening with a statement. ABC News agrees that we should not have reported that Philip Morris and Reynolds add significant amounts of nicotine from outside sources. That was a mistake that was not deliberate on the part of ABC, but for which we accept responsibility and which requires correction. We apologize to our audience, Philip Morris and Reynolds . . .

Interviewer: [To Paul Friedman, Executive Vice President, ABC News] In view of the fact that you had the former surgeon general of the United States in your corner, there had been mock jury trials which upheld the network position, how do we account for the—the willingness to—to—to sort of back down at a time when you seemed to have all the cards in your hand?

Friedman: You've used the words "backed down." I don't—

> **Interviewer:** And I use the words—
>
> **Friedman:** —accept them.
>
> **Interviewer:** Well—
>
> **Friedman:** I don't accept them. It's the policy of ABC News to apologize when we make a mistake. We made a mistake. We also said that the principal focus of that piece was to talk about whether cigarette companies control the amount of nicotine in the cigarettes to keep people smoking and we have not backed away from that central focus or from the people who did the work.

Which is an excellent example of how to use doublespeak to make the best of a bad situation. Translated: "It was a mistake for us to claim that the cigarette makers add extra nicotine to their products and we apologized, but that doesn't mean we backed down from our 'central focus,' which is whether or not they control nicotine content." This is as safe and nonlibelous a statement you could make. As we have seen, *of course* the companies control the nicotine content of cigarettes. How else could they make them?

Also appearing on "Frontline" was Ron Motely, an attorney specializing in suing tobacco companies.

> **Motley:** The reason they settled the case, as far as I'm concerned, is very simple. It's clear as the big nose on my face. They—they had a concern about the jury, had a concern about the judge, but they thought they would prevail eventually, four or five years down the line, in the U.S. Supreme Court. That was a factor, but the overriding factor was the immediacy of the takeover of ABC by Disney.

According to Schorr, the sale of ABC was quite financially beneficial to the network's top executives. News president Eric Ober received almost a million and a half dollars in stock options and chief counsel Ellen Kaden more than $1 million in stock options and $3.7 million more from a salary buyout and other benefits.

So we are asked to believe that after all the trouble ABC had gone to in preparing for trial, the brass at newly merged ABC/Disney simply decided to forget the whole thing as a matter of corporate convenience. Even though the network had "documents" in its possession proving its case, the brass decided they had bigger fish to fry. In other words, business imperatives took precedence over exposing the truth about how those deceitful tobacco companies play fast and loose with the health of Americans.

It's interesting that no other news organization has since taken up ABC's deserted cause. Is it from fear of a similar lawsuit, which can indeed be enormously expensive even if you eventually win, or the knowledge that ABC was simply wrong?

The whole idea behind ABC's "revelation" was based on the superficially logical but faulty reasoning that because nicotine is "addictive," the more there is of it in a cigarette, obviously the more "addicted" the smoker will be and the more cigarettes he will smoke. Thus the allegation that cigarette makers "spike" their products to increase that addiction.

The following year, *Wall Street Journal* reporter Alix Freedman was awarded a Pulitzer Prize for her coverage of the tobacco industry, which included an article based on confidential company documents that showed how cigarette companies use ammonia-based chemicals to "boost" the potency of nicotine. Her editor praised her "relentless reporting" that had "changed the terms of debate on one of the greatest public-health issues of our time."[61]

But the "terms of the debate" weren't changed; they were the same old ones the media had been using for years, as for example in an editorial in *The Atlanta Journal-Constitution* which spoke of the "mounting evidence that cigarette makers have been boosting the nicotine content of their products."[62]

All of which prompts me to suggest another entry in our updated *Devil's Dictionary*:

Mounting evidence — When used in connection with tobacco or smoking, this term does not refer to an actual increase in any evidence but rather to the mounting number of repetitions of the *claim* that such evidence exists. Cf. **"mountain of evidence**." Cf. "**irrefutable proof**."

Yet for one reader of the AJC, there was no doubt in her mind that she was a tool of the cigarette makers:

> I recently became a nonsmoker . . . Smoking was one of my closest friends. Always there when I needed it, always listened, was unjudgmental, accepted me for who I am. I, in turn, embraced

> it every chance I got . . . Am I happier? Of course. I am in control of my life. I am not angry with my friend; it was as innocent as I was. What pushes my button is hearing how I might have been manipulated by an industry that regulated nicotine levels to sucker me in. I resent when my choice to smoke is threatened. Do not take my right of choice away by doctoring a product.[63]

I am still trying to figure out what the writer was saying in that last sentence. That if the industry hadn't (allegedly) doctored their product with nicotine she would have freely chosen to smoke? Or would freely have chosen not to? Or that she wouldn't have chosen to stop smoking? Or that if they stopped (allegedly) doctoring their product with nicotine she would start smoking again?

THE "DAY ONE" FLAP came a little more than a year after the FDA's Kessler made a second appearance before the House Subcommittee on Health and the Environment. In June 1994, three months after the appearance mentioned above, he revealed a project undertaken by the Brown and Williamson Tobacco Company to develop a variety of tobacco, code-named "Y-1," with a nicotine content "significantly higher than any normal variety of tobacco grown commercially."[64]

The story began, he said, with the FDA's discovery of a Brazilian patent for this new variety. In 1983, B&W contracted with a company called DNA Plant Technology, in whose laboratories, greenhouses and fields much of the developmental work on Y-1 took place. In 1991, B&W filed an application with the U.S. Patent Office and deposited sample seeds of Y-1 with the National Seed Storage Laboratory in Fort Collins, Colorado. In 1994, however, the FDA learned that the company had withdrawn both the application and the seeds. DNA Plant Technology also told the FDA that Y-1 was never commercialized.

Ah, but by dint of assiduously digging through a mountain of invoices filed with the U.S. Customs Service, FDA sleuths discovered two invoices revealing that more than half a million pounds of Y-1 had been shipped to B&W from Brazil in 1992. And only four days before Dr. Kessler's appearance before the subcommittee, B&W told him that three and a half million pounds of Y-1 were currently being stored in company warehouses in the United States. Even more damning, B&W admitted that Y-1 had in fact been used in five brands of cigarettes in

1993—Viceroy King Size, Viceroy Lights King Size, Richland King Size, Richland Lights King Size and Raleigh Lights King Size.

When asked by the FDA why they were interested in developing a high-nicotine variety of tobacco, B&W officials said they wanted to reduce tar while maintaining nicotine levels. However, Dr. Kessler didn't say whether the FDA had ascertained what the actual nicotine levels were in those five brands, or if they were higher than usual.

Skip ahead three years. Like Inspector Javert, the Food and Drug Administration doesn't give up in its relentless pursuit of the tobacco industry. On January 7, 1998, hit with a "criminal information" filed against it by the FDA, DNA Plant Technology agreed to plead guilty to conspiring to violate the Tobacco Seed Export Law (which, incidentally, had been repealed in 1991). An unnamed tobacco company (guess who) was cited as an unindicted co-conspirator.[65]

Thus once again, as far as newspaper readers knew, another cigarette company had been caught "spiking" nicotine in its cigarettes in order to hook smokers.

(Interestingly, all the while he was busily sleuthing out Brown and Williamson, Administrator Kessler was also nickel-and-diming the American taxpayer with padded expense-account vouchers. An Associated Press review of some $17,377 in federal reimbursements that Kessler claimed on travel vouchers from mid-1990 through spring 1995 found them riddled with inflated claims. No really big stuff, though. More than a third, for example, were for taxicab fares for which he had no receipts and which were often two or three times higher than actual costs. Kessler said the errors were unintentional and that he had written a check for $850 to cover anything he owed the government.[66])

Back to 1994. Having informed the congressmen of the Y-1 "plot," Kessler moved on to another issue, the chemical manipulation of nicotine.

He noted that when six major American tobacco companies released a list of ingredients added to tobacco, nicotine was not among them. "But Mr. Chairman," he said, "a number of chemicals on that list increase the amount of nicotine that is delivered to the smoker." One of the "most striking" ways is the use of ammonia. He quoted from one tobacco company's 1991 handbook on leaf blending and product development:

> [Ammonia] can liberate free nicotine from the blend, which is associated with increases in impact and "satisfaction" reported by smokers . . . This means that at the same blend alkaloid content, a cigarette incorporating [ammonia technology] will deliver more flavor compounds, including nicotine, into smoke than one without it.

Skip ahead four years again. TRIAL REVEALS HOW AMMONIA FUELED CIGARETTE SALES was the banner headline in the middle of page one of the February 9, 1998 *Atlanta Journal-Constitution.* The story by Steve Karnowski of the Associated Press told readers how Brown and Williamson found out why Philip Morris's Marlboro brand started surging ahead of B&W's Winston brand in the 1970s. "The secret of Marlboro is ammonia," said a subpoenaed B&W document revealed at the trial of Minnesota's lawsuit against the industry (more on that suit in Chapter 12.)

A Mayo Clinic authority on nicotine addiction and a Stanford University chemical engineering professor testified that the purpose of ammonia was to boost the addictive power of "free nicotine" while lowering tar and actual nicotine content in cigarettes. "What the industry was concerned with, in the face of lowering tar, is the problem they would face if nicotine levels dropped" below the level needed to keep smokers hooked, said Channing Robertson of Stanford.

Well, shame again on Philip Morris for trying to produce a cigarette with reduced tar that still delivered satisfaction to smokers. Readers of this shocking story had no way of knowing that the FDA was well aware of ammonia at least as early as 1994 or that an industry handbook, which was hardly a secret and suppressed document, had described its use three years before that. Nor did the AJC remind readers that in 1994 it had reported ammonia as an ingredient in cigarettes (see below).

Back to 1994 again and Dr. Kessler:

"Why spend a decade developing through genetic breeding a high-nicotine tobacco," Dr. Kessler rhetorically asked the subcommittee, "if you are not interested in controlling and manipulating nicotine? Why focus on enhanced delivery of free nicotine to the smoker by chemical manipulation if you are not interested in controlling and manipulating nicotine?"

Beats me, commissioner. All I can say is, the people who run tobacco companies are obviously nothing but a bunch of rotten, dirty rats. It couldn't possibly be because they wanted to enhance the delivery of nicotine in cigarettes—which, after all, is what people smoke them for—while minimizing the bad stuff that goes along with the nicotine. I can, however, pose a question of my own to Dr. Kessler, as well as to Drs. Henningfield and Benowitz, John Banzhaf, Michael Pertschuk, Stanton Glantz and the whole host of antis who are so concerned about the well-being of their fellow Americans:

Why in the name of sanity, gentlemen, are you not encouraging the tobacco companies to produce cigarettes with the highest consumer-acceptable levels of nicotine so that we "addicts" could smoke fewer *of them to receive the same effect while ingesting* less *of the allegedly harmful toxins in tobacco smoke?*

Yet here again, despite the evidence Dr. Kessler presented to the subcommittee on March 25 showing that different people require different levels of nicotine in their smokes—*and stay at that level*—he and the other antis continue to promote the myth that the more nicotine there is in a cigarette, the more addicted the smoker becomes.

It is also worth asking why Dr. Kessler was so worked up about nicotine addiction but never, so far as I know, criticized the pharmaceutical companies for the way they push habit-forming drugs on millions of people through aggressive advertising in medical journals that doctors read. According to one authority, "More than 20 million Americans take Prozac, Ritalin, Xanax, Valium, or other potent psychotropic drugs prescribed on the basis of DSM labels [the American Psychiatric Association's "Diagnostic and Statistical Manual"] . . . In short, doctors are beginning to treat normal life problems with drugs—exactly what drug users do."[67]

Or why he never worried over the fact that a million and a half children and young people ages 5 through 18 are being doped with Ritalin for so-called "Attention Deficit Disorder (ADD)," a psychiatric term for "hyperactivity" or sometimes simply fidgetyness.[68*]

*"Fifteen years ago, no one had ever heard of ADD. Fred A. Baughman, Jr., a California pediatrician, contends that ADD 'was invented, in committee, at the American Psychiatric Association in 1980.' In its brief history it has been called Hyperkinetic Child Syndrome, Hyperactive Child Syndrome, Minimal Brain Damage, Minimal Brain Dysfunction in Children, Minimal Cerebral Dysfunction and Minor Cerebral Dysfunction."[69]

Says one physician: "I have seen so much psuedo-ADD that I have be-

As for that list of once-secret ingredients in cigarettes (whatever the number of them is; I've seen it given as anywhere from 599 to as high as 800) that Dr. Kessler referred to and which the companies, under pressure from Congress, released on April 13, 1994, tobacco opponents still weren't happy. They complained that the cigarette makers "continued to hide" how much of those chemicals a smoker gets in each puff.[76]

One has to sympathize with the antis for the difficulties they labor under. Apparently they have no research facilities of their own with the ability to analyze the chemical content of cigarettes but are utterly dependent upon what the tobacco industry tells them (or, more usually, what some disgruntled industry whistleblower "reveals").

The FDA evidently has the same problem. Of those 599 (or whatever) ingredients, eight of them are most questionable as to safety but the FDA apparently has formed no opinion about them, according to a

---

gun to question attention deficit disorder as a diagnosis whenever I have a new patient who hasn't shown significant improvement on Ritalin, or other type of stimulant."[70]

According to Dr. Mark Riddle, director of the division of child and adolescent psychiatry at the John Hopkins Medical Institutions, anxiety disorders, including "separation anxiety, generalized anxiety and social phobia," are more widespread in children than pediatricians had thought and can be treated pharmacologically. Unfortunately, he adds, Ritalin can actually increase nervousness and anxiety in many children.[71] So what's a shrink to do? Why, look for another magic pill. The National Institute of Mental Health, in conjunction with Solvay Pharmaceuticals of Marietta, Georgia, launched a study using 200 children to assess the effectiveness of the drug fluvoxamine to treat anxiety disorders in children.[72]

An even more serious problem with Ritalin, in at least one city, is that it "is increasingly being snorted or injected by metro Atlanta schoolchildren in search of a quick high . . . Because the drug is legally prescribed to many of their classmates, kids mistakenly think Ritalin cannot harm them. But when abused, the drug produces stimulating effects similar to those of amphetamines," said Dr. Gaylord Lopez, director of the Georgia Poison Center. According to the Drug Enforcement Administration, Ritalin overdoses in children ages 10 to 14 went from 40 in 1990 to 400 in 1995.[73]

Interestingly, Utah, which has the lowest percentage of smokers, has four times the national level of Ritalin consumption and nearly twice that of the next highest state.[74] Nationally, Ritalin is prescribed *250 times as frequently* in the United States as in Western Europe.[75]

list published by *The Atlanta Journal-Constitution*[77] (all emphases added):

— **Megastigmatrienone**. A flavoring that tobacco companies contend is found naturally in grapefruit juice and is considered safe by the food industry. *The FDA couldn't confirm that.*

— **Dehydromenthofurolactone**. A flavoring that tobacco companies say is found in peppermint and is considered safe by the food industry. *The FDA couldn't confirm that.*

— **Ethyl furoate**. Found naturally in coffee, kiwi fruit and peanuts. The food industry considers it safe. *The FDA hasn't formally ruled on it.*

— **Maltitol**. A sweetener used in chewing gum and candy for diabetics. The food industry considers it safe, but *the FDA hasn't ruled* on a petition questioning its safety.

— **Sclareolide**. A synthetic form of a naturally occurring tobacco element. The food industry considers it safe.

— **Tobacco extract**. Used to boost the flavor of reconstituted tobacco. Contains a small amount of nicotine.

— **Ammonia**. A processing aid. The FDA considers certain forms of ammonia safe in food but *couldn't comment* on the type used in cigarettes.

— **Methoprene**. An insecticide that toxicologists say is biodegradable. Tobacco companies say the FDA allows it in dried fruit, but *the FDA couldn't confirm that.*

"The FDA couldn't confirm." "The FDA hasn't ruled." "The FDA couldn't comment." Obviously, the agency needs a bigger budget so it can hire more investigators.

Something not so curious happened when R. J. Reynolds launched an advertising campaign telling smokers that it had reformulated its Winston brand to remove any and all of the chemicals, flavorings and other compounds normally used in mass-market cigarettes. The company was immediately attacked by John Garrison, chief executive of the American Lung Association, who foamed: "We demand evidence to substantiate the claim that these cigarettes are safer than other cigarettes. Smokers will grab for anything they think might be less harmful, and Reynolds has an obligation to its customers to prove these new Winstons are any less dangerous than other cigarettes."[78]

The company of course had made no such claim. Commented *The Wall Street Journal*:

> Three years ago [1994] the anti-smoking triumvirate [American Lung Association, American Heart Association and American Cancer Society] denounced the use of additives in cigarettes, claiming that they were a toxic soup of carcinogens. Now a tobacco company has done nothing less than to heed their advice and remove the additives. But there is no rejoicing among the triumvirate's pooh-bahs. Instead, they are demanding that the tobacco companies come up with evidence that the additive-free cigarettes are less dangerous than the toxic-soup variety.
>
> If there is no proof that the additives are harmful, then why did the triumvirate denounce additives three years ago? Are they now suggesting that they had no evidence for their claims? Or is it that, having used the issue of additives as a wedge, they aren't about to let Big Tobacco get off the hook with any additive-free nonsense?
>
> If additives are harmful, then the pooh-bahs should be happy that smokers have an option that reduces their risks, if only marginally. If the additives are not harmful, then the pooh-bahs should apologize for having suggested that they were.[79]

Anybody who expects antismokers to ever apologize about anything, let alone require them to use logic, has a very long wait. For what it's worth (about $12 in 1997), I tried a carton of the new Winstons and couldn't detect anything at all different about them.

To close this topic, the following is a cute poem a letter writer sent to *The Atlanta Journal-Constitution*:

> The manufacture of tobacco products
> Is easily the greatest miracle yet:
> They cram 700 additives
> Into one little cigarette.
> It all seems kind of whacko [*sic*].
> Is there still room for the tobacco?[80]

IF SOME DOCTOR OR medical researcher might in a weak moment concede that nicotine is *maybe* a wee bit less harmful to the human body than a number of other drugs that could be named, would any doctor be so crazy as to suggest that nicotine, or possibly something else in tobacco smoke, might actually be beneficial?

Smokers are fond of pointing out that nobody has ever rammed a car into a crowded school bus under the influence of nicotine. Nobody has ever beaten his wife in a nicotine-induced rage. Nobody has ever checked into the Betty Ford Clinic for nicotine detoxification. And certainly nobody has ever employed nicotine addiction as a defense in a criminal trial, much less won the sympathy of the court with such a stratagem.

(It's happened, though, with another popular mood-altering "drug"—sugar. The most notorious example is the murder of Harvey Milk, a member of the San Francisco Board of Supervisors and one of the first openly gay elected public officials in the United States. Milk, along with San Francisco Mayor George Moscone, was shot to death on November 18, 1978 by a disgruntled and apparently antigay former supervisor and former police officer, Dan White. To the shock and amazement of many, a San Francisco jury found White guilty not of murder but of manslaughter, judging him to have acted out of "diminished capacity" partly from having eaten too much junk food—the so-called "Twinkie Defense." The enraged San Francisco gay and lesbian community reacted with one of the worst civil disturbances in the city's history, known as the "White Night" riots.[81]

(More recently, a judge in Florida ruled that one Wesley Shaffer could use a defense plea of insanity caused by cotton candy after the accused burglar claimed that skyrocketed blood sugar caused him to break into a home in Boca Raton and steal a bag of jewelry.[82])

It may be stretching a little to call the absence of an intoxicating effect from nicotine a "benefit," yet it ought to be legitimate to pose this fact as a counter to those who lump nicotine into the same category as the narcotic drugs. Incidentally, although we call the pathological dependence on alcohol "alcoholism," I have never seen the corresponding word "nicotinism" used in connection with tobacco, even by the antismokers, although there is such a term, coined at the end of the last century. Perhaps it has fallen into disuse because, like another 19th-century affliction, "spermatorrhea," which doctors warned was a consequence of masturbation, the term is now recognized as unscientific and useless.

Smokers have also frequently claimed that smoking increases their mental alertness. This is not just their subjective impression; numerous studies have backed them up.

For example, in 1995, three researchers presented a paper before the annual meeting of the Canadian Society for Brain, Behavior and Cognitive Science in Halifax, Nova Scotia, which stated:

> Smokers' reports of increased mental alertness due to smoking are supported by the findings of improved performance on a host of cognitive tasks following smoking . . . This enhancement is generally attributed to the pharmacological effects of nicotine. The types of tasks in which smoking/nicotine improves performance include rapid visual information processing, memory tasks, motor tasks and choice reaction-time (RT) tasks. The varied nature of these tasks indicates that smoking/nicotine has positive effects on performance through its actions on several neural systems.[83]

Unfortunately, two of the three authors were associated with the R. J. Reynolds Tobacco Company, so we'll have to throw out their report, along with 21 supporting studies they cited. (Antismoking researchers, of course, are *never* influenced by anything other than the facts.)

But the previous year a team of research scientists from the Medical College of Georgia had concluded from clinical studies that nicotine enhances both short-term and long-term memory, at least in rats trained to solve a test involving opening a door to receive a reward, and may offer potential for treatment of degenerative diseases like Alzheimer's.[84]

The goal of such research, said team leader Dr. Alvin Terry Jr., was to find a way to help Alzheimer's patients by delaying progression of the disease, if not the actual onset of it. Although nicotine is known to be addictive, it would be much better to be hooked on a drug than to keep losing memory, he said.

Others have located the cellular mechanism in the brain that is activated by nicotine. Nicotine stimulates the release of a chemical that transmits signals from one cell to another in many parts of the brain, a team of researchers at Columbia-Presbyterian Medical Center in New York told readers of the August 8, 1996 issue of *Science*, the journal of the American Association for the Advancement of Science.[85] Anyway, it did in chicken brain cells the researchers kept alive in test tubes.

"[Nicotine] produces a profoundly more active connection. It enhances interaction between cells," wrote Lorna Role, senior author of the study, adding that this may also explain why smoking is such a difficult habit to break. "The brain has a way of saying, 'That was good, do it again.'"

(The brain likes a lot of things. For example, chocolate, "which temporarily helps relieve symptoms such as mood swings and anxiety," says Cindy Deversa, a dietitian at St. Jude Medical Center in Fullerton, California. "Simple sugars make it easier for the amino acid tryptophan to cross the blood-brain barrier. Trytophan is a precursor to serotonin, a neurotransmitter that gives you a calm, sedated feeling."[86])

Unlike the Georgia researchers, however, those in New York weren't looking for therapeutic uses for nicotine. Rather, they hoped their finding would aid development of a drug that blocks nicotine's addictive effects and thus help smokers kick the habit.

According to an article in the British journal *New Scientist*, epidemiologists began to find "apparently beneficial effects of smoking " in the late 1960s, when a study of American military veterans found that those with Parkinson's disease were less likely to be smokers. "The weight of evidence suggests that smokers are 50 percent less likely* to develop Parkinson's disease than those who have never smoked."[87]

That claim was later confirmed by Dr. David Morens of the University of Hawaii Medical School who reported in the June 1995 issue of the journal *Neurology* that he found cigarette smokers are half as likely to develop Parkinson's disease as nonsmokers. Parkinson's, which affects some one million Americans, is a neurological disorder that causes tremors, impaired motion, stiffness and difficulty in breathing.

Morens was honest enough to say that he was skeptical going into the study but was finally persuaded because the data "were overwhelmingly in favor of a protective association." He suggested that "It could be that something in the smoke stimulates an enzyme to break down chemicals in the smoker's brain that causes Parkinson's."[88]

*Fairness requires me to warn readers that a 50 percent "*less* likely" risk (or relative risk of 0.5) in a study favorable to smoking is subject to the same reservations as a 50 percent "*more* likely" risk (relative risk 1.5) in a study not favorable to smoking. The same goes for other percentage benefits of smoking cited in this chapter. It bears repeating that relative risks so close to 1, whichever side of it they are on (below 1, less risk; above 1, more risk) are not considered to be statistically significant.

Could it possibly be nicotine itself? One bit of evidence that it might be is that when someone with Parkinson's chewed nicotine gum, Morens found, "a transient [less than half-hour] suppression of diagnostic Parkinson's disease signs" occurred.

There have been other studies suggesting (which is really all that research into smoking usually does) that "something" in cigarette smoke may also prevent or delay or ameliorate the effects of the dreaded Alzheimer's disease. Still other studies suggest that that "something" may also help prevent ulcerative colitis.

But if medical science on rare occasion giveth a bit to tobacco, it quickly taketh it away. Researchers at the Brookhaven National Laboratory in Upton, New York, don't think cigarette smoke directly prevents Parkinson's. Rather, they reported in the February 22, 1996 issue of the British journal *Nature*, "something" in the smoke, other than nicotine, breaks down an enzyme called monamine oxidase B, or MAO B, which destroys dopamine. (Dopamine is a pleasure-enhancing chemical that is activated by a lot of things, including cocaine, heroin, sex, chocolate bars and a raise in salary.) Smoking thus increases the amount of dopamine in a smoker's brain, intensifying addiction, they say.[89]

Their study found that smokers have about 40 percent less MAO B than nonsmokers. As a result, they have more dopamine, and since Parkinson's is aggravated by a shortage of dopamine, that, the researchers suggest, may be why smokers may have a lower risk of developing that disease. But far from recommending that Parkinson's victims take up smoking, the Brookhaven folks believe that other drugs currently being used to treat this disease could help smokers quit smoking by reducing the drop in dopamine that results from quitting.

Interestingly, the previous week's issue of *Nature* reported that researchers had found "a statistical link" between dopamine receptors in the brain and whether a person acts detached and cold. Testing all of 24 people, they discovered that the lower the density of a type of receptor called D2, the higher the likelihood that the person would avoid closeness and warmth in relationships with people.[90] (Maybe that explains why smokers are such friendly, outgoing people.)

Yet another team of researchers, this time at the University Hospital of Wales in Cardiff, reported in *The New England Journal of Medicine* (NEJM) that nicotine appears to relieve the symptoms of ulcerative colitis, a chronic inflammation of the colon. They studied 72 patients with the affliction, half of whom wore a nicotine patch for six weeks and the other half wore a dummy patch. For about half of those using the real patches, symptoms of ulcerative colitis—bloody diarrhea and abdominal pain—went away. (But that was also true for a quarter of those with the dummy patches. The "placebo effect"?)[91]

Lest anything good be said for nicotine, however, an accompanying editorial in the NEJM criticized the study for not taking "objective data" from the patients instead of relying solely on their reports. It also questioned whether the "mood-altering" effect of nicotine could change their perceptions of symptoms. In other words, because the researchers didn't personally examine the stools of the 18 patients who reported that their symptoms disappeared, it could have been just a nicotine-induced illusion in the minds of those patients. I'm not aware of the NEJM ever criticizing any of the thousands of studies linking smoking to this or that disease because they relied on the subjective reports of the subjects studied.

That wasn't the first time the NEJM had reported on a possibly beneficial nicotine-ulcerative colitis connection. According to the American Smokers Alliance, both that journal and *The Journal of the American Medical Association* ran articles in 1981 and 1983 on studies which found that colon cancer and ulcerative colitis seem to be about 30 and 50 percent respectively less frequent among smokers. The latter journal also reported in 1985 that endometrial cancer of the womb in smokers occurs at around 50 percent of the rate among nonsmokers. And the government's first Health and Nutrition Examination Survey found that osteoarthritis is five times less likely to occur among heavy smokers than nonsmokers.[92]

PARKINSON'S DISEASE shares a number of pathological and neurochemical characteristics with the even more harrowing scourge of the elderly, and sometimes not so elderly—Alzheimer's disease. According to *New Scientist,* in the United States Alzheimer's affects 20 percent of people over 80 and 10 percent of those between 60 and 80, "which is, in absolute numbers," says one researcher, "far more than cancer and atheroma deaths related to smoking."[93] (Atheroma is fatty deposits on arterial walls.) In the case of this disease there is again evidence of the beneficial effects of smoking.

The *New Scientist* article cited above went on to say that in the mid-

1980s a nicotine effect similar to that for Parkinson's was spotted for Alzheimer's. Some studies found that smokers were 70 percent less likely to develop the disease than nonsmokers, while other studies found no advantage for smokers. The most consistent finding is a reduced risk for smokers in inherited Alzheimer's disease. The article quoted Peter Whitehouse, director of the Alzheimer's Center at University Hospitals in Cleveland, Ohio:

> The epidemiological evidence suggests that there is something in cigarette smoke, in the nicotine, that directly relates to the manner in which brain cells die. It's not just supporting the cells that are there . . . but preventing the cells from dying in the first place.

Up to April 1992, 17 studies on Alzheimer's disease and smoking had been reported (which is really infinitesimal compared to the multitude of studies of other diseases allegedly caused by smoking). Thirteen found a reduced risk among smokers and the remaining four found no difference between smokers and nonsmokers. None found an increased risk among smokers compared to nonsmokers.[94]

According to Elaine Perry of the MRC Neurological Pathology Unit at Newcastle General Hospital, also quoted by *New Scientist*, if you administer nicotine to a damaged animal brain, it recovers much faster. "This backs up the notion that nicotine prevents the degeneration in Alzheimer's disease."

Here again, "suggestions" that nicotine or "something" in cigarette smoke could have medical benefits of great importance to millions of people. "Some free citizens might prefer to take the smoking risk of cancer and of atheroma rather than that of Alzheimer's disease," says one scientist.[95] They might if they knew the facts, or if the medical establishment were more devoted to finding out the facts about nicotine.

Why, the *New Scientist* article asks, should medical researchers be so reluctant to study the apparent positive effects of smoking? It quoted Jeffrey Gray, professor of psychiatry at the Institute of Psychiatry in London: "If the same information was available about any other compound, it would have been headline news a decade ago."

One reason for the "reluctance" is that epidemiological studies are often conflicting. But that is an argument for more research into the possible benefits of nicotine or smoking, not less.

Another reason—excuse, rather—used by those who dismiss the potential benefits of nicotine for Parkinson's patients is the claim that smokers die of smoking-related diseases before developing Parkinson's. But Parkinson's typically occurs at a much younger age than smoking-related deaths.[96]

The argument that smoking would kill you before it helped you might have some superficial validity when it comes to Alzheimer's, which is most often a disease of old age, and smokers aren't supposed to reach that stage in life. But if that's so, one wonders where anyone was able to find enough elderly smokers to compare them with elderly non-smokers, as they did in those 17 studies referred to above.

The real reason medical science has been "reluctant" to investigate the possible beneficial effects of smoking and why the general public has been told little about those studies which have been conducted is, purely and simply, antismoking bias. Again quoting from *New Scientist*:

"When the first results appeared everybody bent over backwards to find reasons it couldn't be true." —Dr. Gray again on the Alzheimer's-smoking link. He likens the efforts of medical researchers to disprove the benefits of smoking to attempts by the tobacco industry to destroy the link between smoking and heart disease. (But only the tobacco industry is accused of suppressing the facts about smoking.)

"When I speak to neurologists handling Parkinson's patients about nicotine they cannot believe it. They cannot imagine prescribing what to them is a dirty drug." —Karl Olov Fagerström, a nicotine researcher and consultant to the Swedish drug company Kabi Pharmacia.[97] (This is not necessarily an expression of abhorrence of nicotine, although it probably is in this case. I've read that in pharmaceutical parlance, a "dirty drug" is one that is so exasperatingly complex and has so many different effects that it can't be easily pinned down.)

So millions of human beings may be needlessly suffering from Parkinson's and Alzheimer's diseases or, at the least, are being denied potentially alleviating treatment because of the dogma that tobacco and nicotine are unmitigated evils. It could be rather a costly sacrifice to be placing on the altar of political correctness.

I have known only one person afflicted with Alzheimer's, a colleague at Newspaper Enterprise Association who later went into public relations. (Despite that defection, we remained close friends.) He was a heavy smoker and heavier drinker, but gave up both habits some 15 years before he died. After he was diagnosed with the disease, its progression was rapid and devastating, taking only a few years to cause his death in his early 60s. His physical death, that is; his mind and everything that had made him what he was had deteriorated beyond retrieval well before that merciful end. I'm sure he would have taken up smoking again had he been aware of any studies into the possible benefits of nicotine. Yet it must be conceded that 30 or more years of prior smoking did not prevent the onset of Alzheimer's in his case.

The hysterical war against tobacco has also either hampered or not encouraged investigations into other valuable uses for the weed. For example, according to John Diana, director of the University of Kentucky's Tobacco and Health Research Institute, "the prospects for developing new products and technology [from tobacco] is enormous." He says tobacco could be used to produce a vaccine for malaria and a tobacco enzyme could be used in paper processing and the food industry. Some 30 other substances, such as pharmaceuticals and food products, have been produced as a result of genetic engineering of the tobacco plant.[98]

Researchers at Virginia Polytechnic Institute have also succeeded in genetically engineering a tobacco plant to create an enzyme, glucocereborsidase, to treat Gaucher's disease, a rare inherited metabolic disorder. The enzyme is currently so difficult to produce that a year's supply for a patient costs up to $300,000.[99]

TO WIND UP THIS chapter on nicotine and addiction, let's ignore the fact that it is not the most dangerous drug in the world. (You can buy it at your local pharmacy without a prescription, remember, and even the famous 1964 surgeon general's report dismissed it as a factor in lung cancer.*) Let's even ignore those studies suggesting that it may actually

*Even so, many people, and at least one scientist, believe or want to believe that nicotine causes cancer. Stephen Hecht, director of research at the American Health Foundation, says that an ingredient in watercress called phenethyl isothiocyanate, or PEITC, has prevented tumors in rats. He found that 11 smokers who ate two ounces of watercress three times a day for three days had a 30 percent decrease in "detoxified" nicotine excreted in their urine.[100] That was evidence, he said, that the PEITC in watercress had

have some useful place in the medical armamentarium. Let's simply agree that (shudder) it causes addiction (leaving aside whatever different meanings different people may attach to that word). Is it still possible that Dr. Kessler and the nicotine-bashing gang are barking up the wrong tree? That just maybe, in their passionate absorption with the physical aspects of nicotine "addiction," they are ignoring the whole panoply of possibly beneficial psychological components involved in smoking?

The antis can trot out any number of ex-smokers who will testify that even 20 years after quitting they still miss cigarettes, proving, they argue, what a powerful hold nicotine has on people—long, long, long after the last of it has been cleared from their systems.

Writer George Autry, who was partially quoted at the beginning of this chapter, went on to say that even after he freed himself from his "slavery" to cigarettes, "I still miss cigarettes, especially when I leave church or the dentist's office. But I also miss them while writing, after a good dinner, and after making love and many of the times in between."

Another writer said that almost seven years after he finally stopped, "[E]very day I want a cigarette. Every day on my way to work I pass a billboard that reminds me of something I want but must not have."[101]

But if it's nicotine and nicotine only these former smokers still crave, I've not heard of them lining up at the drugstore counter to buy nicotine-laced chewing gum or patches.

For their part, smoking defenders can trot out witnesses who will maintain that things are just not that simple. The pleasure of tobacco goes far beyond what nicotine does to the system, says Joe Dawson:

> It's a way of life. What the smoker enjoys is the whole experience, the routine of handling the pack and the cigarette, lighting up, gazing into the flame, the oral satisfaction of drawing, the taste and the smell. Eating and drinking are synergistic with smoking; they each enhance the taste of the smoke, and smoking enhances the contemplation of food and drink.
>
> Nicotine plays a part, but a small one. It can no more substitute for a smoke than No-Doz tablets could replace a good cup of

---

prevented the nicotine from metabolizing and becoming cancer-causing. I've never seen anything more about this "discovery" and it remains the only reference I have ever come across alleging a carcinogenic effect in nicotine.

> coffee. That's why nicotine patches and chewing gum aren't very effective when it comes to quitting. Of *course*, it's hard to give it up. [Emphasis in original.] So are many other things which are not physiologically addicting. Your right arm, for example. Or your spouse. If either is taken away you will experience a severe psychological withdrawal. Using "dependence" as a criterion, millions of people are addicted to Monday Night Football.
>
> In the not-too-distant past, smokers would freely admit that they were addicted and even joke about needing a "fix." Now, however, the most many of them will admit to is a habit. Whether it's a habit or an addiction would be merely a semantic argument, except that most anti-smokers seem to think that addiction gives them the moral right to step in and pass laws or otherwise control the "addict's" behavior without his consent. It doesn't.[102]

This is of course a smoker's opinion. However, a report by the Congressional Research Service, a branch of the Library of Congress which works exclusively for Congress by analyzing legislation and providing information to congressional committees and their staffs, says much the same thing:

> [T]he fact that individuals engage in hazardous or dangerous activities does not mean that they are making bad choices. Individuals are presumed to choose activities, in accordance with their subjective tastes and preferences, that make them the happiest. This choice does not necessarily mean that they will maximize their health or their lifespan. Individuals engage in all sorts of behaviors that impose some danger in exchange for benefit (driving small cars or riding motorcycles, working in risky jobs, eating unhealthy diets, engaging in risky sports). Thus, nothing in economy theory precludes the notion that individuals smoke because their enjoyment of the activity outweighs the sum of the actual costs of purchasing cigarettes and the internal health costs . . .
>
> [S]imply because individuals engage in behavior that involves habit formation or addiction does not mean they are making a mistake, as long as the individual recognizes the difficulty of modifying behavior in the future and the possibility of a need for such modification. Individuals make many decisions that are difficult to change (and that they are probably aware are difficult to change)—marriage, job, purchasing a home, locating in a given area—*without those decisions being seen as bad choices and appropriate targets for government intervention* . . . [Emphasis added.]
>
> That smoking is habit forming is essentially beyond dispute. There is also a substance in tobacco, nicotine, that is physically

> addictive to some degree. A very large number of smokers say they would like to quit, and quitters experience a high rate of recidivism . . . Other observations suggest, however, that *addiction is not serious enough to make smoking decisions significantly different from many other decisions in which the government does not intervene.*[103] [Emphasis added.]

So much common sense exhibited by "faceless bureaucrats" is as refreshing as it is uncommon.

A fact of life that seems obvious to me but which I have seldom seen pointed out anywhere is that no one becomes addicted to, or a habitual indulger in, something that does not give him pleasure or some kind of reward, whether that something is a substance or an activity. The pleasure may be only transitory; there may be unpleasant consequences, such as the binge drinker's next-morning hangover or the drug user's comedown from his "high." But *no one* becomes addicted to that which provides *no* pleasurable benefits whatsoever.

Lest that be dismissed as merely my own uninformed opinion, let me quote someone who is probably as much of an expert on the subject as Drs. Koop or Kessler. Referring to a statement by Atlanta Braves pitcher Greg Maddux that he would like to quit his chewing-tobacco habit, especially after fellow player/chewer Brett Butler was diagnosed with throat cancer, but couldn't because "it's an addiction," Mark A. Moore wrote: "Having conducted a number of stop-smoking seminars for a national organization, I am convinced that people who *can't* quit actually *choose* to continue because they like tobacco and are not willing to pay the price of quitting, which is surprisingly cheap if one analyzes the venture . . . The cost of quitting is some temporary discomfort. The benefits make a lengthy list."[104] [Emphases his.]

To put it another way, many smokers who make the socially obligatory statement that they would like to quit but are unable to because their addicted bodies won't let them really don't *want* to quit.

Moore's opinion might possibly be dismissed too, for he is a retired professor of economics at Georgia Tech, not a physician or shrink. But if only members of the medical profession were considered qualified to make pronouncements regarding tobacco, the ranks of the antismoking movement would be barren. Stanton Glantz, for example, was trained as a mechanical engineer, although the media always refer to him as a "professor of medicine." John Banzhaf, the founder of Action on Smoking and Health, is a lawyer, as is Michael Perchuk of the Coalition on Smoking OR Health. It's too bad the latter two didn't go into medicine instead of law, considering all the antitobacco litigation they have fomented. Banzhaf is the Jesse Jackson of the antismoking movement; he pops up everywhere he can get his name or his organization in the news.

That there are many simple pleasures associated with smoking (or other uses of tobacco) and that it is not purely a matter of "addiction" to or "dependence" upon nicotine or an indication of some personality problem is a fact which seems to elude many members of the research community. They keep dreaming up studies to probe the psyches of smokers.

For example, maybe smokers are too smart (or think they are) for their own good. Psychologists at Iowa State University tested 174 smokers to try to find out why they persist in the habit despite "overwhelming evidence" that it is dangerous. The researchers rated the subjects on a self-esteem scale and interviewed them before, during and after an attempt to quit smoking. Those who were assessed with having very high self-esteem and who relapsed reported a significant decline in their perception of the risks of smoking.

Dr. Frederick Gibbons, lead author of the study published in the *Journal of Personality and Social Psychology*, concluded (based on this purely anecdotal evidence) that people who consider themselves smarter than the average bear and who have high self-esteem "have difficulty admitting that their behavior has been unhealthy and/or unwise."[105]

But on the other hand (there's always at least one other hand), high self-esteem can lead to healthier, longer lives, a group of researchers at the University of Wisconsin in Madison reported (also on the basis of anecdotal evidence). The authors of a study published in *Archives of Family Medicine*[106] surveyed 154 patients at a midwestern family practice clinic on their perceptions of themselves and then compared those perceptions with health and behavioral histories.

In men, low self-esteem was "related to personal loss, *smoking*, alcohol use, and exposure to dangerous situations," the researchers discovered. In women, a low self-image was "related to weight, *smoking*, and alcohol use." [Emphases added.]

"Self-esteem was positively related to seatbelt usage, perception of overall health, greater social support, life satisfaction, and projected longevity. Those with greater self-regard were predicted to live longer, while those with poorer self-esteem achieved shorter predicted longevity."

They "achieved" longer or shorter "predicted" longevity? Since none of the subjects had actually died, were the longevity predictions based simply on the presence or absence of certain perceived "risk factors," such as smoking? If nobody had yet fulfilled the predictions, and wouldn't for a number of years, of what real validity was this study?

Indeed, the authors inadvertently rendered useless their own findings by cautioning that it is still not clear which comes first—self-esteem or physical well-being. Furthermore, "It can be assumed neither that individuals who choose to smoke do so because they have low self-esteem, nor that they have poor self-esteem because they smoke."

So much for the smoking/self-esteem question. Obviously more research is needed. But hey, what's the good of all that grant money lying around if it isn't used for something?

IN THE SOMEWHAT more distant past, specifically 1947, before smokers became the object of society's opprobrium (and before all that grant money was available to study them), Ernest Dichter, a pioneer in the field of "motivational psychology," wrote a book called *The Psychology of Everyday Living*, one of whose chapters was titled "Why Do We Smoke Cigarettes?"[107]

One of the first facts he discovered in talking to several hundred people was that advertising played little role. "None of the much-flaunted appeals of cigarette advertisers, such as superior taste and mildness, induces us to become smokers or to choose one brand in preference to another . . . Smoking is as much a psychological pleasure as it is a physiological satisfaction. As one of our respondents explained: 'It is not the taste that counts. It's that sense of satisfaction you get from a cigarette that you can't get from anything else.'" Dr. Dichter then listed some 17 categories of satisfaction. Among them (comments in brackets are mine):

Smoking is fun. "You sometimes get tired of working intensely," said an accountant, "and if you sit back for the length of a cigarette, you feel much fresher afterwards."

Smoking is a reward. The first and last cigarette of the day are especially significant rewards. The first one, right after breakfast, gives the smoker a little consolation prize in advance and at the same time manages to postpone the evil hour when he must begin his hard day's work. The last cigarette of the day is like "closing a door." It is something quite definite. "I nearly always smoke a cigarette before going to bed," said one smoker. "That finishes the day. I usually turn the light out after I have smoked the last cigarette and then turn over to sleep."

Smoking is oral pleasure. Oral pleasure is as fundamental as sexuality and hunger and functions with full strength from earliest childhood. There is a direct connection between thumbsucking and smoking. "Whenever I try to stop smoking for a while, I get something to chew on, either a pipe or a menthol cigarette," said another smoker. "You just stick it in your mouth and keep on sucking. And I also chew a lot of gum when I want to cut down on smoking . . . " [Or today when you're forced to cut down because of the increasing number of situations where you aren't allowed to smoke, as one heavy TV advertiser of chewing-gum-as-consolation is aware.]

The satisfied expression on a smoker's face when he inhales is ample proof of his sensuous thrill. The immense power of the yearning for a cigarette, especially after an enforced abstinence, is acknowledged by habitual smokers. Said one, "When you don't get a cigarette for a long time and you are kind of on pins, the first drag goes right down to your heels."

The cigarette is a modern hourglass. Frequently the burning down of a cigarette functions psychologically as a time indicator. A smoker waiting for someone who is late says to himself, "Now, I'll smoke one more cigarette, and then I am off." A cigarette not only measures time, but also seems to make time pass more rapidly. That is why waiting periods almost automatically stimulate the desire to smoke. Cigarettes may also have a psychotherapeutic effect on nervous anxiety. Soldiers, waiting for the signal to attack, sometimes value a cigarette more than food.

"With a cigarette I am not alone." The companionable character of cigarettes is reflected in the fact that they help us make friends. [Don't forget, this was back in 1947!] In many ways, smoking has the same effect drinking has; it helps to break down social barriers. One middle-aged lady related how, "a long time ago" during a steamer cruise she wanted to meet a boy but there was no one to introduce them. "The second day out, he was sitting at a table right next to me, and I was puffing away at my cigarette. The ashes on my cigarette were getting longer and longer, and I had no ashtray. Suddenly he jumped up and brought me one. That's how the whole thing started. We are still happily married." [Today, of course, any right-thinking young man would disgustedly turn his back on a young woman who smoked.]

"I like to watch the smoke." In mythology and religion, smoke is full of meaning. Its floating intangibility and unreal character have made it possible for man to see therein mystery and magic. Even for us moderns, smoke has a strong fascination. Just as most people like to watch their own breath on cold winter days, so they like to watch cigarette smoke, which similarly makes one's breath visible. "Smoke is fascinating," said one person. "On a rainy day, I sort of lie in a haze in the middle of the room and let my thoughts wander while I smoke and wonder where the smoke goes." [Well, today we know where the smoke goes—it goes right through the walls and into the lungs of the neighbors in the next apartment, dooming them to an early death. (See Chapter 7. For another kind of fascination with cigarette smoke, see Chapter 9.)]

Other satisfactions smokers mentioned to Dr. Dichter included: the friendly gesture of lighting another's cigarette; memories of certain moments in their lives closely linked with cigarettes; expressing one's mood through smoking mannerisms—the way the cigarette is lit and held and the smoke blown out; smoking as an aid to thinking and relaxing.

But enough already. If some of the statements above could be cited by the antismokers as proof of the addictive or compulsive nature of smoking, they also illustrate aspects of human psychology the antis seem totally incapable of understanding or appreciating.

As could have been expected back in 1947, Dr. Dichter's respondents seemed little concerned about the potentially harmful effects of smoking, yet at the same time all of them worried about smoking too many cigarettes. This is shown, he said, by the fact that nearly everyone has tried, at one time or another, to "cut down" on smoking. Some give it up entirely for a period of weeks or months. "Periodic abstemiousness of this kind indicates an underlying feeling of guilt," he wrote. "Such individuals really think that constant smoking is not only harmful, but also a bit immoral. Efforts to reduce the amount of smoking signify a willingness to sacrifice pleasure in order to assuage their feeling of guilt." Much of this guilt, he adds, can be traced directly to one's first cigarette, "which the older generation remember as a forbidden and sinful thing."

Thou shouldst be alive today, doctor. This sense of guilt weighs on the current generation of smokers more heavily than ever. Indeed, in the art of confessing to sins, the graduates of a Communist "re-education" program have nothing over smokers.

"I am a smoker," someone wrote to Dear Abby. "It's not something I'm proud of, and yes, I'm aware of the damage I may be doing to my health. I also live with the guilt of possibly hurting others with my smoke."[108]

"Smokers establish associations: a cigarette with coffee, a cigarette after meals, so forth," wrote *Atlanta Journal-Constitution* television critic Phil Kloer. "For some of us, smoking goes with guilt. Guilt for the few times I've been out walking with Amanda [his daughter] and I try to exhale the smoke away from her but the wind whips it around into her face. Guilt for the tiny burn marks in the front seat of the car . . . And the big one: guilt that this addiction will take its inevitable toll and leave Heather [his wife] without a husband and Amanda without a dad before it might otherwise have been."[109]

Guilt. It's this feeling of self-condemnation for harming not only themselves but others that the antis have so successfully instilled in the minds of many smokers that, in my opinion, goes a long way toward explaining why they have meekly let themselves be pushed around, not only figuratively but quite literally, by the moralists and healthists. But even guilt has its limits.

Dichter's words closing that chapter of his book bear repeating in full to close this chapter of this book:

> During the seventeenth century, religious leaders and statesmen in many countries condemned the use or tobacco. Smokers were excommunicated by the Church and some of them were actually condemned and executed. But the habit of smoking spread rapidly all over the world. The psychological pleasures derived

> proved more powerful than religious, moral, and legal persuasions. As in the case of the prohibition experiment in the United States, repressive measures seem to have aroused a spirit of popular rebellion and helped to increase the use of tobacco.
>
> If we consider all the pleasure and advantages provided, in a most democratic and international fashion, by this little white paper roll, we shall understand why it is difficult to destroy its power by means of warnings, threats, or preachings. This pleasure miracle has so much to offer that we can safely predict the cigarette is here to stay. Our psychological analysis is not intended as a eulogy of the habit of smoking, but rather as an objective report on why people smoke cigarettes. Perhaps this will seem more convincing if we reveal a personal secret: We ourselves do not smoke at all. We may be missing a great deal.

Dr. Dichter's next-to-last sentence underscoring the objectivity of his research into the reasons people smoke is a little curious, for on a television program about the history of public relations and "motivational psychology" I caught sometime in 1997 on, I think, the A&E channel, he was shown in an old clip from an interview holding a pipe in his hand. Maybe it was just a prop; pipes are, or used to be, associated with professorial intellectualism. Whatever, everything he reported about smoking and smokers back in 1947 remains true today.

Notes

1. George Autry, "The Psychology of Cigarettes," a review of *Cigarettes Are Sublime*, by Richard Klein. *The Atlanta Journal-Constitution*, February 20, 1994, p. N10.

"In my view, drug addiction—that is, the habitual use and craving for a drug—is not something that happens to a person unwittingly, against his will; it's something he does to himself, generally by practicing assiduously how to use—and enjoy—a particular substance. The idea that a single experience with a drug . . . makes one a 'slave' to it, makes one unable to exist without it, is simply not true." — Psychiatrist Dr. Thomas Szasz in an interview in *Reason*, October 1974.

2. Stanton Peele, *Diseasing of America* (Boston: Houghton Mifflin, 1989), p. 117.

3. In a study of 396 men and women who averaged 38 hours a week "on line," psychologist Kimberly Young of the University of Pittsburgh-Bradford found that heavy Internet users met the psychiatric criteria for clinical dependence applied to alcoholics and drug addicts, leading her to coin the description, "Internet addiction disorder." — Marilyn Elias, "Net overuse called a 'true addiction.'" *USA Today*, August 4, 1996. At www.usatoday.com/life/cyber/tech/ct071.htm.

"Unlike stamp collecting or reading, computers are a psycho-stimulant, and a certain segment of the population can develop addictive behavior in response to that stimulant," according to Dr. Howard Shaffer of Harvard University Medical School. One interviewer reported that 22 out of nearly 100 computer users experienced "a cocainelike rush" from their mastery of on-line technology. — "Addicts Defer to Greater Power: The Computer." *The Atlanta Journal-Constitution*, March 12, 1995, p. D2. From *The New York Times*.

And as could be expected, "Online support groups such as Webaholics and Interneters Anonymous have sprung up to help Net surfers overcome their addictions to cybersex or information overload."— Carolyn Poiroti, "Internet addiction is more than hooked on feeling." — *The Atlanta Journal-Constitution*, October 25, 1998, p. P12. From *The* (Fort Worth) *Star-Telegram.*

4. *Smoking and Health.* Report of the Advisory Committee to the Surgeon General of the Public Health Service, U.S. Department of Health, Education and Welfare, Public Health Service Publication No. 1103, p. 350.

5. Ibid, p. 352.

6. Richard Kluger, *Ashes to Ashes: America's Hundred-Year Cigarette War, the Public Health, and the Unabashed Triumph of Philip Morris* (New York: Alfred A. Knopf, 1996.) pp. 244, 245.

7. Ibid, p. 257.

8. *Smoking and Health*, p. 351.

9. Loc. cit.

10. Ibid., p. 353.

11. *The Health Consequences of Smoking.* A Report of the Surgeon General. Department of Health and Human Services publication (CDC) 88-8406, 1988. Abstract, p. 10.

12. Ibid, p. 9.

13. Steele, p. 174.

14. *The Health Consequences of Smoking*, p. 7.

15. Ibid, p. v of Preface.

16. "The Twelve Steps of Nicotine Anonymous." At www.slip.net.

17. Quoted in John Blake, "Just Get Over It." *The Atlanta Journal-Constitution*, February 7, 1998, p. B1.

18. Peele, p. 143.

19. Jerome Jaffe, in *The Pharmacological Basis of Therapeutics*, Alfred Goodman Gilman and Louis S. Goodman, eds. (New York: Macmillan, 1980), pp. 547-48. Quoted in David Krogh, *Smoking: The Artificial Passion* (New York: W. H. Freeman, 1991), p. 72.

20. Amanda Husted, "Cancer Society asks smokers to break their habit today." *The Atlanta Journal-Constitution*, November 19, 1992, p. C3.

21. Ibid.

22. Bill Hendrick and Amanda Husted, "Many alcohol abusers find their own solutions." *The Atlanta Journal-Constitution*, July 19, 1996, p. T2.

23. David A. Kessler, "The Control and Manipulating of Nicotine in Cigarettes." Statement before the Subcommittee on Health and the Environment, Committee on Energy and Commerce, U.S. House of Representatives, March 25, 1994. From the University of Pennsylvania's OncoLink page at www.oncolink.upen.edu.

24. Quoted in "Throwing Away Those Cigarettes." Kaiser Permanente (Atlanta) Partners in Health newsletter, Winter 1993-94, p. 15.

25. Philip J. Hilts, "Is Nicotine Addictive? It Depends on What Criteria You Use." *The New York Times*, Science Section, August 2, 1994.

26. Kessler, op. cit.

27. Alix M. Freedman, "Former Philip Morris Scientist Alleges Company Knew Nicotine Acts Like A Drug." *The Wall Street Journal*, March 18, 1996, p. A3. Courtesy of the Advocacy Institute.

28. Edward McNamara, "FDA Regulation of Tobacco Could Cause More Deaths." From www.interaccess.com/lumpen/edmc/fdacig.html, quoting from *The New York Times* of May 2, 1994.

29. "The Nicotine War." Transcript of "Frontline" Show No. 1306, January 3, 1995, p. 3.

30. "Eye on America." CBS News With Dan Rather, November 4, 1996.

31. Richard J. Grandpre, "What's the Hook? Smoking Is More Than A Chemical Bond." *Reason*, January 1997, pp. 47-48.

32. McNamara, op. cit.

33. Editorial. "Getting A Grip on Nicotine." *The Atlanta Journal-Constitution*, April 15, 1994, p. A14.

34. Reagan Walker, "Nicotine-free Cigarette Made of Lettuce." Cox News Service, September 23, 1997. At http://nytsyn.com:80/live/Week/266_092397_19005_ 27426.html.

35. "The Nicotine War," loc. cit.

36. Figures cited in John Carey, "It's Time for Regulators to Stop Blowing Smoke." *Business Week*, March 14, 1994, p. 34.

37. Joe Dawson, "Essays on the Anti-Smoking Movement." At www.tezcat.com~smokers/issues1.html.

38. "Addiction to Nicotine." Undated ASH release at www.setinc. com/ ash/.

39. Thomas W. Laquer, "What the prohibitionists don't understand about tobacco." *The New Republic*, September 18 and 25, 1995, p. 42.

40. Gene Borio, "Capsule History of Tobacco." The Tobacco BBS at www.tobacco.org/.

41. Garry Trudeau, "Doonesbury." May 16, 1993.

42. Brad Rodu, "We Already Knew the Smoking Secret." *The Washington Times*, December 29, 1995. From www.forces.org/.

43. Ibid.

44. Lacquer, op. cit.

45. National Cancer Institute Press Office release, July 13, 1995. From OncoLink at www.oconlink.upenn.edu/.

46. "Nicotine Addictive, FDA Panel Rules." *The Atlanta Journal-Constitution*, August 3, 1994, p. A1. From the Associated Press.

47. Anita Manning, "Nicotine Patch Sold Over the Counter." *USA Today*, June 18, 1996. At www.usatoday.com/life/health/smoking/prevent/ lhspr005.htm.

48. Comics section. *The Atlanta Journal-Constitution*, March 17, 1997.

49. "A Dose of Nicotine." *The Atlanta Journal-Consitution*, August 2, 1996; "Nicotine Spray Aims to Halt Smoking." *The New York Times*, March 26, 1996, p. C7; "New Nicotine Nasal Spray Approved to Stop Smoking." *The Wall Street Journal*, March 26, 1996, p. B4; Anita Manning, "Quitters' New Tool: Nicotine Nasal Spray." *USA Today*, March 26, 1996, p. A1; Associated Press, "FDA Allows Nicotine Nasal Spray." *The Washington Post*, March 26, 1996, p. A3. Sources courtesy of The Advocacy Institute.

50. Philip J. Hilts, "Anti-Smoking Groups Move to Keep a Low-Smoke Cigarette Off U.S. Market." *The New York Times*, November 30, 1994, p. A18. Courtesy of the Advocacy Institute.

51. Kaiser Permanente, "Throwing Away Those Cigarettes."

52. "NCI Smoking Study 'Failure' May Boost Smokers' Suits." At www. setinc.com/ash/pr/failnci.htm.

53. "AMA blasts low-nicotine cigarettes." *The Atlanta Journal-Constitution*, September 30, 1992, p. C3.

54. "Tobacco Trade Journals Brag of Nicotine Levels." *The* (Cleveland, Ohio) *Plain Dealer*, June 26, 1994. From Scripps Howard.

55. John Schwartz, "Tobacco Executives Defend Chemical Mixing Practices." *The Washington Post*, cited at http://the-tech.mit.edu/V4/N21/ tobacco.21w.html.

56. "ABC Settles Lawsuits With Tobacco Giants." *The Atlanta Journal-Constitution*, August 22, 1995, p. A3. From the Associated Press.

57. "ABC gets bad ratings for settling tobacco suit." *The Atlanta Journal-Constitution*, August 24, 1995, p. G9. From staff and wire reports.

58. Ibid.

59. Philip J. Hilts, "The Tobacco Wars." Luncheon address to the Joan Shorenstein Center on the Press, Politics and Public Health Policy, November 14, 1995.

60. "Frontline." Show Number 1413, air date April 2, 1996.

61. "Wall Street Journal's Freedman Wins Pulitzer Prize for Tobacco Reporting." *The Wall Street Journal*, April 10, 1996, p. A2. Courtesy of The Advocacy Institute.

62. Editorial. "Let FDA Regulate Tobacco." *The Atlanta Journal-Constitution*, March 5, 1994, p. A18.

63. Joan Pressman, "A friendship gone up in smoke." Letters. *The Atlanta Journal-Constitution*, September 14, 1996, p. A13.

64. David A. Kessler, "The Control and Manipulation of Nicotine in Cigarettes." Statement before the Subcommittee on Health and the Environment, Committee on Energy and Commerce, U.S. House of Representatives, June 21, 1994. From www.oncolink.upenn.edu.

65. Michael J. Sniffen, "Plot to grow high-nicotine tobacco revealed." *The Atlanta Journal-Constitution*, January 8, 1998, p. A10. From the Associated Press.

66. Nation in Brief. *The Atlanta Journal-Constitution*, November 2, 1996, p. C5.

67. Sydney Walker III, M.D., *A Dose of Sanity: Mind, Medicine, and Misdiagnosis* (New York: John Wiley & Sons, 1996), pp. 54 and 88.

68. *Pediatrics*, the Journal of the American Academy of Pediatrics, December 1996. Cited by *The Atlanta Journal-Constitution*, December 11, 1996, p. B3.

69. Quoted in Michael Skube, "Ritalin not a cure but just a symptom of a nation that cannot compose itself." *The Atlanta Journal-Constitution*, July 16, 1996, p. E3.

70. John Lochridge, M.D., "Anxiety and depression can masquerade as ADD." The Cobb Medical Report advertising supplement, *The Atlanta Journal-Constitution*, February 20, 1997, p. T4.

71. Bill Hendrick and Amanda Husted, "Study to test drug against anxiety disorders in kids." *The Atlanta Journal-Constitution*, February 11, 1997, p. C3.

72. Ibid.

73. Beth Burkstrand, "Teens abusing Ritalin." *The Atlanta Journal-Constitution*, May 11, 1997, p. G1.

74. Steele, p. 131.

75. Dr. Dominic L. Mazza and Nancy Reddington Parlo, "Drugs Alone Not Answer for Attention Disorders." *The Scranton Times*, August 2, 1997, p. C3.

76. "Cigarette makers reveal secret list of additives." *The Atlanta Journal-Constitution*, April 14, 1994, p. A1. From the Associated Press.

77. Ibid, page 10.

78. "Additive-free Smokes." *The Wall Street Journal*, August 27, 1997. Quoted at www.junkscience.com/news/additives.html.

79. Ibid.

80. L. Chavarria-Aguilar, "Last Gasp." Letters. *The Atlanta Journal-Constitution*, April 15, 1994, p. A14. The author was identified as a retired professor of Sanskrit and linguistics.

81. At http//headlines.yahoo.com/planetout/stories/8491139304.html.

82. "Cotton candy drove him to crime, burglar contends." *The Atlanta Journal-Constitution*, November 8, 1996, p. C4, from the Associated Press; "Sweet defense." *The Atlanta Journal-Constitution*, November 14, 1996, p. A6.

83. Michael E. Houlian et al., "Can Smoking Speed Cognitive Processing?" Presentation to the Canadian Society for Brain, Behavior and Cognitive Science in Halifiax, NS, Canada, June 23-24, 1995. Posted on Wake Forest University Internet site.

84. Bill Hendrick, "Nicotine Ingestion Might Help Memory." *The Atlanta Journal-Constitution*, November 17, 1994, p. D20.

85. "Scientists Zero in On Reason for Nicotine Cravings." *The Atlanta Journal-Constitution*, September 22, 1995, p. B1. From the Associated Press; Doug Levy, "Nicotine's Power On Brain Tied to Smoker's Alertness." *USA Today*, August 8, 1996. At www.usatoday.com/life/health/smoking/research/lhsrh002.htm.

86. Julie Bawden Davis, "Happy memories, brain chemicals feed the desire." *The Atlanta Journal-Constitution*, September 10, 1997, p. D3.

87. Ian Mundell, "Peering through the smoke screen: Cigarette smoking appears to protect against a number of diseases, but researchers have been reluctant to ask why." *New Scientist*, October 9, 1993. Posted on the Internet by American Smokers Alliance at www.smokers.org/alzheimer/05-peering_through.html.

88. Roger Field, "Stunned Docs Discover Cigarettes Stop Parkinson's." *The New York Post*, June 15, 1995, p.18. Courtesy of The Advocacy Institute. See also Ekin Holmstad, "Cigarettes linked to reduced risk of Parkinson's." *Milwaukee Journal Sentinel*, June 17, 1995. At www.smokers.org/research/alzheimer/03-cigarettes—parkinsons.html. Also Associated Press, "Parkinson's Drugs May Lessen Nicotine's Effect." *The Washington Post*, February 22, 1996, p. A15; Doug Levy, "Linking Smoking, Lower Parkinson's Risk." *USA Today*, February 22, 1996, p. D1. Sources courtesy of The Advocacy Institute.

89. Warren E. Leary, "Brain Chemical Said to Play Role in Cigarette Addiction." *The New York Times*, February 22, 1996, p. 22.

90. Amanda Husted, "Report links dopamine, personality." *The Atlanta Journal-Constitution*, February 13, 1997, p. E2.

91. Amanda Husted, "Study: Nicotine patch may alleviate ulcerative colitis." *The Atlanta Journal-Constitution*, May 24, 1994, p. C4.

92. American Smokers Alliance, "Behind the smoke screen." At www.smokers.org/research/alzheimer/01-behind_screen.html.

93. G. Mathé, "Cancer versus Alzheimer risks: Health is not moral." Institute de Cancerologie et d'Immunolgie, Hospital Suisse de Paris. Posted on the Internet by American Smokers Alliance at www.smokers.org/research/alheimer/02-cancer_v_alzheimers.html.

94. "Alzheimer's Disease: The Real Plague." Fact sheet from the Freedom Organisation for the Right to Enjoy Smoking Tobacco (FOREST). Posted on the Internet by American Smokers Alliance at www.smokers.org/research/alzheimer/04-fact_sheet.html.

95. G. Mathé, op. cit.

96. Holmstad, op. cit.

97. Mundell, op. cit. A similar situation exists with "Schedule II" drugs such as morphine. So great is the stigma attached to the narcotic drugs, and the fear surrounding them, that many people are suffering needless pain because their doctors underprescribe them or don't prescribe them at all, lest their patients become addicted or the doctors get into trouble with federal and state drug watchdogs. See Jacob Sullum, "No Relief in Sight." *Reason*, January 1997, p. 22. Stigma and fear have also hindered investigation into the possible medicinal uses of marijuana.

98. Gil Lawson, "Kentucky research institute seeks new tobacco uses." *The Louisville Courier-Journal*, February 22, 1995. From Mercury Center on the Internet.

99. Amal Kumar Naj, "Tobacco Plant in Lab Tests Produces A Medicine Used in Gaucher's Disease." *The Wall Street Journal*, October 3, 1995, p. B8. Courtesy of The Advocacy Institute.

100. Anne Rochell, "Watercress may block nicotine risk." *The Atlanta Journal-Constitution*, March 27, 1996, p. A13.

101. Eric Ringham, "Death by Inhalation." *The Atlanta Journal-Constitution*, March 30, 1994, p. A15. From *The* (Minneapolis-St. Paul) *Star Tribune*.

102. Dawson, op. cit.

103. Jane G. Gravelle, Dennis Zimmerman, "Cigarette Taxes to Fund Health Care Reform: An Economic Analysis." CRS Report for Congress 94214E, March 8, 1994, pp. 17-20.

104. Mack A. Moore, "No excuses: Kick the tobacco habit in a few easy steps." *The Atlanta Journal-Constitution*, May 27, 1996, p. A15.

105. Bill Hendrick and Amanda Husted, "High self-esteem can make quitting smoking harder." *The Atlanta Journal-Constitution*, January 27, 1997, p. C7.

106. *Archives of Family Medicine* (1997;6:67-71). Posted on Reuters Health Line January 28, 1997, at www.reutershealth.com/news/rhdn/100701/1997012808.html.

107. Ernest Dichter, "Why Do We Smoke Cigarettes?" *The Psychology of Everyday Living* (New York: Barnes & Noble, Inc., 1947), pp. 86-99.

108. "Dear Abby." *The Atlanta Journal-Constitution*, May 17, 1993, p. C2.

109. Phil Kloer, "Smoking Is A Puff of Pleasure Amid A Cloud of Smoke." *The Atlanta Journal-Constitution*, January 17, 1995, p. B1.

Chapter 5

THE FOUR-HUNDRED-THOUSAND-PEOPLE QUESTION

The great masses of the people . . . will more easily fall victims to a great lie than to a small one.

— Adolph Hitler[1]

One of the most startling differences between a cat and a lie is that a cat has only nine lives.

— Mark Twain[2]

I do not mind lying, but I hate inaccuracy.

— Samuel Butler[3]

IT MAY SEEM EXTREME to lead off a chapter in which I intend to examine the second most outrageous lie that has ever been said about smoking*—that it kills 400,000 (or more) Americans a year—with a quotation from one of the worst murderers of truth, as well as of human beings, who ever polluted the earth (although Hitler was also an avid hater of tobacco). Because a lie is a *deliberate* falsehood, it may also seem unfair to the many nonsmokers who in all sincerity repeat what they believe is the truth. But as for the more prominent leaders of the anti-smoking movement who ought to know better, one can only conclude that either they are capable of infinite self-persuasion about the perils of smoking or that much of their propaganda does indeed consist of intentional lies, or what I have called "pious falsehoods." By virtue of their promulgating and operating upon those lies, it is not without

*In terms of its baleful effects on human social intercourse in late 20th-century America, the Number One outrageous lie is the one about the danger of secondhand smoke, which is the subject of the next three chapters.

basis that they have been called "health fascists." In fact, if we believe the numbers of people they claim have been killed, are being killed and will eventually be killed by tobacco, the toll makes Der Fuehrer look like a chump.

For example, according to Dr. H. Nakajima, M.D., Ph.D., Director-General of the World Health Organization (WHO): "Since the middle of the twentieth century, tobacco products have killed more than 60 million people in developed countries alone. In another three decades, unless the trend changes drastically, we can expect about 10 million people to be killed each year by tobacco products, with 70% of these deaths occurring in developing countries." He adds that "the risks of tobacco use are underestimated[!] by the public, and even by many of those who are responsible for protecting and promoting public health."[4]

If so, maybe a doubling of his numbers, which could readily be done simply by forming one's lips and uttering them, would get more people to pay attention. Sixty million, schmixty million—it's all pulled out of a hat anyway.

In the meantime, according to another authority, "Nearly nine million people, mostly infants and children, die each year from diseases associated with impure water."[5] Even if this figure is also inflated, even if it may be only a few million deaths around the world due to impure water, these are *actual* deaths, not somebody's guess about how many people—adults, not children—might die from smoking three decades from now. But it is smoking that exercises the director-general.

I discuss numerous other lies (or to put it most generously, "inaccuracies") in this book. But the Hitlerian great lie I want to deal with in this chapter, a lie that has become firmly entrenched in the popular mind and is endlessly repeated, is: *"Smoking kills 400,000 Americans a year."* A more popular variation is: *". . . more than 400,000 Americans a year."*

When did this lie first appear? The earliest clipping I have that mentions it dates to 1991, in an article in *The Washington Post*,[6] which stated that according to the Centers for Disease Control and Prevention (CDC), "more than 434,000 Americans died in 1988 from health problems caused by smoking." This was an 11 percent increase over the 1985 total, said the article, and constituted one-fifth of deaths from all causes, including, presumably, old age and simple wearing out.

The article further explained that the 434,000 figure was calculated using 1988 death rates from illnesses "for which smoking is a well-established risk factor" combined with 1988 smoking rates for men and women according to race and age group. The figure included deaths from various cancers, heart disease, high blood pressure, stroke and lung disease, as well as burn deaths and infant deaths allegedly caused by mothers smoking during pregnancy.

It also included (exactly) 3,825 deaths caused by "passive smoking" (secondhand smoke) and would have been higher except that the CDC chose to include only passive-smoking deaths from lung cancer but not from heart disease because "the link between passive smoking and heart disease has been less extensively documented." (As for just how "extensively documented" the link between passive smoking and lung cancer is, see Chapter 6.)

Thus the CDC emphasized that the new figure represented the "minimum" number of deaths caused by smoking. "This is a conservative estimate," said then director William Roper. "We believe the real numbers are higher."

Think about it, he said. "Eleven Marines died in a fight in the [Persian] gulf. [Actually, it was in Somalia—D.O.] That's a terrible tragedy people have on their minds. Think about almost half a million people who died in 1988 due to smoking. These are real people who died needlessly . . . Somehow, we don't seem to make the same connection."[7]

How many "real" people Roper's figure represented I'll look at later. But notice how easily 434,000 is rounded off—upwards—to "almost half a million." And ah, people, especially those in the media, did quickly make the connection. The 400,000 (or whatever) figure was, as I said, to be repeated endlessly in the coming years. Most of the following examples are from *The Atlanta Journal-Constitution* (AJC) because that is the newspaper I read every day, but they could be multiplied by similar examples that could be cited from any of the country's newspapers and news syndicates, not to mention TV and radio news programs and the many antismoking sites on the Internet.

In 1992:

"Tobacco use is blamed for 500,000 annual premature deaths."[8] (This was from a report by the Associated Press, which did not give its source for that figure, so I don't know who is responsible for improving on Roper's "almost" 500,000.)

In 1993:

"Smoking caused more than 400,000 deaths in 1990, according to the Centers for Disease Control and Prevention."[9]

In 1995:

". . . smoking-related illnesses that kill more than 400,000 people in this country annually."[10]

Now the tempo begins to step up (or maybe it's just that I was becoming more conscientious about collecting newspaper stories and Internet downloads).

In 1996:

"Smoking is directly linked to over 400,000 deaths due to cancer, stroke and cardiovascular disease every year in the U.S."[11]

"The latest reading of the leaves looks good for those of us who would like to see the wilting of an industry whose product, when used as intended, *kills more than 400,000 Americans each year and harms millions more."*[12] ["Intended" emphasized in original.]

". . . a product that kills an estimated 400,000 Americans per year."[13]

". . . you have tens of millions of people who smoke, you have 400,000 a year who die from it . . . "[14]

"Some 400,000 Americans die of smoking-related illnesses each year."[15]

". . . a $50 billion industry . . . causing the deaths of more than 400,000 Americans per year."[16]

"Couldn't somebody make the argument that this [nicotine] *is a drug that doesn't do anybody good, and kills 400,000 people a year, then you must prohibit all sales, outright?"*[17]

". . . an industry whose product kills more than 400,000 Americans a year . . ."[18]

Finally, just one from 1997:

" . . . the tobacco industry kills almost 500,000 Americans each year. This includes more than 50,000 nonsmokers; more than those who are killed by vehicle accidents, all crimes (including guns), AIDS, and illegal drugs."[19]

Five hundred thousand is such a nice round figure, and "almost 500,000" is almost as nice. The last citation is from Action on Smoking and Health (ASH), which gleefully reports, and elaborates on, any bad news (or fabricated bad news) about smoking. Even so, the inclusion of 50,000 deaths of innocent nonsmokers from "secondhand smoke" is quite an inflation of the CDC's already inflated 3,825. ASH no doubt got it from prominent antismoking activist Stanton Glantz, who is "credited" with the figure of 50,000 second-hand smoke deaths.*

Among the most convinced believers in that 400,000-a-year smoking deaths figure (or somewhere in that ballpark, give or take a few tens of thousands) are those twin sisters of empathy and advice, Abigail Van Buren and Ann Landers. They can be counted on to remind readers of this tragic toll every time they comment on a letter about smoking, and always on the anniversary of the "Great American Smokeout" each November.

In 1993, answering a request from the president of the American Cancer Society to alert her readers that it's Smokeout time again, Abby says, "I'll do it gladly . . . Tobacco claims one life every 13 seconds. An estimated 149,000 will die of lung cancer in 1993 . . . [E]mphysema, chronic bronchitis and heart disease. This year an estimated 424,000 will die from one of these."[21]

One hundred forty-nine thousand smoking-caused deaths from lung cancer plus another 424,000 smoking-caused deaths from emphysema, chronic bronchitis and heart disease add up to 573,000 dead smokers in one year, well over Roper's "almost half a million" and the Associated Press's full half million. That's some ballpark! But something doesn't quite compute. There are 31,536,000 seconds in a year. If one smoker dies every 13 seconds, slightly over 2,425,846 smokers should have died in 1993, which would have been more than the total of deaths from *all* causes that year in the United States. Abby must have been referring to the worldwide smoking death rate, although that is usually given as one death every 10 seconds. Where she came up with one every 13 seconds I have no way of knowing and it's not important except that she doesn't tell her readers that this is the (alleged) smoking

*According to Joe Dawson, Glantz arrived at this figure by starting with the fact that some one million Americans die each year from heart disease. He then "reasoned" that if the fatty arterial buildup claimed by researchers to be attributable to environmental tobacco smoke was only one-20th as thick as that required to cause a heart attack, then it must be producing a 20th of the total heart attacks, or 50,000 of them. "This is like saying that if a million people cross a body of water 10 feet deep and 100,000 of them drown, then 1,000 would drown if the water were an inch deep," comments Dawson.[20]

death rate for *the entire world*, not the United States. (How many people bothered to check her statement with a calculator?) I'm sure she wouldn't intentionally mislead her readers, but it's a rather careless bandying about of statistics, to say the least.

A reader asks Ann: "How can I get my loved ones to stop smoking? We are shocked by a disaster such as the earthquake in Japan or a tragic airline crash. But I cannot understand why, when 419,000 people die each year from smoking, it is accepted as 'inevitable.'" Ann lets the writer's number stand without correction or comment, saying only, "Smoking is an addiction. Some say that tobacco is harder to kick than heroin."[22]

In 1994, answering a request from the president of the Illinois chapter of the American Cancer Society to remind her readers that it's Smokeout time again, Abby, updating her 1993 column, tells us: "An estimated 157,000 people will die of lung cancer in 1995. Tobacco claims one life every 13 seconds . . . [E]mphysema, chronic bronchitis and heart disease. This year, an estimated 435,000 will die from one of these."[23]

Now in only two years we're up to a total of 592,000 dead smokers, an increase of 19,000 over 1993. (I don't know what happened to 1994.) Abby does again use the qualifying word "estimated" and only a cynic would suggest that she's either playing rather fast and loose with numbers or giving little thought to what she's actually saying. But note also that while this is the *total* of estimated deaths that will (allegedly) occur from these diseases in 1995, Abby leaves her readers to infer that each and every one will be due to smoking. She's also still citing that 13 deaths-per-second figure as if it applied to the United States.

Just one year later, though, the smoking death toll has inexplicably shrunk by no less than 142,000! Asked again by the Illinois ACS to remind her readers that it's Smokeout time again, Abby writes: "An estimated 450,000 Americans will die from smoking-related diseases in 1996. That means tobacco will claim 51 lives every hour in the United States. An estimated 158,700 of them will die from lung cancer."[24]

A decline in smoking-related deaths of 142,000 in one year (subtracting 450,000 in 1996 from 592,000 in 1995) sounds like good news to me, which Abby would have realized if she had bothered to dig up her 1994 column. It's also *fantastically* good news that the smoker death rate is down to only 51 lives every hour—or roughly one death every seventy seconds—although this still yields the unprovably high figure of 446,760 annual smoking-caused (or "related") deaths in the United States. Abby didn't mention emphysema, chronic bronchitis and heart disease this time, but since lung cancer deaths were predicted to increase by 1,700 over the previous year (158,700 in 1996 vs.157,000 in 1995), that suggests that deaths from these other diseases would be reduced by some 140,300 in 1996. (I get that by taking 592,000 total "smoking-related" deaths in 1995, subtracting 450,000 total "smoking-related" deaths in 1996, then adding 1,700 additional "smoking-related" lung cancer deaths in 1996). Wasn't that more good news?

Incidentally, as for lung cancer deaths, Abby never says whether the figures she cites include nonsmokers. A conservative estimate is that some 10 percent of lung cancers occur in nonsmokers but she leaves the impression that the figures apply to smokers only. I'm sure she doesn't know or even thought to inquire if the estimates also include nonsmokers. If so, she shouldn't be repeating statistics she hasn't looked at closely. (Not that it really matters of course; you can always blame a nonsmoker's lung cancer on secondhand smoke.)

I've picked on Abby and Ann not only because millions of people are faithful readers of their columns but by way of illustrating how ridiculous and meaningless are the smoking-death statistics Americans are bombarded with and how uncritically they are accepted by intelligent people. Abigail Van Buren and Ann Landers may be excused their gullibility; they merely repeat in good faith what the supposed experts tell them, and anyway the actual figures apparently don't matter to them—it's the thought that counts! But even such a knowledgeable writer as Michael Fumento, who has done, and continues to do, yeoman work in exposing the fallacies behind supposed environmental perils as well as the motives of those who promote them, casually repeats the "400,000-a-year" lie.

In his book *Science Under Siege*, which I draw upon in Chapter 11, Fumento refers in one passage to ". . . smoking/tobacco health risks, known to cause several hundred thousand deaths per year . . ."[25] After I read the book I found his e-mail address in *Reason* magazine, to which he contributes frequent and valuable articles, and sent him a message expressing my "disappointment" in that statement, especially since the rest of his book was so well-researched and documented.

He replied: "You're probably right about the 400,000 figure being very amorphous and too high. Whether it's AIDS infections or cancer deaths from smoking, all of these things are politically influenced. On the other hand, the figure is probably as good as any and the point is made, even were it, say, 250,000."[26]

I e-mailed him again, telling him that I was writing a book about smoking and planned to quote from his reply, italicizing "*the figure is probably as good as any and the point is made, even were it, say, 250,000.*" I asked him if he was happy with that sentence as it stood. I said that it sounded very much like something Marc Lalonde or Stanton Glantz would say to justify the propagation of dubious, if not wholly false, antismoking statistics. Again he was good enough to reply:

> Mr. Oakley: You're right, that last line did come out a bit Glantzish. What I meant was that while the 400,000 [figure] is undoubtedly the highest figure they could possibly justify, a more accurate number—were it ascertainable—would probably be lower. I say this based not on medicine but on knowledge of the way the political process works. That said, I think it is also clear that the number of smoking-related deaths is probably extremely high, with "extremely" probably making it the leading cause of self-induced death. In other words, I don't think there's any policy difference between 250,000 deaths a year and 400,000 in this case. Also, keep in mind that the 250,000 figure is something I pulled out of a hat. I don't want anybody citing me as a source for that being mine or anybody else's estimate.— Mike Fumento[27]

Okay, Mike, I'll emphasize that: you did *not* state as a fact that smoking causes 250,000 deaths a year. You *couldn't* have, for the simple reason that neither you nor I nor anybody else has a clue in the world as to how many people smoking may actually kill.

Fumento was not writing about smoking in *Science Under Siege* and seized on that 400,000 figure only to argue that deaths allegedly caused by poisons in the environment are insignificant in comparison to a real, "proven" peril like smoking. But the unfortunate fact is that most people don't distinguish—indeed, are not aware that there *is* anything to distinguish—between "politically influenced" statistics and truthful statistics, especially in regard to smoking, where they have been primed to accept anything and everything bad that is reported about the "deadly" habit. My wife, for instance, who after smoking heavily for half her life is a very youthful and healthy woman in her 80s, pretty much believes everything the activists and crusaders say about smoking but is not impressed by the opposing arguments I offer. Most people, however much they may distrust their elected officials, still place great faith in the folks who work in the various government agencies charged with looking out for the general health and welfare. These are, after all, dedicated public servants and not the bought-off minions of deceitful corporations with self-serving axes to grind. The same holds true for those in the medical and healthcare and public-advocacy fields. Why would they ever lie to us?

To most people that 400,000 figure is absolute, gospel truth. But while most people would not see the "policy difference" between that number and any other number that might be tossed up, it *would* be vastly significant to them if a more accurate figure for smoking-caused deaths—"were it ascertainable"—turned out to be 250,000 instead of 400,000. What if it was actually 200,000 or 100,000? What if it was even lower? What if, in fact, it was far, far lower? (One would hope that healthcare professionals at least, if not the policymakers, would also be intensely interested in a more accurate figure but, alas, the hope would be in vain.)

As for making the "point" that smoking is (probably) the leading cause of self-induced death, does that mean that any old figure is justified, so long as it makes people sit up and take notice (because, of course, it's "for their own good")? Shouldn't the "point" be the truth? How do we know that smoking is, or may be, the leading cause of self-induced death if we really *don't know* how many people are actually killed by smoking and not only that, really have *no way* of knowing?

Antismoking activists are not the only ones who inundate the public with frightening pseudostatistics that bear little relation to reality; health activists, in and out of government—yes, even our trusted civil servants—do the same thing. For only one example, in a 1975 broadcast of the CBS Evening News, anchorman Dan Rather informed his millions of viewers that "The news tonight is that the United States is number one in cancer. The National Cancer Institute estimates that if you're living in America your chances of getting cancer are higher than anywhere in the world."[28]

This was nothing but a purely political statement that someone, unidentified, at the NCI had fed to the media. The truth was that the United States was then, and doubtless still is, one of the healthiest nations in the world in terms of cancer. According to a 1973 study of 35 industrialized nations, which was the best *nonpolitically influenced* estimate that had been made up to the time of the NCI release, the U.S. ranking was eighth for black Americans and 24th for white Americans.[29] Later estimates by the World Health Organization placed the United States, in 1977, 18th in cancer mortality out of 44 nations, both industrialized and semi-industrialized, and, in 1979, 22nd out of 44 nations.[30] (I don't trust anything WHO says about the "global tobacco epidemic" but in this case it would have no reason to jiggle with cancer statistics to make any particular country look good, or bad.)

This information never made a headline or a news broadcast. It is not the "sexy"—i.e., alarming—kind of story that sells papers or enhances ratings. As for the NCI's motive in publicizing that particular lie, caring bureaucrats apparently believe that their mission is to do everything they can to guard Americans from lulling themselves into a false sense of security with the idea that they are *not* surrounded by and immersed in all kinds of cancer-causing perils and are *not* dropping like flies. If that requires feeding the public unfounded and exaggerated statistics, well, it just has to be done; it is, after all, "in a good cause." (Again, only a cynic would suggest that this kind of numbers game played by the bureaucrats also just happens to magnify their importance and indispensability in guarding the public weal and helps persuade Congress to increase their budgets.)

Rarely do those who disseminate inflated statistics to "make a point" admit to their motives. One exception, however, involved a claim by the Atlanta Task Force for the Homeless that 188 people died in homeless shelters or in hospital emergency rooms or out on the city's streets in 1991. When the Centers for Disease Control and Prevention, which doesn't like anybody else butting into the business of putting out phony figures, looked into the claim, the Task Force could produce only 37 death certificates. A "clarification" by Adam Fuerstein, spokesman for the group, has to be admired for its ingenuousness: "I don't think we ever say for sure that ours is the exact number of homeless deaths. We're doing it mainly as a political statement."[31]

SO JUST WHERE *does* that 400,000 (or whatever) figure come from? The proximate source is the August 27, 1993 Morbidity and Mortality Weekly Report (MMWR) published by the Centers for Disease Control and

Prevention, which compiled statistics for smoking-attributable deaths in the United States in 1990 from data provided by state health departments.* At the time of this writing (1998) it still remains the most recent such report. (I reproduce the table from it on page 246.) But how does the CDC arrive at its calculations from those state reports? At least one enterprising reporter, Nickie McWhirter of *The Detroit News*, tried to find out. Her article was posted on the Internet by the American Smokers Alliance. She wrote:

> I recently read that 435,000 Americans die every year from smoking-related illnesses. That sounds like a rock-hard, irrefutable fact, and pretty scary. How are such statistics determined? I phoned the American Lung Association's Southfield office to find out.
>
> No one there seemed to know. However, a friendly voice said most such numbers come from the National Center for Health Statistics. That's a branch of the National Centers for Disease Control. The friendly voice provided a phone number in New York City.
>
> Wrong number. The New York office collects only morbidity [the rate of occurrence of a disease] data, I was told. I needed mortality data [the death rate].
>
> Several bureaucratically misdirected calls later, I spoke with someone in Statistical Resources at NCHS. He said his office collects mortality based on death certificates. Progress! Data is categorized by race, sex, age, geographic location, he said, but not smoking. Never. No progress.
>
> He suggested I phone the Office of Smoking and Health, Rockville, Md., and provided a number. That phone had been disconnected.
>
> Was I discouraged? No! Ultimately, and several unfruitful phone calls later, I found a government information officer in Washington, D.C., with a relatively new phone directory and a helpful attitude. She found a listing for the elusive Office on Smoking and Health in Atlanta.†

*The MMWRs deal with far more than smoking statistics, of course. For instance, the August 27, 1993 report also included an investigation of toxic effects in three children who ingested tablets of Jin Bu Huan, a Chinese herbal medicine, in Colorado in 1993, and surveillance for cholera in the Department of Cocabamba, Bolivia, from January to June 1992.

†Part of the Centers for Disease Control and Prevention and not to be confused with Action on Smoking and Health (ASH), the antismoking group founded and led by Washington lawyer John Banzhaf.

Bingo! Noel Barith, public information officer, said the 435,000 figure probably came from its computers. S&H generates lots of statistics concerning "smoking-related" stuff, he said. It's all done according to a formula programmed into the computers.

Really? Since I had already determined that no lifestyle data on individual patients and their medical histories is ever collected, how can the computer possibly decide deaths are smoking related? Barith didn't know. Maybe the person who devised this computer program knows. Barith promised to have a computer expert return my call.

The next day, SAMMEC Operations Manager, Richard Lawton, phoned. SAMMEC, I learned, is the name of the computer program. Its initials stand for Smoking Attributed Morbidity, Mortality and Economic Cost.

The computer is fed raw data and SAMMEC employs various complex mathematical formulas to determine how many people in various age groups, locations, and heaven knows what other categories are likely to get sick or die from what diseases and how many of these can be assumed to be smoking related.

Assumed? This is all guesswork? Sort of. Lawton confirmed that no real people, living or dead, are studied, no doctors consulted, no environmental factors considered.

Lawton was absolutely lyrical about SAMMEC and its capabilities, however, provided one can feed it appropriate SAFs. What are SAFs?

"That's the smoking attributable fraction for each disease or group of people studied," he said. It sounded like handicapping horses. Lawton began to explain how to arrive at an SAF, using an equation that reminded me of Miss Foster's algebra class.

"Wait a minute!" I commanded. "I don't need to know that. I need to know if the SAFs and all the rest of this procedure yield valid, factual information. To know that we must know if sometime, somewhere, some human being or human beings actually looked at records of other human beings, smokers and nonsmokers, talked to their doctors, gathered enough information from reality to BEGIN to devise a mathematical formula that MIGHT be applied to large groups of people much later, without ever needing to study those people, and could be expected to yield TRUE FACTS within a reasonable margin of error. Who did that? Can you tell me, Mr. SAMMEC expert?" [Caps in original.]

Nice guy, Mr. Lawton, but he didn't have a clue. He said he thought the original work concerning real people, their deaths and evidence of smoking involvement was part of work done by a couple of epidemiologists, A.M. and D.E. Lilienfield. It's all in a book titled *Foundations of Epidemiology*, published about 1980 by

> Oxford University Press, he said. SAMMEC came later, based on the Lilienfield's [*sic*] work. Maybe. He wasn't sure.
>
> I was unable to find the book, or the Lilienfields.
>
> So there you have it. Research shall continue, but so far it has only revealed that no one churning out statistics knows anything about smoking and its relationship, if any, to diseases and death. A computer knows everything, based on mystical formulas of unknown origin, content and reliability. Raw data in, startling statistics out. SAMMEC speaks, truth is revealed! Oh, brave new world.
>
> Are there 435,000 smoking-related deaths per year in America? Maybe. I can tell you this with absolute certainty, however: No human beings are ever studied to find out.[32]

In an editorial in *Modern Pathology*, the official journal of the U.S. and Canadian Academy of Pathology, editor Bernard Wagner, M.D. commented on McWhirter's article:

> I continue to be amazed and amused at the numbers thrown around regarding causes of death. Now that everybody has a computer, the name of the game is "What can we feed it?" The old axion [*sic*] "GIGO"—garbage in, garbage out—seems to be lost as the complexities and wonders of computation overwhelm us. The incredible need to quantify everything in life, from what you think to what you eat, continues to engulf us. Does anyone notice we may be drowning in a sea of quantified nonsense? Well, Nickie McWhirter, a reporter for the Detroit News does, and her experience poses a lesson for those who cherish numbering things.

The editorial then reprinted McWhirter's article in almost its entirety, after which Dr. Wagner concluded:

"Pathologists are constantly quoting statistics as regards cause of death. The next time you do, ask yourself this question, 'Where and how were the numbers obtained?'"[33]

Would that there were more medical mavericks like Dr. Wagner. As for *Foundations of Epidemiology*, by Abraham M. and David E. Lilienfield, it does exist; it is in the Library of Congress Catalog under Call Number RA 651.L54 1980. Whether it would be worth anyone's while to obtain a copy and read it is problematic.

Pending such an endeavor, let's look at the smoking-related diseases Ms. McWhirter learned were the meat that SAMMEC feeds on. The CDC has identified 27 of them. The list below is from the State of Maryland's Tobacco Page on the Internet:[34]

Cancers:

Lip, Oral
Esophagus
Pancreas
Larynx
Trachea, Lung, Bronchus
Uterine Cervix
Urinary Bladder
Kidney, Other Urinary

Cardiovascular Diseases:

Ischemic Heart Disease
Pulmonary Heart Disease
Aetherosclerosis
Aortic Aneurysm
Cerebral Vascular Disease
Pulmonary Heart Disease
Rheumatic Heart Disease
Other Heart Disease
Other Arterial Disease

Respiratory Diseases

Asthma
Respiratory Tuberculosis
Bronchitis/Emphysema
Pneumonia/Influenza
Chronic Airways Obstruction
Respiratory Distress Syndrome
Respiratory Condition Newborn

Other:

SIDS (Sudden Infant Death Syndrome)
Low Birth Weight
Burn Deaths

I have attempted to rationalize the list, which was presented in rather haphazard fashion, by placing the entries in what would seem to be their obvious categories. (For those I put under "Cancers," the source merely named the organs and I have assumed that cancer is the chief disease they are prone to, although I'm sure there are other diseases or infections that qualify as "Urinary Bladder" or "Kidney, Other Urinary." I don't think it really makes much difference for propaganda purposes.) I discuss a number of these "smoking-related" diseases at various places in this book, some of which, it must be admitted, appeal to one's common sense as being possibly caused by or related to or aggravated by smoking. This is especially true of the respiratory diseases. For some of the others, however, such as rheumatic heart diseases, which is caused by a bacterial infection and usually occurs in children, imputing a causative association with smoking requires great imagination combined with a basic prejudice against smoking..

Any way you slice it, this is one hell of a roster of diseases and afflictions (plus one type of accident) that are "related" or "attributable" to smoking. Did the CDC miss any? The terms "*Other* Urinary," "*Other* Heart Disease" and "*Other* Arterial Disease" would seem to cover any possible loopholes.

Is there *any* ailment that human flesh is heir to that *isn't* "smoking-related"? Well, there may be two at least—stomach cancer and gastric ulcers. According to another source:

> Smoking was falsely blamed for ulcers and stomach cancer actually caused by *Helicobacter pylori* infection. Smoking supposedly caused from two to five times greater risk of these diseases, and the anti-smokers concocted theories that smoking increased stomach acid to cause ulcers, and produced supposed "evidence" of this, and invoked carcinogens in cigarette smoke for stomach cancer. But ulcers and stomach cancer were recently ever-so-quietly removed from the Centers for Disease Control's list of so-called "smoking attributable" diseases. They didn't wish to publicly discuss the reasons.[35]

Readers unsympathetic toward smoking may dismiss this because it was published on the World Wide Web by the American Smokers Alliance,* a "smokers' rights" organization. However, there would re-

*Both the ASA and the NSA (National Smokers Alliance) were initially created with help from the tobacco industry, although they are now mainly supported by members' dues. If this renders them suspect, it should be remembered that the antismoking industry is crucially dependent upon a sector that has little say in where its money goes: the public. Antismoking groups like the American Cancer Society and the American Lung Association as well as individual researchers receive tens of millions of dollars in grants from such federal agencies as the Centers for Disease Control and the Environmental Protection Agency, which are themselves of course tax-funded. Stanton Glantz's book, *The Cigarette Papers*, was made possible by a grant to his employer, the University of California. (It should really be called *The Purloined Cigarette Papers* since it consists of stolen internal Brown and Williamson Company documents passed to Glantz by a "Mr. Butts.") In California and Massachusetts, smokers pay for the very propaganda that is used against them in the form of a surtax on cigarettes, which raises millions of dollars that various antismoking groups scramble for. Every other smokers' rights group I know of is entirely supported by private individuals, including some nonsmokers who distrust Big Brother more than they dislike smoking.

main the question of why stomach cancer and ulcers are *not* on the CDC's list when just about everything else imaginable is. (Of course, antismokers can still argue that smoking "probably" encourages and assists this bug in its work.)

For a long time the medical establishment pooh-poohed the idea that ulcers were caused by a bacterium. Today *Helicobacter pylori* is recognized as "the leading cause of chronic gastritis and peptic ulcer disease and a primary risk factor for gastric adenocarcinoma" and "is one of the most prevalent infections of humankind."[36] As noted in Chapter 3, it is now implicated in heart disease as well.

As for those diseases, ailments, afflictions and one accident still on the CDC's list, the Maryland Tobacco Page explains that each of them has a risk relative to smoking called, appropriately, the relative risk, or RR. An RR is the ratio at which smokers and former smokers allegedly die from a smoking-related disease compared to those who never smoked. RR estimates applied to smoking prevalence (smoking rates, wherever they are derived from) result in the smoking attributable fraction, or SAF. Then, as Ms. McWhirter was told, the SAFs are used by SAMMEC to calculate mortality, mortality costs, years of potential life lost (YPLL), morbidity costs and healthcare costs (the latter which you, the innocent nonsmoking taxpayer, are forced to shoulder because smokers are getting a free ride—never mind the billions in tobacco taxes they pay, never mind the personal health insurance premiums they pay, never mind the money they save Medicare and social security by dying early, as the medical profession says they do, and never mind that nonsmokers also sometimes get sick).

But now the question is: where do the relative risks—the RRs—come from? Which brings us back to the CDC's August 27, 1993 Morbidity and Mortality Weekly Report. (Apparently the SAMs—Smoking Attributable Mortality figures—are what SAMMEC regurgitates after it's fed the SAFs—Smoking Attributable Fractions.)

I have reproduced the MMWR on the next page in reduced size. For those who may be interested, this MMWR, as well as others dating back to 1993, are available for viewing or downloading in Adobe Acrobat Portable Document File (PDF) full-page format at the CDC's Website at www.cdc.gov/epo/mmwr/mmwr.html.

In an Internet posting by San Francisco-based FORCES, Martha Perkse examined this MMWR and made the following comments:

Cigarette Smoking — Continued

TABLE 1. Relative risks* (RR) for death attributed to smoking and smoking-attributable mortality (SAM) for current and former smokers, by disease category and sex — United States, 1990

	Male			Female			
	RR			RR			
Disease category (ICD-9 code)†	Current smokers	Former smokers	SAM	Current smokers	Former smokers	SAM	Total SAM
Adult diseases (persons aged ≥35 yrs)							
Neoplasms							
Lip, oral cavity, pharynx (140–149)	27.5	8.8	5,033	5.6	2.9	1,442	**6,475**
Esophagus (150)	7.6	5.8	5,668	10.3	3.2	1,616	**7,284**
Pancreas (157)	2.1	1.1	2,667	2.3	1.8	3,447	**6,114**
Larynx (161)	10.5	5.2	2,379	17.8	11.9	611	**2,990**
Trachea, lung, bronchus (162)	22.4	9.4	81,179	11.9	4.7	35,741	**116,920**
Cervix uteri (180)	NA§	NA	NA	2.1	1.9	1,294	**1,294**
Urinary bladder (188)	2.9	1.9	3,046	2.6	1.9	980	**4,026**
Kidney, other urinary (189)	3.0	2.0	2,866	1.4	1.2	353	**3,219**
Cardiovascular diseases							
Hypertension (401–404)	1.9	1.3	3,299	1.7	1.2	2,151	**5,450**
Ischemic heart disease (410–414)							
Persons aged 35–64 yrs	2.8	1.8	26,431	3.0	1.4	7,701	**34,132**
Persons aged ≥65 yrs	1.6	1.3	38,918	1.6	1.3	25,871	**64,789**
Other heart diseases (390–398, 415–417, 420–429)	1.9	1.3	23,295	1.7	1.2	12,019	**35,314**
Cerebrovascular diseases (430–438)							
Persons aged 35–64 yrs	3.7	1.4	4,557	4.8	1.4	4,114	**8,671**
Persons aged ≥65 yrs	1.9	1.3	10,421	1.5	1.0	4,189	**14,610**
Atherosclerosis (440)	4.1	2.3	3,737	3.0	1.3	2,675	**6,412**
Aortic aneurysm (441)	4.1	2.3	5,913	3.0	1.3	1,382	**7,295**
Other arterial disease (442–448)	4.1	2.3	2,032	3.0	1.3	1,115	**3,147**
Respiratory diseases							
Pneumonia and influenza (480–487)	2.0	1.6	11,292	2.2	1.4	7,881	**19,173**
Bronchitis, emphysema (491–492)	9.7	8.8	9,324	10.5	7.0	5,541	**14,865**
Chronic airway obstruction (496)	9.7	8.8	30,385	10.5	7.0	18,597	**48,982**
Other respiratory diseases (010–012, 493)	2.0	1.6	787	2.2	1.4	668	**1,455**
Pediatric diseases (persons aged <1 yr)							
Short gestation, low birth weight (765)	1.8		285	1.8		222	**507**
Respiratory distress syndrome (769)	1.8		219	1.8		141	**360**
Other respiratory conditions of newborn (770)	1.8		214	1.8		160	**374**
Sudden infant death syndrome (798)	1.5		288	1.5		182	**470**
Burn deaths ¶			863			499	**1,362**
Environmental tobacco smoke deaths **			1,055			1,945	**3,000**
Total			**276,153**			**142,537**	**418,690**

*Relative to never smokers.
†*International Classification of Diseases, Ninth Revision.*
§Not applicable.
¶Source: National Fire Protection Association, 1993 (*6*).
**Deaths among nonsmokers from lung cancer attributable to environmental tobacco smoke (Environmental Protection Agency, 1992 [*7*]).

(1) The relative risks in the MMWR are based on smoking-related data from an unpublished American Cancer Society study called "Cancer Prevention Study-II" (CPS-II).*

(2) The diseases listed in the MMWR are "known to be caused by or associated with smoking in adults." But "associated with" means "occurs with." It does not imply causality. For instance, according to the Sudden Infant Death Syndrome Alliance, SIDS is associated with being born twins or triplets. This does not mean that being born twins or triplets *causes* SIDS. Likewise, just because some of the diseases listed on the MMWR are associated with smoking (e.g., pneumonia and influenza) does not mean that smoking caused the reported deaths from those diseases.

(3) Almost half the relative risks reported by the MMWR are less than 2. For example, the RRs for Ischemic Heart Disease for persons 65 or older are 1.6 for male current smokers, 1.3 for male former smokers and ditto for female current and former smokers.

(4) CPS-II did not consider confounding factors such as diet, alcohol, occupation, socioeconomic status, etc. The MMWR itself stated that the estimates "in this report are not adjusted for confounders (e.g., alcohol), which may lower the estimates for laryngeal and certain upper gastrointestinal cancers." In other words, if confounders had been considered, the estimates would no doubt have been lower.

Perske quotes Dr. Ernst Wynder of the American Health Foundation, who points out that smokers have a lower intake of fresh fruits and vegetables than nonsmokers, consume more fat and more red meat and have a higher serum cholesterol because of the high fat intake. "[You have] clearly got to think about fat as a confounder to tobacco consumption," he says.

*In its introduction to the MMWR, the CDC says that estimates for adults and infants were based on 1990 mortality data, the 1990 prevalence of smoking among adults, 1989 data on smoking prevalence among pregnant women from the CDC's National Center for Health Statistics, and from "unpublished data." I asked Mrs. Perske about CPS-II. It is a massive ongoing study involving about 1.2 million selected volunteers. According to epidemiologists T. D. Sterling, W. L. Rosenbaum and J. J. Weinkam, the study's participants are unrepresentative of the general population and its figures of lives lost due to smoking are "an illusion."[37] Perske says she has found it impossible to obtain information about the data base used in CPS-II, either from the American Cancer Society or the CDC.[38]

She also quotes Dr. Michael Siegel of the CDC's Office on Smoking and Health, who says that one of the most important things to consider in lung cancer risk is diet.

Finally, she quotes CDC epidemiologist Ann Malarcher, who says that "many factors . . . are causally related to cardiovascular disease . . . They include, but are not limited to, cigarette smoking, hypertension, elevated serum cholesterol, obesity, genetics, diabetes, physical inactivity, socioeconomic status and diet."

"If 'many factors' are causally related to cardiovascular disease, why did the CDC examine just one: smoking?" Perske asks. "And if diet is one of the most important things to consider in lung cancer risk, as Dr. Michael Siegel and others say it is, why did the CDC not consider it? How does the CDC know smoking caused 1,294 deaths from cervical cancer if other factors such as early and frequent intercourse, multiple sexual partners, pregnancy at an early age, and the presence of sexually transmitted diseases (to name a few) were not considered?"[39]

Well, of course, the answer is that the CDC is "making a point," so why confound the public's understanding with "other factors"?

IF NOBODY KNOWS how many, if any, people are being killed by smoking, there is documented evidence that at least one person has been killed by smoking *research*. In 1996, a college student taking part in a study on the effects of smoking and air pollution on the lungs died from an overdose of the anesthetic lidocaine. Hoiyan Wan, a 19-year-old sophomore from New York City had undergone a bronchoscopy at the University of Rochester Medical Center. This is a procedure in which a tube is inserted down the throat and wind pipe to retrieve or study lung cells. "Obviously too much lidocaine was given" to suppress the young woman's cough reflex, said Dr. Jay H. Stein, the medical center's provost for health affairs. An investigation showed twice the acceptable amount of lidocaine in her blood stream.[40]

That unfortunate accident really has nothing to do with the subject of this book or this chapter, of course, but the following, from *The Atlanta Journal-Constitution*'s "Q&A on the News" feature, is more than a little pertinent.

A reader asked: "Why do the Japanese smoke more than Americans, yet have lower rates of lung cancer?" The AJC replied:

> This is but one instance in which commonly held medical advice concerning cause and effect does not hold true statistically in other countries. And there are many studies under way and numerous theories as to why these disparities exist. It has been theorized, for instance, that wine consumption by the French may be why they, despite a diet loaded with saturated fat and serum cholesterol, have a lower rate of heart disease than Americans.
>
> Tea consumption has been called a possible reason for the lower lung cancer rate in Japan. Rutgers University researchers found that drinking green tea at concentrations normally consumed by people blocked up to 87 percent of skin cancers, 58 percent of stomach cancers and 56 percent of lung cancers in mice.
>
> Garlic may also play a part. The largest garlic consumption is in Japan, China and Korea, and studies show they have an entirely different cancer susceptibility than Americans and do not suffer from colon, breast and lung cancer to the extent that Americans do.[41]

In other words, any explanation will do as long as it doesn't exonerate smoking. My explanation as to why smoking is not the "killer" in certain other nations that it is in this country is that these other nations have not (yet) developed the kind of powerful antismoking movement we Americans enjoy. Only in those nations which *do* have strong antismoking movements—chiefly Canada, Great Britain and Australia—is the "havoc" wrought by smoking on a par with that in the United States.

The AJC's answer to the question was reasonably straightforward and factual. Yet in its frequent reiterations of the 400,000 deaths-from-smoking figure, the newspaper has never mentioned the existence of possible confounding factors. As far as its readers are told, all these deaths are due to smoking, and smoking alone. The media as a whole not only accept without critical examination every new allegation or "finding" against smoking but almost never report dissenting views or other research that contradicts or questions these revelations. This is not because of any antismoking conspiracy, I'm sure, but simply because belief in the evils of tobacco has been so ingrained in the media's thinking, as it has in the public's, that any evidence to the contrary is simply not taken seriously. (Also, bad news sells better than good news.)

An example of how quickly antismoking claims become part of the received wisdom was the announcement in late 1996 that scientists had at long last found the "smoking gun"—the precise physical mechanism by which smoking causes lung cancer. (I examined this claim in

Chapter 2.) This immediately became established truth. To quote from the AJC again, in an editorial about new air-quality standards proposed by the Environmental Protection Agency it wrote:

> [Scientists] disagree about how low the standards ought to be because there is no clear line that separates the safe from the unsafe. Scientists are also wary of claiming certainty about the link between pollution and health problems because they don't know how the damage occurs. In a similar case, scientists did not learn until last year exactly how cigarette smoke caused cancer. So for decades, tobacco lobbyists used that loophole to claim that the link between smoking and cancer had not been proved.[42]

Thus did another piece of antismoking propaganda become "common knowledge." The paper's readers have never been informed that the "smoking gun" turned out to be not so hot after all and that the "loophole" remains unfilled.

To digress further, what are we to make of the U.S. surgeon general's 1996 report, *Physical Activity and Health*, which, echoing the warnings on cigarette packages, stated that "Lack of physical activity is detrimental to your health"? The report estimated that 250,000 Americans die prematurely each year due to lack of physical activity. In fact, a sedentary lifestyle, it claimed, was as bad as smoking a pack of cigarettes a day. According to then Acting Surgeon General Audrey F. Manley, M.D., "This report is nothing less than a national call to action. Physical inactivity is a serious nationwide public health problem, but active and healthful lifestyles are well within the grasp of everyone."[43]

Perhaps unbeknownst to Dr. Manley, a couple of concerned academics, both economists, had already called for "action." In their opinion:

> It is somewhat ironic that the government discourages smoking and drinking through taxation, yet when it comes to the major cause of death—heart disease—and its spiraling health-care costs, politicians let us eat with impunity . . .
>
> [W]e should have a progressive tax on the saturated-fat content of food . . .[W]e believe it is time to rethink the extent to which we allow people to impose their negative behavior on those of us who watch our weight, exercise, and try to be as healthy as possible.[44]

Shame, shame, I say, on those politicians who "let us eat with impunity." What do they think we send them to Washington for?

Just how the acting SG knew that inactivity ever killed any one person, let alone is killing a quarter of a million persons every year, is a good question. Because I'm an exercise freak myself, however, this is one case—the *only* case—where I think a surgeon general has talked sense, notwithstanding a certainty that that 250,000 inactivity-deaths figure was plucked out of the same thin air as its 400,000 smoking-deaths counterpart.

This too immediately became established truth and was very quickly buttressed by scientific studies, one of which, published in the *Journal of the American Medical Association* (JAMA), found that "low fitness is a risk factor on the same order as smoking."[45] Men who were most fit—even though they had high blood pressure and high cholesterol and *even though they smoked*—had a 15 percent survival advantage over the least fit who *didn't* smoke. But heaven forbid, this finding should by no means be construed as a license for those who exercise to smoke or eat fatty foods, the study's authors cautioned.

The JAMA article was duly editorialized upon by *The Atlanta Journal-Constitution*, although only in a mildly admonishing tone. It encouraged the potatoes to get up off their couches, but did not call for a national campaign to stigmatize or ostracize them or demand that the makers of snack foods fork over billions of dollars to the states to make up for the medical costs the consumers of their products impose on all us fit people. The surgeon general's report was also seized upon by at least one chain of exercise centers. "Living Without Exercise Is Like Smoking A Pack of Cigarettes A Day," said an ad for Australian Body Works in *Atlanta Sports and Fitness Magazine*,[46] using smoking as a health benchmark again.

A quarter million Americans (another nice round figure) die from lack of exercise? Why aren't we alarmed about this? Why is there no organized anticouch-potato movement? I for one am tired of paying their doctors' bills. Why has not the government launched a massive "intervention" effort or "remedial" actions to get these nonsmoking lazybones off their duffs? Why has not the medical community heeded former Surgeon General C. Everett Koop's impassioned plea that "Physicians can no longer sit on the sidelines as America's obesity epidemic reaches crisis levels"?[47]

It's not as if his is a voice crying in the wilderness of American dietary self-indulgence. At the annual meeting of the American Association for the Advancement of Science in Philadelphia in February 1998, president-elect M.R.C. Greenwood stated that "With as much as 30 percent of the adult population considered to be obese, obesity has, in recent years, become as big a public health hazard as nicotine and smoking." (There they go again.)

He was seconded by Judith Stern, a nutritionist at the University of California-Davis: "We are in the midst of an obesity epidemic that costs us upwards of $100 billion a year, and the toll is increasing. With 5.4 million children now considered to be obese, this should be considered a national emergency."[48]

And no doubt Greenwood was thirded and fourthed by others.

Lazy, overweight nonsmokers: sneer while you can at us socially outcast smokers. Your time is coming.

Interestingly enough, though, a few weeks before the AAAS meeting, an editorial in the prestigious *New England Journal of Medicine* had cautioned that "Although some claim that every year 300,000 deaths in the United States are caused by obesity, that figure is by no means well established. Not only is it derived from weak or incomplete data, but it is also called into question by the methodologic difficulties of determining which of many factors contribute to premature death . . . *The medical campaign against obesity may have to do with a tendency to medicalize behavior we do not approve of.*"[49] [Emphasis added.]

It has never occurred to the editors of the NEJM that the same kind of skepticism might possibly be useful in regard to that other medical campaign that claims that smoking causes "more than 400,000" deaths in the United States every year.

The JAMA article calls to mind a 20-year study started in 1975 by the U.S. Public Health Service—the Multiple Risk Factor Intervention Trial (MRFIT), nicknamed "Mister Fit." More than 12,000 men between the ages of 35 and 57 who were thought to be at risk of heart disease because of their rate of cigarette smoking, cholesterol consumption and their blood pressure were divided into two groups. Those in the "intervention" group were encouraged to stop smoking and eat less fat and were given drugs for their blood pressure. Those in the "control" group were left alone.

After seven years those who did not do any of the "healthy" things had a death rate of 40.4 per 1,000. The death rate among the intervention group stood at 41.2 per 1,000. Death rates from heart disease and other illnesses, including lung cancer, were no different in either of the groups. For cancers other than of the lung, the intervention group had 60 deaths compared to 48 in the control group.[50]

In 1990, the MRFIT study produced another report on the same two groups. It turned out that there were more deaths from ischemic heart disease in the intervention group, or what Lauren Colby calls the "nagged" group, than in the control group—96 vs. 86 deaths. Moreover, there were more deaths from cancer of the respiratory and intrathoracic organs in the "nagged" group than in the control group—66 vs. 55.[51]

Because the men in both groups had a history of smoking, I'm not sure just what this study proved, except that there are limits to what well-meaning people can accomplish by "intervening" in other people's lifestyle choices.

If you add laziness-caused deaths to smoking-caused deaths you're accounting for a sizable percentage of all deaths in the United States each year. Let's imagine that we could magically eliminate the accumulated damage today's smokers have done to themselves and put them on a health par with nonsmokers. Let's further imagine we could transform the couch potatoes into clones of Richard Simmons and Jane Fonda. Let's also assume that it is true that smoking shaves 20 years off a person's life, and that the same is true of inactivity. That would mean that by saving 650,000 lives a year, 20 years from now there would be 13 million extra Americans hanging around who wouldn't otherwise have been there. Obviously they wouldn't live forever (it would just seem like they had). I can see the 21st-century headlines:

DEATH TOLL AMONG ELDERLY RISES TO HIGHEST
LEVEL IN HISTORY, CDC REPORTS

OLD AGE NOW LEADING CAUSE OF MORTALITY IN U.S.

CITING CRISIS, SURGEON GENERAL CALLS FOR ACTION

On the other hand, it's possible to "prove" that smoking adds to a person's life. Epidemiologist Theodore Sterling and his colleagues took the mortality rate for smokers in the American Cancer Society's CPS-II study and applied it to the entire U.S. population in 1986. They came up with 1,675,123 deaths. This was 277,621 fewer deaths than the 1,952,744 deaths from all causes that actually occurred that year.[52] Does anyone believe that if every American smoked we'd *prevent* more than a quarter million deaths a year?

You can have a lot of fun with statistics.

BACK TO SAMMEC. One of the most outspoken critics of SAMMEC is Rosalind B. Marimont, described in an article posted on the Internet in 1996 by FORCES USA as "a retired mathematician and scientist who did research and development for the National Bureau of Standards, now the NIST [National Institute of Standards and Technology], for 18 years until 1960, and at the National Institutes of Health for another 19 years. She retired in 1970. She started in electronics defense work during World War II at the NBS, then went on to the logical design of the early computers during the fifties. In 1960, she moved to the NIH, and there studied and published papers on human vision, speech, and other biomathematical subjects. Since her retirement she has been active in health policy issues—first, the treatment of chronic pain by integrated mind/body methods, and second, the dishonest war on smoking which has corrupted scientific research and gravely distorted the nation's health priorities."[53]

I don't know if Ms. Marimont is a smoker, ex-smoker or never-smoker, but she makes no bones about her low opinion of SAMMEC and its uses:

> That smoking causes 400,000 deaths annually is now widely promoted as a statistical truth. The recent campaign against teenage smoking asserted that one out of three teenagers who smoked would be killed by this habit. These numbers are a gross misinterpretation of the CDC SAMMEC results, and a gross overestimate of the importance of smoking as a cause of death. Another mantra of the Anti-Smoking Partisans (ASPs) is that smoking kills more people than alcohol and drugs combined. This latter piece of disinformation has been used to justify neglect of the shocking rise in teenage binge drinking and driving.* Neither candidate for president [in 1996] has even mentioned teenage drinking, and the Clintons have hardly mentioned drugs until the Republicans made an issue of it.
>
> The 400,000 plus estimate is the result of logical and epidemiological blunders and a lack of scientific integrity by the anti-

*An excellent point. I return to it later in this chapter.

> smoking lobby. The CDC estimate is described as the number of deaths *associated* with smoking, not *caused* by it. [Emphases hers.] This is not a semantic distinction, because a death can be associated with many factors. Among risk factors for heart disease, for example, are hypertension, high serum cholesterol, obesity, sedentary life style, smoking, and genetic factors. If we ran SAMMEC computations for each of these factors, we could estimate the number of heart disease deaths associated with each of these factors. But suppose that John Smith, who died of heart disease, had all of these factors. He would have contributed 6 deaths to the total associated deaths. So that when we sum up these results to arrive at the total deaths, we find that our total is *much larger than the number of people who actually died of the disease.* [Emphasis mine.]

This kind of overcounting is not the only problem with the SAMMEC system, she says. In estimated risk ratios that compare deaths of smokers to those of nonsmokers, the ratios would be true estimates of the risks of smoking only if the two groups were identical in all other respects than smoking. This is of course not true since the measurement is done without controls. For this reason epidemiologists rarely take seriously risk ratios of less than 3. But, she points out:

> In the SAMMEC report, of the 102 risk ratios of smoking for various diseases, only 40 are greater than 3. If we consider only risk ratios equal to or greater than 3, the number of deaths is cut in half, to about 200,000. Even if we reject only those less than 2, the number is cut by about one third, to about 270,000. And these corrections still leave a number of serious confounders.

(I don't know what SAMMEC report she's referring to here. I count only 82 relative risks, or risk ratios, for current and former smokers, male and female, in the August 27, 1993 MMWR, of which 28 are greater than 3. Her essential point remains valid, however.)

One of the most serious confounders in smoking studies, she points out, is the inverse correlation of smoking with socio-economic status (SES). An abundance of studies have found that low SES is one of the best predictors of disease and early death.

And finally, no attention is paid to the benefits of smoking. For some conditions, such as obesity, the risk ratio of smoking is less than 1, since smokers are less likely than nonsmokers to be obese. Also, smokers are less likely to have ulcerative colitis. "It is of course heresy to suggest that smoking can have any good effects, but like caffeine, nicotine is known to improve alertness, and allay depression and anxiety. There is recent evidence that smoking may provide some protection against Alzheimer's disease and Parkinson's. [See Chapter 4 in this book.—D.O.] These good effects are rarely mentioned for fear of being branded a tool of the tobacco companies." She concludes:

> It has been said that truth is the first causality of war. The deceptions of the war on smoking have done incalculable harm to the nation. The grossly overstated dangers of smoking to health have distorted the nation's health priorities. To equate smoking with alcohol or drugs as teenage dangers is obviously absurd, and would never have happened if the health dangers of smoking had been accurately reported. The war on smoking has become a crusade of good against evil, and logic and science have been prostituted to attain its objective.[54]

In my opinion, the most telling argument against SAMMEC is, as Ms. McWhirter learned, that the raw figures fed into the CDC's computers are based on death certificates from state sources and the cause of death listed on a death certificate can itself be subject to physician bias or error or guesswork. I have heard one estimate that 40 percent of death certificates may falsely attribute the cause of death because so few autopsies are conducted. Beyond that, the state figures are unaccompanied by lifestyle data about any *actual* person or persons who died. The relative risks—which, once established, are engraved on stone—are simply applied to the (guesstimated) total of deaths from any given disease to arrive at the smoking-attributable figures.

It would of course be impossible to conduct autopsies on or investigate and compile the medical histories of every person who dies in the United States. Fortunately, since we *know* that smoking is associated with almost every disease, it is infinitely easier to give a computer a bunch of raw numbers and RRs and let it do the work.

Reputable people willing to speak out publicly against the misuse of science in the service of antitobaccoism are regrettably few and far between and their voices seldom heard, except on a few prosmoking sites on the Internet. Thus I must again turn to Rosalind Marimont and a somewhat intemperate letter she fired off to Steve Lapham, editor of *Science*, the magazine of the American Association for the Advancement of Science (AAAS). The letter, posted by FORCES Canada, is dated June 19, 1996:

> Dear Mr. Lapham: Part of the American scientific community is excommunicating a group of its members—ostensibly those who accept research money from tobacco companies ([Special] Report, "Tobacco Money Lights up a Debate," Jon Cohen, Science, 26 April, 1996). The anti-smoking crusaders (ASC), led by Stanton Glantz, have won again. In a long and brilliantly effective campaign, the ASC have transformed the discussion of a public health issue into a holy war against smoking. To do this they have established 3 major dicta.
>
> (1) Smoking kills 440,000 Americans annually.
>
> (2) Environmental tobacco smoke (ETS) kills 50,000 Americans annually.
>
> (3) Anyone who questions the validity of (1) or (2) is a tool of the tobacco industry.
>
> Dictum (3) is necessary because serious scientists recognize that (1) is questionable and (2) preposterous.
>
> Good scientists encourage criticism of their results. By honest give and take they refine their theories and advance knowledge. The ACSs, unable to defend their often shoddy science, have changed the subject to attacking the tobacco industry and impugning the motives of scientists who accept its funding. The real or alleged evildoing of the tobacco industry is irrelevant to the public policy of the dangers of smoking. No money will corrupt an honest scientist, and Federal money (Stanton Glantz' specialty) will corrupt a dishonest scientist as thoroughly as tobacco money.
>
> The war on smoking has obviously become part of political correctness, or the American form of Lysenkoism. Lysenkoism, the subjugation of science to ideology, is named for Trofim Lysenko,* Stalin's favorite scientist, who suppressed all genetic research in the Soviet Union and damaged Soviet science and agriculture for decades. It is easy to see why genetic research should be anathema to Stalinists, but can anyone enlighten me as to why smoking is the abomination of the politically correct?
>
> . . . Defaming one's critics is a durable technique of crusaders, from Lysenko in the USSR to our own Salem witch hunters,

*Trofim Denisovitch Lysenko (1898-1976) was a Soviet agronomist who maintained that acquired characteristics could be inheritable. Josef Stalin found this congenial to Communist philosopy because it meant that the traits of the "new Soviet man" would be passed on to succeeding generations. Scientists dissenting from this dogma were ruthlessly suppressed.

> Senator Joe McCarthy, and now Stanton Glantz and his fellow ACS.
> If Glantz' lucrative and effective propaganda has been able to harm the career of so distinguished an epidemiologist as Theodor[e] [T.] Sterling,* I can see why young scientists are afraid to protest. But where are the leaders of the AAAS, or other retirees, like me, who are free to speak out? For 37 years I was proud to be [a] Federal government scientist . . .
> The 1993 EPA [Environmental Protection Agency] report [on environmental tobacco smoke] was merely embarrassing, but the current surrender to Lysenkoism is shameful and frightening.
> —Rosiland Marimont.[55]

Actually, there were five Special Reports by Jon Cohen in the April 26, 1996 issue of *Science*, Vol. 272, No. 5261, on pages 488,489, 490, 492 and 494, all dealing with the subject of tobacco industry funding of scientific research.

In one, Cohen reported that funds from tobacco companies are a major and growing source of support for academic biomedical research in the United States and that this has set off a big debate in the scientific community. On the one hand, many researchers believe there is nothing wrong with this as long as the recipients are entirely free to conduct and publish their research. They also argue that tobacco money can be a key source of support for important work at a time when traditional funds are scarce. On the other hand, critics charge that the industry uses the fact that it is supporting prominent researchers "to sow doubts about the health hazards of smoking." (Your old "smokescreen" again.)

Another report said that Philip Morris was funding a new institute in La Jolla, California, "focused on the hot topic of cell signaling" to the tune of $15 million a year for 15 years. The institute is headed by famed molecular biologist Sydney Brenner, who said that Phillip Morris

*Professor emeritus of computational epidemiology at Simon Fraser University in Burnaby, British Columbia, who claimed that the methods used by the U.S. surgeon general, the U.S. Office of Technology Assessment and the World Health Organization to estimate deaths from tobacco use are based on faulty assumptions contained in two American Cancer Society Studies, CPS-I and CPS-II (see Note 37 to this chapter.) According to FORCES Canada he was attacked for this by the "politically-correct-on-tobacco establishment" and has since remained silent.

would have no say in research decisions. Again, however, some critics found this source of support "unacceptable." As a result of such flack, in February 1996, the institute's name was changed from the "Philip Morris Institute for Molecular Sciences" to the "Molecular Sciences Institute."

In another report, Cohen said that a number of institutions are debating whether to accept tobacco industry money because of growing opposition to this source. Again on the one hand, some institutions, such as Harvard Medical School, have decided that it would be an infringement of academic freedom to bar tobacco funds. Others, such as Massachusetts General Hospital and the M. D. Anderson Cancer Center at the University of Texas, have decided to spurn such funds on the grounds that tobacco companies can cite their support of academic researchers as proof that they are still seeking evidence that smoking causes diseases. (More "smokescreen.")

The debate's also going on among scientific journals, Cohen reported. In December 1995, two journals published by the American Thoracic Society, an affiliate of the American Lung Association, began refusing to review papers that resulted from work sponsored by the tobacco industry. Again, some researchers argue that the quality of the work is the only thing that matters and the source of support is irrelevant. At least one highly respected journal, the *British Medical Journal*, attacked the society's decision.

Finally, we learn that the Council for Tobacco Research, which is the chief source of tobacco industry funds for individual researchers, has sponsored some 139 special projects that were selected by tobacco companies and their lawyers, even though the council "prides itself on supporting only peer-reviewed, independent research." Here the critics charge that the projects involved "sensitive topics related to smoking and health" and that the companies have sometimes tried to prevent their disclosure under the guise of "attorney-client privilege." Cohen notes that at least one judge (at the time hearing Mississippi's suit to recoup medical expenditures for alleged smoking-caused illnesses, to which the tobacco industry eventually capitulated, see Chapter 12) has agreed with the critics.

As I state elsewhere in this book, it's a shame that the American scientific community is apparently so strapped for funds that it cannot conduct its own independent research into "sensitive topics relating to smoking and health" but must rely on the tobacco industry for financing, and then must take the companies into court to learn the results of their "secret" research. It is perhaps an even greater shame that tobacco has become so stigmatized that in the minds of many the merest whiff of it taints scientific research that may have nothing to do with smoking and health simply because it might make the industry look good.

In any case, *Science* never published Rosiland Marimont's letter. At least I couldn't find it in the table of contents of issues from June through December 1996. Since Cohen didn't mention Stanton Glantz and nobody was defamed, it was probably a wise editorial decision. *Science* didn't publish a letter from anybody else on this subject either. I don't think this particular case is an indication that "politically incorrect" people are being silenced but rather that this respected journal has a more important function than to serve as a forum for endless and useless debate.

WHEN I FIRST BEGAN researching for this chapter and learned that the famous 400,000-deaths-from-smoking figure originated in a Centers for Disease Control and Prevention "Morbidity and Mortality Weekly Report," that of August 27, 1993, I assumed that these figures were updated regularly. But in viewing every MMWR available on the CDC's Website, from January 7, 1993 through March 21, 1997, a total of 215 of them, I discovered to my surprise that, although there are many MMWRs dealing with various aspects of smoking, not only is that of August 27, 1993 the most recent report on *total* smoking-caused deaths in the United States broken down by diseases but that it was based on 1989 and 1990 data. Whether feeding more current data into SAMMEC would result in a figure somewhat higher or somewhat lower than 418,690 is probably of little consequence though. "The point" is the important thing, and it really doesn't matter how long ago it was first made.

In my search of the MMWRs, however, I did find substantiation for Rosiland Marimont's complaint that, in it is obsession with teenage smoking, the medical establishment is ignoring the problems of teenage drinking and driving. Between the dates mentioned above, out of the 215 MMWRs I found only 17 dealing with alcohol in some way. These 17 MMWRs contained 25 separate entries, the majority reporting statistics of alcohol involvement in fatal motor vehicle crashes. There was but one entry concerning alcohol and youths and young adults, and this too had to do with traffic crashes and fatalities, not binge drinking.

In contrast, in 31 of the 215 MMWRs there were 43 entries on the subjects of smoking and tobacco, of which no less than 12 were specifically concerned with young people. The subjects included: the accessibility of minors to tobacco products in several states, exposure of persons greater than 4 years of age to tobacco smoke, reasons for the use of tobacco and symptoms of nicotine withdrawal among adolescents and high school students and young adults, and projected smoking-related deaths among youths in the United States.

(There were two other entries I have not included in the count: the ingestion of cigarettes and cigarette butts by children in Rhode Island between January 1994 and July 1996 and the prevalence of cigarette smoking among secondary students in Budapest, Hungary, in 1995. But the fact that the CDC considers the last two worthy of inclusion in an MMWR is further evidence of what its major preoccupation is.)

This is a score of at least *twelve* MMWRs in a period of four years devoted to various aspects of smoking and youths, *one* on drinking and youth (motor vehicle accidents) *zero* on binge drinking and youths (which is a serious problem at many colleges and universities) and *zero* on marijuana or hard drugs and youths (even as illicit drug usage has soared).

The CDC devotes an MMWR or part of it to observance of "The Great American Smokeout" each November and "World No-Tobacco Day" each May, where it recites progress made in eliminating smoking since the surgeon general's 1964 report, re-emphasizes the toll of human life, potential years lost and monetary cost due to smoking, and exhorts the necessity for continuing efforts to end this plague. There is no "Great American Drinkout," no "Great American Drugout." There is no "World No-Alcohol Day," no "World No-Drugs Day." Does this say something about priorities?

I am certainly not against the reasonable, pleasurable use of alcohol; I imbibe some of the stuff every day. Nor would I wish to see the alcohol industry villainized the way the tobacco industry is. But the young people who kill or injure themselves in automobile accidents because of drinking (or drug use, not to mention others they may kill or injure, not to mention property damage); the young people who die of alcohol poisoning from binge drinking (not to mention the young women who are sexually abused in an intoxicated state)—these are *real* people, not numbers manufactured by a computer. They have names. They had hopes and dreams. They had their whole lives ahead of them.

Consider also that:

- Ethyl alcohol is the number one cause of death for American youth 15 to 24 years of age.
- The use of alcoholic beverages is the leading cause of preventable birth defects in the United States and one of the foremost causes of mental retardation in the Western world.
- Nearly one and a half times as many American school-age children begin using alcoholic beverages each day than begin cigarette use.
- Alcohol use in the United States causes 20 percent more loss of potential life before age 65 than does the use of tobacco.
- The use of alcoholic beverages is the most common factor associated with violence, crime and family sociopathy in the United States.[56]

Why don't we see a slew of MMWRs on these subjects? Maybe it's because we are constantly reminded that "tobacco is the only substance which, when used as intended, is harmful to the health," while there is evidence that moderate amounts of alcohol are beneficial to the heart. (But Alcoholics Anonymous tells us that there is no such thing as the moderate or " normal" use of alcohol for the alcoholic or recovering alcoholic. In fact, many substances, when "used as intended," can be harmful to some people—sugar and diabetics, for example.) Maybe it's simply because people who smoke in the United States today are far outnumbered by people who drink. "Everybody" is against smoking but most people like a little nip now and then. No doubt many members of the staff of the Centers for Disease Control and Prevention do. Many reporters, editors, health activists, officials of the lung and cancer societies and directors of federal health agencies probably do.

All right, that was a cheap shot. Yet it just seems to me that alcohol and drug use among young people ought to occupy a level of concern in the national consciousness at least *approaching* that of tobacco use among young people.

In fairness to the CDC, however, I hasten to add that it published 19 other MMWRs in this four-year period containing articles dealing in general with health and behavioral risks to the nation's youths. Items included sexual behaviors and drug use, adolescent homicide, suicide and attempted suicide; also teenage pregnancy and birth rates and the prevalence of overweight among adolescents. Also available to the healthcare community are periodically published CDC "Surveillance Summaries" which track such youthful behavioral risks as alcohol and other drug use, sexual behaviors, fighting, carrying of weapons, unhealthy dietary behaviors and physical inactivity, as well as smoking and smokeless tobacco use.

In one of these 19 MMWRs, dated June 18, 1993, an entry entitled "Mortality Trends and Leading Causes of Death Among Adolescents and Young Adults" reported on alcohol use and drug use among young people, along with seat belt and helmet use or nonuse, and fighting (as well as, needless to say, smoking).

What interested me was that in this report the CDC stated that nearly 15,000 persons between the ages of 10 and 24 are killed in motor vehicle accidents every year. Not all these deaths, or even most, are due to somebody's drinking, of course. But if it is true—as we are told again and again—that 3,000 young people take up smoking every day and 1,000 of them will die because of it maybe 20 or 30 or 40 years later, it seems safe to say that *no* persons between the ages of 10 and 24 die from smoking in *any* year. Aren't 15,000 *actual* deaths a year a little higher than *zero* deaths a year and of more immediate import than X number of *guess*timated deaths a generation in the future?

And what about this? According to Carol Statuto, a spokesman for the National Council for Adoption, 2,000 children die every year at the hands of their own parents or other care-givers.[57] Again, alcohol or drugs are not always involved in these tragedies, but these victims too are actual people, with names. I'm not aware of any surveillance by the CDC of this national tragedy, nor the similar one of spousal abuse.

LEST ANYONE BE left with the impression that I have been attempting to impugn or denigrate an institution which, *when pursuing its original function*, has contributed enormously to the nation's health and well-being, I'll end this chapter by quoting extensively from one more MMWR which I think should be of interest to everyone. It was published June 28, 1996 on the occasion of the CDC's 50th anniversary:

> The Centers for Disease Control and Prevention—CDC—traces its roots to an organization established in the southeastern United States during World War II to prevent malaria among personnel training on U.S. military bases. On July 1, 1996, CDC formally celebrates its 50th anniversary as a federal agency dedicated to ensuring the public's health through close cooperation with state and local health departments and with other organizations committed to improving health in the United States and throughout the world.
>
> . . . The Communicable Disease Center was organized in Atlanta, Georgia on July 1, 1946; its founder, Dr. Joseph W. Mountin, was a visionary public health leader who had high hopes for this small and comparatively insignificant branch of the Public Health Service (PHS). It occupied only one floor of the Volunteer Building on Peachtree Street and had fewer than 400 employees, most of whom were engineers and entomologists. [As of 1997 the CDC had some 6,000 employees.—D.O.] Until the previous day, they had worked for Malaria Control in War Areas, the predecessor of CDC, which had successfully kept the southeastern states malaria-free during World War II and, for approximately one year, from murine typhus fever. The new institution would expand its interests to include all communicable diseases and would be the servant of the states, providing practical help whenever called.
>
> Distinguished scientists soon filled CDC's laboratories, and many states and foreign countries sent their public health staffs to Atlanta for training. Any tropical disease with an insect vector and all those of zoological origin came within its purview. Dr. Mountin was not satisfied with this progress, and he impatiently pushed the staff to do more. He reminded them that except for tuberculosis and venereal disease, which had separate units in Washington, D.C., CDC was responsible for any communicable disease. To survive, it had to become a center for epidemiology. Medical epidemiologists were scarce, and it was not until 1949 that Dr. Alexander Langmuir arrived to head the epidemiology branch. He saw CDC as "the promised land," full of possibilities. Within months, he launched the first-ever disease surveillance program, which confirmed his suspicion that malaria, on which CDC spent the largest portion of its budget, had long since disappeared. Subsequently, disease surveillance became the cornerstone on which CDC's mission of service to the states was built and, in time, changed the practice of public health.
>
> The outbreak of the Korean War in 1950 was the impetus for

> creating CDC's Epidemic Intelligence Service (EIS). The threat of biological warfare loomed, and Dr. Langmuir, the most knowledgeable person in PHS about this arcane subject, saw an opportunity to train epidemiologists who would guard against ordinary threats to public health while watching out for alien germs. The first class of EIS officers arrived in Atlanta for training in 1951 and pledged to go wherever they were called for the next 2 years. These "disease detectives" quickly gained fame for "shoe-leather epidemiology" through which they ferreted out the cause of disease outbreaks.
>
> The survival of CDC as an institution was not at all certain in the 1950s. In 1947, Emory University gave land on Clifton Road for a headquarters, but construction did not begin for more than a decade. PHS was so intent on research and the rapid growth of the National Institutes of Health that it showed little interest in what happened in Atlanta. Congress, despite the long delay in appropriating money for new buildings, was much more receptive to CDC's pleas for support than either PHS or the Bureau of the Budget.
>
> Two major health crises in the mid-1950s established CDC's credibility and ensured its survival. In 1955, when poliomyelitis appeared in children who had received the recently approved Salk vaccine, the national inoculation program was stopped. The cases were traced to contaminated vaccine from a laboratory in California; the problem was corrected, and the inoculation program, at least for 6- and 7-year olds, was resumed . . . Two years later, surveillance was again used to trace the course of a massive influenza epidemic. From the data gathered in 1957 and subsequent years, the national guidelines for influenza vaccine were developed.
>
> CDC grew by acquisition . . . When CCD joined the international malaria-eradication program and accepted responsibility for protecting the earth from moon germs and vice versa, CDC's mission stretched overseas and into space.
>
> CDC played a key role in one of the greatest triumphs of public health: the [worldwide] eradication of smallpox . . . CDC also achieved notable success at home tracking new and mysterious disease outbreaks. In the mid-1970s and early 1980s, it found the cause of Legionnaires [*sic*] disease and toxic-shock syndrome. A fatal disease, subsequently named acquired immunodeficiency syndrome (AIDS), was first mentioned in the June 5, 1981 issue of MMWR.

This is a proud and admirable record by the "disease detectives," whose adventures have inspired at least a couple novels and movies I can think of (scary and farfetched though they are). To it should be added the CDC's tracing of an outbreak of disease in the southwestern United States to the hantavirus in 1993. Also admirable is the candor exhibited in the following paragraph from the same MMWR:

> Although CDC succeeded more often than it failed, it did not escape criticism. For example, television and press reports about the Tuskegee study on long-term effects of untreated syphilis in black men created a storm of protest in 1972. This study had been initiated by PHS and other organizations in 1932 and was transferred to CDC in 1957. Although the effectiveness of penicillin as a therapy for syphilis had been established during the late 1940s, participants in the study remained untreated until the study was brought to public attention.* CDC also was criticized because of the 1976 effort to vaccinate the U.S. population against swine flu, the infamous killer of 1918-19. When some vaccinees developed Guillain-Barré syndrome, the campaign was stopped immediately; the epidemic never occurred.

To conclude:

> As the scope of CDC's activities expanded beyond communicable diseases, its name had to be changed. In 1970 it became the Center for Disease Control, and in 1981, after extensive reorganization, Center became Centers. The words "and Prevention" were added in 1992, but, by law, the well-known three-letter acronym was retained. In health emergencies CDC means an answer to SOS calls from anywhere in the world, such as the recent one from Zaire where Ebola fever raged.
>
> Fifty years ago CDC's agenda was noncontroversial (hardly anyone objected to the pursuit of germs), and Atlanta was a backwater. In 1996, CDC's programs are often tied to economic, political, and social issues, and Atlanta is as near Washington as the tap of a keyboard.

Unfortunately, perhaps sometimes a little too often and too closely tied to those economic, political and, especially, "social" issues, and too near Washington. As noted in my Introduction, only one of the CDC's seven centers is still involved in the original—and, to repeat, admirably performed—mission of tracking down and eradicating infectious dis-

*On May 16, 1997, President Clinton formally apologized on behalf of the United States to the survivors of this "deeply, profoundly, morally wrong" experiment.

eases, and that center accounts for only about 10 percent of the CDC's budget. Thanks to its success in that mission, the agency has had to look for other "public health" areas to enter to justify its existence and, as a consequence, today seems itself to be infected by a "disease" which, to borrow from Chapter 2, I'll call "antitobaccosis." The "shoe-leather epidemiologists" are wearing out a different article of clothing these days: not their shoes but the seats of their pants from prolonged sessions at computers.

In the same month as it celebrated its 50th anniversary, and upon the unanimous recommendation of the Council of State and Territorial Epidemiologists (CSTE), which is the Centers' primary collaborator for determining what diseases or conditions the states report, the prevalence of cigarette smoking was added to the list of conditions designated as reportable to the CDC. It was the first time that a risk *behavior*, rather than a disease or illness, had been included. Such is the overarching importance of the tobacco menace.

But while the CDC has escaped criticism for its obsession with smoking, the agency has been forced to back off from two other "epidemics" it attempted to inspire crusades against. One was the role of guns in violent deaths; the other was AIDS. Both issues happened to come to a head in the CDC's golden anniversary year.

In the 1980s, noting that injuries were killing more young people than some diseases, the CDC's National Center for Injury Prevention and Control (NCIPC) began awarding grants for research into this problem, including a number of major gun studies. In 1987, NCIPC director Mark Rosenberg claimed that 8,600 homicides and (exactly) 5,370 suicides could be avoided each year if all guns were confiscated from the general population. (As if people determined to kill themselves or someone else wouldn't find other means.) In 1994 he told *The Washington Post*, "We need to revolutionize the way we look at guns, like what we did with cigarettes. Now it [smoking] is dirty, deadly, and banned."[58]

One CDC study in particular aroused the wrath of the powerful National Rifle Association, as well as some physicians. The study, conducted by Dr. Arthur Kellerman, director of Emory University's Center for Injury Control and published in *The New England Journal of Medicine*, claimed that homes with guns were five times more likely to be the scene of suicides and three times more likely to be the scene of homicides than homes without guns. Calling the NCIPC "politically biassed," the NRA said Kellerman's study was flawed because it didn't take into account people who have defended themselves against injury and death because they had a gun in the house.

One physician, Dr. Miguel Faria, clinical professor of neurosurgery at Mercer University School of Medicine in Macon, was asked to resign as editor of *The Journal of the Medical Association of Georgia* after he published editorials and articles challenging the premise that guns are a health threat.[59]

CDC director David Satcher (who became U.S. surgeon general in 1998) underwent grilling from gun ownership supporters on Capitol Hill at a House subcommittee hearing on the CDC's $2.2-billion budget request for fiscal 1997, during which it was suggested that his agency was using research into violent death and injury as a pretext for a campaign to make firearms socially unacceptable in America. Shortly thereafter, the CDC quietly announced that it would no longer seek new firearms-related research proposals, saying that the decision "reflects new priorities."[60]

(This is far from the end of that issue, however. Inspired by the success of the states in plundering the tobacco industry [see Chapter 12], several cities, including Philadelphia, Chicago, New Orleans and Atlanta, have filed or plan to file suits against the firearms manufacturers to recover the costs of gun-related violence.)

It was also back in the 1980s, specifically 1987, that "federal health officials made the fateful decision to bombard the public with a terrifying message: Anyone could get AIDS," said an article in *The Wall Street Journal* that launched another firestorm against the CDC.[61] The message was highly misleading, said the *Journal*, pointing out that the CDC's own research showed that the risk of contracting AIDS from a single act of sex was smaller than the risk of being hit by lightning. It further charged that the CDC was spending most of its AIDS prevention budget on combating the disease among low-risk groups, such as heterosexual women, rather than those at high risk—homosexuals, bisexual men and intravenous drug users. So successful was the CDC's fear campaign, said the article, that by 1988 69 percent of Americans believed AIDS "was likely" to become an epidemic.

But that rampant and unwarranted fear was not a bad thing, in the opinion of many anti-AIDS activists, who credited it with achieving profamily goals that no amount of moralizing could do. "I don't see much downside in slightly exaggerating" the risk of AIDS, said John Ward, chief of the CDC branch that tracks AIDS cases.[62]

That statement reminds me of the crusade against tobacco and the pious falsehood syndrome. So there's some "slight" exaggeration about the risk of AIDS. It's in a good cause, isn't it?

The WSJ article moved columnist Marie Gallagher to cry out: "The CDC knows the truth [about AIDS]. Yet this year, its education program is once again aimed at the general population. The ultimate casualty of the CDC's lies will be Americans' faith in public health officials, heretofore generally exempt from our growing mistrust of government."[63]

Somehow, neither Ms. Gallagher nor other antismoking columnists are able to see that the same thing is true for the crusade against smoking but instead swallow the official line without question. And while the Centers for Disease Control and Prevention has toned down its gun-violence and misdirected AIDS campaigns, one is left with only the faint hope that it will someday overcome its terrible addiction to tobacco.

I HAVE WANDERED afar from what started out as a discussion of the 400,000 smoking deaths lie but I think I've made *my* "point" as well as I am able: the figure is a myth, at least as much of a myth as *The Myth of Heterosexual Aids*, the title of another reality-check book by Michael Fumento. Unfortunately, while he acknowledges that the 400,000 figure is a "political statement," he still believes the true figure is "probably" somewhere in the hundreds of thousands.

It's time now to take a look at the Number One most outrageous lie against smoking and another federal agency that has done far more to damage the fabric of American society, and far less to benefit it, than anything the CDC could be charged with.

Notes

1,2. *Dictionary of Quotations*, Collected and Arranged and With Comments by Bergen Evans (New York: Delacorte, 1968), p. 387.

3. *The Viking Book of Aphorisms*, A Personal Selection by W. H. Auden and Louis Kronenberger (Dorset, 1966), p. 336.

4. Message from the Director-General of the World Health Organization for "World No-Tobacco Day, 1997." At www.who.ch/programmes/psa/toh/Alert/4-96/E/ta1.htm.

5. Arun Elhance, senior fellow with the International Peace Academy, a nonprofit research group in New York that works closely with the United Nations. Quoted in Bob Davis, "Ted Turner's gift: Despite mogul's donation, U.N.'s money woes remain." *The Atlanta Journal-Constitution*, September 21, 1997, p. A3.

6. Susan Okie, "Smoking-Related Deaths up 11% to 434,000 Yearly, CDC Reports." *The Washington Post*, February 1, 1991, p. A1.

7. Ibid.

8. "Unhealthy habits, violence cost $42.9 billion annually to treat." *The Atlanta Journal-Constitution*, February 23, 1992, p. A1. From the Associated Press.

9. Anne Rochell, "Great Smokeout targets 46 million puffers." *The Atlanta Journal-Constitution*, November 18, 1993, p. B6.

10. Editorial. "It's a good day to be a quitter." *The Atlanta Journal-Constitution*, November 16, 1995, p. A14.

11. Christopher R. Johnson, MS IV, and Mark S. Gold, M.D., "Nicotine Addiction." *The Journal of the Florida Medical Association*, February 1996. From the Internet at www.medone.org/consumer/journal/february.html.

12. John Head, "A smoking gun: Almighty tobacco shows its first weak spot." *The Atlanta Journal-Constitution*, March 22, 1996, p. A16.

13. John Head, "Smoke screen: Tobacco tycoons put a positive spin on death." *The Atlanta Journal-Constitution*, April 5, 1996, p. A14.

(I assume that Mr. Head, who is the AJC's most frequent author of signed columns condemning smoking, and probably its antismoking editorials as well, does not write his own headlines, otherwise one would hope he could have come up with something more original than "a smoking gun" or "smoke screen.")

14. Statement by John Grisham in Katy Kelly, "Grisham's smoking gun: 'Runaway Jury' paints picture of devious tobacco industry." *USA Today*, April 29, 1996, Book Section. (That "smoking gun" again. What would writers do without it?)

15. Anne Rochell, "CDC using state reports to track smoking rates." *The Atlanta Journal-Constitution,* June 28, 1996, p. C6.

16. Editorial. "Tobacco industry's judgment day." *The Atlanta Journal-Constitution*, August 15, 1996, p. A18.

17. Question asked of Food and Drug Administration commissioner David Kessler in a "Q&A" column by Jeff Nesmith. *The Atlanta Journal-*

Constitution, August 30, 1996, p. A2. (Kessler's answer: "Prohibition will not work. It will not be effective. It is not correct to say we would have to do something that would not be effective." But how he must have wished that he *could* outlaw smoking.)

18. Editorial. "Buying friends for tobacco." *The Atlanta Journal-Constitution*, September 11, 1996, p. A10.

19. Action on Smoking and Health (ASH), at http://ash.org/mar97/3-04-97-01.html.

20. Joe Dawson, "Essays on the Anti-Smoking Movement." At www.tezcat.com/~smokers/issues1.html.

21. "Dear Abby." *The Atlanta Journal-Constitution*, November 17, 1993, p. B2.

22. "Ann Landers." *The Atlanta Journal-Constitution*, March 5, 1995. p. B2.

23. "Dear Abby." *The Atlanta Journal-Constitution*, November 15, 1995, p. D12.

24. "Dear Abby." *The Atlanta Journal-Constitution*, November 20, 1996, p. C12.

25. Michael Fumento, *Science Under Siege: How the Environmental Misinformation Campaign Is Affecting Our Laws, Taxes, and Our Daily Life* (New York: William Morrow, 1993), p. 339.

26. Personal communication to author.

27. Personal communication to author.

28. Dan Rather, "The American Way of Death." CBS Evening News, October 15, 1975.

29. Cited in Edith Effron, *The Apocalyptics: Cancer and the Big Lie: How Environmental Politics Controls What We Know About Cancer* (New York: Simon and Schuster, 1984), pp. 449-450.

30. Loc. cit.

31. Anne Rochell, "CDC's homeless-deaths tally far lower than task force's." *The Atlanta Journal-Constitution*, September 24, 1993, p. D4.

32. Nickie McWhirter, "Computer blows out smoking-related death figures with no real human facts." *The Detroit News*, October 18, 1992. From American Smokers Alliance at www.smokers.org/research/articles/10-computer_blows_out.html.

33. Editorial. "The 'Cause of Death' is Dying." *Modern Pathology* 6(3):237 (May 1993).

34. At http://sailor.lib.md.us./docs/tobacco/samexp.htm

35. Carol Thompson, "Deconstructing the Anti-Smoking Movement." From FORCES Canada, an affiliate of San Francisco-based FORCES (Fight Ordinances & Restrictions to Control & Eliminate Smoking), at www.forces-cdn.com/ca-decon.htm.

36. Thomas P. Monath, M.D. et al., "The Search for Vaccines Against *Helicobater Pylori.*" *Infec Med* 15(8):534-535;539-546, 1988. From Medline at

www.medscape.com/SCP/IIM/1998/v15.n08/m3316.mona-01.html. Also Jerry E. Bishop, "Study Suggests Causes and Cure for Ulcers." *The Wall Street Journal*, May 1, 1992, p. B1.

37. T. D. Sterling, W. L. Rosenbaum and J. J. Weinkam, "A Non-technical Discussion of 'Risk Attribution and Tobacco Related Deaths.'" An authors' summary for the layman of a paper published in *The American Journal of Epidemiology*, Vol. 138, No. 2, 1993. At www.forces-cdn.com/sterling/theo.htm.

38. Personal communication to author.

39. Martha Perske, "Does Smoking Really Cause Over 400,000 Deaths Per Year in the U.S.?" At www.forces.org/pages/marta2.htm.

40. "Study halted after student volunteer dies." *The Atlanta Journal-Constitution,* April 4, 1996, p. A9. From the Associated Press.

41. *The Atlanta Journal-Constitution,* February 16, 1994, p. A2.

42. Editorial. "New rules to clear the air." *The Atlanta Journal-Constitution,* February 22, 1997, p. A12.

43. "Historic Surgeon General's Report Offers New View of Moderate Physical Activity." Department of Health and Human Services press release, June 11, 1997, at www.cdc.gov.

44. Jack A. Chambliss, professor of economics at Valencia Community College, and Sarah C. McAlister, an economics major at the University of Central Florida, in *The Orlando Sentinel,* December 22, 1996. Quoted in *Reason,* June 1997, p. 16.

45. Susan Gilbert, "Poor fitness may rival smoking as early death risk." *The Atlanta Journal-Constitution,* June 17, 1996, p. A1. From *The New York Times.*

46. *Atlanta Sports and Fitness Magazine*, May 1996, p. 47.

47. "Koop's Kooky Crusade." FORCES Weekly Tobacco News, October 1996, at www.forces.org.

48. Mike Toner, "Obesity called 'a national epidemic.'" *The Atlanta Journal-Constitution*, February 12, 1998, p. D.3

49. The Week That Was, December 29-January 3, 1997, an update from The Science & Environmental Project, at www.junkscience.com/news/singer10.htm.

50. Fact Sheet on Lifestyle Studies. From FOREST (Freedom Organization for the Right to Enjoy Smoking Tobacco) at ftp://ftp.demon.co.uk/FOREST.

51. Personal Communication to author.

52. T. D. Sterling et al., "A Non-technical Discussion of 'Risk Attribution and Tobacco Related Deaths.'"

53. Rosalind B. Marimont, "The Blunders of SAMMEC—400,000 Killed by Smoking???" At www.forces.org/pages/sammec.htm.

54. Ibid.

55. Letter to *Science*, June 19, 1996. Posted at www.forces-cdn.com/articles/roz-03.htm.

56. From an August 5, 1995 open letter to FDA Commissioner David A. Kessler from Cyrus J. Stow, D.D.S., a retired private citizen and former smoker concerned about the FDA's misdirected campaign against tobacco. Published by FORCES Canada at www.forces-cdn.com.

Stow cites as his sources: Daniel Pollock et al., "Underreporting of Alcohol-Related Mortality on Death Certificates of Young U.S. Army Veterans." *Journal of the American Medical Association*, July 17, 1987, pp. 345-348; Robert W. Amler and Donald L. Eddins, "Cross-sectional Analysis: precursors of premature death in the United States." *American Journal of Preventive Medicine* 1987;3(suppl):181-187; J. Michael McGinnis and William H. Foege, "Actual Causes of Death in the United States." *Journal of the American Medical Association*, November 10, 1993, Vol. 270, No. 18, pp. 2207-2212; "Cigarette Smoking Attributable Mortality and Years of Potential Life Lost—United States, 1990." CDC Morbidity and Mortality Weekly Report, August 27, 1993, Vol. 42, No. 33, pp. 645-649; "Advance Report of Final Mortality Statistics, 1991." CDC National Center for Health Statistics Monthly Vital Statistics Report, August 31, 1993, Vol. 42, No. 2(suppl), pp. 1-61; Jane Ellen Stevens, "Treating Violence as an Epidemic." *Technology Review*, August/September 1994, pp. 12-30; Surgeon General's Advisory on Alcohol and Pregnancy, FDA Drug Bulletin, July 1981, Vol. 11, No. 2, pp. 9-10; "Fetal Alcohol Syndrome and Other Effects of Alcohol on Pregnancy Outcome." Seventh Special Report to the U.S. Congress on Alcohol and Health, 1990, Department of Health and Human Services Pub. No. (ADM) 90-1656; pp. 139-155; "Update: Trends in Fetal Alcohol Syndrome—United States, 1979-1993." Morbidity and Mortality Weekly Report, April 7, 1995, Vol 44., No. 13, pp. 249-251.

57. Quoted by columnist Mona Charen, "Republicans can step in to save kids." *The Atlanta Journal-Constitution*, April 9, 1997, p. A17.

58. Quoted in Don B. Hates, Henry E. Schaffer and William C. Waters IV, "Public Health Pot Shots." *Reason*, April 1997, p. 26.

59. R. Robin McDonald, "Are Guns a Health Menace?" *The Atlanta Journal-Constitution*, August 27, 1995, p. Q1.

60. Jeff Nesmith, "A debate on guns and health"; Anne Rochell, "Funding ends for study that drew fire of gun lobby." *The Atlanta Journal-Constitution*, May 2, 1996, p. A13; Bill Hendrick and Anne Rochell, "CDC defends its research on guns, AIDS." *The Atlanta Journal-Constitution*, May 4, 1996, p. A1.

61. Amanda Bennett and Anita Sharpe, "AIDS Fight Is Skewed By Federal Campaign Exaggerating Risks." *The Wall Street Journal*, May 1, 1996, p. 1.

62. Ibid.

63. Maggie Gallagher, "The ultimate AIDS fraud." *The Atlanta Journal-Constitution*, May 3, 1996, p. A15.

Chapter 6

ETS AND THE PROSTITUTION OF SCIENCE

> *Why should I have to have someone kill me* [with cigarette smoke]*? What if someone came up with a gun and said, "Why don't you try this bullet?"*
>
> — Larry Hagman[1]

> *I smell the cigarette's smoke as it wafts through the air, and I freeze, consumed with as much fear as if the smoke were a man with a gun on a dark street . . . The smoker walks toward me. I am trapped by courtesy.*
>
> — Susan Gilbert McGuire[2]

CIVIL SOCIETY HAS come to a sorry pass when a person smoking a cigarette is likened to someone holding a gun in his hand, and is considered equally as menacing. Although it is not usually expressed in such melodramatic terms as in the two quotations above, the belief that a cigarette, or rather the smoke from it, is potentially lethal to everyone within its radius is fervently held by millions today. That millions do so believe is testimony to the most successful mass brainwashing campaign of modern times. It is the result of more than 30 years of unrelenting antismoking propaganda, the last 10 or 15 years of which have hammered on the dangers of "secondhand" smoke, otherwise known as "environmental tobacco smoke" (ETS). The alleged danger of ETS to innocent bystanders is also implicit in the loaded terms "passive smoking" and "involuntary smoking."

Sadder yet, this campaign could not have been successful without the collaboration of scientists who were willing to compromise the ethics of their profession, or turn a blind eye and remain silent when others did so, in the cause of a "smoke-free society."

Larry Hagman, a reformed smoker, would not allow smoking on the set of "Dallas," even as alcohol was destroying his liver. Yet drinking, or the simulation of it, was a constant in nearly episode of that television series. Hagman is alive today only thanks to modern medical science, which gave him a replacement liver. What is the damage that his former smoking, or somebody else's smoking, did to him? He's never said, as far as I know.

But it wasn't secondhand smoke that was killing Susan Gilbert McGuire's husband at the time she wrote an article that was reprinted in *Reader's Digest*, although she obviously believes in its lethality; it was his own smoking. She writes:

> My husband received a diagnosis of metastasized lung cancer. He had smoked heavily but quit five years ago. I'd hoped he would escape the disease that killed my grandfather when I was a teenager. My loathing of cigarettes began as I watched my 250-pound grandfather waste away to 136 pounds in one year . . .
>
> Since the diagnosis over a year and a half ago, my husband had: chemotherapy and radiation therapy; his right lung and nine cancerous lymph nodes surgically removed; more chemotherapy; hair loss; pneumonia; surgery to remove fluid from around his heart; and a 49-pound weight loss from his perfect, muscular body. I cry at the thought of what he endures . . .
>
> After eight months of treatment, my husband was scheduled for more tests. As we drove up to the hospital, three employees stood outside the entrance, smoking and laughing. So bad were their addictions, so effective was the tobacco industry's claim on their lives, that they stood in the cold, braving wind and rain, to smoke.

Notice the assumption underlying that last statement: anyone with half a brain knows that smoking will kill you; therefore anyone who persists in doing so, even under circumstances of semiexile and harsh physical discomfort that a wise and caring society has inflicted upon him, is obviously a slave to tobacco and those who sell it to him.

To DIGRESS A moment already (as readers who have stuck with me this far are aware that I am prone to do), the segregation of smokers from decent society may have benefits that go beyond the protection of innocent nonsmokers from disease, disability and premature death. For example, in a posting to the alt.smokers "user group," "SipePL@po5.pl.unisys.com (Particle Man)" wrote:

> An observation: the more nonsmokers push for smoke free environments, the more smokers end up together. Smoking, talking, trading notes.
>
> When I started smoking there was very little, if any, community spirit among smokers. You smoked at your desk, or wherever, and never really felt any association with other smokers . . . But now, we have our own sections. Our own lounges. And our own user group . . .
>
> The really interesting thing about the outdoor smoking area where I work is how many problems get solved there. I work in an engineering organization. The smoking "lounge" attracts people from every discipline for one simple reason: they are addicted to nicotine. But hey, here are mechanical engineers, electrical engineers, device driver types, application types, Unix, MS Windows, OS/2, managers, janitors, net-hackers, physicists—and they are all there having a cigarette or cigar or pipe, and looking at each other. Guess what? A LOT of tough problems get solved there, more than I've ever seen in multi-functional meetings called by management.

From *NSA Voice*, the National Smokers Association newsletter:

> Workplace smoking prohibitions have created "unlikely friendships with co-workers whose paths they might never cross," reports the *Newark Star Ledger*. As a result, new lines of communication are being formed as these "smoke-break buddies" from various levels and different departments gather in the doorways and on loading docks of their companies to smoke.
>
> "Go out and smoke, and you'll learn lots of things," said Janet Saporito, a South Orange, N.J., smoker interviewed by the newspaper. "You do meet people you'd never know otherwise."
>
> Stanley Deetz, professor of communication at Rutgers University, commented on this social phenomenon. "A lot of companies have tried to invent these types of connections, yet here's one that has emerged spontaneously," said Deetz. "It has this uncontrolled, spontaneous quality which makes it creative and useful."
>
> Julie Wiegel of West Orange, N.J., for example, found her new buddies useful in her search for a new job. "You find out different jobs that are open," said Wiegel, whose position at her company was being eliminated. "You'll hear, 'My friend works here, and they're hiring.'"
>
> Others have benefited by meeting company executives. "I've

had some great conversations," said Frank Petrock of Belleville, N.J. "There are people who come out here at a higher level."[3]

More ironies from the overflowing files of the cockamamie antisecondhand smoke crusade:

According to *The Resistance*, another NSA publication, in Des Moines, Iowa, employees of Wellmark Blue Cross and Blue Shield are forbidden from smoking cigarettes within 100 feet of the Ruan Center. To make sure they don't, all outdoor ashtrays have been removed from the area. Across the street, employees of Norwest Financial are likewise forbidden from smoking in front of their building.

So on their smoke breaks, the Blue Cross/Blue Shield people cross over to the Norwest building and the Norwest people cross over to the Ruan Center. The two groups exchange greetings as they pass.[4]

In Seattle, Washington, smokers attending a game at the Kingdome, a large indoor stadium, are obliged to go outside to smoke, says the writer of a letter to *Philip Morris Magazine*. "On the other hand," he says, "when we watch our college team—which plays in an outdoor stadium—we are forced to go inside to enjoy a cigarette. Perhaps there is consistency here: Has someone decided that nobody can smoke while sitting down?"[5]

Makes a whole lot of sense, doesn't it?

Abigail Van Buren ran this letter in her column a few years ago:

> Dear Abby: My daughter, in her 20s, had terminal breast cancer and she never smoked. I am a smoker, and we smokers are such amicable and gracious people that we do not lambaste others.
>
> When my daughter was in the Shands Hospital in Gainesville, Fla., it was the smokers who came by her room asking if I needed anything from town. At Emory, where my daughter received her bone marrow transplant, the smokers found a place for me to stay—at no cost—and smokers were welcomed!
>
> Smokers have a special comradeship. Wherever you non-smokers put us, we huddle together and share our experiences as "social outcasts." My friends who have quit smoking are now grossly overweight and miserable. When I get to heaven, I'll ask to be in the smoking section because that's where all the fun people will be.—Janice Wingard, Proud Smoker.[6]

Abby's comment, if she made any, was not included in the column I saw. But the perfect rejoinder would have been to tell the writer that if she continued smoking she'd get to heaven long before the nonsmokers. Assuming, that is, that smokers are allowed into heaven.

Abby did comment on a follow-up letter from another reader, one Oren M. Spiegler of Pittsburgh, who took issue with Ms. Wingard's description of smokers "as 'amicable and gracious.' Don't make me laugh! How about selfish and inconsiderate? . . . Society owes no accommodation to those who choose an addiction."

"Dear Mr. Spiegler," Abby replied. "You must be a new reader or you would know that I have little patience and even less compassion for smokers."[7]

Glad Abby cleared that up. Fairness, however, compels me to acknowledge that there may be a downside to the forced comradeship of smokers. Aldrich Ames, the CIA employee who sold secrets to the Soviets, says that he was able to pass such a variety of information along to the KGB because he picked up the info while standing outside CIA headquarters shmoozing with other smoking agents.[8] Talk about selfish and inconsiderate!

Because I retired in 1985 I never had to put up with this kind of outcast treatment, though no doubt my former employer has long since banned smoking in the office. I did however have occasion to see one of these "smokers' ghettos" in January 1997 at Northside Hospital in Atlanta (as a visitor, not a patient). Smokers were allowed to indulge outside in a kind of well that was below the ground-level entrance and unroofed. It was pleasant enough because the weather was good, but if it had been cold or raining— tough luck. I don't know if any doctors or nurses frequented the ghetto but I did meet a couple nurse's aides. But doctors and nurses could be seen chowing down fat-filled hamburgers and french fries at a McDonald's restaurant inside the hospital. I heard a lot of jokes about that. I just hope that when they have their heart attacks it will be before they're eligible for Medicare. I don't want my tax dollars going to pay for their foolish lifestyle choices!

Kennestone Hospital in Marietta also has a smokers' ghetto in the form of a cute gazebo in one corner of the grounds. The problem is that it is entirely enclosed, except for the entrance. Doesn't the hospital care that by confining smokers this way it is forcing them to breathe in their own secondhand smoke in unnecessarily heavy quantities?

* * *

RETURNING TO MRS. McGuire, who concludes her sorrowful story:

> We are told that tobacco-related diseases kill one person every ten seconds. But there are even more victims. How many children weren't born because a smoker died early? How many can't afford college because a family's financial future was destroyed by cigarette-related cancer? How many widows and widowers have been left alone?
>
> How many young people around the world start smoking because Hollywood still portrays "cool" by showing stars with half-closed eyes and voluptuous lips pursed lazily around a cigarette? We should have learned something from Humphrey Bogart and Gary Cooper, who both died from smoking-related cancers.
>
> What would their deaths do to their families? As they inhale the smoke deep into their lungs, do they wonder if they'll die decades before old age? They would if they'd spent the past year and a half with my husband.

Oh dear and my, my. To address the first two of Mrs. McGuire's questions, most people who die from cancer (whatever caused it) are past their procreative years, so I doubt if there are a whole lot of children going unborn because of smoking. And since cancer is predominantly a disease of old age, the children of its victims should be long since out of college. Anyway, nonsmokers have to pay for smokers' illnesses (so we're told), so smokers aren't depleting their children's college funds.

As for her husband's lung cancer, I have no way of knowing what caused it (not to mention Humphrey Bogart's and Gary Cooper's). But there is reason to question that it was due to smoking, or smoking alone. A "metastasized" cancer is one that had its origin in some organ of the body and later moved through the blood vessel and lymphatic systems to another organ, very frequently to the lungs, as in his case.*

Cancer is a terrible, often seemingly random-occurring disease, and its treatment is almost as terrible (and, for lung cancer, usually futile). Thus victims and their loved ones desperately need an answer to *"Why?"* Even if it can't be conclusively proved that smoking was the

*"Metastases to the lungs are common from primary cancers of the breast, colon, prostate, kidney, thyroid, stomach, cervix, rectum, testis, and bone, and from melanoma."—*The Merck Manual of Diagnosis and Therapy*, Sixteenth Edition, page 732.

culprit in any given instance, study after study has shown that smoking is bad for the health. So it is an easy and obvious and all-too-human leap of logic to conclude that if cancer occurs in a smoker or former smoker . . . well, there's your answer.

When cancer strikes smokers or former smokers and they are convinced that it was caused by their smoking, they have only themselves —or the tobacco companies—to blame. But when the victim has never smoked at all, the belief that somebody else's smoking caused her death can be positively heartrending, as witnessed by the following letter to Ann Landers that was reprinted in *Breathers' Digest*, the newsletter of AIRSPACE Non-smokers' Rights Society in Vancouver, British Columbia:

> Dear Ann Landers: This is in response to the woman who was upset because her brother and his wife would not allow her to smoke in their home . . . Millions of people who consider themselves non-smokers should think again. If they allow smoking in their homes, they are smokers whether they like it or not.
>
> I have never smoked, but I have been exposed to second-hand smoke since early childhood. Last fall I was diagnosed with lung cancer. I had major surgery followed by five horrific months of chemotherapy. My weight dropped to 92 pounds. I lost all my hair, had hallucinations, nightmares and wanted to die. To have gone through all this hell when I've never smoked a cigarette has made me very bitter. I experienced no symptoms. My cancer was discovered during a routine medical examination. Several weeks ago I was told to get my life in order because there isn't much time left. I am the mother of two young children and I don't deserve to die this way because I have never smoked, at least that's what I thought—Lynn Van Horne, Edmonton.

Anne replied in part, "Dear L.V.H.: You have written a powerful letter, one that is sure to be clipped and sent to smokers who insist on lighting up in the presence of those who do not smoke. It is not unrealistic to say that you have probably saved some lives today."[9]

Equally as heartrending was a letter Lynn Van Horne's sister, Heather McDonald, sent to *The Edmonton Times*, which was also republished in *Breather's Digest*:

> Today was my sister's birthday. Year after year, I would call her up anonymously and play the "Happy Birthday" tune from a little toy music box . . . On April 27, 1992, I would call her for the last

> time. She was in the hospital, dying of cancer. When I came by to see her that day, I brought along the little music box and stopped briefly in the lobby to place that important phone call. When I appeared moments later in the doorway of her room, she smiled and said to me softly, "I got the call. Whoever it is didn't forget and somehow knew where to find me." At that, we laughed and we cried as I shared the secret. Six weeks later she was gone.
>
> Like the senseless murder of Edmontonian Barbara Danelesko, Lynn Van Horne's death almost two years ago was front-page news. Like Barb, my sister was married and had two young sons at home . . . And like Barb, she too was defenseless. But here the similarities of their tragic and untimely death end.
>
> Arrests were made in Barb's death. There is mounting public outrage that innocent people are not even safe in their own homes any more.
>
> Lynn was a lifelong non-smoker who developed smoker's irritant lung cancer from inhaling the tobacco smoke of others. In her case, those responsible for her death were not held accountable. There was no public outcry that non-smokers are not safe in the workplace and in public where they are forced to go, simply because smoking continues to be socially acceptable, albeit increasingly less so than in the past.
>
> My sister knew that she didn't have long to live, and petitioned legislators for protection for workers from involuntary exposure to second-hand tobacco smoke. The ministers of health and safety and the environment, at the time, all acknowledged that second-hand smoke is a cause of preventable death among non-smokers. However, nothing was done.
>
> It is absolutely reprehensible that our government leaders must be forced to care, but unless we intensify our demands for legislation to protect the innocent, nothing is going to change.

This reprehensible situation *has* changed; Canadians today are as frightened of, and have instituted the same repressive measures against, secondhand smoke as their southern neighbors.

Breathers' Digest appended this note to the letter:

"Heather McDonald . . . played a leadership role in getting smoke out of her workplace, McDonald's Restaurants. Now we know what motivated her and why she did not back down. On November 7th, 1994, Heather's legal claim with McDonald's Restaurants was settled. On November 22nd, 1994, Heather McDonald died of cancer."[10]

The *Digest* did not say that Heather also died of lung cancer, but presumably she did. However, the fact that cancers took both these sisters suggests a possible genetic explanation that is at least as reasonable to suspect as their assumption—nay, their firm conviction—that their cancers were due solely to secondhand smoke. Be that as it may, Heather's frustration and anguish over the fact that no identifiable person or persons could be held responsible for her sister's death is particularly moving.

I hold the organized antismoking movement and its alarmist propaganda directly accountable for fostering such wholly unnecessary anguish. That propaganda, by the way, has not shrunk from revising history.

In my Introduction I wondered whether the constantly smoking character in the film "Jurassic Park" was supposed to convey a prosmoking or an antismoking message. Since then, after viewing another film by Steven Spielberg, I have to conclude it was the latter.

In one scene in "Schindler's List," as I recall it, Schindler and his chief accountant are going over the names of Jews they think they can save from the Nazi gas ovens. Schindler paces and puffs constantly. "How many cigarettes have you smoked this evening?" the accountant asks. "Too many," replies Schindler. Says the accountant, "Every time you smoke one, I smoke half."

I find it rather sad that in one of the most important movies ever made about one of the greatest tragedies in human history, someone felt it necessary to interject an antismoking message, an anachronistic one at that. In any case, secondhand smoke was the last thing Schindler's Jewish accountant had to fear.

Another example of historical revisionism was the James Dean commemorative stamp issued in 1996. In the original photograph used for the stamp, the actor's trademark symbol of rebellion, a cigarette, was dangling from his lips. This was deleted on the stamp. Commented *The Tampa Tribune*:

> When the U.S. Postal Service issued its James Dean stamp and promotion poster a month ago, it zapped Dean's ever-present cigarette.
>
> "We removed the cigarette . . . so we would not be in a position of promoting or being accused of promoting cigarettes," spokesman Mark Weinberg said Wednesday.
>
> "We're in an era of political correctness," said Lenny Prussack, who manages a gift shop at the James Dean Gallery in Fairmount, Ind., Dean's hometown. "It's kind of tampering with history."

The Postal Service had "censored" another stamp in 1994, eliciting this comment from Joe Urschel in *USA Today*:

> Each generation may indeed write its own history. But never before has a generation rewritten the past with such Orwellian glee.
>
> So when blues musician Robert Johnson was honored with a stamp last week, he was politically correctified by the U.S. Postal Service to comply with the new moral code of America. The cigarette was airbrushed out of the picture from which the stamp was taken.
>
> That such a brazen alteration of fact was not met with howls of protest from freedom-loving Americans is either a sad nod of acquiescence to puritanical censorship, or confirmation that we have in fact all turned into gumptionless Pollyannas who really do believe we can remake the world into the perfect setting we wish it would be.[11]

The Book-of-the-Month Club did the same thing to a photograph of writer and novelist Ayn Rand in a mailing to its members offering three of her books.[12] And Columbia Records altered the cover of a CD retrospective set called "Old Friends" by Simon and Garfunkel. In the original photo the two were sitting on a stage, with Paul Simon holding a cigarette to his lips. The evil weed was deleted for the new, politically correct, cover.[13]

I also understand that Franklin D. Roosevelt's famous cigarette holder (with cigarette) is nowhere to be seen in his memorial on the Mall in Washington. The Soviet Union may be dead, but Big Brother's "memory hole" is in full operation in the land of the smoke-free and home of the fearful.

The antismokers would not only bend history to their purposes but the laws of physics themselves, or at least severely strain plausibility. Consider "Esther's story," which I found at the World Wide Web page of Smokefree Air for Everyone (S.A.F.E.), "a network of individuals who have been injured or disabled by secondhand smoke," located in Newbury Park, California:

> I used to be a teacher until I was injured by secondhand smoke. It drifted into my classroom from an employee lounge *so distant* [emphasis added] that I did not understand what was happening to me until it was too late. In April, 1992, I received a Workers' Compensation settlement of $29,999, but it is a sad story since my

> lung damage is too severe for me to teach anymore or hold a full time job.
>
> The smoke came from a small employee lounge that was set up in September, 1987. *The smoke traveled down a long hall and up a flight of stairs* propelled by air currents in the building. [Emphasis again added.] Other teachers smelled the smoke; they complained of headaches and eye irritation.
>
> I, however, was more vulnerable because I have asthma. It became difficult for me to breathe and project my voice. I would become so hoarse that by the end of the day, I could not produce sounds. My medicine did not help me. I did not believe what was happening to me. In my doctor's office and at home I did not have symptoms . . .
>
> By April of 1989, I could no longer force myself to get out of bed and go to work. In May, a lung specialist provided a diagnosis of severe, progressive and irreversible chronic obstructive airway disease in addition to asthma. According to my physicians, the condition had probably been developing for years. (My parents had both smoked when I was a child with asthma.) The secondhand smoke had aggravated the existing respiratory problems . . .
>
> Now I am worried about my children who also have asthma and allergies. My son has just had to quit two jobs in succession because exposure to tobacco smoke made him ill. How long will innocent people continue to be hurt?[14]

Not to make fun of this unfortunate woman's suffering (but I will), I can visualize those evil tendrils of death creeping along the long hallway and then, like vengeful ghosts in some English castle, floating up the stairs in search of their distant victim. *"Es . . . ther . . . we know where you are . . . We're com-ing-g-g for you . . ."*

(Strange, but just the opposite happens in my house. The smoke drifts out of my office when I'm puffing away at the computer, crawls along a hallway and then *down* the stairs in search of my wife, who is innocently reading or watching television in the family room.)

It's hard to beat "Esther's story" as an example of the amazing penetrating power of cigarette smoke but the following one comes close. It was posted on "Smoker's Home Page" on the Internet by one Tom Farrell in response to a challenge to produce an example of a smoker's rudeness and lack of consideration for a nonsmoker:

> I was in my apartment, in bed, reading. I smelled cigarette smoke strongly and started coughing. I realized that my next door neigh-

> bor was indulging his habit of standing around in the hallway outside my apartment door and chatting on his cordless phone (I think it was because there was a loud party going on in his apartment and he couldn't hear there) while smoking a cigarette. I put on a bathrobe, opened my door, found him standing right there, smiled, and said (just loud enough to be heard over the noise of the party), "excuse me, but would you be so kind as to extinguish your cigarette?" He then started screaming and yelling at me, and as I was backing into my apartment to make room for the door to close, he was raising his fists and moving in my direction. At that moment two people happened to be arriving (apparently to the party), saw him, grabbed him, and dragged him off to his apartment. I went into my apartment and locked the door.[15]

That was pretty rude and inconsiderate, all right (but on whose part?).

Consider this: people have been asphyxiated or burned to death in apartment house and hotel fires because they unwittingly and unsuspectingly opened their door to the hallway and found heavy, billowing, choking smoke or even a raging inferno *they didn't know was there.* But this guy is in his bedroom, presumably some distance from his door, and not only smells cigarette smoke coming through the door but the fumes thereof are strong enough to make him cough. *Pu-lease.*

Yet Esther's and Tom's stories must be true. For according to John Howard, M.D., chief of the California Division of Occupational Safety and Health, in testimony before a California Assembly committee on October 20, 1994, "Tobacco smoke travels from its point of generation in a building to all other areas of the building. It has been shown to move through light fixtures, through ceiling crawl spaces, and into and out of doorways."[16]

Let us all pray that Saddam Hussein doesn't hear about this. He could forget about stockpiling nerve gas or biological weapons and simply switch to tobacco-filled bombs that would ignite upon impact.

Fortunately for Mr. Farrell, though, his neighbor's smoke apparently doesn't penetrate his bedroom wall, just the door, unlike some other unfortunate victims of secondhand smoke whose stories I'll tell in the next chapter. (Loud party noises do, but that isn't what bothers him.) He also doesn't say whether his neighbor's smoke has harmed his health in any way. For some examples of that, here is a list of physical problems allegedly triggered by airport smoking as reported by Action on Smoking and Health (ASH) in its January-February 1997 "Review" and reprinted by FORCES Canada:[17]

— Angina resulting in a temporary inability to walk, talk, or carry luggage
— Inability to breathe normally for about 3 days after exposure
— Throat constriction to the point of being unable to speak
— Eye irritation severe enough to cause near blindness
— Severe pain after deviated septum surgery
— Coughing up black or grey matter
— Illness that required 2-3 days for recovery
— Collapsed on the floor
— Burning of sinuses
— Weeks of suffering from upper respiratory problems and sinus coughing spells lasting many hours
— Heart pain which can result in heart damage
— Caused me to throw up several times
— Prostration virtually to the point of unconsciousness
— Bleeding from ear, nose, or throat
— Eyelids swollen shut

ASH also reported the following experiences of nonsmokers at specific airports:

Norfolk, VA: "Waiting at the gate the air was full of tobacco smoke, and my operated [on] eye was irritated. By the time I arrived in my home in Virginia Beach felt sick and I had excruciating pain in my eye. I gradually lost sight in the eye until it became completely blind. The diagnosis was optic neuritis. I believe this condition was caused by the tobacco smoke eliminating oxygen preventing blood flow to the nerve and killing it."

Detroit, MI: "The smoke completely stopped my air sacs."

Atlanta, GA: "Asthma attacks as well as severe breathing and allergy problems, had to use my inhalers."

Cincinnati, OH: "My allergy and asthma symptoms were so severe that the airline finally decided to allow me to pre-board while the aircraft was being serviced."

De Moines, IA: "Eye and mouth mucous membranes irritated by tobacco smoke."

Charlotte, NC: "My eyes and throat became irritated."

Philadelphia, PA: "Had an asthma attack."

Wyoming: "I started vomiting as soon as I took off and vomited all the way to [destination]. I was sick the whole time we were there, and that spoiled my husband's job interview."

Strange, comments FORCES Canada, how no one noticed these reactions to secondhand smoke for decades!

Obviously the people at FORCES are too young to remember the trouble we smokers used to have climbing over the prostrate bodies of nonsmokers when getting on and off airplanes.

Okay, ignore that as another poor attempt at humor. I've reserved serious discussion of other nonsmokers' brushes with death, disease, discomfort and disability because of secondhand smoke, as well as comment on the subject of asthma, for the next chapter.

HOW DID SUCH beliefs about secondhand tobacco smoke—which are unquestionably sincere—become implanted in people's minds? When and how did all this nonsense get its start?

At the beginning of the 1970s, cigarette packages had been carrying warning labels for four years. Cigarette commercials were soon to be banned from the airwaves. Six years after the "landmark" 1964 surgeon general's report (which hadn't mentioned secondhand smoke at all), polls showed that increasing majorities of people not only believed that smoking was bad for the smoker's health but thought it probably wasn't exactly good for people around them either. For the most part, though, nonsmokers were content to let smokers indulge their self-destructive habit in peace, and to the dismay and frustration of the anti-smoking activists, millions of smokers continued to do just that. Cigarette company profits were soaring. Clearly, people were not "getting it."

It was about this time that the antis realized that there was at hand a lever by which they could move the world of public opinion: *Environmental tobacco smoke! Secondhand smoke! Passive smoking! Involuntary smoking! My God, why didn't we think of that before?* All they needed was a fulcrum, some kind of (pseudo)scientific justification, upon which to rest the lever.

What this lever could, and did, accomplish is summarized by Richard Kluger in his encyclopedic book, *Ashes to Ashes*:

> Besides stigmatizing smokers, the ETS issue brought with it a fresh rationale for interventionist programs. If smokers were now viewed as violators of the social contract by imposing the unhealthful consequences of their pleasure-taking on others, then it might be quite acceptable to quarantine or even punish them as part of the broader social movement to cleanse the environment. Smoking near someone else was no more excusable than poisoning streams with industrial runoff or fouling the air with toxic smokestack emissions.[18]

Kluger, to say the least, is not favorably inclined toward smoking, either firsthand or secondhand, although he does criticize the antis for their overemphasis on the latter. Another observer takes a more far-reaching view. John Luik, a senior associate of the Niagara Institute, wrote in Boston University's *Bostonia* magazine:

> For most of the twentieth century the campaign to delegitimize smoking has employed two major weapons: science, particularly epidemiology, and morality, within the general conceptual framework of what can be called health paternalism . . . [Once] it was established that smoking increased the risks of ill health in smokers, the groundwork was laid for a series of moral arguments that purported to show that subjecting oneself to these risks was both so irrational and immoral as to justify government efforts to prevent one from assuming the risks . . .
>
> But, however closely aligned to science, the ability of health paternalism to secure all of the public-policy objectives of the anti-smoking movement was always constrained by the fact that, at least within democratic societies, the justifications for government intervention to protect adults from themselves—to coerce "healthy" lifestyles—would continue to have a totalitarian flavor about them that would ensure significant and widespread opposition. It is only by demonstrating the dangers from smoking transcend the smoker and extend to innocent bystanders that the anti-smoking movement could move beyond obvious health paternalism and enlist unambiguous support for public-policy measures designed to restrict, ban, and criminalize public smoking.[19]

But this much-desired and eventually achieved goal of the antis was a long time coming, for there was little science, not even much "junk science," to back up claims about the dangers of ETS. Nevertheless, in the surgeon general's 1972 report, "The Health Consequences of Smoking," the sixth in the series, Surgeon General Jesse B. Steinfeld officially raised the specter for the first time. It was, however, purely his own opinion, based upon his reasoning that since smoking causes lung cancer and 10 to 20 percent of lung cancer deaths occur among nonsmokers, many of the latter undoubtedly must have been caused by exposure to someone else's smoke at some time or another.

More years passed, and still no scientific evidence was forthcoming. It didn't matter; the ETS seed had been planted and was beginning to flourish. Thanks to petitioning by that people's guardian, good old Ralph Nader, the Civil Aeronautics Board in 1972 decreed separate smoking and nonsmoking sections in airliner seating. The following year the Interstate Commerce Commission did the same for interstate buses. In 1975, Minnesota enacted a Clean Indoor Act prohibiting smoking in confined public places, with few exceptions. Public opinion was being moved, bigtime.

The Minnesota ordinance was considered a model of its kind that other jurisdictions began copying. I saw it in action when my wife and I visited the Mall of America in Bloomfield, near Minneapolis, in 1996. Signs informed that smoking was prohibited except in designated spaces, but I could find no such space anywhere in the huge complex. How pathetic, I thought, that in this vast and cavernous and anything but confined public place there was not even a little corner set aside where smokers could smoke. There was, however, a bar called the Alamo on, I think, the third level, where smoking was evidently permitted. Peeking through the windows, I saw ashtrays on every table.

The Seventies also saw the litigation-minded beginning to gear up on the ETS issue. The earliest reference I have seen for someone claiming injury from secondhand smoke, a tiny harbinger of the deluge that was to come, is an item in the chronological "Capsule History of Tobacco" on Gene Borio's Tobacco Bulletin Board on the World Wide Web:

> 1976: Donna Shimp sues New Jersey Bell Telephone for not protecting her from secondhand smoke. Ruling in her favor, the judge said, *"if such rules are established for machines, I see no reason why they should not be held in force for humans."* [20] [Emphasis in original.]

The Bulletin Board doesn't say what kind of protection from secondhand smoke, or reparation for the previous absence of such protection, Ms. Shimp received from New Jersey Bell.

Fast forward to 1978. In that year physicist and antismoking activist James L. Repace—who later joined the Indoor Air Division of the Environmental Protection Agency and became a driving force, if not *the* driving force, behind the anti-ETS crusade—conducted studies of "respirable suspended particles" in various smoky settings, such as restaurants, cocktail lounges, a bowling alley, etc., and compared them with levels in nonsmoky settings. "Respirable suspended particles" (RSP) are thingies in the air that are small enough to reach the deepest recesses of the lungs. Researchers disagree about the size limit for an RSP but do agree that tobacco smoke is one. Repace computed the risk of exposure to lung cancer from the ETS levels he obtained to be 250 to 1,000 times above the acceptable level as set down by federal guidelines for carcinogens in air, water and food.[21]

At last, something solid, or seemingly so, on which to rest the lever. Or was it? Other scientists were to severely criticize Repace's methodology and findings. In any event, whatever the levels of ETS he claimed to have found, there was still no evidence that anyone was being harmed.

Along with a chemist named Alfred Lowrey, Repace published his study in *Science*, claiming that "indoor air pollution from tobacco smoke presents a serious risk to the health of nonsmokers . . . [that] deserves as much attention as outdoor air pollution."[22] In 1985 both men published another article in *Environment International* which went so far as to assert that exposure to ETS was a greater risk than "all regulated industrial emissions combined."[23]

Regarding this article, the following year the *American Review of Respiratory Diseases* editorialized that "Despite the simplifying assumptions of the risk estimates and the flaws in the epidemiological data from which they are derived, Repace and Lowrey's figures remain the best current estimates of lung cancer deaths and passive smoking."[24]

Talk about praising with faint damns. Yet this is also in keeping with the "Lalonde Doctrine": the need to educate the public about the dangers of smoking is so urgent that we have to ignore the fact that the studies may be scientifically questionable.

About this time, antismoking leaders, most notably John Banzhaf of ASH, began petitioning the Occupational Safety and Health Administration (OSHA) to ban smoking in all workplaces in the nation. In an unusual display of common-sense caution for a regulatory agency,

OSHA resisted the demand, citing the lack of evidence about the dangers of secondhand smoke.

Rewind to 1980. In that year the grandfatherly pediatrician C. Everett Koop, whose antismoking mischief-making was to cause more shredding of the social contract than any amount of environmental tobacco smoke, was appointed surgeon general. Over the next seven years, each annual report issued under his aegis told Americans more about the terrible toll of disease and death caused by smoking, but essentially hashing and rehashing previous reports. In 1984 Koop announced the goal of making America "smoke-free" by the year 2000.

Then at long last, in 1986, came his report entitled "The Health Consequences of Involuntary Smoking," in which it was flatly and unequivocally stated that "Involuntary smoking* is a cause of disease, including lung cancer, in healthy nonsmokers."[25] Well, not entirely unequivocally. Koop acknowledged that nobody knew how many people actually fell victim to ETS but he was sure we would eventually find out from future studies. The National Academy of Science (NAS) also issued a report in 1986 implicating ETS as a cause of lung cancer.

(Four paragraphs later, however, Koop noted that "Several studies have reported small decrements in the average level of lung function in nonsmoking adults exposed to ETS . . . but it seems unlikely that ETS exposure, by itself, is responsible for a substantial number of cases of clinically significant chronic obstructive lung disease."

(This puzzles me. I would think that lung cancer, which is almost always fatal, is a somewhat more serious disease than what is usually termed chronic obstructive pulmonary disease, or COPD. It seems a little strange that secondhand smoke would cause the former but would be "unlikely" to cause the latter.)

Koop's pronouncement regarding ETS, like that of his predecessor, Dr. Steinfeld, was largely his own opinion and went well beyond the findings of his own scientific advisors or the NAS. According to Richard Kluger, when asked about it by "one prominent investigator on

*Dr. Koop explained that "Nonsmokers' exposure to environmental tobacco smoke is termed involuntary smoking in this report because the exposure generally occurs as an unavoidable consequence of being in proximity to smokers, particularly in enclosed indoor environments."[26] This cynical writer suspects it could also be because the term "involuntary smoking" conveys a lot more punch than the blander "environmental tobacco smoke."

the dangers of smoking," Koop replied that "as the nation's ranking public-health advocate, he had to be forceful in warning of the ETS threat in order to win the public's attention."[27]

Here was the Lalonde Doctrine again in its naked purity: the end—the elimination of smoking—justifies the means, even if it involves bad science or, at best, only tentative science. Health messages must be "loud, clear and unequivocal" even if the scientific evidence doesn't support them. Here was a pious falsehood par excellence.

Even Kluger is critical:

> [W]ithout a doubt Koop was *on the side of the angels*, but without much doubt, either, he was in this instance using dubious means—shaky science—to justify the worthy end of achieving a healthier society."[28] [Emphasis added.]

And later:

> Only one or two nonsmokers per thousand died of lung cancer, while fifty to one hundred smokers per thousand succumbed to it: by stressing the risk of ETS exposure, the smoking control moving was effectively trivializing the risk from direct smoking, which was thirty to forty times greater. It was an incendiary, effective, but questionable tactic for those *on the side of the angels*.[29] [Emphasis added.]

Would that we had been spared the "touch" of such angel-helpers.

The 1986 report, and its conclusions, were based on 13 epidemiological studies, 11 of which showed "a positive association" between lung cancer and involuntary smoking and six of which reached "statistical significance."

I have only seen a summary of the 1986 report, so I don't know what the actual "statistically significant" relative risks reported in the six studies were. But a "positive association" is merely any fraction of a percentage point higher than unity. A relative risk at unity, or 1.0, means no risk at all. In epidemiological practice, for a risk to achieve a level of "statistical significance" that is not due merely to chance it must at least approach 2.0. (A relative risk of 2.0 would mean that nonsmokers exposed to ETS had twice the risk of developing lung cancer than nonsmokers not so exposed—statistically, that is, not necessarily actually—and the risk would still be barely "significant.") Since only six of the 13 studies apparently reached, or exceeded, that level, the other 11 could be dismissed.

But again it doesn't matter because it was not the 1986 surgeon general's report that really set the ETS panic in motion. What did it was a report which, although even more suspect and controversial than Koop's, carried far more impact and was to have profound social consequences that have not yet run their sorry course.

For the background, Richard Kluger again:

> What the antismoking movement most needed was a finding by the Environmental Protection Agency that ETS qualified as what the EPA termed a Group A [also called Class A—D.O.] carcinogen, meaning that it was found to cause at least 1 death per 100,000, the measure by which asbestos, radon, and a dozen other substances were branded human killers and thus subject to government regulation. By such a finding, ETS would be elevated to an official public menace, given the all but universal exposure to it by the American public, *and it would hardly matter how relatively slight the risk from it might be for any healthy individual*; in the process, the industry's chief defense—that ETS had not been shown to be a legitimate health risk but was, for some, a source of annoyance, readily mitigated by courtesy on both sides—would be destroyed.[30] [Emphasis added.]

What the antismoking movement wanted, the antismoking movement got. And the story of how it got it forms the next part of this chapter.

ON JANUARY 7, 1993—29 years almost to the day after the surgeon general's famous 1964 report (long since transfigured into Holy Writ) and with repercussions second only to that report—the Environmental Protection Agency released at a much-publicized press conference a long-awaited 510-page report on environmental tobacco smoke: "Respiratory Health Effects of Passive Smoking: Lung Cancer and Other Disorders." In it the EPA officially announced that it had classified ETS as a Group A or "known" human carcinogen that, from lung cancer alone, was killing 3,000 Americans a year. ETS also wasn't good for little kids, to the tune of 150,000 to 300,000 annual cases of lower respiratory tract infections in infants up to 18 months of age.*

*"For 10 years the EPA, following the lead of the International Agency for Research on Cancer, has classified chemicals in an alphanumeric scheme that range from A—substances known to cause cancer in humans—to E—

The announcement set off a new wave of hysterical smoking bans around the country on federal, state and local levels—in offices, in restaurants and bars, in shopping malls, in airports, even in open-air sports stadiums and public parks, even private homes where nonsmoking spouse confronted smoking spouse. As far as the public knew from what the media reported, environmental tobacco smoke was now a proven killer.

(It also resulted six months later in a suit filed in federal court by a group of tobacco growers and tobacco manufacturers challenging the scientific basis of the EPA report and demanding that the agency be required to recall it. I'll discuss the court's decision later.)

Typical of the media's absolute faith and trust in the EPA and their enmity toward the tobacco industry was an editorial in the *Atlanta Journal-Constitution*:

> EPA for the first time has declared secondhand smoke a cause of cancer in humans, putting it in the same class with such dangerous substances as asbestos, benzene and radon . . .
>
> Tobacco industry lobbyists have attacked the "flawed science" used by the panel that wrote the report. Hmmmm. Who can be trusted on this one? A group of scientific experts, or the cigarette makers whose multibillion-dollar market shrinks with each confirmation of the dire health consequences of using their product?[32]

Never mind that EPA-engineered scares over asbestos, benzene and radon are also based on dubious science (see Chapter 11). Never mind that antismokers may also have their own agendas. What the AJC, and probably the rest of the media in the country, didn't report, at least not prominently or in any detail, was the follow-up reaction from numerous independent scientists who disputed the EPA's finding and pointed out its serious shortcomings. But why confuse people? Nor did

---

substances for which there was evidence of noncarcinogenicity in humans. In practice, the important substances were those classified as A, B1, or B2. Substances classed as A were known human carcinogens; substances classed as B1 were known animal carcinogens with some evidence of carcinogenicity in humans; and substances classed as B2 were known animal carcinogens with no evidence of carcinogenicity in humans. The EPA calculated a carcinogenic potency factor for each A, B1, or B2 substance, and the potencies were used to set limits on human exposures. Substances rated C and below essentially dropped from view." [31]

many reporters feel it necessary to confuse people with too many details about what the EPA based its conclusion on.

It was based on a combination ("meta-analysis") of 30 independently conducted epidemiological studies that compared disease rates of nonsmoking wives married to smoking husbands with the disease rates of nonsmoking wives married to husbands who didn't smoke. *No studies* on second-hand smoke in the workplace were included nor did the EPA do any original research of its own. Eleven of the studies were conducted in the United States and 19 in other countries. Most of them found "positive associations" between lung cancer and women exposed to ETS, but only six studies were "statistically significant." Nine studies actually found a *reduced* rate of lung cancer, but these were not "statistically significant."*

The bottom line was that the EPA estimated that a woman who lives with a smoker has a relative risk of 1.19 of developing lung cancer. That is, a woman married to a smoker has a 19 percent greater chance of developing lung cancer than a woman living with a nonsmoker.

Sounds like a lot, doesn't it? Especially when you extrapolate it to the entire U.S. population, which is what the EPA did to come up with the "estimate" of 3,000 annual lung cancer deaths due to ETS. Yet that relative risk (RR) of 1.19 is lower than the EPA-alleged 50 percent greater chance (RR=1.50) of getting cancer from the chlorine in drinking water, over which the agency has not (yet) launched a national scare campaign. (Unfortunately, it inspired such a campaign in Peru, to the great harm of that country's health. See Chapter 11). It is below the 2.6 relative risk the EPA calculated for diesel emissions, which it classed as only a Group B or "probable" human carcinogen. It is far below the 4.45 relative risk that Canadian researchers estimated in a study linking high occupational exposure to electric fields with cancer—which translates into a 445 percent chance![34]†

*"The studies EPA looked at were all surveys of women married to smokers, many of them conducted over the phone. They asked the women to give a very rough estimate of their exposure. Often, the women weren't available, and an acquaintance answered the questions. Unfortunately, most of the surveys didn't gather adequate data about other factors that might bias the results ('confounding factors'), like the diet, or income of the women."[33]

†According to the American Smokers Alliance, some studies have put

In an article in *Forbes MediaCritic*, Jacob Sullum, an editor of *Reason* magazine, quoted James Enstrom, a professor of epidemiology at the University of California-Los Angeles: "You're talking about ratios so close to 1.0 that it's really beyond the realm of epidemiology . . . You're basically down in a noise-level situation, and whether you can really see a true signal above the noise is doubtful."[35]

(Sullum's article was widely reprinted in newspaper advertisements by the tobacco industry, for the reprint rights of which he was paid $5,000 by R. J. Reynolds. Sullum's employer, the Reason Foundation, also received a $10,000 donation from Philip Morris. Thus in some eyes everything he said will be disregarded, no matter how true it was. But see other comments about the EPA report untainted by a whiff of tobacco money under this note in the Notes section.)

The EPA's official release of its report on January 7, 1993 was not really news because draft versions had been circulating since 1990. Most of what follows in this chapter is based on a statement that Rep. Joseph Bliley Jr. (R-VA) presented to the Health and Environment Subcommittee of the House Committee on Energy and Commerce, dated July 21, 1993.[36] Bliley was then ranking minority member of the Energy and Commerce Committee and when the Republicans swept into control of Congress after the 1994 elections became its chairman.

In his statement Bliley takes us back to our friend, James Repace. In 1989, he says, Mr. Repace "prompted" the EPA to publish a "Fact Sheet" on environmental tobacco smoke, which "[D]espite its name, 'Indoor Air Facts Number 5,' made extravagant claims about ETS going far beyond the conclusions of the 1986 reports of the National Academy of Science (NAS) and the Surgeon General" and "took certain statements in the 1986 Surgeon General's report out of context to claim a consensus that 'passive smoking significantly increases the risk of lung cancer.'"

To Bliley, the Fact Sheet, plus other documents the EPA subsequently published, plus statements by EPA officials, made it clear that the agency had already reached a conclusion regarding ETS—that it

---

the relative risk of developing a disease from eating pork chops once a week at 2.12; that of drinking three glasses of whole milk a day at 2.14; that of eating pork sausage once a week at 2.42, and that of a nonsmoker keeping pet birds at 6.70.

had "started with the restrictive policy it wanted to promote" and was working "backward to 'develop' the scientific conclusions necessary to justify that policy."

In June 1990, the first draft of an ETS "risk assessment" was released by the EPA for public comment. The drafts were also transmitted to the agency's Scientific Advisory Board (SAB), which by statute is intended to be an independent review body composed of experts from outside the agency serving as a check on the agency's use of science to formulate regulatory policies.

Early in 1991 the SAB sent the risk assessment back to the EPA "with directions that it be revised extensively," records Bliley. "After major rewriting, a second draft was released in June 1992 and a second SAB hearing was held." Eventually, the much transmogrified final risk assessment was released to the public on January 7, 1993.

FOR A LITTLE INSIGHT into the revising and rewriting process, another digression may be in order here. In March 1992 the EPA sent its draft report to its Office of Research and Development-Environmental Criteria and Assessment Office in Cincinnati (ECAO-CIN), where a team of epidemiologists gave it a look-see. Their reports back to EPA headquarters in Washington were not intended for publication, but San Francisco-based FORCES somehow obtained a copy of two of them and put them on its Website.[37] In the first, dated March 23, 1992, Patricia A. Murphy commented:

> Although we were asked to review specific proportions [*sic*] of this document, it is our collective opinion that this is a scientifically inadvisable means of approaching the issue. We found that we were repeatedly forced to either accept certain statements and assumptions at face value or go back to the previous chapters to seek out the information needed for a thorough assessment of the validity of some of the analytical approaches which were taken.
>
> . . . If, however, commonly used formulae have been adusted or manipulated in any way, it becomes impossible to evaluate their validity if they are presented without supporting documentation and references for the various assumptions implicit in their use. . .
>
> Some parts of this chapter [Chapter 3] bear a rather striking resemblance to an article by Brian Leaderer (1990). Risk Analysis, Vol 10, pp. 19-26. In some cases, the wording is identical. It may be that this person also authored this chapter. If not, this could be

a source of embarrassment, as there are surely many people familiar with this article who will also be reading this EPA document in some capacity. This should be looked into by the authors.

... Appendix A: ... What is lacking is a clear statement of why these particular studies were selected for review. Was any attempt made to include non-published studies (which are likely to have non-positive findings) in this review? Chapter 5 uses these studies as the basis of a meta-analysis, but it is not really clear to me how the process of data abstraction took place, i.e., the specific pieces of information which were being sought from each study to form the data set for re-analysis.

... Chapter 5. This might be better titled REintepretation of studies based on REanalysis of published data. Meta-analysis is repeatedly alluded to but it is never clearly stated what the purpose and form of this data analysis really is.

... [T]here is no discussion or mention of the "file drawer problem,"* i.e., the existence of unpublished studies showing no positive effects, which may bias the results of the data pooling in the direction of finding a positive effect.

... The discussion of bias and confounding in the individual studies is pretty thorough, but there is no mention of the potential for residual confounding in or misclassification of erroneously measured variables used for the purpose of confounding adjustment. It is known (see Greenland, 1987 for citations) that this type of error can result in a variety of types and directions of misclassification bias of unknown magnitude. This might seem to be an overly picky comment but I believe it should be discussed because I'm sure some outside critic will cite this source of potential error as possibility for the positive findings in these studies.

In the last part of Chapter 5, I feel that the case for a clear causal relationship between lung cancer and ETS is somewhat overstated ... It is alluded to that adenocarcinoma seems the most strongly related to ETS exposure—is it not curious that among active smokers squamous cell carcinoma is usually found in abundance and the relative risks for adenocarcinoma among active smokers are dwarfed in comparison .. ? ... I recall 7 or 8 years ago when it was first noted that adenocarcinoma seemed to occur with greater frequency in women compared to men. At that time, the theory was that these adenocarcinomas were likely due to domestic radon exposure; now they are being attributed to ETS. This

*This is also known as "publication bias." Only studies that come up with the results the researchers are looking for tend to be published in peer-reviewed journals; studies that turn out negative are "filed."

issue should be better addressed before a causal relationship is "confirmed."

Appendix D: Incomplete as received. Sections D.2 and D.3 are missing, which makes it impossible to review the methods for calculation of the attributable risk estimates which form the basis of Chapter 6.

The second document, dated March 24, 1992, was written by Terry Harvey and reads:

As you will note from the comments, no one liked the 11 day time allotted for review and thus a very quick product is attached as best we could accomplish in the time available. I suggest the document manager(s) consider more time for evaluation to balance the seriousness of this document as applied to the public health and the intrinsic value of doing it right on this key health topic.

I have personally reviewed only the "Summary and Conclusions" and have these comments:

1. I am concerned with the extrapolation of data from females to males in the married never smokers (p. 1-3). There are sex differences for both cancer and non-cancer health effects. I suggest clarification of this variable to affirm inadequate male data and reinforcing the EPA cancer guideline proviso where inadequate data exists.

2. It is confusing to the reader to skip back and forth from "ETS" to "passive smoking" (pg. 1-1). I suggest an improved scientific description is "PETS" or "Passive Exposure To Tobacco Smoke." In any case, use one set of terms and define it upon first usage.

3. To be technically accurate and avoid confusion, the document summary (pg. 1-1) should not use the generic term "cancer" unmodified as to the type . . , e.g., squamous cell carcinoma vs. adenocarcinoma. Great confounders will emerge if this is not carefully articulated (see Pat Murphy, Pg. 5). If you can technically show causal association, do; where you can't, don't infer it.

4. The non-cancer asthma effect must be clarified medically to show effects primarily in [the] sensitive asthmatic subpopulation having pre-disposition component-like genetic risks and not displayed as public health risk to the general non-predisposed population.

5. I suggest a full discussion of category A vs. B, based on the absence of definitive data on PETS in humans. Like it or not, EPA should live within its own categorization framework or clearly explain why we chose not to do so . . .

> ECAO-CIN will be most happy to spend further time improving the quality of this document. Let us know how we can be of further help.

"Once again," says FORCES, "one can see evidence of the disagreement within the EPA's own organization about classifying secondhand smoke as a Class A carcinogen. Once again, the comments of the reviewer are about sloppiness, inaccuracy, data spin doctoring, and the great rush to push it through."

As far as the general public knew, however, or at least the readers of the *Atlanta Journal-Constitution*, the EPA's delay in releasing the report was because of "a massive tobacco industry lobbying campaign."[38]

According to Jacob Sullum, between May 1990 and February 1994, *The New York Times, The Los Angeles Times, The Wall Street Journal* and *The Washington Post* ran more than 100 news stories about ETS, of which about 45 focused on the EPA report in its various versions.[39] Most of those stories no doubt were duplicates. But from my own file of newspaper clippings for those years, 1990 through 1994, I count no fewer than 129 articles, editorials, columns and letters dealing with ETS, all but a handful from one newspaper alone, *The Atlanta Journal-Constitution.* Adding 1995 through May 1997, the total comes to 160. (This is not counting "general" antismoking articles, columns, etc.)

Two of the clippings dealt with the makeup of the EPA's Scientific Advisory Board and both cast doubt on its "neutrality."

The first one, from 1990, reported that:

> Six of the 16 members of a newly appointed Environmental Protection Agency panel considering the health risks of secondhand cigarette smoke have ties to a tobacco industry research organizations . . .
>
> "They've stacked the deck with people who have close ties to the tobacco industry." said Dr. Alan Blum, a founder of the antismoking group Doctors Ought to Care. "It's pathetic."
>
> "We were concerned about the appearance of conflict of interest," said Donald Barnes, staff director of the EPA's scientific advisory board. But he said the link between the panel members and the tobacco industry "does not cause any question to be raised about their technical capabilities."
>
> The panel's task is to review the scientific accuracy and objectivity of two forthcoming EPA reports on the health effects of passive smoking.

> Six members are connected with the Center for Indoor Air Research of Linthicum, Md. . . . The center is financed by Phillip Morris, R. J. Reynolds Tobacco Co. and Lorillard Corp., three of the nation's largest tobacco companies.
>
> The chairman of the EPA's passive-smoking panel, Morton Lippmann of New York University, is on the science advisory board of the tobacco industry center.[40]

The second clipping, two years later, reported that:

> A draft Environmental Protection Agency report linking cigarette smoke to lung cancer in non-smokers and respiratory infections in children faces review today by a panel of scientists that includes some with financial ties to the tobacco industry . . . The panel was assembled by the EPA to provide an unbiased critique of the EPA report on second-hand smoke. Since the panel last met in December 1990, one of its members has accepted a $1.2 million grant from the Phillip Morris tobacco company.
>
> The researcher, James E. Woods of Virginia Polytechnic Institute in Blacksburg, Va., also recently became the second member of the EPA smoking panel to join the board of a tobacco industry research organization. The first was Morton Lippmann of the New York Medical Center, who is chairman of the EPA panel . . .
>
> The EPA report found that second-hand cigarette smoke is a proven cause of lung cancer in non-smokers, leading to about 3,000 deaths annually . . .
>
> The Tobacco Institute, the industry's lobbying arm, held a news conference Monday to denounce the EPA report, saying it "has employed questionable scientific standards, selectively used data and has ignored the agency's own guidelines."
>
> Robert Axelrad, director of the EPA's indoor air program, said the report has been extensively rewritten during the past year and a half and has been substantially strengthened. "I think the report is both stronger, as well as more solid scientifically," Mr. Axelrad said. "The one thing that has not occurred is foot-dragging because of industry pressure."[41]

The complaints to the press by Dr. Blum and other antismoking spokesmen about the makeup of the SAB panel can be seen as a kind of insurance policy that put them in a couldn't-lose position. If an EPA review panel that was allegedly "stacked" in favor of the tobacco industry, and whose chairman himself, Morton Lippmann, had "ties" to the industry, were to uphold the draft report condemning secondhand smoke, that would mean that the panel found the evidence overwhelming and indisputable and the industry would be left simply "blowing smoke" (forgive me). But if the unthinkable happened and the panel returned a Scotch verdict of "not proven," it would obviously be because of pressure from the industry, Mr. Alexrad's having averred the contrary notwithstanding.*

Actually, however, if the SAB panel was "stacked," it was hardly in the industry's favor. Three of its members were selected by EPA staff member Dr. Steven Bayard, with input from James Repace and Axelrad. The first two were well-known antismoking activists. None of the candidates suggested by the tobacco industry was appointed to the panel, while three out of six candidates suggested by antismoking organizations were.

Before the first review hearing in 1990, EPA administrator William Reilly had promised Rep. Bliley that antismoking activists on the SAB would be "balanced" by individuals "who could represent the opposing point of view." That ain't what happened.

Says Bliley:

> Despite Mr. Reilly's promises, the SAB panel meeting on December 4-5, 1990, was conducted in a manner that effectively prevented scientific viewpoints critical of the two draft ETS documents from being given anything resembling a full and fair hearing. Less than two hours were allowed for presentations by scientists critical of the report. Certain attendees who had personally requested time from the Chairman were foreclosed from speaking under the agenda that had been formulated. The input of several critical points of view was lost, as well as the opportunity for the panel to ask questions and to conduct a dialogue with other scientists. In contrast, twice as much time was given to antismoking organizations . . .
>
> No presentations were permitted on the risk assessment chapter dealing with the respiratory health of children. Without providing any opportunity for public comment, EPA had transmitted to the SAB a new "draft report with a detailed description and analysis of 26 studies" on childhood exposure to ETS. Not surprisingly, the document failed to discuss any studies that did not support the EPA's preferred conclusion. By inserting it at the

*"[I]t's not that I'm a tool of industry," Dr. Lippmann told *The Los Angeles Times*. "I'm a bigger tool of government. I've been working for the EPA longer. I have more to lose by offending the EPA than industry."[42]

> last moment and preventing public discussion of the topic at the hearing, meaningful scrutiny of the Agency's conclusion was excluded.

Dr. Lippmann, chairman of the SAB panel, presented the panel's report to the SAB's Executive Committee in April 1991. Curiously, says Bliley, the SAB concluded that the worldwide epidemiology data on ETS were too weak and inconclusive to support the draft risk assessment's conclusion that ETS is a cause of lung cancer in nonsmokers. He continues:

> [H]owever, the SAB could not bring itself to take the logical, if politically unpalatable, next step and reject the EPA's conclusions regarding ETS and lung cancer among nonsmokers. Instead, the SAB endorsed the conclusion that ETS is a "Group A" carcinogen while taking the extraordinary step of urging the EPA staff to attempt to "make the case" against ETS by extrapolating from data concerning active smoking. In essence, the Agency was being encouraged to do the science backwards—to maintain its conclusion while going about the task of finding support for it . . .
>
> The SAB's report feebly suggested that the panel "had some difficulty in applying the 'Guidelines for Carcinogen Risk Assessment,' as they are currently formulated," to the ETS data. Particular attention was given to the report's statement that "[I]f the guidelines for Carcinogen Risk Assessment can be used to cast doubt on a finding that inhalation of tobacco smoke by humans causes an increased risk of lung cancer, the situation suggests a need to revise the guidelines" (SAB Rep. 28).
>
> This prompted one member of the SAB Executive Committee to note that it sounded a little like saying "if the data doesn't fit the guidelines, the guidelines should be changed." Nevertheless, the Committee adopted the panel's Group A designation despite the clear failure of the data to satisfy the Agency's own guidelines.

Also curiously, following the Executive Committee's meeting, Dr. Lippmann again candidly told reporters that in his view the risk due to ETS exposure is "probably much less than you took to get here through Washington traffic."[43]

For next year and a half, the EPA labored to "make the case" against ETS and finally, on June 18, 1992, issued a revised risk assessment of over 600 pages. Incredibly, says Bliley, the EPA gave the public just nine days to comment on it, even though the report had doubled in length "and a whole new set of flaws had been introduced." The second draft was even more curious than the first, he says:

> As an EPA health scientist who contributed to the draft admitted, the Agency staff had engaged in some "fancy statistical footwork" . . . to "fashion [an] indictment" of ETS.[44] In the prior draft, EPA's calculations had showed that the epidemiological studies based on U.S. populations showed no statistically significant association between ETS and lung cancer among nonsmokers. In order to reach a statistically significant result in the first draft, EPA therefore had included in its calculations all of the studies of ETS conducted worldwide to tilt the balance in the favored direction. Both the EPA and the SAB rejected out of hand arguments by critics that the risk assessment should have considered only U.S. studies.
>
> When EPA staff was revising the risk assessment, however, it was confronted by the Wu-Williams/Blot study, which had been conducted in China and reported a statistically significant negative association* between marriage to a smoker and lung cancer among nonsmokers—the exposure scenario relied upon in the initial risk assessment draft. Inclusion of the Wu-Williams/Blot study in EPA's analysis would have forced EPA to reverse its conclusions about ETS and lung cancer. At the same time, however, EPA had obtained preliminary data from a large U.S. study that, with some massaging, could be used to support its calculations of risk based exclusively on the U.S. studies.
>
> Accordingly, the EPA entirely reversed course and decided in the second draft to disregard the non-U.S. studies. Instead, EPA used the U.S. studies only . . .

That "massaging" Bliley refers to was to lump all the U.S. studies into a "meta-analysis," a procedure that is meaningful only when a number of different studies are closely similar in structure—which was not the case in this case. Writer Michael Fumento, who is no friend of smoking, explains that "meta-analysis [is] the pooling of results of numerous studies which by themselves are too small to be definitive. Meta-analysis is controversial because inevitably it mixes studies done by different researchers under different conditions. Like oil and water, they can be thrown together but not really combined. Further, good epide-

*Which—if it had any application to the real world—would mean that secondhand smoke actually protected nonsmokers from lung cancer!

miology builds on studies that have gone before. Meta-analysis wipes this out, because it weighs the first study as heavily as the last."[45]

This time the SAB allowed only a mere two days of public hearings on the revised risk assessment in July 1992 and in October submitted its report approving it. Bliley again:

> The panel's conclusions make absolutely clear that it was unconcerned with the scientific soundness of the report's underlying rationale. A brief comparison of the SAB's actions following its first and second review of the risk assessment confirms that the SAB actually disregarded its earlier findings in order to embrace the desired conclusion.

To summarize Bliley's comparison:

In its first review the SAB had concluded that the epidemiological data were too weak to support the inference that exposure to ETS causes lung cancer in nonsmokers and recommended that the EPA use data extrapolated from active smoking studies. But in its second review the SAB decided that active smoking data didn't help either.

Again, in its first review, the SAB concluded that all studies of ETS and lung cancer conducted worldwide should be included. But in its second review the SAB decided that the EPA need only include the U.S. studies because, had the EPA and SAB stuck with their original decision to use all the ETS studies, the meta-analysis would not have shown a statistically significant risk.

Despite all this, says Bliley, "the SAB decided that the total 'weight of evidence' supported a Group A classification."

Following the SAB's October 1992 report, the EPA rushed to revise and release the absolutely final risk assessment, that of January 7, 1993. (Again curiously, during that revision, the rejected foreign studies somehow crept back in.) The reason for the EPA's haste—at least according to critics—was the release in November 1992 of the Brownson study,[46] the largest case-control study of ETS ever conducted up to that time, which found *no* association between ETS and lung cancer. Inclusion of that study would have completely invalidated the EPA's conclusion. "Rather than face this embarrassment," says Bliley, "EPA rushed to release the report without considering the Brownson study on the pretext that 'it had to stop somewhere.'"

Unfortunately, Mr. Bliley also apparently decided it was time to stop. Despite his knowledge of the statistical and other shenanigans the

Environmental Protection Agency had employed in order to brand secondhand smoke a menace, despite the powerful position he later obtained as chairman of the Energy and Commerce Committee, he did nothing I am aware of about this most egregious example in modern U.S. history of the prostitution of science for a political end except submit a blistering statement to a House subcommittee, where it was buried from public view.

Perhaps it was because he was already dubbed "R-Phillip Morris" since his district encompasses Richmond, the home of the nation's largest tobacco company. To have called the EPA on the congressional carpet to expose its fraudulent behavior in public hearings before his committee could have solidified the perception that he was a "tool of Big Tobacco." Maybe I wrong him. But whatever the reason for it, Bliley's silence after the release of the EPA's secondhand smoke report would seem to qualify as something less than a profile in courage.

THE EPA'S DUBIOUS use of a meta-analysis was only one pirouette in its "fancy statistical footwork." In order to arrive at the relative risk of 1.19 mentioned above, the EPA had to change the "confidence interval" of its calculations.

As explained in Chapter 1, a confidence interval, or CI, is a convention of statistics which gives epidemiologists, well, confidence that whatever relative risk they come up with in a given study is reasonably reflective of actuality and is not due to mere chance. It's a range of relative risks, the lower end of which usually must be above 1.0 (no risk) in order to be "statistically significant." Traditionally, the accepted confidence interval in the field of epidemiology is 95 percent, meaning that there is only a five percent possibility that a result occurred by chance. But in a virtually unheard of departure from accepted practice, the EPA lowered its confidence interval to 90 percent, in effect doubling the possibility that its conclusion regarding the danger of environmental tobacco smoke was purely due to chance.

Even using the lower standard, the confidence interval the EPA came up with for spousal ETS risk was 1.04-1.35. (The much-publicized relative risk of 1.19 is in the middle of that range.) The lower end of the confidence interval was just barely within "statistical significance."

"The gold standard in epidemiology has always been a 95 percent confidence interval," says Fumento. "Curiously, the Agency rejected that, in what appeared to be a rigging of the results. It was like moving the goal post to the three yard line because the football had fallen two yards short of a touchdown."[47]

I don't think it's curious at all, seeing that the EPA already knew what verdict it wanted. And to say that it "appeared" to be a rigging of the results is putting it all too mildly. To state it plainly, the Environmental Protection Agency committed what scientists consider the cardinal sin (or used to, before the antismoking crusade began): it *cheated.*

It is one thing for antismokers to make extravagant claims based on personal prejudices and flimsy scientific evidence. It is even forgivable if scientists, who are, believe it or not, only human, tend to emphasize the data that supports whatever they are trying to prove and ignore the data that questions it. But it is quite something else to prostitute science itself by distorting the evidence, if not falsifying it outright, to forward a cause, no matter how noble one may believe the cause to be.

Pshaw, or words to that effect, says Stanton Glantz. To criticize the EPA for changing the confidence interval is a kind of "hairsplitting that only professors care about . . . There is nothing magical about [the 95 percent CI]. I know that scientifically it's widely used, but there is a strong body of thought that people are too slavishly tied to 95 percent."[48]*

To which Fumento responds with his football analogy again: "[C]ritics say[ing] that noting the original selection of 95 percent was arbitrary misses the point. It was arbitrary to make a football field 100 yards long, but once that's the standard, you can't change the length in the middle of the game."[50]

What we're dealing with here is a little more serious than a ballgame, however. Writes Matthew C. Hoffman, a policy analyst with the Competitive Enterprise Institute:

*Possibly because of all the flack it has been subjected to on this issue, the EPA is thinking of dropping the requirement for "statistical significance" entirely in future studies. At least that is the reading by two critics of new "Guidelines for Cancer Risk Assessment" the agency proposed in 1996.[49] If the requirement were to be dropped, it would mean that a risk would simply be whatever the EPA says it is—which, come to think of it, would not be all that great a change from the present situation!

> Those who see smoking as a social evil may be apt to dismiss the relaxation of scientific standards at EPA as a little white lie, a well-intentioned measure to eliminate a nasty and unhealthy habit. But if the EPA succeeds, nonsmokers may find to their chagrin that its new license extends beyond the confines of benign nannyism. Already, the EPA is rummaging through a plethora of potential domestic health hazards, including substances in the steam emitted during hot showers, and the electromagnetic fields generated by common household appliances. Allowing EPA bureaucrats into the private lives of smokers may open new vistas for "environmental protection," at the expense of individual rights.[51]

Mr. Hoffman doesn't seem to appreciate that the EPA bureaucrats are also "on the side of the angels" and if they sometimes go off the deep end, it is only out of concern for "our own good."

Ironically, the EPA's attempt to make a case against ETS by hook or by crook was actually somewhat of an embarrassment to the tobacco companies. For 29 years they had been claiming that the evidence against direct smoking was purely statistical; now they were claiming that the evidence against secondhand smoke was *not* statistical. As Fumento puts it in another analogy, "In a sense, it was the boy who didn't cry wolf—the guy who year after year saw a wolf and claimed there was no wolf there. When he says, 'Look, there's no wolf there,' the media are not going to be quick to believe that."[52]

Of course, the tobacco industry's historic "inability" to acknowledge any direct-smoking wolf does not mean that the reported ETS wolf is real or that it has any fangs. Anyway, if antismokers can get away with "spin-doctoring" every study about smoking to their advantage, I think the industry can be cut a bit of slack once in a while.

AS MENTIONED, a few scientists spoke out, directly or indirectly (but not too loudly), against the EPA's misuse of epidemiology (see again Note 35 to this chapter in Notes section). But perhaps the most authoritative voice was that of Alvan Feinstein, M.D., professor of medicine and epidemiology at Yale University and editor of the *Journal of Clinical Epidemiology*, who in a journal called *Toxicologic Pathology*[53] wrote scathingly of the studies that formed the basis of the EPA report:

> In the investigations of [ETS] . . . the various studies are contradictory, some going in positive directions and others not. The

> inconvenient failure of the evidence to comply with a prime requisite of scientific reasoning for causality, however, has not inhibited the causal accusations. The "prosecution" has simply ignored the inconvenient results and emphasized those that are (in a memorable term) "helpful."

As for the implications this had for the future of research on smoking, Feinstein wrote:

> [I]n the current fervor of anti-smoking evangelism, what young scientists would want to risk their career and what older scientists would want to risk their reputation by doing anything that might be construed as support for the "bad guys" of the tobacco industry? What governmental agency would fund research in which the established "accepted" anti-smoking doctrines were threatened by a study proposed by someone—an obviously deranged skeptic—who wanted to do an unbiased, objective investigation?
>
> [T]he "bad guys" . . . are not always right, but if they are denied a fair and proper scientific hearing, neither society nor science will benefit. Society is entitled to make decisions based on advocacy. The scientific basis for those decisions, however, should depend not on political advocacy, but on scholarship—no matter how it is produced or by whom.

In the same article, Feinstein reported that he had "recently heard an authoritative leader in the world of public health epidemiology make the following statement [regarding the EPA report]: 'Yes, it's rotten science, but it's in a worthy cause. It will help us get rid of cigarettes and become a smoke-free society.'"

Elsewhere, at a toxicology forum in which the subject of environmental tobacco smoke came up, Feinstein characterized the EPA's manipulation of data in even stronger language, calling it "a perversion of science."

Jennifer Jinot, one of the authors of the EPA report, was present and was understandably rather offended by that remark. Dr. Feinstein "apologized" to her in these words:

> I certainly meant no personal slights in my term "perversion of science". . . I have no doubt that you and your colleagues probably devoutly believe in what you have done, and that, alas, has been true of all of the great blunders throughout the history of medical science. They have been devoutly believed in. It is not

> that people were committing fraud. It is not that they were doing misconduct. It is not that they were trying to sell delusions to the public. They, themselves, honestly believed their own delusions, and you and I would have to spend a lot more time talking with one another to go over some of the details that we disagree upon.[54]

Another important critique of the EPA's report was released in November 1995 by the Congressional Research Service (CRS),[55] an investigative agency that conducts research and analysis at the request of Congress. Its report was produced in response to a proposed Occupational Safety and Health Administration ruling, based on the EPA's findings about environmental tobacco smoke, that would ban smoking in federal workplaces. Because the conclusions of the CRS are expressed in the tentative language of good science—unlike the practice at the EPA—both prosmoking and antismoking groups have been able to claim that it supports their positions.

Probably the best authority the antismokers have on their side is the primary author of the report, C. Stephen Redhead, who surely ought to know what the report tried to say. Upset by tobacco industry "misrepresentations" that the report discredits the EPA's finding that secondhand smoke is a Group A carcinogen, Redhead maintains that the report in fact supports the finding.[56]

On the other hand, another CRS analyst, Jane G. Gravelle, principal author of another CRS report[57] on the use of cigarette taxes to fund health care, released in March 1994, told a congressional committee that "Our evaluation was that the statistical evidence does not appear to support a conclusion that there were substantial health effects of passive smoking."[58]

Well, No. 1, does the Congressional Research Service support the EPA or doesn't it? And, No. 2, does it really matter?

1. Does it or doesn't it?

Everyone has biases, and given the cautious—I would even say, timid—language of the Redhead/CRS report, it's easy to pick and choose excerpts to prove whatever one wants to prove. But my own (admittedly biased) reading of it is that while it hardly brands the EPA's secondhand smoke report as the fraud that it is, it certainly does not validate it. A few of my favorite excerpts (with all emphases added):

"[A]bout one-third of the studies reviewed by EPA for dose response* behavior show a statistically significant (at the 95 percent level) upward trend. While there is evidence of an upward dose response trend, the results are not definitive. And even at the greatest integrated exposure levels, the measured risks are still *subject to uncertainty*." (Page 2)

"T]he amount of nicotine inhaled by a nonsmoker working in a relatively smoky restaurant for eight hours is equivalent to smoking one-eighth of a cigarette." (Page 17)

"Even when overall risk is considered, it is a *very small risk* and is *not* statistically significant at a conventional 95 percent level." (Page 25)

"[T]he two largest U.S. studies [released since the EPA report]—Fontham and Brownson—found in one case a positive risk that was *barely significant* and the other *no risk at all*." (Page 25)

"[S]moker misclassification could explain all the measured risk even at high exposure levels even for studies such as Fontham and Brownson." (Page 41)

"It is clear that misclassification and recall bias plague ETS epidemiology studies . . . It is possible that more research on the general question of misclassification will reduce the *uncertainty* now present in these ETS results, but such research will be difficult to perform because its methods, too, appear to be subject to *considerable uncertainty*." (Page 45)

"In general, smokers are less health conscious than nonsmokers. They tend to drink more alcohol, eat less healthy diets, exercise less, and have a lower socioeconomic status. The degree to which non-smoking spouses of smokers share their partner's unhealthy lifestyles has not been studied extensively, but it is likely that some of the risks are shared." (Page 68)

And the best one of all:

"[I]t is possible that *very few or even no deaths* can be attributed to ETS." (Page 55)

*That is, the more exposure to secondhand smoke (the "dose") and the longer the exposure (measured in pack/years), the more cases of lung cancer.

I may be guilty of doing a little cheating myself: (1) my liberal sprinkling of italics above, although no words were changed; (2) the passage from page 17 is not really germane because the EPA did not use any studies dealing with secondhand smoke outside the home, mainly because such studies are extremely difficult to conduct and fraught with even greater "uncertainties," and (3) the statement from page 55 was part of a highly technical discussion of the Fontham and Brownson studies which were not included in the EPA's meta-analysis, though I believe the statement also applies to the EPA's official finding.

But at least I'm trying to be honest. Before you sue me, listen to Rep. Henry Waxman's "spin" on the same report:

"The new [CRS] *report vindicates the conclusions of the Environmental Protection Agency. It shows that secondhand tobacco smoke is a dangerous human lung carcinogen."*[59] [Emphasis mine.]

Unfortunately, Mr. Waxman, the man who dragged seven tobacco company CEOs before his committee in 1994 for a kangaroo-court-style inquisition (see Chapter 12) didn't tell us where in the CRS report (which he obviously didn't read) such vindication can be found. He couldn't, because there wasn't any.

Even one member of the SAB's review panel, Dr. Geoffrey Kabat, says that "the EPA is making a stretch when they call ETS a Class A carcinogen." Kabat, an epidemiologist with the Albert Einstein College of Medicine, conducted his own study on ETS, with funding from the National Cancer Institute, and reported in the July 15, 1995 issue of the *Journal of Epidemiology* that he found little association between ETS and the risk of lung cancer from women living with smoking spouses.[60]

Of the EPA report he said, "If these were data on something else—risk factors for ingrown toenails or something like that—people would look at it and say, 'Well, it's really not too impressive . . . '"[61]

But the EPA report didn't deal with toenails, unfortunately; it dealt with secondhand smoke, and I'm quite convinced that many people, for various reasons, desperately *wanted* to be told that secondhand smoke was dangerous.

If the Redhead/CRS report can, by a similar "stretch," be construed to support the EPA, the earlier Gravelle/CRS report mentioned above does not lend itself so easily to that procedure—which may be why, in several years of surfing the many antismoking sites on the World Wide Web, I have never seen it referred to. Although the Gravelle report was concerned with the question of whether an increase in cigarette taxes to fund health care was justified on the basis that smokers' illnesses are a burden on society (see Chapter 12 for a fuller discussion of that issue), it also examined the EPA's secondhand smoke report. Again operating from my own bias, I have selected the following passages from pages 47-49 and have again supplied all emphases:

> [I]t is unusual to return to a study after the fact, lower the required significance level and declare its results to be supportive rather than unsupportive of the effect one's theory suggests should be present.
>
> However, this characterization masks the critical issue raised by the change in the statistical significance standard. The test of statistical significance used in these [EPA] studies answers the following question: *How large a chance, statistically speaking, are we willing to take that we accept existence of a passive-smoking effect when in fact a passive smoking effect does not exist?* In effect, EPA changed the standard from accepting a chance of two-and-a-half percent to accepting a chance of five percent.
>
> These studies do not have (and indeed *cannot* have) very precise estimates of exposure from environmental tobacco smoke. The data are based on interviews of the subjects or their relatives. If errors in measurement occur in a systematic way that is correlated with development of the disease, the effect would be to bias the results. An example would be if those individuals who developed lung cancer (or relatives of those individuals) remembered or perceived their exposure differently from those who did not develop the disease.
>
> Another concern is the possibility that some nonsmokers are actually current or former smokers and that such current or former smokers are more likely to be married to husbands that smoke. While EPA made some adjustment for this effect, it is not possible to correct precisely for this problem. That is, it remains possible that a relationship observed might reflect the effects of active rather than passive smoking.
>
> In addition, while EPA considered the presence of confounding factors in its evaluation of the studies, this issue is not laid to rest. If wives of smokers share in poor health habits or other factors that could contribute to illness that are not or cannot be controlled for, statistical associations found between disease and passive smoking could be incidental or *misleading*. This effect could presumably be correlated with exposure levels.
>
> These limitations of studies are often inevitable, but they impart *some degree of uncertainty* to the results, especially when relatively small risks are estimated.

Finally, there is the question of smoker misclassification due to the possibility that some women reporting themselves to be nonsmokers were actually current or former smokers. (Two reasons may be because of guilt about smoking or because they lied to their life insurance companies in order to get a lower rate.) As Gravelle notes, the EPA "adjusted" its mathematics to allow for this effect. But between the release of its first draft report in 1990 and the final 1993 report, the agency adopted a different formula recommended by A. Judson Wells, a consultant to the Occupational Safety and Health Administration, which lowered the adjustment for smoker misclassification and resulted in a higher relative risk for passive smoking.[62] Without this change, together with the lowering of the confidence interval, the EPA would have been unable to come up with the famous risk estimate of 1.19 (which even so, remains barely "significant").

2. Does It Really Matter?

No. Not a bit. Not in the slightest.

For one thing, most people have probably never heard of either of the two CRS reports, and even if they have heard of them are unlikely to have the technical knowledge needed to make much sense of them, much less the desire to try to.

But most important, and overriding everything else, is the fact that the belief that secondhand smoke is "a dangerous human lung carcinogen," as Waxman said, and a cause of all kinds of other human afflictions as well, has become firmly ingrained in popular thinking. That "secondhand smoke kills" is now "common knowledge." It has become so much a part of the accepted wisdom that I don't know what could change that perception, except maybe the passage of time and the emergence of a medical/scientific establishment more concerned with scientific integrity than obsessed with chasing the bogeyman of smoking.

THIS CHAPTER TO this point was written before the long-awaited decision in the tobacco industry's suit against the EPA was finally handed down. Yet even though that decision held in favor of the industry and embodied every criticism Rep. Bliley had made (but not too loudly) against the agency's secondhand smoke report and the devious means by which it had been arrived at, everything I said in the immediately preceding paragraph still holds. The decision won't change a thing.

On July 17, 1998, five years—*five years*—after the suit was filed, during which time the belief that secondhand smoke killed innocent bystanders became ever more firmly entrenched in the popular mind, Judge William Osteen of the U.S. District Court for the Middle of North Carolina vacated virtually all of the EPA's report.[63]

In a scathingly worded memorandum opinion, Osteen found that:

"EPA publicly committed to a conclusion before research had begun; excluded [the tobacco] industry by violating the [Radon] Act's procedural requirements; adjusted established procedure and scientific norms [by lowering the confidence interval—D.O] to validate the Agency's public conclusion, and aggressively utilized the Act's authority to disseminate findings to establish a de facto regulatory scheme intended to restrict Plaintiff's products and influence public opinion."

(The Radon Act, passed by Congress in 1986, established guidelines the EPA is supposed to follow in making health risk assessments for radon, asbestos and other potentially harmful environmental pollutants.)

Further, said Osteen:

"In conducting the ETS Risk Assessment, EPA disregarded information and made findings on selective information ["cherry picking" among studies—D.O.]; did not disseminate significant epidemiologic information; deviated from its Risk Assessment Guidelines; failed to disclose important findings and reasoning and left significant questions without answers . . . Gathering all relevant information, researching and disseminating findings were subordinate to EPA's demonstrating ETS a Group [A] carcinogen."

It was just as Bliley and other critics had claimed all along. The EPA established its conclusion first, then bent the rules and the evidence to try to validate it.

Again media reaction was predictable. *The Atlanta Journal-Constitution* did indeed report the decision on its front page of July 20, 1998 under the subheading: "Judge rejects secondhand cancer link." However, its headline, in type so large that it took up fully one-third the space of the entire story, was: "EPA says smoking bans stay." By so doing, in one stroke it minimized the importance of the decision and reassured readers that nothing was going to change. Not on that day or on any following day did the AJC print an editorial commenting on the decision. It was simply ignored.

It takes no imagination to guess what the reaction would have been—in this newspaper, in every other newspaper in America, on every television news broadcast, by every organ of the media—had Judge Osteen ruled the other way.

I found a few comments from other newspapers and from antismoking spokesmen like ASH's John Banzaf on the Web, and they all generally agreed—approvingly—that the decision changed nothing. And they're right, of course.

Businesses and city councils are not going to reverse their bans against smoking. Smoke-free restaurants are not going to permit smoking once again. Nonsmokers are not going to welcome smokers into their homes. Nonsmoking spouses are not going to stop nagging smoking spouses. Not in what remains of *my* generation's lifetime.

Wouldn't you think that antismoking groups would be glad that the evidence against second-hand smoke is far from conclusive? asks Bruce Herschensohn, a distinguished fellow at the Claremont Institute in Claremont, California, and a member of the board of advisors of the National Smokers Alliance. Wouldn't you think that if the health of others, including their own health, is really their concern, that they would hope "secondary smoke" is not harmful?

"Not at all," he writes. They want it to be a killer. That gives righteousness to their cause that, without such justification, is nothing more than dictating the choices of others. And they know it."[64]

That goes to the heart of the ETS issue and the whole antismoking movement itself. It is *control* over the behavior of others the antismokers want, and if it requires the perversion of science to accomplish that end, well, so much the worse for science.

I'll close this chapter with another quote from John Luik's *Niagara* article:

> The debate about Environmental Tobacco Smoke, though ostensibly a debate about smoking, is really a debate about much more than smoking. It is a debate about the legitimacy of perverting science and public policy on science in the interests of a particular ideology. It is a debate at bottom about the worth of a health paternalism that guarantees to leave all of us substantially less free but not less ill.

To which I will add two comments: Mr. Luik is a nonsmoker, and you'll never see his article reprinted in *Reader's Digest.*

Notes

1. Interview of the actor in the *Dallas Morning News*, August 17, 1986, Section E.

2. Susan Gilbert McGuire, "A Smoker's Wife." *Reader's Digest*, November 1995, p.35. From *The Chicago Tribune*.

3. National Smokers Alliance newsletter *NSA Voice*, November/December, 1996, p.3

4. "Absurdity Meets Resistance." Nation Smokers Alliance newsletter *The Resistance*, October 1997, p. 5.

5. *Philip Morris Magazine*, Fall 1991, p. 22.

6. "Dear Abby.""Happy smokers have no plans to kick the habit." *The Atlanta Journal-Constitution*, April 7, 1993, p. B2.

7. "Dear Abby." *The Atlanta Journal-Constitution*, August 9, 1993, p. B2.

8. Molly Ivins, "Blowing smoke over 'oppression.'" *The Atlanta Journal-Constitution*, August 6, 1994, p A14.

9. "Second-hand smoke becomes death sentence." *Breather's Digest*, February 1995. At www. seercom.com/airspace/bd295.

10. Ibid.

11. "Making a photograph lie." *The Tampa Tribune*, August 10, 1996; Joe Urschel, "Post office blows away history in a puff of smoke." *USA Today*, September 30, 1994. Both sources cited in personal communication from Martha Perske.

12. "NSA Takes on Book-of-the-Month Club; Charges Censorship." *The NSA Voice*, April 1995, p. 2.

13. "Paul Simon's cigarette airbrushed off cover of Old Friends box set." FORCES Georgia, at www.forces.georgia.org/national/oldfriends.html.

14. "Esther's Story: A Little Bit of Secondhand Smoke Can Go A Long Way." Posted on the World Wide Web by S.A.F.E. (Smokefree Air For Everyone) at www.pacificnet.net/~safe/story.html.

15. From Smoker's Home Page at www.tezcat.com/~smokers/alt_smokers.html#farrell.

16. Quoted by S.A.F.E. at www.pacific.net/~safe/news.html.

17. From FORCES Canada at www.forces-cdn.com/trash.htm.

18. Richard Kluger, *Ashes to Ashes: America's Hundred-Year Cigarette War, the Public Health, and the Unabashed Triumph of Philip Morris* (New York: Alfred A Knopf, 1996), p. 506.

19. John C. Luik, "Pandora's Box: the Dangers of Politically Corrupted Science for Democratic Public Policy." *Bostonia* magazine. No date given. Posted on the World Wide Web at www.forces.com/pages/pandora.htm. An associate of the Niagara Institute, Luik is a professor of philosophy and politics.

20. From www.tobacco.org/History/Tobacco—History.html.

21. Kluger, p. 495.

22. A.H. Lowrey and J. L. Repace, "Indoor Air Pollution, Tobacco Smoke and Public Health." *Science*, vol. 208 (1980), pp. 464-472. Cited in Bliley, Note 36 infra.

23. J. L. Repace and A. H. Lowrey, "A Quantitative Estimate on Nonsmokers' Lung Cancer Risk from Passive Smoking." *Environment International*, vol. 11 (1985), pp. 3-22. Also cited in Bliley.

24. *American Review of Respiratory Diseases* vol. 133 (1986), pp. 1-3. Quoted in Kluger, p. 498.

25. "The Health Consequences of Involuntary Smoking." A Report of the Surgeon General, U.S. Department of Health and Human Services, 1986, p. 13.

26. Ibid, page 10.

27. Kluger, p. 503.

28. Loc. cit.

29. Ibid, pp. 690, 691.

30. Ibid, p. 691.

31. Michael Gough and Steven Milloy, "EPA's Cancer Risk Guidelines: Guidance to Nowhere." Cato Institute Policy Analysis No. 263, November 12, 1996.

32. Editorial. "EPA shows need for smoking bans." *The Atlanta Journal-Constitution,* January 11, 1993, p. A10.

33. Matthew C. Hoffman, "Smoking Signals, Secondhand doubts." *The Washington Times*, April 5, 1994. Hoffman is a policy analyst for the Competitive Enterprise Institute.

34. Steven Milloy, "More on the Importance of Statistical Significance." At www.junkscience.com/news/emf/data-dredging.html.

35. Jacob Sullum, "Passive Reporting on Passive Smoke." *Forbes MediaCritic*, March 1994.

FORCES Canada has published a raft of similar comments from other scientists at www.forces-cdn.com/index.htm. A few of them (can they all be "tools" of the tobacco industry?):

"In epidemiologic research, relative risks of less than 2 are considered small and are usually difficult to interpret. Such increases may be due to chance, statistical bias, or the effects of confounding factors that are sometimes not evident." (Press release, U.S. National Cancer Institute, October 1994.)

"Small associations below 2.0 may be beyond the limits of reliable epidemiological inference." (J. Peto, 1992, International Agency for Research on Cancer [IARC], part of the World Health Organization.)

"In general, I think it's a general opinion, and my opinion, that if a relative risk figure goes below about three, then the significance of that result becomes open to question. The relative risks we are talking about with ETS are well below three, and most of them well below two. If it was anything else but ETS I think people wouldn't bother with it at all. They wouldn't discuss it. The relative risks are far too low." (Professor John Robert Ashford, Managing Director of Exeter Health Information Services, commenting on a proposed Occupational Safety and Health Administration [OSHA] rule on Indoor Air Quality, 1995.)

"Differences in risk of 50% (relative risk of 1.5) are small in epidemiological terms and severely challenge our ability to distinguish whether it reflects cause and effect or whether it simply reflects bias." (Lynn Rosenberg, Boston University School of Medicine quoted in a press release from the U.S. National Cancer Institute, October 26, 1994.)

"Epidemiological studies in general are probably not able, realistically, to identify with any confidence any relative risks lower than 1.3 . . . " (Dr. Eugenia Calle, Director of Analytic Epidemiology, American Cancer Society, *Washington Post*, October 27,1994.)

"The statistical evidence does not appear to support a conclusion that there are substantial health effects of passive smoking." (Dr. Jane Gravelle et al., Senior Specialist in Economic Policy, Congressional Research Service, in testimony before the Subcommittee on Clean Air and Nuclear Regulation, Committee on Environment and Public Works, U.S. Senate, May 11, 1994.)

"The totality of data on ETS and lung cancer does not support the claim made in the draft EPA report that ETS is responsible for an increased incidence of lung cancer in the United States. There is no scientifically valid basis for conducting a risk assessment on ETS or classifying ETS as a known carcinogen or even probable human carcinogen." (Dr. W. Gary Flamm, Science Regulatory Services International, former director of the Office of Toxicological Sciences, U.S. Food and Drug Administration.)

" . . . It seems that the epidemiological database as it stands today does not support an association between ETS exposure and lung cancer. The workplace data reports no elevation in risk and the spousal exposure data reports either no increase in risk or an increase that is so small that it can be entirely accounted for by bias and confounding factors that have not been properly addressed in the studies." (Dr. Hitoshi Kasaga, Tokai University School of Medicine, Japan, in *Environmental Tobacco Smoke*, H. Kasuga, ed., Springer-Verlag, 1993, p. 84.)

"The ETS lung cancer epidemiological data provide no scientific basis for government regulation of smoking in the workplace." (Le Vois, M.E. et al., "Inconsistency Between Workplace and Spousal Studies of Environmental Tobacco Smoke and Lung Cancer." *Regulatory Toxicology and Pharmacology*, 1994.)

"The EPA has manipulated selected portions of the existing literature until it produced the desired result." (Kent Jeffreys, "Science, Economics, and

Environmental Policy: A Critical Examination," a research report by the Alexis de Tocqueville Institution, August 11, 1994.)

36. Rep. Thomas J. Bliley Jr., Statement to the House Committee on Energy and Commerce Health and Environment Subcommittee, July 21, 1993. From www.pipes.org/Articles/Bliley.html.

37. From www.forces.com/pages/epa-epid.htm and www. forces. com/pages/epa-asse.htm.

38. Jess Nesmith, "Secondhand smoke data may trigger tough curbs." *The Atlanta Journal-Constitution,* January 6, 1993, p A1.

39. Sullum, op. cit.

40. "7 on EPA smoking panel linked to tobacco industry." *The Atlanta Journal-Constitution*, November 9, 1990, p. A6. From the Associated Press.

41. "Smoking report goes to EPA panel with tobacco ties." *The Atlanta Journal-Constitution*, July 21, 1992, p.A5 . From the Associated Press.

42. Quoted in "Impartial Panel for Smoking Study Proves Hard to Find." *Los Angeles Times*, November 24, 1990, p. A27. Cited in Bliley.

43. *Washington Times*, April 18, 1991, p. A3. Cited in Bliley.

44. *Science*, vol. 257, p. 607 (July 31, 1992). Cited in Bliley.

45. Michael Fumento, "Consumer Report's False 'Truth' about Secondhand Smoke." From *Reason* magazine's Website at www.reasonmag.com.

"[D]rawing conclusions from meta-analytic studies is like having your cake and eating it too." Ray Hyman, "Psychic Functioning: Claims vs. Reality." *Skeptical Inquirer*, March/April 1996, p. 24.

46. R. C. Brownson et al., "Passive Smoking and Lung Cancer in Nonsmoking Women." *American Journal of Public Health*, vol. 82, pp. 1525-1530 (1992). Cited in Bliley.

47. Michael Fumento, "Ignored Report Says EPA Wrong On Passive Smoking." At www.reasonmag.com.

48. Quoted in Michael Fumento, "Is EPA Blowing Its Own Smoke?" *Investor's Business Daily*, January 28, 1993. Republished by the American Smokers Alliance at www.smokers.org/research/ articles/08-epa_ blowing _ smoke html.

49. Michael Gough and Steven Milloy, "EPA's Cancer Risk Guidelines: Guidance to Nowhere." Cato Policy Analysis No. 263; November 12, 1996. At www.cato.org/pubs/pas/pa-263es.html. Michael Gough is director of science and risk studies at the Cato Institute. Steven Milloy is executive director of The Advancement of Sound Science Coalition in Washington, D.C., and edits the Junk Science Page at www.junkscience.com.

50. Michael Fumento, "Is EPA Blowing Its Own Smoke?"

51. Matthew C. Hoffman, "Smoking Signals, Secondhand Doubts." *The Washington Times*, April 5, 1994.

52. Quoted in Sullum.

53. Alvan Feinstein, in a critique of a review article, "Environmental Tobacco Smoke: Current Assessment and Future Directions." *Toxicologic Pathology*, vol. 20(2), pp. 303-305 (1992). Quoted in Bliley.

54. The Toxicology Forum, 1993 Annual Summer Meeting, held at the Given Institute of Pathobiology, Aspen, Colorado, pp. 339, 340 of transcript. Posted on the Web at www.forces.org/pages/alvan.htm.

55. C. Stephen Redhead and Richard E. Rowberg, "Environmental Tobacco Smoke and Lung Cancer Risk." CRS Report for Congress 95-1115 SPR, November 14, 1995.

56. Quoted by the California Center for Health Improvement (CCHI) at www.webcom.com/cchi/PUB/tobaccosmoke.html.

57. Jane G. Gravelle and Dennis Zimmerman, "Cigarette Taxes to Fund Health Care Reform: An Economic Analysis." CRS Report for Congress No. 94214E, March 8, 1994.

58. Quoted in Joyce Price, "EPA takes heat on Hill for passive-smoke report." *The Washington Times*, May 12, 1994. From American Smokers Alliance at www.smokers.org/research/articles/03_epa_takes_heat.html.

59. In a statement released on Nov. 15, 1995. Quoted in Martha Perske, "Are Anti-Smokers Attempting to Manipulate the Public?" American Smokers Alliance Website at www.speakup.org/perske.html.

60. FORCES, at www.forces.com/pages/kabat.htm, which cites as its source *Indoor Pollution News: The Bi-Weekly Newsletter on Regulation, Legislation, and Litigation* (Silver Spring, MD), August 21, 1995, p. 135.

61. Quoted in *The Resistance*, a newsletter of the National Smokers Alliance, January 1998, p. 3.

62. Letter from A. Judson Wells to Steven Bayard, project officer for the EPA's environmental tobacco smoke study, September 28, 1990. Copy in possession of Martha Perske.

63. Order and Judgment in the United States District Court for the Middle District of North Carolina, Winston-Salem Division, re Flue-Cured Tobacco Cooperative Stabilization Corporation, the Council for Burley Tobacco, Inc., Universal Leaf Tobacco Company, Inc., Philip Morris Inc., R.J. Reynolds Tobacco Company and Gallins Vending Company, plainiffs, *v.* United States Environmental Protection Agency and Carol Browner, Administrator, defendants, 17 July 1998.

64. Bruce Herschensohn, "It's Time to Choose Sides." *The NSA Voice*, May/June 1997, pp. 5-6.

Chapter 7

FUN WITH ETS

A thoughtful man, even if he is a nonsmoker, carries a lighter or matches so he can light a woman's cigarette.

— Amy Vanderbilt (1958)[1]

Irrational emotions against smoking and the return of puritanism under the guise of political correctness have thus, at least in America, contributed to the decline of civility.

— Pierre Lemieux (1996)[2]

THE PREVIOUS CHAPTER ended on rather a somber note. Let's start this one by looking at some more adventures folks have had with environmental tobacco smoke, or ETS, and some of the ways in which the crusade against smoking has contributed to the decline of civility in late 20th-century American life.

As we learned in Chapter 6, cigarette smoke penetrated the closed door of a man's apartment with enough effect to make him start coughing even though he was some distance away in the bedroom, and cigarette smoke disabled a teacher in a room on a floor above and also some distance away from a smoking lounge. These are by far not the only instances of this phenomenon. In 1992 a couple in Chesapeake, Virginia, took their landlord to court asking that he be forced to seal off their apartment from the smoke-laden air of their next-door neighbors on the ground that it was a health hazard the landlord had a duty to prevent. It was the first such suit in the state, according to Virginia GASP (Group Against Smoking in Public).

Pamela and David Billings said they began smelling cigarette smoke after a family with two smokers moved next door. David Billings testified that several times he had "gagged . . . walking into my own bathroom." Pamela Billings, who has a form of asthma, testified that she suffered burning eyes and breathing problems. Four other current or former residents of the complex testified that they had the same problems.

A city inspector found a half-inch hole under a flange behind a kitchen pipe and a four-inch hole under the bathroom sink, cut out to give access to a shut-off valve. Under questioning by the landlord's attorney, the inspector agreed that the holes could be blocked with masking tape.

Unfortunately for the plaintiffs, they came up against an unreconstructed judge who smoked and was less than sympathetic to their plight. He not only threw the case out but terminated the Billings's lease. He did not even allow testimony from GASP regarding the medical dangers of ETS.

As the president of the rental company summed it up, "Being strident and a tough guy isn't always the best thing to do."[3]

Another couple living in a Dover, New Jersey, co-op were a little less strident when they took their downstairs neighbor, a 60-year-old widow, to court. Although they claimed, among other things, that the defendant's smoking had caused the wife to have an unfortunate ectopic pregnancy,* they merely demanded that the widow be required to refrain from smoking after four in the afternoon so that, presumably, the air would be cleared by the time they came home from work.[4] I don't know how that case came out.

Not so easy to make a judgment call on, though, is a case where a smoker did indeed pose a hazard to others, and himself as well. One John Womack, a smoker for more than 50 of his 67 years, was given 10 days to vacate his apartment—not because of his smoking but because the new owner of the complex learned that he smoked six cigarettes a day even while hooked up to an oxygen tank for his emphysema.

*To say the least, that would be difficult to prove. But who knows? According to a report in the *New York State Journal of Medicine*, one-millionth of a gram of tobacco smoke in a cubic yard of air "poses an unacceptable hazard."[5] A whole gram is one 350ths of an ounce. If a mere millionth of a gram of tobacco smoke is dangerous, then anything is possible.

Anna Corcoran, the apartment owner, said she wasn't aware that the man had just been told he had two months to live when she served the notice, but insisted she was only looking out for the welfare of the other tenants. Although Womack had been on oxygen for four years without an explosion or fire, there was certainly that possibility. Womack said he would stop smoking, which should be easy enough for someone down to only six cigarettes a day, but Corcoran countered, understandably, that there was no way to enforce the promise.[6] I don't know how this came out either.

Not to digress already (but I will), one's next-door or downstairs neighbor's smoking is bad enough, but we can pass laws against that or haul them into court. What if he snores? (I say "he" because this usually seems to be a male problem.) I caught part of an "Oprah" show on the subject of snoring, aired in the Atlanta area on May 29, 1997, in which it was said that somebody, somewhere, snored so loudly that the neighbors called the police. I didn't hear the rest of the story. But what're you gonna do—ask the court to order the guy not to sleep after four P.M.?

Or what if you bought a house whose previous owner kept cats? A couple moved into a $317,000 home in Fairfield Township, New Jersey, near Newark, in 1994 only to find (somehow they hadn't noticed it before) that their dream house not only reeked of cat urine but that the urine had seeped through the carpets, staining walls, rusting baseboard heaters and damaging electrical wires, all at a cost of $125,000 in repairs. It was so bad that when they ran the dishwasher, "a yellow substance came out with a strong smell," they told an appellate court.[7]

Now *that's* a cat-astrophe (pun stolen from source), compared to which secondhand smoke pales to insignificance. In this case, however, no alleged ectopic pregnancy due to cat urine was involved.

According to the National Smokers Alliance, we have only seen the tip of the cigarette, so to speak, in this litigation-ripe matter of our neighbors' smoking. It reports that Action on Smoking and Health (ASH), a prominent antismoking group, has developed guidelines on how to force condominium associations and apartment buildings to ban smoking throughout their buildings, including in individual units.

ASH recommended these steps: 1) Examine your lease or condominium agreement; 2) Obtain medical documentation if possible; 3) Seek out other nonsmokers for support; 4) Seek help from local antismoking organizations; 5) Reassure management that there is no right to smoke; 6) Consider and propose different remedies; 7) Consider advising management of potential liability; 8) If all else fails, consider legal action; 9) Know, and tell others, about the health dangers.[8]

And it appears that some are following ASH's advice. In Los Angeles, for example, a man filed suit against his downstairs neighbors to stop them from smoking. Claiming that he became physically ill and emotionally distressed, Roy R. Platt also sued his homeowners' association, asking that smoking be banned or restricted in his complex.

Some city and state governments are getting into the act. In Salem, Massachusetts, in 1996, a city council member attempted to prohibit smoking inside residents' apartments in the city's elderly housing complexes, which prompted one 69-year-old resident to comment: "Who the hell are they to dictate what someone can and cannot do in their own home? That's an invasion of civil rights." (He was 69 and he smoked and he wasn't dead? How could that be? Oh, never mind.)

The Ft. Pierce, Florida, Housing Authority passed a no-smoking policy that required all new public housing tenants to agree not to smoke in their own homes. The policy would be a term of all new leases; current tenants would not be affected.

In Utah, state Senate President Lane Beattie asked legislators to draft laws that would help nonsmokers whose apartments and condominiums are invaded by tobacco smoke from nearby dwellings. According to *The Salt Lake Tribune*, experts at the Department of Health and others have been assigned the task of developing potential solutions to the "problem" of smoking in private residences. The results were to be introduced in the 1997 legislative session.[9]

"It's the nanny state run amok," commented Roger Pilon of the Washington, D.C.-based Cato Institute.[10]

As for how Ft. Pierce Housing Authority would enforce the new policy, Commissioner Richard Sneed admitted that, "I don't know how we will go about policing it, but as a commission it is not our job to do that."

They just make the laws, ma'am. But no doubt the public-spirited citizens in Ft. Pierce can be counted on to keep an eye on their neighbors and report infractions. After all, it takes a village to raise the collective consciousness.

Some are not amused. We're becoming "A Nation of Meddlers,"

wrote Charles Edgley, professor of sociology at Oklahoma State and Dennis Brissett, professor of behavioral science at the University at Minnesota Medical school, in an article with that title.

"These days . . . people are not only known by what they don't do, but also by what they don't tolerate: 'I don't drink, smoke, use drugs, or eat the wrong foods' is not enough. Now self is preserved by adding emphatically: 'and I don't tolerate those who do!' If the meddlee seems to be happy, interesting, fun-loving, and (perhaps even healthy, satisfied, and fulfilled), this only increases the grim-faced challenge offered the meddler."[11]

Just how far are the nanny state or local communities and their meddlesome supporters prepared to go in the crusade against secondhand smoke? The antismokers are now laying claim to the wide-open spaces themselves of this great country as their very own.

Homeowners in little Rolling Hills, California, were apparently among the first in the nation to have the right to smoke in their own backyards taken away by ordinance.[12] In Flemington, New Jersey, however, only persons under 18 are prohibited from smoking in public or possessing tobacco products.[13] That law is aimed at curbing youth smoking rather than ETS, but Friendship [*sic*] Heights, Maryland, considered trying to stop everybody from smoking outdoors.

A measure before the village council would have subjected anyone smoking, using smokeless tobacco or discarding tobacco products anywhere in Friendship Heights to a $100 fine.[14] According to the mayor, Dr. Alfred Muller, who is also an internist, the ban would convince children that smoking is not acceptable and would create a "smoke-free generation." It wouldn't infringe on anybody's civil liberties because smokers could still smoke in their homes, out of view of impressionable youth or nonsmoking adults who might be offended at the sight of somebody enjoying a cigarette, pipe or cigar—if they weren't dispatched in their prime by the secondhand smoke, that is.

As for his critics, the kindly physician was quoted in *The Washington Times* as saying, "Eventually, they [smokers] are going to die out. I think they should smoke as much as they like—that will cut down their membership quickly."

Because Friendship Heights is unincorporated, however, the ordinance was subject to oversight by the Montgomery County Council, whose Health and Human Services Committee for some strange reason (perhaps a fit of sanity?) voted three-to-one to kill the measure.[15]

This was only a minor setback. According to The Advocacy Institute, an antismoking group which monitors the nation's news media:

> An article in the *New York Times* reports that local laws banning outdoor cigarette smoking appear to be gaining momentum. The tobacco industry says these measures illustrate tobacco control advocates' "prohibitionist zeal."
>
> Particular attention has been drawn to a measure banning cigarette smoking from public parks in Bellaire, Texas. Thomas Lauria of the Tobacco Institute said, "This is tobacco apartheid at its worst. They're saying that a taxpayer cannot smoke a cigarette while walking his dog in the park? It's totally absurd." The city also bans dogs and open alcohol containers in its parks.
>
> The California cities of Palo Alto and Davis and the Massachusetts town of Sharon have also instituted outdoor smoking bans. Davis and Palo Alto both prohibit individuals from smoking within 20 feet of a building's entrance that's open to the general public. Sharon's law prohibits smoking in any of the town's municipal recreation areas.
>
> No attempts to repeal the outdoor smoking bans have been successful and none of the outdoor smoking bans have been legally challenged. According to the article, the American Civil Liberties Union (ACLU) has not decided whether it would support a constitutional challenge to the bans.[16]

The ACLU has, indeed, been conspicuous by its absence in cases involving smokers' rights, or alleged rights. In fact, Ronal Madnick, director of the Worcester County, Massachusetts, chapter of the organization, defended smoking regulations passed in Fitchburg and Leominster. Echoing Friendship Heights's Dr. Muller, he said, "There is no civil liberties issue here. The smokers' right is overruled by the right of the person who doesn't want to be exposed [to ETS]."[17]

There is a certain logic to this. After all, many things are illegal to do in public. Having sex, for instance, which is considered harmful to the public morals. Every country has some sort of law against that and few people (with the possible exception of English train riders, see below) would claim it is an infringement on their civil liberties. Most people would rather engage in this activity in private anyway. (Yet some states still prohibit certain kinds of sexual activities even in private between consenting adults.) As for smoking, however, the logic falters when you consider that people have been doing this in public for 400 years to no one's terrible distress—and all of a sudden the authorities decree, upon trumped-up evidence, that it is harmful to innocent bystanders. At the very least, there would seem to be a civil liberties issue involved in telling owners of private property, e.g., restaurants, bars, etc., that they may not permit smoking on their premises.

Davis and Palo Alto are actually very liberal. When I accompanied my ailing, never-smoked-a-day-in-his-life brother-in-law to the University of Massachusetts Hospital center in Worcester for some tests a few years before he died, a sign warned, "No Smoking Within 50 Feet of Building Or Entrances." The prohibition was being observed in the breach by a number of smokers clustered right by the main entrance.

I could understand how a wisp of cigarette smoke might enter the building when somebody opened a door. But were the brick walls that porous?

According to ASH, however, which always takes the most extreme position possible, to a sensitive nonsmoker "a cloud of tobacco smoke contamination constitutes as great a barrier to access [to a public facility] as flights of stairs present to a disabled person in a wheelchair."[18] As such it's a violation of Title III of the Americans With Disabilities Act, ASH claims. Indeed, the U.S. Court of Appeals for the Second Circuit in New York has ruled that sensitive nonsmokers are entitled to protection from secondhand tobacco smoke under that rubric.[19]

Funny, I didn't see any indication of this accessibility problem at the hospital in Worcester. Everyone who entered did so with no observable difficulty. Some of them surely were nonsmokers.

But what about the barriers sensitive antismokers—sensitive to nobody's rights but their own, that is—are erecting against smokers? The Daut family was turned away from a Best Western Motel (my source doesn't say where) because the manager noticed a pack of cigarettes in Mr. Daut's possession. He wouldn't rent a room to nonsmoking Mrs. Daut or their nonsmoking children either because their clothing might exude the smell of smoke.[20]

Most smokers, one hopes, have learned to be considerate of nonsmokers. What about consideration for a smoker—me—not for his smoking but for his sensitivity to loud, obtrusive music everywhere he goes? I have had more than one dining-out experience spoiled by the blare of so-called music, sometimes from a speaker right over my head. I can't be the only one.

When I worked at a Wal-Mart store after my retirement from editorial writing, the incessant "mood" music used to drive me nuts and I would sneak into the back to the control panel and turn it down. Inevitably, one of the managers would turn it up again. At an exercise spa I used to go to I had to use earplugs. There are young men who live in my neighborhood whose cars can be heard (felt, actually) a block away because of the BOOM-BOOM-BOOM of their stereo amplifiers, even through closed doors and windows.

Music, or the noise that's called music today, isn't a threat to health like ETS, you say. Well, it makes me very irritable and agitated, and that isn't good for my mental health. I could have a nervous breakdown or even develop a manic-depressive illness, and you nonsmokers would have to pay for my treatment. According to the National Institute of Mental Health, manic-depressive illness, or "bipolar disorder," cost the nation a staggering $45 billion in 1991 for in-patient and out-patient care and the lost productivity of wage-earners and homemakers, among other things.[21] That is not markedly inferior to the alleged cost of smoking-related illnesses.

All right, I'm being funny (?). The point is that people do a lot of things that bother other people. Where it causes merely annoyance, or even personal discomfort, but where there is no clear-cut, demonstrable, provable harm to others—as there is *not* in the case of ETS—should we call for laws and ordinances prohibiting the annoying or discomforting behavior simply because we may have the majority clout to do so, or should we find ways to get along with one another?

Unfortunately, in the case of ETS, that is the essence of the "accommodation" solution put forward by the always suspect tobacco industry, and it's the unaccommodating, uncompromising, true-believing antismokers who are currently in the saddle. Onward then with laws, ordinances, prohibitions and bans.

Desirable as a smoke-free society may be (and what the healthists will want to "free" us from after that is a whole other subject), the road to that utopia promises to be anything but smooth. For the most part smokers have meekly let themselves be pushed outside, as well as around, with little protest. But sad to say, in 1993 one smoker was evidently pushed all the way over the edge.

It happened in San Pablo, California, where Daphnye Luster lit a cigarette in the nonsmoking section of a restaurant. Four women at another table complained and she was asked to leave. The 20-year-old mother of four did so, only to return with a shotgun with which she killed one of the women, Rachell Rashan Houston, aged 22.[22] Thankfully, that is the only incident of its kind that I'm aware of.

In Cincinnati, however, in a decision reinstating an antismoking activist's lawsuit against a local radio station, the 1st Ohio District Court of Appeals held that tobacco smoke itself could qualify as battery because it fell within the state supreme court's definition of "offensive contact." In this case, Ahron Leichtman of Citizens for a Tobacco-Free Society had gone on a WLW-AM talk show on the eve of the 1991 "Great American Smokeout" to discuss the dangers of secondhand smoke, during which broadcaster Andy Furman allegedly deliberately blew cigar smoke in Leichtman's face.[23]

More recently, in Smyrna, Tennessee, officials were investigating three suspicious fires at the Cambridge Medical Center. They believed the fires may have been set by residents of the nursing home protesting a new no-smoking policy.[24] After the third fire, three residents and five employees were treated for smoke inhalation, which I would guess was a little more serious than anything a resident's secondhand smoke might have done to them.

By way of evening things up, though, a 60-year-old patron was bounced from a New York City restaurant by five waiters, who allegedly kicked, punched and threw him out into the street for the crime of smoking.

The office of the Manhattan District Attorney defended the restaurant's right to "use physical force . . . to eject abusive customers." Although the man was in a coma (for how long, I don't know), the D.A. claimed there was "insufficient evidence that excessive force was used [since] the only physical injury was to the back of the man's head."[25]

On a happier note, those who believe that bans on smoking indoors are saving lives can cite one at least case in proof.

According to a report in the Hanover, Virginia, *Herald-Progress*, one Roscoe Wingfield stepped out onto the loading platform of the Ashland Milling Company for a smoke. When he heard cries for help coming from the nearby South Anna River, Wingfield ran to the water and pulled out a handicapped man who had been fishing from a wheelchair and had accidentally rolled into the current. If Wingfield hadn't been smoking outside, the man would probably have drowned.[26]

With more and more people becoming vulnerable to secondhand smoke, and with the unlikelihood of the Environmental Protection Agency ever succeeding in removing the last molecule of unhealthy "particulate matter" from the nation's air, something more needs to be done to prevent further episodes of violence like those recounted above, other than merely banning smoking indoors. That will solve neither the problem of ETS pollution outdoors nor that of industrial and automotive pollution outdoors (which in the EPA's eyes gets worse the more it gets better).

I'm happy to report that there may be a solution. A company called Environmed Research, Inc., has developed a "personal air-purifying respirator" (APR). As described in a release posted on the World Wide Web on March 23, 1997,[27] an APR consists of three basic components: a face mask, a filter and/or cartridge to remove dust, smaller particles and mists, and a cartridge filter to remove chemical gases. The company admits that:

> The personal use of APRs at home, work, on the street, and in cars is not yet common or fashionable but it will be—very soon. A good APR looks weird at first glance—it certainly is not inconspicuous because it requires two large canisters on either side of the face mask. The mask also has to be supported by a neck strap and two elastic straps that go over the top of you head and mess with your hair. Until more people wear APRs and everyone is used to them, we can safely say that if you strap one on to go to work, or walk the dog, most people will say "it looks weird!"
>
> But looks aside these devices are a solution to an ever increasing problem of contaminated air. An APR can protect you and make you feel a lot better when there are airborne problems and you have to breathe. We predict they will become fashionable.

An added benefit, it occurs to me, is that if the use of personal air-purifying respirators ever did become fashionable, it would be easy to identify smokers and avoid them: they'd be the ones walking around *without* the respirators.

Environmed's enthusiasm for its product notwithstanding, I don't think there's much future for it. The physical condition of nonsmokers is already precarious at best (as we saw in Chapter 6, one whiff of secondhand smoke can prostrate them) and I doubt that many would want to be burdened with carrying around a personal respirator when it's so much easier to pass regulations to curb smoking.

There may be another solution, however. In Canada, where the antismokers are as much a social plague as they are in the States, a couple of enterprising people have successfully pioneered the first "oxygen bar."

"We offer a breath of fresh air, " says Shamilia Hunter, who along with Lissa Charon opened the O2 Spa Bar in Toronto. "People work a lot. They're stressed. They have headaches, especially in the summer when the air quality gets so poor. They can come in here for 20 minutes, breathe pure oxygen [definitely no smoking there!—D.O.] and relax. By the time they leave, their head's clear, they feel great, they have more energy."[28]

Whether or not the idea of an oxygen bar will ever fly, the mania surrounding ETS *has* proven to be a boon to manufacturers of smoker shelters, as more and more employers send smoking employees out of doors to indulge their vile, nasty, disgusting, revolting and deadly-to-everyone habit. One of them is Duo-Guard Industries, Inc., a small company in Detroit, which since at least 1994 has been making and shipping prefabricated shelters to dozens of states. There of them were installed by the VA Medical Center in New Orleans in that year so that men and women who served their nation in its various wars could smoke away their remaining days in peace without infringing upon their fellow citizens' right to life, liberty and the pursuit of smokers.[29]

I ALMOST STARTED to get somber again with that violence stuff. Ann Landers and Abigail Van Buren always make me laugh, whether they intend to or not, and usually they don't, when they write about smoking. Here are two examples from Ann.

A reader wrote that he had seen a story in the *Times* of London that awakened him to the fact that "hatred for smokers is a worldwide problem." He relates:

"It seems that a young English couple was having sex in a nonsmoking section of a train. Fellow travelers did not object to the fact that they were openly indulging in the most intimate of human activities. Only when the couple lit up cigarettes afterward did the other passengers complain. The fine was $142 each for smoking in a nonsmoking area.

"Apparently it's O.K. to fornicate in public as long as you don't smoke. Does that prove my point or what?—Billy in Bangkok."

Commented Ann: "It does indeed. How very British!"[30]

In another column, Ann informed her readers that "The New York Transit Authority recently ruled that bare-breasted women on subways should be arrested ONLY if they create a disruptive or dangerous situation. In fact, police spokesman Al O'Leary said, 'If a woman were sitting on a subway bench, topless, SMOKING A CIGARETTE, we would take action.' [Caps in original.]

"So, folks," said Ann, "I guess it's O.K. to go half-naked in public in New York, just don't smoke while you're doing it."[31]

We'll certainly be on the lookout for topless women in New York, Ann, smoking or not.

Speaking of indecent exposure, or what used to be considered indecent, burlesque may be dead in the Big Apple but much more than mere toplessness is routine in the legitimate theater these days, not only in that depraved city but elsewhere in the country. However, it wasn't nudity or even simulated sex, violence and foul language that offended a member of an audience at a performance of a play called "Unidentified Human Remains and the True Nature of Love" at Actor's Express in Atlanta. According to artistic director Chris Coleman, the only patron to walk out did so because he was offended by the smoking that occurred in the play.[32]

Another from the theater of the absurd: In New Haven actress Judy Geeson was playing a chain-smoking woman in the play "Faith Healer." Suddenly a man stood up and shouted, "This is disgraceful! You're going to kill yourself with the amount you smoke!" He then walked out, muttering that smoking was not permitted in the theater in the first place.[33]

It's also not permitted in theaters in Boulder, Colorado, or any other public building in that politically correct city. The Boulder Dinner Theatre was putting on a production of the Broadway musical "Grand Hotel," which includes a one-minute scene where a couple characters smoke. An irate patron called the police, who ordered the owner of the theater to eliminate the scene or face ninety days in jail and a $1,000 fine. This put the owner between a rock and a hard place because copyright law forbade him from altering the play at the risk of civil litigation.

"It's so funny," said the copyright owner. "In these censorious times, everyone goes home and sits around the dinner table and talks about how great it is to live in a free country."[34]

Apparently it's easier to get away with murdering a child in Boulder, Colorado, than it is to smoke a cigarette in public.

Nor was smoking permitted inside the Richmond County Civic Center in Augusta, Georgia—until the authorities decided that forcing concertgoers to go outside to smoke between numbers was even more dangerous to their health than their smoking: it put them at risk of being mugged or robbed. They voted to relax the ban to allow smoking in the concourse area of the main arena.[35]

Such solicitude for smokers is rare indeed these days.

This next item has nothing to do with smoking but it qualifies for inclusion here under the headings of political correctness and protecting children from bad influences.

Cellist Anne Conrad-Antoville quit the Eureka, California, symphony orchestra rather than perform Prokofieff's "Peter and the Wolf," the classic children's musical work with narration which, if I remember aright, is sympathetic to wolves. But Conrad-Antoville huffed and puffed that it teaches children "to hate and fear wolves and to applaud a hunter who kills a wolf." She called on the public to boycott the performance. As it turned out, her protest actually gave ticket sales a boost.[36]

This doesn't have anything to do with smoking either, but I'll strain to make that connection anyway. During a concert in New York City (my clipping doesn't say where but probably at Avery Fisher Hall), New York Philharmonic conductor Kurt Masur threw down his baton in disgust in midplay because of all the coughing from the audience. "The coughing was so strong, I could hardly hear the strings' pianissimo," he said later.[37]

Let's think about that. In view of the drastic decline in the number of smokers, and the fact that smoking was certainly not allowed wherever this happened, the audience could not have all been smokers, even though we know that only smokers ever cough. The only explanation is that people had had to pass by smokers congregated outside when they entered the place and were only clearing secondhand smoke from their lungs during the concert. (Then again, it could possibly have been caused by "sick building syndrome" about which more later.)

One last item from the performing world, which this time is not entirely unrelated to smoking. One Jeanine Fleming wrote to *The Atlanta Journal-Constitution*:

"I attended the back-to-back productions of 'Angels in America' at the Alliance Theater. My experience was marred by the inconsiderate playgoers seated around us who had drenched themselves in strong perfume and aftershave. We were surrounded by so many different, intrusive scents that it make me feel sick to my stomach and made my companion's eyes water . . . [T]his is as bad as sitting next to me and lighting up a cigarette."[38]

Than which there is nothing badder! But I sympathize with the writer, for I too have been offended by the strong odor of perfume or aftershave in enclosed places. I particularly remember a fellow who rode the bus I used to take into Washington who must have drenched himself in Aqua Velva each morning, causing us scent-sensitive fellow passengers to gag. To paraphrase from the surgeon general's 1964 report on smoking, "Perfume and Aftershave Are A Health Hazard (Well, A Personal Annoyance Anyway) of Sufficient Importance in the United States to Warrant Appropriate Remedial Action."

Truly, personal scents may well be next on the anti-everything hit list. An organization called the Human Ecology Action League has declared that "Perfume is going to be the tobacco smoke of tomorrow."[39] The University of Minnesota's School of Social Work has adopted a "scent-free policy" banning perfumes, colognes, shampoos and other products from certain areas that could cause discomfort to those who suffer from "multiple chemical sensitivities."[40] Commenting upon this, *The New York Times* suggested that it may mark the beginning of a national "chemical correctness" revolution.[41] (As Steven Milloy has remarked, "Ah, so much to ban. So little time.")

"No one should be wearing perfume to the theater," says Julia Kendall of the Chemical Injury Litigation Project. "Why should we have brain damage because people are wearing toxic chemicals?" Explaining the aptly named organization's agenda, she says, "Basically, we want to destroy the fragrance industry."[42]

Statements like this suggest to me that brain damage can occur even in the absence of toxic chemicals.

Speaking of personal odors reminds me that back in 1991 the National Cancer Institute (NCI) reported on a study which found that "people who regularly use alcohol-containing mouthwashes may [note that "may"—D.O.] have a 60 to 90 percent higher chance of developing cancer in the mouth or upper throat than those who don't use such products."[43]

According to Dr. William J. Blot, who headed the study, these two forms of cancers strike nearly 30,000 Americans each year and kill about 9,000 of them.

At the time I was just beginning to get concerned about all the "revelations" regarding secondhand smoke and actually started writing a funny(?) piece of satire on the newly discovered mouthwash peril in which I pretended to recount the history of this unfolding public-health menace. Soon after the NCI study, I wrote, other studies started coming in not only confirming the oral cancer "link" but implicating the inadvertent swallowing of mouthwash as a cause of esophageal, colorectal and other cancers. Then came the first study "suggesting" a link between the *secondhand breath* of mouthwash users and cancer in innocent bystanders. There quickly followed a pronouncement by the surgeon general that mouthwash-induced cancer was the second most preventable cause of death in the United States (next to smoking, of course). Mouthwash users became social outcasts. Eventually the government issued rules prohibiting them to appear in public without face masks, and finally banned alcohol-containing mouthwash entirely.

All of which was thoroughly silly—although who would ever have imagined how far the ETS madness would go? I did expect that there would be more studies on the mouthwash-cancer connection but I never saw any mention of it again until in the course of writing this chapter I came across a reference to the NCI study on Steven Milloy's "Junk Science" site on the Internet. It quoted from an article in the *American Journal of Epidemiology* in which the authors, apparently using the mouthwash study as an example of how not to do epidemiology, pointed out that the study was flawed because it did not take into account such "confounders" as heavy alcohol and tobacco use and that the failure to do so could have produced the spurious relationship between mouthwash and oropharyngeal cancer.[44]

I've brought this up only to demonstrate another point, and that is that when you read that something you do or use or breathe or eat gives you a higher chance of developing this or that kind of cancer, the alleged chance is usually minimal to the point of nonexistence. In the case of mouthwash, even the higher chance—90 percent—only meant that the researchers found a "relative risk" of 1.9 for people who used alcohol-containing mouthwashes compared with people who didn't. To say it again, in epidemiology a relative risk of 1.0 is no risk at all and anything less than 2.0 is not considered to be "significant." Even a relative risk of 2.0, which translates into a scary 100 percent greater chance, is just barely "significant" and may tell us nothing at all about any actual risk in real life, whether or not the risk "suggested" by the particular study was "confounded."

Nevertheless, as with ETS, where the estimated risk of 1.19 is practically at the no-risk level, the National Cancer Institute had felt it necessary to inform the public about the potential "danger" of mouthwash and at least one newspaper reported it as !!PAGE ONE NEWS!!

THE SUBJECT OF SCENTS and odors requires a section all its own in this chapter, for next to being killed by ETS, what rabid antismokers and otherwise tolerant nonsmokers alike hate most about other people's smoking is the *smell.* Witness two representative e-mails that were sent to the smokers' rights organization FORCES:

"Smoke your deathsticks as you please, just keep the stench away from those who haven't asked to smell it."

"What if I developed a habit for spraying foul-smelling aerosol into the air at random? Why should I not be able to? What about spraying toxic chemicals into your face as you are permitted to blow your cancerous smoke into mine?"

Or consider the following two messages posted on a variety of "alternate" newsgroups on the Internet, including alt.smokers and alt.support-nonsmokers:

"I do not blow my exhaust into a restaurant where people are eating, into a workplace where people are working or any public place where I would be normally arrested for trying to hook my exhaust up to."

"I've been in the situation where minutes after I got out of the shower and left to go somewhere, I ended up in a public place where I had to briefly pass by a smoker, only to find that my hair and clothes picked up the smell which I either have to carry around with me for the rest of the day, or immediately return home for another shower at the risk of encountering another smoker anyway."

All that from just "briefly passing by" a smoker? Now *that's* sensitivity. And think of the damage smokers are forcing this person to do to his or her skin by removing essential oils with so many showers.

Again, as always, there's Ann Landers, to whom "Sad in Baltimore" wrote:

"I met the girl of my dreams. She was beautiful, witty and bright and had a great sense of humor. We had a wonderful time together, but I had to pull out of the relationship. Her smoking turned me off.

"'Miss X' made a big effort to keep from lighting up around me, but the smell of rancid smoke was in her hair and on her clothes. Her apartment stank like an old railroad station. I left a sweater there one night and had to take it to the cleaners before I could wear it again."[45]

(I used to know a girl, a nonsmoker, who had a pet lap dog she cuddled and nuzzled and even kissed on the mouth. That, and the doggy odor, turned me off. Which goes to show how weird *I* am.)

I'd say that "Miss X" was one lucky girl to be shut of that guy. At least "Sad" was able to salvage his sweater, unlike a teenager whose story of addiction to cigarettes was reprinted in *Reader's Digest.* She writes that, although she can no longer smell tobacco on herself, "I remember one time before I smoked. I left my jacket at a friend's house. Both her parents smoked. When I got the jacket back, I had to throw it away because it smelled like an ashtray. So I feel sorry for those who don't smoke and have to put up with my odor all day."[46]

Hmm . . . Somehow her dislike for the odor of tobacco smoke didn't keep the girl from taking up smoking herself. One wonders why.

Something is definitely wrong with me. For an odor that clings to one's clothing, wood smoke far surpasses tobacco smoke in my opinion. When my son was in the Boy Scouts I went on camping trips with him. There was always a nightly sing-song around a bonfire, and when I got home my clothes would reek from the smoke. But a washing or just a tumble in the dryer got rid of it and I didn't have to throw anything away.

Why can I smell wood smoke on myself but not tobacco smoke? My wife tells me I don't smell it, let alone realize how *awful* it is, because I still smoke, and she certainly has a point. In 1995 some students at the University of South Carolina conducted a research project into popular beliefs about smells and one of the areas they investigated was the effect of smoking on olfactory acuity.

They reported that, according to the "1986 National Geographic Smell Survey," of the people polled, smokers rated the intensity of androstenone [human sweat], cloves, and gas as weaker than those [ratings] of nonsmokers, while banana and musk were perceived as stronger by smokers. However, smokers and nonsmokers did not differ in their detection of the rose scent. Additionally, smokers were less confident in their own ability to detect odors. As expected[!], smokers' responses to the survey demonstrated a lowered sensitivity to odor quality. Smokers found the odors rated as unpleasant by nonsmokers to be less offensive, and indicated a decreased appreciation of the pleasant odors, as well.

In an additional study conducted at the University of Indiana, 100 students were asked to use their noses to locate their own shirts from an assortment of shirts. Seventy-four of the 100 students were able to correctly identify their own shirts by scent alone. However, of participants that smoked more than 10 cigarettes per day, almost half were unable to correctly identify their own shirts.[47]

Moderately interesting and probably totally meaningless. Presumably the students were blindfolded for the shirt search, but were they allowed to handle them or just stick their noses in them? As with everything connected with smoking, obviously "more studies are needed." But I question the finding that smokers are less sensitive to odors that nonsmokers rate as unpleasant (with the exception of tobacco smoke, of course, which the National Geographic survey apparently didn't cover), as well as being less appreciative of pleasant odors. (Another question is, why should the National Geographic Society care about people's smelling ability in the first place?) I think my sense of smell is pretty normal, except, again, when it comes to tobacco smoke.

When my wife and I visit friends in Florida, who have an automatic lawn sprinkler that uses ground water, every morning when the sprinkler turns on at 6:30 A.M. the strong smell of sulfur in the water wakes me up without fail like an alarm clock. Yet the sulfur smell doesn't waken my wife. I would also note that it took at least several years after she stopped smoking for her aversion to tobacco smoke to develop—coincidentally, or perhaps not so coincidentally, about the time the antis discovered the ETS issue.

Be all that as it may, why doesn't the smell of wood smoke send people to extremes of panic and vituperation? It contains all the carcinogens present in tobacco smoke.

In 1996 my wife and I stopped at a welcome center somewhere. I think it was in Hannibal, Missouri, on a visit to Mark Twain's boyhood home. Although it was in the middle of summer and no fire was burning, a strong and rank smell from the fireplace permeated the entire building and I was glad when we left. There's nothing like the stink of a dead fireplace. But no one complained; after all, the stink wasn't coming from cigarette butts in an ashtray, of which, of course, there were none in the welcome center.

On another trip, an active fire was burning in a large fireplace in a restaurant in Merrifield, Virginia, where we and a former neighbor couple had dinner. I could smell the smoke as soon as we entered. Interestingly enough, the fire was in the nonsmoking section which, of course, is where we went. (Our friends knew I was a smoker but it did not occur to them to ask, nor did I expect them to ask, if I would prefer the smoking section, for it goes without saying that the smoker must always accommodate the nonsmoker.) While we were eating I jokingly complained about how offended I was by the odor from the fire. Everyone thought that was very funny.

The smell of wood smoke actually *was* fairly strong. Had it been tobacco smoke, there would have been complaints from everybody in the room, and *not* in jest.

Or take barbecues. Many a weekend chef looks forward to standing over his smoking charcoal broiler, breathing in far more carcinogens than he would get in a room full of cigarette smokers. But people like the smell of barbecue smoke, and were the chef to light a cigarette while cooking, his guests would chide him about the grave risk to his health.

I grew up during what can now be seen as the golden age of smoking. I was aware of the society around me. I read the newspaper, listened to the radio. I had close nonsmoking friends, shared college rooms and army barracks with them, and observed countless nonsmokers. Not once did I hear, or hear of, a complaint about the smoke from a cigarette, mine or anybody else's. If it can sneak up stairways today, crawl along hallways and penetrate closed doors to sicken innocent nonsmokers or block their access to a building entirely, why did it never happen in the old days?

Well, there was one incident, the only one I can recall, and the person involved was myself. Many years ago I was eating a meal at a diner counter and a guy on the stool next to me was obliviously smoking a cigarette. What we now call "sidestream smoke" naturally drifted in my direction (as it always does to the person not smoking) and over the food on my plate. I thought it was rather inconsiderate of him not to be aware of this and at least hold his cigarette down below the counter between puffs..

A cigarette after a good meal is one of life's little pleasures, one that is becoming increasingly forbidden in public eateries. Personally, though, I have never cared to smoke *while* eating. Yet this other guy's smoking while I was eating was such a minor annoyance that I don't remember where or when it occurred. I grant you of course that if this happened to me, it must have happened to many other people. Even so, you never heard any complaints.

I can also recall only one incident from the old days in which a nonsmoker, or a person I assume was a nonsmoker, berated a smoker, and this too involved myself. One day in 1955 I was in the card catalogue room in the library at the University of Chicago when I encountered an attractive coed of my acquaintance. We sat down on a bench and started chatting. Thoughtlessly, I took out and lit a cigarette.

Almost immediately an irate librarian, your stereotypical sour old maid (though she may have been on her third husband for all I knew) descended upon me. She could have smiled and said chidingly, "You know you can't smoke in here." Instead, she spat out those words with a devastatingly fierce glare. I was already operating on only half a wit by virtue of sitting next to a pretty girl and was so startled and suddenly guilt-ridden that I dropped the cigarette to the floor and stamped it out. This elicited another glare and the woman walked away.

I have seen this same guilty reaction in other smokers. A few years ago my wife and I and our son and his then fiancée were in a restaurant in Richmond, Virginia. Our table was on the edge of a section that was slightly elevated above the main floor. A man was standing just below smoking a cigarette and the smoke drifted (naturally) in my son's direction. Normally a very polite and tolerant person, he could have smiled and said gently, "Excuse me, sir, but would you mind blowing your smoke elsewhere." Instead, he reached down and tapped the fellow on the shoulder and, frowning, flicked his hand a couple times at the smoke, as if brushing away a fly. The guy got the message instantly and almost jumped away.

It goes without saying that I don't smoke in my son's presence or my stepson's, whether in their homes or in a restaurant with them. I refrain both out of consideration for them and because their disapproval, and that of larger society, has taken the pleasure out of smoking in what used to be congenial settings. The comfort of nonsmokers supersedes everything else today, of course. Too often, though, the pure air they demand reeks of a strong odor of sanctimoniousness.

I think that the superior attitude of many nonsmokers partly reflects a kind of self-justification or smug self-congratulation on their part, either for an early decision not to start smoking or a later decision to stop smoking. Many ex-smokers, especially, have wholeheartedly embraced everything bad said about smoking, to the point that they have persuaded themselves that they never really liked to smoke and are oh so glad they quit, and frequently have become even more fanatical and intolerant on the subject than people who have never smoked at all.

But by "the old days" I don't necessarily just mean my youth or early adulthood. It was not until 10 or 15 years after the surgeon general's 1964 report that one started hearing protests from nonsmokers about being subjected to secondhand smoke. It was in 1978 that I personally first became aware of it, during one of those "if-it's-Tuesday-this-must-be-Belgium" tours of Europe my wife and I took. There was a middle-aged lady across the aisle on the bus who put a handkerchief to her face and started making tiny little gasps the first time I lit a cigarette. I thereafter either didn't smoke on the bus or did it the rear, where the tour group—including myself, I'm ashamed to say—had banished a fellow who liked cigars.

Little did I dream, not in a million years would I have dreamed, that my two-pack-a-day wife would one day manifest that same ultrasensitivity to cigarette smoke as that pathetic lady on the bus. Why didn't one ever encounter such people in the old days? Because they stoically kept silent? But though the lady on the bus didn't say anything; her gasping into a handkerchief was demonstrative enough. Why did I never see that kind of reaction in even one person in my three-plus decades of smoking up to that time? Today there are *millions* who cannot tolerate cigarette smoke and their ability to detect it would put a cocaine-sniffing DEA dog to shame. Where were those millions before the antismoking propaganda machine cranked up?

WHICH TAKES ME back to what I started to say. It's almost as if there has been an evolutionary leap forward in our ability to detect health-threatening odors, or maybe a regression to the supposed olfactory sensitivity of our protohuman ancestors. As a result, we also seem to have developed a new instinctual survival mechanism or an enhancement of the body's autonomic nervous system. Just as a person will instantly remove his hand from a hot surface without having to make a deliberate decision to do so, the merest scent of tobacco smoke will put a nonsmoker into protective flight mode without the necessity of conscious (or rational) thought on his part.

The problem with this line of speculation, however, is that this new sensitivity or "instinct" has appeared in just the past couple decades and evolution doesn't work that fast. Moreover, in the case of tobacco it has manifested itself only in nonsmokers or reformed ex-smokers. Active smokers, who are at greatest risk from tobacco smoke, strangely exhibit neither the odor sensitivity nor the aversive reaction. At the same time there has been a corresponding increase in the number of people afflicted with various breathing difficulties, especially asthma, along with claimed outright allergy to tobacco smoke, and this is also manifested only in nonsmokers. Some poor souls today are even disablingly allergic to *everything*—victims of so-called "multiple chemical sensitivity," or MCS—and a whole branch of medical (mal?)practice has arisen devoted to treating them.

Speaking of MCS, no less than that supreme guardian of the public health, the Environmental Protection Agency itself, was being sued as of this writing by 19 of its own employees to the tune of $40 million because, they said, the air inside the EPA building at Waterside Mall in Washington made them sick. One of them, Amy Svoboda, claimed to have been permanently brain-damaged by the air she breathed in her office. According to an article by her sister in *Spin* magazine,[48] her symptoms included hearing loss, swollen joints, burning lungs and nose, stomach aches, nausea, loss of coordination and huge welts on her abdomen. She can't go out to a restaurant unless the place is relatively free of hair spray, perfume, deodorant, burning candles, makeup, aftershave, cleaning agents, pesticides, new furniture, gas fumes, the residue of recent renovation and, of course, cigarette smoke. As for other employees described in the article:

"Kirby Biggs, an analyst in the EPA's Superfund section, found he could no longer read a spreadsheet. 'Looking at a report felt like I was making a paper cut across my eyeballs,' he says. He lost 45 pounds in six months. Carol Bass, a national expert in hazardous waste, had trouble walking and talking. Her hair turned snow white when she was 44. Sometimes she cannot dial a phone, though she was once a concert violinist. Steve Spiegel, chief steward of the union local, passed out inexplicably on numerous occasions between 1988 and 1990 . . . Environmental scientist Emily Roth says she had difficulty figuring out how to get dressed in the morning. Susan Watkins went to an emergency room four times while working at Waterside Mall, once by ambulance. 'My throat felt like I was breathing fiberglass. I couldn't remember my name, and my right leg started dragging,' she says. She retired on disability—at age 50 . . . Independent tests showed that mice put in a chamber with EPA carpet samples died within four hours. Almost a hundred workers quit, retired on disability, went on leave, or began working at home."[49]

Talk about anecdotal evidence! But it must be the explanation for all the crazy programs and cockamamie regulations the EPA has been imposing on Americans: the people who work for it are brain-fogged, if not mentally and physically disabled altogether! Interestingly, and most appropriately, one of the victim participants in the lawsuit was Mr. James Repace, he of "particulate matter" fame and one of the instigators of the EPA's phony report on ETS, whom we met in the previous chapter.

What goes around comes around, EPA.

Since there are probably few if any smokers working for the EPA, and certainly none smoking inside the building, what do these employees and former employees blame for their symptoms? Besides cheapo government-issue carpeting, the alleged culprits include cheapo pressed-wood furniture saturated with formaldehyde, chemical-exuding photocopiers, fax machines and computers, and new man-made pesticides and air fresheners, the toxic emanations from all of which were exacerbated by poor ventilation in an insulated, air-tight building that was a legacy of the 1970s "energy crisis."

And what did the EPA have to say in response to the suit? More or less that it was all in the complainants' heads—which for once is an instance where the agency was probably right.

Truthfully, the best thing that could happen to this country would be if the Environmental Protection Agency were abolished outright, all its programs dismantled and its employees placed elsewhere in the federal bureaucracy. Even if they were all retired on millionaires' pensions the nation would still save billions of dollars that the EPA's phantom environmental scares are costing it.

Think I'm exaggerating? According to Tammy Tangs et al. at the Harvard Center for Risk Analysis, the median cost for every life (presumably) saved by the EPA is $7,629,000. The second highest figure for a federal agency, the Occupational Safety and Health Administration, is $88,000. For the Federal Aviation Administration, which I think millions of airline travelers would consider to be one of the most essential federal agencies, it is only $23,000.[50]

It would be one thing if the EPA's activities actually did save some lives, but once again we are talking about statistical projections (guesses), not real people. But there is no doubt that the agency is costing Americans huge sums of money, as well as great inconvenience, to no purpose. The following item printed in *The Atlanta Journal-Constitution* in 1994 speaks for itself:

> A 1991 federal regulation requires cities to remove at least 30 percent of "organic waste" from incoming sewage before treating it. According to a *Washington Post* story in May, the Environmental Protection Agency refused to exempt Anchorage, Alaska, from the regulation, even though the city has so little organic waste coming in that its incoming waste is cleaner than most cities' outgoing waste. Required to comply anyway, Anchorage solved the problem by paying fish processors to purposely dump fish byproducts into the sewer so the city will have enough organic waste to remove.[51]

BUT I HAVE DIGRESSED again. Pending confirmation by science that there has been a fundamental change in the human physiology, it has to be assumed that 30 or 40 years ago, when smoking was widespread in society, human beings possessed the same degree of olfactory acuity and the same breathing apparatus and nervous systems as they do today. Then as now, most people didn't smoke. I ask again: why weren't the millions of nonsmokers annoyed by tobacco smoke long before now?

It may be suggested that people didn't know about the dangers of secondhand smoke back in those dark ages. Like children too young to be able to read and understand the warning label on a bottle of poison, they were simply unaware of the peril ETS presented.

Even so, if it stinks now, it stank then, didn't it?

The answer of course is that people have been conditioned to *expect* to be offended and feel threatened by someone's smoking. And this is the truly great and historic triumph of the antismoking movement, the necessary prelude to the ultimate victory—total tobacco prohibition.

Not to belabor the matter (but I will), you never heard complaints about it back in the old days, when nearly half the population smoked and did so just about anywhere they pleased (although you were never allowed to smoke in elevators or department stores when I was growing up in Pittsburgh). There were no such things as nonsmoking motel or hotel rooms or nonsmoking sections in restaurants. When I was in college, smokers and nonsmokers shared dorm or fraternity rooms as a matter of course. At Carnegie Tech, when I was studying music, I would often smoke in one of the small, closed practice rooms while I listened to a fellow student playing the piano or violin, and there was no problem. I visited nonsmoking friends in their homes and they were glad to provide me with an ashtray. Never once in the decades of my life before ETS became an issue did I experience personally, or hear or read about, any objections to tobacco smoke.

I ask again, if it stinks now, it stank then too, didn't it?

In 1961 I attended a science symposium for journalists at the University of Michigan in Ann Arbor and roomed with the editor of *Today's Health*, a general readership magazine published by the American Medical Association. He was a very stocky fellow about my age, and a nonsmoker. It didn't bother him a bit when I smoked in the room.

Today he'd surely comment about my smoking and the dangers thereof. If he did, I could make some kind of riposte like, "Well, I'd rather take a chance with smoking than be a big tub of lard like you, buddy." (I wouldn't, of course; I'd just not smoke in the room.)

Were nonsmokers simply too polite to complain? Maybe so, but surely somewhere, sometime in all those years, I should have observed at least a subtle indication of dislike or disapproval. Or did people complain and I was just too dense to be aware of it? I hardly think so. Yet I know that as far back as 1911, something called "The Non-Smokers' Protective League" was certified in New York State. Since people didn't "know" back then that secondhand tobacco smoke kills, what the league desired must have been simply "protection" from its respiratory annoyance and odor.

Today, even the tobacco companies have conceded that tobacco smoke stinks and, of course, have tried to use that concession to their advantage. For example, a few years ago I saw billboards around Atlanta announcing "Horizon—the first cigarette that smells good." I don't remember what company made them but I bought a pack. As I anticipated, they had the same cloyingly sweet odor of a brand of pipe tobacco called, I believe, "Cookie Jar" that my father smoked occasionally. The sun quickly set on Horizon.

R. J. Reynolds is doing the same thing with its Eclipse cigarette, which it claims generates 80 percent less secondhand smoke and produces no ashes or "stains." "With Eclipse, you get a great-tasting cigarette that leaves virtually no lingering odor on your clothes or in your home. So now you can enjoy being a smoker, without smelling like one," the company advertises.

In effect, Reynolds is disparaging its own regular brands in order to promote the new less offensive brand. Somehow, I don't think they are going to rack up many points with nonsmokers with that tactic.

Wait a minute. There *was* one incident in my early experience that demonstrated what to me was the uncanny ability of one nonsmoker to detect the odor of tobacco smoke. It was back in the 1940s. My best friend in school, Bob F., and I used to sneak smokes together. One evening we had gone to some function at the YMCA and were walking back to his house. I had a pack of cigarettes on me that I had procured somewhere, probably from the vending machine in the Colonial bowling alley, and suggested that we indulge.

"We can't," he said. "My mother would smell it on us."

I told him he was crazy and persuaded him to light up with me. Sure enough, when we were sitting in the living room chatting with his mother, she sniffed and said she smelled cigarette smoke.

"Oh *that*," we said. "That must be from people smoking at the Y."

"People smoked in the Y?"

Yes, we assured her, some adults had. She looked at us dubiously and I could tell she was thinking: surely that nice Mrs. Oakley's boy wouldn't sit there and look at me with a straight face and lie, would he? Fortunately, her disbelief that I would or could lie prevailed and we got away with our crime. That, I can truthfully say, is the only instance in my experience of anyone remarking about the odor of tobacco smoke back in the old days.

In 1995 I saw Bob at our class's 50th anniversary reunion for the first time since graduation. Considering all the antismoking flit that had hit the shan in the past half-century, I was surprised to see he still smoked, one of two members of the class besides me who did. He was in fine health, he told me, and he looked it. His mother was long gone, of course, but his children wouldn't let him smoke in their homes, he said.

In an article about popular mass delusions, Australian sociologist Robert Bartholomew notes that they "all involve a rapid spread of false, but plausible, exaggerated beliefs that gain credibility within a particular social and cultural context . . . [E]veryday objects, events, and circumstances that would ordinarily receive scant attention become the subject of extraordinary scrutiny. Ambiguous agents are soon redefined according to the emerging definition of the situation, creating a self-fulfilling prophecy."[52]

Among contributing factors he lists the mass media, group conformity, and reinforcing actions by such authority figures as politicians or by institutions of social control.

Bartholomew was not talking about environmental tobacco smoke but about documented episodes of mass delusion—witch hunts ("moral" or real), belief in the widespread existence of satanic cults, visitations from space aliens, Communist infiltration scares and unfounded fears about the casual transmission of AIDS, to name a few. But I believe that what he says applies to the late 20th-century fear of ETS, and in this case the authority figures contributing to and reinforcing the "emerging definition of the situation"—i.e., that secondhand smoke kills—are the medical community, government regulatory bodies and the whole antismoking establishment.

In the opinion of another writer, the belief in the harmful effects of tobacco is an example of "the social construction of reality."[53] That is, we didn't know these harmful effects existed until various institutions of society began telling us they did.

There is also what Michael Fumento calls "the nocebo effect":

> A nocebo is a negative placebo. That is, while a placebo pill makes you feel better though unbeknownst to you it's only made of sugar, a nocebo makes you feel bad though physiologically speaking it shouldn't be able to . . .
>
> When a newspaper at which I worked moved to a new building somebody told the librarian that there was formaldehyde in her new library bookshelves. Formaldehyde is a suspected human carcinogen and the librarian knew this. Soon she was suffering

from a headache, aching joints, and labored breathing—all classic psychosomatic symptoms.

But then she heard there was no formaldehyde in the shelves. Suddenly the symptoms disappeared. Apparently the final word on the shelves was that they did contain formaldehyde but the librarian remained blissfully ignorant of this and hence symptom free.[54]

Fumento also cites the examples of Love Canal, breast implants and, more recently, the "Gulf War Syndrome"—none of which became a "problem" until the media said there was (and liability-suit lawyers latched onto them), and in none of which there has ever been any credible evidence of harm to anyone.

While Fumento, an antismoker, would not be likely to acknowledge a "nocebo effect" when it comes to complaints about environmental tobacco smoke, a striking example of it from the smoking warfront has been provided by Pat Michaels, a reporter for the Newport Beach, California, *Newport News*:

Anti-cigarette smoking has reached a fanaticism bordering on hysteria. It could be dangerous to your health. To prove that point, this fearless reporter used one of those smokeless cigarettes made of plastic that look like a real cigarette. They can't be lit, though, and are normally supposed to hold some kind of inhalant to discourage smoking.

My first stop was at the Newport Harbour Elks Lodge and a seat at the piano bar in the smoking section. A lady at a nearby table kept getting up and opening a window that blew blasts of cold air on me. After I'd closed the window three times, and the woman had opened it an equal number, she said to me: "I'll make you a deal; if you stop smoking, I won't open the window anymore." I told her I hadn't smoked in 20 years and my "cigarette" couldn't smoke. I also pointed out she was seated in the smoking section of the room reserved for smokers. "I don't care," she screamed, ignoring my statement, "It's my table, I'm sitting at it, and you are making it impossible to enjoy my dinner." It looked like her purse was about to swing in my direction so I left.

I went to Bandera in Corona del Mar. A waitress greeted me at Bandera's door and immediately noticed my "cigarette." "You're not coming in here with that," she said firmly. I told her it wasn't a cigarette. She claimed she knew a cigarette when she saw one and wasn't about to examine "that dirty thing." She said Bandera's rules prohibited cigarettes, cigars and pipes of any kind. Out!

At Marie Callender's a woman in the next booth complained to

> the management she couldn't breathe because of my "cigarette" and wanted me thrown out of there too.
>
> A similar incident occurred at McDonald's on Coast Highway. And, you should have seen the excitement my phony cigarette caused at the Harbour Municipal Court building—something you felt could quickly degenerate into a lynch mob. No sir! If you're a smoker today, you're about as welcome in some local places as Arafat in Tel Aviv . . . [55]

No doubt Michaels employed a modicum of dramatic license in that story. But call it mass delusion or the nocebo effect, the fact is that popular perceptions about smoking have changed, or have *been* changed. It can be seen not only in ordinary people but in scientists themselves, as evidenced by an interesting experiment reported by George Carlo et al. in the journal *Risk Analysis.*

The experiment divided some 1,460 epidemiologists, toxicologists, physicians and general scientists into two groups. The first group was read a vignette that reflected "mainstream" scientific thinking on secondhand smoke. When queried, 70 percent of the scientists and physicians said that ETS was a serious environmental hazard, and 85 percent felt that public health intervention was necessary.

The second group was read the same vignette, but was told that it had to do with "substance X." Only 33 percent of these scientists and physicians thought that "substance X" was a serious health hazard, even though it was actually secondhand smoke, and only 41 percent felt that it warranted public health regulation.[56]

Such an almost superstitious attitude toward ETS on the part of scientists represents another great accomplishment by the antismoking movement, as brilliant as its success in inciting the general public's panic over secondhand smoke in the first place, with the consequent transformation of smoking into a socially unacceptable, if not yet illegal, behavior.

ALAS, I'M AFRAID this is as funny as this chapter is going to get. What is possibly the most lamentable consequence of the ETS mania—one being fostered by that most fanatical of antismoking organizations, Action on Smoking and Health—involves child custody suits, where bitter divorced, divorcing or just plain bickering parents have been handed a new weapon to use against each other.

MOTHER MAY LOSE CUSTODY OVER SMOKING, EVEN IN KENTUCKY was the capitalized headline on one ASH press release posted on its World Wide Web site.[57] It reported that "Even in Kentucky, a mother may lose custody of her two sons because she allegedly subjects them to secondhand tobacco smoke.

"She now has primary custody of a six-year-old son who has allergies and must get shots, and a nine-year-old who, like his younger brother, has frequent throat and ear infections. Her former husband is seeking primary custody, claiming that her smoking is a major factor in causing these medical problems and other risks to his children."

The case is hardly the first, said ASH, since in at least 15 states courts have held that subjecting children to secondhand smoke can be a factor in deciding custody. In another posting,[58]ASH cited 18 custody cases involving parents who smoke. Among them:

1988. Pizzitola v. Pizzitola. (Texas) Custody awarded to smoke-free father.

1989. Wilke v. Wilke. (Missouri) Custody awarded to smoke-free mother.

1989. Badeau v. Badeau. (Louisiana) In LaPlace, an appeals court upholds a lower court decision reducing a father's visitation rights because his smoking aggravates his child's bronchial problem.

1991. Mitchell v. Mitchell. (Tennessee) In this divorce case, the father had been awarded custody because the child suffered from asthma. On appeal, the court refuses to return custody of the child to its mother, even though she had joined a smoking cessation program.

1991. Brett Lee Bryant/Department of Social Services v. Wakely et al. (Michigan) The Michigan Court of Appeals upholds the decision of a civil court that placement of a child with his grandmother who smoked would not be in the child's best interest. The child had respiratory problems and it was recommended that he live in close proximity to a hospital in Traverse City (where his grandparents were unable to relocate) and that he should live in a smoke-free environment. (Where the poor kid ended up, ASH didn't say. No doubt in some non-smoking foster home. After all, blood isn't as thick as tobacco smoke.)

1992. Sulva v. Isaacson. (Illinois) Judge William Ward signs an order barring Mr. Isaacson from smoking when he visits his son, the first such order in the state. The son, Alex, suffers from bronchitis and it is alleged that his father's smoking might aggravate his condition. One smoke in front of his son could lead to a contempt citation and a jail sentence of up to six months, Isaacson is warned.

1992. John Doe v. Jane Doe. (South Carolina) Court awards custody of asthmatic child to father to prevent exposure to mother's tobacco smoke.

1993. Masone v. Tanner. (California) A county judge grants a nonsmoking father's request to remove an 8-year-old girl from the custody of his ex-wife because she continues to smoke despite an earlier court order that she not do so around the child. A doctor testifies that the girl has only 43 percent of her breathing capacity and would end up in an emergency room if her exposure to tobacco smoke continued.

Sometimes the court merely issues a warning:

1988. Roofeh v. Roofeh. (New York) Nassau County judge Ralph Diamond issues order forbidding Elizabeth Roofeh to smoke in front of her husband and three children. Mrs. Roofeh is also directed to confine her cigarette smoking to a small television room in the couple's King's Port mansion.

1990. De Beni Souza v. Kallweit. (California) Judge David Stirling orders Anna Maria de Beni Souza not to smoke in front of her five-year-old son, ruling at the request of the boy's father, Manfred Kallweit, who had complained of health risks associated with inhaling second-hand smoke. Custody case pending.

1993. Montfar v. Navot. (New Jersey) Judge Orlanda grants post-judgment relief to a nonsmoking father, whose child, aged 10, is exposed to tobacco smoke by his mother and maternal relatives. The order states that the custodial mother shall provide the child a complete nonsmoking environment, which means: no smoking by her or other residents in the home or by visitors; all smoking must be carried out outdoors; remove the child from any situation or location where he is exposed to ETS; remove the child from the grandparents' presence if they are smoking; no smoking in any vehicle in which the child is a passenger.

And sometimes both parents lose:

1989. In Denton, Maryland, a judge places a three-year-old girl with severe asthma in a foster home because her parents ignored medical advice to protect the child from their tobacco smoke.

The two 1993 cases were the most recent ones cited by ASH, but it is not, one may be sure, because there haven't been any others since then. What a great contribution the antismokers have made to "family values." All you have to do is tell a judge that your child has asthma or some kind of respiratory problem and you can really stick it to that damned spouse or former spouse of yours if he or she smokes!

All of which causes great glee in the halls of ASH, whose director, John Banzhaf, urges not only parents but physicians, school nurses and grandparents—any nonsmoker, in fact—to file or to testify in custody disputes involving smoking. His organization, he says, stands ready to assist them.

A spokesman for the Tobacco Institute contends that such court actions are an invasion of privacy. "We have to ask ourselves where this would stop," says Bill Wordham. "Is a parent who habitually takes a child to McDonald's or otherwise feeds that child unhealthy food any less deserving of custody? What about a parent who allows his child to watch long hours of television?"[59]

Another of your typical tobacco industry "smoke screens," obviously. They just don't get it, do they? Yet even self-identified "virulent nonsmoker and hard-core tobacco hater" columnist Ellen Goodman has similar qualms:

> If we award divorced kids a smoke-free home, then why not take all the children of smokers out of their dangerous environment? If so, where do we put them?
>
> If health care becomes the pivotal issue in a custody fight, why stop at smoking? An evaluation of mom and pop should include a lead-paint check, a radon test, a nutritional balance sheet, a search for dangerous weapons and a knowledge of parental seat-belt habits . . .
>
> And what about mental health? Is smoking a better criteria for deciding custody than what we used to call emotional attachment? We're into some very smoky territory.[60]

"Parents exposing their children to secondhand smoke is the most common form of child abuse in America," says Banzhaf, who looks forward to the day when it won't take a custody battle to rescue the children. "I am certainly not suggesting that every time a parent lights up in the same room, we're going to cry child abuse. But the same protection will eventually be extended to children in ongoing marriages through child-neglect proceedings."[61]

In other words, when that great day comes, instead of being forced to wait until divorcing parents take each other to court, antismoking zealots will be able to intervene directly to shatter *intact* families—or even to prevent the formation of families in the first place. A Dr. Fleming in Great Britain advocates screening prospective adoptive parents for their smoking habits (see next chapter). Former Surgeon General C. Everett Koop goes even further than Banzhaf and predicts, with apparent happy anticipation, that the day when criminal charges will be filed against smoking parents "can't be far off."[62]

Koop and Banzhaf were both born a little too late and in the wrong country for them to realize their full fascistic potential. Yet there's hope. America is becoming more and more totalitarian when it comes to health issues. All we need are brown shirts and jack boots. A lot of people are ready and willing to don them.

ASTHMA IS MENTIONED so frequently in association with ETS that this chapter can't end without taking a look at that phenomenon. I call it a phenomenon because, even as the nation's air has become cleaner and the prevalence of smoking has drastically declined, the incidence of asthma has soared. In the last decade alone, the number of reported asthma cases has increased by 42 percent, and the mortality rate for people under 35 has risen by 40 percent.[63] Depending upon whom you read, it afflicts either one out of 40 or one out of 20 Americans, most of whom develop the symptoms in early childhood. According to the Centers for Disease Control and Prevention, asthma affects 4.8 million children in the United States. It says the death rate among young people more than doubled from 1980 to 1993, with fatalities among blacks six times higher than among whites.[64]

An asthma attack is characterized by spasms in the muscles of the bronchial walls, which narrow the airways to the lungs and cause the typical gasping for breath in a severe attack. An attack can also be mild, with only wheezing and shortness of breath, but can progress all the way to complete respiratory failure. It can be triggered simply by exertion, as well as by just about any kind of irritant, such as animal dander and plastic fumes, or by viral colds, emotional stress or drugs, and especially by allergic reactions to substances in the air, including pollens and house dust and—allegedly, if not actually—by cigarette smoke, all of which factors infinitely complicate this phenomenon.

The fact is that nobody really knows what causes asthma, other than the suspicion that susceptibility to it may have a genetic basis. A study published in *Science* in 1997 suggested that the clean living conditions of Western society are associated with the increase in asthma observed over the last several decades. Ironically, childhood respiratory infections might "paradoxically protect against asthma" rather than cause it. But because of the eradication or control of such infections, children's immune systems are not being "challenged," and this predisposes them to asthma later in life.[65]

Another study reported in the *Journal of Clinical Investigation* "suggests" that asthmatics wheeze not because of irritants in the air but because their muscles can't relax normally. A team led by Dr. Alkis Togias believes that asthmatics and nonasthmatics both have the same air-blocking reaction to lung irritation. Nonasthmatics overcome this by breathing deeply to relax the lung muscles, but asthmatics lack this ability.

To test the theory, the researchers gave nonasthmatics an inhalant drug, methacholine, which acts as an irritant and causes breathing problems in asthmatics. They then told the nonasthmatics not to breathe deeply, with the result that they developed asthmalike breathing problems.[66]

Yet another study blames cockroaches, at least in the case of inner-city children. Researchers from the National Cooperative Inner-City Asthma Study studied 476 such children from the Bronx, East Harlem, St. Louis, Washington, Baltimore, Chicago, Cleveland and Detroit and found that more than one-third of the children were allergic to cockroach allergen. Home visits showed that more than 50 percent of the children had high levels of cockroach allergen in their bedrooms. Children who were both sensitive to cockroach allergen and exposed to high levels of it had 200 percent more hospitalizations per year, more unscheduled medical visits for asthma, more days of wheezing, more missed school days and more nights with lost sleep than other children.[67]

Still yet another study, this one presented at an American Lung Association/American Thoracic Society conference in San Francisco in May 1997, "suggests" that exposure to violence "may" be associated with increased severity and occurrence of asthma among inner-city children. The preliminary data from the study by Dr. Rosalind Wright of

Brigham and Women's Hospital in Boston "suggests" that children exposed to violence in their neighborhood (such as hearing gunshots, or witnessing physical violence, often involving weapons), were twice as likely to experience wheezing and to use bronchodilator asthma medication for wheezing, and almost three times as likely to be diagnosed with asthma compared with children not exposed to violence.[68]

To repeat, nobody knows what causes asthma. Thus researchers theorize, conjecture, "suggest."

It's possible that some supposed cases of asthma that don't respond to medications may not be asthma at all but vocal cord dysfunction, or VCD, says Dr. Kenneth Newman, director of the Asthma, Allergy and Sinus Center at the University of Cincinnati, writing in the *American Journal of Respiratory and Critical Care Medicine.*

The symptoms of VCD—wheezing, coughing, shortness of breath —are similar to asthma and lead to incorrect diagnoses, he says. "Many doctors haven't heard of vocal cord dysfunction and those that have think it is a rare disorder, so they don't screen for it."

Newman studied 95 patients referred to the National Jewish Center for Immunology and Respiratory Medicine in Denver because their apparent asthma did not respond to treatment. Fifty-three of them were found to have both VCD and asthma while the others, predominately young women, were diagnosed as having VCD only.[69]

All of this is far removed from my area of "expertise" which, to say it not for the first time, is simply a lifetime's observation of people who smoke and people who don't smoke. I wonder, though, how many of those who base their objections to secondhand tobacco smoke on the claim that they "have asthma" really do have it or, as with the newfound aversion to the odor of tobacco smoke, they have *learned* to experience adverse respiratory reactions to ETS. By the same token, how much of the increase in the incidence of asthma is due to "detection bias"—that is, the sheer assumption that the explanation for a person's reported respiratory distress must be due to asthma because asthma is rather an "in" thing today among doctors as well as among laymen? I am not qualified even to guess, but I read somewhere that doctors actually used to recommend smoking to asthmatics.

In his book, *In Defense of Smokers*, Lauren Colby says that a friend of his who has asthma told him that "smoking cigarettes soothes the lungs and relieves the attacks."[70]

The only asthmatic I know personally is my brother's wife, who walks around with a cigarette in one hand and an inhaler in the other.

The surgeon general's 1964 report briefly looked at the subject of smoking among asthmatics and concluded that "it is clear that cigarette smoking is of no importance as a cause of asthma." Theoretically, it said, smoking may not be advisable for asthmatics "on the basis of the physiologic alterations induced in the tracheobronchial tree by tobacco smoke. Nonetheless, substantiation of worsening from cigarette smoking in asthmatics has not been reported frequently."

The report did note, however, that "In rare instances, allergy to tobacco products has been ascribed a causative role in asthma." It cited five studies, dating as far back as 1917. But the advisory committee did not delve into the subject.[71]

They didn't even think about the possible effects of somebody else's smoking on asthma in nonsmokers because the term "environmental tobacco smoke" had not been invented yet (nor had the term "junk science"), so nobody complained about ETS back then. Thus their finding of a null effect on asthma in active smokers is irrelevant today. All that matters today is that nonsmoking asthmatics *know* that ETS aggravates their asthma, and nobody is going to tell them differently.

Mention should also be made of the complaint by many nonsmokers that they are "allergic" to tobacco smoke. This too is something that did not exist 30 years ago. Yet one researcher claimed in 1974 that eight million people were clinically sensitive to tobacco smoke.[72]

That is pure junk science, says Carol Thompson of the Smoker's Rights Action Group in Madison, Wisconsin. "There is no tobacco smoke antigen."

She bases *that* claim on a 28-page article, with 227 references, in the *American Review of Respiratory Disease*, the journal of the American Lung Association, which reported that "Although many human subjects have a positive skin test reaction to or a specific IgE* against antigens extracted from tobacco leaf, only a much smaller number display these forms of response to smoke extract." And "antigenically cross-

*Defined in my dictionary as a class of antibodies that cause allergic reactions in response to certain foreign antigens. An antigen is any substance that can stimulate the production of antibodies and combine specifically with them.

reactive material was found in a number of vegetables, including tomatoes and peppers. Skin test reactivity to tobacco smoke or leaf extract does not appear to be correlated with smoking status, so IgE produced in response to other plant antigens may be cross-reacting with tobacco proteins. There is no firm evidence that allergy to tobacco smoke occurs . . ."[73]

Another study found no correlation between claimed smoke sensitivity and skin-test reactions or IgE antibodies: "None of the serum samples tested contained detectable IgE antibodies to smoke extracts."[74]

Again, unfortunately, this is also irrelevant to today's nonsmoker who, thanks to antismoking propaganda, ***knows*** he is allergic to tobacco smoke.

As Thompson writes, ". . . the anti-smoking demagogues have encouraged public belief in 'tobacco allergy' as a 'useful lie' [a.k.a. "pious falsehood" —D.O.] to use against smokers. They want everybody to blame their runny noses and all their other symptoms on tobacco smoke, instead of on the food they eat or other real allergens, and lay guilt trips on us and pass oppressive laws. If the demagogues had any genuine concern about this supposed allergy, the least they could do is warn people against tomatoes and pepper. But we all know they don't tell the people about this."

I still have a lot more to say about ETS and the unfortunate consequences this manufactured peril has had on American society. It will take one more chapter to do it.

Notes

1. An example of outdated etiquette in Martha Woodham, "Vanderbilt revision makes sure manners don't die with chivalry." *The Atlanta Journal-Constitution,* February 6, 1995, p. C3.

2. Pierre Lemieux, "Smoking and Liberty." Translation from the "Liberty and Society" colloquium held by *Les Amis de la Liberté* in Montreal, May 3, 1996.

3. "Smoke fight lost in court, at home." Roanoke, Virginia, *Times & World News*, July 25, 1992, p. A6.

4. "Dust-up in Dover." *The New York Times*, April 28, 1994. From www.forces-cdn.com/backya1.htm.

5. Rebecca Perl, "Fear of secondhand smoke may push smokers outdoors." *The Atlanta Journal-Constitution*, September 9, 1991, p. A1.

6. Ranae Merle, "Ailing smoker on oxygen faces eviction."*The Atlanta Journal-Constitution*, June 12, 1997, p. A18. From the Associated Press.

7. "Cat-astrophe suit reinstated." *The Atlanta Journal-Constitution*, December 4, 1996, p. A4.

8. "Smoking Problems in Condominiums and Apartment Buildings." At www.setinc.com/ash/papers/h110.htm.

9. *The NSA Voice*, November/December, 1996, p. 4; also "Smoke and ire." *The Atlanta Journal-Constitution*, July 6, 1996, p. A16.

10. Quoted in *The NSA Voice* April, 1996, p. 4.

11. *Society* magazine, May/June 1995, p. 36. Excerpts posted at www.forces.org/.

12. At www.forces-cdn.com/backya1.htm.

13. Evelyn Nieves, "Calls for Bans As Students Keep Puffing." *The New York Times*, March 10, 1996, p. 33. Courtesy of the Advocacy Institute.

14. Michael Janofsky, "No smoking on the green, green grass of home." *The Atlanta Journal-Constitution*, October 6, 1996, p. B6.

15. "Mad Doctor Thwarted." The FORCES Weekly Tobacco News, October 1996, at www.forces.org/.

16. Sam Howe Verhovek, "As Indoor Fights Smolder, Combatants in Smoking Wars Take Battle Outdoors." *The New York Times*, May 5, 1996, Section 1, p. 14. Courtesy the Advocacy Institute.

17. Andy Baron, "Civil Libertarian: Nothing Illegal in Smoking Ban." the Fitchburg, Massachusetts *Sentinel & Enterprise*, March 1, 1996, p. A3. Courtesy the Advocacy Institute.

18. "The Americans With Disabilities Act As Applicable to Nonsmokers." Undated ASH release at www.setinc.com/ash/papers/h211.htm.

19. "U.S. Appeals Court Says Nonsmokers Can Sue for Smoking Ban." April 6, 1995 ASH release at www.setinc.com/ash/pr/2ndcir.htm.

20. Linda Stewart, "Smoking and Civil Rights." At www.forces.org/pages/linda.htm, citing as her source *The Wall Street Journal*, December 8, 1994.

21. "Update on Bipolar Disorder." At www.medscape.com/Medscape/MentalHealth/1997/vo2.no6/mh3205.bowden/mh3205.bowden.html

22. "Angry smoker allegedly kills eatery patron." *The Atlanta Journal-Constitution*, September 30, 1993, p. A4.

23. "Just a stogie? Or maybe a smoking gun." *The Atlanta Journal-Constitution*, January 30, 1994, p. A4. From the Associated Press.

24. "Up in smokes." Region in Brief. *The Atlanta Journal-Constitution*, March 3, 1997, A7.

25. FORCES Canada at www.forces-cdn/beat1.htm, citing *The New York Post*, February 14 and April 6, 1995.

26. "Good Samaritan Smoker." *Philip Morris Magazine*, Winter 1991, p. 25.

27. From www.webdirect.ca/zeno/apr.htm.

28. Bill Manson, "Oxygen bar targets coffee crowd." *The Atlanta Journal-Constitution*, June 8, 1997, p. C5. From *The London Observer.*

29. Evan Wilson, "New Orleans provides shelter for smokers." About the South. *The Atlanta Journal-Constitution*, May 1, 1994, p. M2.

30. "Ann Landers." *The Atlanta Journal-Constitution*, September, 22 1992, p. M5.

31. "Ann Landers." *The Atlanta Journal-Constitution*, November 27, 1994, p. M4.

32. Maureen Downey, "Peach Buzz-Talk of our Town." *The Atlanta Journal-Constitution*, June 12, 1994, p. C2.

33. Chuck Shephard, "News of the Weird." *The Atlanta Journal-Constitution*, July 15, 1994, p. E6.

34. Linda Stewart, op.cit., citing as her source *The Philadelphia Inquirer*, April 28, 1996.

35. *The Atlanta Journal-Constitution*, November 19, 1993, p. CO5.

36. Nation in Brief. *The Atlanta Journal-Constitution*, October 6, 1994, p. F2.

37. "That cacophonous coughing must go." Entertainment News. *The Atlanta Journal-Constitution*, May 28, 1993, p. F7.

38. Letters. *The Atlanta Journal-Constitution*, October 28, 1995, p. A15.

39. Quoted in Richard Klein, "Get A Whiff of This." *The New Republic*, February 6, 1995, p. 18.

40. "Good 'Scents'?" *NSA Voice*, March 1995, p. 3.

41. Klein, op. cit.

42. Quoted in Michael Fumento, "Sick of It All." *Reason*, June 1996, p. 26.

43. Charles Seabrook, "Mouthwash hazardous to health?" *The Atlanta Journal-Constitution*, March 20, 1991, p. A1.

44. Samuel Shapiro, John Castellana and J. Michael Sprafka, *American Journal of Epidemiology* 1996;144:1091-1095. At www.junkscience.com/news/mouthwash-cancer.html.

45. "Ann Landers." *The Atlanta Journal-Constitution*, January 2, 1994, p. M5.

46. Sabrina F. Hall, "So Young, So Addicted." *Reader's Digest*, January 1995, p. 69. Condensed from *Newsweek*.

47. Anne Kitchell, Sharon Lynn and Shiva Vafai, "Does Smoking Affect the Sense of Smell?" At http://zebra.scarolina.edu/smell/ann/myth7.html.

48. Terese Svoboda, "Every Breath She Takes." *Spin*, December 1996, p. 111.

49. Ibid, p. 117.

50. Cited in Kenneth Green, "Fancy Figures." *Reason*, October 1997, p. 23.

51. Chuck Shepherd, "News of the Weird." *The Atlanta Journal-Constitution*, August 12, 1994, p. F6.

52. Robert Batholomew, "Collective Delusions: A Skeptic's Guide." *Skeptical Inquirer*, May/June 1997, p. 29.

53. Joseph R. Gusfield, "The Social Symbolism of Smoking and Health," in Robert L. Rabin and Stephen D. Sugarman, eds., *Smoking Policy: Law, Politics, and Culture* (New York: Oxford University Press, 1993), p. 54. Gusfield borrowed the term from *The Social Construction of Reality: A Treatise on the Sociology of Knowledge*, by Peter Berger and Thomas Luckman (Garden City, NY: Anchor Books/Doubleday, 1967).

54. Michael Fumento, "How the Media and Lawyers Stir Up False Illness." At www.reasonmag.com/.

55. Pat Michael, "Inside Newport." At www.forces-cdn.com/michael.htm. Also, "Testing the Hysteria." *NSA Voice*, March/April 1997, p. 4.

56. Jerry Taylor, "Cancer Risks for Thee, But Not for Me." *The Wall Street Journal*, January 3, 1995. Reprinted in *The NSA Voice*, February 1995, p. 4.

57. At www.set.inc.com/ash/kentucky.html.

58. At www.setinc.com/ash/papers/h11.html.

59. Quoted in Andrea Sachs, "Home, Smoke-Free Home." *Time*, October 18, 1993, p. 55.

60. Ellen Goodman, "Smoker's rights: Puffers can at least be parents." *The Atlanta-Journal Constitution*, November 29, 1993, p. A9.

61. Sachs, op. cit.

62. Quoted in Joshua Wolf Shenk, "California puts an end to the smoke-filled bar." *Business Week*, December 22, 1997, p. 56.

63. Mary Garner Ganske, "Breathless: Is asthma becoming epidemic?" From an article downloaded from Compuserve, September 1995.

64. Joan Kirchner, "CDC: Asthma death rate higher for young blacks." *The Atlanta Journal-Constitution*, May 4, 1996, p. F5. From the Associated Press.

65. *Science* 1997;275:41-42, 77-79. Cited on Stephen Milloy's Junk Science page at www.junkscience.com/news/challenge.html. Also Bill Hendrick, "Less infection may mean more child asthma." *The Atlanta Journal-Constitution*, January 3, 1997, p. A1.

66. John Hendron, "Study: Asthmatics suffer from muscle malfunction." *The Atlanta Journal-Constitution*, October 30, 1995, p. A8. From the Associated Press.

67. Steven Milloy, www.junkscience.com/news/roaches.html, citing David L. Rosenstreich et al., "The National Cooperative Inner-City Asthma Study." *New England Journal of Medicine* 1997;336:1356-1363; Thomas A.E. Platts-Mills and Melody C. Carter, *New England Journal of Medicine* 1997;336:1382-1384.

68. Jim Augustine and Elizabeth Hlinko, "New Studies Suggest Role of Violence In Asthma and Higher Than Expected Asthma Rates In Inner City." American Thoracic Society press release, from www.thoracic.org/pres_ic.html#ic1.

69. "Masquerading disorder." New Port Richey, Florida, *Suncoast News*, March 20, 1996, p. HN30.

70. Lauren Colby, *In Defense of Smokers.* Self-published 1995, p. 40. Also available on the Web at www.lcolby.com.

71. *Smoking and Health.* Report of the Advisory Committee to the Surgeon General of the Public Health Service, U.S. Department of Health, Education and Welfare. U.S. Government Printing Office, 1964, p. 276.

72. Cited in Carol Thompson, "There Is No Tobacco Allergy." At www.forces-cdn/com/carol2.htm, citing B. M. Zussman, "Tobacco sensitivity in the allergic population. A specific allergic entity." *J Asthma Res* 1974;11(4):159-167).

73. Ibid, citing G. T. O'Connor et al., "The role of allergy and nonspecific airway hyperresponsiveness in the pathogenesis of chronic obstructive pulmonary disease." *Am Rev Respir Dis* 1989;140:225-252).

74. Ibid, citing S. B. Lehrer et al., "IgE antibody response of smokers, nonsmokers, and 'smoke-sensitive' persons to tobacco leaf and smoke antigens." *Am Rev Respir Dis* 1980;121:168-170).

Chapter 8

KIDS, SIDS AND ETS

We will never now how many smokers' lives we prolong . . . when we force them to do the right thing for themselves.

— Glenn Barr of Americans for Nonsmokers' Rights[1]

The trouble with aggressive nonsmokers is that they feel they are doing you a favor by not allowing you to smoke. They seem to think that one day you'll look back and thank them for those precious fifteen seconds they just added to your life. What they don't understand is that those are just fifteen more seconds you can spend hating their guts and plotting revenge.

— David Sedaris[2]

THE CRUSADE AGAINST smoking has contributed marvelously to the disintegration of social harmony among Americans. But as the second quotation above illustrates, not only does at least one smoker fiercely resent the self-righteous meddling of "aggressive nonsmokers" (which is another term for antismokers), implicit in his statement is the acknowledgment that the antis are right: smoking kills. The loss of lifespan can in fact be measured down to a matter of seconds.

Without the silent complicity of smokers who, having bought the antismoking line along with everyone else, are guilt-ridden and apologetic about their habit, the crusade could not have achieved the success that it has. Some smokers have even bought more than is being peddled. Prochoice writer Martha Perske told me she met a woman, a smoker, who was surprised to learn that the official, medically endorsed line was that one out of three smokers dies prematurely from some "smoking-related" disease. The woman had thought it was three out of three and was quite relieved to hear otherwise. One out of three seemed like pretty good odds to her.

But ah, that was the old estimate (although it continues to be used to frighten teenagers who smoke). A newer figure is one out of two. Famed British epidemiologist Richard Peto told the 10th World Conference on Smoking OR Health held in Beijing, China, in August 1997, that based on "more recent data," lifelong cigarette use, particularly if begun before age 20, kills at least half of all smokers. Moreover, at least 25 percent die in middle age (36-69), losing on the average over 20-25 years of life.

Based upon these new data, Peto now estimates that smoking will kill more than 100 million people over the next 20 years, even if no new smokers take up the habit. (But around 50 million people die every year, which means that over the next 20 years, 900 million nonsmokers will die. Over the next 100 years, nearly every one of the five billion-plus human beings alive today will die. Why doesn't anybody worry about that?) Yet it could be worse. Even if a smoker quits in middle age, before getting incurable cancer or other serious disease, he will avoid most of the later risk of premature death, Peto said.[3]

Mrs. Perske's friend might still consider one out of two reasonably good odds, depending upon how hopelessly "addicted" she is to cigarettes. But ah again, the antis aren't going to let her get away with even that faint hope.

According to more "more recent data," a study conducted at the University of Pittsburgh "suggests" that long-term smoking triggers a biological change that increases the risk of lung cancer *permanently*, even for ex-smokers. Smoking the equivalent of a pack of cigarettes every day for 25 years "appears" to encourage both healthy and mutated lung cells to multiply, increasing the odds of developing cancer, no matter how long ago a person stopped smoking.

"Once this switch is turned on, it appears to be permanent, which may explain in part why long-term ex-smokers who have not had a cigarette in over 25 years are still at high risk for getting lung cancer," said Jill Siegfried, director of the study, which was published in the August 1997 issue of the *Journal of Respiratory and Critical Care Medicine*.[4]

The researchers found an abnormal protein on the surface of lung cells from heavy smokers. The protein, a gastrin-releasing peptide receptor, attracts a type of hormone that stimulates cells to divide. "The more cell growth you have, the greater the chance that one of those mutated cells will be the one that grows," Siegfried said.

The harmful protein was not present in light smokers, but Siegfried said a larger survey would be needed to determine when irreversible damage sets in. (Translation: more grant money.) Other researchers said Siegfried's findings were "significant."

Commenting on the study, Vincent Miller, a lung cancer researcher at Memorial Sloan-Kettering Cancer Institute in New York, said it is the first to explain why ex-smokers are twice as likely to develop lung cancer as those who have never smoked.

Also commenting, Frank Cuttitta of the National Cancer Institute said that many smokers mistakenly believe that when they stop, their lungs will eventually become healthy again. This study shows why that doesn't happen, he said.

This Siegfried study confirms an earlier one that was presented before a meeting of the American Society of Clinical Oncology in Los Angeles in 1995. In an analysis of 685 lung cancer patients seen at Brigham and Women's Hospital in Boston between 1988 and 1994, Dr. Gary Strauss reported that 41 percent of the victims were current smokers and 51 percent were former smokers. The former smokers diagnosed with lung cancer had stopped smoking an average of six years before, and a quarter of them had been off cigarettes for more than 20 years.[5]

(Which prompted a reader of *The Atlanta Journal-Constitution* to write: "A recent article titled 'Half of lung cancers strike former smokers' left me unable to decide whether I'm sorry I ever started smoking or sorry I quit. So instead, I decided to be sorry I let the statisticians suck me in again."[6])

So there we have it. It *couldn't* be worse. Mrs. Perkse's friend might as well just smoke and enjoy; she's doomed whatever she does. (Does it never occur to antismokers that pushing their propaganda to the ultimate extreme might backfire?)

IN NO AREA HAS the crusade against smoking achieved greater success, among smokers and nonsmokers alike, than in the matter of ETS—so-called "environmental tobacco smoke," also known by the emotion-laden terms "secondhand smoke," "passive smoking," "involuntary smoking." As early as 1992, a year before the Environmental Protection Agency officially released (as opposed to leaking) the infamous study that was the subject of Chapter 6, an Associated Press telephone poll of 1,000 adults found that fully two out of three of them were worried that exposure to secondhand cigarette smoke could cause serious health problems, especially cancer. A slight majority, 54 percent, also favored bans on smoking in public places.

"The public is clearly sensitized to the health effects of secondhand tobacco smoke," commented Scott Balin, a spokesman for the Coalition on Smoking OR Health, made up of the American Heart Association, the American Cancer Society and the American Lung Association.[7]

"Sensitized to" is an understatement in light of developments since that poll was taken. "Hysterically panicked about" would be closer to the mark today.

When the ETS issue was discovered—make that invented—by the antismokers, I used to wonder why, if secondhand smoke was so bad for nonsmokers, it wasn't even worse for smokers. After all, the latter not only breathe in firsthand smoke but their own secondhand smoke on top of it, and not just occasionally but more or less all day long. Thanks to medical science's dedicated and indefatigable researchers I learned the answer. According to a study in the April 5, 1995 *Journal of the American Medical Association*:

> Regular smokers are chronically and continually adversely affecting their cardiovascular systems which, in turn, adapt to compensate for all of the harmful effects. Nonsmokers do not have the benefit of this adaptation, which offers some protection. This means that nonsmokers exposed to secondhand smoke are actually more vulnerable to injury from secondhand smoke than regular smokers.[8]

But this only raises other questions in my mind. The fact is that *all* smokers were at one time nonsmokers, and at least 99.999 percent of them must have been exposed to secondhand cigarette smoke to some degree before they became smokers, which means during their childhood years when presumably they would be most susceptible to the adverse health effects. Even if they miraculously escaped such exposure, they were certainly exposed to their own secondhand smoke when they first started smoking, also usually at a young age. How did they escape the injury to which even adult nonsmokers are allegedly more vulnerable than smokers? Were they injured by secondhand smoke but the injury was somehow repaired or mitigated when they became regular smokers? If regular smokers can "adapt" to firsthand smoke, which is infinitely more concentrated with suspected poisons than secondhand smoke, why can't nonsmokers "adapt" to the latter? Might they possibly benefit from *more* rather than less exposure to secondhand smoke?

The real answer, of course, is that the antismokers will go to any lengths, however, illogical, to promote fear of tobacco smoke among nonsmokers.

My wife and I travel a lot around the country, and everywhere we stop I like to get a copy of the local newspaper to catch up with the latest antismoking news. (News about smoking is always antismoking news.) Invariably, wherever we stop, small city or large, if there is not an article reporting "the latest study" about smoking there is an editorial or an op-ed column or a letter to the editor. In 1992, the year of the AP poll, we were in California, where I found the following letter from a reader of the *Conejo Valley Daily News*:

> It is high time that smokers realize that our land of freedom includes the right of nonsmokers to our health. We don't invade the private right of smokers to inhale carbon monoxide—thereby devastating their bodies in their homes—but we ask them not to deprive us of our pleasures.
>
> Why should we be exposed to the smokers' lifestyle and have to put up with secondary smoke inhalation and smelly clothes? It is well known by now that thousands of people die of lung cancer due to the smoking habits of others, plus the fire dangers in homes and forests. It is only fair that nonsmokers demand that public places be free of smokers' intrusions on our rights.[9]

Conejo Valley is hard by Los Angeles, which is not renowned for the purity and health-enhancing quality of its air. One wonders if the writer was as concerned about the tons of carbon monoxide (not to mention the formaldehyde, sulfur dioxide, benzene, polycyclic hydrocarbons, butadiene and on and on) which, despite California's strict emission requirements, are spewed into the environment around the clock by the "driving habits of others" (and probably by his as well), the proud owners of the millions of automobiles that populate the area.

More than likely, though, he would agree with a fellow who sent a letter to the Sarasota, Florida, *Herald-Tribune*:

> I must take issue with the letter writer from Bradenton who questions the danger of secondhand smoke but feels pollution from smokestacks, cars, etc., is more of a problem. Nothing could be further from the truth.
>
> Nothing compares to the deadliness of secondhand or passive tobacco smoke. Chemical analysis shows it to contain not only carbon monoxide and nicotine but also 43 known carcinogens, or cancer-causers. If tobacco were a new product today, it could never pass the safety tests required by either the Environmental Protection Agency or the Food and Drug Administration. Tobacco is the only "legal" product that not only kills the user but also the innocent bystander when used as directed.[10]

The famous Dr. Pavlov, who conditioned dogs to salivate at the ringing of a bell, had nothing on our modern antismokers. They've got people so frightened of secondhand smoke that the mere mention of it starts "innocent bystanders" foaming at the mouth.

It was also in the course of our travels, long before I dreamed of trying to write a book about smoking, that I first encountered what to me was a curious and silly thing—nonsmoking motel rooms. When or where this was I don't remember, but my family and I had stayed at dozens of motels over the years, with ashtrays and matches as standard furnishings in every room. Now, all of a sudden, people were demanding "smoke-free" rooms? I half-suspected that it was really nothing more than catering to the propaganda-inspired prejudices of nonsmokers. Surely, I thought, if a room was properly cleaned and aired, no one could tell that it had been smoked in by a previous occupant.

Of course, this was before I became aware of the amazing ultrasensitivity to tobacco smoke that was manifesting itself in the nonsmoking population. Later, a former neighbor of ours, an ex-smoker who frequently traveled by automobile on business, assured me that he could indeed tell if a motel room had been smoked in. "I can smell it on the pillows," he said. I didn't ask him what kind of establishments he frequented that didn't change the bed linens between customers. But then, such is the penetrating power of tobacco smoke that it evidently impregnates and contaminates the pillows themselves, not to mention the mattress, the carpet and the very walls. Funny, though, that nobody ever noticed this years ago, or if they did, said nothing about it.

I ask again: where *were* these sensitive people before a string of surgeons general told us that tobacco smoke kills, both the user of tobacco and the innocent bystander alike?

Could people *really* tell that a room has been smoked in the day before? I put this question to the clerk at an Econo Lodge in Bloomington, Minnesota, in 1996. A lady ahead of me had been upset that smoking rooms were the only ones currently available. She reluctantly agreed to stay in one only on the promise that she would be transferred to a nonsmoking room the next day. Yes, the clerk told me, they can tell. I could only shake my head in wonderment. I have detected a lot of strange smells in motel rooms and, although I am obviously desensitized to tobacco smoke, I think I would rather put up with that than a number of other odors I could name.

Today, as simple good business, just about every motel and hotel in the country offers nonsmoking and smoking rooms (the latter, I have observed, usually way down toward the rear of the building at motels or on an upper floor). And today, while I have learned to request a smoking room, I carry my own ashtray with me just in case. On one occasion, in Richmond, Virginia, I had reserved a smoking room at a Comfort Inn, only to discover after we had deposited all our belongings that it was nonsmoking. Rather than to have to go to the desk and try to get another room and move everything to it, I simply used my ashtray. Did the next occupant have a conniption and was the room thereafter rendered unfit for nonsmokers? I will never know.

A car that has been smoked in is also evidently forever tainted. (It's sort of like the "B.O. Entity" that infected Jerry Seinfield's car in one episode of his TV show and was impossible to get rid of.) This is another phenomenon that began to come to my attention in the early '90s—smoke-free rental cars. "[T]he smoke-free rental car has roared into South Florida, one big parking lot for some of the world's largest rental car fleets," said an article in my trusty *Atlanta Journal-Constitution* (you can trust it to report anything unfavorable to smoking).[11] The article continued:

> The latest: No. 1 Hertz, where 80 percent of the fleet has gone smokeless in recent months. Customers, the company concluded, had a burning desire to rent cars never befouled by the smothering stench of a stogie, cigarette or pipe.
>
> "Yep, that was the whole motivation," said Susan Carney, a Hertz

> spokeswoman. "Customers wanted it. And we like happy customers."
>
> In the beginning, Thrifty was the only smoke-free chain, offering smoke-free cars in the late '80s. The company even takes out the cigarette lighters.

What if someone smoked in a nonsmoking Hertz rental car? "We just take the car and put it in our smoking fleet," Ms. Carney said.

(That mention of cigarette lighters relates to another development in our smoke-free world—the manufacture of cars without ashtrays. In 1993, Saab announced that it was going to charge buyers of its new 900 model $45 if they wanted ashtrays.[12] The following year Chrysler announced that its Dodge Stratus and Chysler Cirrus models would offer ashtrays only as an option.[13] Happily, however, there will always be cigarette lighters, or at least receptacles for them, because the outlets can be used for other purposes, such as the ubiquitous cell phone, which as a precipitator of accidents has already probably eliminated more cars from the nation's active fleet than any amount of smoking in them.)

As Florida went, so, unfortunately, went the nation. After my brother retired and moved from Ohio to California in the mid-1980s, he and his wife operated an Avis agency for several years. They did the same thing; if they found evidence of smoking in a returned nonsmoking car, they simply reassigned it as a smoking car. The evidence, of course, was butts in the ashtray and/or burn marks on the upholstery. Because both he and his wife are smokers, they are physiologically incapable of detecting lingering tobacco smoke odor. (They've also told me stories of cars returned by smokers and nonsmokers alike showing far worse abuse than having been smoked in, but that is outside the scope of this book.)

This suggests something we smokers can do to FIGHT BACK! Let's all rent a nonsmoking car and smoke up a storm in it. If enough of us do it, and do it often enough, there won't be any nonsmoking cars left and the poor nonsmokers will be up the proverbial creek without a paddle—or without wheels anyway.

Here again, as throughout this book, my own experience runs counter to the commonly known "facts" about the consequences of smoking. In 1994, after I traded in my '88 Olds "88" for a new one, having smoked in it for six years and 60,000 miles, I got a call from the new owner, who had apparently obtained my telephone number from the dealer. He had bought it as a second car for his wife and he just wanted to tell me how pleased she was with the good shape it was in. The interior looked like it had never been used, he said.

This told me that the new owners either were smokers themselves or olfactorily impaired nonsmokers. Or maybe it simply testified to my diligence in cleaning up the car for trade-in. (But if I could do it, why couldn't rental agencies?) Fortunately, I'd never dropped a cigarette on the carpet or seat to leave a telltale sign that the car had been smoked in. Unfortunately, however, shortly after taking possession of my '94 "88," I not only did drop a cigarette, leaving a burn mark on the floor mat on the driver's side but, while throwing a butt out the window, left a scar on the sun visor. Which means that when the time comes to trade this car in, the dealer will be stuck with it unless he can sell it to a smoker—assuming dealers will continue to accept trade-ins from smokers, assuming there will be any smokers left.

WHICH ALSO PROMPTS the first and only digression in this chapter. Cigarette butts. The careless disposal of them is something for which smokers are rightly criticized. Though I have never emptied an ashtray in a parking lot, as far too many smokers seem compelled to do, I would routinely and unthinkingly use the public roadway as a convenient receptacle for a burned-down cigarette, until one time a few years ago I was admonished about it by my wife. Since then I have faithfully used the ashtray, which I periodically empty into the garbage can in our garage.*

The fact that we live on a corner lot at an intersection with four-way stop signs has also raised my consciousness on this subject. Along with causing drivers to slow their heady pace just a bit, the stop signs

*It's not just a litter problem or a forest fire danger but, at least in California, has other untoward consequences. According to a posting I found on the World Wide Web, "Lit cigarette butts . . . fly through open windows into cars or land in the back of trucks. In a column in the *Los Angeles Times*, readers described how they or their cars were burned by these missiles. One driver had a butt fly into her car and burn her leg. Another had her truck destroyed when a butt landed in the back which was loaded with furniture."[14] The article included the author's e-mail address, so I wrote and asked him for the date of the newspaper column but never heard back from him. I can, again, only express wonderment that flying cigarette butts was never a reported hazard before we learned that smoking kills.

also seem to alert them that this is a good place to dispose of their cigarette butts, which the prevailing winds blow onto my property. (Most of them are Marlboros—another crime that can be laid to the door of Phillip Morris.) Even so, I'd rather pick up cigarette butts off my lawn than deal with the frequent calling cards left by some of my fellow neighbors (by their dogs, that is) as they stroll by with their pets, many of whom (the owners, that is) are possibly nonsmokers and none of whom has apparently ever heard of a pooper-scooper.

Coincidentally, at the very time I was writing this chapter, a Sunday edition of the comic strip "For Better or For Worse" revolved around both issues. It showed a couple walking their dog along a beach and conscientiously collecting its dropping in a bag and disposing of it in a trash container. Then they stroll past another couple who are sitting on a log smoking. Dozens of cigarette butts litter the sand at their feet. As the first couple passes, one of the smokers comments: "Man, if there's one thing I can't stand, it's guys who take their dogs to the beach!!!"[15]

The message of course was that smokers are a messy, inconsiderate lot. But it also illustrated something else that the author probably did not intend: even where smokers are allowed to smoke outside—and the number of such places is dwindling—butt cans are seldom provided for them. (One would have been handy by that log because that one couple couldn't have been responsible for all those butts.) Whether or not most smokers would use such receptacles is an open question. The fact remains that they are simply not provided. In any case, are cigarette butts worse than discarded beer bottles and soft drink cans?

This wasn't as much of a problem when most cigarettes were unfiltered. When I was in the Army we were required to "field strip" our butts under penalty of having to police the drill area. First you'd knock the coal off, then tear open the cigarette and scatter the tobacco to the wind, then roll the paper into a tiny ball about the size of a BB and flip it away. I don't know what the Army does now if you drop a filtered butt on the ground. Probably court-martial you.

Smokers have been making life difficult for nonsmokers in other ways as well, as indicated by a letter to *The Atlanta Journal-Constitution* from a citizen of Marietta, Georgia:

> I, for one, am simply no longer willing to sit in a restaurant trying to eat dinner while someone blows smoke in my face; to

> have my silk blouse burned by a careless smoker waiving [*sic*] their arm to gesture; to have match heads pop in my lap by a client at lunch; or to have to send everything I had on to the cleaners because I attended a business function after work.
>
> Thank you to all of the places where I do business because you are smoke-free facilities.[16]

Popping matchheads. Now that's a hazard I never thought of. (And, incidentally, how come cleaners can remove the odor of tobacco smoke from clothing but motels and car-rental agencies can't remove it from rooms or cars?) Of course, most of the problems the writer encountered could be minimized, if not by the spirit of "accommodation" between smokers and nonsmokers that the hapless cigarette companies advocate (and for which they are sneeringly ridiculed simply as a matter of course), at least by providing separate smoking and nonsmoking sections in restaurants.

This has been the solution in most parts of the country, where it is left to the proprietors of such establishments to decide, on the basis of their customers' preferences and what they consider is best for their own businesses, whether or not to have such sections. Two major exceptions are Maryland (the "Free State"), where smoking is universally banned in restaurants, and California, where on January 1, 1998 its restaurant ban was enlarged to include even bars.

But according to comedian, musician, song writer, author, raconteur and all-around genius Steve Allen (that's a sincere compliment), to say that customer preferences should rule on this issue is to embrace "the marketplace fallacy"—the argument that the marketplace (that is, the people who patronize restaurants) should determine whether nosmoking sections are desired. There are some important problems with this argument, he says:

"The marketplace should not decide public health problems. We don't let the marketplace decide about outdoor air pollution, and shouldn't let it determine the quality of air indoors. The issue is health—not preferences. When it comes to health, governments are obligated to protect people."[17]

He cites the examples of child safety seats in automobiles, laws regulating the removal of asbestos from buildings and mandatory immunizations for children entering school.

A lot depends, however, on whether some perceived "public

health" problem really is a problem that can only be handled by laws and regulations, and on where you draw the line between the legitimate role of government and nanny-state health paternalism. In the case of secondhand smoke, the real and only problem with it is the corrupt science behind the official statistics, which Allen and others who hate smoking eagerly accept at face value.

(As for outdoor air pollution, even here there are certain marketplace solutions, such as allowing industries that perform better than federal standards to sell their emissions permits to other companies, thus giving all of them financial incentive to clean up their acts.)

Allen further argues that banning smoking in restaurants, as well as in workplaces, actually does a favor for smokers. For one thing it helps them to quit. For another, "smokers don't like being asked not to smoke when they light up; nonsmokers' rights laws eliminate that problem."[18]

So you see, smokers, at bottom the militant nonsmokers really have your convenience at heart. Isn't that nice of them?

By making that statement Allen demonstrates that he embraces a rather arrogant fallacy of his own—the idea that all the restaurants in the country are community property and are and of right ought to be exclusively for the enjoyment of nonsmokers.

Inevitably, the adamant refusal of antismokers to countenance reasonable accommodation for smokers will inspire restaurants and bars to come up with ingenious solutions. One example is in California, exemplar for the nation with its all-encompassing public antismoking law.

> "[A]t least one Bay Area brewpub is taking the lead in figuring out how to get around the stringent Schmoking Ist Verboten law that went into effect in California last week," wrote Bill Citara, food and wine critic for the *San Francisco Examiner.*
>
> Down in San Mateo, Barley & Hopps brewery-restaurant-night club has spent $30,000 constructing a classy (and thoroughly legal) Cigar Bar & Smoking Lounge. . .
>
> In order to comply with provisions of the law that prohibit indoor smoking in the presence of employees, the lounge is equipped with an intercom system that patrons can use to place orders at the bar. Their order is then delivered outside the lounge door, where customers can step out of the room to pick it up. Not exactly the epitome of service, but, hey, we've all gotten used to pumping our own gas, and we'll eventually get used to this, too.[19]

* * *

THE FOREGOING NONSENSE about rental rooms and cars and cigarette butts, and even restaurants, is of less than earthshaking importance. Not so the accelerating tide of smoking prohibitions in offices and other places of work. While the Associated Press poll cited above reported that two-thirds of those polled were concerned about the danger of secondhand smoke and 54 percent favored bans against smoking in public, it also reported that another slight majority (more than 500 out of the 1,000 polled anyway) believed that smoking bans in the workplace should be decided by employer and employees, not by law.

This shows how outdated that poll is. Today there is no such thing as accommodation in the workplace. (Well, possibly a few places where it is not prohibited—so far—by the law's majesty.) It is in this area of American life that the antismoking crusade, fueled by the hysteria over ETS, has attained to the uttermost reaches of insanity.

It is one thing for smokers to be continually and continuously chided, criticized, chastised, castigated and condemned for their nasty habit. They can live with that. It is quite a different thing to deprive them of one of the basic rights accorded every other American of whatever race, creed, political persuasion or mental or physical handicap. I don't mean the right to smoke anywhere or anytime they want. There never was such a right. I mean the simple right to earn a living.

A list of companies that refuse to hire smokers, or which make a pledge of not smoking, *even at home*, a condition or precondition of employment, would be as long as this chapter. In Atlanta, the entire Ted Turner empire—CNN News, Turner Television and its subdivisions—is one. Lockheed Aircraft in nearby Marietta is another. Elsewhere in the nation there was Motorola, which tried to forbid smokers from smoking in their own cars in the company parking lot, until employee complaints and adverse publicity forced them to reverse the ban.[20] The case is notable in being one of the few times the American Civil Liberties Union (ACLU) has taken a stand on behalf of smokers. Motorola employees still must go outside to smoke, however.

At Pratt & Whitney in East Hartford, Connecticut, employees cannot smoke inside any of the company's buildings and are restricted to where and when they can smoke outside on company property, and only on their lunch hours and before and after their shifts. They are not allowed to smoke on other breaks. Smokers are also charged $500 more a year for health insurance than nonsmokers.[21]

At the New Brunswick Scientific Company, a maker of biotech equipment in Edison, New Jersey, the company's chairman, David Freedman, says he allows any of his 350 employees to smoke outside the building on the company property, but he was thinking of banning that because "People who smoke spend a lot of their time outside smoking, so they have a great deal more time off than the nonsmokers." His company also charges smokers more for their health coverage.[22]

It has apparently never occurred to Mr. Freedman that a smoking lounge inside the building could help cut down some of that wasted time. But a properly ventilated smoking lounge that would meet federal standards would cost money; it's much easier simply to ban smoking entirely. After all, given a choice between smoking in poverty or not smoking and earning a living to support his family, even the most addicted smoker would rather work than smoke. As for allowing people to smoke on the job at their desks or work stations, even if the company would benefit from higher productivity—don't be ridiculous. Those days are long gone.

I can't explain how it ever happened (maybe the "all-powerful" tobacco industry is behind it), but according to Action on Smoking and Health (ASH), in reaction to this kind of unjustifiable discrimination some 28 states and the District of Columbia have passed laws that prohibit companies from refusing to hire smokers,[23] a development the American Cancer Society calls "unfortunate." In other states, however, such legislation has been defeated.

In Florida, Gov. Lawton Chiles vetoed a smokers' rights bill, saying he saw no reason to bring smokers under the same umbrella that protects people from discrimination in employment and housing. "We should not trivialize people's fundamental civil rights with an unnecessary new class of 'smokers,'" he declaimed.[24]

In Virginia, Gov. L. Douglas Wilder used similar language in vetoing a similar bill. "It is creating a special class of people that would be given protection that others were not entitled to," he said.[25]

Apparently these two governors felt it was all right that existing antidiscrimination law had created all kinds of special classes of people, just as long as they weren't smokers.

In Georgia, a bill that would have prohibited companies from hiring or firing people on the basis of whether they smoked or not was passed by a committee on the House side of the legislature but didn't go any further. Introducing a similar bill in the Georgia Senate, its sponsor conceded that it would be defeated, but antismoking spokespeople testified against it for three hours anyway.[26]

More importantly, the courts, which usually have the final say, have ruled that requiring smokers to stop smoking as a precondition of employment is perfectly legal. Two examples cited by Action on Smoking and Health:

In *Grusendorf v. City of Oklahoma City*, 816 F.2d 539 (10th Cir. 1987), the U.S. Court of Appeals held that it was constitutional for a city agency to require employees to sign an agreement as a precondition of employment that they will not smoke a cigarette, either on or off duty, for a period of one year from the time they began work. (Does this mean they can start smoking again after the year is up?) It also held that the city was justified in firing a trainee firefighter for smoking a cigarette during his lunch break because its no-smoking regulation had a legitimate purpose in promoting health. (Had the guy been caught eating a bag of fat-and-cholesterol-rich potato chips, he'd still have his job.)[27]

In *City of North Miami v. Kurtz*, 653 So.2d 1025 (1995), the Supreme Court of Florida held that it was constitutional, under both the U.S. and the Florida constitutions, for the city to adopt a regulation requiring job applicants to sign affidavits, as precondition of having their applications considered, stating that they had not used tobacco in the preceding year.[28]

Surely such decisions would not stand up on appeal to the big guys in Washington, you might think. Think again. On January 3, 1996 the Supreme Court of the United States let stand the Florida Supreme Court's decision in the North Miami case. According to "The Daily Report of Tobacco News" on the Internet:

The case was brought before the [Florida Supreme] court on behalf of Arlene Kurtz, a smoker who in applying for a clerk-typist job with the city (population 50,000) refused to sign a newly required statement averring she had not smoked or used any tobacco products during the previous 12 months. Her interview was terminated, and she was not hired.

The 1990 policy, applicable to new hires only, was adopted to save money on medical coverage, due to smokers' costlier medical bills, according to the city. Ms. Kurtz, 52, had been smoking for 30 years and challenged the policy as embodying constitutional violations of privacy and due process. She won her case in appellate court but lost when it was brought before the Florida Supreme Court in 1995.

The justices in that case ruled 5-2 that Kurtz had no expectation of privacy as a smoker—smokers are constantly asked to disclose their habit, as in hotels and restaurants. Furthermore, the court said, the city's interest in reducing medical costs was a valid reason for the rule.[29]

Florida rivals California in antismoking idiocy (too much exposure to the sun?). When in July 1997, Brian Morrison, 23, applied to the police force in Boca Raton, which bans tobacco use by its employees, a polygraph test revealed that he had puffed on a cigar six months before, thus dooming his chances of becoming a police officer.[30]

"I figured the rule applied to smokers, and I'm not a smoker," said Morrison. "I had a cigar at my [college] graduation and at a friend's birthday party. I didn't think it counted."

Morrison's tobacco use was the primary reason he was disqualified, said police spokesman Eric Lawrence, but added that even without that he would have been disqualified for other reasons. No doubt that made the young man feel a little better about his reckless behavior.

What if a smoker is healthy and able-bodied, as Ms. Kurtz evidently was, even after 30 years of smoking? It doesn't matter, for incontrovertible (yeah, right) studies have proved (sure) that smokers as a class cost employers money because of absenteeism due to "smoking-related" illnesses, as well as accidents. Thus smokers are the only people in America, other, perhaps, than homosexuals, against whom it is legally permissible to discriminate as individuals on the basis of the popular stereotype of the group to which they belong.

The U.S. Supreme Court's refusal to hear the Kurtz appeal does not necessarily set a precedent (individual states can still pass smokers' rights laws), though it certainly does not bode well for any smoker who dares to challenge a firing or a nonhiring. Yet it could be worse. That is, we have not yet reached the point where a potential employee is required to swear, à la suspected Communist sympathizers in the McCarthy era, under penalty of fine and/or imprisonment or at least loss of career, reputation and livelihood: "I am not now using nor have I *ever* in my life used a tobacco product." But be patient.

In fact, it's already worse in other ways. Not only do smokers have no right to work. Not only do smokers have no expectation of privacy. But even though every medical authority in the known universe agrees that smokers are addicted to their habit, smokers have no right to claim such addiction as a "handicap"—even though nonsmokers have been allowed to claim that their *aversion* to tobacco smoke is a "handicap" and have been accorded "accommodation" (that is, the right to stick it to their employer or the taxpayers) for such claims. Again I am indebted to ASH for the following information:

The Americans With Disabilities Act (ADA) of 1990 (42 USC §§ 12101 et seq.) is one of two federal employment laws which protect the disabled, says ASH. The other is the Rehabilitation Act (RA) of 1973 (29 USC § 794), which specifically applies to handicapped persons. "The terms 'disabled' used in the ADA and 'handicapped' used in the RA were described by the Congressional (House) Committee concerned as 'comparable.'

"The following are examples of cases where a federal court or federal agency decreed that a sensitive nonsmoker was a disabled (then termed 'handicapped') person who was eligible to ask for reasonable accommodation under the Rehabilitation Act. Such cases are precedents for similar requests under the Americans with Disabilities Act."

Parodi v. Merit Systems Protection Board. 690 F2d 731 (9th Cir. 1982). "The U.S. Court of Appeals for the 9th Judicial Circuit held that a sensitive federal government employee who suffered from exposure to tobacco smoke in the workplace was entitled to disability benefits unless the government could show that an appropriate substitute position was available. As no appropriate position was available, the case was settled on the basis of the employee receiving a disability retirement pension plus a $50,000 lump sum payment."

Vickers v. Veterans Administration, 548 F. Supp. 85 (1982). "A federal District Court held that a federal employee whose hypersensitivity to tobacco smoke limited his capacity to work in any environment which was not completely smoke-free was a 'handicapped person' for the purpose of the Rehabilitation Act, but that his employer had, in fact, made reasonable accommodation."

Flaniken v. Office of Personnel Management, U.S. Merit Systems Protection Board, Dallas Field Office. No. DA831L1001 (1980). "The MSPB found that a sensitive federal government employee was entitled to a disability retirement annuity where [*sic*] she had contracted chronic laryngitis caused by cigarette smoke and environmental pollution."

Pletten v. Department of the Army, U.S. Merit Systems Protection Board Nos. CH07528010099, CH01520 2901 (1981). "The MSPB found that a tobacco-smoke sensitive civilian Army employee was a 'handicapped person' for the purpose of the Rehabilitation Act and that he was accordingly entitled to reasonable accommodation to [*sic*] his handicap."[31]

Antismoking case law is accumulating in the private sector as well. For example, in Des Moines, Iowa, a furniture salesman named David Chico was awarded unemployment benefits after he quit his job because of his coworkers' smoking which, ruled an administrative law judge, created "unsafe, intolerable and detrimental working conditions attributable to the employer."[32]

So it would seem that the rights of the tobacco-smoke-sensitive nonsmoker are pretty well established. As for the rights of the "addicted" smoker, again from ASH:

> A New York [State] appellate court has ruled unanimously that smokers are not entitled to protection against discrimination as "addicts" or as "disabled persons," even if they only smoke in their own homes and not on the job.
>
> The ruling reversed an order requiring the Fortunoff department store chain to pay $10,000 to a job applicant who smoked at home.
>
> The court said that the defendant's status "as a smoker outside the workplace," standing alone, is not enough to establish a disability under state anti-discrimination law. The court's decision was also based upon:
>
> ☐ an opinion issued by the U.S. Office of Contract Compliance, the agency responsible for enforcing the federal Rehabilitation Act, that a smoker is not a "handicapped" person;
>
> ☐ the New York State Attorney General's position in another suit that, under the anti-discrimination statute, smokers are not disabled;
>
> ☐ a separate statute designed to cover this specific situation.
>
> Action on Smoking and Health (ASH), a national nonsmokers' rights organization, hailed the ruling, saying that it may help put an end to claims that there is some kind of right to smoke—whether the smoking occurs in public, in a private office, *or even in the home* [emphasis added]—or that there is some requirement that smokers be protected or accommodated . . .[33]

"We have a right to make a decision to protect the health and well-being of our customers and associates," said Louis Fortunoff, explaining the smoking prohibition at his family's chain of New Jersey housewares stores.[34]

Mr. Fortunoff certainly has that right. But just how a potential employee's smoking at home would threaten the health and well-being of his company's customers and associates is not clear. It's not as if smokers were modern Typhoid Marys bearing communicable diseases.

What *is* clear is that the antismokers can neatly have it both ways. They can claim that smokers are hopelessly addicted to their habit when it suits one purpose—charging the cigarette companies with inducing, manipulating and maintaining that addiction. They can claim that smokers are *not* addicted when it suits another purpose—denying them the right to participate in the same game nonsmokers enjoy: picking somebody else's pocket.

Am I alone in this, or is it not passing strange that the courts have ruled in some cases that an employer may not refuse to hire someone with a criminal record, or have required an employer to rehire a worker who was fired because he had a "disability" that prevented him from showing up for work on time, yet the terrible, terrible addiction to nicotine is not allowed as a "disability"?

The ASH press release also doesn't give the date of the New York court's decision, but it was in December 1995 that the U.S. Labor Department set a precedent in the field of workers' compensation law. That month the department ordered the Veterans Administration to pay the widower of a deceased VA nurse $21,500 year—half her salary—until his own death.

According to the Associated Press report, "For 18 years, Mildred Wiley was a nurse in the psychiatric ward at a Veterans Affairs hospital, caring for patients who smoked so much that she often worked in a blue haze."

Mrs. Wiley was a nonsmoker. The Labor Department ruled that secondhand smoke was partly to blame for her death from lung cancer in 1991. It was the first workers' compensation case in the nation linking secondhand smoke to a cancer death.[35]

What proof did the department have that secondhand smoke contributed to Mrs. Wiley's death? Another silly question. No proof was needed, for we *know* that secondhand smoke kills nonsmokers. The EPA has told us so and the EPA never lies, it just promulgates untruths.

Unfortunately, now that smokers have been nearly universally banished from the workplace and from public life, it is going to become more and more difficult for other nonsmokers, or their survivors, to get in on this lucrative game. But that's one of the prices that will have to be paid for a "smoke-free society."

As THE PRATT & WHITNEY and other examples above suggest, one of the excuses for discrimination against smokers in the workplace is their alleged higher health costs. This is a subject I address in Chapter 12. The real rationale (and I apologize for using that word to describe acts of pure unreason) behind it, the fundamental motivating factor, is purely and simply the fear of ETS. And nowhere has that fear been taken to the uttermost extreme than by a company in the little town (population less than 2,000) of Wilton, New Hampshire (one of the states with an apparently meaningless "smokers' rights" law). Rather than paraphrase, I'll repeat the whole story as it was posted on the World Wide Web by San Francisco-based FORCES[36] (parentheses in original):

> New Hampshire, August 6, 1996—It has recently come to light that a private company, Kimball Physics, a manufacturer of high-tech components such as electronoptics and ultra-high vacuum equipment, has had not only a no-smoking ban in place in the workplace, but something far worse.
>
> According to the Rules (listed in full below), they forbid any employee or visitor to enter the plant that has smoked within two hours of entering the facility because they have been "tobacco contaminated" and may have tobacco residue on their persons.
>
> According to Dr. Chuck Crawford of Kimball Physics, the policy has been in place for nearly three years (since 1993). Prior to that, they had an indoor smoking ban only. However, some of their employees "claimed" that they were getting headaches and asthma attacks from the residual smell of smoke on smokers. In response to this, the management and employees opted to go to their current policy of not allowing anyone into the plant that has been tobacco contaminated within two hours of entering the plant.
>
> Crawford said that the policy was put in place to protect employees' health. He said "new data" show the residuals from tobacco are more dangerous than anyone believed (more dangerous than the smoke itself). He stated that he has this from the best scientific source—papers published by Dr. James Repace of the EPA.
>
> When Dr. James Repace at the EPA was contacted, he told our source that he had never published a paper nor written a report on

the topic . . . "But it's true," he said. "Nicotine itself is not a carcinogen . . . it's toxic. Everyone knows that." He also stated that he never sent Dr. Crawford anything written but maybe told him this information over the phone.

The problem with Kimball's company policy is that it is not based on "scientific" fact. They are using anti-smoking bias to control the lives of their employees by extending the ban outside the company. They do this by using the "tobacco residue" excuse to further limit smoking of their employees outside company time.

What is even more distressing it that Dr. Repace (an avid anti-smoker) is using his position at the EPA and his "expertise" to promote anti-smoking bias and unscientific facts. Dr. Repace should be held accountable for expousing [*sic*] such personal opinions as facts to use against smokers and the civil liberty to smoke.

Through our information network, there is no study ever researched or report ever written about the toxicity of tobacco residue. Dr. Crawford at Kimball Physics and Dr. James Repace should produce evidence of such a misleading and dangerous statement. They should be held accountable for any untrue scientific statement that may have deep ramifications of [*sic*] innocent people because of this.

How far will the anti-smoking agenda go to eliminate smoking—as far as it takes to achieve that. Even if it means lying and propaganda to achieve this goal.

FORCES then posted the rules adopted by Kimball Physics and its frightened employees:

(1) No tobacco use is permitted inside any Kimball Physics building, structure, or motor vehicle. Further, no tobacco product, by-product, or product accessory shall be brought into any Kimball Physics building, structure, or motor vehicle. No tobacco use will be permitted at any Kimball Physics function, party, trade booth, off-site meeting, or other sanctioned gathering under company control.

(2) No tobacco use is permitted outside of Kimball Physics buildings or structures on Kimball Physics owned, co-owned, or leased property. Proscribed areas include entry areas, parking lots, grassed areas, fields, woods, and all other areas where Kimball Physics exercises legal control. No tobacco use is to be permitted inside any motor vehicle while on Kimball Physics property, irrespective of whether such vehicle is in motion or parked, and irrespective of who the owner of such vehicle may be.

(3) Except as provided below, no tobacco contaminated person or object shall be permitted inside any Kimball Physics build-

> ing, structure, or motor vehicle. A person or object emitting the characteristic residual particulates or vapors associated with tobacco combustion shall be considered a-priori [hyphen in original] contaminated. A person who is a tobacco user, and who has used a tobacco product within the previous two hours, shall also be considered a-priori contaminated. This rule shall not apply if: (A) An emergency of any sort is in progress; (B) It can be shown that protective measures have been implemented, such that others are not exposed to the tobacco residues (and management, in its sole discretion, agrees as to the efficacy of those measures); or (C) Some suitable corrective action is in progress (such as a person changing clothing, or using company showers to wash contaminated hair).
>
> (4) The tobacco exclusion rules shall apply equally to co-workers, managers, customers, vendors, and visitors, while in the buildings or on the property as defined. All persons entering the property shall as far as practical, be politely informed of the existence of the rules. It is the responsibility of each manager and co-worker to inform visitors under their control as to the substance of the rules. Persons unwilling or unable to abide by the rules will be requested to temporarily transact their business elsewhere. Persons who repeatedly violate the tobacco exclusion rules, or who willfully expose others to tobacco, tobacco combustion products, or to low level tobacco residues, will be permanently expelled from the property.

"*No tobacco product, by-product, or product accessory*"? Not even a fresh, unopened pack of cigarettes, or does even unburned tobacco give off toxic emanations? Not even a cigarette lighter?

"*No tobacco contaminated person or object shall be permitted inside any Kimball Physics building*"? What happens if a cigarette-smoking deliveryman has a package for the company? Both he and the package would be "contaminated," wouldn't they? Evidently he'd have to leave the package outside until it "decontaminated" itself. As for the exception allowing for emergencies, presumably if Kimball Physics caught on fire one can assume that management would not first sniff out responding firefighters for tobacco residues on their persons before allowing them to enter the building. Or would they?

This is another example of how antismokers never know when to stop. First they force people to go outside to smoke. Then they won't let them back inside if they smoke outside. Finally, they can't smoke outside even if they don't come inside.

How does Kimball Physics "know" that the molecular residue of tobacco or tobacco smoke (it's not quite clear which) is so dangerous? Thanks again to dear old ASH, here is the company's "rationale" behind its rules:

> Tobacco combustion products are now classified as Group A carcinogens by the Environmental Protection Agency. In terms of number of lives lost, pain and suffering, economic loss, and consequential damages, tobacco is an extraordinarily serious problem.
>
> According to the U.S. Surgeon General, smoking is the largest single avoidable cause of death; with many millions of lives already having been lost. Environmental tobacco smoke (second hand smoke) has become a serious ancillary problem, causing illness and distress to millions and death to thousands.
>
> Even trace quantities make many people sick. As with most carcinogens, there is no low-level threshold below which exposure becomes safe. [Presumably they mean carcinogens in tobacco smoke or "tobacco residues," not nicotine. Repace said nicotine isn't carcinogenic. So why did he bring up nicotine when queried by FORCES? Just what did he tell Mr. Crawford?—D.O.]
>
> Tobacco use is a legal activity (although a most unwise and unhealthy one); and what legal activities individuals choose, on their own time and in their own space, is (and should be) largely their own choice. Organizations under most circumstances, have neither the right nor the need to intrude on the private legal activities of individuals. [I say again, be patient.—D.O.]
>
> On the other hand, no individual (or group of individuals) has the right to knowingly cause random deaths, or to cause serious illnesses, or even to thoughtlessly make others mildly sick.
>
> The OSHA Cancer Policy (OSHA 29 CFR Ch.XVII) states that exposures to all Category I (Group A) carcinogens (the most dangerous types) are to be reduced to the minimum levels consistent with continued operation of a facility. At Kimball Physics, the minimum tobacco carcinogen levels consistent with continued operation are zero.
>
> Accordingly, tobacco and tobacco combustion products, including the lower level residuals, are to be excluded down to a minimum practical trace level throughout the entire Kimball Physics work environment. The goal is to protect co-workers and all others from some particularly dangerous substances.[37]

As a manufacturer of "electronoptics" and other high-tech equipment, Kimball Physics must use a lot of plastics and other synthetic materials in its business. Does it worry about the effect of all the chemical residues and emanations and whatnot from these materials on the health of its employees? Wanna bet?

It would stretch the satirical talents of a Mark Twain or an H. L. Mencken to deal properly with this kind of idiocy. Unfortunately, both gentlemen are no longer with us. I can only stand aghast. The entire Kimball Physics policy, and that of other companies (though not as extravagantly ridiculous as Kimball's), are based entirely on suspect if not outright fraudulent "science." Yet people can't be blamed if they take the antitobacco, antismoking ball they have been handed by such august agencies of the U.S. government as the Environmental Protection Agency and Occupational Safety and Health Administration and Centers for Disease Control and run with it completely off the field of reason. They have never been told the other side of the story, or even that there is another side. (And, alas, so ingrained in the popular mind has the belief in the dangers of tobacco become that they wouldn't believe it anyway, which means that this book is an exercise in futility). The shame is that of the EPA, of OSHA, of the CDC and of the entire medical establishment and those scientists who let the antismokers get away with just about anything because, after all, it forwards the desired goal of a "smoke-free society."

SAD AS ALL THIS discrimination against them is, smokers, as I said, can live with it (which is not very long, according to the accepted medical wisdom). It is when they are made to believe they are hurting not just themselves and other adults by their habit but the most innocent and most helpless ones of all—little children, *babies*—that the true meanspiritedness, if not total lack of conscience, of the antismoking crusaders shines through in all its ugliness.

Here, in chronological order, are the headlines from just some of the articles I clipped from my local newspaper, *The Atlanta Journal-Constitution*:

— "Cancer risk double for kids of smokers" (Banner headline on page one, September 6, 1990.)

— "Smoking affects infant's breathing" (May 21, 1992.)

— "Kids' behavioral problems linked to moms' smoking" (September 4, 1992.)

— "Passive smoking raises kids' risk of heart disease" (November 15, 1994.)

— "Secondhand smoke is linked to SIDS" (March 8, 1995.)

First lines from other articles from the same source:

— "Smoking during pregnancy may increase the risk of cleft palate, a birth defect, as much as six-fold in some children, according to a study."* (April 3, 1995.)

— "Mothers who smoke cause the deaths of nearly 6,000 babies and 115,000 fetuses in the United States each year, according to researchers." (April 12,1995.)

— "Cancer-causing chemicals in cigarette smoke pass from mother to unborn baby, whether the mother smokes or not, a study† suggests." (April, 23, 1996.)

From the World Wide Web:

— "Mothers who smoke at least ten cigarettes per day cause their children under five to have nicotine and other cancer-causing chemicals in their bloodstream." (University of Pennsylvania OncoLink, September 21, 1994, at http://oncolink.upenn.edu/news/smoke_child.html.)

(Never mind that nicotine, whatever can be said about it, is not a carcinogen. Even James Repace says so.)

— "Children of parents who smoke have more respiratory symptoms and acute lower respiratory tract infections, as well as evidence of reduced lung function, than do children of nonsmoking parents." (National Cancer Institute's CancerNet, April 1995, at www.oncolink.upenn.edu/pdg/600039.html.)

— "Millions of American children fall ill each year from exposure to second-hand tobacco smoke, but there are currently no regulations to protect them, according to a study‡ released on Tuesday." (University of Arizona NicNet, April 9, 1996, at http://hinet. medlib. arizona. edu/~pubhlth/ 04109602.htm.) This one deserves fuller quoting:

"'Four million children are sent to a doctor each year because they are affected by second-hand smoke,' Dr. Joseph DiFranza [whom the reader may remember from Chapter 3—D.O.] told Reuters. 'If a soft drink or breakfast cereal caused four million children to get sick it

*See Chapter 2 for one statistician's caution about "a study" or "one study."

†Ditto.

‡Double ditto.

would be taken off the market within minutes,' said DiFranza of the University of Massachusetts in Worcester. He co-authored the study, which appeared in the April issue of the journal *Pediatrics*, with researcher Robert Lew of Brigham and Women's Hospital in Boston.

"Although many studies have linked second-hand smoke with bronchitis, asthma, pneumonia, coughs, ear infection and even death in children, DiFranza said the results have not been combined or tallied . . .

"'A lot of smokers are in denial. And many grew up in households where they were exposed to smoke. But until now the magnitude of the problem has not been understood.'"

Just what kind of "regulations" he had in mind, the good doctor didn't say. But since there is little smoking today around children in schools or day care centers or anywhere in public, the only place left to "regulate" is the home—and the antis are getting around to that by attempting to characterize parental smoking as a form of child abuse.

It is also curious that the doctor didn't wonder how so many parents could have been exposed to smoking in the home when they were children, yet grew up to become functioning adults. As for their being "in denial," that of course means only that they disagree with him.

Two more examples. One from the popular literature:

— "As a result of studies associating smoking with miscarriage and sudden infant death syndrome (SIDS), pregnant women are usually advised by their doctors to kick the habit." ("Nicotine plays deadly role in infant death," *Science News*, July 15, 1995, p. 39.)

One from the medical literature:

— "A number of epidemiological studies have reported a relationship between maternal cigarette smoking and SIDS. The relation between maternal smoking during pregnancy and SIDS has been confirmed in numerous studies." ("The Effect of Passive Smoking and Tobacco Exposure Through Breast Milk on Sudden Infant Death Syndrome," *Journal of the American Medical Association* (JAMA), March 8, 1995, pp.795-798.)

In the face of all this, which is but a tiny sampling of articles on the subject of smoking and children that could be cited, is it any wonder that everyone believes that cigarettes are nasty, deadly things? Even as intelligent a person as Dr. Joyce Brothers swallows the allegations without gagging and regurgitates them on demand. Witness her reply to a husband who wrote to her and said he was worried about his wife's smoking, especially now that they had a baby:

> Dear O.N.: She might be interested to know of a report in the July issue of the Archives of Pediatrics and Adolescent Medicine that states that more young children are killed by parental smoking than by all unintentional injuries combined.
>
> The report also said that 2,800 infant deaths were linked to low birth weights, which were thought to be the result of pregnant women smoking.
>
> According to this research, 2,000 deaths were attributed to sudden infant death syndrome caused by secondhand tobacco smoke, and more than 1,000 deaths were related to respiratory infection. This research from the University of Wisconsin Medical School should frighten your wife enough to seriously join millions of others, like yourself, who have kicked the habit.[38]

More children are killed by parental smoking than by *all unintentional injuries combined?* No physician whose diagnostic skills have not been compromised by antismoking propaganda can possibly know whether or not tobacco smoke was a factor in a child's death. Sadly, thousands of children are victims of accidents each year, but at least in virtually every case the cause is there for all to see.

As for "linking" low birth weights to 2,800 infant deaths, Dr. Brothers obviously is unaware that this is a matter of *fractions* of an ounce and that low-birth-weight babies quickly catch up with normal infants. As for Sudden Infant Death Syndrome (SIDS), I discuss that subject in the last part of this chapter.

No survey of the "literature" dealing with parental smoking and the effect on children would be complete without turning once again to Action on Smoking and Health, if only because this organization is so frequently quoted by the media.

Following is an article posted by ASH on its Website July 30, 1996:[39]

> PARENTS ARE DELIBERATELY MAKING THEIR KIDS SICK; AT WHAT POINT DOES IT BECOME CHILD ABUSE OR ENDANGERMENT?
>
> Still another study shows that many parents are deliberately making their children sick by needlessly exposing them to tobacco smoke.

> As a result, they suffer excessive and unnecessary colds, flues [*sic*], bronchitis, and pneumonia, and miss 7 million more school days than classmates who are able to breathe smokefree air at home.
>
> Other results of this new study from the federal Centers for Disease Control:
>
> — more than 10 million children (31.2%) are still being exposed to cigarette smoke in their homes, despite study after study showing how dangerous it is to their health.
>
> — an additional 2 million (5.8%) are exposed less often.
>
> — kids exposed to smoke miss more than 28 million days of school, one third more than kids from smokefree homes.
>
> — these children also have 1.7 million more colds and acute respiratory infections, 10% more than kids who are not exposed.
>
> — kids exposed to tobacco smoke also suffer over 10 million days of restricted activities, such as missing sports practice, 21% more than unexposed kids.
>
> Not surprisingly, children in homes with low income and educational levels are far more likely (48%) to be exposed than kids in homes with high income and educational levels (28%).
>
> Exposure also differs by region. Almost half of the kids living in the Midwest (40%) are exposed to tobacco smoke, as compared with 24% in California, where the dangers of secondhand smoke are driven home by statewide bans on smoking in the workplace.

In case some readers were hard of seeing, ASH concluded its article with this capitalized advice:

> PLEASE SHARE THIS INFORMATION WITH ANY FRIENDS OR NEIGHBORS WHO SMOKE AND HAVE CHILDREN LIVING AT HOME.
>
> IF THEY CAN'T QUIT, AT LEAST ASK THEM TO STEP OUTSIDE TO SMOKE, OR TO CONFINE THEIR SMOKING TO A SEPARATE ROOM (SUCH AS A BEDROOM) WHICH THE CHILDREN DO NOT FREQUENT.
>
> YOU MAY ALSO WISH TO TELL THEM THAT SOME PARENTS HAVE LOST CUSTODY FOR EXPOSING THEIR CHILDREN TO TOBACCO SMOKE, AND A GROWING NUMBER OF STATES CONSIDER SMOKING BY A PARENT IN DECIDING WHICH PARENT SHOULD BE AWARDED CUSTODY.

Martha Perske has effectively rebutted the ASH release by reporting just what the CDC study "found." Actually, there were two "findings" (make that "nonfindings"). She writes:

<u>The first finding:</u> The study found no statistically significant association between kids' exposure to tobacco smoke in the home and acute or chronic respiratory illnesses. ASH made no mention of this finding.

ASH also ignored the following statement from the study pertaining to exacerbations of chronic respiratory conditions: "We did not detect an increase in reported exacerbations of asthma and chronic respiratory diseases among children exposed to ETS (environmental tobacco smoke)." To misrepresent and omit important scientific data should be called what it is: misleading the public (the very thing groups like ASH accuse the tobacco industry of doing.)

<u>The second finding:</u> The CDC study reported that children exposed to tobacco smoke in the home had, on average, 1.87 more days of restricted activity, 1.06 more days of bed confinement, and 1.45 more days of school absence per year than children who were not exposed.

CDC extrapolated those numbers (1.87, 1.06, 1.45 more days) to the entire U.S. population of children aged 1 to 10. This, of course, resulted in huge numbers, and it is those huge numbers that ASH uses (e.g., "kids exposed to tobacco smoke suffer over 10 million days of restricted activities . . . 21% more than unexposed kids.").

ASH would no doubt say that these findings are due to kids' exposure to tobacco smoke, but to make such a claim would be going beyond what the data are capable of showing. All we know is that these children lived with a smoker(s). We don't know how (or if) those smokers might have differed in other ways from nonsmokers, or what effect those differences might have had on their children's reported school attendance, bed confinement, or restricted activities . . .

Not mentioned by ASH is the fact that all results from the study were based on telephone interviews back in 1991, and there was no attempt to validate answers given by parents. It also seems important to point out that this CDC study was accepted for publication in an anti-smoking journal, *Tobacco Control* [published by the British Medical Association—D.O.]. Since it was solely about kids, why was it not published in a pediatric journal?

Not only should we be up in arms over ASH's attempt to portray smokers as child abusers (thus trivializing true child abuse), we should also be outraged at the attempt to make it appear that the CDC study gave credence to such a heinous accusation . . .

It is reprehensible enough to threaten smokers with possible loss of custody of their kids, but to misrepresent a federal study in order to heighten the intimidation certainly seems to border on fraud.[40]

Well, you may say, isn't this just Mrs. Perske's personal slant on the CDC study? On what basis does she charge Action on Smoking and Health with fraudulent misrepresentation of the study's findings? After all, she's a smoker and . . . and . . .

The best answer to that is to quote the CDC itself, as Perske does at the end of her article:

"Children who are exposed to environmental tobacco smoke had a higher incidence of acute respiratory illnesses (relative risk [RR]=1.10, 95% confidence interval [CI] 0.95 to 1.26), and all chronic respiratory diseases (RR=1.28, 95% CI 0.99 to 1.65) than children who were not exposed, although both CIs <u>included</u> <u>unity</u>, and chance cannot be ruled out as being responsible for these findings." [Underlining added by Ms. Perske]

She points out that when confidence intervals (CI) "include unity," it means the findings (relative risks) were not statistically significant and, as the CDC itself concedes, may have been due simply to chance.

"Even if they had been statistically significant, relative risks of 1.10 and 1.28 are extremely weak, and are generally not grounds for excitement (let alone charges of child abuse). For example, an American Cancer Society study found that drinking one glass of whole milk each day resulted in a statistically significant relative risk of 1.62 for lung cancer, yet it would be absurd to accuse parents of child abuse for giving their kids whole milk. ("Milk Drinking, Other Beverage Habits, and Lung Cancer Risk," Curtiss Mettlin, published in the *International Journal of Cancer*, 43;608-612, 1989)."

"Unity," as I first explained in Chapter 1, is a relative risk of 1.0, meaning that there is neither any risk of contracting some disease from ingesting or being exposed to some agent, nor any protection against contracting some disease from such ingestion or exposure. In other words, a wash. The fact that the CDC's confidence intervals straddled unity would tell any statistician that its "findings" are essentially meaningless.

Unfortunately, statisticians too often remain silent about such misuses of statistics in the cause of a smoke-free society, and anyway it wasn't them the CDC was trying to influence but rather the scientifically unsophisticated and trusting general population. Thus, as Perske points out in a footnote, "The CDC presents its findings in terms of relative risks and confidence intervals. In other words, the CDC chose not to state in plain English that it found no statistically significant association between kids' exposure to tobacco smoke in the home and acute or chronic respiratory illnesses."

The ordinary person has probably never heard about the Mettlin study, in which the relative risk of children's developing lung cancer from drinking whole milk—RR 1.62—was *higher* than the lung cancer risk alleged by the EPA in regard to exposure to tobacco smoke—RR 1.19—as well as being *much* higher than the respiratory disease risks announced by the CDC—RR 1.10 for the acute and RR 1.28 for the chronic versions. Even if some health columnist did write about the Mettlin study, he almost certainly did not mention that drinking milk is (statistically) riskier than breathing secondhand smoke.

Something else I have never seen anywhere is a study that looked into the effects of marital discord on children's health, although in 1991 two researchers did survey 92 divorce studies and concluded that "Parental divorce (or the factors associated with it) lowers the well-being of children." A "National Survey of Children," which conducted interviews with the same parents and children in 1976 and 1981, "suggested" that children from high-stress, intact families are more likely to be depressed, impulsive, hyperactive and misbehaved than children from divorced families.[41]

Is it not possible that the lowered well-being of children of troubled families, whether broken or intact families, might also account for some of the respiratory problems and missed school days that are attributed to parental smoking? Kids have also been known to "get sick" and stay home from school for a lot of reasons, like avoiding a test or maybe a bully who is tormenting them.

But things like that would not only be difficult to ascertain from a telephone questionnaire but could be treading onto "sensitive" ground.

Not to delve into that can of worms (no-fault divorce, feminism, working mothers, abortion rights, etc.), but when "one study" found that "women who . . . had an abortion had a 20 percent higher rate of breast cancer than women who had no abortion" and that "women who had never had a child and had a first-trimester abortion had a 100 percent higher rate of breast cancer," even the study's own authors minimized it in these words:

"Although a positive association [between breast cancer and abortion] has been seen in a number of studies that have focused on young women, the overall magnitude is not so great that the possibility of bias . . . can be excluded."[42]

"Funny," commented that eagle-eyed deflator of medical nonsense, "the Junkman" Steven Milloy, "I remember how a reported 30 percent increase in lung cancer associated with second-hand smoke was SO definite and meaningful to the public health research crowd. But a 100 percent increase in breast cancer from abortion 'is not so great'?"[43]

'Tis the same with investigations into what makes kids sick. It's so much more politically correct, not to mention much more convenient, to blame it on parental smoking.

It's also all too easy to trash ASH. So let me give it the benefit of the doubt by saying that when it accused parents of "deliberately" making their kids sick, it didn't mean that parents *want* to make their kids sick. At least I hope not.

ALL THE FOREGOING is just for starters for this, my final chapter dealing with environmental tobacco smoke. Now we come to the truly tragic and heartrending consequences of secondhand smoke mania.

It's distressing enough for a woman who has suffered a miscarriage to be led to believe she may have caused the death of her baby in the womb because she smokes, or once smoked, or allowed herself to be subjected to secondhand smoke. It's distressing enough for parents to be harried by the guilty knowledge that they may be responsible for their child's cleft palate or ear infection or chronic colds and other respiratory ailments because they smoke. But to foist on the disconsolate parents of a SIDS baby the terrible burden of thinking that they may have killed their baby outright while still in the cradle—as effectively as if they had purposely smothered it—because they smoke? That is pretty unconscionable in my opinion. It is in this matter of SIDS that the want of ordinary compassion, let alone devotion to the truth, on the part of the militant antismokers is revealed at its tawdry best.

What is SIDS (sometimes called "crib death" or, in Britain, "cot death")? The initials stand for "Sudden Infant Death Syndrome." According to the same issue of JAMA cited on page 388, SIDS is defined as "the sudden, unexpected death of an apparently healthy infant that remains unexplained after a death scene investigation, case report, and an autopsy. In the Western world, SIDS is the most common cause of death of infants between 1 month and 1 year of age and accounts for approximately 50% of deaths of infants between 2 and 4 months of age."[44]

The key word is: *unexplained*. Although numerous studies have found "statistically significant" associations between a mother's smoking before, during or after pregnancy, as well as smoking by the father or other people in proximity to a baby, studies have also "suggested" a host of other possible factors and SIDS remains *unexplained*.

To date, the most that the health establishment has been able to accomplish in the fight against SIDS has been with a public education campaign called "Back to Sleep," launched in 1994 by the U.S. Public Health Service, the American Academy of Pediatrics, the SIDS Alliance and the Association of SIDS Program Professionals, which urged parents of healthy babies to put their infants on their backs or sides to sleep. Similar campaigns in several countries had reduced the rate of SIDS by 50 percent of more.

Yet the continued absence of any really fundamental explanation for SIDS doesn't slow the antismokers down. For the last time in this chapter, I turn to an ASH press release, posted on the Internet in July 30,1996.[45] (At least this time there was no "deliberately" in the headline):

> SMOKING PARENTS ARE KILLING THEIR INFANTS
>
> British researchers Thursday blamed parents who smoke for more than half of crib deaths and said babies should not be exposed to tobacco smoke at all.
>
> More than 60 percent of crib deaths, also known as sudden death syndrome (SIDS) could be prevented if people stopped smoking around their babies and pregnant women, the report in the *British Medical Journal* said.
>
> "The recent research makes it clear that fathers who smoke are also a problem," Joyce Epstein of the Foundation for the Study of Infant Deaths told a news conference.
>
> "If we could remove all smoking from a baby's environment, we estimate that cot deaths would fall by 61 percent," she said, adding the findings were in line with studies underway in the United States, New Zealand and Scandinavia.
>
> If a mother smoked before as well as after the birth, the risk rose, and the more a baby was exposed to smoke after birth, the higher the risk.

> For example, Fleming said babies whose parents smoked, but who were never put into a room where anybody smoked, were still twice as likely to die of SIDS than babies of nonsmokers. Children of smokers who spent eight hours a day in a room where someone sometimes smoked were eight times more likely to die.
>
> "The risk increases crudely by 100 percent for every hour a day a baby spends in a smoky atmosphere. This is startling," Fleming said. "Please don't allow anybody to smoke in a room where the baby sometimes goes."
>
> Fleming said the team had successfully disproved arguments that it was the behavior of smokers that was to blame, not the smoke itself.

In an accompanying article, ASH belatedly identifies "Fleming" (whom I mentioned briefly in Chapter 7) as Prof. Peter Fleming, a professor of infant health at Bristol University and the author of the study.

"Fleming," said ASH, "believes adoption agencies should question would-be parents more closely about their smoking habits because of the cot death risk to babies by asking them whether they or anyone else in the home smoked.

"A spokesman for British Agencies for Adoption and Fostering said adoptive parents were already asked about their smoking habits and Professor Fleming's recommendations would be considered by its medical committee when their suitability was being considered."[46]

Presumably, "their suitability" refers to the adoptive parents, not to Fleming's recommendations. But if adoptive parents in Britain were already being asked about their smoking habits, what "recommendations" by Fleming was the medical committee of the BAAF going to consider? Make them promise to stop smoking or don't let them adopt a child?

Thanks to another female writer who doesn't let the antismokers get away with anything if she can help it, Sara Mahler-Vossler, we can safely say that the Fleming/*British Medical Journal* (BMJ) study is sheer baloney. Her dissection of it was posted on both the FORCES USA and FORCES Canada Web sites, accompanied by graphs from the U.S. Department of Health and Human Services. I'm going to quote from it at length as another illustration of how a nonscientist can easily find the holes in an antismoking study if she is familiar with epidemiological methods (and antismoker tactics) and is not blinded by antismoking prejudice. Mahler-Vossler writes (all emphases in original):

• The BMJ research is an example of a study where the researcher starts with an observation of the outcome (infants who died from SIDS). They compare this group of babies who died to a group of babies who are alive, and try to figure out what caused the different outcomes. But the factors that caused the deaths have already occurred, so the researcher does not have *control* of them. He can only go back among the possible causes, and try to disentangle them. The danger in this is the fallacy of believing as a cause something that merely happened earlier in time—like believing that the rooster's crowing causes the sun to rise.

• Another problem is that the sample was not chosen at random. This always leaves a hole for other related factors to crawl through unnoticed, and these—unknown to the researcher—may be the "real" cause of any relationship found.

• The authors say they collected information that included medical histories, and social and demographic data. This would show if the two groups—the babies who died from SIDs and the babies who were alive—are similar in these things. But none of this information was reported, and without it, we really can't be expected to accept their conclusions.

• The authors state they adjusted for socio-economic status. But, they only mentioned in passing the fact that the families of the babies who died from SIDS were relatively "socially deprived" with respect to the comparison group. So, it seems that [the] authors acknowledged the importance of socio-economic status as a correlate of SIDS, but didn't give us any specifics.

• The racial makeup of the sample was not reported. There was no mention of whether the sample was racially homogeneous or not. But the attached graph shows that the SIDS death rate for blacks is over twice than that for whites. It is similar in the U.K.?

• Boys have a higher rate of SIDS than girls but there is no information in BMJ about the sexual makeup of the sample, or whether they adjusted for sex.

Given the omissions described above, how can we be confident that the results on smoking aren't spurious (false) and, in fact, primarily the result of differences in race and/or sex—or other unreported factors? . . . The researchers took only a snapshot at one point in time, and only seemed to match on age. No follow-up was reported to determine if the comparison babies, who were alive at this one point in time, all survived their first year.

> On top of this, the age distribution of the babies in the sample was not reported. This could be important, because, if you look at the attached graph, you see that the rate of SIDS begins to rise sharply at around three weeks of age, and peaks at about 3 months. It then drops sharply, reaching a relatively low level around six months, then continues to decline gradually for the rest of the year
>
> . . . The results from a statistical analysis—like that used in the BMJ study—can be changed by varying the instructions given to the computer. For example, you might tell the computer to alter the sequence in which it enters the factors on different runs of the same data. You can also vary the decision rules for evaluating and handling the data . . . So, you can "fiddle" with the data until you get the "best" result . . .
>
> The authors operated from assumptions that ignored the sum of knowledge about SIDS. The study design, though widely used, has weaknesses—but these weren't acknowledged. Important information about the sample was missing—which could account for much, if not all, of the relationships . . . A bunch of numbers, that would have shown important things, weren't there, and we don't know what the authors actually did when they ran their statistics.
>
> And yet, a "prestigious" medical journal published this, and pretends it's valid science. Only in the irrational throes of "political correctness" could something like this happen![47]

The amazing thing is that the *British Medical Journal* published the study despite its own reservations about it. As Mahler-Vossler notes:

"[E]ven an editorial about this study, in the same issue of this journal, cautions that 'lingering doubts remain that the association [between parental smoking and SIDS] may be due, in part, to the association of parental smoking with other infant care practices, which might vary by socio-economic status.'

"'The editorial goes on to state that the authors 'have not helped to resolve this issue,' and criticize the study for not having performed a sufficiently rigorous analysis on the postnatal smoking data, nor reported enough details on how they did their statistical analysis."

Yet it published it anyway, in keeping with the "LaLonde Doctrine" that smoking is such a threat to humanity that even scientifically untenable studies should be reported.

The same kind of criticism could be made about a multitude of other smoking studies "proving" this or that about smoking. Unfortunately, there are far too many studies and far too few people like Sara Mahler-Vosser or Martha Perske or Lauren Colby or Steve Milloy who try to keep the researchers honest, and only the smokers' organizations publish them anyway. Whatever questions other scientists voice are usually confined to letters or editorials in the journals, like the editorial in the BMJ partially quoted above, and the public never hears about them either.

In case anyone would dismiss Mahler-Vosser's analysis as the biased nitpicking of another "prosmoker," I'll end this chapter by quoting from a December 4, 1996 letter to ASH from an organization that is certainly no defender of smoking but which certainly ought to know something about SIDS—The Sudden Infant Death Syndrome Alliance, headquartered in Baltimore, Maryland:

> John F. Banzhaf III, Esquire
> Executive Director
> Action on Smoking and Health (ASH)
> 2013 H Street NW
> Washington, DC 20006-4207
>
> Dear Mr. Banzhaf,
>
> We at the SIDS Alliance applaud your efforts to bring to the attention of the American public the hazards associated with smoking and smoke exposure; we must, however, object to your organization's use of misleading data and terminology when linking Sudden Infant Death Syndrome to your cause.
>
> Statistically, passive smoke exposure is a recognized, significant factor for SIDS. To date, no direct causal relationship has been established. In fact, the vast majority of infants born to smoking parents do not die of SIDS. And, since many SIDS deaths occur in a smoke-free environment, we must refrain from making smoke exposure appear to be linked to all SIDS deaths.
>
> The sensational heading for one of your recent Internet reports, "Smoking Parents Are Killing Their Infants," has gone too far. Avoiding known risk factors for SIDS may reduce its incidence for some babies, but offers no guarantee for every baby. Risk factors alone do not cause SIDS.
>
> It is likely that SIDS may be caused by a subtle developmental delay, an anatomical defect, or a functional failure. The first year of life is fraught with periods of rapid growth and development, during which a baby's system may become unstable; during such periods any baby may be vulnerable.

It is also important to realize that SIDS can claim any baby, in spite of parents doing "everything right." Insensitive generalizations about SIDS broadcast through print or the electronic media serve only to perpetuate the public's misconceptions. The last thing we need to do to parents who suffer this tragedy is stigmatize or marginalize them. The simple truth is that many SIDS victims have no known risk factors; and, most babies with one or more risk factors will survive.

Your literature states that smoking "kills more than 2,000 infants each year from SIDS." Any published figures are sheer speculation, or guesses, not grounded in actual experimentation. The best we can do at this juncture is talk in terms of attributable risk—and there is no consensus on what that might be . . .

[W]e respectfully request that you adjust your message as far as SIDS is concerned. While we support your cause, we cannot do so at the expense of the tens of thousands of families we represent . . .

Sincerely,
Phipps Y. Cohe
National Public Affairs Director[48]

ASH did not "adjust" its message about SIDS (antismokers never admit to errors or excessive zeal) but it did it reply to Mr. Cohe—after a fashion (see below).

In the meantime, one Barry S. Brokaw, a member of the SIDS Alliance in Sacramento, California, also attacked the ASH release in a letter to *The Los Angeles Times* on August 2, 1996 in response to a July 26 article in that newspaper titled "Smoke Makes SIDS Risk Soar":

Recent reports of research on sudden infant death syndrome conducted in the United States and Britain hailing the success of "Back to Sleep" campaigns in reducing the SIDS rates (placing the infant on it back rather than on its stomach) and linking smoking and other environmental factors to an increased "risk" for SIDS seem to underplay or leave out entirely the most fundamental point about the status of SIDS research efforts.

Researchers don't know what causes this leading killer of babies between the ages of 2 weeks and 1 year. Because the underlying causes of SIDS remain unknown, all newborn infants are potentially at risk for SIDS. Babies placed on their backs to sleep still die of SIDS. Babies not exposed to cigarette smoke still die of SIDS. Babies who are breast fed, who have had wonderful prenatal care, who were full term and of normal birth weight, who have

> parents who have not abused drugs, in short, who have no known risk factors, still die of SIDS.
>
> As a result of the way these research studies are presented, the public may come to view SIDS as somehow "preventable" if we simply alter the child's environment. Of even greater concern to me is the effect of those reports on families who have lost a child to SIDS, and they still number around 500 a year in California, and between 4,500 and 5,000 nationally.
>
> The last thing we need to do to parents who suffer this tragedy is to stigmatize or marginalize them. The simple truth is that SIDS can, and does, claim any baby, in spite of parents doing "everything right."[49]

The fact that Mr. Brokaw's and Mr. Cohe's letters use similar phraseology indicates that the SIDS Alliance was pretty upset with ASH.

The Washington Times also published an article that ruffled ASH's feathers titled "Infant death link to smoking hit as 'misleading' data," which quoted a SIDS spokesperson, and to this ASH did respond. The response, posted on its Website,[50] did not give the date of the *Times* article or the name of the spokesperson or tell readers that she represented the SIDS Alliance, saying only that she was with "a Baltimore-based SIDS organization."

In a preface to its posting, ASH immediately adopted an *ad hominem* posture, characterizing *The Washington Times* as "a newspaper which frequently takes a pro-tobacco stand" and suggesting that "the spokesperson seems to be a lay person rather than a physician or scientist, and neither the article nor the letter written to ASH about the matter cites any scientific or medical authority for the critic's views."

Then followed ASH's brief letter to the editor of the *Times*, repeating that "neither the critic nor the reporter cited any medical support for questioning the smoking-SIDS death link." ASH then said that its "Smoking Parents Are Killing Their Infants" posting was based on a report by the Reuters news agency (Reuters was not mentioned in the posting), then cited an article in *The Journal of Family Practice* blaming parental smoking for 1,900 to 4,800 deaths from perinatal disorders and 1,200 to 2,200 deaths from SIDS, then a headline from *The San Diego Union*—"2nd-Hand Smoke Can Kill Babies," based upon a report published in the *Journal of the American Medical Association*—as if a newspaper article reporting a study was proof of its validity.

The ASH release concluded with: "As one of the leading researchers in the area recently put it, at least three times as many infants die of SIDS caused by maternal smoking as are killed as a result of homicide or child abuse."

The "leading researcher" was not identified—not that it matters. When it comes to antismoking propaganda, one lies (well, grossly exaggerates) and the other swears to it.

Killing two birds with one stone, the same Web posting reproduced "ASH's Letter to the Complainant" who was also not named but was Mr. Cohe since it refers to "your letter of December 4, 1996."

Again ASH stated that its report was based on a story by "the impartial and highly respected Reuters news organization.

"Thus while your organization may well disagree with this conclusion, it is hard to claim that ASH's report on the news item was not accurate, or that ASH should be held to a higher standard than a major new organization employing specially-trained medical writers and proofreaders."

Mr. Cohe of course made no such claim nor demanded any such standard on ASH's part. As for the "specially trained" medical writers and proofreaders at Reuters, I am not able to comment (although I would remind the reader of the journalistic maxim: "Bad news sells."). And again, the fact that a news organization reports about a study hardly qualifies as substantiation of the truth of the study.

Then, after repeating much of the report Cohe criticized and again attributing it to Reuters, ASH went on: "Thus persons who read ASH's report are more than adequately advised of the conclusions of the British researchers, regardless of the particular terms used in the very brief heading ASH used . . .

"Indeed, one of the persons ASH quoted is, like you, a representative from an organization devoted primarily to the problem of Sudden Infant Death Syndrome. Thus it is unlikely [*sic*!] that such a person would be biased or uninformed regarding this issue, and it is entirely appropriate for ASH to quote such a person in its news report."

ASH was here evidently referring to Joyce Epstein of the Foundation for the Study of Infant Deaths. But Mr. Cohe did not question anybody's bias or qualifications. (Also, ASH didn't quote Ms. Epstein; it quoted Reuters quoting Ms. Epstein, although it didn't say so.)

ASH then drove the rapier home by turning Mr. Cohe's words against him:

"Although 'the vast majority of infants born to smoking parents do not die of SIDS' and 'many SIDS deaths occur in a smoke-free environment,' this does not prove that smoking is not a cause or SIDS. [Cohe never said it wasn't.—D.O.] One could as well argue that, since the vast majority of people who smoke in bed don't start fires which kill their children, and many children are killed by fires in homes where parents don't smoke in bed, smoking in bed doesn't cause fires that kill children. That conclusion is, of course, absurd."

Talk about non sequiturs. The causes of fires are fairly easily identified in most cases; the cause or causes of SIDS remain ***unexplained.*** One could as well argue that because the majority of traffic accidents do not involve drunken drivers, and many drinking drivers never cause an accident, drinking and driving doesn't cause traffic accidents. ASH's analogy is what is absurd.

"Your organization," ASH continued, "is, of course, free to dispute or to characterize the findings of the British study in a different manner, or to question the statistical conclusions which they support. [ASH inadvertently got that right: the conclusions of the BMJ study support the findings, not the other way around!—D.O.] But your dispute seems to be with those researchers and the other foundation, and not with ASH for simply reporting those conclusions fairly and in an unbiased [*sic*!] manner."

Finally, ASH cited no less than 40 journal articles or studies linking smoking with SIDS—as if Mr. Cohe was not already probably aware of them, as if they had any bearing on the damning headline of ASH's article and his objection to the whole tenor of it as unnecessarily stigmatizing or marginalizing the parents of SIDS babies.

Nowhere did ASH identify to visitors to its Website the names and titles of Mr. Cohe or the Baltimore spokesperson or their organizations ("protobacco" FORCES USA did). That would have credentialed them in readers' eyes (as well as being ordinary courtesy).

Talk about "smoke screens." Ash then erected a straw man by insinuating that its (unnamed) critic disputed the link between smoking and SIDS—and then knocked it down because he offered no medical evidence to back up his disputing what he had not disputed at all. Of course, Mr. Cohe could not have offered evidence that parental smoking does not cause SIDS because none exists, just as no evidence exists that parental smoking does cause SIDS.

It erected a second straw man by insinuating that its (unnamed) critic accused ASH of inaccuracy when all it did was innocently repeat a story it got from Reuters and of holding ASH to a higher standard than its source—all of which again Cohe did not do.

Finally, ASH erected a third straw man by insinuating that its (unnamed) critic unfairly impugned ASH's integrity when all it did was quote a respected SIDS authority (Ms. Epstein or Prof. Fleming)—and insinuating to boot that its (unnamed) critic also questioned the impartiality of this spokesperson—when again Cohe did no such thing.

In short, ASH evaded Mr. Cohe's central point entirely and thus, like Pontius Pilate, considered its hands washed clean. Where did I ever get the impression that this organization is hopelessly biased and untrustworthy?

Notes

1. Dr. Thomas J. DiLorenzo, "California's Proposition 99: Pork Barrel for Anti-Smoking Groups." At www.forces.org/pages/prop99.htm. Quote taken from written transcript of a three-day conference titled "Revolt Against Tobacco" held in Los Angeles in September 1992.

2. David Sedaris, *Barrel Fever* (New York: Little Brown). Quoted by Smoker's Last Resort at http://joe.law.pace.edu/staff/ub/smoklit.html.

3. "Smoking More Dangerous Than Previously Thought; Kills Half of All Users, Many In Middle Age." At www.ash.org/august97/8-24-96-6.html.

4. "Sad News for Former Smokers; Permanent Biological Change May Have Already Occurred." At www.ash.org/august97/8-22-97-6.html, quoting from a story in *The Washington Post.*

5. "Half of lung cancers strike former smokers." *The Atlanta Journal-Constitution*, May 24, 1995, p. A1. From the Associated Press.

6. Letters. *The Atlanta Journal-Constitution*, May 30, 1995, p. A6.

7. "Poll: Where there's smoke, there's fear." *The Atlanta Journal-Constitution,* March 25, 1992, p. B2.

8. Cited in Dr. Joel R. Cooper, "Secondhand Smoke: Irritating Annoyance or Serious Threat?" CIGNA HealthCare of Colorado Report at www.cigna/healthcare/.

9. Pierre Van Wessel, "Nonsmokers have rights." Letters. *Conejo Valley Daily News*, January 21, 1992.

10. Stan Geiser, "Secondhand smoke is the deadliest pollution." Letters. Sarasota *Herald-Tribune*, Venice/AM Edition, January 26, 1993.

11. "Put out that pipe and drive: Rental cars go smoke-free." *The Atlanta Journal-Constitution*, November 4, 1991, p. S2.

12. "Saab to charge for ashtrays, lighters." *The Atlanta Journal-Constitution*, August 13, 1993, p. S2.

13. Ellen Creager, "Are ashtrays going up in smoke?" *The Atlanta Journal-Constitution*, January 29, 1994, p. G35. From Knight-Ridder Newspapers.

14. Paul Eiser, "The Dangerous Habit of Throwing Cigarettes Out Car Windows." At www.pw2netcom.com/~captains/butts.html.

15. Lynn Johnston, "For Better Or For Worse." Comics section. *The Atlanta Journal-Constitution*, August 31, 1997.

16. Dottie Dow, "Smoke-free facilities get a big 'thank you.'" Letter in "Cobb Extra" section of *The Atlanta Journal-Constitution*, August 4, 1994, p. JF6.

17. Steve Allen and Bill Adler Jr., *The Passionate Nonsmoker's Bill of Rights* (New York: William Morrow, 1989), p.111.

18. Ibid, p. 120.

19. Bill Citara, "Time to light up and pick up." *San Francisco Examiner*, January 7, 1998, page ZZA2.

20. "The Irony of 'Libertyville': A Case Study in Corporate Excess." National Smokers Alliance at www.speakup.org/motointr.html; "Motorola Lightens Tough Smoking Ban." Weekly Tobacco News, August 1996, at www.forces.org/pages/news0896.htm.

21. Martha Nolan McKenzie, "Earning It: So Don't Even Think About Smoking Here." *The New York Times*, November 29, 1996. Reprinted in "Cutting Smoking Costs Despite Smokers' Rights Laws." At www.ash.org/important/company.html.

22. Ibid.

23. Ibid. The figure is attributed to John Banzhaf, executive director of ASH.

24. "Chiles vetoes bill protecting smokers from discrimination." The South in Brief. *The Atlanta Journal-Constitution*, April 12, 1992, p. A5.

25. "Rights bill for smokers KO'd in Va." *The Atlanta Journal-Constitution*, March 31, 1993, p. A11. From the Associated Press.

26. Steven Harvey, "House bill broadens rights of smokers." *The Atlanta Journal-Constitution*, March 1, 1991, p. F3.

27. McKenzie, op.cit.

28. Ibid.

29. "Smoker Hiring Ban Upheld." At http://dx.com/tobacco/Tobacco_Daily.html#aamor.

30. Karla Schuster, "Cigar stubs out hopeful's chances; Boca police candidate puffed stogie at party." Fort Lauderdale *Sun-Sentinel*, July 24 1997. From FORCES Canada's Theater of the Absurd at www.forces-cdn.org.

31. "The Americans With Disabilities Act As Applicable to Sensitive

Nonsmokers." Action on Smoking and Health at www.setinc.com/ash/papers/h211.htm.

32. "Ex-smoker quits job, wins fight." *The Atlanta Journal-Constitution*, August 3, 1994, p. A4.

33. "Smokers Are Not Entitled to Legal Protection." At http://setinc.com/ash/protection.html.

34. "Up In Smoke," the very original heading for an item in Business Report. *The Atlanta Journal-Constitution*, July 28, 1990, p. F2.

35. "Man wins secondhand smoke claim." *The Atlanta Journal-Constitution*, December 16, 1995, p. C2. From the Associated Press.

36. "Private Company Forces Control of Employes with Unfounded 'Scientific Facts.'" FORCES Weekly Tobacco News, August 1996, at www.forces.org/pages/news0896.htm.

37. "Cutting Smoking Costs Despite Smokers' Rights Laws." At www.ash.org/ important/company.html.

38. Joyce Brothers, "Dangers of Smoking Around Babies." At www.ash.org/nov97/11-16-97.5.html.

39. "Parents Are Deliberately Making Their Kids Sick." At www.ash.org/kids/parents.html.

40. Martha Perkse, "Anti-Smoking Organization Goes Too Far." At www.forces.org.

41. Nick Gillespie, "Family Ways." A review of three books on divorce. *Reason*, October 1997, p. 64.

42. A study by Janet R. Daling, Louise A. Brinton, Lynda F. Voight, Noel S. Weiss, Ralph Coates, Kathleen Malone, Janet Schoenberg and Marilie Gammon in the *American Journal of Epidemiology*. Cited in Steven J. Milloy, "Abortion Contortion." At www.junkscience.com/news/abortion.html.

43. Ibid.

44. Editorial, "Sleep Position and Sudden Death Syndrome." *Journal of the American Medical Association*, March 8, 1995, p. 818.

45. "Smoking Parents Are Killing Their Infants." At http://ash.org/kids/parents.html.

46. "Plea for Adoption Rules." Ibid.

47. Sara Mahler-Vossler, "Smoke Police Sink to New Depths: Flawed Study on Infant Death is Misrepresented to Frighten and Intimidate Parents." At www.forces/org/sara-art.htm.

48. "The Sudden Infant Death Syndrome Alliance's Letter to ASH on Smoking and SIDS." At www.forces.org/pages/cohe01.htm.

49. Quoted in "You Should be ASHamed." FORCES Canada at www.forces-cdn/ashamed.htm.

50. "ASH Attacked for Posting Smoking-SIDS Link." At http://ash.org/ashsids.html.

Chapter 9

'CIGARETTE SIRENS': THE EROTIC ANGLE

> *I am 6'1" tall, 180 lbs. black haired, brown eyes male. I very much enjoy watching women smoke. I am also very submissive. If you hate housework and want me as your slave to do cleaning, washing, ironing and what ever esle* [sic] *you ask i* [sic] *will. If all you want is to use me as a house slave fine, if you want me for sex i will do as told. All i ask is after i have served you, you will allow me the honour to watch you smoke while i worship at your feet. Age, size, race are unimportant, just an understading* [sic] *of my fetish. Any intrested* [sic] *ladies should e-mail me. 1lb@toronto.ark.com. For your referenced* [sic] *i am located in Toronto, Canada.*

A CURIOUS PHENOMENON that may or may not be causally related to the antismoking crusade is the recent emergence of a subculture whose adherents (victims?) are obsessed with images of women smoking—the younger and more attractive the woman is (clothed or unclothed), the longer the cigarette or larger the cigar she wields and the denser the clouds of smoke she generates, the better. At least one newsletter, now growing into a full-fledged magazine, is devoted to the subject, as well as an Internet newsgroup called alt.sex.fetish.smoking, to which the plea above was posted.

Whether this subculture is a consequence of the antismoking crusade is problematic; most of those who belong to it have had the fetish from a very early age, before they became sexually conscious and presumably before they were bombarded with or became susceptible to organized antismoking propaganda. But it is also problematic whether they would have the fetish if smoking were still as socially acceptable as it once was.

That the antismoking movement has played some role in fostering this subculture's growth, however, is suggested by the following excerpt from "my own personal story of my sexual fascination with women smoking" posted to alt.sex.fetish.smoking by "ideslovr@aol.com":

> I can't recall when the attraction first started. In growing up, like most children, I considered smoking as not only taboo, but also "nasty," partially as a result of all the antismoking propaganda delivered in schools . . . Perhaps like drinking and messing around with girls in the backseat, smoking was attractive because of the taboo. I began to see smoking by the opposite sex as attractive.

Those who share this attraction invariably say that their first intimation of it came at a young age, usually in the preteen years but sometimes even earlier, as witness a letter to *Smoke Signals*, "A Monthly Newsletter Devoted to the Smoking Fetish":

> I still do not know how those of us with this fetish acquired it. I know that I have had it since I was a very young child, because I remember seeing one of my mom's friends, who was attractive, smoke when I was a small child, and having a funny feeling in my genitals. This was long before I even knew what sex was! As a teenager, before I had any interest in sex, I remember watching one of the high school girls smoke, and it made my penis hard. I didn't know what was going on!

Confesses another:

> My fetish comes from watching my aunt Eva, when I was 4 or 5 years old. I would play with her and after we stopped, I would watch her smoke white, non-filtered cigarettes. My aunt was a beautiful woman and beautiful smoker; one time she kissed me and my heart started pounding away! I would look forward to her coming over so I could watch her smoke.

"Confess" is used advisedly. Wrote the editor/publisher of *Smoke Signals* in its inaugural issue in September 1994: "Nobody knows how many men (or for that matter, women) are keeping this terrible 'secret' to themselves. But whenever a person who is captivated by the sight of a sexy smoker finally discovers a kindred spirit, the reaction is always the same: 'I thought I was the only one!'"

I first stumbled across *Smoke Signals*, and the fetish, while surfing the many smoking links on the World Wide Web in the course of researching for this book. I sent $5 for a sample copy to the Providence, Rhode Island, address of the publication and received the December 1995 issue—a 12-page newsletter consisting of six individual sheets of paper stapled together at the top left corner, probably printed on a desktop printer, probably in the publisher's home. (Nine months later the newsletter was still only 12 pages but commercially printed, the cover glossy stock, the pages gutter-stapled and folded over magazine style and the editor hopeful that it might eventually be available on newsstands. The magazine also now has a site on the Web.)

The first page and a half were taken up with an eminently sensible editorial I will quote from in Chapter 10. The next two pages carried letters from subscribers. For example:

> Dear *Smoke Signals*: I don't smoke myself, but I agree with you that watching women smoke is an incredible turn-on. I think most men (and women) believe that smoking is erotic but are afraid to admit it. It's certainly a phallic image. Nothing gets me hotter than being on a date with a beautiful woman and discovering she smokes, when she reaches into her purse and comes out with a cigarette. Women in sexy lingerie who smoke are particularly hot, especially when they wear high-heel pumps. —Scott

The reaction of nonsmoker Scott stands in vivid contrast to that of a young fellow portrayed in an antismoking message I saw on television a few years ago. He is standing among a group of young people, at a disco or party or something, when he spots an attractive girl across the room. Just as he is about to approach her, however, she takes out a cigarette and lights it. His interested expression is immediately transformed into one of disappointment and disgust and he turns away, clearly writing her off as someone he might want to know.

As well as foregoing the chance to speak to the girl about the terrible thing she was doing to her body, and perhaps assist her in breaking her health-threatening habit, the boy in this antismoking ad might also have missed another opportunity with her, as suggested by another letter:

> Dear *Smoke Signals*: In a recent letter from Duane, he had a theory that women smokers could be more likely to do 'naughty' things. There is no question that this is true. This makes more

> sense than ever, considering that in this day and age smoking is perhaps the ultimate naughty behavior. A 1992 survey of young women ages 14-21 found that 81.6% of young women smokers were sexually active while only 33.3% of their nonsmoking counterparts were sexually active. This is an absolutely stunning difference! —Jason.

Jason didn't identify the survey but there is no reason not to believe it's as valid as the multitude of surveys cited by antismokers. Didn't there use to be a saying that "a girl who smokes cigarettes is a girl who will do anything"?

Next in the sample issue of the newsletter came "This Month's Smokin' Story!" This was a two-and-a-half-page tale, apparently nonfiction, by an anonymous writer who described how he acquired the fetish as a child watching his mother and female relatives smoke, a behavior he found "fascinating and exciting."

On page nine was "This Month's Reviews" of videotapes and photo sets. First of two featured was a tape by "Selena - 30 minutes - various brands - no sex or nudity. $29.95 plus $5.00 shipping. Coherent Light Photography, 60 E. 15th St. #184, Edmond, OK 73013-4301. Smoking videos and photos are available. They also have an artist available for custom smoking art."

The second was "Wicked Leather, " a photo set by "Miss S." "Because we've gotten such a strong reaction to the photos done by Miss S., we're reviewing a new set that she's just produced. In 'Wicked Leather' she shows a more dominant side, posing in a leather outfit, with garters and chains and heavy makeup, while smoking long cigarettes, of course! There are several close-up shots of Miss S. in mid-french inhale or exhaling through her nose."

"Wicked Leather" consisted of "10 photos - 120mm cigarettes - no nudity. $15.00 (cash, money order or check payable to Smoke Screen Productions, P.O. Box 221, Dept. S, Bridgeport, PA 19405. Various photo sets available; $15 for ten pictures; $25 for twenty pictures. Custom sets (20 photos) for $40. Miss S. has also completed her first video, which is available for $40."

Below this information was a black-and-white photograph of the somewhat less than stunning Miss S. "with a mouthful of smoke." That's what the caption said; the smoke was not discernible in the poor quality picture.

I guessed correctly what a "french (or French) inhale" was. (Why do we always identify the French with eroticism?) As for a "snap inhale," which I came across later, I wasn't sure until early in 1996 when *The Wall Street Journal* discovered the existence of the fetish and defined both terms (see below).

Following the video and photo review was "December's TV and Video Rental Guide," a listing of mainstream movies on tape and on cable TV in which even the briefest instance of a woman smoking, or just *holding* a cigarette, was called to the attention of the fetishists.

For example, under the heading of "Don't Miss - Rentals" was the movie "Dolores Claiborne" in which "Jennifer Jason Leigh chain-smokes; as usual, she's not an outstanding smoker, but this entry is better than her earlier work."

"Mad Love": "Drew Barrymore smokes throughout; there are many deep inhales, although the exhales aren't great. The director has also unfortunately mastered the technique of cutting away just as Drew starts to take a drag."

"Malicious": "Even though the producers use her smoking to show that Molly Ringwald is a villain, there are a few outstanding scenes in this one."

"Swimming with Sharks": "One very nice sequence by Michelle Forbes, including several nose exhales."

Under the category of "The Best of the Rest - Rentals" were:

"Cover Me": "One very quick drag." "Mirage": "One incidental shot." "New York Cop": "One drag on a joint."

As for whether any of these films were worth watching for the *story*, that apparently was of no interest to the readers of *Smoke Signals*.

Next came "This Month's Best Smoking Shots" in magazines:

"*Us* for December has a fabulous full-face color shot of Elizabeth Shue, in mid-french inhale; thick, creamy smoke covers her lips. There's also a nice posed head-and-shoulders shot of Mira Sorvino holding a cigarette, with a pack of Shermans on the table in front of her (proving she's a *real* smoker!).

"The winter issue of *Cigar Aficionado* is out, and there is a lovely photo spread (with text, of course), on the growth of cigar smoking among the 20-something generation. Needless to say, there are several young ladies in their 20s who were more than happy to participate (alas, no good exhale shots, though).

"The usual foreign fashion magazines fall short this month, unfortunately. There *are* six shots in *Italian Glamour* for November, and also six shots in November's *Italian Vogue*; they're nice, but certainly not of the caliber that can drive you to actually consider laying out the twenty bucks or so it costs to buy the magazines in the States."

The last page was an ad for two more videos, with accompanying photos:

"Cathy. This lovely brunette is a wonderful smoker. She chain smokes long white cigarettes in a holder, often french-inhaling, popping her hits [I'm still not sure what *that* means—D.O.] or taking double drags. And she obviously loves every single drag! See May's *Smoke Signals* for review."

"Zerina Dreams. Porn star and exotic model Zerina Dreams (64FF-26-36) smokes cigars as she changes lingerie and outfits in this outstanding video from the nation's number-one producer of cigar fetish videos. See June's *Smoke Signals* review.)"

It amazed me that men would actually lay out $35 or $40 for a half-hour video of not especially beautiful or even pretty women smoking a cigar or cigarette. If they really wanted to see women smoking all they had to do was watch some of the movies from the '30s, '40s and '50s on American Movie Classics on cable TV. But perhaps those movies don't appeal to them because, back when these films were made, the smoking by the actresses was natural and unposed; their smoking was purely incidental, not the whole focus of the film.

SPEAKING OF LAYING out good money, this one issue of *Smoke Signals* should have been enough for me. But chiefly because of the rationality demonstrated by the publisher in his editorial I quote from in Chapter 10, I was still curious about the kind of people who were wrapped up in this fetish, so I sprang for the ridiculous sum of $39.95 for a year's subscription to the newsletter. However, each issue proved to be much the same as the sample one, differing only with such new features as The Question of the Month ("Describe your ultimate fantasy smoker." "Describe your best 'sighting,'" etc.) and lists of both well-known and less-well-known actresses who not only smoke in films but are IRL ("in real life") smokers. It seems to be very important to the fetishists to know—or to think—that a celebrity *really* smokes, not just pretends to.

Only two months later, in the February 1996 issue, the publisher could proclaim that "By the time you read this, our fetish may already have been put into the national (and international) spotlight. If all goes according to plan, the fetish will be showcased in, believe it or not, both *Playboy** and *The Wall Street Journal*, both of which are working on what they see as a fascinating story . . . Almost all of us remember the 'I thought I was the only one' feeling, and remember how long it took us to find out how wrong we were. Imagine how many smoking fetishists will see these articles, and will join our growing fetish community!"

The Wall Street Journal did indeed alert the world to the fetish on January 31 with a story headlined: "Drag Queens: Paula Puffs and Her Fans Watch, Enraptured." Under that: "'Smoxploitation' Films Signal That Smoking Is Becoming a Fetish Among Many."

Wrote staff reporter Suein L. Hwang: "Cigarette smoking, it seems, has fallen so far out of the mainstream that it has entered into the nether world of fetishes and erotica." She quoted Dian Hanson, editor of *Leg Show*, a popular fetish magazine claiming a circulation of about 250,000: "Smoking is the fetish of the '90s. Anytime anything becomes widely condemned and taboo, it will be eroticized."

But the eroticism has limits. "Unlike some fetishists—those into underwear or shoes, for example," Ms. Hwang reported, "many smoking fetishists don't want overt sexual content muddying up the scenes . . . Smoking technique is paramount." She quotes *Leg Show's* Ms. Hanson again: "'The exhale is very important—seeing smoke actually exiting the mouth. [Viewers] don't want to see a long ash on [a cigarette]; they want to see lipstick on a cigarette.'"

They also want to see mastery of a technique called the "French inhale," which Ms. Hwang described as an actress letting smoke out of her mouth and inhaling it through the nostrils, and the "snap inhale,"

*Some time after writing this chapter I happened to be browsing through the February 1998 issue of *Playboy* (looking for an article, of course) and came across a small ad at the bottom of page 147 placed by a company offering videos of "Gorgeous female models, elegantly dressed, smoking cigarettes and cigars!" I wonder how many readers of a mainstream men's magazine like *Playboy*, who are usually interested in elegantly *undressed* models (as well as the articles, of course), would be attracted to the smoking fetish. I've never seen the ad again in subsequent issues (while looking for articles, of course.)

in which she allows a puff of smoke to emanate from her mouth before quickly drawing it back in.

Unfortunately, the smoking art—or at least a filming session of it—is long and life is short.

"Paula, now an Oklahoma college senior who won't reveal her last name, quit smoking just two weeks after shooting her namesake video," the article ends. "'I smoked a pack of cigarettes in three hours and it's pretty sickening,' she says. 'I was tired of it by the end of filming. I was just green.'"

Some people will find the smoking fetish pretty weird and even disgusting. Others, less condemnatory, will consider it merely silly and essentially harmless morally, if not harmless from a health standpoint. But even with "normal" people, smoking has always been associated to some degree with sex, whether it is the proverbial cigarette enjoyed in the afterglow of intercourse or simply the idea of "naughtiness" or daring, which for many if not most of us enhances sexual feeling.

What might be called a more normal combination of smoking and sex is described in a message found in Robert Wagner's Internet pages, alt.smokers.faq ("frequently asked questions"). From "laszlo@ alpha1.csd.uwm.edu (Tyson F Nuss)":

> I hold my cigaret to her lips, and she takes a full drag and inhales. We then press our lips together in a sensual, moist, insistent French kiss. While kissing, I inhale while she exhales, so that I draw my breath from my lover's lungs. Then I return the same breath, and we continue sharing the same air until one of us is gets too dizzy to continue.
>
> Another variation: She takes a drag, inhales, and we bring our lips very close together, but without touching. She exhales a plume of smoke as if blowing a kiss, and I inhale, receiving her air-kiss. This is very subtly, insidiously sensual.

I say this is "more normal" only because I can personally relate to it. On one occasion, many, many years ago before we were married, my wife-to-be and I were sitting and smoking in my car in a park. For some reason we began to blow smoke into each other's faces as we alternately smoked and kissed. This progressed to where, similar to the procedure described above, we would each take a deep drag and then blow it gently into the other's mouth, then receive the smoke back in like manner, again and again until a fresh infusion of smoke was needed.

I suppose it was erotic, but for both of us it was simply a spontaneous, different and fun thing to do. It was certainly not an essential component of or precondition for sexual arousal and we never repeated it.

As I said above, subsequent issues of *Smoke Signals* were much the same as the first, but each one provided a little more insight into the fetish, and those consumed with it. In January, for example, "Dar" wrote that "I am glad that smoking videos are produced without porn and sex. The porn stuff is frankly uninteresting. What is exciting is [*sic*] the close-ups of women's lips, their hands holding the cigarette to their lips, and most of all, the smoke itself!"

To which the editor/publisher commented: "Most of the readers we've heard from regarding sex in smoking fetish videos agree with you, but there are still quite a few who like to see some more explicit action in their videos. Our read is that people who have a strong and exclusive smoking fetish find the sexual action distracting; those who have the fetish as just one part of their sexuality, prefer a more 'varied diet.'"

Makes sense to me. Yet as seems to be the case in other aspects of life, those who find "explicit action" not just distracting but offensive are the ones most vocal about it. Wrote "Christian" in a later issue: "I was very disappointed when I received my May issue and saw the review of a video that included nudity and masturbation. Please! I realize that you are trying to offer items that appeal to everyone; however, I have no desire to watch a woman masturbate or play with her breasts (yuck!). I hope that in the future you will offer more videos of women who are fully clothed while they smoke. That turns me on more than anything."

SO JUST WHAT IS it about seeing women smoking, with or without clothes, with or without engaging in explicit sex, that turns the fetishist on? "From the Publisher" in the February 1996 *Smoke Signals* may provide some insight:

"I was asked by *Playboy* for some thoughts on the fetish," he began. "Not knowing how much (if any) of that material they'll use, I thought it might be worth sharing the material with you. I hope it reflects, in some way, the thoughts and feelings of our readers, gathered after years of speaking with and hearing from hundreds of you. There are many opinions and theories as to why many men (AND women!) find smoking attractive, sexy and alluring."

He then suggested the following:

• Women who smoke are self-confident, sophisticated and socially adept; they handle their smoking with confidence and style.

• Women who smoke are "naughty"; they deliberately do something that is sometimes (today, more than ever!) viewed as unacceptable, unfeminine or just plain "wrong."

• Women who smoke are more relaxed, carefree, fun-loving and not as uptight; many guys see smoking as a reflection of the attitude: "I do what I like."

• Women who smoke are more often confident of their sexuality; they may even use their smoking as a "tool" or "prop" to attract attention.

• Finally, many can't even explain the reason for their attraction to women who smoke, any more than some guys can explain why they're attracted to women with long hair or nice legs. Plain and simple, it just turns them on.

"There are also some 'deeper' aspects of the fetish or attraction that we hear at times," the publisher of *Smoke Signals* continued. "Some with the fetish are attracted to dominant women who smoke, with the smoking one symbol of their dominance (it seems that those who feel this way are less likely to smoke themselves, increasing the symbolism of the woman in charge who's 'allowed' to smoke). Less common aspects that we also hear involve a Freudian oral fixation . . . or an attraction to women who are heavy smokers dependent on their habit (we're not quite sure what the psychological basis is for that, but there probably is one)."

As for what exactly it is that fetishists are attracted to, he lists the three most common answers:

• The exhale—French inhaling, inhaling through the nostrils, blowing smoke rings, etc. "It's quite sensuous and alluring, particularly when women are 'accomplished' or 'talented' smokers."

• The manner—how they handle their cigarettes and their inhaling and exhaling.

• What's being smoked—women who smoke long cigarettes, women who smoke cigarettes with white filters or brown filters, women who smoke strong cigarettes, women who smoke cigars or women who use cigarette holders.

He concludes:

> Those who might claim that the tobacco industry perpetuates the "myth" that smoking is attractive or sexy totally ignore the social history. Obviously, dating back to the early days of women taking up smoking in America, there was a sexual mystique surrounding women who smoke (a recent book of postcards from the era 1890-1930 clearly demonstrates that fact), and the way that female smoking was portrayed in early American films (I'm sure most people have very clear memories of the way smoking was portrayed in the black and white films of the '30s and '40s) makes it clear that there has always been a 'sexual component.' The Virginia Slims ads of the '60s, to use one example, didn't CREATE that perception, they REFLECTED it. [Caps in original.]

In the second anniversary issue of *Smoke Signals*, September 1996, the publisher reprinted part of his editorial in the very first issue, in which he had quoted from a magazine called *Platinum* that "if you want to draw a bead on the American psyche, look no further than American cinema—the who, what, where and why of how we live our lives is all right there. If it happens on the street, it happens on the screen . . . Bogart, Davis, Dietrich, Dean. In countless scenes and studio publicity photos, smoke forever curls from the lips of our favorite stars. Whatever the image desired by the studio, the history of film is a history of smoking." Commented the publisher:

> It should not, then, come as any surprise that many people have fixated on smoking as an object of sexual desire or arousal. For some, it is just preference that their partner smoke. *For others, it is a necessity.* [Emphasis added.] That difference is crucial, when it comes to understanding some people's fixation on a link between smoking and sex . . .
>
> [S]tudies in psychological and psychiatric journals have found smoking to be a common focus of this sort of sexual behavior. Further, most studies conclude that there is little or nothing that can be done to 'cure' any sort of fetish, and a wide variety of experts has concluded that as long as the fetish is one without a victim, there's no reason to try to change it.
>
> So, what does this say to people who are attracted to smokers or have a smoking fetish? Basically: relax, accept it as just one of many parts of your identity, and enjoy it!

AT RISK OF BELABORING the subject, a few more reader comments from other issues of *Smoke Signals*:

> My personal preference is for girls and young women who look way too sweet and innocent to be smokers. —Bob

In response to a Question of the Month—"Describe the first sexy smoker you can ever remember seeing"—an unidentified reader wrote:

> My first memory of a sexy smoker was at a wedding reception which I attended when I was 12. The woman was the cousin of [the bride]. This woman was in her early to mid 20s and was absolutely gorgeous! She was seated directly across from me at a small table which sat only six people, so I wasn't more than three or four feet from her for the entire evening. She wore very heavy dark red lipstick, had beautiful long dark red fingernails, and smoked Herbert Tareyton Cork Tips.
>
> . . . I watched her smoke cigarette after sexy cigarette all night long. She must have known that she was turning me on, because she frequently looked directly at me and smiled as she dragged, or inhaled, or exhaled. Sometimes she would blow the thick smoke in my direction as she smiled at me. Until that night I was kind of an anti-smoker. Suddenly, I didn't mind cigarette smoke as long as it was an attractive woman or girl who was smoking.

On the other hand, "Michael" thought that "Even a plain Jane can be suddenly transformed into a beautiful, alluring creature with the addition of a long, thick, good-quality cigar."

In response to "Describe your most memorable sighting," another unnamed reader wrote:

> The sighting I still remember most was during the spring before I turned 12. Up until that point, I had followed the household party-line—viciously anti-smoking all the way. But then, while I was on an application tour at a private school, at some kind of official function at the end of the day, I saw one of the mothers, and my life changed forever. Striking red hair, impeccably dressed (imagine a woman coming out of a Wall Street boardroom and you'll have the right image), appeared to be smoking B&H [Benson & Hedges] or VS [Virginia Slims] or something similar, executing a perfect nose exhale. I think it was at that moment that sexual attraction became something more than just theoretical for me (even though she was easily three or four times my age).

If watching a beautiful woman smoke can cause even a "viciously antismoking" guy to defect from the ranks, no wonder the antis are so upset when attractive people are shown smoking in movies or on television. (It's okay for the villain to smoke, although that's bad enough.) It is no accident that television news broadcasts about the "latest smoking study" are invariably illustrated with unflattering closeups of homely people sucking on the weed.

In another issue of *Smoke Signals* the question was asked, "If you met your dream woman, but her smoking was only ordinary, what advice would you give her to make her smoking perfect?" One reader responded:

> No single factor can alone make a truly glamorous smoker, but one possibly underappreciated factor might be the tip and ash management. I like a nice, rounded tip, slightly pointy, and to observe an orange glow as much as possible. It turns me off when the tip is uneven and blackened, as if it is about to burn out. The single most important thing, of course is *never ever* use thumb and forefinger. [Emphasis in original.]

So much for male smoking fetishists. Are there any female ones? Well, there is at least one, unnamed, who submitted a first-person story to the August 1996 issue of *Smoke Signals*. I think it's worth quoting in full:

> I always used to think that my feelings about cigarettes and smoking were unusual, but thanks to your publication, I now know that I am not as unique or bizarre as I had believed. Obviously, untold numbers of people share the smoking fetish.
>
> For me, the association of smoking with extreme pleasure and sexuality began when I was still in grade school. I remember thinking how attractive and pretty a long, white cigarette looked when held gracefully between a woman's fingers. My best friend had an older sister named Valerie, a very gorgeous and very mature girl who was in her teens, and I was so impressed by her and her girlfriends, all of whom smoked and seemed so cool to me. In my eyes, they were fully developed young women who got to wear makeup, go out on dates, and right along with that, they smoked cigarettes, almost as if to say, "I'm not afraid of anything." I was so intrigued by the image of these "naughty" girls, participating in what was obviously a rebellious, even forbidden, gesture.
>
> Valerie always wore bright pink lipstick and shiny lip gloss to accentuate her full lips, and I would gaze in total fascination and be hypnotized as I watched her perform the smoking ritual. She would tap a pack of cigarettes, open the box and pull out one long, white filter-tipped 120 [millimeter] cigarette, and put it between her pretty lips. She looked to me so wild, young and hungry, sucking deeply,

> taking all that lovely warm white smoke deep into her lungs. She exhaled with a sly pout that spoke volumes: "ah, pure pleasure . . ," she seemed to say. I loved everything about it, the softness of the filter tip, the long white length, the heat and glow of the orange tip which would brighten with each hard pull her mouth took on it. To this day, I am still captivated by this very sexy, erotic act. Oddly enough, I am a non-smoker, as my boyfriend dislikes the idea of my smoking. I like it this way, because I will never become immune to the pleasant sensation smoking gives me, and it will always be reserved for special occasions. Occasionally I will have a cigarette, always in private. I usually smoke it very slowly and deliberately, and wow! Do I enjoy every deep drag! It actually makes me feel amazingly good like nothing else.
>
> My closet fetish has changed my life in the sense that I am always on the lookout for sexy pictures or films of women smoking. I must confess to enjoying lunch hour in the city where I work. Because of the no-smoking ordinances, attractive young women huddle together in all kinds of weather, greedily smoking away in little cliques, sucking in nicotine hungrily. It looks like a real bonding experience shared by lady smokers, like a secret club, which I think is adorable. I guess it all goes back to the days when Valerie and her teenaged girlfriends who looked so pretty and were so "cool" would fill the room full with cigarette smoke, looking so mischievous and sexy as they practiced french inhaling and chain-smoked together for hours. Thanks, *Smoke Signals*.

What a refreshing contrast that letter is to the dismal propaganda of the antismokers, who are incapable of appreciating the true virtues of the noble weed!

I also found a couple messages of a different nature from females on alt.sex.fetish.smoking, which is another treasure trove of material on the fetish. One wrote: "Hi guys, I love to smoke during all kinds of sex. Send me some hot e-mail and tell me what you like.— Kim." Another: "I love to give head to smokers. I'd love to talk about it.—LuAnn."

Lest anyone be tempted to contact these ladies(?) I've deleted their e-mail addresses, both in the interest of upholding American morality and because women, and sometimes men posing as women, have been known to use the Internet to promote scams aimed at the sexually desperate.

Another long message was posted on April 28, 1996 by "Jenny" on alt.sex.masturbation and alt.sex.stories, as well as alt.sex.fetish.smoking It was prefaced by a challenge to story writers to some up with the best learning-to-smoke and sexual-awakening story based on an electronic conversation she had with "Margo" via what is called Internet Relay Chat. What follows has been edited for length only:

jenny: hi
margo: hi jenny
margo: where are you
jenny: palo alto
jenny: lez or bi
margo: i'm in seattle
margo: lez you??
jenny: lez
jenny: is 19 your age
margo: are you really 15???
jenny: just turned 16
margo: happy birthday
jenny: thanx
margo: you are welcome sweet
jenny: is 19 your age
margo: yes i'm 19
margo: what are you doing up at this time of morning
jenny: can't fucking sleep
margo: alright
margo: would you like to talk??
jenny: fuck yes
margo: i'm in the middle of puget sound on this computer
margo: is your family sleeping
jenny: mom is out with her gf [girlfriend] i'm alone
margo: cool
jenny: r u in school
margo: yes u of w [University of Washington]
margo: i assume you are to
jenny: soph in HS [high school]
margo: doing well???
jenny: pretty good
margo: glad to hear that
jenny: i'm 5'2 long blonde hair blue eyes small tits
jenny: so what do you look like
margo: i'm 5' blonde hair blue eyes 95lbs 34-25-36
jenny: :) [an Internet "icon" indicating a smile viewed sideways]
margo: small can be beautiful
jenny: speaking of small how big are your tits
margo: i have a 34c
jenny: i'm barely a 32b but I dont wear a bra anyway

margo: probably don't need one i don't wear thos things either
jenny: cool
jenny: i need t get some matches brb [be right back]
jenny: i'm back
margo: :)(: [smile, frown]
jenny: do you smoke?
margo: yeah nasty habit but life without vice would be very dull indeed
jenny: i smoke vs120's
margo: me winston lights but i think i'm going to try to quit before i get in too deep
jenny: my gf kelly got me started when I was 13 she said it made me sexier she fucking started at 12
margo: tell me about kelly
jenny: well she's about 5'4 very thin maybe 90 lbs, very small tits maybe 30a, long sandy brown hair, brown eyes, she looks like she's still 12, but she smokes 2 packs a day and says fuck in almost every sentence, and masturbates twice as much as me—if you can fucking believe that.
margo: you believe it makes you sexier???
jenny: kind of like how i look in the mirror
margo: well alright
jenny: what about u
margo: what do you mean
jenny: you believe it makes you sexier?
margo: smoking? not really ever have a cigerette [*sic*] during sex?
jenny: not really but I smoke when I masturbate in front of the mirror
margo: do you??
jenny: yes
jenny: do you smoke when you masturbate?
margo: i get too excited to smoke i'd probably burn the place down
jenny: I masturbate a fucking lot usually three times a day
margo: i do it a lot if i don't have a girlfriend

There were no more references to smoking. The balance of the conversation dealt with the girls' masturbation frequencies and techniques and their lesbian experiences.

I encountered another Jenny on the World Wide Web, Jenny G., the author of "Jenny's Teen Smoking Page" (www.eccentrica.org/teensmoke). This site featured photographs of wholesome-looking young girls smoking cigarettes, evidently sent in by the girls themselves. Other pages carried letters from fans of female smoking, mostly from males. (Jenny G. also hosts, or used to host, another Website called

"Jenny's Teen Lesbian Page." Why so many young female smokers seem to be lesbians, I couldn't say.)

Links from Jenny's smoking page took me to other teen smoking Websites, letters to which I quote from in Chapter 10, as well as several run by adult female smokers, including "Sabrina's Smoking Chat House," Ciara's "ciara2sexy/Personal WBS Home Page" and Suzy's "suzysmokesex/Personal WBS Home Page." Here's how the latter introduces herself:

> Hello, I'm Suzy and I am your ultimate smoking fetish. I'm a student at an eastern university and I am a professional cigarette smoker. I'll blow smoke in your face. I'll ash your carpet and I'll burn your furniture. You'll be so aroused by my luxurious smoking style you'll be unable to control yourself. I enjoy being with women as much as I do men but men will submit to me and my sexy cigarette and my collection of long, sophisticated holders. Once you see me smoking in my leather outfits, heavy make up and bright red lipstick you'll know I'm a woman of class and elegance. I've made a few home videos of myself smoking which is only appropriate since I model part time when I'm not attending classes and I may offer my smoking videos for sale in the near future so you must "cum" visit my site often.

On alt.sex.fetish.smoking, "p006778b@pbfreenet.seflin.lib.fl.us (J.C.)" revealed to the news group what happened when his wife started smoking:

> She tried smoking during sex, and we fucked like hell and she masturbated to a hot, hot cum! Next day she bought her first pack, and in about 3 days she was hooked. Smokes about half a pack a day now and masturbates plenty, and does girls as well. Any other girls start smoking recently and notice increase in your sex drive?

As these examples suggest, for some reason that shrinks might want to look into, a lot of female smokers, both "professional" and amateur, seem to be inclined towards all kinds of sex, both heterosexual and lesbian. Does smoking activate their libidos, as J.C. asks, or do they smoke because they are already highly charged sexually?

It is also evident that if some females are turned on by smoking, it is their *own* smoking or that of other women. Others may be turned on by the knowledge that their smoking excites men. In all my explorations of this subject, however, I have yet to come across a female who is excited by a *male's* smoking. For good reason has the smoking fetish been called a new form of pornography, which historically has been almost exclusively a male interest. (Heterosexual pornography, that is; smoking does not seem to play any erotic role in gay pornography.)

But what if you've got a girl (and the fetish) and she doesn't smoke? "Choralmike@aol.com (Choralmike)" posted this message on alt.sex.fetish.smoking:

"Any advice out there for me? I'd love to get my girlfriend to start smoking. Problem is, she's shy, straightlaced, and 'semi' antismoking. I think she'd do just about anything to please me sexually, but I haven't a clue how to even get started on this idea. Please e-mail me or post here with any ideas/advice. Thanks."

"Jay Messersmith rhvohvo@popd.ix.netcom.com" replied:

"I was in the same boat. And my girlfriend is very similar to the qualities you describe. But after a lot of playing guessing games, I finally came out to her. We tried VSL (Virginia Slims Lights) 120s, but she couldn't get used to the taste. It was thru this newsgroup that I learned about, and decided to try, clove cigarettes. It was the best decision I ever made. She's been doing this for me for about five months now, and learning how to French inhale. I enjoy teaching her, and the effects of everything else too. Although she doesn't like 'real' cigarettes, she says the cloves make her feel sexy, and it's kind of like 'her' brand."

"kfenske@fast.net (Ken)" agreed that "Cloves are a great way to get a girlfriend to smoke. They are really good tasting from the start and a semi-anti can be easily convinced that it's not a 'real' cigarette."

However, "Brian Murphy CA 1clbmurph@compapp.dcu.ie" cautioned: "You should be real careful when trying to introduce your partner to a personal fetish at the best of times but when it's something that could, at an extreme, harm her health then you should really ask how important it is to you."

Brian evidently decided it was very important to him, however. He continued:

> I've been with my girlfriend for many years now and it's only recently that I've managed to fully share this fetish with her. I guess I started by gently letting it be known that I'd like it if we could share a cigarette together at times . . . For me, my girlfriend is now what I would call a social smoker. If somebody offers she will take a cigarette and when we're alone she'll sometimes smoke. She knows

> I find it attractive and she really hasn't got a problem with it. But it took me years of thinking about how to go about introducing her to this wonderful habit to get where we are today. Today, she's quite happy to smoke in bed and even during sex. I guess she knows that it's a power she has over me.

Ah, but the rewards of giving one's girl that power are great. Writes "y7mark@aol.com (Y7 Mark)":

> My girlfriend always told me she would never smoke. Then one day she said, "I'm so glad you don't smoke." To which I replied, "It wouldn't bother me if you smoked."... Later that night, I bought her cigarettes, on the premise that it was a joke.
>
> It started a whole new page in our relationship. Later that night we had the greatest sex while she smoked a cigarette. Now she masterbates [*sic*] while smoking and tells me about it later ... The greatest thrill I had is one day when she was in the shower. I was looking for a pen and found a pack of cigarettes that she had purchased on her own. She was becoming a fullfledged smoker ... And then just a few weeks ago, we were going out and she was out of cigarettes but said she had another pack in her glove compartment. I got an instant hard-on.

On the other hand, some people who are heavily into sex are turned off by smoking, by females and males alike. For example, people who advertise in "swingers'" magazines specifying they wish to meet nonsmokers only. ("You can sleep with my wife, just don't smoke in her presence.")

A mail-order catalog for pornographic videotapes I happened to see, from a company called Leisure Time Products, had several one-page articles on various sexual subjects interspersed among its offerings. They were thoughtful and well-written, even had scholarly references. One of the pages roundly condemned smoking as a dirty and disgusting habit and totally unerotic. The article was surrounded by dozens of pictures of women with their faces splattered all over with semen.

As they say, different strokes for different folks.

Later, quite fortuitously, I ran across a site on the World Wide Web which evidently was the source of these articles. A disclaimer stated that the sexual content of the site was not intended to appeal to the prurient-minded. It's name: "Kinkysex.com."

* * *

GETTING BACK TO the voyeuristic aspects of the fetish, in a posting to alt.sex.fetish.smoking, "75110.1153@ compuserve.com (Ken)" asked anyone who had pics of pregnant smokers to "please post them!" He told about a pregnant smoker who was a coworker of his a few years before:

> I worked at a computer center and most of the operators smoked in the computer room, those were the days! Anyway, this one woman was about 5 foot 2, thick and brown hair. She was quite attractive and smoked constantly. She was never without a cig and must have smoked almost 3 packs a day of Marlboro Reds. She became pregnant and I was surprised that she didn't alter her consumption at all. It was really nice to come in every day and talk to her about her pregnancy and whatnot while she had a cig hanging out of her mouth. Near the end she even seemed to increase her consumption to combat the stress of the pregnancy.

Then, with words to make a pediatrician roll his eyes heavenward:

> She returned for a visit during maternity leave with a beautiful baby boy in fine health. She said she was breast feeding and she was obviously still a heavy smoker. I would have loved to see her breastfeed while enjoying a smoke.

I can hear the antis saying, "Sure, maybe the baby *looked* healthy, but it was probably underweight and mentally retarded and will develop all kinds of physical and psychological problems later." Today, indeed, such a mother's behavior might even be grounds for taking her child away from her (see Chapter 8).

I had an experience similar to Ken's when I worked for a time in a new Wal-Mart store in Roswell, Georgia, during my third retirement. The district manager, a reformed smoker but not the type who demanded that everyone follow his example, ordered the employees' break lounge to be partitioned off to give us smokers our own room. (Nonsmokers would occasionally stick their heads in the door and cough elaborately.) One of the denizens of this den of iniquity was a very pregnant young woman. I never had the nerve to ask her if she was aware of all the warnings about smoking during pregnancy, much less ask her why she ignored them. I never saw her again after she left to have the baby, so I don't know if it was healthy or not. Skeptical of the antismoking medical establishment as I am, and especially since seeing the studies of smoking and pregnancy from Wanda Hamilton's bibliography that I cited in Chapter 3, I would bet that it was. That's just a guess, of course, as my personal knowledge on this subject is limited by the fact that my wife stopped smoking while she was carrying our son. He was, however, unaffected by exposure to the secondhand smoke of two parents after his birth and all through his childhood.

In one of the most imaginative letters I saw in *Smoke Signals*, "George" made the following suggestion:

> I just had an idea. While stories and videos are great turn-ons for us, we all really crave the excitement of being in the presence of a sexy lady smoker, smelling the smoke, even receiving smoky kisses. One of the best things about this fetish is that it allows us smoking spectators to basically engage in sex in public in a perfectly legal manner. This may even extend to watching underage smokers. No one gets hurt, and all we're doing is watching a legal activity. Well, because smoking is sexual to us and perfectly legal, I thought it might be interesting to set up services in various locations where your readers live that would have sexy women (18 or over) smokers perform in person, one on one, with a client. For a fee, the smoker would smoke, even share smokey [*sic*] kisses and it's all legal as long as no other sex goes on. The client could request certain techniques like nose exhales, smoke rings, cigarette holders, cigars, specific brands, etc. As this would be legal, you could advertise for women smokers to participate and make money, and you could actually run a personal-ad type section for men wishing to make these connections. It may sound a bit weird at first, but think about it. What could be a better nirvana for us?

Smokehouses instead of cathouses? Sorry, George, the antis would never allow it. And remember what happened to Paula, the fetish-video star.

Another idea to facilitate the "legal" observation of smoking women was suggested by another posting by "Ken" on alt.sex. fetish.smoking:

> It occurred to me that a great place to see women smoking heavily is one of those smoking cessation programs where they make you smoke continuously for an hour . . . It might be a great way to chain smoke in public with the women really getting off. Afterwards you can hang around and perform a public service by helping people off the wagon and perhaps pick someone up and

> give them whole new reasons to smoke. I think that people who go into these things are misguided anyway, they've gotten into a rut and need something to make smoking exciting again.

You can always dream, Ken.

An anonymous contributor to this news group related how he watched two women smoking in a restaurant:

> One, a delicately pretty and nicely attired blond of maybe 35-40, caught my notice in particular. Immediately upon being seated, she reached for a Va Slims Light 100 . . . Then, adeptly and nonchalantly, she broke the filter off it and lit the no-longer filtered end. She smoked with a wonderful demureness—slow, steady pulls, reasonably long and deep breaths of the strong smoke, slow exhales, discarding the end only when it was down to an inch or so. After a while she enjoyed another, same lovely unfiltered technique.

He concluded, "There are some good things about this trend of separate smoking areas in restaurants."

Finally, from "sksmk@aol.com (SKSMK)", the most unusual variation on the fetish I have seen (emphases in original):

> I've seen through this newsgroup that this fetish takes on many forms. Here's another. As a nonsmoker with the fetish I've experimented for several years with "smoke pumps" that produce smoke and that I employ in various fantasies (I'd never dream, or so I thought, that I'd ever devulge [*sic*] any info about my fetish to anyone). Well a friend figured out what turned me on and got me to tell her all about it. She doesn't smoke but has seen me watching women smoke for years. She wanted to know all about the smoke pump. Finally I agreed to show it to her. We went to a secluded place where I could show her how it worked. It smokes several large cigars (cigarettes are used up too soon and cigar smoke is *much* more effective.) The pump uses up to twenty cigars at once and can produce large quantities of very thick smoke.
>
> She was really turned on by the thought of using the thing on me and, unknown to me, had procurred [*sic*] some very heavy restraints. I set it for her, not expecting, but hoping that something would develop. Before I knew it, after the pump was producing smoke she was taking off my clothes. She forced me down onto a bed in the very same room (with little resistance from me) and proceeded to restrain me until I was unable to move. Then she started repositioning the hoses from the smoke machine so they

were aimed strategically at me. Then much to my ectasy [*sic*], dense, soft smoke began coming for me. Soon the entire bed was covered with a thick fog. She puffed smoke over me again and again until she couldn't take it anymore either and mounted me. While I struggled under her, the smoke kept puffing down over me while she stayed on me. Needless to say things went *very* well and we'll be repeating the whole event soon.

REGRETTABLY, THE ADVICE of the publisher of *Smoking Signals* to "relax and enjoy" notwithstanding, there is a dark side to the smoking fetish. While many, perhaps most, enthusiasts of smoking videos or photographs seem to be satisfied with this form of voyeuristic sex-by-suggestion or sex-by-proxy, others are gravely burdened by a life-complicating and often frustrated need for smoking plus *real* sex with a *real* woman. One rather pitiful example was an anonymous posting to alt.sex.fetish.smoking in April 1996:

I have had a fetish about smoking women since my teenage years and am now in my early forties. Throughout those 30 years I have found it has varied from being very exciting to something relatively unimportant, but nevertheless always there. It is something that I have never felt entirely comfortable with, and despite the excitement I have felt that I know regular readers of this group can readily relate to, it is something that I would rather not have, if I am honest with myself. Particularly now, as it is fundamental to problems I am having in my marriage. Let me explain.

Anonymous (who apparently does not smoke himself) states that we must first go back 20 years, to a time when "I, like many others who have posted here, thought I was abnormal and a bit weird":

It was then that I met the woman who was to become my wife. I fell in love with her as a complete person and it didn't seem to be much more than a bonus at the time that she was also a smoker. It wasn't long before she started to notice that I had a bit of a "thing" about watching her smoke. I would try very gently to bring the "thing" to the surface more and more. This was a very gradual process taking years rather than months. After being together 6 or 7 years, she let me take some pictures of her smoking, albeit somewhat bashfully in the process. They would be quite appreciated in this group, I can tell you! This was the golden era of the relationship in some respects, because at this stage she was a confirmed smoker who quite readily admitted she loved smoking.

After being together 10 years, she became pregnant with our first child. She knew she ought to quit, but she was addicted and still liked smoking, so she continued to smoke, albeit a bit less than usual. As time went on after the birth [presumably normal?—D.O.], her smoking consumption soon returned to its previous level. It was around that time that I began to notice a change in her smoking. Before the child was born, she used to just smoke for pleasure in a relaxed way, but she was now often to be seen smoking fast and furious in the breaks between tending to our child. Instead of sitting down to smoke with a drink, book or TV, she would grab a cigarette while doing something like putting dishes away. She would now start to take a drag, remove the cigarette to inhale, then put the cigarette back in her mouth while exhaling so she could carry on working. She had become a stress smoker as well.

Our second child was born 6 years ago and this one was quite demanding on being fed during the night [but otherwise also normal?—D.O.]. After one of the many feeding sessions in the middle of the night, my wife came back to bed with a cigarette. Being the typical man, I usually slept through all this, but something made me stir into that semi-awake state. I leaned over to kiss her and got to her lips as she was in mid-exhale. She tasted delicious. I came to and said I wanted to make love. She asked if I could wait until she had finished her cigarette. I said that I couldn't wait and, yes, after 14 whole years I at last made love to my wife while she smoked. It was wonderful and I told her so.

For the next 5 years she would often smoke while we made love. At long last I had achieved what I had always wanted, and she said she was quite happy doing it some of the time, but not always. I was happy too.

Then a year ago, out of the blue, she said she was going to quit smoking. She felt ashamed of the kids having to grow up with a smoking mother and the bad influence it represented. Besides, she had been smoking for 20 years and that was long enough. I knew what she was saying made perfect sense, but I also felt devastated about the prospect of losing something that excited me and I loved. By this time I had discovered alt.sex.fetish.smoking and realized I was not alone in my fetish. I decided to lay all my cards on the table and explain how I felt. She seemed to understand.

During the ensuing seven months Mrs. Anonymous somewhat reluctantly agreed to occasional smoking during or as a prelude to sex to please her husband.

But then came "another bombshell." Anonymous "lost out badly in a company restructure" and became very agitated. An additional business venture he and his wife had started was not doing well, adding to his agitation.

> So my wife chose the very same time to give up smoking. This time she didn't warn me—she just did it. She said we needed to save some money, and this was the only way she could do it. Besides, as I was so agitated about other things anyway, she might just as well get everything over with together. Despite all the sense I knew it made, I still flipped.

Anonymous begs his wife to delay quitting until after all their other problems had subsided. He tells her he will find some means of ridding himself of his fetish, perhaps through hypnotherapy, when they could afford it. He endures three weeks of her not smoking, the longest she had ever abstained.

> But it didn't last. Her addiction was too great and she gave in, but no way did I ask or persuade her to start again. Things were different now. She banned smoking in all upstairs rooms, and included our bedroom as her smoking there would encourage my fetish, and that was no good, so she said. But she continues to smoke in the lounge and kitchen. She is back to the same level of smoking as before, but there is going to be no return to the way things used to be.
>
> I feel hurt and rejected by this action. O.K., if she had totally given up, that would be one thing and I would at least know where I stood. But she still smokes, and although she knows I miss it, she is standing her ground. We haven't made love since. Not because I couldn't do it without her smoking. I thought she understood when I came clean a year ago, but she can't really have, and that's what hurts.
>
> So let's face it, this fetish is now hell to live with. I don't have any others, but I tell you it is agony to live with someone who said she was happy to indulge it, and then withdraw the indulgence without warning, yet I still have to see her smoking. Wouldn't life be so much simpler without it? I could encourage her in giving up like I know I should without any of the feelings of rejection and resentment that I have experienced for the last 3 months.
>
> The marriage is beginning to creak as a result of this. I have realized that ridding myself of the fetish may possibly be the only way to pull things round. But what can I try? And will it work? Remember, we are talking 30 years experience here! And what about the other extreme? Supposing I am to totally remove the fetish and I then find my wife's continuing to smoke repulsive?

> I hope some of you have persevered this far. For those that have, I am sorry that this is such a negative thing to post in a group that primarily wishes to enjoy the smoking fetish. Many of you will be like I was 20 years ago and you feel excited to see women smoking and even more so when you start dating a smoker. You will feel you want to explore your interest with her, and to those I say good luck, but tread carefully! Others may feel that the fetish is more of a burden than a pleasure to live with. Well, what do you do about it, and how do you cope?
>
> Despite the recent events, I still love my wife and don't want this to be the start of us breaking up. But the situation will need to be resolved. Constructive replies especially welcome!

Anonymous's appeal elicited several sympathetic responses to alt.sex.fetish.smoking. For example, the following from "huh@where.com (RJ)," who, even though he has the fetish, says his wife's smoking is actually a turn-off for him. He finds his satisfaction from the newsgroup and from girl-watching. He tells Anonymous:

> What you describe is a tragedy in the making . . . however, there is a way around the trouble . . . I love my wife for what she is and not what she does. We have shared my fetish in other ways. For instance, she keeps an eye out for gorgeous women smokers when we are out on the town and calls my attention to them. Later, if I'm in the mood, she will assist me in creating [a] fantasy of words and we will stimulate each other. I've been married 14 years and have done this with my wife from the beginning. Don't be afraid to move the fetish in the direction of fantasy. Fantasy can help [you] survive reality . . . Good luck. Our prayers are with you.

From "kfenske@fast.net (Ken)," whom we met previously:

> I read your post and was immediately concerned about your plight. In a way you have a [smoking fetishist's] worst nightmare, you've come out of the closet to the most important person in your life and now her knowledge of it had [*sic*] become a negative between you . . . You need to understand your wife's motives to understand that she still loves you. You can make love to your wife without cigarettes as soon as you realize that she's not doing this to you. It's the anger that's keeping you apart, not cigarettes . . . Your marriage sounds strong but she needs to understand how deeply your fetish goes and you have to understand how strong her desire to quit is. People who decide to quit are almost religious about it because it requires a complete redefinition of your self image and

a lot of will power, which our society sees as a virtue. You cannot rid yourself of a fetish.

Ken goes on to say that he is 36, has smoked since he was 14 and has had the fetish since he was younger than 8.

I have no intention of quitting smoking but that doesn't mean I'll always feel that way. A person can have and enjoy the fetish without smoking themselves, it's just harder. The health aspect of our fetish does concern me but not enough to give it up yet. I smoke a pack a day and don't feel that that is excessive . . . My wife [is] older than me and smokes 1+ pack a day of light 100s. Again, I don't feel that this is excessive and she shows no signs of harm from it. She quit for a 10 year period so today it's like she's only been smoking for about 8 years. She loves smoking as much as I do and has enjoyed our explorations of smoking and the fetish over the last year. She is also concerned about the long-term health effects. She'd like to quit but doesn't feel too strongly that she must quit now, that could change. For now it can wait and that's OK with me. I'll love her just as much if she smokes or doesn't smoke. I do love to watch her smoke. Sometimes I just stand behind her and watch her put the cigarette in her mouth, then watch the plume of smoke that rises above her head. If she came to me tomorrow and said, "Ken, it's time for me to quit and I want you to quit with me," I don't know what I'd do . . .

We tried twice together about a year ago but once she gave in and once I did and we know that we have to quit together if we're ever going to be successful. Problem is that since discovering ASFS [alt.sex.fetish.smoking] I've really gotten into the fetish community and the resources available and I love it too much to quit now. I even set up the first ASFS gathering in NYC where 11 of us got together last September and for the first time we were all in a situation where our smoking and fetish were positive. It gave me a whole new outlook on life. We're having another in May if you're interested, perhaps your wife would find it interesting too. My wife enjoyed it and really liked some of the people we met. Best of luck to you and please write.

In a somewhat less sympathetic response, "mkohary@u.washington.edu (Mike)" addresses Anonymous's problem from a "tough-love" approach (all emphases in original):

At the end of this post, you welcome constructive replies. I assume that means that you're asking for advice. I have some for you; any psychology I engage in here is amateur (I'm a biologist,

> not a psychologist), but it is educated as I have done research in psychological issues (not pseudoscientific, though; no parapsychology or repressed memories here!) and a great deal of research into fetishism in particular, since I have a vested interest in that subject . . .
>
> Let me start by saying that much of what you say makes sense, but you clearly need a paradigm shift because much of what you say is also nonsense. Please don't take that personally; I'm simply trying to be frank . . . [Y]our statement that it [the fetish] is "something that I have never felt entirely comfortable with" is *key* . . . Also, your fetish, believe it or not, is *not* the fundamental problem in your marriage. Furthermore, you can't choose to have it or not . . .
>
> Let's clear up one fantasy that I think most of us entertain. While it is true that many smokers claim to truly enjoy smoking and the like (and I'm sure many are telling the truth), the fact is that most smokers do not smoke because they enjoy it. They smoke because they are addicted to the nicotine contained in tobacco, and because it has become a habit, and they thus far lack the discipline or "willpower" to quit . . . Chances are your wife smokes out of habit and not because she enjoys it. Disengage your selective thinking (you *want* to believe she smokes because she enjoys it) and perhaps you'll see this.

Mike seems to have forgotten that Anonymous said he knew his wife smoked only because she was "addicted." Continuing, he refers to the five years Anonymous speaks of during which his wife would often smoke while they made love, and "at long last I had achieved what I had always wanted" and his wife said she was quite happy doing it—some of the time:

> This is a little unclear. Did she like it or not? Doesn't matter; your sex life at this point became dependent on the satisfaction of your fetish, which was bad news, as you now know. This is why masturbation and fetishism can be a problem for some; some let them replace the intimacy that provides for a good relationship. Suddenly, the pleasure of sex has little to do with the partner you're having it with, and more to do with the inanimate object that comprises your fetish. It's ok to have sex that involves a fetish, but if you begin to require it then it's all downhill from there.

He tells Anonymous that his job problems are irrelevant: "You will always have other problems, and you were using this as an excuse for her to wait to quit. If it hadn't been that particular problem, it would have been another. Remember it's her body, and for you to want her to smoke for your sake is selfish. Sorry."

He also advises Anonymous not to waste his money on hypnotherapy.

> You cannot "rid" yourself of the fetish, and the sooner you accept that, the better off you'll be. You are who are, and you are not responsible for your feelings, only your behavior. Again, your statement that you're not comfortable with this is key. Are you starting to figure out what your *real* problem is yet? I can tell you that it has little to do with your wife . . .
>
> Instead of focusing on something you can't control, why don't you focus on something you can? That something would be your *behavior*, or the way you act on your fetish. There is more than one way to satisfy it, you know. Most of us thrive on pictures, stories, our imagination, you name it. But the more you beat yourself up for having something you can't get rid of anyway, the less productive your nonproductivity becomes. Stop focusing your energies on something that can't be helped, and focus your energy instead where it can be put to good use . . . I would bet my life savings (a high five figures!) that you have other problems in your marriage besides this one, and I'd bet my house that most of them are more immediately threatening than this one. Look to those things first, because your fetish problem is just that: YOURS. It is not your wife's problem, and it's not something she can deal with or help you to deal with. . . You are creating nonexistent problems for yourself, probably in order to avoid or deny the real problems that you're having. The key is to practice some critical thinking, and discard the garbage that's clouding the issue.

Mike's analysis is at least as useful as Anonymous would get if he paid a therapist 200 dollars an hour to listen to his story. (Any right-thinking psychologist would surely second the assertion that smoking is an addiction and that nobody *really* enjoys it—more's the pity). The sympathetic advice from his fellow fetishists is in fact probably even more helpful to Anonymous than that which a professional shrink could give him because they share and understand his fetish. They have "been there."

Is THIS FETISH something new under the sun? That is, has it emerged only in the past 30 or so years since the surgeon general's report and the ensuing onslaught of antismoking propaganda? Or did it exist back in "the old days" too? If it did, was it as "secret" and as guilt-inducing as it is today? It would be interesting to know.

To end this subject, one last letter from *Smoke Signals*, from "Kevin":

> I would also like to offer a comment on the current anti-smoking movement and how it relates to my own smoking fetish. It seems that every time I hear of some new plan or law whose ultimate purpose is to eradicate smoking from society altogether, I experience a very uncomfortable emotional mix of resentment and anger, and then guilt for feeling that way in the first place. I think that we smoking fetishists are in the unique and somewhat unfortunate position of having as our primary source of sexual excitement something which at one time society indicated was perfectly acceptable and "good" but is now deemed to be unacceptable and "bad" . . .
>
> I often wonder what it would be like if even half of the adult male population had a smoking fetish. I wonder where that would put our contingent of anti-smoking fascists. I wonder what it would be like if *I* didn't have a smoking fetish.

Well, Kevin, I share your resentment of and anger toward the antismoking movement. But unlike you, I don't feel guilty about my anger. I just get angrier, and feel only sadness that young people like you today have no memory of how it used to be, when smoking, if not necessarily deemed to be "good," was a perfectly normal and socially acceptable thing.

The emotional confusion that many of the smoking fetishists seem to suffer is another consequence of the demonizing of tobacco and smoking. How much better off everyone would be if people could simply enjoy smoking—without guilt, without shame, without health worries, with or without fetishes.

Chapter 10

THOSE UNTAMABLE TEENS

We've got a major problem with young people smoking in this country. If we're going to do something as a society to make it more difficult for young people to smoke, we've got to intervene directly.

— William Roper[1]

If teens want to smoke, they're going to smoke, whether the government or parents like it or not!

— Allison, age 13[2]

IF UMPTEEN THOUSAND studies reporting the health dangers of smoking haven't been enough to convince more than four-fifths of Americans not to smoke; if millions perversely persist in this self-destructive practice even at the cost of being made outcasts from polite (and politically correct) society and virtually relegated to second-class citizenship through employment discrimination and draconian restrictions on smoking in public places; if despite everything we are still as far from a "smoke-free society" as when former Surgeon General C. Everett Koop proclaimed the goal, there is yet another—perhaps the ultimate and most insidious—stratagem of the antismokers that even the most hardened smoker can scarcely disapprove of: *Save the Children.*

The first clipping I have on this aspect of the antismoking crusade—though certainly not the first I could cite had I begun collecting them earlier—dates back to July 1992.

(Fortunately for the length of this book, I did not start prowling the Internet until 1995 and thereby gain access to the electronic archives of some 120 newspapers in this country and abroad, as well as to a plethora of smoking sites—overwhelmingly anti, only a few pro—on the World Wide Web, or my pile of smoking-related articles would be even higher. It has been hard enough to choose which ones to cite and which ones to pass over out of literally hundreds.)

"Frustrated CDC [Centers for Disease Control and Prevention] urges states: Raise legal age for buying cigarettes to 19" was the heading in an *Atlanta Journal-Constitution* article, from which the quotation above by then CDC Director William Roper was taken.

In addition to declaring 19 as the legal age for smoking, the CDC would urge the states to create agencies for licensing and monitoring the sale of tobacco to teens, Roper announced. (And, purely incidentally, create a lot of new employment opportunities for deserving bureaucrats along the way).

At that time, every state but two had set 18 as the legal smoking age. It was 17 in Georgia and Montana didn't regulate minors' access to tobacco at all. New Mexico regulated only smokeless tobacco. But only six states had laws penalizing underage teens for cigarette possession, and selling to a minor was merely a misdemeanor in all 49 states where teenage tobacco use was regulated, although the penalty in Washington for selling to a minor was severe: up to a year in jail and a $5,000 fine.

Despite the laws, the CDC found that "at least" 70 percent of the country's 2.6 million smokers younger than 18 had successfully bought cigarettes or other tobacco products "at least once" in 1989 (the latest year for which statistics were then available).[3] Of those 2.6 million, more than half—1.5 million—regularly bought their own cigarettes, and of that number 84.5 percent purchased them at small stores or gas stations. Only 14.5 percent reported ever getting cigarettes from vending machines.

(Two years later, though, the Food and Drug Administration would report that "Vending machines are a primary source of tobacco products for young smokers," with 22 percent of 13-year-olds using them compared with two percent of 17-year-olds.[4] Whether that meant that more of the youngest youngsters were getting their cigs from vending machines, possibly because they couldn't pass for 18 like 17-year-olds could and buy them at the store counter, or whether it's simply a matter of different antismoking axes being ground in different ways by different people at different times, your guess is as good as mine.)

The children's crusade began to get rolling as 1993 dawned. In Sunday papers on January 3, cartoonist Garry Trudeau took up most of his "Doonesbury" strip with a sign which his character Mr. Butts urged boys and girls to cut out and tape to the window of their favorite store "to show your appreciation" for the risk the store takes by illegally purveying tobacco to them. "This Store Sells Cigarettes to Minors! A Mr. Butts Salute!" the sign read. Be sure to make lots of copies, Mr. Butts advised, in case the store owner takes the sign down.[5] (To his credit, Trudeau didn't use the loaded words "kids" or "children.")

In February, the Associated Press reported that the CDC had given Georgia, New Mexico and Montana until September to make 18 the legal age for buying tobacco products or lose federal health funds. Noncompliance would cost those states $3 million, $7 million and $3 million respectively.[6]

In April 1993 I clipped the first of a continuing series of articles alerting Americans to the increasing use of smokeless tobacco by teens and warning about the dangers thereof.[7] As for smoking though, it wasn't until late 1993 and early 1994 that the warning bells began to be rung in earnest. In December, John Pierce of the University of California-San Diego, reported at the first scientific conference of the California Tobacco-Related Disease Research Program in San Francisco that "while adults have dropped it like a stone," smoking by teenagers suddenly began to rise in 1988 after declining about one percent a year over the previous 15 years.[8]

Even worse, in February 1994, in a survey of some 50,000 teenagers in grades eight, 10 and 12 at more than 400 schools, University of Michigan researchers found that not only was teenage tobacco smoking up but marijuana use was two to four percentage points higher in 1993 than in 1992. The use of stimulants, LSD and inhalants had also risen in all three grades.[9]

"These findings . . . are an urgent alarm we must heed at once," said Department of Health and Human Services secretary Donna E. Shalala.[10]

I later came across an editorial in an offbeat—*way* offbeat—newsletter called *Smoke Signals* (see Chapter 9) that critiqued either this or some other University of Michigan study in greater detail and is worth quoting from at length.

The writer first cited some figures from the study, which he said were widely disseminated by Action on Smoking and Health (ASH): that smoking among eighth graders increased 30 percent between 1991 and 1994 (from 14.3 percent to 18.6 percent), smoking among tenth graders increased 20 percent (from 20.8 percent to 25.4 percent), and that the rate of smoking among high school seniors now exceeded the adult smoking rate, increasing from 27.8 percent to 31.2 percent during the three-year period studied.

He then commented (all emphases in original):

> Of course, what *isn't* said by ASH is also interesting. For example, they don't define 'smoking' in their writeup. Are these students smoking every day? Every week? Every month? Or is it defined, as is often the case in these surveys, as having *tried* smoking? They don't mention that in 1976, nearly *40* percent of high school seniors smoked (meaning that over the past twenty years, smoking among high school seniors has *declined* nearly 25 percent), nor do they offer similar statistics for previous decades when Joe Camel wasn't around to bear the blame . . .
>
> They blame "cartoon characters in cigarette ads, more smoking in movies and on TV, low prices of brands kids like, and universal availability to kids." Somehow, this seems a bit disingenuous at best. Can they cite one other example of behavior that's been drastically affected by cartoon characters? (Perhaps an incredible rise in the use of Acme dynamite to blow up coyotes in the 60s?) Do they really believe there's more smoking on TV now than in the 50s, or more smoking in movies now than in the 40s? . . . And do they really think that cigarettes are more available to kids now than in the 50s and 60s? Give us a very large break.
>
> Finally, the study attacks tobacco advertising, because the students surveyed believed that ads promote the benefits of smoking. Among 16- and 17-year-olds surveyed, 76.2 % said ads show smoking as enjoyable, 73% said ads show smoking as relaxing, and 67% said ads show it as a way to reduce stress. Imagine that. How dare the tobacco companies use their advertising to show positive aspects of their product (and aspects to which many, if not most, smokers would attest)! Obviously, we've just missed seeing beef and egg industry ads revealing cholesterol levels and automakers' ads dealing with pollution and crash rates. And do the anti-smoking forces really *believe* that cigarette advertising today goes further than the endorsement ads by doctors in the 40s, or the beautifully done TV ads of the 60s?
>
> What's our point? Just a suggestion that, in addition to being delighted (as we are) to see smoking rates increasing among young

> people, we should notice the lengths to which the anti-smoking forces will go, and whenever possible, make sure that simplistic statements by the anti-smokers don't go unchallenged."[11]

I can't vouch for the writer's counter-statistics, but it is an unfortunate fact that the statistics put forward by the antis, much less their logic, are *never* challenged in the mainstream media.

THE AMERICAN MEDICAL Association soon joined the rising chorus. In the eighth annual tobacco issue of its *Journal* (JAMA) in February, the association reported on a study that found that children in some areas, predominantly minority neighborhoods, were buying single cigarettes called "loosies" for 25 cents each at the corner store. The study involved 206 retail stores, 49 percent of which sold single cigarettes and 93 percent of those cigarettes to children.[12]

Another study cited in that issue of JAMA claimed that Virginia Slims advertising and other campaigns aimed at adolescent girls had pushed smoking rates for girls aged 11 to 17 up by 110 percent from 1967 to 1973.

I can believe this. At least, I seem to see young girls smoking everywhere these days, something I haven't seen for a long time. For example, a few years ago, during a visit to Richmond, where our son then lived, my wife and I were having lunch in the Cloverleaf Mall food court. I watched two very pretty and very young girls (pardon, young women), not teenagers but no older than their early 20s, smoking cigarettes as they chatted at a nearby table. By the time we left, one girl had lit a second cigarette. Just like the old days, I thought. (The Cloverleaf Mall, by the way, is one of the few left in the country that still permit smoking, at least at this writing. Could it be because Richmond is the headquarters of Philip Morris?)

When we got home I dug up the yellowed manuscript of a novel I had started several decades before while in college and had never finished about a boy's coming of intellectual age. ("Write what you know," the writers' magazines always advised.) In one chapter my protagonist, Tom, makes his first visit to the Student Union at his university. To one side of the entrance he found a large room, with every table filled with students either eating food obtained from a snack bar at one end or playing bridge.

> Tom looked at the girls. There was little to distinguish them except for variations in sizes and shapes. They were all dressed nearly identically—sweaters, skirts and bobby socks. Some were what could properly be called "sweater girls," but for the most part their forms were shrouded in the large, bulky coverings. They were not much different from high school girls, Tom thought, though probably they would have been offended by the comparison. For they were *college* girls, and they could smoke, he observed . . . He was just a little shocked to see these nice little high school girls sitting around playing cards and smoking.

Not that my protagonist disapproved of smoking, by girls or by anybody else. Far from it. It was just that he had never seen so many girls smoking in one bunch. Or rather, *I* hadn't (it was—what else?—a semiautobiographical first novel). Fast forward 50 years. No doubt many of those girls who smoked cigarettes in their youth have joined the dear departed. Derive from that whatever lesson you wish.

It was on another trip, a visit to my wife's sister in Marlborough, Massachusetts, in the summer of 1997 that I saw four preteen girls flourishing what looked like skinny cigarettes outside the Wayside Country Store on Route 9 near Sudbury. They were holding them in their fingers and up to their mouths just like cigarettes. I realized they were candy cigarettes. I hadn't seen them since I was a child myself and didn't think they were made anymore.

I asked one of the girls where they'd gotten them and she said inside the candy store. Sure enough, there were several different "brands" of candy cigarettes behind one counter, made by a company in Brooklyn, New York. One with an all-red box was a dead ringer for Pall Mall, except that it was called "King's." Others (aping the "Marlboro Country" theme?) were "Round Up" and "Stallion." For 20 cents I bought a box with the most cigarette-sounding name—"Lucky Lights." Inside were 10 sticks of hard candy, about the length of a regular cigarette. They were just as I remembered them, including the red coloring at their tips to simulate a lighted cigarette. There was a "Nutrition Facts" label on the box that hadn't been there in the old days, but no surgeon general's warning.

It did my heart good to see those young girls practicing "smoking." There were two women with them, presumably their mothers, who did not seem to be at all concerned about it. Maybe there's a future for smoking after all.

JAMA's report prompted the Coalition for Smoking OR Health —composed of the American Medical Association, the American Cancer Society, the American Heart Association and the American Lung Association-March of Dimes—to reiterate a call for the Federal Trade Commission to ban advertising targeted on children. "This isn't toothpaste we're talking about," said chairman Scott D. Ballin, "but a product that's addictive and deadly."[13]

The biggest event of 1994, of course, was the release in February of the 314-page surgeon general's report: "Preventing Tobacco Use Among Young People."[14] This, the 23rd edition in the series "Smoking and Health," chronicled, among other things, the marketing practices of the tobacco industry from the candy cigarettes of yore* to the sponsorship of racing cars and the peddling of cigarette lighters, T-shirts and other paraphernalia emblazoned with brand logos.

"Smoking is not just an adult habit," said Surgeon General Joycelyn Elders. "It is an adolescent addiction."[15] (Although Dr. Elders later got the boot because of a remark on teaching teenagers about masturbation—*about* it, not how to do it—it may have been just as well that she resigned. Any surgeon general who calls smoking among adults merely a "habit" is not fit to wear the uniform of the U.S. Public Health Service.) The report issued under her aegis stated that more than 70 percent of persons who become daily smokers do so by age 18.[16]

This revelation falls a bit short of terrifically surprising. By age 18, most adolescents have initiated all kinds of adult behavior—driving cars, working at jobs and opening their own bank accounts, voting, joining the services, embarking on college and careers, even marrying or otherwise having (or obsessing about) sex, and so on.

Dr. Elders did not have the benefit of more recent "knowledge" about teenage smoking. It's not just an "adolescent addiction" anymore but a "pediatric disease," with the definition of "pediatric" having been expanded to include, at a minimum, everybody too young to vote or join the military services.[17]

*Evidently the surgeon general wasn't aware of what was going on in Marlborough, Massachusetts, and still going on as late as 1997. I hope I haven't inadvertently alerted the antismoking movement that at least one company is still making candy cigarettes. But then, the antis wouldn't read this book anyway.

She also said that teenagers who smoke run higher risks of experimenting with alcohol and drugs, doing poorly in school, fighting, engaging in unsafe sex and even attempting suicide. Again, more recent "research"—or is it just entrenched antismoking prejudice?—backs her up. From the February 1996 *Journal of the Florida Medical Association*:

> [C]igarette smoking by youth is alarming because it is highly correlated with other problem behaviors that contribute to premature morbidity and mortality. Tobacco is generally the first drug or gateway substance used by young people.
>
> Adolescent users also are more likely than nonusers to be concurrent users of alcohol and illegal drugs. In addition, youth smokers are statistically more likely to get into fights, carry weapons, attempt suicide, and involve themselves in high-risk sexual behaviors.[18]*

Since that issue of the journal was devoted to the grave problem of smoking in Florida, especially among youths, it is worth noting that according to one prosmoking (or, more accurately, anti-antismoking) writer, that same year a nationwide state-by-state ranking of children's well-being in terms of rates of juvenile crime, teen pregnancy, poverty and education placed Florida's children *third from the bottom* of the 50 states. "Were it not so tragic it would be ludicrous to focus our resources on teen smoking when national statistics show the depth of the truly serious problems facing our children," she commented.[20]

If all this stuff about smoking leading to antisocial or self-endangering behavior is true, these problems should have been worse back when teenage smoking was more prevalent than it is today. Maybe teenagers were different when I was one, but I don't recall any connection between smoking and kids who were poor scholars, or with fighting. The only fights I was ever in were in grade school, long before any of us could be said to have become "addicted" to cigarettes. As for alcohol, I don't recall any of that either. I didn't taste my first beer, let alone hard liquor, until I was in college, though that may have been because my parents didn't drink. Of the thousands of kids who passed through

*The American Cancer Society puts it the other way around: "Statistics . . . show that students who use other drugs, get in fights, carry weapons, attempt suicide, and engage in high-risk sexual behaviors are more likely to smoke."[19] There is, I think, a subtle but important distinction.

Avalon High between 1936 and 1948 when my siblings and I attended, none ever attempted suicide. The only death in all that time was of a boy killed during football practice. And with a possible exception or two that had nothing to do with smoking, back in the dark ages when I grew up there was no sex at all for teenagers, safe or unsafe.

Drug use was also unheard of among teenagers, of course, so I cannot say that if illegal drugs had been as easy to obtain as they apparently are today I would not have been tempted to fool around with them. But if today's teenagers who smoke are really more liable to experiment with drugs, that may be less a matter of cause-and-effect than due to the antis' elevation of tobacco to an evil on a par with hard drugs—and in the process unwittingly minimizing the dangers of the latter. If a hit of nicotine is just as bad as a hit of marijuana or cocaine or heroin, if all are equally taboo, it should not be surprising if those youths rebellious enough to smoke cigarettes might go through the "gateway" and try the others too—especially in view of their omnipresent availability, which years of antidrug efforts and millions of antidrug dollars expended by the federal government have not been able to stem and in fact have made the drug problem worse.

I have seen only one chapter of the surgeon general's 1994 report on tobacco use among young people, Chapter Four: "Psychosocial Risk Factors for Initiating Tobacco Use." But just that one examined every aspect of teenage smoking down to the proverbial gnat's eyelash. It cited various studies which found, for examples: that low educational attainment among fathers was predictive of smoking onset in middle-school youth; that both adolescent females at all grade levels and adolescent males in grade 9 through 11 who smoked had parents with fewer years of formal education than the parents of nonsmoking peers (but the educational attainment of parents of 7th- and 8th-grade males was not predictive of anything), and that starting to smoke in childhood is "associated" with living in a single-parent home (page 127). Further, that adolescent girls who smoke are more socially skilled than their nonsmoking peers (page 128); that adolescents with parents who currently smoked were more than twice as likely to smoke as those whose parents had never smoked, yet, curiously, that those whose parents had quit smoking were *three* times as likely to smoke (page 129).

To refine it even further, one study documented that adolescents who reported that their parents were generally supportive of them were less likely to begin smoking or to become regular smokers than those who perceived that their parents were generally not supportive of them (page 132). Also, that among the youngest subjects—10 through 12 years old—those who perceived that their parents were more strict than other parents were more likely to begin smoking but that among the oldest subjects—14 through 16—those who perceived that they had stricter parents were *less* likely to begin to smoke. As for kids aged 13 to 14, for some reason they apparently were not affected by parental strictness, or the absence thereof (page 133).

Make of it all what you can. But note the word "reported" above. As in all studies about smoking, the researchers are entirely dependent upon what the subjects tell them. I can visualize them passing out questionnaires to a group of kids with questions like: "Do you smoke cigarettes? If yes, how often—Once a month, Once a week, Every day?" Followed by: "Do you think your parents are too strict with you—Always, Sometimes, Never?" And Johnny whispering to the boy next to him, "*Psst*, what'd you put down for number four?"

Then of course there is the matter of influences other than the parental. For example, the SG's report noted that a 10-year longitudinal* study found a positive relationship between an older sibling's smok-

*There are three main types of epidemiological studies: 1) cohort, or prospective, in which a group of people with different levels of exposure to a particular health risk are followed over a period of time to see what happens to their health; 2) case control, or retrospective, which investigates the past exposure of a group of people with a particular health condition and those without it to infer why certain subjects (the "cases") became ill and others (the "controls") did not; 3) cross-sectional, or longitudinal, which compares groups of people in terms of their current health and exposure status and assesses their similarities. (There is a fourth kind of study, the occupational, whose subjects are working people with particular jobs or exposures and which can be either cohort, case control or cross-sectional.)

According to Dr. Daniel J. Wartenberg of the Environmental and Occupational Health Sciences Institute at Rutgers University, the cohort study "is a desirable design because exposure precedes the health outcome—a condition necessary for causation—and is less subject to bias because exposure is evaluated before the health outcome is known. It is also expensive, time-consuming and the most difficult logistically of all the studies . . . The main advantage of the case control study is that it enables us to study rare health outcomes without having to follow thousands of people, and is therefore generally quicker, cheaper, and easier to conduct than the cohort study. Primary disad-

ing and a younger sibling's beginning to smoke (page 130). In another study, best friend's cigarette use was predictive of the first try at smoking, whereas having a majority of friends who smoke was predictive of the second cigarette (page 131). As for the third cigarette, the surgeon general sayeth not. Obviously, further studies were in order.

By way of adding to the world's store of worthless knowledge, one team of researchers cited by the SG proposed the theory that adolescents "construct shared social environments in which they perceive themselves and other(s) [parentheses in original for some reason—D.O.] as having mutual cognitive, emotional, and valuative reactions . . . [T]he intersubjectivity created by sharing generates a sense of wellness. This sense of mutuality enhances the attractiveness of the group and may lead to incorporation of the self-image of the others into the image of one's own self" (page 131).

Translated from the "sociologese": kids make friends with kids, kids share kid interests, kids like to pal around with other kids, kids imitate each other. Sounds much like what adults do with other adults.

In what may have been one useful, if hardly surprising, revelation in the report, several studies reached the conclusion that "Knowledge of the long-term health consequences of smoking has not been a strong predictor of adolescent onset . . . perhaps because . . . many adolescents feel inherently invulnerable in their characteristically short-term view" (page 135).

So much for the value of all those warnings.

In response to the surgeon general's report, R. J. Reynolds issued a statement claiming that peer influence and parental example "are the reasons why youth smoke . . . If we believed Camel advertising caused youth to start smoking who otherwise would not, we would voluntarily pull the campaign without any outside urging."

Sure they would. Reynolds later did retire Joe Camel, but apparenly

---

vantages: There's a greater potential for bias, since we know the health status before the exposure is determined." As for the cross-sectional or longitudinal study, "the main advantage is that [it] is a particularly easy study to conduct, as we do not have to wait for the health outcome to occur or estimate what the level of exposure was likely to have been years ago. Its main disadvantages are [*sic*] that *we can't infer a cause* because we're only looking at current health and exposure."[21] [Emphasis added.]

because he had outlived his usefulness, not because he was seducing youth.

On February 21 the company released a Roper poll it had commissioned showing that 90 percent of kids aged 10 to 17 recognized such ad icons as the Energizer Bunny and the Keebler elves, compared with 73 percent who recognized Joe Camel, and only three percent of those who recognized Joe said they liked cigarettes or that smoking was okay.[22] Of course, anything a tobacco company says is even more worthless than my personal anecdotes.

To jump briefly to 1995, on August 28 of that year then FDA Commissioner David A. Kessler, M.D. was a guest on National Public Radio's "Talk of the Nation" discussing smoking with a group of teenagers. He asked them to name the most heavily advertised brands of cigarettes and the answer was Marlboro, Camel and Newport. And what where the most popular brands among teenagers? Same answer.

"Do you think that's by accident?" he said. He then asked them to name the most common brands among adults, and answered for them: "The generic brands. Adults want to buy the cheapest cigarette."[23]

Which may be presumptive evidence of the power of cigarette advertising over teenagers. But it should also be acknowledged that teenagers are brand-name conscious in just about everything, from shoes to underwear to designer jeans, all of which are heavily advertised. Teenagers favor Marlboro over discount cigarettes for the same reason they buy Reeboks or Nikes instead of cheaper knock-off brands. And having fewer financial responsibilities than adults, like meeting the monthly mortgage payment, they also tend to be less frugal than adults.

(Speaking of teaching kids about the dangers of smoking, one Damien Christopher Xaros was arrested in Wilson, North Carolina, on charges of recruiting teenage boys for sadomasochistic sex acts and "slave parties." Police said Xaros, 22, lured teenagers to his home in Port Lucie, Florida, while preaching to them "that alcohol, cigarettes and drugs were harmful."[24] Let's hope the court took that into consideration.)

While steadfastly maintaining that their advertising is solely designed to persuade adult smokers to switch brands (or remain loyal to their current brand),[25] the tobacco industry later climbed on the save-the-children bandwagon with great alacrity, announcing programs to prevent youth smoking. Probably the most loudly trumpeted in newspaper ads was Phillip Morris's "Action Against Access," which among other things called for the licensing of cigarette retailers and cutting off marketing support to stores convicted of selling to minors.

Not only were smoking opponents less than impressed by this but the company's own retailers accused it of shifting the blame for kids' smoking from itself onto a convenient scapegoat. "It is disappointing that the priorities of the largest tobacco manufacturer in the nation have degenerated to posturing blame," someone at the National Association of Convenience Stores wrote Phillip Morris. "Your plan will certainly punish our industry for these events, but it will not solve the problem."[26]

To the antismokers, of course, "Action Against Access" was merely another tobacco industry "smoke screen." Advertisements publicizing an R. J. Reynolds youth smoking prevention campaign moved columnist Ellen Goodman to write: "I have built up some resistance to hypocrisy over the years. But the offer to help kids resist peer pressure is too much even for my immune system. Peer pressure doesn't come out of the ozone. These guys created it in their marketing lab."[27]

Backing up Ms. Goodman, the same month her column appeared researchers at the University of California-San Diego claimed that "Tobacco promotions, not peer pressure, have the most powerful influence over teenagers who become new smokers."[28] If so, then the question is, why should tobacco promotions be so much more influential than antismoking promotions aimed at teens?

The researchers tracked four major cigarette marketing campaigns over the past 100 years and found that, "In each case, the start of the campaign was associated with increasing number of those who were targeted—either adolescent boys or girls—taking up smoking."

One can only marvel at their ability to discover the number of boys or girls taking up smoking a century ago. One also wonders how much is in the eye of the beholder. For instance, Bob Gordon of the "San Francisco Gay Lesbian Bisexual Transgender Tobacco Free Project" (I didn't make that up!) thought he saw ads that targeted young gays.

"In this one ad that's up in a grocery store in the Castro, a life-size Joe Camel looks like a gay guy," he said. "Joe Camel is pictured wearing jeans and boots, looking cool and gay."[29]

And as long as we're in the City by the Bay, we might mention the emotional complaint of San Francisco Supervisor Angela Alioto, who called for a ban on outdoor advertising of tobacco-related products near schools, playgrounds and recreation centers.

"It's criminal the way the tobacco industry has preyed on young people, enticing them with cartoon figures like Joe Camel. Well, Joe Camel won't die of lung cancer, but our young people will."[30]

(Other people claimed that Old Joe was a deliberate phallic symbol—his nose looked like a penis. This is something that I, in my innocence, have been unable to discern.)

The cigarette companies' programs ostensibly aimed at discouraging teenage smoking were, of course, initiated with the hope of taking some of the heat off themselves. It would also seem to have been a can't-lose proposition for them because they know intuitively something that the antis seem constitutionally unable to recognize: the more something is made taboo, the greater its attractiveness to young people.

One exception may be Dr. Joseph R. DiFranza of the University of Massachusetts Medical School, who alerted us back in Chapter 3 about all those smoking-induced miscarriages. Tobacco industry campaigns advising children "to make mature decisions about smoking" and "portraying smoking as an adult activity actually encourage children to smoke by making smoking appear to be a desirable 'forbidden fruit,'" he said.[31]

So once again we see that the industry can't win for losing, no matter what it does.

At the time of this writing an intramural argument was going on among antismoking activists over the wisdom of so much concentration on youthful smoking, but not for the reason alleged by Dr. DiFranza.

According to Robin Hobart of Americans for Non-Smokers Rights, "When you reframe the goal from a smokefree society to not wanting kids to smoke, it really narrows what you can do about issues like secondhand smoke."[32]

No less than Stanton Glantz warned: "The antitobacco movement has careened off the narrow path because they know it's noncontroversial. But it is probably counterproductive. A kid-centered program is doomed to fail."[33]

And in an editorial in the tobacco trade journal, *Tobacco International*, Editor-in-chief Frank Bocchino wrote, "At times it seems like the anti-smoking forces are actually trying to encourage smoking among teenagers." He contended that warning teenagers about the dangers of smoking is a subtle attempt to make it more appealing to them because if everybody stopped smoking the advocates would be put out of work.[34]

That may be reaching just a wee bit far, but the antis should certainly not be privileged against questions about their true motives and no doubt many of them would have to look for other employment if smoking were eliminated. There are others, who are neither antismoking activists nor dupes of Big Tobacco, who argue that the campaign against teenage smoking is wrongheaded.

In an article posted on the Heritage Foundation's Web page,[35] Edwin Feulner, president of the foundation, lit into the Food and Drug Administration's proposed regulations to ban cigarette vending machines and self-service displays in stores, the use of tobacco brand names on T-shirts, hats, keychains and lighters and to prohibit brand-name sponsorship of sporting events such as the Virginia Slims tournament. He cited the warning of a former Heritage Foundation intern, Jennifer Murray, that these regulations, far from preventing teens from smoking, "by focusing additional attention on the forbidden, could actually entice them."[36]

This is the same FDA, Feulner reminded, "that conducted the 1991 raid that captured 24,000 half-gallons of Citrus Hill 'fresh choice' orange juice because the agency didn't like the way the o.j. was labeled! Are the food and drug police now going to swoop down on every mom and pop grocery store to make sure teen employees aren't smoking in the boy's room?"

To say it yet again, all I know about smoking is based on personal experience and observation. My wife says that it was her best friend who introduced her to smoking at age 16. For myself, if any one thing influenced me, and probably all my contemporaries who smoked, it was simply what seemed to be the near-universality of smoking in the society we grew up in. I realize in saying this that I'm lending support to the antismoking activists who maintain that cigarette advertising does precisely that: gives youngsters the impression that more people smoke than actually do and that smoking is acceptable behavior. But it wasn't advertising, it was adult example. I still remember one of our teachers, Mr. Dean, a very handsome young man and an assistant football coach whom all the girls adored, standing in front of class with a package of cigarettes visible in his shirt pocket. No doubt he eventually quit smoking, as most of his generation did, but in any case he lived long enough to attend my sister's 50th high school reunion, so his youthful smoking did not seriously shorten his life.

(That reminds me that when I was about 10, one of my sister's boyfriends came to our house. He had been to Havana and brought back some Cuban cigarettes. They were unusual in that the paper was either coated with or impregnated with sugar. He let me touch my tongue to one of them to taste the sweetness.)

"Peer influence" and advertising were part of that picture, but while they may have been reinforcements toward smoking, they were not *causes* in and of themselves. Yet people my age, even nonsmokers, can probably remember some of the old cigarette advertising campaigns: "Chesterfield, they satisfy." "I'd walk a mile for a Camel." "Not a cough in a carload"—also Camel, I think. On radio, bellboy Johnny's "Call for Philip *Moor . . . iss*." On television, the dancing Old Gold packs and the May West-like suggestion by the Muriel cigar to "Pick me up and smoke me sometime." Several slogans by Lucky Strike still stick in my mind, the first from way back: "Life in the raw is seldom mild"—vividly illustrated in one magazine ad by the Romans' rape of the Sabine women (I wondered what rape meant); "So round, so firm, so fully packed, so free and easy on the draw"; "LS/MFT—Lucky Strike means fine tobacco"; "Tear and compare"—which urged smokers to see for themselves how firmly packed a Lucky was by tearing a strip down the length of one. Not only was I never a Lucky Strike smoker but even if I had been I certainly wouldn't have wasted one by dismantling it!

I can state categorically that it wasn't because of parental example. My mother never smoked and my father quit cigarettes for cigars and pipes, which I didn't like, long before I wanted to smoke cigarettes. The only thing that might be construed to have been parental influence was the absence of an outright condemnation of smoking by them. (What they did condemn was the prevalence of drinking in the movies we attended as a family every Monday evening on "Bank Night," especially "The Thin Man" series starring William Powell and Myrna Loy. My father didn't live to see "Dallas" on television). Obviously, having parents who smoke could encourage a young person to try smoking himself. Yet both my son and stepson grew up (healthy, by the way) in households where both parents smoked, and neither of them has ever smoked. They are both, in fact, staunch smoke-haters.

I can't explain this in my stepson, who was an adult before I married his mother. But for many years I thought I may have been the direct cause of my son's aversion to smoking. One day, back when he was just a toddler, I was sitting in my chair and had just lit a cigarette when he suddenly climbed onto my lap and was struck by the full force of both my initial exhale and fumes from the match I'd used to light the cigarette. His little face contorted and his eyes closed and he coughed and he quickly scrambled away from me.

I felt very bad about that and when I later read about an "aversion therapy" in which smokers trying to quit were forced to smoke continuously in a closed room, breathing in their own firsthand and secondhand smoke until they were thoroughly sickened, I wondered if that episode with my son explained his intense dislike of smoking.

Turns out it wasn't that, however. Only recently he told me that the reason he had never started to smoke was having been shown a picture of a smoker's diseased lungs in the fifth grade. Was it really a smoker's lungs and was the damage really caused by smoking? Who knows, but it worked for him.

Had I been born in 1977 instead of 1927 and been subjected throughout my growing-up years to such antismoking images and messages, I really can't say if I would be a smoker today (although I'd probably have taken it up just to spite the moralists). But I was always very respectful of authority and no doubt I would have believed—at least until experience and observation told me otherwise—everything the antismokers said. Let me quote some of the things today's youngsters are being told:

One example appeared in the "You Can" science-for-kids panel that runs in Sunday newspaper comic sections and also has a site on the Web. Among children who were awarded microscopes by "You Can" for coming up with things to research was one girl who "studied the stinking, lousy, tragic, self-loathing, dirty, disgusting addiction of cigarette smoking."[37]

Another was a 1995 Dave Barry column in which he gave this argument against smoking: "It's a repulsive addiction that slowly but surely turns you into a gasping, gray-skinned, tumor-ridden invalid, hacking up brownish gobs of toxic waste from your one remaining lung."[38] (Surely you made that one up, Dave.)

I also suspect a wee bit of exaggeration in a testimonial by Maria Mastriana, age 16, that appeared in the "Fresh Voices" feature in *Parade* magazine: "Yeah, I do enjoy it [smoking]. But I actually coughed up black chunks, which was really bad. Tar, piece of lung, whatever. So I basically cut down."[39]

My spit used to be black after I had shoveled coal into the coal bin when I was a kid back in Pittsburgh, but I've never coughed up "chunks" of tar or a piece of lung, whatever. It just goes to show that kids can be as inventive as adults when it comes to antismoking horror stories, especially when they know that's what the adults want to hear.

For an extreme example of antismoking propaganda, there was a letter in Ann Landers's column in March 1996. A mother wrote that she "got the scare of my life" when the principal of her daughter's school called and said that her daughter had fainted in class and to please come and get her. It seems that the girl's health and hygiene class had showed a film about what happens to people who smoke, with "very graphic photos" of diseased lungs and cancer-ridden patients. The mother was furious with the school for making her daughter sick and asked Ann's opinion of this.

"I think it's wonderful," said Ann. "I wish more young students would get sick and faint from such pictures. Then perhaps fewer adults would die from lung cancer and heart disease."[40]

In other words, if reason and logic don't work, try terror. That letter to Ann reminds me of a film they showed us in Army basic training graphically illustrating the physical and mental effects of tertiary syphilis. We considered it a welcome and entertaining break from drill.

In 1995, as a feature of that year's "Great American Smokeout," the American Cancer Society launched on the World Wide Web its "first-ever national anti-smoking event targeted at teens—The Great American SmokeScream . . . One of the main attractions of the site is sure to be Clungs!"[41]

The game of Clungs! presented multiple-choice questions about smoking. After each correct answer, the blackened lungs of teen characters "Lisa" and "Larry" were gradually cleared out, and through the wonders of digital technology, they became a healthy pink.

"By the time the lungs are back in good shape, those who have played the game have learned some great (and fun) facts about smoking and why they are 'too smart to start,'" said Steve Dickinson, national vice president of public relations for the society.

Speaking of "fun facts" about smoking, my brother in California found some in his local newspaper and sent them to me.[42] Among those that parents could tell their teenagers were:

• Tobacco contains nicotine, which is used in blowguns to kill moneys in the jungle.

(Dumb me, I always thought it was curare. Of course, pure nicotine would do the same job but I don't know if the natives in the Amazon have access to it.)

• Cigarettes contain acetone (nail polish remover), ammonia (used to clean toilets), arsenic (a poison), cadmium (in rechargeable batteries), carbon monoxide (in car exhaust fumes), DDT/dieldrin (insecticides), formaldehyde (preserves body tissues and fabric) and hydrogen cyanide (gas chamber poison).

(Antismokers of course don't tell teenagers that a host of chemicals that would be deadly in large quantities are also found naturally in the ordinary foods they eat. "An innocent-looking leaf of cabbage, for example, contains 49 natural pesticides and metabolites, with huge, ominous-sounding names like 4-methylthiobutyl isothiocynanate and 3-indolylmethyl glucosinolate."[43])

• Tar from cigarettes blocks the entrances to air sacs in the lungs, causing air sacs to pop.

(After 53 years of smoking I wonder how many more sacs I have left to pop.)

• Smoking makes you weak because the carbon monoxide in cigarettes robs your body of oxygen.

(You would have to smoke a couple packs of cigarettes to equal the amount of carbon monoxide you would breathe in from automobile exhaust during a stroll down a busy street.)

• Chewing tobacco and dipping snuff cause bad breath and wear down the surface of your teeth.

(I can't address this one. All my lifelong dental problems, beginning when my teeth first appeared, have obviously been caused by smoking, not chewing.)

• Smoking is a leading cause of impotence in men because nicotine constricts the blood vessels.

(The Baby Boom was a myth? All those cigarette-smoking GIs who came home from World War II merely *seemed* to be fecund? All those millions of babies were found under cabbage patches?)

• Women who smoke will get wrinkles faster than those who don't.

(Those who don't what? Who don't wrinkle or who don't smoke? All right, I'm being a smartass, but I can't help myself when I read this kind of fear propaganda fed to children.)

BUT I HAVE DIGRESSED again. To get back to 1994, it was on April 1 that Natick, Massachusetts, became, to my knowledge, the first community to ban cigarette self-service displays and vending machines (even if they were locked and required an adult attendant to operate them). It also required the town's tobacco sellers to purchase a special permit. Despite the date, this was no joke. Violations for selling cigarettes to minors carried fines up to $500 and revocation of permits.[44]

The Natick Board of Health, which promulgated the regulations and apparently runs the place, didn't have to rely on violations to swell the town's coffers. Permits were set at $100—to cover the program's "administrative costs." This was on top of the fee for a regular license to do business. The merchants also stood to loose additional hundreds of dollars in money the tobacco companies paid them to display their products.

"One way to look at it is it's the cost of selling death, I guess," said Health Director Roger Wade.

There was some grumbling from the 40 affected merchants, both over the loss of income and also over the fact that the new law was imposed on them without warning or prior consultation with them. But how could they complain? After all, it was in a good—nay, a noble, life-protecting, medically correct—cause.

(It's the same kind of reasoning used by the teenager who initiated a successful petition to have smoking banned in Cobb County, Georgia, schools, even by teachers. She told the *Atlanta Journal-Constitution* that she sometimes throws away her aunts' and uncles' cigarettes. "They don't get angry with me because they know I'm doing it out of caring."[45]

(As long as I'm inside parentheses, this is a good place to quote from a sign I saw at the checkout counter in a drugstore in Buford, Georgia:

("A person less than 18 years of age who purchases, attempts to purchase, or offers to purchase smoking material or smoking paraphernalia to [*sic*] a person less than 18 years of age is subject to a fine of up to $500 and imprisonment for up to six months."

(Does that mean it's lawful in George for a person *more than* 18 to purchase smoking material or paraphernalia for a person less than 18? More likely it means that the state's education system failed the person who wrote the sign.)

Lest anyone get the impression that the Natick Board of Health was unconcerned with the effect on small businesses of its righteous rule-making, it should be mentioned that it also considered banning smoking in restaurants but decided to wait until adjacent towns did the same so that local restaurants wouldn't lose patrons over the borders.

This was to say, in effect: "We know that many people like to have a cigarette or two when they dine out, enough of them that it would hurt our local restaurants if they went elsewhere. But if they don't care about their health or that of people around them forced to breathe in their noxious emanations, *we* care, and when it becomes feasible for us to do so we will take steps to stop them from causing any more harm."

And no doubt they did not too long after.

As for the ban on open displays of packages of cigarettes, it was because they were easily shoplifted, director Wade explained. But displays of other easily shoplifted products were not banned.

This was to say, in effect: "We know kids are going to shoplift, but we can at least make sure that in the future they'll only be able to steal harmless things, like candy bars or lipsticks or ballpoint pens or other such pocketable items."

Or maybe I'm wrong. Maybe forcing delinquents to go out of town to steal cigarettes resulted in a decline in petty thievery of all kinds in Natick. Somehow, though, I doubt it.

(Four years later the Natick Board of Health was to institute another high-handed measure by deciding it was time the town started fluoridating its drinking water. Whereas its vending machine ban and vendor licensing requirement seems to have upset only those merchants selling cigarettes, the idea that Natick should join the rest of the country by polluting its water with "dangerous" fluoride created a great deal of opposition among the citizenry, judging by letters I read in the local *Middlesex News* during a trip to Massachusetts in November 1997. This has nothing to do with smoking, but serves to confirm my impression that Natick, Mass., is something less than a model for the nation.)

A Mr. Birney Montcalm of Douglasville, Georgia, thinks open displays are a plot by the tobacco companies "to get cigarettes in the hands of children while protecting convenience store clerks from being arrested for selling them to minors: Let 'em steal them!"

The obvious strategy, he wrote *The Atlanta Journal-Constitution*, "is to allow these forbidden treasures to be easily shoplifted by budding nicotine addicts who can't legally purchase them. The tobacco companies simply write off any losses under their advertising and promotions accounts, while gaining newly addicted, life-long (as opposed to long-life) customers in the bargain."[46]

The tobacco companies must fondly wish that were so, Mr. Montcalm. Those villains, of course, are capable of anything. But be that as at may, if any teenager gets caught swiping cigarettes, in Natick or Douglasville or anywhere else, he can cite in his defense a case in Lynnwood, Washington. In something less than a landmark ruling, Judge Robert Schillberg imposed a fine of $1 on a shoplifter who had admitted stealing two packs of cigarettes from a Safeway store, then paid the fine himself and released the defendant because, he said, "the store is more culpable than [he] is" for selling such dangerous products in the first place.[47] So much for personal responsibility.

Inevitably, all this emphasis on preventing minors from buying cigs has inspired a number of sting operations in which an underage person, who is of course picked because he or she looks older than his or her years, is used to entrap a store owner or, more usually, a clerk who himself or herself may not be old enough to smoke (legally).

One such sting that struck close to home for me was conducted in Cobb County, Georgia, in 1995 at the request of a state legislator and a "cancer risk educator" at Promina Cobb Hospital, both of them on the board of directors of the local American Cancer Society chapter. Three female checkout clerks in three stores out of five that were visited were charged with the misdemeanor of selling cigarettes to a 15-year-old girl working as an undercover agent for the county solicitor's office. The offenses were recorded by TV news camera crews who just happened to be at the stores.[48]

"We wanted to do something to draw people's attention to the fact that kids can still buy cigarettes," said one of the ACS directors.

Attention drawn, the assistant solicitor who oversaw the operation said that the charges would be dropped if the three women read a copy of the ordinance, told their coworkers not to sell tobacco to minors and signed affidavits to that effect. Otherwise, it would be penalties up to a year in jail and $1,000 in fines.

The Atlanta Journal-Constitution, in a display of common sense regarding smoking notable for its rarity in this newspaper, blasted the whole operation. That is, the morning *Constitution* reprinted a column that had previously run on the editorial page of the afternoon *Journal.*

(Although the two papers have separate editorial staffs and their own comics and other features, they are essentially the same newspaper and in fact run combined editions on weekends and holidays.)

Wrote Jim Wooten, editorial page editor of the *Journal,* in a signed column, "It is shocking that a public official would allow the enforcement authority of the state to be used as a prop for the promotion of the Great American Smokeout and, furthermore, that unwitting clerks would be held hostage for lectures by self-appointed lifestyle police from the American Cancer Society.

"It's one thing to enforce the law. It's another to take it on a public-relations junket . . . [W]hen do-gooders and police consort to terrorize and preach, the freedom-loving should grow alarmed and wary."[49]

Sad to say, Mr. Wooten seems to be the only member of the AJC family who exhibits common sense, skepticism and balance when it comes to the subjects of tobacco and smoking.

In a variation of a sting operation, a 14-year-old "tobacco control advocate" illegally purchased a pack of cigarettes from a vending machine in a U.S. House of Representatives office building, even though she was wearing a T-shirt saying, "I am 14 years old."

This roused the easily aroused Scott Ballin of the Coalition on Smoking OR Health to say that "Congress's failure to implement their own law [banning vending machines from all federal buildings] . . . smacks of not caring much about the issue, not being willing to take the tobacco industry on."[50]

Congress routinely exempts itself from the laws it requires everyone else to obey and this is about the only case where I'm pleased to learn it did. But was someone supposed to stop the girl? I wouldn't have tried. You can get in deep trouble these days for approaching 14-year-old girls, especially if you try to peer at their chests, even if it's just to see what's printed across them.

Mr. Wooten's concern over the do-gooders' threat to freedom was not unwarranted. For a few months cigarette sting operations were institutionalized in these United States of America—not by any law, not by the enforcement authority of the states, not by vote of the people, but by edict of the Food and Drug Administration. Beginning March 1,

1997, anyone who sought to purchase tobacco products who "appeared" to be younger than 27 was required to produce photo ID proof that he was at least 18. How a clerk was supposed to distinguish between someone who was 26 and someone who was 27 wasn't clear.) And because the guardians of teenage health were prepared to send in undercover agents in their early or mid-20s who "appeared" older than their actual age, the safest thing for merchants would have been to card *everybody.* But it was in a good cause, and no patriotic Americans would object to this autocratic measure. Anyway, most of them don't smoke, so why should they care?

"It's going to take an army of citizens," said John Banzhaf of Action on Smoking and Health (ASH), whose organization began enlisting thousands of Hitler Youth—oops, concerned young people—to report suspected lawbreakers to an FDA hotline.[51]

Fortunately, in August a panel of the U.S. Fourth Circuit Court of Appeals in Richmond, Virginia (a hotbed of cigarette manufacturing), struck down The FDA's regulations in their entirety, ruling that the agency had no jurisdiction to regulate tobacco products.

The decision was reported in *The Resistance* ("The Active Voice of the National Smokers Alliance").[52] I saw no mention of it in any newspaper.

BUT BACK TO 1994 again, which was a banner year for the burgeoning children's crusade.

As an explanation of why smoking rates among young adults had stopped declining, in May Dr. Corinne Husten of the Centers for Disease Control and Prevention (CDC), offered that "There's been an increase in the marketing of deep discount brands, so cheaper tobacco products are available."[53]

One wonders if she apprised commissioner Kessler of this. But it's another example of smoking foes having it both ways. On the one hand they are concerned about the omnipresence of R. J. Reynolds's old Joe Camel and Phillip Morris's heavy advertising of Marlboro, which has certainly helped make it the leading brand among smokers—of all ages. On the other hand it's alleged that more young people are smoking because of the availability of cheaper brands.

First, Camel and Marlboro are not cheap, let alone "deep discount," brands. I would like to smoke Marlboros, but I am not going to pay four or five dollars more for a carton of them than for a carton of a discount or generic brand.

Second, discount brands are little advertised. A few, like Cambridge and Basic are, but I would classify them not as discount but as second-tier name brands, somewhat cheaper than the top tier.

Third, discount or generic brands are hardly a recent development. I have been smoking them for at least 15 years.

Continuing our trek through 1994, in June Mississippi closed a loophole in its law that had allowed minors to buy tobacco products if they had their parents' permission.[54]

In August, the Centers for Disease Control and Prevention refined our knowledge of the link between teenage smoking and attempted suicide mentioned by Surgeon General Elders: high school students who smoked were 18 times as likely as nonsmokers to attempt suicide, it reported.[55]

This didn't mean that smoking *causes* suicide, said CDC psychologist Kenneth Carter, but rather that smoking may be an indicator of depression or hopelessness and that some youngsters may use tobacco to gain relief from those feelings.

There's that "times as likely" business again I discussed in Chapter 1. Without telling us the baseline figure—the frequency with which teenagers attempt suicide—the number is meaningless. As I wondered back then, does it really mean that for every nonsmoking teenager who attempts suicide, 18 smoking teenagers do? How many teenagers attempt suicide anyway, and how does anybody know whether they smoke or not, or if they do, how much they smoke?[56]

And if smoking doesn't cause suicide but is merely a concomitant of some teenagers' depression and despair, shouldn't we be addressing the *sources* of their angst rather than focusing on just this one indicator of it, if it is an indicator? If smoking doesn't cause suicide or attempted suicide, why mention it at all?

On the other hand, drugs *do* cause suicide, as witness a prominent example, that of the son of actor Carroll O'Connor. Drug users frequently die from overdoses as well, something that never happens with nicotine. If antismokers are grieved by such tragedies, it doesn't seem to bother them enough to persuade them to reorder their priorities regarding the welfare of the nation's youth. All the antismoker can see in his monomania is tobacco, tobacco, cigarettes, cigarettes.

To me, now, psychologist Carter's statement was an indicator itself, one of the first signs of a drive by some antis to have smoking declared to be not only an addiction but a full-blown pathology. Another indicator, which I found on the Internet, was in the form of a dialog between a father and his beginning-smoker son. After a discussion of whatever dubious and short-term benefits of smoking there might appear to be, versus the obvious long-term health disadvantages, the father concluded with, "[I]t seems to me that if an ordinary, healthy young person, aware of the facts and intelligent enough to understand them, deliberately decides to smoke, then *this suggests the existence of a personality disorder, requiring extensive counseling.*"[57] [Emphasis added.]

A more recent report from the Centers for Disease Control and Prevention stated that 70 percent of all deaths among school-age students result from car crashes, other injuries, homicide and suicide.[58] In fact, life expectancy has increased for every age group of Americans except for 15- to 24-year-olds because of drunk-driving fatalities. Drunk driving is the number one cause of both deaths and injuries in this age group, according to yet another CDC report.[59]

"Too many high school students are participating in a variety of behaviors that put them at risk both today and in the future," said Laura Kann of the CDC's Division of Adolescent and School Health.[60]

The chief "future risk" pointed to by the CDC was, of course, cigarette smoking, which should make everyone feel a little better about all those actual, current, violent deaths.

In September, the prestigious Institute of Medicine came out in vigorous support of the Food and Drug Administration's plan to regulate tobacco as a drug, first broached by commissioner Kessler in February. The institute did so after spending a year and a half studying how to combat teenage smoking and concluding that education and state laws just weren't cutting the mustard.[61]

"Tobacco needs supervision and regulation right away," declared Dr. Paul Torrens of the University of California, Los Angeles, a cowriter of the Institute's report.

As if tobacco was not already one of the most supervised and regulated products in the country.[62]

Although it was the alleged "manipulating" of nicotine in cigarettes by the tobacco industry that was the purported reason for the FDA's assertion that tobacco should be brought under its authority to regulate drugs (see Chapter 4), the need to curb teenage smoking quickly became the most frequently cited rationale for doing so. (Smokers knew of course that Dr. Kessler's *real* desire was to ban tobacco entirely.) And it was then that the Clinton administration's mantra that "3,000 teenagers get hooked on smoking every day and a third of them will die because of it" began to reverberate throughout the land. It is a testimony to President Clinton's shrewdness that he recognized that it was with teenage smoking, not teenage drug use, that political hay was to be made, although he belatedly took up the latter cause as well when he came under intense criticism from the Republicans during the 1996 presidential campaign.

AS THE CRUSADE TO save the children gathered momentum, media commentators were to fall uniformly fallen into line, even those who otherwise espoused antiregulatory views. For example, said Don Feder in the *Boston Herald*: "I too worry about government becoming the national nanny, telling us exactly what to ingest and mandating a health regimen. But here we're talking about children courting death."[63]

And that renowned conservative, William F. Buckley: "It is in the interests of the tobacco companies to permit Clinton his intervention. The part of his program that calls for banning advertising especially designed to attract teens just might be challenged on constitutional grounds, but again, this is not a judicial contest the tobacco companies should want to be seen as winning. The other side can come up with 300,000 corpses, the harvest of a million teenagers dispatched by Philip Morris." [64]

Well, *ahh*, Mr., *ahh*, Buckley, that's an arresting image but it has, *ahh*, one fatal flaw. By the time today's smoking teenagers start showing up as corpses they'll be senior citizens and it's unlikely that those who will then be busy running the country will much care. Or do you really believe that people die in their teens from smoking?

At least Buckley used the words teens and teenagers, not children or kids. Contrast that with an outburst from Scott D. Ballin, spokesman for the American Heart Association: "They've [the cigarette companies] been robbing the cradle of America's kids for too long."[65] Robbing the cradle? Evidently these vile companies can't even wait until the "kids" are toddlers before attempting to hook them.

"Kids" is a very emotion-laden term, which of course is why the antismoking movement uses it so often, as in:

> If current tobacco-use patterns persist, five million *kids* nationwide who are 17 are younger will die because of a smoking habit, the CDC said in its weekly report . . . In Georgia, more than 400,000 *kids* will become smokers, the CDC said, and one-third of those will die from it.[66] [Emphases added.]

The CDC's frightening figures were repeated a couple months later by the Washington-based National Center for Tobacco-Free Kids in a three-quarter-page ad in *The Atlanta Journal-Constitution.* In bold black letters it proclaimed that "The Lives of Five Million Kids Are About to Go Up In Smoke." That's nearly the entire population of Georgia, the Center pointed out. It did not, of course, explain that when these five million die they will be several decades beyond the "kids" category.[67]

Fourteen months later the Center was back, this time with a full-age ad, at the top of which was the face of a Marlboro Country-type cowboy with a cigarette between his lips looking over a field of tombstones. "Every Day Without Action on Tobacco, 1,000 Kids Will Die Early," the ad proclaimed in big black type. Again, the impression left with the reader—intentionally—was that "kids" will die from smoking even before they reach adulthood.[68]

When was the last time you saw a newspaper ad proclaim: "If the current drunk-driving trend continues, X number of kids (*real* kids) will die prematurely in automobile accidents"? For that matter, when was the first time?

At least one nationally syndicated columnist wasn't fooled by all that kid's stuff, however. Wrote *The San Diego Union-Tribune*'s Joseph Perkins: "The president's real aim is to kill the cigarette industry through draconian government regulation. And he's using kids as a smoke screen."[69]

In October, Christian, Jewish and Muslim members of the Maryland-based Interreligious Coalition on Smoking OR Health, expressing their "moral outrage" over the advertising of tobacco, seconded the administration's call for a $2 a pack tax on cigarettes.[70]

"The slaughter of the innocents must stop," proclaimed Roy Branson, cochairman of the group.

Which slaughter of which innocents? If smoking kills people, it may not be until their 50s or 60s or later. The violence engendered by the illegal drug traffic kills them in their teens and 20s. So does binge drinking and drunk driving, especially the combination of the two. According to the Centers for Disease Control and Prevention, between 1988 and 1995, more than 68,000 fatal automobile crashes involved young drivers. Of those, 18,600 had blood-alcohol levels of 0.1 or higher, which constitutes legal intoxication in most states.[71]

Yet it was smoking alone that "outraged" the Coalition.

Voices questioning the nation's and the Clinton administration's fixation on teen smoking are so rare that one of them, that of syndicated columnist Maggie Gallagher, warrants quoting:

> Cigarettes are a bad habit, no question: an unhealthy, disgusting but essentially minor vice. Smoking may yellow your teeth, wrinkle your skin and cut a few years off your life, but it does little or no damage to the body politic . . . Compare teenage smoking with teen pregnancy, which the president also has publicly deplored. Pregnancy of unwed teenagers has far more immediate and devastating consequences. Between 1985 and 1992, births to single teenage moms leaped 44 percent. Over the same period, the juvenile violent-crime arrest rate jumped in 49 out of 50 states. Twenty percent of our nation's kids live in poverty. Seven percent live in neighborhoods in which the majority of families are female-headed. So where is the bold new Clinton plan to cut unwed teenage pregnancy in half in seven years?. . .
>
> Suppose the president succeeds in cutting teen smoking in half. How much better off would America's children really be? . . . [T]he squalor America's youngest citizens face would remain, unaffected and unaddressed by our latest misguided choice of moral crusades.[72]

This elicited three letters to *The Atlanta Journal-Constitution*, where I saw Gallagher's column, tasking her for "belittling" the problem of teen smoking. Not one letter supported her.

A few days after the Interreligious Coalition on Smoking OR Health vented its outrage, the plain old Coalition on Smoking OR Health (those "OR"s are very cute), joined by no fewer than 74 other national organizations, announced that they would begin circulating petitions demanding that the government enact stronger regulations to keep cigarettes away from the young.[73]

In November, contrary to R. J. Reynolds's argument, as well as the surgeon general's report, a study of students in five high schools, published in the *Journal of Personality and Social Psychology*, questioned the importance of peer pressure in leading teenagers to smoke. In fact, since the vast majority of teenagers studied were nonsmokers, peer pressure tended to work the opposite way. Thus they concluded that teen smokers were more likely to be social outsiders than their nonsmoking peers.[74]

"It could be that smoking is a result of social isolation," said the study's authors, Susan T. Ennett of the Center for Social Research and Analysis and Karl E. Baumann of the University of North Carolina. "Perhaps isolates have social inadequacies, and smoking is a coping mechanism."

"Could be." "Perhaps." It could also be that with messages about the evils of tobacco constantly being drummed into kids from an early age, those who do smoke, for whatever reason, find themselves automatically isolated. Again, what is cause and what is effect?

In this same vein, a later study also seemed to contradict the surgeon general's finding that girls who smoke are more socially skilled than their nonsmoking peers. A study published in the February 1996 issue of the *American Journal of Public Health* found that teens who experience emotional unrest such as depression, panic attacks or irritability are more likely to smoke regularly and that girls who smoked were twice as likely as boys to report greater psychiatric problems, at least in Australia.

Psychiatrist George Patton of the University of Melbourne led the study of more than 60,000 students enrolled in grades 7, 9 and 11. He advised that tobacco control strategies aimed at high school girls should focus on alternative coping strategies for dealing with stress and anxiety.[75]

I don't know what to make of this study. Those girls I saw smoking in the Cloverleaf Mall in Richmond didn't look anxious or stressed out. (Well, I do know what to make of it, but who's going to believe me?)

Finally, to bring 1994 to a close, in December I clipped another article about teenage use of smokeless tobacco. Based on the then latest statistics (1993), the American Cancer Society reported that 55 percent of teenage males had tried smokeless tobacco and 40 percent claimed to be regular users.[76] Since then there has been a host of studies into the consequences of chewing tobacco—throat cancer, cancer of the jaw, etc. But this is a whole other front of the antitobacco campaign which I won't go into since I have no experience with chewing the stuff.

The length of this chapter would be more than doubled were I to continue past 1994 to cite studies of the causes and consequences of teenage smoking from my pile of clippings and Internet downloads. I have already referred to some of them above, but for the most part they are a rehashing of earlier studies or alarums. However, there is one other aspect of teenage smoking that is worthy of mention, a finding in 1995 that "the rate of black teenagers who smoke has dropped dramatically in the past 20 years, from 26 percent to 4.4 percent."[77]

The experts were at a loss to explain this. They offered such theories as that sports are especially important to black youths; the influence of Muslim groups, which forbid smoking; that black parents are less willing than white parents to let their children smoke in the house; that black girls are less weight-conscious than white girls, and that blacks tend to view smoking as a "white thing."

Whether or not black teens are still shunning cigarettes today, an unfortunate fact is that too many black youths also seem to view academic study as another "white thing" and if fewer of them are killing themselves (slowly) with cigarettes, the TV evening news in every city I've been in usually leads off with the latest drug-related murder or other crime in the black community. Call me crazy, but there are worse things to worry about than teenage smoking.

IT HAS BEEN SEVERAL generations since antismokers claimed in articles and sermons and books, especially works of fiction, that cigarettes could turn even the brightest and most promising young man into an indolent, neurasthenic mess, robbed of all drive and ambition. Smoking was seen as a threat to youth rivaling the danger of "self-abuse" or "self-pollution" that also exercised the professional worriers and moralizers of a bygone era. (Young women were seldom mentioned because so few of them smoked. As for masturbation, females were not believed to possess sex drives, or if they did it was not something one acknowledged in polite society.)

To show how much our aesthetic standards, if not our prejudices, have improved since the early part of the 20th century, *The New York Times* in 1911 actually reviewed one of those moralistic and contrived novels, *The Tyrant in White*, in which a 16-year-old youth, seduced by the tyranny of the (white) cigarette, starts down a path that culminates in suicide.[78]

"[S]eekers after the values and mysteries of life will do well to avoid it [the book]," the reviewer advised. ". . . But doubtless it will prove pleasant reading for all those who hate tobacco."

I came across the review in the course of doing research for a project entirely unconnected with smoking. Like so many other things I was unaware of before I started writing this book, I didn't realize that *The Tyrant in White* was a typical antismoking screed, one of many in the early years of the century.

Lauren Colby, author of *In Defense of Smokers*, came across an old magazine called "The Youth's Instructor" edited by two concerned ladies, Fannie Dickerson Chase and Adelaide Bee Evans. He posted on his Website[79] some sample pages from Volume XLV, No. 35, published in Washington, D.C., on August 28, 1917.

One cartoon shows a boy waving off a hand that holds out a pack of cigarettes as he walks confidently up the road labeled "Success" with the sun rising at the top of the hill. Three disreputable-looking fellows, two with cigarettes in their mouths and one with a bottle in his hand, are taking the downhill path labeled "Failure."

An item reports a warning by the Postal Life Insurance Company of New York that "Tobacco covers nearly the whole range of human ills, dyspepsia, catarrhal troubles of the nose and throat, heart disturbances, nervous irritability, trembling, and impaired eyesight."

Luther Burbank, as famous a plant wizard as Thomas A. Edison was a wizard of invention, "absolutely refuses to employ cigarette users in his garden, for he says tobacco destroys the delicacy of touch necessary in his budding [no pun intended, I'm sure.— D.O.] work."

(Edison also refused to employ cigarette smokers in his laboratories. He liked cigars, though.)

In a foretaste of today's secondhand-smoke nonsense, and as an example of what happens when a scientist pontificates outside his area of expertise, Hudson Maxim, the inventor of improved explosives and younger brother of Hiram Maxim, inventor of the machine-gun, is quoted as saying:

> Tobacco is one of the greatest evils of the modern world. It is one of the great degenerators of the race.

> None of my direct ancestry, as far back as I am able to trace, ever used tobacco, consequently tobacco is unusually poisonous to me through lack of immunity. Up to the time I was thirty-six years old I found the use of tobacco by others an insufferable nuisance. Frequently I would become so poisoned by tobacco smoke as to be ill for days. One time in London while attending a dinner I was made sick for six weeks.

(What happened at age 36? Mr. Maxim didn't say. Maybe he developed "adult onset acquired tobacco smoke immunity"?)

The founders of the Spencerian Business College, on the basis of 30 years of observation of young people, said that:

> The effects of this narcotic are premature age, shattered nerves, mental weakness, stunted growth and general physical and moral degeneracy; and therefore we decline to receive into our institution any who use this noxious weed.

From the Life Extension Institute:

> Nine-tenths of army rejections are said to be due to tobacco heart. It has been proven that the excessive use of tobacco —
>
> Checks Growth
> Causes tobacco heart
> Promotes Cancers
> Injures eyesight, frequently causing blindness
> Impairs Intellect
> Lowers scholarship
> Injures nerves
> Destroys sensitiveness of taste
> Predisposes to tuberculosis
> Impairs work of kidneys
> Seriously interferes with circulation and respiration
> Weakens morals
> Excludes religion
> Offends society
> Makes criminals
> Lessens business efficiency
> Unfits for athletic sports
> Creates craving oftentimes for liquor
> Poisons family

All this (and more of the same) was published four months after the United States had entered World War I, in which two million of the youths Fannie and Adelaide were trying to save from the scourge of tobacco were thrown into the maw of hell in Europe. (When asked what the boys "over there" most needed, General Pershing replied: "Cigarettes. Send us more cigarettes.") Sixty-three thousand of those boys never came home; 204,000 returned with shattered bodies. Hiram Maxim lived to see the first two years of that war. Hudson Maxim, who lived until 1927, saw it all. Did it ever occur to either of them that their inventions had killed, and would go on to kill, vastly more millions than even the World Health Organization (a product of the Second World War) attributes to the deadly weed?

Cigarettes were also vital to the morale of American soldiers, seamen and airmen in World War II. Can you believe—the Army actually used to include them in field rations! Lucky for them, a lot of Germans and Japanese were addicted to cigarettes as well; that evened things up on the score of physical and mental fitness. Lucky for democracy, Adolf Hitler, a famous tobacco-hater, couldn't do anything about that. We might all be sprechen Sie deutsch today.

ALTHOUGH TODAY'S antis say little about the "moral" aspects of smoking, they still focus on many of the same physical consequences of the habit their counterparts alleged way back when. (But while the modern antis are now armed with "proven" medical arguments against smoking, unlike their predecessors who were simply voicing their personal, prejudiced opinions, these arguments too are at bottom inspired by and infused with a great deal of moralism.)

The antis are entirely correct when they maintain that in order to survive the tobacco companies must depend upon young people taking up smoking. But this is merely a truism on the order of saying that sports car manufacturers depend upon new generations of drivers coming into the market, or that the makers of disposable diapers depend upon new crops of babies being born. Every business—indeed, every profession, every calling—needs new blood as population cohorts move through life toward the inevitable end.

Automobiles and diapers are useful things, you say, cigarettes aren't. Even if that were true, it is beside the point. Some portion of the population is going to smoke, come what may, and that is what is so frustrating to the antis.

Even so, one must ask how it can be that despite being taught, from the time they enter kindergarten or first grade, about the health consequences of smoking, and despite present-day society's disapproval of smoking, so many young people do start to smoke. It is all too facile to blame it on "addiction," much too simplistic to say that, whether it's out of rebelliousness or just curiosity, once they smoke that first cigarette they're hooked for the rest of their (allegedly) shortened lives.

Most teenagers have probably tried cigarettes at some time or other and most teenagers don't become smokers, just as, ever since the weed has been around, most people have been nonsmokers.

So why does *any* teenager start? The shrinks continue to try to psyche them out.

Again, it's because of advertising, claims yet another researcher. "Kids come out of elementary school ardently against smoking," says John Pierce of the University of California-San Diego. "That resolve gets weakened in middle school. Tobacco marketing is the primary influence in weakening the ardent anti-smoking resolve of the very young adolescent."[80]

That is one more all-too-convenient explanation. Another is that many teens today have "a sense of hopelessness about the future; a feeling that there's not much of a future to look forward to." So thinks Dr. Michael Eriksen, director of the CDC's Office on Smoking and Health. "There's a cynicism, a sense of fatalism, among kids . . . Teens now take solace in cigarettes and it's pathetic that we as a society have reached the point where teens see cigarettes as their friends."[81]

There may be something in that—not much, but something—and if there is something, then, as I said before, we should be doing studies of teenage malaise and angst rather than teenage smoking. But a much more likely reason, I think, is suggested by Ken Resnicow of the Emory University School of Medicine: an overload of fear messages.

"In the age of AIDS, cholesterol and fitness, there are so many things that can kill you, we may have saturated our youth with fears. As a result, warnings may be falling on numb, not deaf, ears."[82]

Not only that, but antialcohol and antitobacco messages aimed at older children could ultimately backfire if they are extremely negative. That was the deduction of University of Washington researchers from an ongoing study of more than 1,000 fourth- through seventh-grade students.

Young children tend to have very negative views of smoking and drinking, but these attitudes become less negative as they get older, the researchers found. "Kids may ignore negative, one-sided messages as they begin to realize some issues are more complicated" than they have been portrayed, they said.[83]

(I sincerely hope that's true. When I retired from Scripps Howard in 1985 I drove a school bus for two years in Fairfax County, Virginia.

There was an official prohibition against smoking on the buses, even when children were not on board. On day I was sitting in front of an elementary school in Reston, defying the prohibition as I waited for my passengers to come out. A youngster walked past the bus on the driver's side. Something about the way he looked at me made me watch him in the side mirror. Sure enough, when he got to the rear of the bus he turned and shouted, "Smoking is bad for your health!" He's a young man now. I wonder if he got over it.)

There may be yet another reason: "Is it possible that some people are born to be smokers?" That was the question asked in another of my clippings. Researchers at the University of Michigan administered doses of aerosolized nicotine to the subjects in the study. Those who react strongly when first exposed to nicotine develop a tolerance to it and become heavy smokers, they reported. Nonsmokers and occasional smokers don't react strongly and don't become tolerant. Thus the researchers "speculated" that nicotine tolerance is inherited and "suggested" that smokers might need medical or psychiatric counseling to help them quit.[84]

This is another of those ridiculous studies no one would pay any attention to if it hadn't involved smoking. Perhaps I do the researchers an injustice because the article gave no details of the study and I haven't seen it referred to elsewhere. Was nicotine sprayed in the subjects' faces? If so, you would think everyone would react strongly, even if the aerosol was only Glade™ room deodorant. If it was sprayed elsewhere, on the arm, say, no one would react, unless it stung, and in that case you would again get a reaction from everyone. Why would those who react strongly to nicotine become tolerant of it and become smokers? It sounds topsy-turvy to me. How old were the subjects, and how many years were they followed to see if they became smokers or not? Or were they followed at all? One can only guess because the article used the present tense: "react," "develop," "become."

Studies of twins conducted some half-century ago by eminent biometrician Sir Ronald Fisher found evidence of a genetic factor in smoking behavior. Data on a series of male twins gathered in Germany showed that about twice as many identical twins were alike in their smoking habits than nonidentical twins—65 percent vs. 33 percent. In another group of female twins in England, 83 percent of the identical pairs were alike in their smoking habits as compared with 50 percent of nonidentical twins. There was an even higher correlation of smoking habits in identical twins separated shortly after their births than in nonidentical twins.[85]

I do believe that some people are indeed in some meaningful sense "born to smoke" (and that furthermore they are in no need of psychiatric counseling). I know of at least two people I would put in that category. When I started writing this book I put my name on a smokers list at "Smoker's Home Page" on the Internet and said I would like to receive e-mail from other smokers. I received two replies. Although the writers weren't teenagers, their personal stories seem appropriate for this chapter.

The first was from Ryan K. in British Columbia:

> Don — Read your entry on the smokers list. I enjoy corresponding with other smokers about the habit we love so much. I am 28 and have been smoking steady since the age of 14. I love to smoke and will smoke for the rest of my life. I smoke Camel Filters and currently smoke about 2 packs per day. I enjoy smoking now more than ever and take pleasure in the fact that my daily consumption is always increasing. I'm sure I'll be up to 3 packs per day in the not too distant future. I find that the more I smoke the more I enjoy it. After 48 years of smoking do you still enjoy it as much as ever? How much do you smoke? It is great to hear about your good health. Have you ever regretted starting smoking? I sure haven't, the amount of pleasure I get from bathing my lungs in smoke is immeasurable, I will never give that up. Do you have children and do they smoke as well? What about grandchildren who smoke? If your children do smoke did you support there [*sic*] decision to start? My parents are both dedicated smokers so when at 14 years of age I told them I was smoking they supported me 100% and actually made sure I always had a supply of cigarettes. I think they enjoyed seeing me smoke and the obvious pleasure I got from smoking. When I have children I will support them in their decision to smoke if they choose to do so, I would actually be pleased knowing the pleasures of smoking like I do. Please write back and tell me about your habit and the key to continuing good health. — Ryan

I wrote back to Ryan to answer his questions but unfortunately couldn't give him the key to good health, although I suspect it's mostly a matter of picking the right parents and grandparents. I told him he had to be the most dedicated smoker I'd ever encountered and was the first person I'd ever heard of who actually wanted to increase his consumption of cigarettes, which I thought was especially amazing for someone living in Canada with its outrageous taxes. (But he's not unusual, I learned later. I'll expand on that below.)

The other response was from Sandy S.:

> Hi Don—I saw your post on the Smoker's page and enjoyed your comments about the book you are writing. It is great to hear from a healthy smoker your age and give [*sic*] me comfort that not all smokers die young! I started smoking when I was eight years old! My Dad let me have one of his and let me continue to enjoy smoking when I was a kid in the 50s. So, let's see, I am 47 now, so I guess I have smoked for 39 years now. I have always been healthy, so hopefully I will get to be your age. Thanks. — Sandy.

I thanked Sandy and told him to keep up the good work.

Some shrinks think they can predict which kids—boys, anyway—will be likely to take up smoking. Two of them conducted a longitudinal study to "assess the usefulness of personality dimensions measured at ages 6 and 10 years in predicting early onset of cigarette smoking, alcohol abuse, and other drug use in boys."

The boys were assessed by teachers' ratings of behaviors. Self-reports of smoking cigarettes, getting drunk and using other drugs were employed to measure the prevalence of substance use. "Discrete-time survival analysis," whatever that is, was used for the statistical analyses. The researchers found that "High novelty-seeking and low harm avoidance significantly predict early onset of substance use (e.g, cigarettes, alcohol, and other drugs) . . . The stability of the prediction between ages 6 and 10 years suggests that the kindergarten assessments may be used for preventive efforts at school entry instead of waiting until early adolescence."[86] [Parentheses in original.]

I wonder what these guys would have predicted about my older brother, who was rather a hellion in his teenage years and whose "personality dimensions" included a high degree of "novelty-seeking" and a very definitely low level of "harm avoidance," not limited to smoking cigarettes. For example, he once climbed the steeple of the Bellevue Methodist Episcopal church to touch a revolving cross at the top at least 50 or 60 feet above the ground. He amused himself by shooting rats in the borough dump with a .22 rifle, and one time was collared by the Avalon police for using the glass insulators on telephone poles as a target. (Fortunately, Ritalin was unknown back then and the police handled such incidents of "novelty-seeking" by having a good talk with the parents instead of hauling a kid into juvenile court.) Even when he was older, just for the hell of it he shot a hole through the door of his Model A Ford, forgetting to roll the window up first. I don't know how old he was when he jumped aboard a barge on the Ohio River at one of the locks, but I remember my mother having to drive down to Emsworth to pick him up where he was thrown off.

For all his lack of respect for property, my older brother was an idealistic and compassionate human being with a pure heart. Unfortunately, his low level of harm avoidance led him to become a paratrooper with the 82nd Airborne Division. He went through the campaigns in North Africa, Sicily and Italy. In England, while the Allies assembled their forces for the D-Day invasion of Europe, he served as an aide to the division's commander, Gen. James M. Gavin. But he still hadn't had enough adventure and asked to be sent back to the line. On June 5, 1944, lst. Lt. William R. Oakley was mortally wounded outside St. Mere Eglise, the first town to be liberated in France.

I have fond memories of my own novelty-seeking and low harm avoidance, and that of my younger brother as well. Our mother would have had heart failure, even though she never smoked, had she known some of the things we did.

For instance, we liked to climb on the cliffs across the boulevard from our house. One time I got caught in a situation from which there seemed no avenue of escape—up, down or sideways. I bargained with God that if he got me out of this predicament I would never climb the cliffs again. It took a second such experience before I kept my part of the bargain.

We also liked to wander the railroad tracks between the foot of the cliffs and the Ohio River. There were four tracks. One day I was walking along the cliffside one when I heard an approaching train. I was afraid to cross all four tracks to the river because I didn't know which one the train was on and it was coming fast. Just my luck—it was on the same track that I was! There were only what seemed like mere inches between the track and the cliff wall. Closing my eyes and holding my breath, I spread-eagled myself against the hard stone. Needless to say, the train passed by harmlessly or I wouldn't be writing this. I don't think I had time to pray that time.

The river was less of a temptation because of its filthiness. I only swam in it—involuntarily—on one occasion. Johnny Z., the boyhood neighbor I mentioned in the Introduction with whom I used to sneak smokes in his backyard shack, was even more novelty-seeking and less harm-avoiding than I. He had built a flimsy boat and wanted to try it out. My younger brother and I accompanied him on a maiden voyage across the river without incident. Coming back, however, the boat started leaking. Halfway across it was almost completely submerged. We were forced to swim the rest of the way, with our clothes on, pushing and dragging the boat along with us.

Undaunted, the builder patched the thing up and used it again, without me or my brother as crewmen; one time on—and in—the river was enough for us. The craft met a sad end, however. Whilst dragging it back across the tracks after one maritime excursion, our friend was caught by another of those pesky trains. He had to abandon the boat on the tracks, where it was smashed to smithereens. He got into a peck of trouble because of that, but again, fortunately, the wisdom of our elders prevailed and he was not sent to juvenile hall or given a criminal record. As an adult, John had a long and distinguished career as a scientist and administrator with the National Aeronautics and Space Administration in Cape Canaveral, Florida. Who could have predicted that?

I SAID ABOVE THAT my e-mail correspondent Ryan was the only person I'd ever heard of who wanted to increase his consumption of cigarettes. Subsequent surfing of the Internet revealed that he is far from alone. I don't know if the kind of youthful smoking behavior discussed in this section falls under the category of "born to smoke" or is an unforeseen consequence of antismoking propaganda, but I suspect the latter because I never encountered such behavior in my own youth. I'm speaking here of the appearance of teenage sites on the World Wide Web, where adolescents not only militantly express their love of smoking but their desire to smoke more and more.

In Chapter 9, I briefly referred to "Jenny's Teen Smoking Page," which featured pictures of young girls smoking, as well as letters and stories about smoking sent to Jenny by other teens. Another is Allisons's "Smoking Home Page for Teens and Pre-teens" at www.member.aol.com/marbsmoker/home.html.

Allison, who was 13 in 1997, says she has been smoking since she was 10, and "luckily, my mother was very accepting of my smoking when she finally found out." She usually smokes Marlboro Mediums or Marlboro Reds, "but once in a while I'll buy a pack of Camels or Winstons. I smoke about a pack and a half a day, usually more on the weekends." Allison even introduced her formerly antismoking 11-year-old sister to the habit.

As for the effect of all the warnings about the health dangers of smoking, Allison says she knows about the risks "but, at least for now, I'm not going to think about them. I like smoking . . . and I know it can happen, and probably will happen to me someday." A heading on her page proclaims: "If teens want to smoke, they're going to smoke, whether the government or parents like it or not!"

I quoted that at the beginning of this chapter and it bears repeating. While Allison, and millions of other young people, thoroughly believe the antismoking propaganda that tells them they are quite probably going to be killed by their smoking—why shouldn't they believe it; they never hear anything else—*they're going to smoke anyway.*

Caution to antismokers: reading the following excerpts from messages posted to Allison could be hazardous to your mental health, or at the least cause elevated blood pressure.

> Hi MarbSmoker: I'm Lisa, a 13-year-old smoker from Ohio. I'd like my message posted on your page, but please don't use my e-mail address because I use my dad's address and he doesn't know I smoke. My parents smoke but don't want me to ever touch a cigarette! . . . I started smoking at 12 by taking a few of their cigarettes . . . I have found a store where the cashier will sell me cigarettes . . . I get an allowance so I can buy two packs a week, which isn't enough but I have a girlfriend [who] steals cigarettes from her mom and she gives me a few if I need them. They are Marlboro Lights, which don't taste as good, but they are 100s. I like 100s becuase [*sic*] they are longer and I get more for my money. I can smoke at my house during the summer when my parents are working, but during school, I have to sneak outside to smoke. I can smoke sometimes at my girlfriends [*sic*] house when her mom works nights. I like smoking a lot. But I wish I could smoke whenever I want to.

> Hi Alison, I'm 26 years old, I started smoking when I was 12 and I still love smoking. I am glad to see that people your age are not being affected by the antismoking propaganda. Smoking is one of the most enjoyable things in life, and it is [a] disgrace that we have people in our country trying to stop young people from smoking.

Sure their [*sic*] are some risks associated with smoking, but they are much less than people believe. I envy you being able to smoke a pack and half a day. I am about to enter marine officer training and I have had to cut down to a pack of Marlboros, so I can run the required 3 miles in less than 20 minutes. Good luck with your page.

Hey Allison! My name is Terry and I'm 15 yrs.old. I think your page is really cool! I smoke Newport and a lot of my friends smoke, but like you said a lot of them need to hide it, and I think that sucks. I wish grown-ups would treat kids like people, and remember what they were doing when they were our age.

Hi, how are you doing? My name is Ana and I'm 16 years old and I smoke about a pack and a half a day. My parents know and they let me smoke in front of them, And I just wanted to give advice to all the girls out there that her [*sic*] parents still don't approve, just keep on smoking and they will quit nagging you one of these days, because they will just realize that you will do the exact oposite [*sic*] of what they say. So, from a girl that accomplished smoking in front of her parents in less than a year (I have being smoking for 6 years, just never got cougth [caught] until last year). Follow my advice and smoke a lot!!!!

Hi, Allison! I'm Amber, 18 yrs old and been smoking since I was 8. At 10 I smoked one pack per day and today I'm smoking 3-4 packs every day and sometimes more. I love it and thinks its [*sic*] very sexy too. Your site is great and I hope that you continue into chain-smoking like me! You and all other smoking girls are welcome to e-mail me! Love & smoke from Amber!

Allison, Your homepage is great. I am an adult now, but started smoking on and off when I was 15 . . . Unfortunately, we had to sneak it as kids (and my parents still think I quit), but you are very lucky you have such an open minded mom. I'm glad your sister is enjoying smoking so much, after being an anti-smoker.

Allison, I am a 26 year old male who started smoking when I was 9. My parents didn't find out until I was 11 and were VERY upset even though they smoked too. Not much they could say so they eventually let me smoke and I have been smoking ever since. I am now up to two packs a day of Marlboro 100s and loving every breath of cigarette smoke I inhale. — Corb

This one is also obviously from a male:

Hi, allison. This is probably a really weird question and you may not know the answer because you're pretty young, but maybe your sister or some of your posters will know. i read a little while ago that girls who start smoking early are more likely to have sex before they're 15 and have it more often and with more than one guy. do you think that's true? i'm not going to say anything about me and sex, but i think it's true about girls that i know. If you or any of the other girls who read your page want to e-mail me, i'd love to hear from them at [e-mail address deleted in the interests of American morality—D.O.].

One more message to Allison, which I'll quote in full:

Hi, I'm Wendy, a 17 year old senior in high school. I cheer for football, play basketball for school and am a sprinter on the track team. I love virginia slims menthol 100s (full flavor). I became a smoker on my 8th birthday and really enjoy it a lot. I love the feeling of the smoke deep inside of me the best. For as long as I can remember, I watched my Mom and Dad enjoy smoking.

I have an older sister (2 years older), Lisa, who started smoking towards the end of 3rd grade. My parents weren't thrilled about it but decided to let Lisa smoke openly since she probably would sneek [*sic*] them anyway. So, I watched my whole family enjoy cigarettes and wanted to be a smoker too. After much pestering, Lisa taught me how to smoke on my 8th birthday. That was the best present she ever gave me!

. . . That was January 7th, 1988 and I only smoked about 5 or 6 a day until that summer. I wasn't hooked on them or anything, but I really enjoyed smoking the[m] 5 or 6 a day. Then, in that first summer, '88, I started to smoke a bit more each day . . . [and] by the end of summer I was up to about a pack a day. I also noticed that I was inhaling my drags longer and deeper and really started to crave them. I stayed at about a pack a day for the [next] 7 years.

In the summer of '95, Lisa was a life guard at an outdoor pool and I got a job there helping out. By then, Lisa was up to 1-1/2 to 2 packs a day and decided to try chaining since we were outdoors and could smoke practically the whole day. Seeing Lisa light one right after the other and enjoying it so made me want to try chaining too. I had been only smoking about a pack a day for 7 years and when I began chaining it was very different. I think because my body wasn't used to so much nicotine, it was almost like starting to smoke all over again.

For the first couple of weeks I would have a real "smoked-out" feeling after smoking 2 then up to 3 packs per day. Lisa's transition into becoming a daily chainer was smoother since she had already smoked more per day than me. Soon, I really enjoyed chaining too

> and by the end of the summer I consistently smoked 3 packs per day.
>
> My cravings for cigarettes by now were intense. Chaining made me enjoy smoking a lot more too. When school started again it was very tough for me. But for the last 2 years, I've smoked 2 packs per day during school and 3 packs per day on weekends and vacations. I grab a smoke between each class in the girls [*sic*] room and chain during lunch. That's the only bad thing about chaining, wanting one all the time. I do know about all the health risks and since I became a chainer have noticed smoking's effect on my body.
>
> I used to be able to run the mile in 7:30 as a frosh. Once I became a chainer, I couldn't do the long distance anymore and became a sprinter. Still, I used to be a super athlete, but now I guess I'm just an average one due to all my smoking. I don't have any regrets though since I enjoy smoking so much.
>
> I'm glad to see a great page here for teens who choose to smoke. I'm very fortunate since my parents have always allowed me to smoke and my Mom buys me my cigarettes. Unfortunately, a lot of my friends still have to hide their smoking from their parents. Smoking isn't for everyone and neither is chaining. But, it is our choice!

If Wendy's message doesn't confound the antismokers, it does confound me. As many smokers and former smokers can attest from their memories of hangovers from too much smoking at a party the night before, the last thing you want to do the next day is to repeat the experience. Yet here are girls who deliberately strive to become "chainers," and the more they smoke the more they want to smoke.

Certain things are clear from these messages, however: regardless of parental or societal disapproval, no matter how punitively high cigarette taxes are raised or how severely cigarette sales to minors or cigarette advertising are restricted, some young people are going to take up smoking come what may. Indeed, the very strong case can be made that the ultimate effect of all these actions against smoking will only be to *increase* the ranks of teenage smokers.

Former surgeon general Everett Koop's hoped-for "smoke-free" society by 2000 could very well be going up in smoke, or be what my father used to call an impractical wish: a "pipe dream." (Not that the good doctor would ever be caught dead with a pipe in his hand.)

One last newspaper clipping and then I'll leave the teenagers in peace:

"We recently discovered that our 16-year-old daughter is smoking with her friends," a parent wrote to family psychologist John Rosemond, who authors an uncommonly commonsensical newspaper column on parenting and also has a page on the World Wide Web. "Neither of us smoke and she knows she's breaking a family rule . . . She makes good grades, she isn't a troublemaker and we don't disapprove of her friends (although we disapprove of them smoking). Apart from this one problem, she's not rebellious. How can we get it through her head that smoking is damaging her health and get her to stop?"

She will stop, Rosemond first says, when she gets it through her head herself that smoking "is slowly but surely damaging her skin, lungs, cardiovascular system and kidneys, not to mention that it causes one's breath, hair and clothing to smell like an ashtray."

But then he makes up for that bit of obligatory propaganda with these wise words:

"Count your lucky stars. Your daughter makes good grades, chooses reasonably good friends and tells you the truth, even concerning smoking. If the only thing she does to disappoint you during her teen years is smoke, you are fortunate indeed."[87]

Amen to that, say I.

Notes

1. Quoted in "Frustrated CDC urges states: Raise Legal age for buying cigarettes to 19." *The Atlanta Journal-Constitution*, July 10, 1992, p. D3. From the Associated Press.

2. See pages 476 and 477.

3. More recently, the CDC has reported that 62 percent of 7,773 underage minors surveyed in 1993 said they bought their own cigarettes, an increase of four percent over the 1989 survey. One in five smokers aged 12 to 15 bought their cigarettes from vending machines, while other teens continued to buy their tobacco products from convenience stores or gas stations. —Reuters/Mike Cooper, February 15, 1996. At clari.news.issues.smoking.html.

Yet a 1995 CDC survey found that only two percent of underage smokers got their cigarettes from vending machines. — "Underage smokers: Machines not top source of cigarettes." *USA Today*, May 23, 1996. At www.usatoday. com/. The National Automatic Merchandising Association (NAMA) reported that nine percent of individuals ages 13 through 17 purchased cigarettes from vending machines. — Raymond J. Keating, "Cost of Another FDA War: Attack on Vending Machines, An Attack on Jobs and Small Business." November 1995. From the Heritage Foundation Website site at www.townhall.com/.

Pick a number, any number.

4. "Children and Tobacco: The Problem." FDA Press Office release, August 10, 1995. Posted on the Department of Health and Human Services Website at www.os.dhhs.gov:80/new/press/p950810.html.

5. Comics section. *The Atlanta Journal-Constitution*, January 3, 1993. By way of illustrating the truth of the old show-business saying that satire is what closes on Saturday night, or Sunday morning in this case, and that someone can always be counted on not to "get it," later that year the AJC ran another "Doonesbury" strip mocking the notion that smoking is "cool," which elicited this response from an indignant mother of a teenager: "I'm disappointed with Garry Trudeau and *The Atlanta Constitution* for running this absurd, uncool, degrading, cancer-promoting strip." Letters. October 12, 1993, p. A6.

6. "Teens and Tobacco." *The Atlanta Journal-Constitution*, February 26, 1993, p. C3. From the Associated Press.

7. "Doctors Predict Oral Cancer Surge for Teens Using Chewing Tobacco." *The Atlanta Journal-Constitution*, April 7, 1993. From *The Washington Post*; also Amanda Husted, "Smokeless Tobacco Use Increasing Among Teenagers, CDC Study Says." *The Atlanta Journal-Constitution*, April 16, 1994, p. F4.

8. "Teenage smoking has begun to rise after long decline." *The Atlanta Journal-Constitution*, December 3, 1993, p. A4.

9. Pat Burton, "Teen smoking, drug use up, survey claims." *The Atlanta Journal-Constitution*, February 1, 1994, p A1.

10. Ibid.

11. "From the Publisher: Statistics and Advertising." *Smoke Signals*, December 1995, Vol. 2 No. 4, p. 1.

12. Amanda Husted, "Youths' cigarette use among top concerns." *The Atlanta Journal-Constitution*, February 23, 1994, p. E1.

13. Ibid.

14. U.S. Department of Health and Human Services, *Preventing Tobacco Use Among Young People: A Report of the Surgeon General.* (Atlanta: U.S. Department of Health and Human Services, Public Health Service, Centers for Disease Control and Prevention, National Center for Chronic Disease Prevention and Health Promotion, Office on Smoking and Health, 1994.)

15. "Adolescent smoking targeted; Surgeon general rips tobacco ads for luring teens." *The Atlanta Journal-Constitution*, February 25, 1994, p. A5. From the Associated Press.

16. Ibid.

17. Robert J. McDermott, PhD, Barbara Clark-Alexander, MPH, and Wayne W. Westhoff, PhD, MPH, MSW, "Tobacco Use Initiation: Future Intentions to Use, and Attitudes Toward Use in Sample of Florida 5th-Graders." *The Journal of the Florida Medical Association*, February 1996. From the Internet at www.medone.org/consumer/journal/february.html.

18. Ibid.

19. "Questions About Smoking, Tobacco, and Health . . . and the Answers." At www.cancer.org/smoking.html.

20. Wanda Hamilton (Vice President, Florida Smokers' Rights Association), "Tobacco and Children: The Truth." At www.forces.org/.

21. Dr. Daniel J. Wartenberg, "Epidemiology for Journalists." At www.facsnet.org/report_tools/guides_primers/epidemiology/. Also personal communication to author.

22. Maria Mallory, "That's One Angry Camel; The heat on RJR's campaign has it breathing fire." *Business Week*, March 7, 1994, p. 94.

23. "Talk of the Nation," Ray Suarez, host. National Public Radio, August 28, 1995.

24. "Sex club arrest." *The Atlanta Journal-Constitution*, March 21, 1997, p. D2.

25. The claim may not be entirely without substance. Even though the consumption of wine and liquor has declined in recent years, at least one company in this field has reported booming sales. "Our revenues are up every year," said Michael C. Carlos, CEO of National Distributing Co. "We are taking business away from the competition because of the brands that we sell." Quoted in Maria Saporta, "Decrease in alcohol consumption hasn't hurt National Distributing." Business section. *The Atlanta Journal-Constitution*, September 22, 1996, p. H7.

26. "Retailers fume over Phillip Morris plan." *The Atlanta Journal-Constitution*, July 30, 1995, p. R6. From *The Wall Street Journal*.

27. *The Washington Post*, October 14, 1995, p. A23.

28. Lee Bowman, "Study: Ads, not peers, spur teens to smoke." *The San Francisco Examiner*, October 18, 1995 p. A19. From Scripps Howard News Service.

29. Julian Guthrie, "Activists to fight illegal selling to kids, ads that target them." *The San Francisco Examiner*, December 20, 1995, p. A15.

30. Steven A. Chin, "Alioto seeks law banning tobacco ads near schools." *The San Francisco Examiner*, October 31, 1995, p. A3.

31. "Industry efforts to curb cigarette sales to kids useless, researcher says." *The Atlanta Journal-Constitution*, September 1, 1992, p. D4.

32. Barnaby J. Feder, "Critic Calls Anti-Smoking Drive Misdirected." *The New York Times*, April 1, 1996, p. A12. Courtesy of The Advocacy Institute.

33. Ibid.

34. "The Antis Are Against Tobacco—Right?" *Tobacco International*, February 1996, p. 3. Courtesy of The Advocacy Institute.

35. Edwin Feulner, "FDA: The Smoking Police." February 23, 1996, at www. townhall.com.

36. Jennifer Murray, "Butt out, Mr. President." *The Atlanta Journal-Constitution*, November 28, 1995, p. A23. From Knight-Ridder/Tribune News Service.

37. "You Can." Comics section. *The Atlanta Journal-Constitution,* September 5, 1993.

38. Dave Barry, "Take it from old Dave: Smoke's no joke, you teens." *The Atlanta Journal-Constitution*, September 17, 1995, p. C3.

39. "Lynn Minton Reports: Fresh Voices." *Parade*, December 11, 1994, p. 20.

40. "Ann Landers." *The Atlanta Journal-Constitution*, March 14, 1996, p. M7.

41. American Cancer Society news release, November 1, 1995. At www. cancer.org/clungs.html.

42. Donna Kennedy, "Send A Signal to Young People That Smokers Are Playing With Fire." Moreno Valley, California, *Press-Enterprise*, October 9, 1996, p. C1.

43. Michael Fumento, *Science Under Siege*. (New York: William Morrow, 1993), p. 62 in Quill paperback edition.

44. Evan Berland, "Assault on cigarettes: Natick outlaws cigarette vending machines, issues sales permits Friday." *Middlesex News*, March 31, 1994. Evan Berland, "Tobacco sellers fuming: Natick bylaws attempt to stamp out teen smoking." *Middlesex News*, April 2, 1994, p. 1A.

45. News for Kids. *The Atlanta Journal-Constitution*, March 29, 1993, p. B3.

46. Letters. *The Atlanta Journal-Constitution*, December 28, 1995, p. A18.

47. Chuck Shepherd, "Did smoke get in judge's eyes?" News of the Weird, *The Atlanta Journal-Constitution*, October 1, 1993, p. C3.

48. Doug Payne, "Cigarette sting targets teen sales." *The Atlanta Journal-Constitution*, November 15, 1995, p. B4.

49. Jim Wooten, "Life, liberty and law's long arm." *The Atlanta Journal-Constitution*, November 19, 1995, p. D7.

50. Peter Hardin, "Congress Holds 'Smoking Gun.'" *The Richmond Times-Dispatch*, March 28, 1996, p. A1. Courtesy of the Advocacy Institute.

51. Quoted in Lauran Neergaard, "Buyers to be carded, even if they look 26." *The Atlanta Journal-Constitution*, February 28, 1997, p. A16. From the Associated Press.

52. *The Resistance*, September 1998, p. 1

53. Anne Rochell, "Smoking decline is fizzling out: Ads, low prices help lure youths." *The Atlanta Journal-Constitution*, May 20, 1994, p. A6.

54. "Mississippi snuffs sale of tobacco to minors." *The Atlanta Journal-Constitution*, June 11, 1994, p. M2. In North Carolina, however, although it is against the law for teenagers to buy or "receive" tobacco and for others to sell or give it to them, it is not illegal for teenagers to use tobacco. Several school systems in that state have, or used to have, smoking areas where 16- and 17-year-olds could smoke if they had their parents' permission. Christopher Quinn, "School Official Defends Smoking Policy for Teens." *The Winston-Salem Journal*, February 29, 1996, p. A4. Courtesy of The Advocacy Institute.

55. "Smoking, suicide linked." *The Atlanta Journal-Constitution*, August 17, 1994, p. C5.

56. The latest suicide statistics I have found are that, according to the CDC, there were 32,410 suicides in 1994, up from 31,230 in 1993. The figure was not broken down by age, but the report stated that suicide rates among young men ages 15-24 remain twice as high as the overall suicide rate in the United States. — "National Data Show Drop in Homicide and Increase in Youth Suicide." National Center for Health Statistics press release, October 23, 1995. At www.os.dhhs.gov/.

57. "Transcript of counselling given to Owen (age 15) by his father, Session 1." The Public Policy Assessment Society, Inc. (Australia), January 1996. From www.peg. apc.org/~polsoc/ ppas_fd2.htm.

58. Anne Rochell, "CDC: High percentage of teenagers in danger." *The Atlanta Journal-Constitution*, September 27, 1996, p. A10.

59. Anne Rochell, "Fatality rate rising for teen drivers." *The Atlanta Journal-Constitution*, December 6, 1996, p. A3.

60. Ibid.

61. Lauran Neergaard, "Scientists urge crackdown on tobacco." *The Atlanta Journal-Constitution*, September 14, 1994, p. A10. From the Associated Press.

62. According to Tom Lauria of The Tobacco Institute, nine federal agencies regulate tobacco products, including two agencies providing oversight of tobacco advertising. In addition, every state has laws governing tobacco, from prohibiting sales to minors to regulating where adults may smoke.

63. *The Boston Herald*, October 25, 1995. From the Tobacco BBS at www.tobacco.org/.

64. *The New York Post*, August 14, 1995. From the Tobacco BBS at www.tobacco.org/.

65. Quoted in Kim I. Mills, "Rising wrath over youth smoking." *The San Francisco Examiner*, October 5, 1995, p. A9.

66. Anne Rochell and Amanda Husted, "CDC warns young Georgia smokers." *The Atlanta Journal-Constitution*, October 8, 1996, p. D2.

67. *The Atlanta Journal-Constitution*, December 18, 1996, p. A4.

68. *The Atlanta Journal-Constitution*, February 22, 1998, p. G4.

69. Joseph Perkins, "Kids are just a smokescreen." *The Atlanta Journal-Constitution*, August 23, 1995, p. A11.

70. "$2 tax on pack of cigarettes urged." *The Atlanta Journal-Constitution*, October 1, 1994, p. E6.

71. Anne Rochell, "Fatality rate rising for young drivers."

72. Maggie Gallagher, "Energy wasted on a 'harmless' vice." *The Atlanta Journal-Constitution*, August 22, 1996, p A11. (Single quotes courtesy the AJC.)

73. "75 groups declare war on tobacco. Top goal: Keep young away from cigarettes." *The Atlanta Journal-Constitution*, October 5, 1994, p. A5. From Scripps Howard News Service.

74. "Teen smokers more likely to be loners." *The Atlanta Journal-Constitution*, November 9, 1994, p. G1. From *The Philadelphia Inquirer.*

75. Sandra G. Boodman, "Teenage Girls Fight Emotional Woes." *The Washington Post*, May 28, 1996, Health Section, p. 5. Courtesy of The Advocacy Institute.

76. Julie A. Njaim, "Some teen statistics to chew on." *The Atlanta Journal-Constitution*, December 19, 1994, p. C3. From the *The Toledo Blade.*

77. "Call it a miracle, call it a mystery, but black youths shunning tobacco." *The Atlanta Journal-Constitution*, August 13, 1995, p. A1. From *The Kansas City Star.*

78. Unsigned review, "A Counterblast Against Tobacco: Mr. Berman in 'The Tyrant in White,' Writes of the Demoralizing Influence of the Cigarette." *The New York Times,* October 3, 1911.

79. At www.lcolby.com.

80. "Study: Tobacco ads induce children to start smoking." *The Atlanta Journal-Constitution*, October 1995, p. A9. From Knight-Ridder Newspapers.

81. Bill Hendrick, "Smoking appeals to world-weary teens, some say." *The Atlanta Journal-Constitution*, August 23, 1995, p. E3.

82. Ibid.

83. Bill Hendrick, "Negative messages backfire?" *The Atlanta Journal-Constitution*, January 10, 1996, p. D3.

84. "Born to smoke." *The Atlanta Journal-Constitution*, November 30, 1993, p. E4.

85. Cited in Carl C. Seltzer, "Why People Smoke." *The Atlantic*, July 1962.

86. Louise C. Mâsse, PhD; Richard E. Tremblay, PhD, "Behavior of Boys in Kindergarten and the Onset of Substance Use During Adolescence." *Archives of General Psychiatry*, 54:62-68 (January 1997). At www.ama-assn.org/scipubs/journals/most/recent/issues/psyc/oa6070a.htm.

87. John Rosemond, "No need to blow your stack about teen daughter's smoking." *The Atlanta Journal-Constitution,* October 25, 1996, p. E3.

Chapter 11

THE FEARMONGER FACTOR

There are scientists in existence today who are deeply distrustful of, or even hostile to, science as well as technology. They are guided by the belief that Western industrial civilization will, if not arrested and reversed, destroy life on earth.

— Edith Effron, *The Apocalyptics*[1]

It is increasingly apparent that there is something fundamentally wrong with much of the science underlying our environmental health regulations, as we have seen in recent episodes on asbestos, dioxin, and PCB, where risks have been dramatically overstated at simply enormous cost to the public.

— Rep. John Dingall[2]

AMERICANS' CURRENT horror of secondhand tobacco smoke is only one in a series of hyped-up menaces they have been taught to fear in the past several decades. Not *big* fears like nuclear holocaust or an earth-destroying collision with an asteroid, but a succession of health and environmental and consumer-product scares that have been perpetrated against a timorous and gullible public.

I use the word "perpetrated" deliberately. These recurring scares have been created—*manufactured*—by so-called "consumer crusaders" or "consumer advocates," both in and out of government, with in most cases little or no hard scientific evidence to warrant them. And in *all* cases—having injured if not destroyed a business, forced the removal of a useful product from the marketplace or prevented it from becoming available in the first place, having cost American industry and consumers untold millions of dollars—without a word of apology when scientific investigation proves their scare-of-the-week to have been unfounded and grossly exaggerated, without the slightest self-doubt of their righteousness and the purity of their motives, these guardians of the public weal eagerly move on to the next "cause."

And like Charlie Brown and the football Lucy promises to hold for him to kick and then always whips away at the last instant, the public continues to be suckered in every time.

More often than not, too, after creating an alarm, the fearmongers are unable to back off when the facts catch up with them. To do that would be not only to admit to deception or incompetence but, almost as bad in their thinking, it might encourage public "complacence" about other scares. It would "send the wrong message." Thus their typical reaction is to minimize or ignore findings that contradict them. This is, lamentably, as true of the people in government agencies as it is of the professional "public-interest" advocates.

At the same time, paradoxically, the fearmongers can never really claim success; they can never say that a peril has been vanquished. This is especially evident in the case of lead in the environment, which I discuss below. Even as blood lead levels in people have fallen drastically in recent years, the campaign against lead has been stepped up. For both public and private crusaders, to announce that a problem has been reduced to a minimal stage (if it even was a problem in the first place) would be to invite funding cuts and questioning of their indispensability as protectors of the nation's health.

Human beings of course have always been fearful of things they don't understand and have no control over, from the mysterious calamities of the natural world attributed to vengeful spirits or punitive gods in the infancy of the race, to the socially revolutionizing technological innovations of the 19th and 20th centuries. Technology is still mysterious to most of us. Thus we are easy prey to those who capitalize on both our general ignorance of science and the scientific method and a vague, nagging apprehension that the fast-changing modern world is a dangerous place fraught with perils. Prey, too, to the media, for which the latest scary allegation is like raw meat but the follow-up facts showing the scare to be unfounded are dull oatmeal and seldom reported.

In my college days, I once had an argument with a freethinking fellow student. He maintained that human beings were every bit as superstitious and credulous as they had been in the Middle Ages. How can you say that? I exclaimed. Look at science. Look at the modern world. We don't burn witches anymore, do we?

I realize now that he was right and I was wrong. Look at junk science. Look at the modern world. No, we don't burn witches anymore (or hang them, as they did in kinder, gentler Salem, Massachusetts, in 1692); today we simply imprison them and destroy their lives and reputations, as witness the notorious and absurd child-abuse witch hunts at day-care centers in Los Angeles and Edenton, North Carolina, and elsewhere in 20th-century U.S.A. Witness the variety of "New Age" nonsense (which is really age-old nonscience) like astrology or the "channeling" of ancient spirits; the widespread belief in abductions by UFO aliens; the popularity of "psychic hotlines"; the mass suicides of the followers of charismatic leaders at Jonestown and of the Heaven's Gate cult members in California, and so on and on.

To be sure, the perils we live with have often been very real. Way back in 1906, Upton Sinclair's book, *The Jungle*, exposed shoddy practices in the meat-packing industry and led to passage of the Pure Food and Drug Act and establishment of the Food and Drug Administration. The "muckrakers," as Sinclair and other early activists were called, were responsible for a long list of needed reforms, from purer foods to child-labor laws.

Today, however, there is such an avalanche of scares-of-the-week that it is becoming more and more difficult to distinguish which social or environmental problems deserve national attention and concerted efforts to remedy them and which are sheer fabrications of the fearmongers. I place the origin of this predicament with the publication in 1962 of Rachel Carson's *Silent Spring*, in which, in lyrical and compelling language, she issued a chemophobic doomsday warning about the deleterious effects of pesticides on us and the other living things with whom we share the world. But what could have been a cautionary wake-up call to a public theretofore confident that there was no end to, and no unforeseen costs to be paid for, "better living through chemistry," became the bible—doomsday myths and all—of the environmental movement, with consequences on American society as fateful as the release two years later of the first surgeon general's report on smoking and health.

It is true that the environmental awareness created by *Silent Spring* helped end the misuse and overuse of the pesticide DDT, which had seriously depleted populations of eagles and falcons and other raptorial birds that live high on the food chain by thinning their egg shells. Unfortunately, the book also led to the ending in 1972 of the entire use in this country of a chemical that had saved millions of human lives since its advent in World War II as a treatment for such diseases as malaria* and typhus.

But like the experience with the tranquilizer thalidomide, which the Food and Drug Administration refused to approve because of suspicions, which were eventually dramatically confirmed, that its use by pregnant women in Europe caused birth defects, the bird-shell lesson of DDT has been learned too well. Critics of the FDA say that because the agency was right about thalidomide does not justify years-long foot-dragging on the approval of other drugs, even when their safety and effectiveness has been demonstrated in other countries. Similarly, the misuse or overuse of DDT does not justify banning all uses of that chemical, much less justify the general fear of all pesticides. "Rachel Carson's legacy is not entirely positive," says Robert Gwadz, a malaria researcher at the National Institutes of Health. "DDT is one of the more benign pesticides known."[4]

It can be argued that books like *Silent Spring* have to be couched in dramatic "the end is near" tones in order to get people's attention, although I think that, like crying wolf too many times, this tactic ultimately defeats its purposes. An example of that is Paul Ehrlich's *The*

*Banning DDT may have been fine in the United States, where malaria has not in the 20th century been the serious problem it is in less developed countries. The seesaw use and disuse of DDT in Mexico provides a good example of the value of this pesticide. In that country, there were almost 140,000 cases of malaria in 1959, before DDT was used. By 1970, when three million houses were being sprayed annually, the number of annual cases of malaria had dropped to about 40,000. By 1973, when the number of households sprayed had decreased to about one million, the number of cases of malaria had risen to more than 100,000. But by 1985, when the number of households sprayed increased to almost seven million, the number of cases of malaria had dropped to less than 10,000. Thanks to environmental concerns, however, DDT use in Mexico declined again in the late 1980s and early 1990s, and the number of cases of malaria again increased.[3]

Population Bomb, which in 1968 predicted worldwide mass starvation by the 1970s that would kill hundreds of millions. Three decades later a similar but much modified warning was issued by Lester Brown, president of the Worldwatch Institute, who warned that "The deterioration of the Earth's ecosystem is slowing growth in world food production during the '90s and ushering in an era of scarcity."[5]

People like Ehrlich and Brown who make these kinds of apocalyptic predictions are often called Cassandras, after the prophetess of Greek mythology who was cursed by Apollo with being always right but never believed. The difference with our modern Cassandras is that they are a curse in reverse—never right but always believed.

Back in 1948, long before Rachel Carson, I read a book I believe was called *This Plundered Planet* that my father got from the Book-of-the-Month Club. I haven't been able to locate that title anywhere, but I do recall being very concerned by its warnings about soaring population growth and the depletion of soil and forests and other natural resources (although, as with my immediate reaction to the surgeon general's 1964 report about smoking, only temporarily concerned). That year I was a freshman at Western Reserve University (now Case Western Reserve) and a professor who taught a required introductory science course for nonscience majors was famous for frequently reminding us students that "where man has lived the longest, there you will find the world's greatest deserts."

Since 1948 (and 1968) the world's population has continued to soar and we continue to be running out of everything, yet most people, including those in the Third World, are living better than ever, or are at least no worse off than they have historically always been. Certainly there is a limit to how many people the earth can sustain and still leave room for a few other species besides Homo so-called sapiens, but somehow "the end" keeps retreating into the future.*

*Actually, it may be *de*population that confronts the world in the 21st century. According to a 1996 projection by the United Nations, based on fertility trends in both developed and developing countries, "global depopulation would commence in a little over four decades. Between 2040 and 2050, the world's population would fall by about 85 million. From then on, world population would shrink by roughly 25% with each successive generation." Moreover, by 2050 the median age of those alive then would be over 42,

It was not until after Carson, however, that the modern environmental movement began to take hold. Human-engineered catastrophe became a theme in movies and books in which the basic premise was to take a trend—any trend, such as population growth—and extrapolate it beyond all plausibility. The 1973 film "Soylent Green," for example, depicted a New York City of the 21st century whose 50 million inhabitants were reduced to eating processed human corpses, and a world in which all life in the oceans was dying.

Another example is a novel I got in the 1970s from the Science Fiction Book Club. I remember the title, *Sheep Look Up,* but I forget the author's name. He was a Brit who apparently disliked the United States very much. He depicted a country in which a malfunctioning microwave oven cooks a fetus in its mother's womb, children playing in their own yards are cut down by buried toxic wastes, acid rain and air pollution are everywhere and young people are deliberately going mad on drugs to escape the horrific world created by runaway industrialization. It was the only book I ever threw in the trash can.

"Soylent Green" and *Sheep Look Up* were pure fantasy, but purportedly realistic scare books continue to be written, including a recent one whose name I won't publicize that alleges that manmade chemicals in the environment are disrupting the body's hormone system, causing everything from cancer to Attention Deficit Disorder, as well as being responsible for allegedly falling sperm counts in industrialized nations.*

More important, and long-lasting, fallout from *Silent Spring,* however, was the great expansion of the federal government's regulatory powers during the supposedly conservative Nixon administration,

---

compared with about 20 in 1900. Such a worldwide aging of populations would have profound social, political and economic consequences in every country.[6]

*Some studies in Finland, France and Britain have reported falling sperm counts, with explanations (guesses) ranging from pesticides to food additives or other chemicals which might affect development of the testes in male fetuses at a critical stage in the womb, to tight pants and hot saunas.[7] On the other hand, other studies have found that semen samples sent to different fertility laboratories can produce counts varying as widely as three million to 240 million sperm.[8] Is the world running out of sperm? Obviously, "more studies are needed."

which saw the creation, among others, of the Occupational Safety and Health Administration, the National Highway Traffic Safety Commission, the Consumer Product Safety Commission and, most regrettably of all, the Environmental Protection Agency. These and a host of other regulatory agencies have been given, or have assumed, rule-making powers affecting the most minute activities of both business and private individuals in America to an extent that a central planner in the defunct Soviet Union would have envied.

Thanks not only to the emergence of the "nanny state" but also to an army of product-liability lawyers, the result has been a disturbing (but, I hope, only apparent) change in the American character, once characterized as one of rugged individualism and self-reliance. Today in our crybaby culture there is no such thing as an accident. Whatever tragedy befalls the individual, it's always someone else's fault, and that someone else must be made to pay.

The tragedies can range from the serious, like leukemia allegedly (and unprovably) caused by the proximity of a toxic waste dump, to the frivolous, like a woman spilling hot coffee in her lap and suing McDonald's for several million dollars. Also in the frivolous category was the "hair-eating" Mattel Cabbage Patch Snacktime doll. The parents of a 9-year-old girl in California sued Mattel for no less than $25.5 million, claiming the entire family was traumatized and would need extensive therapy and counseling because the doll "attacked" the girl.[9]

A child could not have foreseen that a doll might attempt to "eat" her long hair, but even adult consumers are no longer expected or trusted to exercise even ordinary common sense in avoiding everyday hazards. Another trivial, but typical, example is a "California Proposition 65" warning I found on a package of manufactured fireplace logs. (Proposition 65 requires the state to publish a list of chemicals "known to cause cancer, defects, or reproductive harm" and requires California businesses to warn the public of potential exposures to these chemicals resulting from the use of their products.)

The warning read:

> Burning fireplace or wood stove fuels, natural gas, and manufactured fireplace logs, results in the emission of carbon monoxide, soot, and other combustion by-products which are known by the State of California to cause cancer, birth defects, or reproductive harm.

> Many factors affect the operation of your fireplace. A properly installed and maintained fireplace and chimney will dramatically reduce the likelihood of combustion products entering your home. An inadequate air supply could cause fireplace malfunction. If you suspect your unit is not functioning properly, a qualified contractor should be consulted.

The sovereign State of California neglected to warn that placing one's hands or head inside a fireplace in which a fire is actively burning could result in severe physical trauma and/or asphyxiation! Asphyxiation from carbon monoxide is of course the greatest and most immediate danger from a malfunctioning fireplace, yet the State of California seems more worried about long-range perils that will probably never happen and which nobody can prove what caused them if they do happen.

I told an e-mail correspondent of mine who lives in California about this label and he sent me a "Public Warning" that was enclosed with his bill from Pacific Gas and Electric Company:

> PG&E uses fossil fuels (natural gas and petroleum products) in its operations. The combustion of fossil fuels can generate by-products such as carbon monoxide, soot, formaldehyde and diesel and gasoline engine exhaust. These chemicals are "known to the State of California" to cause cancer and birth defects and reproductive harm . . .
>
> PG&E conducts sandblasting at compressor stations, which can release sand. Sand naturally contains crystalline silica, a chemical "known to the State of California to cause cancer."
>
> Natural gas, in its original state, contains radon and benzene, chemicals "known to the State of California to cause cancer." It also contains toluene, a chemical "known to the State of California to cause reproductive harm." [All quotation marks in original.]

And so on. For some reason, the State of California doesn't post sand warning signs along its famous beaches. Doesn't it care about the millions of swimmers, surfers and sunbathers who are exposed to all that dangerous silica?

In short, despite the fact that people are healthier than ever and living longer than ever, we have been conditioned to believe that life is becoming more and more dangerous, with hidden hazards lurking around every corner. Time and chance no longer happeneth to us all. To bring Ecclesiastes up to date, when shit happeneth today, when accident or disease strike, *somebody* is responsible. And since you can't take Mother Nature to court, the only remedy is to sue that somebody, usually a corporation with deep pockets, and pass more laws. (Never mind that the ultimate pocket that is picked is not the corporation's but that of users of its products, who wind up paying more for those products as a result of the litigation.)

SILENT SPRING REMAINS the holy writ of the environmental movement, just as the surgeon general's 1964 report, *Smoking and Health*, is the scripture that continues to inspire and infuse the antismoking crusade. Though both are no longer read (if, indeed, the SG's report ever was), their alarmist messages of present and imminent threats to the public's health and well-being—threats which, their authors contended, demanded concerted national "remedial" efforts—still resonate throughout daily American life. To my mind, however, it was in 1965, with one man and one book (also no longer read), that the danger-is-everywhere, the consumer-is-always-innocent, the culpability-in high-places, the corporate-greed-and-malfeasance and the government-must-protect-us-from-everything school really got its biggest boost: Ralph Nader's *Unsafe at Any Speed*, the most notorious chapter of which was the trashing of a fine little car, the Chevrolet Corvair.

At the time, I still shared what seems to be a built-in bias of journalists against big business and was as guilty as the rest of the media in elevating Nader to hero status. Here was a young unknown David of a lawyer daring to take on one of the world's largest corporations, General Motors, even more of a hero when that Goliath blunderingly stooped to trying to impugn the character of the man instead of refuting his allegations. Nader became *the* Consumer Crusader, a demigod status he still enjoys today among his admirers and imitators.*

*Evidence of that status and of the devotion, as well as dismay, Nader still engenders in people was a page I found on the Internet posted by *The Nation* magazine when Nader was running for president in 1996.[10] (More accurately, when he *allowed* himself to be put forward as the candidate of the tiny, 83,000-member Green Party of California. A man who refused to campaign or to file with the Federal Election Commission or to disclose his personal finances or political expenditures or even to stand on the Green Party's platform could hardly be said to have been "running.") On that page there

In 1964 I was writing editorials for Newspaper Enterprise Association in New York City, having been transferred early that year from Cleveland. Living in Manhattan I had no use for a car but had decided that if I ever got one again it would be a Corvair, America's first mass-produced rear-engine automobile and GM's most innovative response to the growing invasion of small foreign cars. That desire was fortified when that fall the redesigned and sharp-looking '65 model was introduced. The following spring I persuaded the company to send me back to Cleveland, and the year after that I did become the proud owner of a 1966 four-door Corvair Monza sedan—despite *Unsafe At Any Speed* and despite reading an article in *Consumer Reports* disparaging the Corvair as "lacking versatility" because it had only two forward speeds and warning that the side windows were a hazard because they had no frames around them. In six years of ownership I never missed that extra gear or gouged an eye out on the corner of a window.

Nader's allegations, of course, involved the 1960-63 models, specifically the alleged tendency of their rear wheels to "tuck under" without warning, throwing the car out of control. Yet in a long technical article about the very first production Corvairs, *Car and Driver* had concluded that except for a tendency to oversteer in a hard turn "that is easily countered by the excellent steering,"

> [the Corvair] is a veritable technical orgy, and a promising basis for a long and useful development life. But most of all it personifies what we feel is important in the field of automotive safety: its fine steering and stable braking restore to the driver of an American car the kind of honest and precise control over his vehicle that he has had to do without for some three fast-moving decades. It has live nerves and quick reflexes that are worth more than all the seat belts and crash pads in the world. In the bargain, it's sparkling fun to drive.[11]

Even discounting this by 50 percent to make allowance for automobile writers' proclivity for hyperbole, it would seem that the Corvair was initially considered to be a pretty neat car.

---

must have been 500 "links" to articles and messages (I lost count at about 200) discussing pro and con every aspect of the Master's candidacy. The key words "Ralph Nader" also produced a minimum of 2,000 links to other pages on the World Wide Web with the AltaVista search engine.

Although I harbored a basic skepticism about Nader's allegations regarding the early Corvairs, along with growing disenchantment with consumer crusaders in general, I was just as glad that my '66 was free of the defect he wrote about. What a great car! So responsive and nimble you didn't need power steering or power brakes. It was the only car I ever really loved and I kept it until 1972, when it was stolen out of a Shaker Heights, Ohio, Rapid Transit parking lot, one of two Corvairs stolen that day, their air-cooled engines probably removed and sold to some honest citizens who were building dune buggys and looking for a bargain.

I don't recall when or how I saw a copy of *Unsafe At Any Speed*, but I do know that I didn't finish the first chapter, which dealt with the Corvair. I stopped at the place where Nader (so I remembered) asked the reader something like, "Have you noticed how many Corvairs have dented rear ends?" The implication was that the damage was caused by the cars going out of control. I knew this to be ridiculous and misleading. The engine air-exhaust grille below the rear bumper of Corvairs was just a thin sheet of metal easily damaged simply by backing into a high curb.

Realizing that my brain has also suffered damage from years of smoking, when I started this chapter I thought it might be a good idea to read *Unsafe* to verify that memory. A number of Nader's books were listed in the Cobb County, Georgia, public library system but not this one.

"Oh, that was about the Corvair, wasn't it?" said the woman in my local library who handled my request for help in finding the book. She'd learned to drive on a 1963 Corvair, she told me, and thought it was a very nice car. I've since learned that my brother's wife had owned a 1961 Corvair before they were married and had also liked it. (It's things like this that make me wonder what's wrong with the people I know or meet. I mean, they smoke and don't get lung cancer . . . they drive Corvairs and don't smash them up . . .)

A copy of *Unsafe* was located at and borrowed from Southern Technical Institute in Marietta. It turned out that the statement I thought I remembered was made not by Ralph Nader but by a sports car racer and writer named Denise McCluggage in an unspecified article Nader had quoted from: "Seen any Corvairs lately with the back end smashed in? Chances are they weren't run into, but rather ran into something while going backwards. And not in reverse gear, either."[12]

Thus I owe Mr. Nader an apology for all the bad thoughts (or at least this one bad thought) I had been thinking about him for all those years. But it is only a semiapology because it obviously served Nader's purposes to take Ms. McCluggage's words literally without allowing for the flashy exaggeration automotive writers indulge in to exhibit their knowledgeability and expertise.

(Nor is Nader above indulging in this kind of alarmist exaggeration on his own. In *The Lemon Book*, a manual on how to handle complaints about automobile defects, jointly authored in 1980 by Nader, Clarence Ditlow and Joyce Kinnard, directors of one of Nader's spin-off consumer advocacy groups, the Center for Auto Safety, this statement appears: "Tires tend to be more defect-ridden than any other single part of a car and the defects generally have more disastrous consequences than other car defects. Evidence of their frequency can be seen along any major highway—chunks of rubber and damaged guardrails are left behind, although the rest of the debris may be towed away."[13]

(Damaged guardrails may very well be evidence of collisions with automobiles that have been towed away, but virtually all the rubber fragments one encounters on every freeway are pieces of retreads thrown off by heavy trucks. I've seen it happen firsthand.)

It also turned out that the copy of *Unsafe* I obtained was not the 1965 edition but a 1972 reprint with a long introductory chapter recounting changes in automotive safety in the previous seven years. Even in 1972 Nader wasn't yet done with the Corvair. In this introductory chapter he marshaled more evidence against it, citing proving-ground tests by both Chevrolet and Ford Motor Company in which prototype and early production models of the Corvair had gone out of control and overturned right and left. Even before I reached the original text, I learned that *all* Corvairs had been dangerous, including my beloved 1966.

Noting that (in 1972) there were "still seven hundred and sixty thousand lethal Corvairs on the highway," Nader told of a suit brought against General Motors in 1962 by a man who claimed to have suffered permanent brain damage as the result of driving long distances in his 1961 Corvair Greenbriar station wagon while breathing in deadly carbon monoxide emitted into the passenger compartment by a defectively designed heating system.[14] Yet in 1971, wrote Nader, in "an incredible agreement" with the National Highway Traffic Safety Administration, General Motors had been permitted to deny in letters of warning to owners of 1961-1969 Corvairs that their cars' heaters had any defect.[15] The NHSTA thereafter prohibited car manufacturers from such "sabotaging" of defect notification letters, he added.

Repair of the heater would have cost $170 and was not even a permanent fix, wrote Nader. GM refused to absorb that cost, "even though the need arose from the company's defective design of the vehicle." In any case, he noted, it was unlikely that any owners of these cars would bother to have the repair made because most of them were "now worth not more than two hundred dollars."[16]

I wonder if it occurred to him just why Corvairs would have such low resale value. I also wonder if my brain damage is the result not of smoking but of driving a closed-up Corvair through six Ohio winters. Or possibly it's a combination of both.

The very title of the book was pure hyperbole. The Corvair (and other cars Nader criticized) were unsafe at *any* speed? The subtitle—"The designed-in dangers of the American automobile"—was even more inflammatory, implying that the automakers not only skimped on safety but *deliberately* made their cars dangerous. It is true that safety was hardly foremost in Detroit's mind back then, yet any car, including today's models embodying the latest safety features, can be dangerous in the hands of a poor or reckless driver. Automobiles will always be dangerous as long as they are driven by human beings.

In the very first sentence in the original preface Nader set the tone for the rest of the book: "For over half a century the automobile has brought death, injury, and the most inestimable sorrow and deprivation to millions of people." With nary a compensating benefit, as far as I was able to find. Nader obviously did not and still does not share, or even comprehend, the depths of Americans' love affair (or maybe it should be called love-hate relationship) with the automobile, notwithstanding all the human sorrow and social and environmental problems it has brought about.

I do believe that GM executives, for all their corporate stupidity in the way they tried to handle Nader's attack on the Corvair, were truly blindsided by him. They did not conceive that they were dealing, not with a con artist or opportunist having ulterior motives for questioning the safety of what they knew was a well-engineered automobile, but with an idealistic young man, a veritable ascetic seemingly devoid of personal vices and above ordinary human failings. General Motors simply did not realize that Ralph Nader was far more dangerous than a con artist: he was a True Believer.

But was the young crusader all that idealistic? As a journalist I was frequently sent books by publishers, although book reviews were not my job. One I received in 1969 was called *The Assassination of the Corvair*, which title naturally intrigued me. Its author, Andrew J. White, founder of Motor Vehicle Research in New Hampshire, had a long list of credentials as an automobile research and testing engineer.

White had had numerous personal contacts with Nader, beginning when Nader was still in Harvard Law School. He tells about receiving one late-evening telephone call in 1965 in which Nader "excitedly" told him that GM had launched a character-assassination plot against him, employing good-looking girls to tempt and compromise him, hiring gumshoes to trail him and interviewing some of his acquaintances in hopes of getting information to discredit him. (White found this hard to believe but it was, lamentably, true.) White said Nader called him again in 1966 seeking confidential file material he could use in a confrontation with General Motors during a scheduled congressional subcommittee hearing into automobile safety in general and the Corvair in particular. White had the feeling that Nader was "brain-picking." He told Nader he was chasing the wrong vehicle and that his claims about the Corvair had no technical foundation. As for *Unsafe At Any Speed,* White wrote:

> Succinctly, this book belongs, in my opinion, in the archives discussing UFOs . . . My impression of Nader's pseudo-technical nonsense was that it tended to create an impression that our roads were strewn with bodies, mangled and crushed in accidents caused by a "killer car" . . . that General Motors Corporation was a giant monster living among our citizens, eating them up when it was hungry and milking them of their money by selling them metal monsters designed to kill them . . . that General Motors had traded safety for profits by designing the Corvair with papier-mâché components and deleting others which would make the vehicle safe to drive . . . that any changes in the design of a vehicle from year to year are prima facie evidence that the manufacturer did not know what he was doing in the first place . . . that the Corvair was described as behaving abnormally under normal driving conditions.[17]

These statements may also warrant a certain amount of discounting, for White was as favorably disposed toward the automobile industry as Nader was in the opposite direction. Essentially, however, they are an accurate description of the tone and intent of *Unsafe*.

Although all attention was focused on the allegations regarding the 1960-1963 Chevrolet Corvairs, *Unsafe* also condemned the 1963 Buick Roadmaster and the 1964 Ford Mustang, and flailed not only General Motors but all car manufacturers, plus the tire manufacturers. For good measure he also questioned the usefulness and/or integrity of the Society of Automotive Engineers, the National Safety Council, the Auto Industries Highway Committee, the American Association of Motor Vehicle Administrators, the National Committee on Uniform Laws and Ordinances, the Automotive Safety Foundation, the Insurance Institute for Highway Safety, the American Automobile Association, the Auto Industries Highway Safety Committee—in short, the entire automobile and highways and traffic safety establishment, both federal and local, private and nonprofit. Not neglected were the media for what he considered to be their uncritical support of the auto industry. As for automobile design in general, enough nits were picked to place the lice population on the endangered species list.

Unlike Andrew White, the salient impression I came away with from *Unsafe* (other than that automobile company executives are strangers to all human decency and compassion) was that automobiles, not their drivers, were always to be held accountable in accidents. Deaths and injuries resulting from accidents were the fault of unsafe vehicle design, not the initiating driver errors. Wrote Nader:

> The failure of the [automotive] establishment to provide some empirical basis for its driver-oriented nostrums is fully consistent with the purpose of concentrating on the driver in the first place. That purpose is to divert attention from the vehicle, not really to understand driver behavior, because a sincere attempt to understand driver behavior would inevitably bring under discussion the engineering of the vehicle. To take a fairly simple example, many drivers respond to an emergency situation by a sudden application of the brakes, which can easily make the brakes lock and lead to loss of steering control. There is substantial evidence that the loss of steering control with locked brakes is highly dangerous and has led to many collisions with other vehicles or roadside objects. There are two approaches to solving this problem; either trying to teach drivers that during emergencies they must not resort to a sudden

> application of brakes which, *because of their design* [emphasis added], will lock; or trying to persuade the manufacturers to provide cars with anti-locking brakes. It is not difficult to choose the more feasible approach. But although anti-locking brakes have been in use in aircraft since the thirties, the automobile makers have done very little research and development in this area—at least, very little that is publicly known.[18]

But how does a driver get into an emergency situation in the first place other than, in almost all cases, because of some kind of error committed by him or somebody else—driving too fast,* following too closely, sheer inattentiveness, etc.? Today, antilocking brakes are either standard equipment or an available option on most new cars, and now we have problems with drivers who don't know how to utilize them properly—by applying firm, steady pressure on the brakes—because they were always taught that you should *pump* the brakes to keep them from locking. Contrary to Nader's assertions, there is only so much that technology can do to save drivers from themselves.

As for teaching drivers the techniques of avoiding emergency situations, Nader had little faith in the value of high-school driver-education courses:

> Even after the elements of the driving task are understood, it may be revealed that the time and resources necessary to upgrade driver control and response to highway situations are not practical and are replaceable by cheaper and more effective engineering innovations which adapt to human limitations.[20]

In other words, in the gospel according to Nader, the most that ought to be expected from the driver of a car is that he know the "elements"—how to start the thing, put it into gear, aim it and stop it. Beyond that, any emergency situation he may get himself into that results in injury becomes the responsibility of the car's designer.

(Even so, Nader told an interviewer that what pushed him "over the edge" into running—sort of—for president in 1966 was President

*In this regard, it is noteworthy that "the most dangerous car on the road today" is another Chevrolet product, the Camaro. It's not because it has any known safety defects but because, says the Insurance Institute for Highway Safety, as a high-performance "muscle car" the Camaro is "frequently driven in such a way that makes it the most lethal set of wheels on U.S. Highways."[19] This was in fact one of the arguments GM used in defending the Corvair.

Clinton's "callous" decision to abolish the federal 55-mile-per-hour speed limit.[21] Which would kind of seem to conflict with his position regarding the role—the nonrole, that is—of drivers in accidents, except that he probably meant that this was another instance of the government shirking its duty to protect us from ourselves. That is, it's not the driver's responsibility to drive prudently. Another implication was that the states were not competent to set rational speed limits on their highways.)

Speaking of nostrums—vehicle-oriented, not driver-oriented—the air bag is a prominent one which Nader and many others championed. On a doom-and-gloom antinuclear power page I found on the World Wide Web, the author quoted President John F. Kennedy as saying in 1963, three months before his assassination, "If even one child loses its life because of nuclear power, it is not worth the cost."[22] Although they had already saved some 1,700 lives at the time I began this chapter, deploying air bags had also killed 54 people, 34 of them young children riding in the front passenger seat. What would Kennedy have said about, not one, but more than *thirty* children losing their lives because of air bags? And the toll has since risen higher.

The air bag is another advance in automobile safety that has necessitated driver reeducation, in this case teaching parents never to let small children ride in the front passenger seat, especially babies or toddlers in rear-facing child-restraint seats, but always to secure them in the back seat. Yet adult drivers too have been killed, although most of them were not using seat belts. Small women, who have to move the seat all the way forward in order to be able to reach the brake and gas pedals, are especially at risk. The National Highway Traffic Safety Administration has also found that elderly drivers are prone to air-bag injury.

Air-bag tragedies, relatively rare though they are compared to the number of lives saved, soon suggested the need for certain "fixes," such as allowing dealers and repair businesses to deactivate the bags upon authorization of the owner, or installing dashboard on-off switches, or to redesign the bags to deploy more gently. (But slower opening air bags would seem to defeat the primary purpose of the bags, which were originally designed to protect an unbelted 170-pound adult in a 30-mile-an-hour collision—and presumably to offer at least some protection in higher-speed crashes—by deploying in a split second.) The NHTSA is also encouraging the development of "smart" bags that can sense the weight resting on the passenger seat. Below a certain weight, that of a small child or perhaps just a package, the "smart" bag would not be activated.[23]

The NHTSA eventually did say it would allow car owners to install an on-off switch (at a cost of about $150)—those, that is, who go through a seven-step process, which includes the filing of a signed pledge documenting why a switch is needed.

It's a small victory for consumers, even though giving people the right, however limited, to decide for themselves whether they want air bags goes against everything the crusaders hold sacred—their mission to protect us from every sling and arrow of outrageous, or even ordinary, fortune whether we want to be protected or not.

It is also extremely costly to replace air bags that have been deployed in an accident, so costly that it is sometimes cheaper for insurance companies to declare a car totaled rather than to pay for repairing it and replacing the bag or bags, even though damage to the car itself may be minimal. This is surely a waste and is something else Nader never considered, and probably doesn't care about. It's not his money. It's never the crusaders' money.

It's also never their own tails on the line. Said Andrew White in testimony before a congressional subcommittee on traffic safety in 1957: "Until any engineer or advocator is willing to endanger his own life in actual crashes, he should be most hesitant to suggest that other human beings place their lives in his hands by following his recommendations."[24]

White was speaking of the use of lap belts, which he believed were more dangerous than no belts at all without being used in conjunction with some kind of shoulder restraint. This was before the shoulder belt/lap belt combination became standard. But his words certainly still apply to the air bags that Nader called a simple and failsafe safety device.

The Naderite view of the world is also reflected in at least one lawsuit involving air bags—the absence of them, that is. The family of one Rebecca Ann Tebbetts, who was killed in an accident in a 1988 Ford Escort, contended that her life could have been saved had the company made air bags available in that model. No less than the Supreme Court ruled that the family could sue Ford because it didn't install every conceivable safety feature in all its cars.[25]

At least one early pioneer of the air bag concept did put his own tail on the line, at least in a laboratory setting. In the mid-1960s, to test proposed air-inflatable seats for Apollo astronauts at Baltimore-based Martin Company, biophysicist Carl Clark was dropped from increasing heights inside a box while lying between two air bags. This led to work on an air bag safety system for automobiles he called the Airstop Restraint System. The bags were reusable because they were inflated by air canisters that could be refilled at a service station, not explosive sodium azinide used in today's air bags.

The automobile manufacturers had also been studying air bags, but (shades of the evil tobacco companies) "their technical work was done in secret," says Clark. ". . . [T]hey didn't want us stirring the pot . . . It was frustrating to see the opposition of the auto companies. They would tell my bosses that their research showed that air bags don't work, at the same time that I was doing work that showed that they worked very well."[26]

Clark is a true Naderite, however, in his belief that there is no reason anyone should be hurt in any kind of car crash. He has patented a solid-fueled, forward-facing retrorocket brake that could slow a car from 55 miles per hour to eight miles an hour in just 23 feet of travel.

"Why is it that we accept a vehicle crashing when the driver has her [or his—D.O] foot on the brake and intends to stop?" he asks.

Why, indeed? Unfortunately, some people drive so fast and so close to the car ahead that they don't have time to hit the brakes, so even retrorockets wouldn't save them. Whoever designed the human nervous system has a lot of explaining to do.

GM's CLUMSY COUNTERATTACK against Nader—which resulted in a $26-million lawsuit filed by him and a congressional hearing at which GM president James Roche publicly apologized to Nader—was actually its second mistake. Its first mistake was settling a prior lawsuit against the Corvair. In the field of product liability, lawsuits beget lawsuits.

By the time *Unsafe* had come out in 1965, more than a hundred such claims had been filed by legal sharks who had caught the scent of a product in trouble. As early as October 1962, an advertisement published in a number of legal journals around the country solicited an exchange of information among attorneys representing plaintiffs in suits against the Corvair.[27] By June 1964, one Los Angeles law firm alone had filed 24 of them. One was *Rose Pierini v. Washburn Chevrolet and*

General Motors Corporation for $300,000 in damages. Ms. Pierini had lost an arm in an accident in her Corvair. Three days into the trial—after the jury had been shown pictures of the unfortunate woman's bloody stump taken at the hospital—GM offered to settle for $70,000, which plaintiff accepted.

This was trumpeted by her attorney as a victory over GM during a television newscast, which included a film showing an overturned Corvair, although the film had not been offered in evidence at the trial. Wire services picked up the story. A Canadian scandal tabloid called *Midnight* screamed: GM CARS ARE DEATH TRAPS; HUSHED UP EVIDENCE REVEALED IN COURT—WOMAN AWARDED 70G FOR LOSS OF ARM IN DEFECTive CORVAIR.[28]

GM fought back after that, and in the next two cases that went all the way to conclusion, juries found for the defense. Although Nader went into detail about the Pierini suit in *Unsafe*, he mentioned these vindications of the Corvair only in passing. He also noted that GM had paid out hundreds of thousands of dollars in other cases, ignoring the probability that many, if not all, of them were nuisance suits that all deep-pocket corporations are hit with and which they consider simply as an inevitable part of the cost of doing business.

Unsafe was published in November 1965. In December, Corvair registrations dropped 42 percent below those of December a year earlier, and subsequently there was never to be a month in which Corvair registrations were able to match those of the year-earlier month.

In 1970 the National Highway Traffic Safety Administration contracted with Texas A&M University to launch an investigation into the 1960-63 Corvairs, and in mid-July 1972 released its final report in which it exonerated the car of all charges, concluding "that the handling and stability performance of the 1960-1963 Corvair does not result in an abnormal potential for the loss of control or rollover and that its handling and stability performance is at least as good as the performance of some contemporary vehicles, both foreign and domestic," and "that no safety related defect exists with respect to the handling and stability characteristics of the 1960-1963 Corvair."[29]

As for that footage of a Ford test driver overturning a Corvair that Nader cited in the 1972 Introduction to *Unsafe*, one Corvair enthusiast and historian, Kent Sullivan, says that "The Texas A&M researchers did a frame-by-frame analysis of the film and found that the driver was intentionally trying to roll the Corvair but not the other cars on the track."[30]

A syndicated financial columnist named Don Campbell wrote on July 26, 1972:

> Nader predictably has labeled the study that he himself insisted on as a whitewash. Which if true, considering the number of governmental agencies, impartial testing groups and educational institutions engaged in it, would have to involve a conspiracy, that in scope, would make the Tea Pot Dome Scandal look like a shakedown on the school playground. The significance of it is a little numbing. The Corvair affair not only catapulted Nader from obscurity into his present role of one of the country's best-known men, but it launched the whole consumer action movement that almost daily makes headlines in every newspaper in the country. And the seed of it all was a charge that present evidence indicates wasn't even true.[31]

But by 1972, of course, it was much too late; the Corvair had already been out of production for three years. Incidentally, Nader somehow omitted mentioning the NHTSA's vindication of the Corvair in his updating introductory chapter to the 1972 reissue of *Unsafe*. While not referring to the report directly, he did however seem to imply darkly that it was part of a deal between the NHTSA and GM. In connection with a suit filed by Ford, Chrysler and American Motors to delay the implementation of a proposed NHTSA regulation regarding air bags, he wrote:

> It is noteworthy that General Motors has not joined the industry law suit. While it has nodded public concurrence with the actions of its colleagues, GM officers have privately been boasting to the NHTSA about advancements in their production model air bag. GM's motivations were mixed. President Ed Cole was said [by whom?—D.O.] to be elated at the price increase he could charge for the air bag, while heaping the blame for the increase on the government. Also, by not actively opposing the embattled agency, GM expected reciprocal sympathy toward the company and its products—in the NHTSA's investigations of Corvair defects, for example, including carbon monoxide leaks from the heater system in 1961-69 models [that means *all* Corvairs ever built—D.O.] . . . Administrator [Douglas] Toms, believing it critically important to success in court for GM not to be a party to the passive restraint suit, has privately played down the urgency of other agency matters

> pending against GM in order to retain the company's good will, naively expecting that this violation of his public trust will serve as a deterrent to GM's doing what comes naturally.[32]

Whether Nader really meant to imply that the NHTSA's investigation into the Corvair's handling and stability was among those "other matters" pending against GM, and that the agency's clearing the car of all charges was a quid pro quo deal between it and the carmaker—the NHTSA would exonerate the Corvair and in return GM wouldn't oppose air bags—only he knows (and will never tell).

The Corvair is but one example of how the media help us "know" things that ain't so. As late as 1997, a program on the History channel on cable TV retold the whole gory story of the unfortunate car. Not a mention of the NHTSA investigation and verdict.

For years I've blamed Ralph Nader for the demise of the Corvair, but recent surfing of Corvair sites on the Internet persuades me otherwise. From one of them:

> The myth that Nader killed the Corvair still pervades the U.S. today, even after 25 years since the last Corvair rolled off the production line. In fact, Nader was probably responsible for keeping the Corvair *alive* [emphasis in original] from 1967 to 1969! The most likely cause of the Corvair going out of production was Ford's introduction of the Mustang in mid-1964 . . . Shortly after the introduction of the Mustang, Corvair development was internally stopped by GM (in early 1965), and development of its replacement (the Camaro) began. Corvair production continued all the way out to 1969 in spite of the deliberate developmental halt by GM, but the production was sharply curtailed by GM (rather than by sales as many have suggested). Some people speculate that Nader's drum-beating, and the flurry of lawsuits, actually prompted GM into keeping the Corvair alive in limited, but decreasing, production in 1967-1969. Without Nader (and his book), the Corvair might have vanished after 1966.[33]

Others have different opinions. About all that can really be said for sure is that Ralph Nader was the right man at the right place at the right time—with the wrong target. Surprisingly—or not so surprisingly, because the Corvair really was a damned fine car—the Corvair yet lives today. There are dozens of Corvair enthusiast clubs all over the country, as well as companies specializing in Corvair parts.

The first Corvair came off the line on July 7, 1959. Between that date and May 10, 1969, when the last one was built, 1,669,482 were sold in this country. "It is interesting to ponder," wrote Andrew J. White in *Assassination*, "why so few people were killed by more than a million six hundred thousand of these alleged 'unsafe monsters.'"[34]

Criticism of the automobile industry is hardly new, though the complaints were usually about the quality of its products, not their safety. In Arthur Miller's play, "Death of A Salesman," Willy Loman muttered about "That goddam Studebaker!" I well remember that in the immediate post-World War II years many people complained that the automakers were using thinner and flimsier sheet metal than they had in prewar cars.

Yet to give Ralph Nader his due, the automobile industry has from its inception kicked and screamed against just about every safety or convenience improvement ever conceived, from windshield wipers to seat belts. If it took the "assassination" of the Corvair to force the automakers to start building better and safer cars, it would have been worth it. (It was actually competition from foreign imports that provided the real incentive to the U.S. industry.) But as for helping instill the fear of *everything* in Americans which, rightly or wrongly, I have given Nader so much credit for, that is something else again.

A final note: in the immediate wake of the Corvair flap, in the spirit of *Unsafe At Any Speed* and in keeping with the popular belief that for every problem there must be a legislative solution, the more far-reaching the better, in February 1966 a bill establishing specifications regarding the lateral stability of automobiles was introduced in the Michigan Senate. Had it been passed into law and enforced, the measure would have banned from Michigan highways every automobile ever made in the United States.[35]

ON THE BASIS OF the fame, and a $480,000 settlement, General Motors bestowed on him, Ralph Nader was established as the patron saint of consumer advocates, going on to attract a corps of idealistic young do-gooders—the accurately named "Nader's Raiders"—and enabled to found at last count some 28 consumer-protection and public-interest groups and lobbies dedicated to ferreting out what he termed "crime in the [corporate] suites."

One of these groups, the Center for Auto Safety (CAS), was to play a prominent role in the hysterical trashing of another fine car, the Audi 5000. The allegation inspiring a host of lawsuits against the Audi was that, for some unknown reason, it would suddenly rocket forward, or backward, even though the driver swore he had his foot on the brake pedal, crashing through garage walls or into trees or other cars. The same "problem" was reported with other makes of cars, but it was the Audi 5000 that became the target of this crusade. Feeding the frenzy was the CBS news program "60 Minutes," on which in a 1986 broadcast reporter Ed Bradley interviewed a grieving mother who, at the wheel of an out-of-control Audi 5000, had crushed to death her 6-year-old son in the family's garage.[36]

It was natural for the CAS to hop on this crusade because the Founder had already been there. In *Unsafe* Nader had cited five cases of what he called "transmission-induced, engine-powered runaway" accidents, the occurrence of which was "rising alarmingly" because of more powerful engines and automatic transmissions. Cars were suddenly jumping forward or backwards, crashing through store windows or into people's backyards, running over and injuring or killing innocent bystanders.[37]

He lambasted the automobile manufacturers for putting the Reverse and Drive positions next to each other on the steering wheel shift quadrant. But that was changed in 1966, with Neutral being placed between Reverse and Drive, so it was not a factor in the later Audi accidents (and probably wasn't in the ones Nader cited). Most significantly, every "sudden acceleration" incident with the Audi began from a dead stop after the driver had shifted into gear. And in every case, the brakes and transmissions and cruise controls and electronics on the cars involved in such accidents were found to be in perfect working order. Audis were torn apart and put back together again, but no cause for this mysterious behavior was ever found, for the simple reason that panicked drivers *thought* they were stepping on the brake but were actually pushing the gas pedal, and the harder they pushed the faster and farther the car went.

The only good thing to come from it all was the introduction of an additional idiot-proofing improvement in the form of transmission shift-locks which require a driver to put his foot firmly on the brake pedal *before* shifting into gear. But it cost Audi millions of dollars in investigating the charge and defending itself in court and settling claims, and millions more in lost sales. It cost other millions to owners of Audis in terms of the reduced resale value of their cars.

Yet even though the National Highway Traffic Safety Administration examined 400 Audi complaints, 300 accident records, 175 injuries and four deaths and eventually gave the Audi a clean bill of health (as it had the Corvair), its finding was dismissed as "incompetent nonsense" by Clarence Ditlow of the CAS. Another one of those government coverup deals and whitewashes, obviously.

Peter W. Huber, who recounts the history of the Audi 5000 in *Galileo's Revenge: Junk Science in the Courtroom*, notes that this car had one of the lowest fatality rates of any on the market, according to both the Insurance Institute for Highway Safety and the NHTSA. He concludes:

> So at the end of the Audi story, only a few numbers remain utterly beyond dispute. Audi lost a few cases and paid millions in damages and settlements. Its sales plummeted, from a peak of 73,000 cars in 1985 to 23,000 in 1988. Where did the 50,000 lost buyers choose to shop instead? Wherever it was, they very likely ended up in less safe cars.[38]

Did Clarence Ditlow or any other consumer crusader apologize to Audi or Audi owners? Silly question. Like antismoking activists, consumer crusaders never admit to overzealousness, much less to error. As for "60 Minutes," when the NHTSA's clearing of the Audi was announced, the show actually reran its tearful 1986 story.

No, consumer crusaders are never wrong and never apologize. And the public admires and honors them.

WHAT HAS ALL OF the foregoing to do with a book that is supposed to be about smoking? Well, one connection is that the day I drove my new Corvair home from the dealer's and looked it over admiringly I discovered that during its assembly someone had tossed a cigarette butt into the trunk—and it had been neatly painted over! That told me something either about Chevrolet's or Fisher Body's quality control at the time or the work ethic of the highly paid members of the powerful but always dissatisfied United Auto Workers. Maybe both.

But the main reason I have written at length about Ralph Nader and automobiles is because (1) it was an automobile that made him famous and because (2) like the antismoking crusaders, he has, in my opinion, exerted, and continues to exert, a malevolent influence upon American society. Nader and those he has inspired to emulate him are responsible in large measure for the public's readiness to believe any and every scary allegation about an endless list of health and safety and consumer product and environmental perils (of which smoking is but one) and to distrust the motives and ethics of large corporations (of which the tobacco industry is only the most prominent example) simply because they are large and wealthy and, presumably, all-powerful.

(For an exhaustive treatment of the most important of these alleged perils in terms of their financial and social cost, and an exposure of the antitechnology mindset of the crusaders who promote them, I recommend Michael Fumento's *Science Under Siege*. His book is a good companion to Huber's *Galileo's Revenge*, which relates how trial lawyers, armed with the weapon of "strict liability," have transformed America's legal system into a battle for the hearts and minds of jurors, a battle waged between cautious, tentative sound-science reasoning and the junk-science argument that if something is remotely possible—like, say, a certain chemical causing cancer—even if it is impossible to prove one way or the other, we ought to give the plaintiff the benefit of the doubt and sock it to the manufacturer or the industry.)

I have also picked on Ralph Nader because he epitomizes the arrogance and hypocrisy and self-righteousness of so many crusaders. A good example of all three traits on Nader's part are the Public Interest Research Groups (PIRG) he set up on a number of college campuses. Just what kind of "public interest research" they did or if they still do it, I don't know, but I first became aware of them in the late 1970s when my son was attending Worcester Polytechnic Institute in Massachusetts. One of the tuition bills I received listed a fee for that school's PIRG. It must have been identified as a Ralph Nader group because I remember being somewhat surprised and a little incensed that Mr. Nader would countenance this method of funding that did not ask a student (or his parent) whether or not he wished to support the PIRG. At the time I was not yet completely disenchanted with Nader and, as I have said, all my years of smoking have damaged my brain, so I don't remember if I did any more than mutter and go ahead and pay the bill. It was only a few dollars.

According to a political action group called Real People for Real Change PAC (political action committee), one school, Penn State, "declined Nader's PIRG group's coercive funding and [its Board of Overseers] voted instead to let students check a box to make a donation . . . a perfectly reasonable compromise. Nader blasted this plan as a 'sabotage technique' and 'tyranny 1776 style' and then announced an investigation of the school's trustees for 'conflicts of interest.'"[39]

Forced payments could have brought in $270,000 a year at Penn State, says Real People, compared to only $30,000 from a voluntary check-off. At least 145 colleges in 20 states were involved with PIRGs in the mid-1970s and these forced payments were raising over a million dollars a year. The actual amount is unknown because Mr. Nader does not reveal information about the finances, or the financing, of his various projects, nor does he appreciate questions about his integrity.

An illustration of the first trait—arrogance—as well as a fourth—insensitivity—on Nader's part can be seen in an exchange between the crusader and Utah Republican Senator Jake Garn during a Senate Banking Committee hearing into the Chrysler bailout in 1979. Nader was demanding that the company be required to promise to make safer cars. To which Garn retorted, "I would suggest that if the American consumer knew what you had cost us in the name of consumerism they would run you out of the country." Then followed this dialogue:

Nader: I suspect, Senator Garn, that some senator's personal tragedy might not have occurred if the auto industry had listened to some of us in the early years to build safer cars.

Garn: Mr. Nader, I take exception to that. I think that is one of the cruelest comments you have ever made. Yes, my wife died in an automobile accident.

Nader: And she could have been saved. She could have been saved with cars that should have been built twenty years ago.

Garn: You always know about everything, don't you? You know the circumstances of the accident, you know how it happened, do you?

Nader: Yes.

Garn: You do?

Nader: Yes.

Garn: Well, tell me about it, then. Let's find out if you do.

Nader: I will tell you when this hearing is finished.

Garn: No; I want to know right now. You made an assertion. Let's put some facts with your assertion.

Nader: It was a crash in Utah, I believe.

Garn: No it was not. It was in Nebraska.

Nader: All right, Nebraska. That's hardly relevant.

Garn: Typical of your research.

Nader: And it was a crash that was under a 60-mile-an-hour collision level, and that level of crash should be survivable.

Garn: It was not a crash. It involved no other vehicle.

Nader: It was a rollover, wasn't it?

Garn: Yes.

Nader: And a rollover is exactly the kind of preventable injury that the auto companies could have designed for, compared to, say, being hit head on by a trailer truck.

Garn: Are you aware she was wearing a seat belt?

Nader: Yes.

Garn: Her seat belt was on and fastened. Are you aware that three of my children happened to be with her, and had no seat belts on at all and had no injuries whatsoever?

Nader: I don't think you are ascribing that tragedy to the seat belt.

Garn: That the personal tragedy of losing my wife of nineteen years . . . to interject that into a hearing. . . . What kind of human being are you?

Nader: A human being who is working to save lives on the highway. Don't try and overemote. I'm saying that safer cars would have saved many Americans, including people in a crash of that kind. And for you to try to pillory me because I am trying to say that your wife could have been saved in a casualty of that kind as you do is irresponsible.[40]

Even if I were a U.S. senator, I would no more argue with Ralph Nader than I would attempt to reason with a dedicated antismoker. So utterly convinced of the rightness of their opinions are such True Believers that anyone who challenges them must be either hopelessly ignorant or operating from ulterior motives.

A MILLION DOLLARS A year (or whatever the figure is or was) raked in by Nader's PIRGs is a piddling sum compared to the tens and hundreds of millions of hidden dollars the public-interest groups and consumer advocates have cost and are costing the American public. It would take an entire book to explore merely the most notorious examples (and Fumento has done just that in *Science Under Siege*), but here are a few of them:

Alar. This was a growth-regulating chemical developed by Uniroyal Chemical Company in the 1960s and approved by the Department of Agriculture for use on a variety of fruits. It was mostly sprayed on apple orchards, however, because it accorded a number of advantages, such as the ripening of the apples in an entire orchard at the same time, more uniform shape and color and longer shelf life. Unfortunately, four highly suspect studies in the 1970s claimed that an Alar breakdown chemical called UDMH induced tumors in laboratory mice. In disregard of the finding of its own Scientific Advisory Panel that the studies were seriously flawed, the EPA (which really stands for "Everything's Potentially Awful" although the official name is the Environmental Protection Agency) listed Alar and UDMH as "possible carcinogens."

That's all it took. The "public-interest" litigation group, National Resources Defense Council (NRDC), launched a campaign against Alar. Ralph Nader got into the act, with his Public Citizen Group joining the NRDC in a suit to force the EPA to ban Alar. When the suit was thrown out of court they switched to public relations (i.e., fear) tactics. CBS's Ed Bradley and "60 Minutes" again did what they could to fuel the alarm by telling Americans on a broadcast on February 26, 1989 that Alar is "the most potent cancer-causing agent in our food supply."

Unlike the short-lived Great Cranberry Scare in the fall of 1959, the Great Apple Scare of 1989 had far-reaching and long-lasting success—if by success one means the elimination of a useful chemical, the unjustified indictment of two industries and the loss of livelihood of many hapless apple farmers. For as the result of "one of the slickest, most cynical fear campaigns in recent American history," writes

Fumento, over 500 schools in California yanked apples, apple sauce and apple juice from their cafeterias, grocery stores across the nation pulled apple products off their shelves and threw out their fresh apples, and panicked consumers stopped buying and eating apples or apple products. The price of apples plummeted. Apple growers in Washington state, which grows more than 50 percent of the nation's apples, alone lost $135 million in 1989 and some small family-owned orchards went down the tubes.

In May of that year the apple industry capitulated and announced that it would stop using Alar, and Uniroyal decided to end both domestic and foreign sales of the chemical (even though, for some reason, Alar never caused cancer, real or imagined, in people or in mice, anywhere but in the United States.) Ah yes, 'twas a great victory in the name of consumer protection. Uniroyal and most of the apple growers will survive but, points out Fumento, "The ultimate victims are those for whom the NRDC claims to be an advocate, the consumers." He sums up the story with this warning:

"The battle against Alar was merely a small part of the war against pesticides in general, which is a small part of the war against man-made chemicals in general, which is a small part of the war against technology in general. And make no mistake, the assailants, the besiegers of science, will settle for nothing short of total victory."[41]

Irradiated foods. Alar is gone and forgotten by most people, but there's another battle—this one not over a product but a process, the irradiation of food— that has been simmering for decades and which the crusaders have so far been winning.

Irradiation is the bombarding of an item of food, say a bag of potatoes or a chicken, with ionizing radiation from various sources, the same kind of radiation used in X-rays, in a special chamber. Most of the radiation passes through the substance, but enough is absorbed to kill insects and the bacteria that cause such nasty and potentially lethal illnesses as salmonella. No radiation remains in the product, any more than an X-ray makes a person "radioactive." Irradiation can also prevent fruits and vegetables from ripening too early. Its greatest virtue is that it greatly prolongs shelf, as long as eight years for a precooked, vacuum-sealed chicken, for example.

Anti-irradiationists point out that the amount of radiation used—

thousands of rads (a rad is a measure of radiation)—would also kill a human being. However, you'd have to climb into the chamber along with the chicken for that to happen. The heat used to prepare a vegetable for conventional canning or the low temperature of frozen-food processing equipment would also thoroughly cook your goose, or freeze it, as the case may be. Opponents—among whose number is the Public Citizen Health Research Group, founded by our old friend Ralph Nader—also contradict their own fear argument regarding the danger of radiation by pointing out that, because no radiation remains in the irradiated product, it has to be sealed in order to prevent post-sterilization contamination. Yet the same is true of *any* preservation process.

Canning and freezing have been around a long time and have served us very well; why do we need another food preservation process? Because of irradiation's superior sterilizing ability, as well as, as stated above, the longer shelf life it affords. As for the "traditional" processes, it's an unusual householder who has never at some time or other reached for a can of, say, stewed tomatoes in the pantry and noticed a suspicious bulge in the can and wisely threw the can away, or who has not retrieved a package of frozen fish from too long a sojourn in the freezer and found the fish had a peculiar odor and the consistency of plastic. Anti-irradiationists also claim that consumers would reject irradiated products, even as they do their utmost to see that consumers never have the opportunity to make that choice.

Irradiation itself has also been around for quite a while. The Army pioneered its development beginning in 1943, but it was not approved for use by the food industry until 1986 when the supercautious Food and Drug Administration finally allowed the process for grains, vegetables, fruits and spices. Up to now, however, it has been used mainly for the latter. (I report this at risk of inciting some easily scared people to shout: "My God, you mean the spices in my pantry have been irradiated all these years? That must be why I have these back pains. Somebody do something!")

Consumers in some 24 other countries can buy irradiated foods. But you can't get them in America unless you're an astronaut. (Crew members aboard the space shuttle eat irradiated food, including steak.) You can't buy them in Maine because that state has outlawed irradiated food completely. In other states you can't buy them simply because the industry hasn't made them available.

And why, pray tell, hasn't the food industry offered irradiated foods as an option to the consumer? Because everybody is waiting for somebody else to go first. They know that whoever goes first will be the target of vicious attacks by the consumer "protectors."

Wrote Richard Rhodes in *The New York Times*:

> Food irradiation would have prevented the illnesses caused recently [August 1997] by contaminated hamburger from Hudson Foods and the several deaths linked to Jack in the Box restaurants in the Northwest in 1993. It could kill the salmonella that infects up to 60 percent of the poultry and eggs sold in the United States; the deadly mutant E. coli strain 0157:H7, which the Centers for Disease Control and Prevention have characterized as a major emerging infectious disease, and such ugly stowaways as beef tapeworms, fish parasites and the nematodes that cause trichinosis in pork.
>
> Yet the new meat inspection system now being phased in by the United States Department of Agriculture does not even mention, much less mandate, irradiation. Neither Agriculture Secretary Dan Glickman nor the Food and Drug Administration invoked food irradiation as a solution to the Hudson Foods situation, preferring instead to press for destruction of 25 million pounds of meat that could have been made edible with the technique.
>
> A petition for authorization to irradiate red meat has languished at the FDA since 1994. Several states, including New York, have responded to pressure from citizen groups by either banning or imposing a moratorium on the sale of irradiated food without reviewing scientific evidence of the technology's safety and value.
>
> Why the gap between promise and application? Because food irradiation—like cancer treatment, medical diagnostics, sterilization of medical isposables, aircraft maintenance and many other technologies—uses radioactivity, which Americans have been taught to fear . . .
>
> Some anti-nuclear and environmental groups have campaigned against food irradiation, even imagining a conspiracy among the Food and Drug Administration, the World Health Organization and the nuclear power industry to use the process to dispose of nuclear waste.
>
> Similarly fanatic resistance plagued the introduction of vaccination, water chlorination, pasteurization and fluoridation—comparable technologies that have reduced disease and saved millions of lives. The unsupported fears of the Luddite opposition are making people suffer needlessly.[42]

After this was written, however, in December 1997 the FDA announced it would finally okay the use of irradiation for red meat.[43] Will anybody buy it? Not if picketing, protesting and propagandizing antis can help it.

In the meantime, by their opposition to irradiation, the antitechnology fearmongers have not only cost Americans millions or billions in dollars but actual deaths and serious illness from food poisoning. Yet they go on, and the public admires and honors them.

Chlorination. When it comes to lives sacrificed on the altar of Absolute Safety, water chlorination, which Rhodes referred to above, and which has been called the greatest triumph in the history of public health, was involved in perhaps the worst example of environmental idiocy in modern history.

It happened in Peru in the early '90s. Aware that studies by the American Environmental Protection Agency in the 1970s had "associated" the drinking of chlorinated water with a one in 100,000 chance of cancer, and under the delusion that the Norte Americanos must know what they were talking about, the Peruvian government decided to stop chlorinating the country's water supplies.[44]

In 1991, an epidemic of cholera broke out in Peru, believed to have been started by bilge water dumped by a ship. The disease rapidly spread to the rest of Latin America and reached the United States in 1992 via an outbreak among 75 commercial airline passengers from Peru. (Ironically, in that same year the EPA decided that the link between chlorinated drinking water and cancer was not scientifically supportable.) The epidemic is reported to have caused as many as *one million* cases of cholera and as many as *10,000* deaths in Latin America.

According to the Centers for Disease Control and Prevention, after the onset of the Latin America cholera epidemic cholera cases reported in the U.S. increased from an average of five cases a year between 1965 and 1991 to 53 cases a year from 1992 to 1994, most of them acquired from abroad.

One Peruvian congressman told Michael Fumento that he hopes the United States can learn from his country's mistake. "We're ahead of the U.S.," said Enrique Ghersi, "and have returned to the Middle Ages as a result."[45]

And did the EPA learn anything? In 1994 the agency proposed—to the distress and alarm of state public health officials—a rule that would require the nation's water systems to eliminate the process known as predisinfection. This unfunded mandate would cost local governments $4 million a year and could force small water systems to abandon chlorination entirely, says Fumento.

As Robert Forbes of the Florida Department of Health and Rehabilitative Services put it, "The reduction or elimination of chlorination of drinking water to reduce the risk of . . . disease is analogous to reducing or eliminating air travel to protect people on the ground from being hit by falling aircraft parts!"[46]

Dioxin. Along with most other people, I always believed that this chemical compound was one of the most toxic substances ever created by man, a mere few ounces of which could wipe out a million people. Or so many "experts" said. It happens that dioxin is another "deadly" substance that is ubiquitous in the environment. It is released by incineration of wastes containing chlorine and is an incidental by-product of a number of different manufacturing processes, such as papermaking. (It may also occur naturally through such a simple act as burning wood in a fireplace, though scientists are in disagreement about that.)

There is actually a family of some 75 dioxins, but one form of it called TCCD is the main culprit involved in the highly publicized Love Canal, New York, and Vietnam War-era Agent Orange episodes. In 1994 the Environmental Protection Agency, on the basis of a few animal studies and once again ignoring the advice of its Scientific Advisory Panel, declared it a "probable human carcinogen." Yet while the residents of Love Canal and thousands of Vietnam veterans reported all kinds of illnesses caused by dioxin (after they were told how dangerous it is), there has ***never*** been a reported case of anyone dying from it. But "probable" or "possible" is all the justification the EPA ever needs to go to work.

Consider the "crisis" in Times Beach, Missouri, where oil containing dioxin had been spread on a road. When the EPA heard about it, it ordered nothing less than the evacuation of the entire population of 2,000 souls and the complete obliteration of the town at a final cost to the taxpayers in the hundreds of millions.

I never thought about what that actually involved until I saw a TV program called "Junk Science: What You Know That May Not Be So,"[47] hosted by ABC investigative reporter John Stossel, one segment of which dealt with dioxin. (Others segments included the scares over salt in the diet, breast implants and "crack cocaine babies.") Stossel* showed people's houses in Times Beach being knocked down, with trucks hauling away the remains, along with dioxin-contaminated soil, around the clock. The whole area looked like something out of a Michael Crichton novel: a once-living town now under quarantine with guarded gates.

For a dramatic contrast with Times Beach, Stossel took viewers to Seveso, Italy, where on July 10, 1976 an explosion in a nearby chemical factory released a cloud of dioxin that fell on the city with a concentration thousands of times higher than anything measured in Times Beach. The U.S. media were full of reports from Seveso of animals "deteriorating," of deformed babies being born and dire warnings of all kinds of diseases the dioxin would eventually cause in the survivors of the accident because their immune systems were damaged. Many birds and small animals were killed by the fallout, but the only problems among humans were temporary cases of nausea, diarrhea, headaches and skin irritations. No one died and no epidemic of diseases has ever happened. Well, the first part of that statement is tragically not quite true: some 90 pregnant women were frightened into aborting fetuses that later were found would have been born as normal, healthy babies.

Today it's all only a memory in Seveso. The dioxin has been buried and a public park planted on top of it. There are no gates or guards. Children happily play there and the birds sing. Meanwhile, in the once-upon-a-time land of the free and the home of the brave, the EPA continues to spend taxpayers' dollars in a continuing effort to ferret out dioxin wherever it is found.

Regrettably, Stossel opened his program with some old TV cigarette commercials, such as "nine out of 10 doctors smoke Camels," and a well-worn film clip of the seven tobacco company CEOs telling a

*Who is a rarity among journalists in that he puts facts before scaremongering and values integrity above sensationalism. Stossel was not always so independent-minded, however. As he told *Los Angeles Times* reporter David Shaw: "[We] consumer reporters approached it [environmental news] from the bias that on the one hand is business, which is greedy and has an ulterior motive and will distort the data, and on the other hand is the noble environmental group, which has no motive other than to help the public. It took me years to realize that their data were often soft, if not absurd, and they had their own venal motives . . . to get on TV, to get famous, to get more grant money."[48]

congressional subcommittee, in turn, "I believe nicotine is not addictive," to illustrate people "knowing" something that isn't so. It apparently did not occur to Stossel that by using the tobacco CEOs as an example of misguided thinking he was tacitly conceding that their beliefs about nicotine, even if in error, were genuine and sincerely held and not "perjured" testimony as the antismokers allege.

The tobacco industry was an easy target and most viewers probably nodded their heads in agreement. It was certainly a safer target than, say, "scientific creationism." But at the conclusion of the program Stossel pointed out that scientific knowledge is continually changing as more evidence comes in and cautioned that some of things he had said pooh-poohing junk-science scares during the broadcast might also be proved wrong in future years. So maybe there's hope for nicotine, although I'm sure he didn't have that in mind.

Fear of dioxin also infected the residents of a predominantly poor and black Pensacola, Florida, neighborhood living near a 50-foot mound of dirt contaminated by residues of the chemical left by a wood treating company and a fertilizer plant when they went out of business. When the EPA started digging up the mound under its Superfund program, which cleans up toxic waste sites, people started getting rashes and coughs. "We pleaded with them to stop digging, but they wouldn't listen," one resident told a reporter.

They also suddenly realized why some of their former neighbors were no longer with them. "Man died of bone cancer in that house," said another resident. "Then that second house, the wife died, both of them cancer. Then you come to our house. My uncle died four years ago of bone cancer."[49]

The only thing these comments prove is that there is a very human need to find the reason—any reason—why dreaded diseases are visited upon us seemingly out of the blue, and why we are prey to those who offer simple answers. Enlisting the help of a national network of "toxic waste activists," the residents finally persuaded The EPA to consider moving everyone out of the area, à la Times Beach.

The EPA's war against dioxin goes on, despite the absence of any scientifically acceptable evidence that anyone has ever been harmed by it, much less died from it. One wonders how many more billions will have been spent before this crusade runs its course. Unfortunately, it is another example of how, when once this overweeningly powerful agency sinks its teeth into some perceived environmental danger, nothing can make it let go.

BECAUSE THE FLORIDA incident above involved a predominately black community, this is a good place for a short break and digression into the subject of "environmental racism." This is the charge that inhuman, profit-grubbing businesses have located, or would like to locate, environmentally dangerous plants in minority neighborhoods, which are usually poor and politically impotent and whose only defenders are the environmental crusaders.

The most recent example of attempted "environmental racism" was a plan by a Japanese petrochemical company, Shintech, Inc., to build a $700-million polyvinyl chloride (PVC) manufacturing facility in Convent, Louisiana, beside another low-income, predominately black neighborhood. A local group calling itself St. James Citizens for Jobs and the Environment petitioned the EPA to block the plant, which the agency did. It ordered the Louisiana Department of Environmental Quality, which had approved the plant, to hold hearings addressing concerns raised under the federal Civil Rights Act.

"We believe it's a tremendous victory and a historic moment," said Pat Melancon, leader of the citizens group.

Nationally prominent black leaders as well as other environmentalists (whose own livelihoods as I have said are never at risk) also hailed the decision. "Right now," said Monique Harden, an attorney with Greenpeace, "you are recording history in that a federal agency is telling a state agency that 'You've got it wrong.' And also that the EPA has concerns about the environmental justice issue as well."[50]

Once again, for a breath of the fresh air of common sense, I turn to Steven Milloy's Junk Science page on the Internet, on which he commented:

> Without scientific evidence that the plant would cause any harm to the local community, [EPA] Administrator [Carol] Browner acted to ensure the community's continued health and economic poverty. Plant construction would provide 2,000 jobs to community residents. Plant operation would provide 165 permanent jobs for which the average wage would be $45,000. The current average income in the area is $5,000. And since we know that "wealth equals health" (wealthier people/communities can afford better medical

> care and have healthier lifestyles), ultimately it is the community residents' health that will pay the price.
>
> So why is Administrator Browner blocking plant construction? Simple. Environmental racism is good politics. And, apparently, the black vote is more important to her than actually doing something beneficial for an impoverished black community.[51]

Eventually, Shintec abandoned its plan and thanks to the environmentalists' "tremendous victory" the residents of Convent, Louisiana, who overwhelming supported the company (but what do they know?), remain mired in the economic backwaters.

I leave it to the reader to judge who are the "environmental racists."

NOW BACK TO THE show. For much of what follows I am indebted to another recommended book, Cassandra(!) Chrones Moore's *Haunted Housing: How Toxic Scare Stories Are Spooking the Public Out of House and Home.* Her description of the role played by the EPA applies to the perils already listed above as well as those below:

"The Environmental Protection Agency has entered the regulatory dance, claiming that the imposition of federal standards can eliminate local threats to health, no matter how small—if they exist at all—and refusing steadfastly to consider the expense involved and the fear evoked."[52]

Radon. From a Utah Division of Radiation Control FAQ (frequently asked questions):[53]

> Radon is a radioactive gas that has no smell, taste, or color. It comes from the natural decay of uranium that is found in nearly all rock and soil. When geologic conditions are favorable, the potential increases for high indoor levels of radon. . . Radon decays into radioactive particles that can be trapped in the lungs when inhaled. These particles release small bursts of energy that damage lung tissue and may lead to lung cancer. *Radon is the second leading cause of lung cancer in the United States.* [Emphasis added.] Only smoking causes more lung-cancer deaths, and smoking combined with radon is a particularly serious health risk . . .

This is a faithful, and uncritical, repetition of the official EPA line on radon. According to the EPA, household radon gas causes 7,000 to 30,000 lung cancer deaths each year in the United States, second only to smoking and is especially a hazard in combination with smoking.

But does it, and is it? According to Moore, "[T[he predicted risks from indoor radon are so small that they cannot be detected in any conceivable residential study."[54]

Fumento again:

> The EPA's claim that radon levels in homes are carcinogenic, like so many of their assertions concerning carcinogenicity, is based on what's called a linear, no-threshold extrapolation. [That is, there is no level of exposure below which a substance is harmless.—D.O.] This theory says that because a substance, such as Alar, or a number of pesticides which the EPA is preparing to ban, causes tumors in lab animals at doses hundreds of thousands of times greater than the doses that humans could possibly absorb, that humans are nonetheless at risk of developing tumors from these chemicals. But radon may turn out to provide the best evidence that this assumption, beyond being scientifically unproven, is demonstrably false.
>
> . . . Happily, there have been a great number of studies on just this . . . Dr. Bernard Cohen,* a radiation physicist of the University of Pittsburgh, has analyzed in repeated studies the relationship between lung cancer and residential radon levels in over 400 U.S. counties. Far from finding higher rates of disease among those with higher exposures, he found lung cancer rates in high radon areas were much lower, prompting his observation that, "The results are contrary to the predictions of the linear, non-threshold theory . . ."
>
> Confirming Cohen's work is that of physicist and radiation consultant Dr. Ralph E. Lapp of Alexandria, Virginia, who compared cancer rates to household radon rates in Morris County. In this area, the EPA shows an average radon screening measurement twice the EPA's recommended maximum allowable level. Using the EPA's own risk calculation, this exposure alone should produce 377 lung cancer deaths per year, over and above smoking-caused lung cancer deaths.
>
> Yet, in all of Morris County, there were only 190 lung cancer deaths in the year Lapp studied . . .
>
> Yet another research team doing testing in Florida reported, "People in localities with the highest radon levels have a lower percentage of malignant neoplasms [cancerous tumors] compared to people from areas with no radon exposure risks.[56]

*Who has also debunked claims about the deadliness of plutonium and once posed a challenge to Ralph Nader: Dr. Cohen volunteered to eat as much plutonium as Ralph Nader would ingest caffeine. Mr. Nader declined.[55]

Moore again:

> Epidemiological studies found that in the three states with the highest mean radon levels in home living areas (Colorado, North Dakota and Iowa), the lung cancer death rate averaged 41 per 100,000, while in the three states with the lowest radon levels (Delaware, Louisiana and California), the rate averaged 66 per 100,000. In other words, the average lung cancer death rate was 29 percent *lower* [emphasis in original] in the states with the highest levels, a result that would give pause to anyone but an EPA administrator.[57]

Far from being deadly, low levels of radon (as well as some chemicals) may actually have a *protective* effect against diseases because they stimulate the body's defense mechanisms. This is called "hormesis." Says scientist Philip Abelson:

> Some experimental data indicate no effect or a beneficial effect from small radiation exposure . . . Moreover, it has been shown that low-level radiations make the cells less susceptible to subsequent high doses of radiation. This adaptive response has been attributed to the induction of a chromosomal break-repair mechanism.[58]

The EPA of course does not recognize the concept of hormesis. Nothing has been able to move the EPA's radon policy a fraction of an inch, notes Fumento. "Why? As Bernard Cohen and a co-author, Harvard Medical School Professor of Medicine Graham Colditz, stated in a 1991 paper, 'A great deal more than radon is at stake here. If the linear no-threshold theory fails for radon, it must surely fail for all other types of radiation, and very probably also for chemical carcinogens.'"[59]

But when did the EPA ever pay attention to data questioning any peril it has proclaimed to be a real and present danger (and which incidentally underscores its indispensability as protector of the health of Americans, as well as creating work for its employees and persuading Congress to increase its budget)? But I forget: environmental guardians can never retract or retreat. The public might start wondering. In the meantime, it is the public that will literally pay, in hundreds and sometimes thousands of dollars, for the cost of radon "mitigation" and/or litigation. According to Moore:

> In response to the perceived threat, 13 states have in fact enacted legislation mandating disclosure [when a house is sold] . . .

> Radon has been a boon to business as firms have emerged to market radon testing kits to provide mitigation should the tests reveal a problem . . . Aided and abetted by rising worry about cancer and health in general, the agency has in essence constructed a house of cards. On the shaky foundation of questionable scientific evidence, it has made a conscious effort to frighten the consumer . . . EPA and Congress, aided and abetted by fear of liability, have succeeded in complicating further the already complicated transaction of a home sale.[60]

Lead. Like radon, this common and useful metal has been around since the earth was formed and has been utilized by humans for at least 5,000 years. Says one source: "The Romans were the first to mine and industrialize its use in the fabrication of sheet lead and pipe for their elaborate water supply systems. They also utilized it in wine casks and eating utensils. Historians tell us today that the Romans may have actually fallen victim to their own progress and their society's decline may be attributable to massive lead poisoning among the population."[61]

Why the successor societies to the Romans didn't decline, I don't know. Maybe because they were already declined and didn't have plumbing or eating utensils. But why history doesn't record massive lead poisoning in Western civilization when lead plumbing was reintroduced in the 19th century, that I also don't know. In any case, according to For Your Disclosure, a Kennewick, Washington, company specializing in environmental hazards:

> Childhood lead poisoning represents the greatest preventable pediatric health problem in our society. [Worse than secondhand smoke?—D.O.] One in 6, or an estimated 3 million preschoolers, are affected by the ingestion of lead. Accidental high exposures cause immediate severe health effects. The rate and severity of accidental high exposures is [*sic*] increasing as more symptoms of the effects of exposure to lead are identified. The legal, health care, and medical costs from lead exposure are increasing rapidly . . .
>
> Even at low levels of exposure, lead can cause reductions in a child's IQ and attention span, and result in reading and learning disabilities, hyperactivity and behavioral difficulties. There is no "cure" for lead poisoning. These effects are forever and cannot be reversed once the damage is done, affecting a child's ability to learn, to succeed in school and to function later in life. Other symptoms of low levels of lead in a child's body are subtle behavioral changes, irritability, appetite suppression, weight loss, sleep disturbances,

> shortened attention span, and difficulties in listening due to hearing impairment. Severe exposures also may cause permanent damage to vital organs such as the kidneys and liver, and in the most severe cases, encephalopathy, coma and even death. A child may show no acute toxic response at all (i.e., asymptomatic) and still be affected. In fact, one of the great dangers of the disease [here comes the really scary part—D.O.] is that its symptoms are so easily confused with childhood "everydays" such as a cold or the flu . . .
>
> How extensive is the problem? An estimated 57 million homes contain lead based paint, and approximately 21 million of these have severe and immediate hazards such as chipping, flaking, or peeling lead based paint and/or excessive levels of lead particulate in household dust. Of these, The Department of Housing and Urban Development (HUD) estimates that almost 4 million are occupied by families with young children who are at high risk of being poisoned.[62]

Even worse, according to the Environmental Defense Fund, lead poisoning is not only "a global environmental and public health hazard" but a veritable "epidemic."[63] (Joining that other "global epidemic," smoking, and about which, of course, Something Must Be Done.)

The Consumer Product Safety Commission also got into the act on October 1, 1996 when it released a report "indicating that public playground equipment *could have* chipping and peeling lead paint, which is a *potential* lead poisoning hazard primarily for children six years old and younger." [Emphases added.]

The CPSC tested and analyzed paint chips from 26 playgrounds in 13 cities and "found that in some of the paint chips from playground equipment, the levels of lead were high enough that a child ingesting a paint chip one-tenth of a square inch—about the size that could fit on the tip of a pencil eraser—*each day for about 15 to 30 days could have* blood lead levels at or above the 10 microgram per deciliter amount *considered* dangerous for children, especially those six years old and younger." Yet despite all the "could haves," the "CPSC has *no reports* of children with lead poisoning from paint on playground equipment."[64] [Emphases again added.]

Interestingly, the lead "crisis" has arisen at the same time as blood lead levels (BLL) in Americans have declined dramatically. A National Health and Nutrition Examination Survey conducted between October 1988 and October 1991 found a 78 percent drop in BLL across all age groups since 1976-1980. The August 5, 1994 Morbidity and Mortality

Weekly Report (MMWR) by the Centers for Disease Control and Prevention reported that the average BLL in infants had fallen from 15 ug/dl (micrograms per deciliter) to 4 ug/dl, a reduction of 73 percent and well below the supposed 10 ug/dl danger point. Most of the decline was attributed to the elimination of lead in gasoline and in solder used in food and beverage cans since the 1970s.[65]

The government's "level of concern" regarding lead was actually set as high as 60 ug/dl back then. Yet even as the amount of lead in the environment began falling, the CDC regularly moved the goal posts by dropping the permissible BLL *six-fold* in the past couple decades.[66] This of course vastly increased the number of children "at risk."

At risk of wearying the reader with my personal anecdoes, I am compelled to note again that my own experience renders me unfit to be alarmed about this crisis. As I mentioned in the Introduction, my boyhood home was right next to a heavily traveled boulevard and we must have breathed in a lot of lead from car exhausts. I never ate any of the "red lead" I helped my Dad paint on the gutters, but we scraped off flakes of the old paint and I got lead dust on my fingers and possibly in my mouth. We also had lead plumbing, as did most houses at that time. My younger brother and I used to melt pieces of lead pipe in a little electric pot to make lead soldiers. (No doubt such a toy would be outlawed today, if only for its potential of causing burns, of which we suffered many. In fact, lead soldiers are probably illegal today.) We didn't eat the soldiers either, but we had to use a knife to scrape off excess lead that had oozed out between the two halves of the casting forms and probably got tiny pieces of it on our persons and clothing. Somehow we survived.

Was there an epidemic of "reduced IQs, shortened attention spans, reading and learning disabilities, hyperactivity and behavioral difficulties, subtle behavioral changes, irritability, appetite suppression, weight loss, sleep disturbances and difficulties in listening due to hearing impairment, damage to vital organs such as the kidneys and liver, etc." among kids in the 1970s (not to mention the '30s and '40s)? Somehow I missed reading about it. Why is it that only in the '90s "Attention Deficit Disorder" and "hyperactivity" have become problems?

As I've conceded, my personal anecdotes, especially those regarding smoking, count for nothing in The Great (Scientific) Scheme of Things. But how much reliance can we put on some of the "scientific" studies that are used to fuel our fears about environmental perils, in this case the peril of lead poisoning?

For example, researchers at the National Institute for Occupational Safety and Health (NIOSH) studied 50 children and reported in the *American Journal of Public Health* that children of lead-exposed construction workers were six times more likely to have a blood lead level of 10 micrograms per deciliter, a higher level than the children of workers in industries where they weren't exposed to lead. As a result, the researchers concluded that children of occupationally-exposed workers are a "high-risk" population. (The "relative risk" of such children was 6.1 at a 95 percent confidence interval of 0.9-147.2)[67]

Fortunately, there's not much that gets past that indomitable debunker of junk science, Steven Milloy. He points out that the reported results are not statistically significant because "the lower end of the 95 percent confidence interval is less than the no-difference-in-risk cutoff point of 1.0. Results that are not statistically significant are usually deemed too flaky to be relied upon." Not only that, but "the reported confidence interval—0.9 to 147.2—is H-U-G-E. Such a wide confidence interval indicates a lot of variability—too much—among the data. This is not unusual in such a SMALL study (only 31 'exposed' children)." [Emphases in original.]

Moreover, he says, "no health effects—e.g., brain damage—were noted in any of the children. This is not surprising given the target blood lead level of 10 micrograms/deciliter is an arbitrary, CDC-defined level that has no basis in science. Even the highest blood lead level measured in the study—17.9 micrograms/deciliter—is not associated with any discernible health effects. So where's the brain damage? In the children or the researchers?"[68]

But want of hard and truly scientific evidence has never stopped a government medicrat from Doing Something. And one thing both the Environmental Protection Agency and the Department of Housing and Urban Development have done has been to require, since December 6, 1996, that the sellers of residential dwellings built before 1978 must disclose any known lead paint hazards. The cost of a lead inspection (if inspection is not waived by the buyer) and "abatement" of the problem by EPA-certified specialists is left to be worked out by the buyer and seller and their agents.

This "lead tax" hits landlords even harder, says *The Wall Street Journal*.

In the People's Republic of Maryland, for example, "landlords must have rental units cleared for lead hazard before they hand keys to tenants. Realtors can also be fined up to $10,000 a day if they fail to warn of lead obligations."[69] The "Lead Poisoning Prevention Act" passed during the Bush Administration has driven down home prices and cut the supply of low-income housing, the paper claims.

And of course the "lead peril" has created a ripe new field for lawsuits. In Massachusetts in 1994, for example, a court awarded damages to a family whose child had a blood lead level of *zero* simply because lead paint was present in the home.[70]

Truly, as For Your Disclosure says, the legal costs from lead exposure "are increasing rapidly." But is it really from exposure to lead, or from exposure to federal regulators and the always-on-the-prowl plaintiffs' bar?

The EPA isn't concerned only about lead in old paint. Lead that's buried in the ground and has never bothered anybody has also been the target of multimillion-dollar "remediation" efforts under the "Superfund" program. When the agency proposed to dig up about one million tons of arsenic- and lead-laced mining tailings in Triumph, Idaho, (population around 50), the residents got up in arms—but not before they were nearly scared to death. EPA officials told them they had dangerously high levels of lead in their drinking water and high arsenic levels in their yards.

"For two months, I was sick over it," said Heidi Heath, a mother of two children, aged 4 and 7. "I thought, 'What have I done to my children?'"[71]

But fear changed to anger when it was realized that people had been living amid the piles of tailings for more than 50 years, without a single known case of cancer, and when urine tests showed no acute health problem in anybody from the metals. The cry became literally, "Not in our backyards, EPA."

(What's this? Joe and Jane Citizen disputing official federal health warnings simply because nothing bad had ever happened to them or anybody they knew? It's like somebody being crazy enough to doubt all the bad stuff about smoking because it had never hurt him or anybody he knew.)

The EPA, of course, had its own reasoning. "We look at risk from a much bigger picture," said David Bennett, EPA National Priority List

Coordinator in Seattle. "We don't guarantee that someone will drop dead from cancer, we look at probabilities."[72]

A state official agreed. "It is true that the biological levels don't pose an imminent health threat," said Pat McGavran, supervisor of the Office of Environmental Health in Idaho. "But they do have elevated levels of arsenic. There is an exposure and there is a potential for health problems."[73]

Ah yes: "probabilities . . . potential . . . "

One resident who led the fight in Triumph, Donna Rose, learned about a similar situation in Aspen, Colorado, where the EPA had found slightly elevated levels of cadmium in the water and where citizens were fighting a Superfund listing because, again, no visible health threat existed. She is now on the executive board of a new national group called Superfund Coalition Against Mismanagement (SCAM), all of whose board members are from Superfund-targeted communities, including Leadville, Colorado, Midvale, Utah, Palmerton, Pennsylvania, and Granite City, Illinois.

The EPA's priorities are mixed up, says SCAM. "The EPA Superfund program too often creates decades-long cleanup programs that are unworkable, unnecessary, ineffective and extremely costly. Billions of dollars are skewed away from the environment and toward the legal industry."[74]

Happily, in Triumph, the EPA eventually backed off to the extent of stating that it would dig up only those yards of residents who wanted them dug up.

Electromagnetic Fields. A single journalist, Paul Brodeur, can truthfully be credited with almost single-handedly manufacturing widespread and unwarranted alarm over something Americans have lived with since the first electric power generator was built, the first transmission poles erected and the first house wired for electricity: the electrical and magnetic fields (EMF) created by this most useful servant of mankind. His articles in *The New Yorker* and his books bore such revealing titles as *Currents of Death* and *The Zapping of America* and *The Great Power-line Cover-up*.

Scores of studies in this country and abroad have failed to establish any real connection between leukemia and power lines. The earth's magnetic field is hundreds of times larger than the field from a power distribution line and natural electrical fields in the body's own cells can be infinitely greater than those from power lines. Even the EPA has minimized the threat, sparing the nation the prospect of having to bury all its power lines at a cost estimated in the trillions. Yet, interestingly enough, some studies have found the power lines-leukemia "risk" to be two or three times greater than the supposed lung cancer risk from secondhand smoke that the EPA felt the country must Do Something about.

Nevertheless, even without the help of the EPA, new court cases against power companies alleging EMF liability are being filed at the rate of about one a month, says Cassandra Moore, signaling, she says "not only the aversion to risk of many consumers but the eagerness of attorneys in a litigious society to file claims."[75] In a landmark case in California in 1988, the U.S. Court of Appeals for the Fourth District awarded damages and litigation expenses to a plaintiff against San Diego Gas & Electric Company as compensation for lost property value.

Affirming a lower court decision, the appeals court held that "the truth or lack of truth in whether electromagnetic projections caused a health hazard to humans or animals was immaterial. Rather the question was whether the *fear* of the danger existed and would affect market value."[76] [Emphasis added.]

As this case and the one involving lead paint in Massachusetts indicate, no actual harm need be proved in court these days when it comes to perceived environmental perils. The simple *fear* of the peril is enough.

<u>Asbestos.</u> To a greater extent even than radon, asbestos, another naturally occurring substance, is everywhere in the environment—not only in the air we breathe but the water we drink and the food we eat. Fortunately, the amounts we absorb are not only minuscule but are generally "white" asbestos (chrysotile), the least harmful of several members of the asbestos family. It was "blue" asbestos (crocidolite) and "brown" asbestos (amosite), heavily used for fireproofing and insulation during World War II, that was diagnosed as the cause of lung cancer occurring years later in World War II shipyard and other defense workers.

That there are different kinds of asbestos and that the most commonly used kind is the least harmful did not matter to the EPA when in

1982 it issued a rule requiring public and private elementary and secondary schools to inspect for asbestos-containing materials. Although the EPA did not mandate their removal, the mere threat of a possible danger was enough. Panicked school officials and parents around the country demanded action.

The city of Houston, Texas, for example, spent some $46 million to remove asbestos from 70 schools. Oakland, Michigan, calculated its costs at $112 million. New York City spent $100 million on inspection and removal.[77]

Belatedly it was realized that stirring up the asbestos used to insulate pipes and heating ducts was creating actual, not presumed, danger, especially to removal workers, and that the best course was simply to seal it in place. But how many books could have been purchased, how many new classrooms built, how many more teachers hired for the amount of money wasted before this lesson was learned? The fear of asbestos remains, however, and of course is one more field for litigation.

Because chrysolite is also no longer used in automobile brake linings, less effective substitutes are also costing Americans more in terms of shorter brake life. Ironically, according to geologist Malcolm Ross, "All the substitutes for asbestos are, in fact, carcinogenic . . . Ceramic fibers, rock wool, fiberglass, all have been found carcinogenic in laboratory animals."[78]

The search for Absolute Safety is never ending.

<u>Global Warming.</u> This chapter has gotten too long, but let me briefly squeeze in one more peril, even though this one bids fair to be the real biggie of environmental concerns in the coming century, dwarfing all the preceding ones in terms of monetary cost, inconvenience and anxiety for the general public. Once again I'm off to a bad start because I remember that only a decade or so ago it was global *cooling* and an impending new ice age that the environmentalists were worried about. I also remember that 1995 was widely trumpeted as the warmest year on record and "proof" that global warming was real—until the data for an unusually cold December came in and 1995 turned out to be only the eighth warmest. (As I write this, 1998 is being proclaimed as the warmest ever.)

Sadly once again, as with most other environmental perils, it's a matter of the Good Guys, who *know* the earth is warming up and that human activity is to blame and who clamor that Something Must Be Done Right Now to slow it down, versus the Bad Guys, which includes anybody who says, "Well, wait a minute. Are we sure about this?" The cast of characters on both sides of the debate was pretty well established in a syndicated newspaper column by Molly Ivins:

> Actually, there's not a debate—in the sense of opposing arguments each backed up with facts . . . What we have is scientific opinion vs. a multimillion-dollar advertising campaign sponsored by corporate interests afraid that the scientists' findings will cost them money . . . But the media in this country treat both arguments as though they were of equal weight and soundness because, you see, we have been trained to assume there are two sides to every story.
>
> . . . [T]he collusion of special interests against the public interest [is] perhaps the brassiest display of greed, lying and self-interest since the time all those tobacco executives solemnly swore to Congress that there was nothing addictive about nicotine.[79]

Where would we be without the example of those greedy, lying tobacco executives? For Ms. Ivins's information, however, a least one patriotic corporation was happy to jump on the global-warming bandwagon. It may only have been a coincidence, of course, that the Dupont company's patent on Freon, used in automobile air-conditioners, was just about to run out at the time the compound was being indicted for causing "holes" in the earth's protective ozone layer and maybe even being responsible for global warming all by itself.

Some foolish scientists disagreed, but because, according to Ivins, there is really only one side to the global-warming debate, Freon was outlawed and every new car built since 1994 has been cooled with "environmentally friendly" and more expensive Freon II—developed by Dupont, it just happens—and prices have soared for the remaining stocks of the old Freon which are allowed to be used on pre-1994 cars only by licensed air-conditioner repair shops until the supply is used up. Another consequence has been the creation of a flourishing black market in the old Freon. (Now who would ever have guessed that banning a product in popular demand could lead to underground traffic in that product?)

At least one poor guy went to jail because he succumbed to the temptation created by this government-decreed transformation of a once-legal compound into an illegal one. Roland Wood, president of

Refrigeration USA in Hallandale, Florida, was sentenced to 37 months in prison for smuggling 4,000 tons of Freon into the country.[80]

I can hardly wait until we outlaw tobacco.

At risk of being accused of suggesting that there could be another side to the global-warming controversy, sheer orneriness compels me to note that "scientists" (I put quote marks around the word so as not to offend Ivins) have reported that total solar radiance—the amount of energy the earth receives from the sun—appears to have been on the rise since 1978. It is more than a little possible that this may have bearing on the current perception that the earth is in a warming trend and the belief that its sole cause is the release of manmade "greenhouse" gases, mainly carbon dioxide, into the atmosphere. A decrease in brightness during the late 1300s is thought to have triggered what became known as the Little Ice Age.

"The total solar radiance trend could produce additional warming of about one degree in 100 years, a potentially significant contribution," says Columbia University climatologist Richard Wilson.[81]

Also totally ignored in the whole debate are benefits that could result from global warming (if warming there is) and increased carbon dioxide levels: more land able to be brought under cultivation, increased crop yields, more vigorous forest growth.

Because I'm a smoker, the medical establishment assures me I won't live to see how this controversy is resolved in the coming decades. Will Charlie Brown America fall for environmental Lucy's latest football trick and wind up on its fanny again?

Thankfully, I'll never know. We smokers take comfort where we can find it. There is no comfort, however, in the fact that while the writers whose words I have borrowed throughout this chapter, as well as others, are doing valuable work in exposing the follies and fallacies of junk science regarding environmental perils, few there are who have directed the same critical attention to the crusade against smoking and some of its preposterous claims.

Notes

1. Edith Efron, *The Apocalyptics: Cancer and the Big Lie: How the Environmental Movement Controls What We Know About Cancer* (New York: Simon and Schuster, 1984), p. 57.

2. Interview in *Insight*, November 11, 1991. Quoted in Dixie Lee Ray with Lou Guzzo, *Environmental Overkill: Whatever Happened to Common Sense* (New York: Harper Perennial, 1993), p. 146.

3. Lizbeth Lopez-Carillo et al., "Is DDT Use a Public Health Problem in Mexico?" *Environmental Health Perspectives* 1996;104(6):584-588. Cited at www.junkscience.com/news/ddt.html.

4. Quoted in Ellen Ruppel Shell, "Resurgence of A Deadly Disease." *The Atlantic*, August 1997, p. 48.

5. "'Era of scarcity' forecast." *The Atlanta Journal-Constitution*, September 21, 1997, p. D6.

6. Nicolas Eberstadt, "The Population Implosion." *The Wall Street Journal*, October 16, 1997. At www.junkscience.com/eberstad.html.

7. From The Electronic Telegraph, January 3, 1997, at www.telegraph.co.uk.

8. Ibid, February 18, 1997.

9. "Attack of the 1-foot doll." *The Atlanta Journal-Constitution*, January 11, 1997, p. A4.

10. At www.thenation.com/cgi.bin/nation/net. thread/bin.net.Thread/pl/message/5.

11. SCI Analysis: 1959 Corvair. At www.caranddriver.com/members/anniv/1959/4corvair.html.

12. Ralph Nader, *Unsafe At Any Speed: The designed-in dangers of the American automobile* (Grossman: New York, 1965 & 1972), p. 10.

13. Ralph Nader, Clarence Ditlow and Joyce Kinnard, *The Lemon Book* (Ottawa, IL: Caroline House, 1980), p. 195.

14. Nader, p. lxvii.

15. Ibid, p. lxiv.

16. Loc. cit.

17. Andrew J. White, *The Assassination of the Corvair* (Readers Press: New Haven, 1969), pp. 27-33.

18. Nader, p. 291.

19. "Camaro's dangers stem from its drivers, GM says." *The Atlanta Journal-Constitution,* November 1, 1996, p. S4. From *The Washington Post.* In 1997, the Camaro again topped the Institute's list of most dangerous cars because of the way it is driven. — Joey Ledford, "Auto study drives home the point: Bigger is safer." *The Atlanta Journal-Constitution,* October 22, 1997, p. B2.

20. Nader, p. 288.

21. Blaine Harden, "In Political Marriage, Nader Dons His Own Shade

of Green." *The Washington Post*, May 21, 1996. At www.nader96/org/m960521.htm.

22. At http://mediafilter.org/MFF/535.Omnicide.html.

23. Department of Transportation, National Highway Safety Administration, 49 CFR Part 571 [Docket No. 74-14; Notice] RIN 2127-AG59. See also 49 CFR Part 595 [Docket No. 74-14; Notice 107] RIN 2127-AG61 and 49 CFR Part 571 [Docket No. 74-14; Notice 109] RIN 2127-AG14. From www.nhtsa.dot.gov/.

24. White, p. 218.

25. *Reason*, April 1996, p. 24.

26. Michael Dorsey, "Stirring the Pot." Worcester Polytechnic Institute *WPI Journal*, Summer, 1997.

27. Statement by Louis H. Bridenstine, assistant general counsel of Chevrolet Motor Division, before the Michigan Senate Highway Committee, February 21, 1996. Cited in White, p. 110.

28. White, p. 113.

29. "Evaluation of the 1960-1963 Corvair Handling and Stability." U.S. Department of Transportation, National Highway Traffic Safety Administration, July 1972. Report DOT HS-820198. Quoted on "Andrew's Corvair Page," no longer available on the Internet.

30. At http://haycorn.psy.cmu.edu/virtualVairs/FAQ/FAQ.1html. Adds Sullivan: "The film was not intended to go outside of Ford, apparently. Maybe someone at Ford leaked it to Nader to hurt Chevrolet—who knows?"

31. Quoted by Robert P. Benzinger, senior project engineer at Chevrolet during the development of the Corvair engine between 1959 and 1962, in a speech at the 1975 CORSA (Corvair Society of America) National Convention in Seattle. From http://haycom.psy.cmu.edu/VirtualVairs/Benzinger.html. According to Benzinger, "The best overall vindication of the Corvair, I think, is in the undocumented, but indisputable, fact that among GM people—employees, executives, engineers—the Corvair was the most popular personal and family car that GM ever built."

32. Nader, pp. lvi and lvii.

33. At http://haycorn.psy.cmu.edu/VirtualVairs/Welcome.html.

34. White, p. 100.

35. Senate Bill No. 773 to amend the Michigan vehicle code, introduced February 1, 1996. Cited in White, p. 102.

36. Cited in Peter W. Huber, *Galileo's Revenge: Junk Science in the Courtroom* (New York: Basic Books, 1991), p. 74.

37. Nader, p. 56. No dates or other details or subsequent findings regarding the five "runaway" accidents are given.

38. Huber, p. 74.

39. "Presidential Candidate Ralph Nader—The Dark Side." At www.realchange.org/nader.htm.

40. Quoted in Michael Lewis, "Campaign Journal: The Normal Person of Tomorrow." *The New Republic*, April 1996. At www.nader96.org/newrep1.htm.

41. Michael Fumento, *Science Under Siege: How the Environmental Misinformation Campaign Is Affecting Our Laws, Taxes, and Our Daily Life* (New York: William Morrow, 1993), pp. 41-44.

42. Richard Rhodes, "Food Safety's Waiting Weapon." *The New York Times*, August 28, 1997. At www.junkscience.com/news/irradiation.html.

43. Curt Anderson, "USDA seeks more authority." *The Atlanta Journal-Constitution*, October 10, 1997, p. A20.

44. "Cholera Epidemic in U.S. Courtesy of EPA 'Science.'" At www.junkscience.com/news/cholera.htm. Based on an article in the *Journal of the American Medical Association*, 1996;276:307-312.

45. Michael Fumento, "Dirty Water." *Reason*, May 1996, p. 53.

46. Ibid, p. 52.

47. John Stossel, "What You Know That May Not Be So." Broadcast January 9, 1997 on the ABC television network.

48. Quoted by columnist Mona Charen, "Rethinking bias in news reporting." *The Atlanta Journal-Constitution*, September 27, 1994, p. A15.

49. Mike Williams, "Noxious neighborhood: Environmental agency offers plan today to move Pensacola residents from shadow of 'Mount Dioxin.'" *The Atlanta Journal-Constitution*, April 20, 1996, p. E5.

50. Jim Yardley, "EPA gives first round to foes of plant in poor area." *The Atlanta Journal-Constitution*, September 11, 1997, p. A4.

51. Steve Milloy, "Carol Browner: EPA Carbetbagger." At www.junkscience.com/news/carpetbagger.html.

52. Cassandra Chrones Moore, *Haunted Housing: How Toxic Scare Stories Are Spooking the Public Out of House and Home* (Washington: Cato Institute, 1997), p. 160.

53. At www.eq.state.ut.us/eqrad/radon.htm.

54. Moore, p. 23.

55. "How Deadly is Plutonium?" Posted on the Internet by Adams Atomic Engines, an energy system design firm, at http://ans.neep.wisc.edu/~ans/point_source/AEI/may95/ plutonium_eff.htmlB.

56. Michael Fumento, "Radon's Real Threat Is to the EPA." At www.reasonmag.com/.

57. Moore, p. 24.

58. Philip H. Abelson, "Radon Today: The Role of Flimlam in Public Policy." *Regulation* 14, (Fall 1991): 95,96. Cited in Moore, p. 16.

59. Fumento, "Radon's Real Threat is To The EPA."

60. Moore, pp. 70-71, 78.

61 "A History of Lead." Posted on the Internet at www.vqinc.com/FYD/epa.htm by For Your Disclosure.

62. Ibid.

63. At www.edf.org/pubs/NewsReleases/1994/Mar/a_leadint.html.

64. "Lead Poisoning Hazard for Children on Playground Equipment." Consumer Product Safety Commission release #97-001, October 1, 1996. At www.Kidsource.com/cpsc/lead. playground.html.

65. "American Water Works Association Comments on the EPA's Proposed Minor Revisions to the Lead and Copper Rule (61 FR 16348)." At www.awwa.org/govtaff/ler_com.htm.

66. Moore, p. 80.

67. *American Journal of Public Health* 1997;87:1352-13550, cited in "Lead Heads" on Steve Milloy's Junk Science Page at www.junkscience. com/news/lead.html.

68. Ibid.

69. "Home Poisons." *The Wall Street Journal*, May 11, 1997. Quoted at www. junkscience.com/news/moore.html.

70. Ellen Ruppel Shell, "An Element of Doubt." *The Atlantic*, December 1995, p. 38. Cited in Moore, p. 133.

71. Steve Stuebner, "Triumph, Idaho, to EPA: *Get Out.*" *High Country News*, September 20, 1993. At www.hcn.org/1993/sept.20/dir/lead.html.

72. Ibid.

73. Ibid.

74. Ibid.

75. Moore, p. 245.

76. Loc.cit.

77. Ibid, p. 187-188.

78. Quoted in Michael J. Bennett, *The Asbestos Racket* (Bellevue, Washington: Free Enterprise Press, 1991), pp. 76-77. Cited in Moore, p. 181.

79. Molly Ivins, "It's getting too hot in here." *The Atlanta Journal-Constitution*, October 8, 1997, p. A19.

80. "Coolant sentencing." *The Atlanta Journal-Constitution*, August 30, 1997, p. B5.

81. "Brighter sun may be bad break for earth." *The Atlanta Journal-Constitution*, September 26, 1997, p. A1.

Chapter 12

THE ANTISMOKING CRUSADE AND THE CORRUPTION OF LAW

When the Puritan righteous among us get their hands on the levers of the state, the property and liberty of all of us are likely soon to be at risk.

— Robert H. Nelson[1]

If there are no smokers, how are we going to pay for health reform? But then again, if we can pay farmers for not growing tobacco, perhaps we can tax nonsmokers for however much they're not smoking.

— Rep. Dick Armey (R-Texas)[2]

Smoking may possibly harm your health, so please be careful not to smoke too much, and please observe good smoking manners.

— Warning label on Japanese cigarette packages[3]

WRITING THIS BOOK has been one of the most difficult and frustrating things I have ever done. Two factors that made the project so hard (as well as so long) are:

1) There seems to be *no end* to the onslaught of antismoking propaganda. Time and again I have had to go back to chapters I thought were finished to add more information or to address yet another "latest study" or some new development in the crusade against smoking.

2) The fear and loathing of tobacco and smoking has become so ingrained in the American mind that there seems to be *no way* that anything I or anybody else says or does can stem, much less halt or reverse, the crusade.

On the first score, it has been almost a decade since, with no real purpose in view, I first began idly collecting antismoking articles from newspapers and magazines and other sources. In the early '90s, however, I began noticing that more and more such articles were appearing. Literally almost every day, either in the papers or on the television news, there was some new "revelation" about the dangers of smoking.

This was not paranoia on my part. Analysts with the Media Research Center reviewed all of the stories about several risky products on the morning and evening news shows on ABC, CBS and NBC, as well as CNN's World News and World Today shows, between August 1, 1995 and July 31, 1996.[4] They found that:

— Tobacco as a risk problem is overemphasized. Tobacco and smoking were the subject of 413 news stories, compared to 136 stories for obesity/fatty foods, 94 for auto safety, and 58 for alcohol. Tobacco even drew more coverage than cocaine, heroin, LSD and marijuana combined, which were the subjects of 340 stories.

In the print media, the disparity was even greater. A Nexis search of headlines in American newspapers found that the terms "tobacco or smoking or cigarette" were employed 9,067 times during the study period. Over the same time period, however, the terms "cocaine or heroin or LSD or marijuana or illegal drugs" were used only 3,875 times. In other words, there were nearly two and a half times as many stories focusing on tobacco and smoking than there were stories focusing on illegal drugs.

"Which is worse," they ask rhetorically, "a legal product that if used over many decades can be life-threatening, or an illegal product that can be of more immediate danger? For America's news media, the answer is overwhelmingly the former."

— The media have allowed the Clinton Administration to use tobacco as a political weapon. President Clinton was the driving force behind a good deal of the tobacco news. Eighty-five stories focused on his efforts to regulate tobacco, portraying him as courageously taking on a powerful industry. Only 45 of the stories about illegal drugs mentioned Clinton, and almost all of these references were positive.

There is a double standard in coverage of tobacco as a political issue. Jack Kemp's flip-flops on affirmative action and immigration were noted in five evening news stories during the 1996 Republican Convention. Al Gore's tobacco flip-flop—politically exploiting his sister's smoking-related death after having boasted in 1988 about his tobacco farming history—didn't receive any evening news coverage during the Democratic Convention.

— **Antitobacco sources far exceed protobacco sources in terms of both quality and quantity.** Reporters ran soundbites from 270 antitobacco/proregulation sources, compared to 116 from protobacco/antiregulation sources. They also gave antitobacco/proregulation sources the last word in 132 stories, compared to only 40 for the other side, and it's the last word that viewers or listeners usually remember.

The analysts elaborate further on their findings, with biting comments, but the foregoing is enough to give the picture.

BECAUSE OF THE nation's media-fed obsession with tobacco and smoking, which began well before 1995, whenever my wife and I visited with friends or family, all of them nonsmokers or ex-smokers, the conversation would always—*always*—turn sooner or later to smoking.

I remember my sister saying, in a reference to the onetime popularity of the habit (in which she had never indulged), "But we didn't *know* back then that smoking was bad." Why didn't we know? For the same reason we never knew that radon in the home or chlorine in drinking water was so dangerous until the Environmental Protection Agency, looking for something to justify its existence, decided they were and told us so. Or why we never knew that a million kids needed to take drugs for "Attention Deficit Disorder" until the psychiatrists (and pharmaceutical companies) told us they did.

When I was a kid, nobody had to tell us that poliomyelitis was bad. The disease was extremely rare; no one in my hometown was ever stricken by it, even during the worst outbreaks in the 1940s. But we saw pictures of people in iron lungs. We knew that President Roosevelt had been paralyzed by polio, though this was seldom mentioned. We read about Sister Kenny (who, like Mother Teresa, could have continued her ameliorating efforts for a hundred years and what she was ameliorating would still have existed).

It didn't require a slew of epidemiological studies or statistical correlations to tell us about polio, for medical science had identified the cause. Polio was caused by a virus, and only by that virus. No "confounding variables" had been involved in the search for the cause and the eventual cure.

Everybody had always known that pneumonia was bad. It carried away my maternal grandmother and other relatives; it had nearly killed me. No fancy statistical footwork like "retrogression analysis" had been employed in the attempt to identify the cause back in the 19th century, only a microscope. If you caught the bacterium, you caught pneumonia, which I did one Saturday on a shopping trip to Pittsburgh with my mother. If someone had suggested to the doctor, who came to our house at all hours of the day or night to treat me, that the disease was "associated" with my father's smoking which had weakened my immune system, he would have considered the knowledge as useful as advice from a shaman to shake rattles over my chest.

The same was true of the other "traditional" diseases—smallpox, typhoid, diphtheria, syphilis—which medical science can cure or prevent, if not eradicate completely. The same is true of new diseases, like legionnaires', hantavirus and AIDS. All have single, identifiable causes (although in the case of AIDS the disease becomes more complex the more we learn about it).

The reason we know what we know about all these diseases is that we know what causes them. The same cannot be said of cancer or, more accurately, cancers. The search for certain causes and sure cures for cancers in all their varieties still goes on nearly three decades after President Nixon proclaimed a war against "it." Ditto for respiratory diseases for which no single causes have been identified—bronchitis/emphysema, asthma. Genes may be involved. Environmental factors may be involved. Just about anything may be involved, and smoking is but one of a host of possible factors.

At the same time, we're learning more about diseases for which smoking has unjustifiably been implicated as the most important risk factor. For example, stomach ulcers, which are now known to be caused by a bacterium. The same bacterium may be a causative agent in heart disease as well.

How did we learn that smoking is bad? Not because we saw it for ourselves but because we were *told* it was bad, that it all by itself *causes* diseases. And once we were told, and because it certainly seems biologically plausible in the case of lung cancer and respiratory diseases, we suddenly realized, why yes, the guy down the street was never without a cigarette and didn't he get lung cancer? Or so-and-so smoked and died of emphysema or something like that. Somebody else had a heart attack, and he was smoker, wasn't he? Eventually every nonsmoker and reformed smoker could relate a horror story about a relative or neighbor or acquaintance or somebody they'd heard about who had been a smoker and had joined the dear departed. Many in the medical profession, few of whose members were trained in epidemiology, were as spooked by the statistics as the rest of us and began to see "smoking-related" diseases or health problems everywhere they looked.

But we kept on being told . . . and told . . . and told about smoking. *What is going on?* I thought. Everybody has known since 1964 that smoking is not good for you. What is the purpose of this incessant hammering on the subject? A lot of things aren't good for you. Why this constant, unceasing preoccupation with smoking?

I didn't know what to make of it. On the one hand was my own lifetime's experience of smoking in good health and the absence of any clear and unmistakable harm done to any other smoker I knew. On the other hand was my ignorance of epidemiology and statistics, which left me in no position to question the flood of studies "proving" over and over and over the terrible and inevitable consequences of this, to me, harmless habit. I didn't even *imagine* that the studies might be subject to questioning. These were *scientific* studies, weren't they? They wouldn't publish them if they weren't true, would they? It never occurred to me that some of the people conducting them might be other than wholly disinterested investigators. I was unaware of the deep and abiding and pure and undistilled *hatred* of tobacco that motivated many of them, as well as the opportunism that motivated others in the form of obtaining grant money for yet another study about smoking.

Something else I didn't appreciate about such studies until I began this book—something that may well be a factor in their findings—was expressed by motivational psychologist Ernest Dichter, whose list of reasons people smoke cigarettes I quoted from at the end of Chapter 4:

> The mind has a powerful influence on the body, and may produce symptoms of physical illness. Guilt feelings may cause harmful physical effects not at all caused by the cigarettes used, which may be extremely mild. Such guilt feelings alone may be the real cause of the injurious consequences.[5]

It that was true in 1947, how much truer must it be today when smokers encounter health warnings, criticism, discrimination and intimidation at every turn, day in and day out?

Not only may smoking be bad for your health; antismoking propaganda that makes you feel bad about yourself may be just as dangerous!

If what I said under 2) at the beginning of this chapter—my inability, as well as that of other people who can write better than I, to stem the antismoking crusade—has resulted in a high state of personal frustration and feelings of hopelessness and futility, what I said under 1) continues to bewilder me. I mean especially the ongoing flood of "new studies" about smoking.

One of the latest that came out while I was writing this chapter was the allegation that smoking reduces the size of the penis. (Somehow this doesn't bother me; I wouldn't have won any prizes in that category even before I started smoking.)

I don't know if this new fear has caused any males to stop smoking, but it's interesting that the study was released about the time the potency drug Viagra came on the market, and that despite reports of a number of heart attack deaths to users of Viagra, the popularity of the drug hasn't been affected. Which goes to show that people will take risks if they value the benefits of something highly enough.

Every time I read some of these smoking studies, with their dozens or scores of references to other studies, I am reminded of nothing so much as the apocryphal village whose inhabitants supported themselves by taking in each other's washing. That is how science is done, of course: scientists build on the work of others. Yet for every paper that represents a true advance in knowledge, whether about smoking or anything else, a hundred others merely recycle old intellectual washing and hang it up on the line as if it were new.

Science is also so specialized today and there are so many thousands of journals[6] that comprise "the literature" that someone reading a paper outside his field may be in no better position to understand it than the ordinary layman. Even if a paper or article is in their own field, I wonder how many scientists have the time, or take the time, to check the multitude of references. Or are they simply impressed by the sheer bulk of them, as the layman is impressed?

But on the futility index, as a septuagenarian with at most a decade or two to live, I am better off than Martha Perske, who has been rendered incapable of pursuing her career as a talented artist, at an age when that career should be in full blossom, because of emotional turmoil and agitation induced in her by the antismokers and their propaganda. She now devotes all her energies to writing articles that expose and counter their most brazen lies.

Adding to her distress is the knowledge that the general public never sees what she writes. Her audience is confined to those who already agree with her—the members of smokers' advocate groups like the American Smokers Alliance or the National Smokers Alliance or FORCES USA and FORCES Canada.

Yet she and a relative handful of others like her persevere. Sometime, somewhere, someone may listen.

NOT TO DIGRESS already, but I will, FORCES USA has posted on its Website the famous quotation by anti-Nazi Pastor Martin Niemuller:

> In Germany they first came for the Communists, and I didn't speak up because I wasn't a Communist. Then they came for the Jews, and I didn't speak up because I wasn't a Jew. Then they came for the trade unionists, and I didn't speak up because I wasn't a trade unionist. Then they came for the Catholics, and I didn't speak up because I was a Protestant. Then they came for me. And by that time, no one was left to speak up.

Some many consider the appropriation by smokers of those words to be a laughable exaggeration of the threat to everyone's freedom that they claim is posed by the antismokers. Yet at least one scholar has—entirely unintentionally, I surely trust, and only in the area of smoking, I emphasize—at least partially rehabilitated the popular image of the Nazis. Robert Proctor, a professor of the history of science at Pennsylvania State University, wrote in the *British Medical Journal*:

> Historians and epidemiologists have only recently begun to explore the Nazi anti-tobacco movement. Germany had the world's strongest anti-smoking movement in the 1930s and early 1940s, encompassing bans on smoking in public spaces, bans on advertising, restrictions on tobacco rations for women, and the world's most refined tobacco epidemiology, linking tobacco use with the already evident epidemic of lung cancer . . .
>
> Franz H. Muller in 1939 and Eberhard Schairer and Erich Schoniger in 1943 were the first to use case-control epidemiological

> methods to document the lung cancer hazard from cigarettes. Muller concluded that the "extraordinary rise in tobacco use" was "the single most important cause of the rising incidence of lung cancer." Heart disease was another focus and was not infrequently said to be the most serious illness brought on by smoking. Late in the war nicotine was suspected as a cause of the coronary heart failure suffered by a surprising number of soldiers on the eastern front. A 1944 report by an army field pathologist found that all 32 young soldiers whom he had examined after death from heart attack on the front had been "enthusiastic smokers." The author cited the Freiburg pathologist Franz Buchner's view that cigarettes should be considered "a coronary poison of the first order."*
>
> After the war Germany lost its position as home to the world's most aggressive antitobacco science. Tobacco-hating Hitler was dead, as were many of his antitobacco underlings. Others either lost their jobs or were otherwise "silenced." Karl Aster, head of the University of Jena's Institute for Tobacco Hazards Research and an officer in the SS, committed suicide in his office on the night of April 3-4, 1945. Reich Health Fuehrer Leonardo Conti, another antitobacco activist, committed suicide on October 6, 1945 in an Allied prison while awaiting prosecution for his role in the euthanasia program. Hans Reiter, the Reich Health Office president who once characterized nicotine as "the greatest enemy of the people's health" and "the number one drag on the German economy" was interned in an American prison camp for two years. Gauleiter Fritz Sauckel, the guiding light behind Thuringia's antismoking campaign and the man who drafted the grant application for Aster's antitobacco institute, was executed on October 1, 1946 for crimes against humanity.[7]

Thus it is hardly surprising, says Proctor, that much of the wind was taken out of the sails of Germany's antitobacco movement (a movement, I would add, that with good reason has never been revived in Germany with anything approaching the power it now exercises in

*Although heart disease among young people is relatively rare and usually caused by a congenital defect, the fact that 32 young soldiers who had been found fit enough to serve in the Wehrmacht died of heart failure on the eastern front might not necessarily be unbelievable, given the stresses of the battlefield. But that it was in every case caused by smoking *is* hard to believe in view of the number of years medical science says it takes for tobacco to work its evil. On the other hand, that this claim was a complete fabrication designed to please Hitler is not at all hard to believe.

these United States). In any event, he says, "The [German] antitobacco campaign must be understood against the backdrop of the Nazi quest for racial and bodily purity, which also motivated many other public health efforts of the era."

That doesn't mean that antismoking movements are inherently fascist, he concludes. "It means simply that scientific memories are often clouded by the celebrations of victors and that the political history of science is occasionally less pleasant than we would wish."

Proctor seems to be saying that it's too bad the Nazis were such bastards that their pioneer research into smoking was forgotten. Well, gee, maybe we ought to uncloud our memories and take another look at the Nazi "science" that proved the inferiority of Jews and Slavs and Gypsies and other "subspecies" of humanity. Just because it was used for an evil purpose doesn't mean they weren't on to something.

The Nazis have become useful to the antismokers in another way. In his book, *Smokescreen: The Truth Behind the Tobacco Industry Cover-up*, Philip J. Hilts "explains" the behavior of tobacco company executives by comparing them with the people who ran the Nazi death camps.

The one rationalizes that people are going to smoke. "What's better? Giving people their small risky pleasures, or prohibition and a civil war over morals?" The other justified what they were doing by asking, "What is better for [the prisoner]—whether he croaks in shit or goes to heaven in a cloud of gas?"

Commented Malcolm Gladwell in a review in *The New Republic*:

> What is grotesque about this passage is not just the casualness with which Hilts enlists the Holocaust in his campaign against the Marlboro Man; Auschwitz, after all, has been cheapened before. It is also the incredible moral and analytical simplification, the obliteration of notions of responsibility, that is required to compare the act of selling people cigarettes to the act of herding people into a gas chamber. At the moment of its greatest victory, the antitobacco movement has begun to acquire a noxious odor of its own.[8]

Some people may consider Hilts's comparison not so much noxious as only a bit overstated. The tobacco company execs don't *deliberately* kill people because, after all, every dead smoker is one less customer. That doesn't mean they are any better than outright murderers, however. That they are in fact no better than murderers was the basis for a March 31, 1998 cartoon by *The Atlanta Journal-Constitution*'s Pulitzer

Prize-winning editorial cartoonist, Mike Luckovich, that was inspired by Florida's execution of the first woman in that state in 150 years. He drew the woman sitting in the electric chair and saying, "Couldn't I just pay a fine, like the tobacco companies?"

Maybe Mike will earn another Pulitzer for that one.

No, "they" haven't come for the smokers—yet. But they *have* come for the tobacco industry. The smokers will be next after the industry that has enslaved them is destroyed. The crusade for a smoke-free America more and more resembles another Nazi campaign that blackened the history of this century—a *Judenfrei* Reich.

It was in early 1994, by which time I had accumulated several bulging folders of material, that then head of the Food and Drug Administration, Dr. David Kessler—"shocked" to have learned that tobacco contains nicotine—took it upon himself to assert that he, one man among 260 million Americans, acting under the statutory authority of his agency, had the right and duty to regulate the nicotine content of cigarettes. It was then that I became seriously alarmed about what was happening in this country and realized that a true crusade against smoking was going on.

As a former journalist familiar with the hyperbolic excesses of the media, I should have known better, but my alarm was fueled by headlines that followed Kessler's announcement:

"The crusade against smoking shifts into higher gear," said *Time* in its cover story, "The Butt Stops Here." "Should Cigarettes Be Outlawed?" asked (suggested?) *U.S. News & World Report* in the title of its cover story. "Tobacco industry fighting for its life," said *The Atlanta Journal-Constitution.*

That same year another little man named Rep. Henry Waxman had haled the CEOs of seven tobacco companies before his subcommittee for the most shameful inquisition of American citizens since the heyday of the infamous House Committee on Un-American Activities. Although the spectacle was televised, at least one member of the media distorted what happened by writing that "One by one they [the CEOs] temporized, fudged and waffled about two simple facts that everyone knows to be true: that cigarettes are addictive and that they cause mortal illness."[9]

But you can hardly "fudge and waffle" if you aren't allowed to speak. It was: "Yes or no. Do you believe cigarettes are addictive?" When they tried to enlarge upon their statements that they did not so believe, Waxman brusquely cut them off.

None dared call it pipsqueakery.

And because the tobacco CEOs—under oath—denied believing what everyone else in the world "knew" to be true, the Justice Department announced it was investigating them for possible perjury charges. The FBI still has a page on its Website "seeking assistance from past or present tobacco company researchers, scientists, product development personnel, or manufacturing officials knowledgeable about the cigarette development and manufacturing process" as part of "an investigation to determine whether tobacco industry representatives made false or misleading statements to Congress or the Food and Drug Administration concerning tobacco, nicotine, cigarettes, the cigarette manufacturing process, or the manipulation of nicotine during that process."[10]

Such "assistance" would be kept confidential, if requested. To do otherwise, of course, would be to accord the tobacco miscreants the traditional right of an accused to confront his accuser. All that's missing from the site are mug shots of the perps.

Within two years, five major grand jury investigations of the tobacco industry were under way in as many cities:

• In the District of Columbia, whether tobacco executives lied to Congress when they stated they did not believe nicotine is addictive.

• In New York City, whether tobacco executives attempted to hide their knowledge of the hazards of tobacco to defraud shareholders.

• In New Orleans, whether Brown & Williamson employees were aware of a scheme to smuggle cigarettes into Canada to avoid that country's cigarette tax.

• In Brooklyn, an investigation of the nonprofit status of the industry-funded Council for Tobacco Research.

• In Alexandria, Virginia, a probe of documents from Healthy Buildings International (HBI) to determine its relationship with the tobacco industry and whether HBI employees falsified data on second-hand smoke during testimony to federal, state and local officials.[11]

In 1996, Action on Smoking and Health chimed in by offering $25,000 "to anyone who provides information leading to convictions for 'cigarette-related felonies.'"[12]

(No one has ever collected that reward nor have any indictments that I'm aware of ever been handed down as a result of the Justice Department or grand jury investigations.)

In short, by 1996 the antismoking crusade had not only shifted into higher gear but had greatly accelerated. If I thought I was ever going to do something within my meager powers to try to influence the course the nation had embarked upon, it was high time to stop collecting and to start writing, and the most feasible way to do that was in the form of a book. Yet so much was there (and still is) to collect, and so hard and fast came (and still come) more developments in the antismoking crusade, that it wasn't until near the end of that year that I actually embarked upon this book.

An addendum of possible interest:

In March 1998, four years after the Waxman inquisition, former Surgeon General C. Everett Koop and David Kessler abruptly canceled scheduled appearances before the House Commerce Committee upon learning that they would be required to testify under oath. Requiring them to take an oath, they said, would be to treat their testimony on legislation to regulate tobacco as comparable to that given by the tobacco company executives.[13] *The Resistance*, published by the National Smokers Alliance, had the unmitigated gall to question the motives of these two noble benefactors of mankind.

Koop, it suggested, might not have wanted to be questioned closely about the basis for his claim that obesity kills 300,000 Americans a year or about the commercial interests and sponsors of a campaign he founded called "Shape Up America!" which is devoted to doing unto overweight people what he was so instrumental in doing unto smokers during his tenure as surgeon general.

Kessler, the newsletter speculated, might have wanted to avoid being asked to explain irregularities in his expense account when he was head of the FDA.[14]

One expects such picky-pickiness from a smokers' rights organization. But things have come to a sorry pass when a committee of the U.S. House of Representatives muzzles two of the most outstanding leaders of the antismoking crusade because of adherence to a silly rule that doesn't differentiate between the good guys and the bad guys but treats them all as if they were equals before the law.

* * *

So now I am at long last arrived at the twelfth and last chapter of this book, which has been the most difficult one of all to write. I began it in early 1998 but because of a flood of new developments in the crusade the constant rewriting of it took up the entire year.

Everything I have written in the preceding eleven chapters pales into relative insignificance compared with what the title of this chapter states is happening in America (although everything that went before has inevitably led up to it). That is the abolishment, by legislative or judicial fiat, of some of the most fundamental rights that have always been accorded defendants in the nation's courts of law—*if* they are tobacco companies.

It occurred to the most outrageous extent in only one state—Florida—and was directed—at that time—at only one defendant, the tobacco industry, and its rationale is something else "everyone knows to be true": that sick smokers are a parasitic drain on state Medicaid funds. But in many of the 39 other states that sued the industry on the same basis, various limits were placed upon the industry's ability to defend itself. Equally as unsavory is that in the recent settlement that embraces all 50 states, the industry voluntarily colluded in the abrogation of whatever rights it once had under the Constitution in the foolish hope that it will be left alone from now on.

In that fateful year of 1994, the Florida legislature revised its "Medicaid Third-Party Liability Act" in a way that, in the words of Robert Levy, "strips tobacco companies of their traditional rights and puts in their place a shockingly simple rule of law: the state needs money; the industry has money; so the industry shall give and the state shall take."

Levy, a senior fellow in constitutional law at the Cato Institute, wrote a masterful analysis of the tobacco-Medicaid litigation scandal that should have been required reading for every member of Congress.[15]

In six essential respects, he wrote, the amendments to the Florida statute tilted the playing field hopelessly against the tobacco industry:

- First: "Assumption of risk and all other affirmative defenses normally available to a liable third party are to be abrogated to the extent necessary to ensure full recovery by Medicaid from third-party resources" (i.e., the coffers of the tobacco companies).

Translation: The tobacco companies may not employ in their defense the argument that smokers voluntarily assume the risks of smoking, a defense which in all but one of the suits filed against them over the past 40 years has resulted in jury verdicts in their favor or denial of damages to the plaintiff (and that one is under appeal).

It was precisely because of the expense and time involved and the uncertainty of obtaining favorable jury verdicts in individual product-liability cases that the plaintiffs' bar turned to class-action suits on behalf of whole populations of allegedly injured consumers—to use a machine-gun instead of a rifle—first with asbestos and breast implants and then tobacco. A further incentive was that because of the immense punitive damages they faced in such suits, targeted industries were more likely to settle for something short of the amount sued for in order to avoid the risk of a jury trial and to get the vultures off their backs.

• Second: "Causation and damages . . . may be proven by use of statistical analysis" without any showing of a link between a particular smoker's illness and his use of tobacco products.

Translation: the state need not demonstrate that any actual Medicaid recipient, anywhere or anytime, was ever harmed by smoking for the simple reason that it is impossible to prove that any person's particular illness was caused by smoking. Therefore the great god Statistics shall rule all.

• Third: The state "shall not be required to . . . identify the individual recipients for which payment has been made, but rather can proceed to seek recovery based upon payments made on behalf of an entire class of recipients."

Translation: it is immaterial how many, if any, Medicaid beneficiaries were or are smokers. The state is entitled to recover for funds dispensed for *all* beneficiaries, whether or not they ever smoked.

• Fourth: In assigning liability to the individual tobacco companies, the state "shall be allowed to proceed under a market share theory, provided that the products involved are substantially interchangeable among brands" (as, of course, cigarettes are).

Translation: It is immaterial what brand of cigarettes a not-to-be-identified Medicaid beneficiary may have smoked, or even if he smoked a brand made by a company not named in the litigation, or even if he smoked in another state and later moved to Florida, or even if stopped smoking before or after moving to Florida. All makers of cigarettes are to be looted.

• Fifth: "the defense of repose [i.e., the statute of limitations] shall not apply to any action brought under [the act]."

Translation: the tobacco industry is to be subject to litigation for all instances of alleged damages to the state, however distant in the past they may be.

• Sixth: if the state recovers damages, it is authorized to pay "reasonable litigation costs or expenses" to an outside private attorney, plus a litigation fee not to exceed "30 percent of the amount collected."

Translation: Bonanzaville for a lucky few of those who were smart enough to go into law instead of something useful to society, like becoming teachers or policemen. (With sincere apologies to all the decent and conscientious lawyers I have known. Yet where were their voices when their Florida brethren were fashioning this legal travesty?)

As far as I know, only one other state, Iowa, considered emulating Florida. There a similar law relieving the state of the burden of proof in its suit against the tobacco industry was proposed but not acted upon.[16]

In March 1996, the Florida legislature came to its senses and passed a bill repealing the Medicaid Third-Party Liability Act, but it was vetoed by Gov. Lawton Chiles and opponents were unable to muster the two-thirds vote needed to override the veto.

I was in Florida at the time and saw how at least one newspaper greeted this event. "Yippee!" said the *Sarasota Herald-Tribune*, or words to that effect. "The forces of good and the forces of greed have combined to deal the tobacco industry a one-two punch which we hope will cut the giant down to size."[17]

Yes, so evil is the tobacco industry that the use of evil by the defenders of the good is justified in combating it.

So is hypocrisy. At the time it filed its suit, Florida had some $285 million in pension assets invested in tobacco stocks. And although it purportedly sought recovery for all "tobacco-related disease," it did not sue cigar companies, perhaps, suggests Levy, because the state is home to the nation's leading producer of high-grade cigars.

Also, for nearly a decade in the 1970s and 1980s, the Florida prison system manufactured unfiltered cigarettes, giving some free to inmates and selling some to local governments. Yet when a prisoner filed a lawsuit seeking access to nicotine patches and other treatment for alleged addiction to nicotine, the state claimed innocence and said it was not responsible for his decision to smoke cigarettes. "Plaintiff is in no way entitled to medical intervention to 'cure' a habit which Plaintiff himself continues to indulge, and over which Plaintiff has ultimate control."[18]

This is another example of the "forces of good" having it both ways. When it suits their purposes, smoking is an "addiction" which is not the fault of an individual but that of the cigarette makers who enslaved him; when the shoe is on the other foot, it's merely an individual's voluntarily assumed "habit."

Even Uncle Sam, whom Americans have learned to beseech for protection of their rights and the redress of their grievances, will turn a deaf ear when the petitioner is a smoker. The Veterans Administration had been paying benefits to veterans who could show that their illness was connected to smoking that began during their military service. But the Clinton administration decided to stop that, and both the Senate and House Budget Committees endorsed the cutoff. The VA estimated it could save $17 billion by denying claims by an expected half-million veterans for compensation for "smoking-related" diseases they incurred because, in the words of Bill Russo of the Vietnam Veterans of America, "the military pushed a dangerous, addictive drug on the troops."[19]

Not that I believe that ill veterans or ill anybody else are entitled to recompense, either from the government or from the tobacco industry, because they smoke or once smoked. I'm merely observing how quickly the hearts of the public's servants turn to stone when "their" money is involved.

A month after the Florida legislature's failure to repeal the Medicaid Third-Party Liability Act, the Florida Supreme Court, ruling on a suit challenging the constitutionality of the act, threw out some of its provisions, such as the abolition of the statute of limitations and the section that authorized the state to sue the tobacco industry without identifying a single Medicaid patient. It otherwise left the statute intact.

Yet in conformity with that part of the ruling requiring the state to identify Medicaid recipients, when trial of the suit began in West Palm Beach, Judge Harold Cohen generously granted the defendants the right to see the medical records of *25* persons picked at random out of *400,000*—with no way of knowing if any of them had ever smoked a cigarette. No wonder the tobacco companies decided to end the fiasco by buying off the extorters.

Although I was incensed and unbelieving at the time—because there was all kinds of evidence the industry could have used to prove that, far from being a drain on Medicaid, smokers actually subsidize the healthcare of nonsmokers, not least or which was a study by the Congressional Research Service—I can almost understand why the industry capitulated and bought off the real parasites to the tune of $11.3 billion. And why it had shortly before done the same in Mississippi—the state that had started a feeding frenzy that was eventually joined in by 39 other states, and which had taken care that its suit *not* be conducted before a jury—by paying its extortionists $3.6 billion (peanuts alongside Florida's take). Or why it next settled with Texas's legal boodlers to the tune of $15.3 billion.

It would be unseemly of me to suggest that the attorneys arguing those suits were not chosen because they were models of probity and idealism and legal acumen and were interested in no reward other than the knowledge that they were fighting the good fight for all of us (plus, of course, modest and reasonable fees). It would be even more unseemly to suggest that political connections and cronyism might be involved.

However, Levy notes that in Mississippi, Attorney General Mike Moore selected his number one campaign manager, Richard Scruggs, to lead that state's Medicaid recovery suit. Scruggs also received a $2.4-million contingency fee for a state asbestos lawsuit in 1992, after contributing over $20,000 to Moore's re-election campaign the year before. In Texas, Attorney General Dan Morales chose five firms to handle that state's suit, four of which contributed nearly $150,000 to Morales's political pot from 1990 to 1995.

In Florida, a Ft. Lauderdale lawyer, one Hugh Rodham, who happens to be the president's brother-in-law, somehow got involved in the negotiations that led to the so-called "global" tobacco settlement with the 40 states. Robert Montgomery, the state's lead attorney in its suit, described Rodham as "one of several 'Johnnie-come-lately's' who have sought to insert themselves into the potentially lucrative tobacco case."[20]

It would also be unseemly to note, but I will anyway, that the Association of Trial Lawyers of America was the third-largest political contributor to the 1996 election campaign, giving $3.5 million, of which 85 percent went to Democrats. Individual trial lawyers gave millions more.[21] It would be unseemly because only the tobacco industry's political contributions, unlike those of any other industry or interest group, are designed to influence legislation in its favor.

Why didn't Florida businessmen hop all over the hypocritical Medicaid Third-Party Liability Act? After all, nowhere did it name the tobacco industry; it applied to any business or industry that sold a product that could conceivably cause injury to someone who used that product—alcoholic beverages, junk food, sports equipment, home appliances, just about anything.

For that matter, any company anywhere in the country that sold a product in Florida could be sued by that state for reimbursement of Medicaid expenditures. Why were they silent? Silly question. It was because it was the hated tobacco industry's ox, not theirs, that was being gored and because gutlessness is not the exclusive property of the cigarette makers.

A group called Associated Industries of Florida, a statewide employers association representing more than 8,000 businesses, did worry about that possibility when the law was being considered, but did not formally protest until *after* it had been successfully used against the tobacco industry. On the very day that the news came of the industry's cave-in, Jon L. Shebel, president and chief executive officer of the AIF, wrote Gov. Chiles:

> As you stated to me shortly after the passage of the law, you were advised by the proponents that the law only applied to tobacco and not any other products; and you subsequently offered to throw your support behind an amendment to the law which would release all of the [other] products and individuals from potential liability.
>
> Now is the time for you to come out in support for a total repeal of this blatantly unfair and unconstitutional law. You have accomplished the goals that you stated to me and to the citizens of Florida [the savaging of the tobacco industry—D.O]. It is now time for you to show that you are the fair-minded individual we have all always believed you to be. I know you must have shuddered at times as to "the end justifies the means" aspect of this law, and now is the time for you to do the right thing.

> Of course, the trial lawyers are "foaming at the mouth" as to the prospects of the next case and subsequent cases. You are well aware of this! This has all gone too far and it is time to bring this terrible inequity to a halt! This has nothing to do with tobacco and your personal feelings for the product; but it has everything to do with fairness, equity and justice for all citizens, individual and corporate, and their right to expect to be able to defend themselves in a court of law in our state.[22]

Fairness. Equity. Justice. What noble and laudable ideals. *Except* when it comes to the tobacco industry. Then "good joins greed" and the end truly justifies the means.

At the end of his paper, Levy quotes from Robert Bolt's play, "A Man For All Seasons," the following exchange between Sir Thomas More, King Henry VIII's Lord Chancellor, and his daughter's intended, William Roper. The latter exclaims:

> "So now you'd give the Devil the benefit of law!"
>
> "Yes. What would you do? Cut a great road through the law to get after the Devil?"
>
> "I'd cut down every law in England to do that!"
>
> "Oh? And when the last law was down, and the Devil turned round on you—where would you hide, Roper, the laws all being flat? . . . [D]'you think you could stand upright in the winds that would blow then? Yes, I'd give the Devil the benefit of the law, for my own safety's sake."

Such quaint, old-fashioned integrity has no place in 20th-century America, not on the part of businessmen or lawyers or legislators, not with the nation in the midst of the gravest crisis it has ever faced: *people smoking cigarettes*. So grave is the crisis and so powerful is the enemy that necessity requires the employment of any means at our disposal, constitutional or not, to combat it.

Another old-fashioned Englishman, the elder William Pitt, had some words about that kind of thinking:

"Necessity is the plea for every infringement of human freedom. It is the argument of tyrants; it is the creed of slaves."

To DIGRESS BRIEFLY again, a better example of hypocrisy and a double standard of justice than Florida's Medicaid Third-Party Liability Act would be hard to find. But there's a close runner-up.

When the U.S. Senate approved a measure that would lower, nationwide, the level at which automobile drivers are considered to be under the influence, from a blood alcohol content of 0.10 to 0.08, the alcoholic beverage and restaurant industries rushed to arms to defeat the measure in the House.

"This is all politics, all about grabbing headlines," declared a spokesman for the American Beverage Institute. (Antismoking rhetoric is never about grabbing headlines.) The National Restaurant Association flew 150 restaurateurs from 40 states to Washington to make their case. Some of the most powerful lobbyists in the capital joined in a veritable blitzkrieg against the legislation, arguing that the proposal would badly hurt restaurant and bar sales, penalize responsible social drinkers and have no effect on the real drunk drivers.[23]

I am entirely neutral on this issue because I am too much of a tightwad to buy more than one drink in a restaurant or bar, so it wouldn't affect me. ("When they came for the social drinkers I didn't speak up because . . . ") I only wonder where the restaurant association and the beverage institute were when Maryland, for example, instituted a total ban on smoking in restaurants and when California banned smoking even in bars.

Well, no, I don't wonder. They said nothing because restaurants and bars don't make any money from cigarettes, except perhaps a cut from vending machines, which are going to be outlawed anyway. (As we all know, it's almost impossible to get a table in a restaurant or a stool at a bar because of the crowds of children lined up at the cigarette vending machines.)

While it's true that individual restaurant and bar owners in some areas, especially in California, have protested that bans on smoking are hurting their businesses by driving smokers away, such protests have amounted to little more than disgruntled muttering compared to the outcry by their representative organizations against a proposal that could *really* hit them in the pocketbook.

A COUPLE MORE items about Florida, and then I'll be happy to leave that state.

In the immediate aftermath of the industry's surrender, Florida lawmakers were in a quandary: how to spend a kitty of $200 million that was separate from the $11.3-billion shakedown and earmarked for antitobacco programs. It had to be spent within two years or they would lose it. (How did the evil industry get away with that provision?)

Gov. Chiles proposed spending $57 million in the then current 1997-98 fiscal year and including the remaining $143 million in the 1998-99 budget. The first year's spending would consist of $18 million for marketing and communications, $17 million for youth programs run by local coalitions, $13 million for education and training, $5 million for enforcement and $4 million for evaluation and research.

("Local coalitions." "Youth programs." One can just see the professional antismokers' ears perk up and their mouths salivate. California wasn't going to be the only "Golden State" for antismokers!)

But Senate Republican Leader Locke Burt of Ormond Beach questioned whether antitobacco programs were effective. "I feel a little awkward about a large appropriation when we don't know what works," he said.

"Unfortunately," admitted Chuck Wolfe, an aide to the governor, "no one in the country knows exactly what works."[24]

But when has the fact that politicians don't know what they're doing ever been an obstacle to grandiose social programs?

Florida Education Commissioner Frank Brogan suggested that some of the money be spent on school construction. Child advocates replied that it would be "hypocritical" for a legislature that voted down tax increases for new schools to look now at the tobacco windfall as an easy solution. It would be "unfair" if lawmakers spent the booty on school construction rather than preventive healthcare and antitobacco programs for kids.[25]

Unfair to professional child advocates, that is. Heaven forbid that Florida should spend its windfall on something that might actually be of real benefit to its children. That would be tantamount to saying that the crusade against smoking is not the most important thing in the universe, or at least not the most important thing in a state that ranks near the bottom in education and in which there were 128,000 reports of child abuse between June 1996 and June 1997, with 62 child-abuse deaths.[26]

(In case it needs to be said again, these kinds of deaths are *real* deaths of *real* children, not statistical projections of "smoking-related" deaths of "kids" several decades in the future.)

What if multimillion-dollar antismoking youth programs, none of which anybody knows if they work, don't work? Florida has another statutory stick. Beginning in September 1997, any person under 18 caught smoking, or just in possession of, cigarettes, could be fined $25 or be sentenced to community service or have his driver's license suspended.[27]

The penalties are far too mild, I say. In Malaysia, students caught smoking can be flogged.[28] Surely Floridians should want to be as progressive as Malaysians.

I won't even go into the fight in Florida over how much the attorneys should get from the settlement, or similar edifying squabbles in Mississippi and Texas over how to spend their ill-gotten gains, or those three states' panic and outrage when the feds said they wanted their share of the Medicaid boodle, to which they are entitled by law. (The federal government provides between 50 and 70 percent of what the states spend on Medicaid.) That would be unseemly too.

But in all this salivating in Florida and everywhere else over multibillion-dollar windfalls, in all the newspaper editorials celebrating the comeupance of the tobacco industry, nobody ever mentions the fact that it is *not* the evil tobacco industry that is being punished but millions of ordinary people who have chosen to smoke cigarettes, for it is *their* money, not the industry's, that is being confiscated.

Another possibly interesting addendum:

Shortly before the tobacco industry capitulated in the Florida Medicaid suit, attorneys for the state announced that they planned to introduce at the trial an incriminating document showing how the industry deliberately targets youth. It was a handwritten, undated memo from the files of the British American Tobacco Company (BAT), the parent of Brown & Williamson, proposing a cigarette that smelled like root beer or fruit juice—a new brand that "'breaks the rules' to appeal to a new generation and shock their parents [and] make conventional brands look bland and weary."[29]

What iniquity! Or was it, as p.r. people say, more like a matter of someone at BAT running a cockamamie idea up the flagpole to see if anyone saluted? Although nothing came of the proposal, the tobacco industry is pilloried not only for anything it has ever done but for anything it has ever *thought* of doing.

MAYBE I'M NAÏVE, but despite the legal raping of "Big Tobacco" (again read: smokers, who will ultimately have to pay) in Florida, Texas and

Mississippi I retain the belief that there must be some kind of ordinary common sense at the foundation of the legal system, some concept of fair play informing the rules of evidence. But consider Minnesota's suit against the tobacco industry, which was getting under way when I began this chapter and was the only one of the 40 to go all the way to trial.

In St. Paul, when at a pretrial hearing a Philip Morris Company lawyer started to introduce the argument that smokers save the state money by dying early because of their health-destroying habit/addiction, Ramsey County District Judge Kenneth Fitzpatrick interrupted him and said he wouldn't allow such a "ghoulish" argument.

"[C]ounsel," said the judge, "can you imagine my sitting here during the trial of this case and allowing you to present what is ultimately a position that you deserve a credit because of the death of people that was premature by reason of smoking?"[30]

I hope I never find myself in the hands of this judge. In the first place, Philip Morris was not seeking "credit" for but simple consideration of the (alleged) fact that smokers die prematurely, thus saving the state monies it would otherwise have to spend later on their healthcare had they survived into old age. In the second place, it is not the to-tobacco industry that has claimed that smokers die prematurely but the antismoking industry. In the third place, it is not the tobacco industry but the antismoking industry that has claimed that smokers pass their healthcare costs on to the rest of society. Shouldn't the tobacco industry be allowed to introduce figures disputing that claim? But again, the forces of good were to have it both ways.*

Judge Fitzpatrick also indicated that he wouldn't permit the tobacco industry to employ another argument—that the state's (alleged, never proven) smoking-related Medicaid healthcare costs should be offset by the $175 million collected annually by Minnesota's cigarette excise tax.

"No courts have ever allowed that," he said.

Let me see if I've got that straight. The industry pays $175 million a year in cigarette taxes to the state. That is, individual smokers do. But

*In their suits against the industry, the states not only pretended that nonsmokers never get sick; they also ignored the fact that long-term nursing-home care for the elderly accounts for 43 percent of Medicaid expenditures.[31] Even antismoking demagogue Stanton Glantz agrees that the supposed excess costs of smoking amount to a mere 4.8 percent of total Medicaid costs.[32]

that doesn't count. Apparently, all that tax money collected from smokers in Minnesota, and the 49 other states, just disappears into their general treasuries. It would be "unfair" to apply any of that money collected from smokers toward helping pay for "smoking-related" Medicaid costs allegedly incurred by those same smokers. Sounds like a kind of double jeopardy to me.

But then, smokers aren't really citizens, are they? Not full-fledged ones anyway. In my former hometown of Cleveland, smokers paid for a new baseball stadium, which they are welcome to enjoy—as long as they don't smoke in it.

The industry would also seem to have had an even better defense against Minnesota Blue Cross/Blue Shield, which was a party to the state's suit. Smokers who belong to this health insurance group pay their own premiums; the money doesn't come from innocent nonsmokers.

Yes, the group could counter, but sick smokers account for a disproportionate share of benefits claims. But even if that were true, is that a problem the sovereign state of Minnesota had to remedy or was it something Blue Cross/Blue Shield should find a way to handle?

To my knowledge, no life insurance company has ever sued the tobacco industry to recoup benefits it has paid to the survivors of dead smokers. They simply charge higher premiums for smokers. No doubt some, perhaps many, smokers lie and say they are nonsmokers. But that does not seem to be a major problem for these companies.

Also not allowed to be considered in the general jubilation over the tobacco industry finally getting what had been coming for it for a long time is the fact, as one observer pointed out, that:

"[Not] one of these states knows how many of its Medicaid patients even smoke or ever have smoked. Not one is prepared to produce a sick Medicaid patient and prove, with scientific evidence, that the patient's illness is a direct result of cigarette smoking . . . The states have no such evidence. They are like a state suing General Motors on the grounds that automobiles are involved in accidents and that victims in accidents have run up the cost of Medicaid."[33]

Actually, it would be much more logical for a state to sue the automobile industry than to sue the tobacco industry because you can count the number of people injured in traffic accidents. You can name their names and tell when and how their injuries happened and you can total their actual medical costs. As for an unknown number of Medicaid recipients who might have incurred health problems because of all the carcinogenic chemicals spewed into the air by automobiles, you could, like Florida in the case of smoking, employ "statistical analysis."

If the automobile industry objected that it was saving the state future heathcare costs by killing thousands of people prematurely, what right-minded judge would allow such a "ghoulish" argument? And if the industry pointed out that individual car owners were already paying millions to the state in gasoline excise and other taxes, what judge would allow a "credit" for that?

This is all fantasy, of course. If any state so much as suggested such a suit, you would see a popular uprising because the money extracted from the industry (perhaps, like Florida, on a "market share" basis) would eventually have to be paid by individual automobile owners in the form of higher prices for their wheels. People may hate smoking but they love their cars. When it comes to gouging the tobacco industry, however, which means gouging smokers, they will stand for—make that go for—anything.

But darn, there I go forgetting again: the gang-up against the tobacco industry was not about filthy lucre but was *in a good cause.* If it happens to enrich a lot of lawyers, surely they deserve that reward for bringing the tobacco industry to justice for all the harm it has done to society. Why can't I get that through my head?

I guess I'm just confused. I keep thinking: if it's really true that "smoking-related" illnesses are a drain on state treasuries, why didn't each state simply take a wild stab at how much and raise its cigarette tax to compensate for it? Why go through the long, drawn-out litigation process and hire expensive attorneys and force smokers to pay them literally billions of dollars that could be used directly to offset Medicaid expenditures? For Florida, Texas and Mississippi alone, the payoff an arbitration panel awarded to those states' lawyers was $8.1 billion!—with more billions to come from the settlement with Minnesota and the rest of the 50 states.[34]

Nobody answers me, so I can only conclude that it's a stupid question and I just don't understand how the world works. Everybody else apparently understands and likes the way it works. It couldn't be because the plaintiffs' bar runs the show.

(Another stupid question: how many states do you think will actually use the money taken from smokers to replenish their Medicaid funds "everybody knows" have been drained by smokers, and how many states do you think will spend their windfalls on all kinds of pet projects? I'll give you a clue: the answers are "zero" and "fifty.")

Initially, the defendants in the Minnesota suit turned over to the court 33 *million* pages of internal company documents. (Why in the world did they keep all this stuff? For that matter, *where* in the world did they keep it? No doubt they now fervently wish they'd shredded it long before, just as Richard Nixon regretted not destroying his Watergate tapes.) The state then demanded, and got by order by the U.S. Supreme Court, 39,000 more documents totaling about 200,000 pages.

These are by no means the first "secret" tobacco company documents unearthed. We've been hearing about them for years. Stanton Glantz published a thick tome of them culled from a bundle stolen from Brown & Williamson. One presumes these selections were the most incriminating of the lot. But I plowed through the whole thing, and nowhere did I find—and nowhere else have I heard of—a single instance of any document revealing that the tobacco industry had ever discovered anything about smoking that was not already known to the medical establishment.

Nothing so well illustrates our national schizophrenia on this issue. One half of the public brain has known since at least 1964 that smoking can be harmful to the health. The other half firmly believes that the tobacco companies suppressed the truth about smoking and lied to us, keeping us in the dark all these decades.

TO DIGRESS AGAIN, will Medicaid or general healthcare nirvana have arrived when America is smoke-free? I'll cite just one study, "ghoulish" though it may be, that predicts an answer to that question.

A nation of nonsmokers might end up spending more, not less, on healthcare, say researchers at the Erasmus University Department of Public in Rotterdam, the Netherlands, in a study analyzed in the October 1997 *New England Journal of Medicine*.[35]

If everyone stopped smoking tomorrow, national healthcare costs would initially be lower than they had been as the incidence of smoking-related disease tapered off. However, as smoking-related deaths decline, they wrote, "the population (as a whole) starts to age. Growing numbers of people in the older age groups mean higher costs for healthcare because the extended lifespan of nonsmokers (relative to smokers) also brings an added risk for the often expensive chronic diseases associated with old age." [Parentheses in original.]

In a theoretical "smoke-free" society, medical costs would begin to exceed those of the old "smoking" society about 15 years after universal smoking cessation, the researchers estimated. In time, "a new steady state is reached in which costs continue to be about seven percent higher than those of populations experiencing current rates of tobacco use."

Of course, they were quick to add, mere dollars should not be the yardstick by which we measure the value of antismoking efforts. Smoking is "a major health hazard" and should be discouraged on that basis alone, they said. (Antismokers only use dollars as a yardstick when they're socking it to smokers.)

The only thing that bothers me about citing a study like this is that in doing so I am tacitly endorsing the thesis that great numbers of smokers die prematurely from expensive illnesses. But again, it's the antismokers who have advanced the claim that smokers are a burden on society and we smokers have no choice but to challenge them on their own ground.

Nor will any other kind of nirvana arrive when the last smoker is dead and everybody else lives forever. "Many of our nation's baby boomers have a time bomb ticking in their heads today," said Stephen McConnell, a spokesman for the Alzheimer's Association, as the group lobbied Congress for $100 million in new research money. Unless ways are found to prevent or cure the disease, the association predicts that by 2050, when the youngest baby boomers will be in their 80s, 14 million Americans could suffer from the disease, compared with four million today.[36]

Epidemiologists are fond of correlations. I'll give them one for free. It's kind of a mirror image of the one between the increase in smoking in the first half of the 20th century and the rise in the incidence of lung cancer. In this case, the dramatic increase in the incidence of Alzheimer's disease in the second half of the century correlates neatly with the dramatic decline in the rate of smoking in the same period.

I am not trying to be cute. There is tantalizing evidence of a protective effect of nicotine against Alzheimer's, as well as Parkinson's. Unfortunately, it is unlikely that researchers will follow up on this because nicotine comes from tobacco, and anything that would make nicotine look good would reflect favorably on tobacco and the smoking of it, and smoking is "a major health hazard." That is all ye know and all ye need to know.

As I MENTIONED in the Preface to this book, the first part of the subtitle I originally chose was "America's Insane Crusade Against Smoking". Besides the fact that the crusade was going off on nuttier and nuttier tangents and occupying more and more newspaper space and television time, I did so for a couple of basic reasons.

One derived from a fundamental commonsense attitude that even if cigarette smoking had been established as a cause, or even *the* cause, of lung cancer (and it is with lung cancer, and only lung cancer, that the epidemiological evidence is at all "statistically significant")—*so what?* If there are risks to smoking, so are there risks to a lot of things we do simply because we like to do them. Skiing can break your legs, or worse. A certain number of people are killed every year while skydiving. *So what?* The vast majority of skiers and skydivers never incur fatal or life-threatening injuries. Similarly, the vast majority of smokers never get lung cancer. And whatever risks there are in any of these behaviors, they are voluntarily assumed.

Unfortunately, the public health establishment quickly moved beyond its legitimate function of alerting smokers to the *potential* dangers of their habit. In the years following the 1964 surgeon general's report, warning was added to warning until in popular thinking the consequences were not merely potential but well-nigh certain. To the ordinary person, "smoking-related" came to mean the same thing as "smoking-caused."*

When exhortation and the ceaseless piling of evidence upon evidence failed to persuade more than 50 million smokers to stop smoking, the next stage was coercion against the stubborn holdouts by making them feel guilty and ashamed that their dirty, self-destructive habit was harming not just them but innocent others, which led easily to the next stage—social ostracization, to which smokers acquiesced without protest because of that very guilt and shame.

*"The leading causes of death are now all listed as smoking-related: heart disease, strokes, respiratory diseases, cancers. That means if you lived all your life on a desert island and never smoked, and died of a heart attack, it could be said that it was smoking-related because heart attacks are listed as smoking-related."[37]

But the main reason I decided that the antismoking crusade was manifesting symptoms of derangement was that the more familiar I became with the multitude of studies associating cigarette smoking with an endless number of health problems, the more I saw how little relation they had to actual cause and effect and the more they revealed themselves to be the product of antismoking bias. This was especially true of those involving "environmental tobacco smoke" (ETS), which became the most effective weapon in the antismoking arsenal, even though there is *not one* study that has shown even close to accepted standards of statistical significance that secondhand smoke has ever harmed anyone. These studies nevertheless have been used as the basis of and justification for all manner of draconian restrictions against smoking and self-righteous discrimination against smokers.

And that's where the "scam" comes from in the subtitle I finally settled on, as well as being the cause of my personal "slow burn" over what was happening in America regarding a habit I had enjoyed for half a century.

At a confab of antismokers in Perth, Australia, in 1990, officially called the Seventh World Conference on Tobacco and Health, Stanton Glantz said, "The main thing the science has done on the issue of ETS, in addition to help people like me pay mortgages, is it has legitimized the concerns that people have that they don't like cigarette smoke. And that is the strong emotional force that needs to be harnessed and used. We're on a roll, and the bastards are on the run. And I urge you to keep chasing them."[38]

(Some smokers jumped all over Glantz's remark about his personal financial benefit from his antismoking activities, but I think he should be given some charity here. I think he was just trying to inject a little humor in his speech. More revealing was his calling the target of his activities "bastards," meaning the tobacco companies. In any crusade or war, the first thing you do is deride and dehumanize your enemy.)

As the '90s unfolded, the antismokers were indeed on a roll and had successfully harnessed "the strong emotional force" of public opinion in pursuance of a relentless crusade against a habit that has given and still gives pleasure to millions, a personal indulgence which like any number of other behaviors may or may not sometime harm them, and only them. Eventually, cigarette smoking was elevated to a matter of crucial national concern over and above anything else—the crime and violence and deaths spawned in the nation's cities by the illegal drug trade and the other insane crusade against it that has only exacerbated it; the creeping down of violent behavior to younger and younger children; child and spousal abuse; teenage pregnancy; unmet educational needs; the approaching crisis in social security; the scandal of political campaign financing, and on and on.

If this is not the picture of a society gone wacko, it is one whose priorities are seriously out of whack.

In the beginning though, I did not conceive that the crusade would reach the point it did in 1997: the attempt to bring the tobacco industry to its knees, if not utterly destroy it, through the threat of perpetual class-action lawsuits unless it submitted to one great massive shakedown, a shakedown on a scale no Mafia don every dreamed of. This was the $368.5-billion "global" settlement arrived at on June 20, 1997 between 40 state attorneys general and the nation's four largest cigarette makers—Phillip Morris, R.J. Reynolds, Brown & Williamson and Lorillard. (The smallest of the majors, the Liggett Group, had set the stage for this sweeping agreement when it made a separate deal with the AGs the previous year.)

It was a settlement, incidentally, from which smokers—the supposed victims of the tobacco industry but who would nevertheless be saddled with the industry's bill—would have received nothing except, as someone put it in reference to smoking cessation programs the industry agreed to finance, "A nicotine patch and a pat on the back."

As for the industry, what it would get (it fondly hoped) would be future "financial certainty" by being freed from the threat of class-action suits—as if, having brought the industry so close to self-destruction the antismokers would stop there. But the people who run the tobacco companies today are no longer emotionally tied to tobacco; there are no figures among them like the "Major James Singleton" of Chapter 1, for whom tobacco was his very life's blood. Today it's just another business, and if it requires the payment of blackmail to the states to stay in business, name your price.

Without doubt, the industry has every reason to fear class-action suits. Inspired by the success of the attorneys general, other groups are looking to get a piece of the action. Hard on the heels of the settlement with the suing states, in September 1997 a coalition of labor union healthcare funds filed lawsuits in federal courts in 21 states claiming that the tobacco industry had been targeting blue-collar workers for years and was guilty of racketeering and conspiring to mislead the public about the health risks of smoking. And just for insurance, in one of the suits that was filed in West Palm Beach, Florida, Jim Ray, whose Washington firm is handling all 21 suits, planned to ask a federal judge to extend to private plaintiffs the protection of the 1994 Florida law that virtually abolished the industry's ability to defend itself against that state's Medicaid lawsuit.[39]

According to coalition spokesman Dave Jewell, a study of the union funds showed that costs continued to rise even as claims by workers had been declining. The fund administrators determined that those extra costs were coming from treatment for smokers. (Sure, the general inflation in medical costs that has been going for years—in no little part because of our readiness to sue doctors at the drop of a syringe—might also have something to do with it. But heck, you can't sue an entire profession. Much, much easier to sue a single industry, especially one everybody hates.)

Even so, I am at a loss to understand how the four companies (who mainly constitute "the industry") could possibly have agreed to the extent of the blackmail. $368.5 billion was a colossal sum of money, even if strung out over 25 years, which was as far ahead as the agreement looked. It was a *stupendous* sum. $368.5 billion is more than total U.S. Treasury receipts in the first 160 years of the nation's existence, from its founding in 1789 through 1949, from the first president, George Washington, to the 33rd, Harry S. Truman. The first time that expenditures by the government of the United States exceeded $368 billion in a single year—for all its agencies and departments and programs, for Congress, the Supreme Court, the armed forces, for *everything*—was not in one of the World War II years, or even all four of those unlimited-spending years, but relatively recently: 1976.

(Of course, if you were to translate the figures for each of those 160 years into 1998 dollars, $368.5 billion might then equal only, say, the government's income for the first 50 or 75 years. That would be offset, however, by the fact that scheduled payments by the industry were to be increased by an inflation factor of three percent a year. According to a study by the Congressional Budget Office (CBO), that would bring the total to about $550 billion over 25 years—if cigarette consumption remained at its current level, which it would not.[40])

Even less, however, did I conceive that when Congress began deliberation on the settlement there would ensue a frenzied "I-am-more-antitobacco-than-thou" rivalry between Republicans and Democrats, inspired not by concern over what was best for the nation but what would be best for them in the next election. As if $368.5 billion were not incomprehensible enough, Arizona Republican Sen. John McCain all of a sudden zoomed the ante to $506 billion! Now we were talking a sum equal to total U.S. Treasury income from 1789 through 1952 and 20 times the cost of the nine-year Apollo moon landing program. Adding in inflation over the next 25 years would put us into a neighborhood approaching a *trillion* dollars.

Just where did McCain or anybody else think all these billions and billions were to come from?

According to various government sources, tobacco industry after-tax profits are currently around $8 billion a year. (This includes all the companies in the industry, not just the big four.) Every penny of that $8 billion would have to be confiscated for the next 63 years to pay out $506 billion. Stanton Glantz estimated the industry's profits could be increased to $30 billion a year if the price of cigarettes were lofted to $4 a pack. (Then we'd only have to confiscate its profits for 17 years.) Such an increase would happily also reduce cigarette consumption by 47 percent, with all the public health benefits that would bring, he said.[41]

But he was figuring that $30 billion on the basis of current consumption. If consumption declined by 47 percent, wouldn't the industry's earnings also decline by 47 percent? And if the companies raised prices again to try to regain some of their lost profits, consumption would decline even further.

This is the kind of cloud-cuckooland these people inhabit. They think they can strangle the smoking goose and still harvest its golden eggs.

Anyway, the McCain proposal called for an increase of $1.10 a pack, not $4. However you slice it, it's a mystery to me how they expected to squeeze $506 billion out of four tobacco companies, or even the original $368.5 billion.

The Congressional Budget Office agreed. After examining the terms of the original settlement, its staff concluded that "[T]here is no plausible set of assumptions under which tobacco companies would actually make payments of $368.5 billion. Even if the settlement was completely ineffective in reducing smoking [through higher prices for cigarettes], the downward secular trend in consumption that has prevailed for many years would lead to a reduction in payments well below that amount."[42]

That certainly applied in spades to McCain's $506-billion grand theft. Does Congress pay any attention to its own researchers?

UNDER THE SETTLEMENT—either the original one or the Senate-revised one—the tobacco companies would also have surrendered their First Amendment right to advertise, except for black-and-white ads with no human or cartoon figures and only in a few magazines that teenagers supposedly wouldn't see. At the same time they would finance propaganda campaigns and programs by the antismoking industry condemning their own product and urging people not to buy it. The settlement earmarked half-a-billion dollars for that, which topped the nearly $490 million the industry spent on advertising in the U.S. in 1996, according to Competitive Media Reporting, a research service, and about equals what McDonald's spent to promote its artery-clogging hamburgers and french fries the same year.[43]

This was another magic bullet against smoking that would misfire. Italy banned cigarette advertising shortly after World War II. Norway banned all tobacco advertising more than two decades ago. Finland instituted a partial ban in 1978. All of these countries have smoking rates comparable to the United States, despite their severe and our comparatively mild (at this time) restrictions.

In New Zealand, 27 percent of adults still smoke, a figure that hasn't changed since 1990 when an advertising ban was enacted. More Canadians are smoking today than did in 1989, when Parliament passed a cigarette advertising ban (later declared unconstitutional, as was a similar ban in, of all countries, Iran!).[44] When I was in Montreal in 1997, it seemed like every third person on the street had a cigarette in his hand.

Doesn't matter. It's an article of the antismoking faith (when it serves their purposes) that people smoke only because they are hooked on it, and they are hooked on it only because of the tobacco industry's pervasive and seductive advertising. Anybody who argues otherwise and brings up something called personal responsibility is either "blaming the victim" or is a tool of the merchants of death.

The industry also agreed to allowing the Food and Drug Administration to regulate the nicotine content of cigarettes about nine years after the settlement went into effect, which if the David Kesslers had their way would mean no-nicotine cigarettes and—*surprise*—a brilliantly lucrative incentive for smuggling and bootlegging. Not without justification was the McCain legislation dubbed "The Lawyers' Enrichment and Bootleggers' Protection Act of 1998." (More about the latter aspect below.)

It got even crazier. The industry agreed to pay penalties (to be capped at a mere $3.5 billion a year) if the rate of teenage smoking wasn't cut by 60 percent in 10 years. Just how the industry was supposed to accomplish this when antismoking propaganda that begins in kindergarten hasn't been able to make much of a dent was not spelled out. This provision of course was based on the myth that advertising creates cigarette smokers. Yet drug use is a continuing, if not worsening, problem among youths, and I've never seen any magazine ads or billboards promoting marijuana or cocaine.

The funny thing is, no cigarette company sells cigarettes to teenagers. Stores do, or the teenagers get them some other way. Every state and the District of Columbia has a law against selling cigarettes to minors, and more of them are enacting penalties against the youths themselves for mere possession of cigarettes. If laws and propaganda can't prevent teens from smoking, how were the cigarette companies supposed to do it?

According to the latest Youth Risk Behavior Survey by the Centers for Disease Control and Prevention, cigarette use by high school students rose by one-third between 1991 and 1997, from 27.5 percent to 36.4 percent. Among black youths, who formerly shunned the habit, smoking was said to have jumped by 80 percent, from 12.6 percent to 22.7 percent.[45]

At first glance, this was the most encouraging news I'd heard in years. Alas, when it comes to lying to the public, the government beats anybody, even the tobacco industry, six ways from Sunday.

Steven Milloy points out that the CDC omitted to mention that teen smoking prevalence was reported to be at 32.3 percent in 1990, which means it went down by nearly five percent in 1991. But the Centers opted to compare the 1991 survey with 1997 because of the larger difference. Considering the survey's error margins, typically in the range of plus or minus two percentage points, it is quite possible that there was no change in teen smoking levels from 1990 to 1997.[46]

Why would the CDC want to make the rate of teen smoking look worse than it really is? For the same reason antismokers ignore studies showing no harm from secondhand smoke: if there is no crisis, there is no need for crisis managers.

One thing we can believe is that when it came time to determine the size of the penalty the industry had to pay because teen smoking hadn't gone down, figures would be found to require the maximum amount. (As David Murray, research director of an organization called the Statistical Assessments Service, says, "There are no real numbers in Washington. There are just useful numbers and nonuseful numbers."[47])

The antismoking industry actually has a vested interest in a high teen smoking rate. I don't mean to intimate that these sour-souled but purehearted folks would sacrifice the nation's youth for their pecuniary advantage. To paraphrase myself, it's just that if we ever reached a point where there was no teen smoking crisis, there would no longer be a need for teen smoking crisis managers.

My local source for antismoking idiocy, *The Atlanta Journal-Constitution*, naturally accepted the CDC's figures without question, as did, I'm sure, every other newspaper in the country. One of the reasons for this reported increase in teen smoking, the AJC editorialized, was the cartoon figure, Joe Camel, who studies have shown is a highly recognizable character to youngsters.

(So is the Energizer Bunny, but the AJC didn't say how much sales of batteries have increased among kids. So is Snoopy, and nobody believes he is being used to peddle life insurance to kids. But logic is tossed out the window when it comes to the cigarette companies.)

Even though old Joe has been retired, concluded the editorial, "his mission continues through ever more sophisticated tobacco marketing."'[48]

I would dearly love to learn more about this "ever more sophisticated tobacco marketing," but the AJC offered no examples. But then, proof is never required in the field of antitobaccoism; allegations alone are sufficient, and the mere stating of them adds to the "mountain of evidence" against smoking and the companies that make the smokes.

Herr Hitler knew that the bigger the lie, the more easily it is swallowed by the public. The antismokers know that the more often a lie is repeated, the more firmly it becomes established as something "everybody knows is true." Isn't it great that the United States has succeeded Nazi Germany as the world's most aggressively antitobacco country?

The Boston Globe also accepted the CDC's figures but took a different approach. That is, one of its columnists did.

"Crunch the data any way you like, the massive anti-teen-smoking crusade has been a disaster," wrote Jeff Jacoby. "Countless millions of dollars have been poured into convincing youngsters not to smoke, yet a larger share of them are smoking every day. It is hard to imagine a more thoroughgoing failure. So will the antitobacco warriors, humbled by such a defeat, call off their jihad? Of course not. They will demand even more restrictions, impose even higher taxes, curse tobacco companies even more loudly. They will insist that the law go even further to deprive smokers of the right to choose. And all, of course, for 'the kids.'"[49]

Jacoby was wrong only about one thing: the antitobacco warriors *want* the teen smoking rate to stay high, again for the same reason they don't want to hear that secondhand smoke is harmless—so that they may continue their jihad against the industry.

Interestingly, in a companion article to the CDC report, *The Atlanta Journal-Constitution* interviewed a number of local teenagers and found that, far from being rebellious delinquents with deep psychological problems, those who smoked were good students and otherwise respectful and obedient children. The paper also reported that some parents felt that as long as their kids made good grades and stayed out of trouble, smoking was not the worst thing they could do.[50]

This *is* encouraging. Like psychologist John Rosemond, whom I quoted in this respect at the end of Chapter 10, some people in this country apparently still retain a sense of balance and proportion regarding smoking.

What about raising the price of cigarettes, as a settlement would have required in some unknown but significant amount? That would surely make teenagers think twice about smoking, wouldn't it?

Sorry, antismokers. Not only do teenagers have much more income at their disposal than many people think, they also have expensive tastes, with high-priced brand names considered to be the "coolest."

The Advocate in Baton Rouge, Louisiana, reported that during the 1997 Christmas season, one teenager spent $129 on a pair of shoes.

Another planned to spend $150 to $200 on two pairs of pants and a shirt, and a third said she planned to spend $150 on sweaters. A *Chattanooga Times* story quoted a 15-year-old as saying she had a $500 Christmas budget and in one hour bought three bottles of nail polish for $12 apiece and two ribbed sweaters. The *Herald-Sun* in Durham, North Carolina, quoted a 17-year-old as having spent more than $200 during one summer, including $70 on football cleats. A senior told the newspaper that he planned to spend $2,000 on a new wardrobe.[51]

"I've been smoking since I was 13," Jeff Adams, 17, told *The Chicago Tribune*, "and even if it costs more I'll still pay. It's worth it."

"Even if they [cigarettes] were $3.50 a pack, I'd still buy them," said Marcia Fountain, 16.

"Price alone won't do it," said Elk Grove Village, Illinois, deputy police chief Larry Hammar. "These kids are smoking because somehow, some way over these last few years it has become fashionable again, cool, for them to seen with a cigarette hanging from their mouths. It's a cultural thing."[52]

Why has smoking cigarettes become fashionable again among teens? Propaganda backlash? The lure of the forbidden? I don't know, but before the end of this chapter I'll tell why I think smoking will never be stamped out.

For whatever reasons teens smoke, a few dollars more for a pack of cigs is not going to deter them. The only people who will be seriously affected by higher cigarette prices are adults with incomes below $30,000 a year, who already pay 53 percent of today's cigarette taxes.[53]

ALL RIGHT, FORGET for a moment about all those billions and billions and billions of dollars involved in the "global" settlement, which the industry finally walked out on anyway. What I really don't understand is why "Big Tobacco" played along with the states attorneys general at all rather than fight them, except in Minnesota where the state at first wouldn't let them settle out of court, apparently because Attorney General Hubert Humphrey III thought his case so strong and the malefactions of the industry so flagrant that truth, justice and the American way demanded a full-scale public trial to expose the wrongdoers.

As noted earlier, in every instance but one in the past 40 years in which a tobacco company entrusted its fate to a jury, the jury found for the company. (This is one reason why the industry agreed to a provision in the "global" settlement allowing individuals to continue to sue it. Another reason, the best one, was that it can outspend and outlast any private plaintiff.)

Once again, however, in Minnesota the industry decided to switch (to being blackmailed) rather than fight. Granted that Florida passed legislation and a pretrial judge in Minnesota delivered rulings that tied the industry's hands behind its back by denying it its best defenses; i.e., that nobody forces smokers to smoke, that their killing themselves prematurely saves the states money and that while they're alive they pay a heck of a lot in taxes that ought to count for something. Surely the industry's clever and highly paid attorneys could have found a way to get those points across to a jury. Or if not, surely jury members would have had enough common sense to perceive those facts between the lines of the state's argument.

Even in the highly emotional and highly subjective area of secondhand smoke, even as the Minnesota suit was proceeding toward trial, a jury in Muncie, Indiana, found that the industry was not liable in the cancer death of a nonsmoking nurse who, her husband claimed, "inhaled smoke constantly" during her 17 years as a nurse in the psychiatric ward of a Veterans Administration hospital.[54]

(In the only other secondhand-smoke suit that has been settled to date, this one also involving a VA hospital nurse, it was the Labor Department's administrative decision, not a jury's, that awarded damages to the surviving husband. See Chapter 8.)

Consider also that most private suits against the industry have claimed damages in the hundreds of thousands of dollars, or at most the low millions ($13.3 million in the Indiana nurse's case). Sought-after damages in class-action suits, which the industry hoped to avoid through the original "global" settlement, are much higher, but even Minnesota claimed only $1.77 billion (which the generous industry upped some nine-fold in the final deal!). Just for the heck of it, put the average state Medicaid claim against the industry at $10 billion. The industry would have had to lose 37 of them in a row before its losses surpassed the $368.5 billion it was willing to fork over in the "global" settlement. And if you consider the length of time it takes for a suit even to reach the court, the industry could have strung them out unto eternity, or at least well into the 21st century.

But the oh-so-shrewd attorneys who run the tobacco companies must have known a lot of things I don't know that persuaded them to settle with Minnesota at the last minute—to the astonishment and dismay of many of the jurors, incidentally. (Speaking of that, did Mr. Humphrey also know something I don't know that persuaded him to abandon his high-minded goal of exposing the evil industry rather than risk putting the suit into the hands of the jury?)

Speculation about the industry's motives is irrelevant, however, because one of the Senate's "improvements" on the original "global" settlement removed a provision giving the industry immunity from class-action suits. Maybe that's why it eventually mustered enough gumption to say to Congress that enough was enough.

AT A NEWS CONFERENCE in Washington on June 20, 1997, some of the 40 states attorneys general assembled to celebrate their victory over the tobacco industry.

The first to take the microphone was their leader, Mississippi AG Mike Moore, who had won fame (or infamy, depending upon your prejudices) as the man chiefly responsible for engineering Big Tobacco's debacle. After congratulating all and sundry for their "courageous" efforts in achieving the historic "global" settlement, this posturing phony told the world what it was all about.

"See, I've got a little boy," he said. "His name is Kyle, and he's 10 years old . . . Also I have a dad. He's about 76 years old, and has been smoking for a real long time. And I worry a whole lot about that. And it's my dad and your dads and your moms and your grandpas and your grandmoms that we did this for."

The next bleeding heart to take the podium was Washington AG Christine Gregoire. After congratulating all and sundry for "making this day possible," she echoed Moore with, "I have been here [at the negotiating sessions] on behalf of an 82-year-old mother who has been smoking since the age of 13. I have been here on behalf of two teen-aged daughters."

Am I the only one who sees the hypocrisy here? Parental example and exhortation and laws against selling to minors can't save Moore's 10-year-old son and Gregoire's teenage daughters from the lure of cigarettes, but the extraction of billions of dollars from the hated tobacco industry—I mean, from smokers—and the transference of much of it to the accounts of law firms representing the states would?

Even famous bank robber Willie Sutton displayed more honesty than these representatives of the forces of good. When asked why he targeted banks, he replied, "Because that's where the money is."

As for Moore's dad and Gregoire's mother, am I the only one who sees the irony here? His 76-year-old dad has been smoking for "a real long time" and her mother has "been smoking since the age of 13"? Just how had they been harmed by all those years of smoking (69 years in Gregoire's mother's case!)? They didn't say. Just how would the settlement benefit their aged parents? They didn't say.

Also putting in a few words was Robert Butterworth, attorney general of the notorious state of Florida. After congratulating all and sundry and Moore in particular, he proclaimed: "With the agreement, Joe Camel and the Marlboro Man will move to the same chapter of our nation's history as asbestos, the Corvair and the Edsel—and you know that's exactly where they belong."[55]

Am I the only one who sees the grandstanding here? Asbestos never was a problem until the Environmental Protection Agency started stirring it up in buildings with its ill-advised and eventually discontinued removal program. The Corvair was the hapless victim of scaremongering by a "consumer crusader." The Edsel was another fine car that simply happened to be the wrong product introduced at the wrong time. It was not the saviors of society who removed it from the scene (it was never charged with any safety deficiencies) but the millions of individual car buyers making their own individual decisions.

Despite the self-congratulation and self-satisfaction of the attorneys general, however, not everyone in the antismoking ranks was pleased with the terms of the settlement. In the public health establishment, only the American Medical Association endorsed it (officially, that is; many of its members demurred). The heart, lung and cancer societies said it was "too easy" on the tobacco industry and a "sweetheart deal" for the merchants of death. "This settlement would grant legitimacy to an industry and its behavior we all find so reprehensible," said John R. Garrison, CEO of the American Lung Association.[56]

Among those sharing such opinions were, of course, the two mad doctors, Koop and Kessler, who issued their own "blueprint" for a smoke-free society under the auspices of a panel they formed called "The Advisory Committee on Tobacco Policy and Public Health." The committee's members included some two dozen representatives from various medical specialty associations and antismoking groups.

Their report[57] is a long and repetitious document that takes up 59 pages in my word processor and whose most frequently used phrases are "should be banned" and "should be prohibited." Most of the actions against the tobacco industry recommended by the committee are —what else?—to be "funded by the tobacco industry."

A clue as to what these people eventually have in mind for cigarettes are their recommendations for "No limitations or special exceptions on FDA authority to regulate nicotine, other constituents and ingredients" and "Consideration of generic packaging of all cigarettes." The second one presumably means plain brown wrappers with just the word "Cigarettes" on them, surrounded by warning messages. Whether the manufacturer would be allowed to put his name somewhere, the report doesn't say.

Where the Koop-Kessler committee talks about a "global" settlement, it *means* global. For example, in case the cigarette companies think they are going to make up their domestic losses by expanding their operations in foreign countries, and in case those supposedly sovereign foreign countries don't know enough to do the right thing:

• "The U.S. should use the broad range of its international activities and influence to actively promote tobacco control, including the adoption of U.S. domestic tobacco control standards as at least minimum global standards."

• "The U.S. must insist that public health concerns overrule trade concerns in all trade negotiations and related proceedings."

• "The U.S. should allocate substantial resources to fund effective international government and non-government institutions engaging in tobacco control activities."

• "Both the executive and legislative branches of the Federal government can do much, within reason [*sic*], to bring about worldwide adoption of tobacco manufacturing and marketing standards at least as comprehensive and stringent as those enforced within the United States."

What I found most revealing about this long document, however, was the committee's concern over what might happen once the antismoking movement achieved all its goals.

"It is, of course, uncertain that current levels of media attention on tobacco and tobacco company behavior will continue indefinitely . . ," they wrote. "[*A*]*t some point the media may run out of newsworthy revelations* [emphasis added] . . . And at some point, other issues and stories will gain attention and dominate the news." This will happen for two reasons, they said:

"1. Passage of such legislation [writing the settlement into law] will convey to most Americans, including journalists, opinion leaders, and policymakers, the impression that the tobacco problem in this country has been 'solved.' Not only that, but the tobacco industry will be seen as a willing partner to the solution. This will mean that tobacco, and the past culpability of the tobacco industry, is no longer 'news' . . .

"2. Passage of such legislation will deflate the tobacco control movement, enervate tobacco control advocates, and shrink funding for tobacco control advocacy. This is true, even though, given the 46 million smokers remaining, tobacco use will remain our number one public health threat for many years, providing a strong rationale for funding tobacco control efforts."

Two paragraphs later:

"Unless the settlement legislation provides for adequate funding to sustain the nation's tobacco control infrastructure, the vital grass roots organizations will be parched for basic resources, and we will have rendered the national tobacco control movement an emaciated watchdog, inadequate to keep pressure on regulators to regulate vigorously, politicians to focus on public health rather than campaign money, and the tobacco lobby from renewing its dirty work."

In other words, if Koop and Kessler and their accomplices could help it, there would *never ever* be an end to the antismoking crusade, not as long as one smoker remained alive. And when the tobacco industry had been bled as much as it could be bled, where would "adequate funding" come from? From you, dear nonsmoker, who by that time will also be paying for the next lifestyle crusade that will be aimed at your dangerous, self-destructive dietary choices.

AT THE BEGINNING of the chapter I said that one of the difficulties I labored under in writing this book was that new developments in the antismoking crusade constantly forced me to go back and add to or revise what I'd already written. Even as I attempted to finish this chapter, and the book, came the industry's announcement that it was withdrawing its support for the "global" settlement because, it said, Congress had gone beyond the original agreement and was trying to punish the companies to the point of bankrupting them.

Had the industry at long last developed some backbone, or was it a tactic to get Congress to soften the terms of the McCain plan? Although there was little chance of the agreement with the state AGs going through in its original form—Congress couldn't back down that far after having raised the ante to the stratosphere—a few concessions to the companies, especially restoring their immunity from class-action suits, might bring them around again.

The immediate response from President Clinton was that he was not trying to put the cigarette companies out of business, just out of the business of selling to children. (It never hurts to repeat a Big Lie.)

"They can be part of it or they can fight it," he said. "I think they ought to rethink their position because we're going to get this done one way or the other."[58]

"We" included the Republicans in Congress as well as the Democrats. As Speaker of the House Newt Gingrich had vowed earlier, "I'm not going to let the president get to the left of me on this."

Congress certainly would have liked to punish the industry, if only because it would be politically popular. But just as certainly it didn't want to kill it outright and deprive itself of all that tax money. Even if it did want to destroy the industry, for all its power Congress still has to operate under the Constitution. Even Congress could not force an agreement down a legal industry's throat—one that would not least of all abrogate its right of commercial free speech (limited though that right is compared to an individual's under the First Amendment)—without that industry's consent. Were it to try, the industry would immediately appeal to the Supreme Court, which I cannot believe would not declare such legislation null and void, despite its being "for the children."

The professional antismokers wanted the harshest possible settlement that would leave the tobacco industry still alive (barely) because it would give them de facto prohibition of tobacco while enabling them to milk the industry in perpetuity. It was their greed that brought them to an impasse with the tobacco industry over the "global" settlement, and it is their greed that will eventually be their downfall.

The antismokers' zeal has caused them to come a cropper before. It was their demand for warning messages on cigarette packages and in advertising back in the '60s that was to provide the cigarette makers with their winning defense against liability suits brought by private individuals in subsequent decades.

But then came another development, forcing another last-minute revision of this chapter. This was the "miniglobal" settlement between the industry and the remaining 46 states not already bought off, to the tune of $206 billion.

Gee, what a deal—only $206 billion instead of $368.5 billion! I'm so glad those tobacco guys are on my side.

This latest and, one presumes, final settlement included most of the provisions in the old "global" settlement by which the industry agreed to cut its own throat: severe limits on its right to advertise, funding of various antismoking programs, allowing individuals to continue to sue it, agreeing to let the FDA regulate nicotine, and the like.

Coming up with that "only" $206 billion will still require steep increases in the price of cigarettes which, combined with piggyback increases added by the cigarette makers and jobbers to enhance their bottom lines, will probably persuade more people to quit smoking than the surgeon general's report did in 1964. And then where will the states get their eagerly awaited windfalls from?

Even while the "global" settlement was still up in the air, cigarette prices started going up sharply—more sharply than even McCain's $506-billion scheme would have required. For example, in the spring of 1998 I bought a couple cartons of Doral for $7.49 at a tobacco discount store in North Carolina, off I-85. When I stopped there again in August, the price was nearly doubled to $14.79. I didn't buy any, but instead chose a still reasonably priced but less desirable generic brand. No doubt it too has doubled in price since then.

Will greed also be the tobacco industry's downfall?

WHY HAVE THE antismokers never been honest about it and demanded the outright prohibition of tobacco? It's not because of the social lessons of alcohol prohibition, America's most famous insane crusade, but because it would be difficult to get money out of an industry that was declared illegal. No government has ever been able to "unaddict" itself from its dependence on tobacco taxes, and tobacco bootleggers wouldn't pay taxes. (I'm sure there are figures somewhere showing how much revenue the states and the federal government lost because of Prohibition, as well as how much it cost them to enforce it.)

Three decades of antismoking efforts have hammered the number of smokers in this country down to a resistant, hard-core percentage of about 25 percent of the population. To force it down much further will take more and more extreme measures. Still, it's hard to believe that Americans would ever be so foolish as to try another "Noble Experiment," this time with tobacco. However, one law professor and specialist on the history of marijuana prohibition predicts we will.

"Why? Because we love this idea of prohibition. We really do. We love it in this country," law professor Charles Whitebread told a group of California judges a few years ago.

He made another prediction: "If we get together here in the year 2005, I will bet you that it is as likely as not that the possession of marijuana may not be criminal in this state. But the manufacture, sale, and possession of tobacco will be."

Why? Because the use of tobacco is increasingly becoming confined to the lower classes of society while marijuana is the drug of choice of the young "elites" who will be the nation's movers and shakers in the coming years, he said. "And cigarettes are no longer going to be three dollars a pack, they are going to be three dollars apiece. And who's going to sell them to you? Who will always sell them to you? The people who will sell you anything—organized crime . . . [W]e will go through the whole darn thing again because I am telling you this country is hooked on the notion of prohibition."[59]

I don't know about marijuana legalization, but California is doing its best to reduce the number of cigarette smokers to the vanishing point. In November, voters there approved, albeit by a razor-thin margin, a 50-cent hike in the cigarette tax, on top of a 25-cent surcharge in place for several years, with the revenue passed on to antismoking groups.

The new tax is supposed to go for some kind of "child development programs" which ostensibly will benefit all the citizens of the state, yet only smokers will be required to pay for them. This was nothing but political bullying by the nonsmoking majority. (And if a significant number of Californians quit smoking because of the tax, again where will the money come from to finance these lovely programs?)

Whitebread's black market scenario is entirely plausible, however, and it won't require tobacco prohibition to make it come true. The exorbitant taxes that some countries have placed on cigarettes already give us a preview of what could happen. (Sources under Notes 60-63 in the following are from a news release by the Libertarian Party posted by FORCES Canada on its Website.)

In Berlin, the capital of Germany, a country where cigarettes cost $3.60 a pack thanks to a 90-percent government tax, "the smuggling of cigarettes [caused] a surge in gangland-style executions and turf wars [that] made Berlin streets more dangerous than at any time since World War II," reported *The Washington Times*. "Authorities fear that cigarette trafficking is leading to crime empires dealing in extortion, prostitution, stolen cars, drugs, and weapons."

"People are being executed in cold blood in their apartments and in broad daylight on the streets, on subway platforms, in front of hundreds of witnesses," said Detlef Schade, a police detective in Berlin.[60]

"Turf battles between the Vietnamese gangs that control street-level sales have been blamed for the deaths of 40 Vietnamese, 15 in Berlin alone [in 1996]," reported *USA Today*. These killings are "the latest episode in a bloody gang war over Berlin's lucrative trade in smuggled cigarettes."

Why the brutal battles? Because a single truck "loaded with 50,000 cartons can net a smuggler $550,000" in profits, said *USA Today*.[61]

In fact, all across Europe, high taxes are resulting in a bonanza for smugglers, reported syndicated columnist Bruce Bartlett. "One-fourth of the world's cigarettes are now smuggled across national borders to evade taxes and tariffs," he wrote. "Governments are already losing $16 billion per year in tax revenues—a figure likely to rise as organized crime becomes a larger player in the business of smuggling smokes. In Italy alone, organized crime is said to make $500 million per year smuggling cigarettes."[62]

Closer to home, says the release, look at what happened in Canada when the government raised tobacco taxes by 146 percent in 1991.

"The result was an invitation to organized crime. Mohawk Indians from tribes along the U.S.-Canada border, biker gangs, and Asian Triads smuggled cigarettes across the border in boats, airplanes, trucks, legitimate courier companies, and snowmobiles. By the end of 1993, nearly one in three cigarettes was contraband.

"Retailers also [became] victims of a crime wave, as it became more lucrative for thieves to skip the cash register and head straight for the cigarettes."

Even more surprising, despite the steep tax hike, "youth smoking did not decrease and many officials ironically argued that high taxes made it more difficult to control youth smoking," reported Erin Schiller of the Pacific Research Institute.

By 1994, shaken by the crime explosion and lost tax revenues, Canadian Prime Minister Jean Chretien said the cigarette tax threatened "the very fabric of Canadian society"—and drastically reduced the tax burden, "which essentially eliminated cigarette smuggling in Canada." Canadian Health Minister Diane Marleau argued the tax cut was needed to "end the smuggling trade and force children to rely on regular stores for their cigarettes"—where purchases could be better controlled.[63]

Even closer to home, because of the disparities in taxes among the states, "Cigarette smuggling is a growth industry," says the *Bergen* (New Jersey) *Record*. "Federal officials report a 300 percent increase nationwide since 1992. But it is expected to explode in New Jersey now that the state's tobacco tax has doubled." That state is also directly on the route from low-tax southern states to New England and Canada.

Never fear. As a counterpunch to the burgeoning crime wave, the federal Bureau of Alcohol, Tobacco and Firearms has created a specialized unit aimed at thwarting the bootleggers. "We're gearing up big-time," said Joseph Green of the ATF's New York regional office in Manhattan.[64]

Elliot Ness, where are you when your country needs you?

One way we might attack this problem domestically would be for the federal government to require the states to place uniform taxes on cigarettes. Or better yet, to give Washington even greater say in local affairs, replace state taxes with a high federal tax, the revenues from which the federal bureaucrats could parcel out to the states—or withhold it from those that weren't doing enough to curb smoking. In either case there would no longer be an incentive to smuggle cigarettes from, say, low-tax Virginia into high-tax New Jersey or elsewhere.

But that would still leave the problem of smuggling cigarettes into Canada (or vice versa if Canadian cigarettes became cheaper than American ones, which they might well) or into the U.S. from Mexico. If we couldn't stop liquor from crossing the border back in the '20s, if we can't stop human beings from crossing the border in the '90s, we wouldn't be able to stop cigarettes, no matter how big-time we geared up the revenuers.

But we're sure gonna try, aren't we? I'm really starting to regret dropping the "insane" from my original subtitle.

THE SECOND PART of the subtitle of this book is "(Why It (the antismoking crusade/scam) Will Fail.)" That's as provocative an assertion as my calling the crusade insane. What makes me think it will fail ?

Well, for one thing, efforts to discourage or prevent smoking on a universal scale have always failed. As mentioned at the beginning of this book, the use of tobacco spread rapidly throughout the world after its discovery by Columbus (its rediscovery; the Indians had always known about it), and even the resort to capital punishment of smokers by some tyrants availed not against it.

For another thing, all crusades eventually run their course. The Crusades (with a capital "C") to capture the Holy Land for Christendom were pursued by Europe and occupied its energies throughout three centuries, but they are now ancient history. I think doctors Koop and Kessler have reason to worry: Americans will eventually weary of the crusade to reach the Holy Land of a smoke-free America and go on to something else.

But I was only joking, or hope I was joking, when I said that the next crusade would be against our eating habits. That would hit too close to home to too many of us. Still, back when half the population smoked, I never dreamed in my worst nightmares that there would be a crusade, in every sense in which that word is understood, against smoking. What the next crusade will be, I wouldn't attempt to predict. But there will be one, and it may well be a crusade to save us from our diets. If, as Prof. Whitebread said, we are hooked on the notion of prohibition, we are just as hooked on *causes*—which is only another word for crusades.

The great appeal of causes are the utopian visions of the future they always project. For example:

> The effects on our physical health are immediate. The incidence of cancer and heart attack, the nation's biggest killers, drops precipitously . . . So do many other diseases . . . So do the neurological disorders and birth defects . . .[65]

The writer is not speaking about a smoke-free America but a meat-free America, which would realize these good things, and more, if only we stopped or significantly reduced our consumption of animal proteins and fats.

The grain we save could feed five times the U.S. population and we could alleviate malnutrition and hunger on a worldwide scale, the writer goes on. The great forests of the world we had been decimating for grazing purposes would begin to grow again. The water crisis would ease as we discovered that ranching and farm factories had been the major drain on our water sources. The change in diet would free over 90 percent of the fossil fuel energy previously used to produce food and our reliance on oil imports would decline, as would the rationale for building nuclear power plants. As expenditures for food and medical care dropped, personal savings would rise. And so on toward utopia.

This may sound like fantasy today, but a growing number of people are turning to vegetarianism, partially or completely. What if they eventually teamed up with animal-rights and environmental groups, which also seem to be growing, both in numbers and in militancy? Numbers plus dedication equals power. And when the time comes to set a crusade for a meat-free America into motion, we can be sure that "studies" will be forthcoming to provide the scientific basis for it. There have already been at least two I've heard of, one in Britain and one in Germany.

"Smoking kills 111,000 people every year (in the U.K)," says vegetarian author Peter Cox, citing these studies. "But that falls into second place behind the 134,000 annual deaths which the evidence suggests could be prevented by a vegetarian diet."[66]

True, the early campaigns against smoking lacked the scientific evidence, valid or invalid, real or trumped-up, that underpins our modern crusade and which has persuaded more people to abandon the habit than any amount of preaching against it ever did or could—although I believe that a moralistic prejudice against tobacco remains the real motive force behind antismoking activism, as it was four centuries ago. Science has merely given antismokers a weapon they never had before.

It is also true that smoking did not become hugely prevalent until after the introduction of the handy cigarette in the 19th century, which ushered in what I call "the golden age of smoking" (and which I will be forever grateful I grew up in).

Even so, how could millions of people over the centuries have embraced such a "nasty, smelly, dirty, disgusting" habit as the smoking of tobacco—or worse, the chewing of it (which, happily, the introduction of the cigarette relegated to a small minority of tobacco users)? Obviously, the noble weed had something going for it, and still does.

There are, first of all, the small peripheral enjoyments attendant to smoking a cigarette or cigar or pipe or preparing to—the sweet aroma of a fresh cigarette or cigar, or the tobacco in a tin or pouch; the tactile pleasure of the ritual of extracting cigarette or cigar from a pack or humidor and handling them, or the scooping of tobacco from a pouch and tamping it down in a pipe; the application of a flame to the tobacco; the taste and all the other organoleptic (sensory) sensations; the visual pleasure of watching the smoke that curls up from the end of a cigarette or cigar or the smoke one blows into the air from cigarette, cigar or pipe.

But aside from that, it is most of all, with cigarettes, the inhalation of the smoke and the feel of it in the throat and lungs and the mild kick of the nicotine that is the reason people smoke and why most of them smoke cigarettes. It is, when all is said and done, cigarettes and the nicotine-induced pleasure they convey that the antismoking crusade is about (although as I predicted in Chapter 1 that they would, the antismokers are now directing their attention to cigars as well). The crusade is not just against the possible and much-exaggerated health consequences of smoking cigarettes. It is against smoking. Period.

The satisfactions attendant to smoking are always there in those little white cylinders any time you want them, so easy and convenient. All you have to do is light one and smoke it. You can smoke when you're relaxing, to add to the relaxation. You can smoke when you're nervous, to allay the nervousness. It stimulates or calms. Whatever your need at the moment, smoking and the nicotine derived therefrom fills it. No other drug can do that, and unlike most other psychoactive drugs, the body does not demand ever increasing amounts of nicotine.

You can smoke while performing complicated tasks (not so with marijuana or other "recreational drugs"), or while doing nothing at all. You can smoke when you're thinking hard or when your mind is idly wandering. Smoking helps you do both. Nothing can do so many things as smoking to enhance the feeling of simply being alert and alive, yet have no psychological consequences other than the wish to smoke again, which of course is why cigarettes are "addictive," just like anything can be that gives pleasure.

Well, maybe nothing except maybe sex, which also has a number of things going for it. But that's another argument in favor of smoking. Like sex, smoking is a pleasurable activity, and anything that provides pleasure the puritan mind fears and abhors.

As with anything that gives pleasure, of course, a lot of people tend to overdo. (But if that is a problem, it is theirs, not society's.)

Again this is especially true of cigarettes because they are so convenient to use, unlike the necessity of cleaning out the bowl of a pipe and tamping in fresh tobacco or unwrapping a cigar and cutting off its tip. Typing away at the word processor, I've often automatically lit a cigarette, only to realize that one I had lit a minute before was still smoldering in the ashtray half-smoked.

For good or ill, human beings are drug-using creatures and cigarettes *are* a drug-delivery device, no question about it. And what they deliver is the most beneficial and harmless psychoactive drug I know of. Of all the drugs in that class, none is as effective and at the same time more benign than nicotine. Until somebody discovers a better drug, smoking will always be with us—but not just because of the nicotine, otherwise millions would be hooked on nicotine patches or gum, but also because of all those peripheral pleasures I mentioned. In a nutshell, smoking satisfies needs that are inherent in both the human physiology and its psychology.

This is one of two reasons why I say smoking will never be stamped out and the crusade against it will fail. The other, no less important, is that any crusade that depends for its success upon scamming people into believing things that "ain't so" cannot last. You can't fool all the people all the time, forever.

IN THE MEANTIME, however, the antismoking crusade has not yet run its course. When or how it will end, I don't know, but it will end. Maybe it will just kind of fade away, like the original Crusades, with the zealous antis trying to re-energize the crusade by continuing to berate and scare smokers but with ever-diminishing effectiveness as the rest of the population, finally realizing that there really are more important things in the world, turns an increasingly deaf ear.

Smoking will never be considered entirely harmless, but maybe the medical profession will eventually begin to recognize that the evidence against it simply proves too much. To quote again Prof. Finch from Chapter 2, if "smoking kills," it does so relatively infrequently, as relatively infrequently as all the other dangers and perils, manmade or natural, behavioral or environmental, that we voluntarily assume or involuntarily encounter in daily life.

Or maybe a new, less self-righteous and less easily frightened generation will bring the crusade to an end sometime in the next century.

In their book *Generations*, William Strauss and Neil Howe examined 18 generations of Americans, from the first colonists to the children of the Baby Boomers, and make a convincing case that there is a recurring cycle of four basic types of "peer personalities" identifying each generation—the Idealistic, the Reactive, the Civic and the Adaptive—that repeat themselves within a grand cycle roughly every 81 years.

As the century ends and as the Civic "G.I" generation dies off, their children, the Idealistic "Baby Boom" generation, are, for better or worse, becoming socially dominant—in terms of political power, not numbers—and will reach their lifetime peak share of national influence around 2005, the authors say (the same year, curiously, Whitebread predicts marijuana could be legalized.) The smaller postwar generation in the middle, the Reactive "Silent" generation to which I belong, has never amounted to much.

Although the Boomers did not initiate the antismoking crusade—the oldest of them were just entering adulthood in 1964—it is they who have caught the torch and are carrying it forward.

Strauss and Howe published their book in 1991, but already, they wrote, "A growing chorus of social critics is noticing a Boom-led . . . 'New Puritanism' in circa-1990 America" that is "beginning to police 'politically correct' behavior." They quoted *New York Times* writer Molly O'Neill's observation that smoking or regular drinking were becoming the "new Scarlet Letters" among the ex-flower children, and one Boomer activist's comment that "There is no such thing as being too rude to a smoker."[67]

As the 90s progressed, they predicted, "Boomer-retooled justice will punish aberrant behavior with growing severity and overtones of moral retribution; Boomer-retooled institutions will strictly regulate conduct (from drug use to parenting) formerly regarded as matters of personal choice [parentheses in original] . . . Looking down the age ladder, elder Silent [that's me!—D.O.] will express dismay at growing signs of tribalism, nativism, social intolerance, and just plain meanness."[68] And as the 20th century gives way to the 21st, "Boomers will become increasingly intolerant, uncompromising, snoopy, and exacting of others. At the same time they will become more dutiful, principled, and demanding of themselves."[69]

But an Idealistic generation is always followed by a Reactive one. These are the children of the Boomers, popularly called the "X" generation but whom Strauss and Howe label "13ers" because theirs is the 13th generation since the United States became a nation. The 13ers actually outnumber the Boomers: 79 million to 69 million in 1991.

Among the 13ers' characteristics:

Parental divorce has struck 13ers harder than any other American generation . . . No other American generation has grown up in families of such complexity . . . No other child generation has witnessed such a dramatic increase in domestic dissatisfaction (and surge to the workplace) on the part of mothers . . . 13er teenagers face a much lower risk of dying from disease than did Silent teenagers 40 years ago, but this advantage has been almost entirely offset by a much higher risk of dying from accidents, murder and suicide . . . As teenagers, 13ers are committing suicide more frequently than any generation since the "Lost" generation of the 1920s . . . Already 13ers have become the most heavily incarcerated generation in American history.

If that is not dismal enough, "during the 13er childhood, America has substantially shifted the federal fiscal burden from the old to the young. Since 1972, older generations have deferred paying for some $2 trillion in current consumption through additional U.S. Treasury debt —a policy five times more expensive (in lifetime interest costs) for the average 15-year-old than for the average 65-year-old."[70] [Parentheses in original.]

Confronted with these facts of life, 13ers have built a powerful survival instinct, wrapped around an ethos of personal determination, the authors say. "In the early 21st century, 13ers will make their most enduring mark on the national culture . . . Controlling the Boom [generation] may indeed emerge as the 13ers' most fateful lifestyle mission. This will be the generation best able to deflect any Boomer drift toward apocalyptic visions. In an age of rising social intolerance, the very incorrigibility of midlife 13ers will at times be a national blessing."[71]

Strauss and Howe make no prediction about the antismoking crusade, but I choose to read in the above that it will be the Americans who are today's teenagers or twenty-somethings who will eventually tell the aging moralistic Boomers to "stuff it." I may not live to see this, but I am going to die in the confident hope of eternal life—eternal life for the venerable habit of smoking, I mean.

Not that I entertain the delusion that smoking will ever return to the "golden age," when people smoked just about anywhere and anywhen they pleased and it was not a serious problem for anyone. The lies about secondhand smoke have so powerfully captured the minds of so many that even their exposure as the lies they are may not be enough to overcome an accompanying conviction the crusade has also instilled in nonsmokers: that tobacco smoke stinks unbearably. I can't think of any habit or behavior that has ever returned to favor once it was deemed socially unacceptable. The most I can foresee is a truce between smokers and nonsmokers that provides for and permits the latter to smoke in peace in areas separated from those who find it so offensive, although those havens could gradually increase in number and acceptance.

Americans have done a number of things in this century out of unreasoning fear and prejudice that they later repented, from the silly—renaming German cabbage "Liberty cabbage" in World War I—to the shameful—interning thousands of loyal citizens of Japanese ancestry in concentration camps in World War II, or conducting witch hunts for Communists sympathizers after both wars and supporting tin-pot dictators in the name of anti-Communism. They may not exactly "repent" the antismoking crusade, but it too will become one of those episodes in history people wonder about and say, "How did they let such foolishness go so far?"

SOME FINAL THOUGHTS:

When I began this book, especially when I began writing about the 1964 surgeon general's report in Chapter 1 (I wrote Chapter 9 first because it was the easiest and most fun), I was still rather in awe of that document because of the sheer bulk of the evidence, or what I assumed must be the evidence, against smoking that it contained, as well as of the credentials of its authors.

Even when I finished Chapter 1, after discovering that the best the SG's advisory panel could do was come up with seven weak studies out of some 7,000 in the scientific literature, I still had a measure of respect for it.

But now, having completed this book, having learned how epidemiology and statistics can be used to serve political or social ends, having become acquainted with the motives and tactics of the professional antismokers, looking back on everything that has happened and is continuing to happen in American society because of that report—the acrimony and division it has caused among Americans but especially the corruption of science and the legal system it has fostered in the cause of a "smoke-free America"—I have come to the conclusion that the 1964 Report of the Advisory Committee to the Surgeon General of the U.S. Public Health Service *is one of the most insidiously harmful documents ever foisted upon a gullible public.*

Let me immediately qualify that: not *intentionally* harmful, and not so much a gullible public as a *trusting* one (though there isn't always much difference between the two).

It is one of the notable and admirable characteristics of American society that its citizens have always had a basic trust in the overall honesty and dedication to the public welfare of those in positions of power and influence and charged with running their governmental and social institutions. That trust has sometimes been abused or betrayed and it will always be a far from perfect Union, but Americans have always retained the bedrock faith that in the long run the democratic ideals upon which this nation was founded will endure and prevail. One of those ideals, the foremost one, is the concept of human freedom, which if it means anything means the right of individuals to make wise or foolish personal decisions.

There can be such a thing as too much trust and faith in institutions, however; it can lead to too much unquestioning dependence on the wisdom and ability of those in authority to guide us in the identification of and solution to our national problems. Throughout this book I've thoroughly tried to abuse one of those authorities, the Environmental Protection Agency. I'll do it one last time.

So used have we become to abiding by the judgment of "those who know best" that we have allowed the EPA to decree how much water our toilets may flush—even though the regulation reducing tank capacity by more than half for new toilets actually wastes water because you often have to flush two or three times. (I've heard that people have begun smuggling "real" toilets into the States from Canada!) But ah, it is the *appearance* that "something is being done" about something—in this case a "water crisis" which, if it exists at all, is strictly localized—that is all that matters to those we have permitted to interpose themselves into even the most personal aspects of our daily lives.

Another only slightly less ridiculous example that I saw: a Food and Drug Administration warning label on a tube of toothpaste containing fluoride advising parents to keep it "out of the reach of children under 6 years of age" and that if you accidentally swallow more than the amount used for brushing to "seek professional assistance" or contact a poison control center "immediately."

Professional assistance! Immediately! Never mind that you'd have to consume hundreds of tubefuls of toothpaste—which alone would kill you—to get anything approaching a possibly harmful amount of fluoride.

These are but two examples of the propensity of the people-protectors to take the well-intentioned authority that was accorded them by Congress to absurd extremes, just as the antismoking movement did with the surgeon general's 1964 report.

One of the reasons Americans decided to embark upon their adventure in freedom and self-government more than two centuries ago was listed in the Declaration of Independence:

"He [King George] has erected a Multitude of new Offices, and sent hither Swarms of Officers to harass our People, and eat out their Substance."

To bring Pogo up to date, in late 20th-century America we have met King George again, and he is us.

For those who may feel that my statement about the surgeon general's report is, at best, outrageous or plain stupid or, at worst, pernicious and insidiously harmful itself—if not indeed blasphemous—I am entirely sure that those who wrote it sincerely believed what they wrote and had the best interests of their countrymen at heart. That very sincerity in fact made their report all the more dangerous and socially destructive. They did not foresee that it would be embraced by swarms of antismokers, in and out of government, who would erect a multitude of new laws and regulations to harass a still sizeable minority of the population and attempt to eat out the substance of a still legal industry they don't have the courage of their own convictions either to outlaw or to face in a fair fight.

The surgeon general's report was an alert to the public about a personal behavior, cigarette smoking, that its authors believed posed significant health dangers. Upon and around that report militant antismokers contrived a dishonest and immoral crusade.

It will fail.

Notes

1. In "Spotted Owls," a review of *In A Dark Wood: The Fight Over Forests and the Rising Tyranny of Ecology." Reason*, June 1996, p. 59. Nelson is a professor in the School of Public Affairs of the University of Maryland and senior fellow of the Competitive Enterprise Institute.

2. *The Atlanta Journal-Constitution*, May 19, 1994, p. A6.

3. Quoted in Gian Turci, "The World Health Organization Attack On Smokers." At www.forces-cdn.com.

4. Timothy Lamer, "Addicted to Tobacco Stories: A One-Sided Portrayal of a Risky Product." Media Research Center Report No. 8, October 7, 1996. At www.townhall.com/mrs/specialreports/tobacco.htm#cont.

5. Ernest Dichter, "Why Do We Smoke Cigarettes?" *The Psychology of Everyday Living* (New York: Barnes & Noble, Inc., 1947), p. 97.

6. "Today there are fifty thousand [specialized science journals] worldwide." — Martin Gardner, "The Internet: A World Brain?" *Skeptical Inquirer*, January/February 1999, p. 12.

7. Robert N. Proctor, "Anti-tobacco campaign of the Nazis: a little known aspect of public health in Germany, 1933-45." *British Medical Journal* No 7070 Volume 313. From http://194.216.217//archive/7070nd2.htm.

8. "Freedom's Smoke." *The New Republic*. November 4, 1996, p. 27.

9. Anna Quindlin, "As tobacco firms fib, the FDA should alter the cigarette." *The New York Times*, May 2, 1994. From www.interaccess.com/lumpen/edmc/anna.html#drb.

10. "Tobacco Industry Investigation." FBI Washington Field Office. At www.fbi. gov/majorcases/tobacco/wfo.htm.

11. David Johnston, "Federal Thrust Against Tobacco Gets New Vigor." *The New York Times*, March 18, 1996, p. A.1. Courtesy of the Advocacy Institute.

12. "Rewards for Tobacco Informants." *USA Today*. At www. usatoday. com/life/cyber-tech/ct082.htm.

13. David E. Rosenbaum, "Objecting to Oath, 2 Smoking Foes Cancel Testimony." *The New York Times*, March 5, 1998. From http://search. nytimes. com/search/daily/bin.

14. "A Tale of Two Citizens." *The Resistance*, March 1998, p. 3.

15. Robert A.Levy, "Tobacco Medicaid Litigation: Snuffing Out the Rule of Law." Cato Policy Analysis No. 275, June 29, 1997. At www.cato.org/pubs/pas/pa-275. html.

16. Robert A Levy, "Forget the law; go for the money." *The Des Moines Register*, September 16, 1997. Infoseek News Center at www.infoseek. com/.

17. Editorial, "Good joins greed." *Sarasota Herald-Tribune*, Venice/AM Edition, March 18, 1996, p, A12.

18. Levy, "Tobacco Medicaid Litigation." Also, "Is Florida Inconsistent on Nicotine Addiction?" Action on Smoking and Health, at www.ash.org/june97/7-02-97-2.html.

19. Bob Dart, "Smoke, ire: Some say VA should cover tobacco-linked ills." *The Atlanta Journal-Constitution*, April 4, 1998, p. A7.

20. "Hillary's brother plays tobacco role." *Sarasota Herald-Tribune*, Venice/AM Edition, April 19, 1997, p. 1A.

21. Jim Drinkard, "Blitzed by suits, business turning attack on lawyers." *The Atlanta Journal-Constitution*, December 12, 1997, p. A12. From the Associated Press.

22. "Florida's Medicaid Third-Party Liability Act Should Be Repealed Immediately, Says Associated Industries of Florida." PRNewswire. August 25, 1997. At www. forces-cdn.com/counterp/florida.htm.

23. Jonathan Weisman, "Lobbyists attack DUI bill." *The Atlanta Journal-Constitution*, March 30, 1998, p. A1. From *The Baltimore Sun*.

24. "Smoke-free campaign: Florida has money to burn on program." The *Florida Times-Union*, January 6, 1998. From www.infoseek.com/Content.htm.

25. Isabelle de Pommereau, "Two States Blow Smoke Over How to Spend Tobacco Booty." *The Christian Science Monitor*, September 25, 1997. At www.csmonitor.com/todays_paper/graphical/today/us/us3.html.

26. Lloyd Dunkelberger, "Battle to end child abuse continues." The *Sarasota Herald-Tribune*, Venice/AM Edition, March 22, 1998, p. 1A.

27. Stephanie Arero, "Florida to penalize underage smokers." *The Atlanta Journal-Constitution*, September 28, 1997, p. C6. From the *Palm Beach Post*.

28. "Smoking penalties." *The Atlanta Journal-Constitution*, May 14, 1997, p. A10.

29. "Latest Revealing Tobacco Document Proposes Root Beer Smelling Cigarette." At www.ash.org/august97/8-15-97-3.html.

30. David Shaffer, "Judge Disallows Argument by Tobacco Industry." *The Pioneer Press*, November 20, 1997. At www.pioneerplanet.com/mfc_docs/009556.htm.

31. Cited in Carol Thompson, "Talking Back to the Media." At www.forces-cdn.org.

32. Stanton A. Glantz, PhD, Brion J. Fox, JD, James M. Lightwood, PhD, attributing the figure to the Centers for Disease Control and Prevention and the Health Care Financing Administration in "Tobacco Litigation Issues for Public Health and Public Policy." *Journal of the American Medical Association*, March 5, 1997.

33. Charley Reese, "No Rational or Legal Basis for States to Sue Tobacco Companies." *Orlando Sentinel*, September 5, 1996, p. A10. Cited in Levy, "Tobacco Medicaid Litigation."

34. "Lawyers' tobacco cut: $8.1 billion." *The Atlanta Journal-Constitution*, December 12, 1998, p. A3. From *The New York Times*.

35. "Health Care Costs of Smoking." Reuters, October 8, 1997, citing *The New England Journal of Medicine* (1997;337(15):1052-1057. From www. yahoo. com/headlines/971008/health/stories/health1.html.

36. "U.S. may face Alzheimer's 'time bomb.'" *The Sarasota Herald-Tribune*, Venice/AM Edition, March 25, 1998, p. 11A. From the Associated Press.

37. Bruce Herschensohn, National Smokers Alliance Advisory Board member, in *The Resistance*, November/December 1998, p. 4.

38. Quoted by Tim White, moderator of a program on secondhand smoke broadcast on National Public Radio, July 11, 1991.

39. "Labor union health-care funds file their own smoking lawsuits." *The Miami Herald*, September 24, 1997. At www.herald.com/florida/digdocs/036843.htm.

40. "The Proposed Tobacco Settlement: Issues From A Federal Perspective." Congressional Budget Office (CBO), April 1998, p.43. At www.cbo.gov.

41. Glantz et al., "Tobacco Litigation Issues for Public Health and Public Policy."

42. CBO report, p. 47.

43. Harry Berkowitz, "New Marketing Scheme for Cigarettes Begins." *Newsday*. From http://library.newsday.com/search.cig?id.

44. "Tobacco: Ad Bans Abroad Haven't Snuffed Out Smoking." *The Wall Street Journal*, June 12, 1997. At www.ash.org.

45. M.A.J. McKenna, "Alarming rise in teen smoking defies national effort, CDC says." *The Atlanta Journal-Constitution*, April 3, 1998, p. A1.

46. "CDC Spins Teen Smoking Rates." At www.junkscience.com/news/cdcteen.htm.

47. Quoted in "Teens telling lies? What a smoke screen." *USA Today*. At www.usatoday.com:80/elect/ew/ew171htm.

48. Editorial. "Joe Camel the last straw in marketing." *The Atlanta Journal-Consitution*, April 6, 1998, p. A8.

49. Jeff Jacoby, "Teen smoking campaign flops." *The Boston Globe*, April 7, 1998. At www.boston.com/dailyglobe/globehtml/097/Teen_ smoking_ campaign_ flops.htm.

50. Bette Harrison, "Growing up in smoke." *The Atlanta Journal-Constitution*, April 3, 1998, p. F1.

51. "Teen Spending Power." *The Resistance*, March, 1998, p. 7.

52. Bob Kemper and Karen Cullotta Krause, "Price alone won't keep cigarette smoke out of their eyes, teens insist." *The Chicago Tribune*. Web-posted September 18, 1997 at www.chicago.tribune.com/print/news/9709/18/news/97091902-44.html.

53. Robert J. Samuelson, "Do Smokers Have Rights?" *The Washington Post*, September 24, 1997, p. A21.

54. Ashley Grant, "Jurors reject tobacco liability in nurse's death." *The Atlanta Journal-Constitution*, March 20, 1998, p. C7. From the Associated Press.

55. "Remarks made by key attorneys general on the tobacco deal at a Washington news conference." From www.forces.com.

56. "Lung Association Opposes Any Settlement." At www.ash.org/07.03.3.html.

57. "Final Report of the Advisory Committee on Tobacco Policy and Public Health." July 1997. C. Everett Koop, M.D., ScD. and David A. Kessler, M.D., co-chairs. Published at www.ash.org/.

58. Steve Lash, "Deal is off, cigarette makers say." *The Atlanta Journal-Constitution*, April 9, 1998, p. A1. From *The Houston Chronicle*.

59. Charles Whitebread, "The Sociology of Prohibition or The History of the Non-Medical Use of Drugs in the United States." A Speech to the California Judges Association 1995 annual conference. From www.pipes.org/Articles/history.html.

60. Erik Kirschbaum, "Vietnamese crime syndicates smoke with German smuggling." *The Washington Times*, February 3, 1996.

61. Paul Geitner, "Smuggling hard to snuff out." *USA Today*, June 13, 1996.

62. Ed Carson, "Tobacco Road." *Reason*, February 1995.

63. Erin Schiller, "Smoking Up North." *The Washington Times*, February 11, 1998.

64. Jerry DeMarco, "Tobacco gains as bootleg choice; State tax hike spurs special ATF unit." *The Bergen Record*, March 23, 1998, p. A01. At www.bergen.com /news/cig199803234.htm.

65. Joanna Macy, in the Foreword to *Diet for A New America* by John Robbins (Walpole, N.H., 1987), p. viii.

66. "Meat Kills More Than Smoking." Press release from the Vegan Discussion Group. Posted on the Internet September 14, 1994.

67. William Strauss and Neil Howe, *Generations: The History of America's Future, 1584 to 2069* (New York: William Morrow, 1991), p. 313.

68. Ibid, pp. 380, 381.

69. Ibid, p. 396.

70. Ibid, pp. 324-327.

71. Ibid, p. 415, 416.